PRINCIPLES OF CALIFORNIA REAL ESTATE

College Edition 4

Kathryn J. Haupt

ROCKWELL
PUBLISHING

Illustrations by Michael D. Duquette

TABLE OF CONTENTS

- Land
- Appurtenances
- Attachments
- Distinguishing Real From Personal Property

- Lot and Block
- Metes and Bounds
- Rectangular Survey
- Other Methods of Land Description

- Wills
- Succession and Escheat
- Accession
- Occupancy
- Deeds
- The Recording System

- Freehold Estates
- Less-Than-Freehold Estates
- Ownership in Severalty
- Concurrent Ownership

- Encumbrances Defined
- Financial Encumbrances
- Types of Liens
- Non-financial Encumbrances
- Easements
- Private Restrictions
- Encroachments
- California Homestead Protection

PREFACE

Principles of California Real Estate offers a thorough overview of the theoretical and practical aspects of the real estate business in California. Originally published under the title *"Fundamentals of California Real Estate,"* it is a "principles and practices" book designed for use in college level real estate courses and professional continuing education programs. In addition, *Principles* serves as an exhaustive reference book for the real estate practitioner and the applicant preparing for the state license exam.

Rockwell Publishing acknowledges the contributions of many individuals in the publication of this book, in particular W. Michael Gough, Real Estate Coordinator of De Anza College, Cupertino, California.

A MESSAGE TO THE STUDENT

Study Aids

Incorporated into this text are several study aids that distinguish it from other books. If used properly, these aids will enable you to consistently identify and make note of the most important information relating to each topic.

Study Aid Number One—Each chapter begins with an outline of its contents. An outline is a useful tool and can help you see "the broad picture," i.e., how various subjects relate to each other. Review of the outline is especially helpful after you have read and become familiar with the concepts contained in the chapter.

Study Aid Number Two—Each chapter contains a section of key terms found within that chapter. These terms were included because of their importance to a thorough knowledge of real estate. In addition, a complete listing of real estate terms appears in the glossary found at the end of the book.

Study Aid Number Three—Important real estate terms are defined in the margins of the book where they appear in the text. This way, you can have the definition of an important or difficult concept as you are reading the pertinent material in the chapter.

Study Aid Number Four—**Boldface type** is used throughout the book to help you identify crucial concepts and terminology.

Study Aid Number Five—We have provided you with wide margins for notes. Researchers have found that notes written on the margins of each page do more to enhance the learning process than do notes made on a separate pad. Placing notes in the margin alongside corresponding topics and explanations makes a review of your notes more productive. For example, if when looking over your notes you find a more thorough examination of a subject is necessary, a detailed explanation is quickly found in the paragraph(s) adjoining the notes.

Study Aid Number Six—At the end of each chapter is a chapter summary and a practice quiz. The chapter summary reviews the material you have just read and the quiz questions are designed to reinforce your knowledge of the information in the chapter. Further, the quiz can help you identify your strengths and weaknesses in terms of comprehension.

Suggested Study Technique

The student should read each chapter carefully, making notes on important material in the margins. We also suggest that you underline important statements. Researchers have concluded that if a reader will underscore just one sentence per paragraph — the sentence he or she thinks is most important — a better understanding of the material automatically follows.

After studying a chapter, take the sample quiz (without referring to the text for assistance). Answers to these questions are found in the answer key which follows each quiz. Any question on the quiz which is answered incorrectly should be reviewed to determine if it was misread, misunderstood, or if you did not know the material well enough to answer correctly.

Finally, we suggest a systematic approach to review. You should review a chapter immediately after reading it, paying especially close attention to the outline, key terms, and your own margin notes and underlined sentences. Also, carefully reread those materials you found troublesome on the practice quiz. Additionally, you should go back over each chapter at various intervals during the period you study this course, to ensure your newly acquired knowledge has been retained.

Chapter 1

NATURE OF REAL PROPERTY

KEY TERMS

realty	personalty
attachments	fixtures
trade fixtures	actual annexation
constructive annexation	emblements
appurtenance	riparian rights
air rights	rule of capture
prior appropriation	subjacent support
lateral support	littoral

CHAPTER OVERVIEW

The term "real property" refers to the actual land as a physical object, plus all of the intangible rights that accompany the land. Ownership of real property includes not just the surface of the earth, but also things under or over the land. This chapter explains and describes the nature of real property and the "bundle of rights" which accompanies it.

INTRODUCTION

Anything that can be owned is considered to be property. There are two types of property: **real** and **personal**.

Realty: the land, everything attached to the land, and everything appurtenant to the land.

Real property (realty) is usually described as the land, anything affixed to the land, and anything incidental or appurtenant to the land. Sometimes it is referred to as that which is immovable. Personal property (personalty), on the other hand, is an interest in things that are movable; it is all property not classified as real property. Personal property items, such as automobiles, furniture or clothing, are occasionally called chattels.

Personalty: items that are movable, e.g., a boat, money.

You are probably more familiar with the term "real estate" than the term "real property." While closely related, there is a technical distinction between the two terms. Real estate is the land and its physical elements, like minerals, airspace and buildings. Real property is a broader term, which includes the land as a physical object plus the intangible rights that accompany it. For the most part, the distinction is an academic one and is seldom made in informal conversation.

LAND AND ITS COMPONENTS

Real property is more than just the surface of the earth; it includes everything attached to it by human acts or the forces of nature, everything beneath it to the center of the earth, everything above it to the upper reaches of the sky, and all of the rights that go along with owning it. Think of real property as land plus a **bundle of rights** which accompany the land. These rights include the right to use, lease, enjoy, encumber, will, sell or do nothing at all with the property.

LAND—THE INVERTED PYRAMID

Not only does a landowner own all of the earth's surface within his or her boundaries, but also everything under it or over it which is of a permanent nature. A parcel of land is seen as an inverted pyramid, with its tip at the center of the globe and its base above the earth's surface.

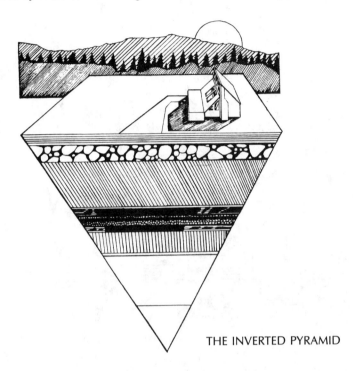

THE INVERTED PYRAMID

THE INVERTED PYRAMID

WAYS TO DIVIDE THE LAND

The land itself can be divided in many ways. A large parcel can be subdivided into smaller parcels which are sold separately. Or various portions of the land, such as the minerals or the airspace, may be sold separately from the surface of the land. In the first instance the land is subdivided vertically; in the second it is divided horizontally. When the rights to a particular mineral are sold, the purchaser automatically acquires an implied easement which allows him or her to come onto the surface of the land and undertake operations to extract the minerals.

APPURTENANCES

An appurtenance is something which goes with or pertains to real property, but is not necessarily part of that property. While it is impossible to describe all types of appurtenances, one basic type is the right

Appurtenance: a right that follows ownership of the property, such as the right to take minerals from the land.

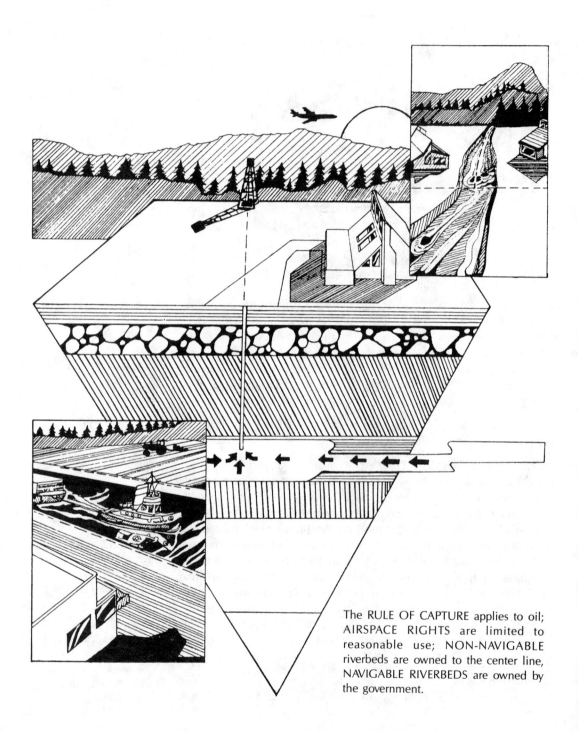

The RULE OF CAPTURE applies to oil; AIRSPACE RIGHTS are limited to reasonable use; NON-NAVIGABLE riverbeds are owned to the center line, NAVIGABLE RIVERBEDS are owned by the government.

to take or use something which is in, on or over the land:

- air
- water
- minerals
- oil and gas
- support
- intangibles

AIR RIGHTS

While in theory, landownership extends to the center of the earth, the owner's boundaries no longer reach the upper limits of the sky. Congress, through the Air Commerce Act of 1926 and the Civil Aeronautics Act of 1938, gave the federal government complete control over our nation's airspace. A landowner still has the exclusive right to use the lower reaches of airspace over his or her property, but may do nothing that would interfere with normal air traffic.

Air rights: the right to reasonable use of the airspace above the surface of the land owned.

If harm suffered from overflights of aircraft is substantial enough, a landowner may recover damages for the actual harm caused. The classic example is the airport built next door to the chicken farm. The noise and vibrations from overflights are so severe that the chickens no longer lay eggs. If the land cannot be used for any other reasonable purpose, the value of the land is significantly diminished and the landowner may be able to force the government to condemn the property and compensate him or her for its fair market value.

WATER RIGHTS

Water is found on the surface of the earth and beneath the surface in porous ground layers called aquifers. Surface water may be confined in a channel or basin, or it may be unchanneled water, such as runoff or flood water. With respect to surface waters which are confined in a channel or basin, there are two types of property rights which may apply: the first is called a **riparian** right, which is the right of a landowner with respect to water which flows through or adjacent to his or her property. A landowner whose property borders upon a lake is called a **littoral** owner. A riparian or littoral owner may never divert water from a stream or lake for use on non-riparian land—land that does not adjoin the lake or stream from which the water is taken or land which lies in a different watershed.

Riparian rights: the right to reasonable use of the water bordering or running over the land owned.

The second type of water right is called an appropriative right. An **appropriative** right is established by obtaining a permit to use the water from the state government. The fact that the water adjoins or does not adjoin a piece of property is completely irrelevant under this system. Once an appropriative right has been established, it may be sold and the water may be used on different land and/or for a different purpose.

Because of its scarcity and its importance for domestic, agricultural and other applications, water has been the source of much legislation and litigation in California. The result is an extremely complex body of laws which regulates the use of water in the state. The unifying theme behind these laws is that water must be conserved by preventing waste and by limiting use to those areas where the water is most beneficial. This goal is promoted by the system of **prior appropriation**, which is the most common method of obtaining rights to water in California.

Almost all water in the state is owned by the state, which grants permits for use of the water to private users. The permits are ranked according to their priority in time and also according to the purpose for which the water is used.

California also recognizes a limited form of riparian rights. Riparian owners may use water flowing past their property, but the use must be reasonable in light of the needs of all other landowners along the stream. Wasteful use of water is never permitted. This same principle of **reasonable use** applies to overlying rights among users of an underground water source (aquifer). Such users do not own the water under their land, but they have the common right to use the water, provided that the use is reasonable in light of all circumstances. The only privately owned water in California is in lakes or ponds which are totally within the bounds of one tract of land or water from natural springs arising on private property.

With respect to surface flood waters, California adheres to the natural servitude principle. A landowner is liable for any harm caused to other property as a result of his or her efforts to block or channel surface flood waters away from his or her property. Various state and federal laws control the use of property in areas of high flood danger.

A riparian owner owns the land under a stream up to the midpoint of the stream, except in the case of navigable streams, where the ownership of the stream bed is held by the government. The public has a right to use navigable waterways for transportation, which means that there is a public easement for right-of-way.

SOLID MINERALS

A landowner owns all the minerals under his or her property. These minerals are considered to be real property until they are extracted from the earth and then they become personalty. Ownership of solid minerals is simple to allocate: one need only determine whether the minerals

Prior appropriation: the right to use water established by a government permit that is not based on riparian rights.

are situated within the "inverted pyramid" beneath a particular parcel's boundaries. If so, they belong to the owner of the parcel.

A property owner can sell his or her mineral rights to another party. The purchaser has an implied easement that allows him or her to enter the property for the purpose of extracting the minerals.

OIL AND GAS

The situation is not so clear with respect to oil and gas. Oil and gas in their natural state lie trapped beneath the surface in porous layers of earth. However, once an oil or gas reservoir has been tapped, the oil and gas begin to flow towards the point where the reservoir has been pierced by the well. This is because oil and gas deposits are under great pressure and, when a well is drilled, it forms an area of lower pressure towards which the oil and gas will migrate. Thus, a landowner could theoretically remove all of the oil and gas from beneath adjoining properties without ever committing a trespass; a drill on one parcel of land can attract all the oil and gas from the surrounding properties.

Because of their fugitive natures, oil and gas are governed by the **rule of capture**. That is, a landowner owns all of the oil and gas which he or she produces from wells on his or her property. The oil and gas become personal property of the landowner once they are brought to the surface. The rule of capture has the effect of stimulating oil and gas production, since the only way for a landowner to protect his or her interest in the underlying gas and oil is to drill an **offset well** to keep the oil and gas from migrating to the neighbor's wells.

Rule of capture: the concept that oil is not owned until it is brought to the surface of the land, when it becomes personal property.

SUPPORT RIGHTS

A landowner has the right to the natural support of the land (which is provided by surrounding land). The right to support is inherent in the land itself and applies to both **lateral support** from adjacent land and **subjacent support** from underlying strata.

Lateral support: the landowner's right to support from adjacent land.

INTANGIBLE APPURTENANCES

Certain appurtenances are concerned with the use of property and do not involve ownership of tangible objects. Examples include easements, covenants and restrictions which apply to the land or to neighboring properties. These types of interests are discussed in greater detail in subsequent chapters.

Subjacent support: the landowner's right to support from underlying strata.

ATTACHMENTS

Attachments: everything
that is permanently
attached to the property
by nature or humans;
part of real property.

Everything that is permanently attached to the land is considered a part of real property. These items are called, simply, attachments. There are two types of attachments: natural and man-made.

NATURAL ATTACHMENTS

Natural attachments are things attached to the earth by roots, such as trees, shrubs and crops. Natural attachments which grow without the help of humans are called fructus naturales and include all naturally occurring trees, crops and plants. They are almost always classified as real property. Plantings cultivated by people are called fructus industriales, and they are also a part of the land. Their crops, however, are treated as personal property. Thus, a cultivated apple orchard would be realty, but the apples themselves would be personalty.

Doctrine of emblements:
a tenant farmer may
reenter land to harvest
crops even after the
tenancy ends.

A special rule, called the **doctrine of emblements**, applies to crops that are planted by a tenant farmer. If the tenancy is for an indefinite period of time and the tenancy is terminated through no fault of the tenant, the tenant has the right to re-enter the land and harvest the crops. The landlord cannot prevent the tenant from exercising this right even if the crops were not ready for harvest until after the tenancy ended. If the crops are an annual product of perennial plants, such as pears or apples, the right to re-enter and harvest the fruit applies only to the first crop which matures after the tenancy is terminated.

MAN-MADE ATTACHMENTS

Fixtures: any personal
property item that is at-
tached to land in such a
way as to become real
property.

Articles attached to the land by people are called **fixtures**. Some obvious examples of fixtures include garages, fences and cement patios. Because fixtures always start out as personal property (e.g., lumber or concrete), it is sometimes difficult to determine whether the item is in fact a fixture (a permanent attachment) or is still personal property. If the item remains personal property, the owner can take it with him or her when ownership of the realty is transferred. However, if it is a fixture, it is transferred to the new owner.

DISTINGUISHING REAL FROM PERSONAL PROPERTY

It is obvious to anyone that in the absence of a legal separation by contract, natural physical elements, such as minerals, trees and water rights clearly run (belong) with the land. However, distinguishing fixtures (man-made improvements) from personal property items is not as simple. Buyers and sellers commonly disagree as to what has been purchased and sold; landlords and tenants disagree over what, once annexed by a tenant, becomes part of the real estate; and real estate lenders and borrowers argue about whether an item is personal property or realty. If it is the former, it can be taken from the land by the borrower; if it is the latter, it is subject to the lender's mortgage lien and would be a part of any foreclosure sale the lender might be obligated to undertake. Where these kinds of differences arise, there are a series of tests which can be applied by the court in its effort to classify the property in dispute. These tests include:

- method of attachment
- intention of the parties
- adaptability of the item to the realty
- relationship of the parties, and
- evidence of written agreement

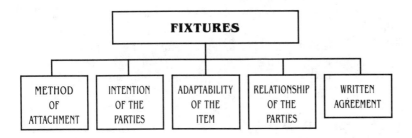

METHOD OF ATTACHMENT. As a general rule any item a person permanently attaches to the land becomes a part of the real estate. A permanent attachment occurs when the item is:

- annexed to the land by roots, as with trees and shrubs;
- embedded in the earth, like sewer lines or septic tanks;
- permanently resting on the land, as in the case of certain types of buildings; or
- attached by any other enduring method, such as by cement, plaster, nails, bolts or screws.

Actual annexation: an item affixed to land by means of physical attachment.

Physical attachment (actual annexation) is not absolutely necessary for an item to be considered a fixture. Often, actual annexation exists even if there is no physical fusion. Mere attachment by the force of gravity may be sufficient, as with industrial machinery which is an integral part of a particular manufacturing operation. Such machinery has been held

Constructive annexation: an item the law considers to be affixed to land, even though not physically attached, i.e., keys to a building.

to be a fixture even though it was not bolted down or otherwise secured to the building. Also, an article may be annexed by virtue of being enclosed in a space so that it cannot be removed without dismantling it or tearing down part of the building.

Even movable articles may be considered attached to the realty. Specialized tools necessary to the maintenance of complex machinerythat is attached to the land have been held to be fixtures regardless of their mobility. This view is based on the doctrine of **constructive annexation**, which applies in the case of movable articles, like keys, which are essential parts of permanently attached fixtures. The constructive annexation doctrine also relates to items which have been temporarily removed for servicing and repair, such as built-in appliances.

INTENTION OF THE PARTIES. Over time, the courts decided that the "method of attachment" test was too rigid and didn't allow for special situations where something permanently affixed would more justly be classified as personal property. The "intent of the parties" test is considered a more important criterion. The court tries to determine what the person intended when he or she annexed the item to the property. Did he or she intend the item to become part of the realty or to remain personal property? Each of the other tests (including method of attachment) is viewed as objective evidence of this intent. For instance, imbedding a birdbath into concrete indicates an intent to make the item a permanent fixture, where just setting it out in the yard would not.

ADAPTABILITY OF THE ITEM TO THE REALTY. Where an unattached article is essential to the use and operation of the land, or if the article was designed specifically for use in a particular location, it is probably a fixture. Examples include items such as pews in a church or storm windows built for a particular building.

RELATIONSHIP OF THE PARTIES. The court will consider the relationship of the parties in its effort to determine intent. For example, it is generally held that a tenant who installs an item, such as a light fixture, probably does so with the thought of removing it at the expiration of the lease. A seller, on the other hand, making a similar installation, is more likely attempting to improve the real property. It is improbable he or she was planning on removing the article at a later date. When a tenant installs items for the purpose of carrying on a trade or business, he or she usually intends to remove them at the termination of the lease. Such articles are called **trade fixtures** and the accepted rule is that they may be removed unless there is a contrary provision in the lease or the fixtures have become an integral part of the land or improvement. If the trade fixtures have become an integral part of the land and the lessee still wants to remove them, it is his or her responsibility to either

Trade fixtures: a fixture installed by a tenant for use in the tenant's business; it remains the property of the tenant.

restore the property to its original condition or compensate the owner for any physical damage resulting from the removal. Trade fixtures that are not removed become the property of the owner.

The same rule applies to items installed by agricultural tenants, such as tool sheds or hen houses, and to articles annexed by residential tenants.

WRITTEN AGREEMENT. Of course, regardless of any of the previous considerations, if there is a written agreement between the landlord and tenant, buyer and seller, or lender and borrower stipulating how a particular item shall be treated—as part of the real estate or as personal property—the court will respect and enforce that agreement. The stipulation would ordinarily be found in the contract made between the parties. For example, if a seller planned to take certain shrubs from the property before the transaction closed, she would include a statement to that effect in the sales agreement since shrubs are normally considered part of the realty.

A controversial area of law is the case of a person who improves real property in the mistaken belief that he or she owns the land. The modern trend is to compensate the innocent improver for the value of the improvement, provided there was no actual knowledge of the mistake before the construction was begun.

> **Example:** Where a person builds a house on another's lot in the mistaken belief that he is the actual owner, most courts will give the improver a lien on the property for the value of the improvement.

Classifying articles as fixtures has added significance in the case of mobile homes. Mobile homes are personal property until they are permanently attached to realty by a landowner who removes the wheels and mounts the unit on a concrete foundation. As personalty, mobile homes may be sold without the need for a real estate license, and the sales are subject to sales tax laws.

CHAPTER SUMMARY

1. There are two types of property: real property and personal property. Real property is the land, anything affixed to the land, and anything appurtenant to the land. Personal property is an interest in things that are movable, such as cars and furniture.

2. Land can be viewed as an inverted pyramid: a landowner owns the earth's surface within his or her boundaries as well as everything beneath the surface and a reasonable use of the airspace above the surface.

3. Appurtenances to the land include: air rights, water rights, mineral rights, oil and gas rights, and support rights.

4. Attachments may be natural (growing) and man-made (fixtures). The tests for distinguishing fixtures from personal property include: the method of attachment, the intention of the parties, the adaptability of the item to the realty, the relationship of the parties, and any provisions in a written agreement.

CHAPTER 1—QUIZ
NATURE OF REAL PROPERTY

1. The two classes of property are:

   a) real & personal
   b) natural & man-made
   c) land & money
   d) appurtenant & in gross

2. Real property is equivalent to:

   a) land
   b) personal property
   c) land, attachments, appurtenances
   d) land and water

3. Items attached to land by people are called:

   a) fructus industriales
   b) fructus naturales
   c) fixtures
   d) emblements

4. A tenant farmer may harvest the crops after the tenancy ends, under the doctrine of:

   a) constructive annexation
   b) emblements
   c) trade fixtures
   d) fructus naturales

5. The opposite of a fixture is:

   a) real property
   b) personal property
   c) land
   d) fructus naturales

6. The most important consideration for determining whether an article is a fixture is:

   a) annexation
   b) annexor's intent
   c) adaptability of the article to the realty
   d) intended use of the article

7. Articles installed in or on realty by tenants for use in a business are called:

   a) fructus industriales
   b) trade fixtures
   c) emblements
   d) easements

8. Articles which are not attached to realty may still be considered fixtures under the doctrine of:

   a) emblements
   b) constructive annexation
   c) adaptability
   d) prior appropriation

9. Something which goes with or pertains to real property, but is not part of the property, is called:

   a) an attachment
   b) an appurtenance
   c) personal property
   d) a fixture

10. Rights to water in a stream which flows through an owner's land are called:

    a) riparian rights
    b) littoral rights
    c) appropriative rights
    d) easement rights

11. Rights to underground water in aquifers are called:

    a) riparian rights
    b) appropriative rights
    c) overlying rights
    d) easement rights

12. The government owns all waters which are:

    a) navigable
    b) riparian
    c) underground
    d) littoral

13. Minerals become personal property when they are:

   a) sold
   b) extracted from the land
   c) taken to a refinery
   d) claimed

14. Rights to oil and gas are determined by:

   a) the rule of capture
   b) offset wells
   c) the Bureau of Land Management
   d) the Department of the Interior

15. The right to lateral support of land is:

   a) an inherent right
   b) an appurtenance
   c) Both a) and b)
   d) None of the above

16. A sale of mineral rights gives the buyer:

   a) a personal property right
   b) an implied easement of access to
      the minerals
   c) a littoral right
   d) a license

17. A landowner whose property borders on a lake is called:

   a) a littoral owner
   b) a riparian owner
   c) an appropriator
   d) a licensee

1. a) Property is either real or personal.

2. c) Real property is made up of land, everything that is attached to the land (e.g., fixtures) and everything that is appurtenant to the land (e.g., water rights).

3. c) A fixture is something attached to the land by people, such as houses, fences, sheds.

4. b) The doctrine of emblements allows a tenant farmer to reenter the land after a tenancy ended and harvest the crops the tenant planted.

5. b) A fixture is real property. The opposite of real property is personal property.

6 b) The intention of the party who attached the item is the primary consideration in determining whether it is a fixture. The other tests are evidence of the party's intention.

7. b) An article installed by a tenant for use in a business is called a trade fixture and remains the tenant's personal property.

8. b) An item which is not physically attached to property, such as a key to a building, is still considered a fixture under the doctrine of constructive annexation. As an essential part of the realty, the key becomes a fixture.

9. b) An appurtenance is a right or interest that goes with the property, even though it is not physically a part of the property. An example would be riparian rights.

10. a) Riparian rights include the right to reasonable usage of the water that flows through a property owner's land.

11. c) The landowner's right to use water contained in underground aquifers is called an overlying right.

12. a) The government owns all navigable waters and the land under navigable waters.

13. b) Once minerals are extracted from the land, they become personal property.

14. a) The rule of capture determines ownership of oil and gas. This rule provides that the landowner owns all the oil and gas removed from a well on his or her property, even if the oil or gas was originally beneath someone else's property.

15. c) The right to support is an inherent appurtenance. If a landowner did not have the right to lateral and subjacent support, his or her ownership rights would potentially be worthless.

16. b) If a person buys the mineral rights from the landowner, he or she has an implied easement to enter the land to remove the minerals. The mineral rights are an interest in real property; minerals do not become personal property until they are extracted from the land.

17. a) A littoral owner is someone who owns land bordering on a lake.

LAND DESCRIPTION

OUTLINE

I. Lot and Block
II. Metes and Bounds
    A. Point of beginning
    B. Tracing boundaries by course and distance
        1. conflicting directions
        2. compass bearings
III. Rectangular Survey
    A. Meridians and baselines
    B. Townships
    C. Sections
    D. Government lots
IV. Other Methods of Land Description

KEY TERMS

plat	lot
block	metes
bounds	monuments
course	point of beginning
rectangular survey	principal meridian
base line	township line
township tier	guide meridian
range line	range
township	government lot
datum	bench mark

CHAPTER OVERVIEW

When land is being transfered from one party to another, it is essential to accurately describe the property being conveyed. An ambiguous or uncertain description is not legally sufficient. Confusion concerning exactly what was transferred could cause problems not only for the parties involved in the original transaction, but for future transactions as well. There are three major types of legal description which will be introduced to you in this chapter: the lot and block method, the metes and bounds method, and the government survey.

INTRODUCTION

California law requires all deeds to contain an adequate description of the land being conveyed. An "adequate" description is one that enables a precise determination of what property is being referred to. The description does not have to be very detailed to be considered adequate, but it must not be ambiguous. For example, a grant of "all my lands in Smith County" may be sufficient because evidence can be introduced to prove exactly what lands are being described. However, a grant of "one of my lots in Smith County" is not sufficient because it is impossible to determine which of several lots is being referred to. An ambiguous or uncertain description is not legally sufficient.

Because a land description is an essential part of the agreement to transfer property as well as being necessary to a valid deed, it is important for real estate agents to understand the basic rudiments of a valid description. A valid description will usually take the form of one of the three major types of land description commonly used today. These are:

Lot: a parcel of property delineated on a plat for reference by the platting method of legal description

- lot and block
- metes and bounds, and
- government survey.

Block: a group of lots surrounded by streets within a subdivision

LOT AND BLOCK

Plat: a subdivision map recorded and filed with the county recorder

The first major system of land description is called the lot and block method. Sometimes it is referred to as platting or the maps and plats system. In this system, land is described by reference to lots and blocks (groups of lots surrounded by streets) which are mapped out by a surveyor on a subdivision plat (map) and subsequently recorded in the county where the land is located. After the map is recorded, any reference made to one of the numbered lots on the specified plat will be a sufficient legal description of the lot. Since a detailed description of the lot is already on file in the recorder's office, that description may be incorporated into any legal document simply by reference.

To find the location and dimensions of the parcel (or any other more specific information about the property), you would merely look in the map book at the county recorder's office.

An example of lot and block description might read as follows:

Lot 2, Block 4 of Tract number 455, in the city of Fresno, county of Fresno, state of California, as per map recorded in Book 25, page 92, of maps, in the office of the recorder of said county.

Plat maps frequently contain a wealth of useful information above and beyond a detailed description of property boundaries. For example, they may include measurements of area, locations of various easements, right-of-way dimensions, location of survey markers, records of conditions and restrictions applying to the land, etc. Nevertheless, a plat map is not a substitute for a thorough title search and should not be treated as such.

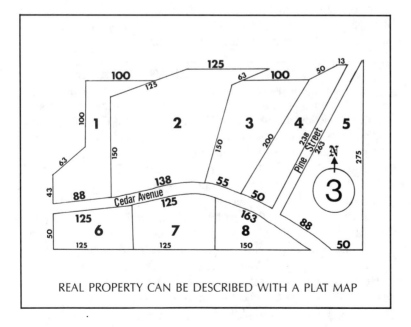

REAL PROPERTY CAN BE DESCRIBED WITH A PLAT MAP

Metes: measurements used to describe land in the metes and bounds method of land description.

Bounds: boundaries used to describe land in the metes and bounds method of land description.

Monuments: a fixed point (e.g., "the old oak tree") used to trace courses and distances

Course: a direction, e.g., northerly

Point of beginning: a monument, or point in reference to a monument, where a metes and bounds description begins

METES AND BOUNDS

The metes (measurements) and bounds (boundaries) system describes a parcel by describing its outline or boundaries. The boundaries are described by reference to three things:

- monuments, which may be natural objects such as rivers or trees, or man-made objects such as roads or survey markers;
- directions or courses, in the form of compass readings;
- distances, measured in any convenient units of length.

POINT OF BEGINNING

A metes and bounds description will start at some convenient and well-defined point along the boundary of a tract of land. It will then give directions which would enable a surveyor to trace the boundaries of the tract all the way around to the point where he or she began. The starting point is referred to as the point of beginning or POB, and will always be described by reference to a monument.

Examples: "The SW corner of the intersection of 1st St. and 2nd Ave.," or "200 ft. north of the old oak tree."

Note that the point of beginning does not have to be a monument itself, it must just be described relative to a determinable reference point, such as the old oak tree in the example above.

TRACING BOUNDARIES BY COURSE AND DISTANCE

Once the point of beginning has been established, a metes and bounds description proceeds by giving a direction to follow and a distance for which to follow the direction. For example, "north, 100 ft." is a course and distance. Both the course and the distance may be described in terms of a monument, for example, "northerly along the eastern edge of 1st St. 100 ft." or "north, 100 ft. more or less to the center line of Smith Creek." Note that a reference to a monument always takes precedence over a course or distance when there is a discrepancy between the two. In the above examples, the first boundary would be along the edge of First Street even if that edge was not in a direct line with north, and the second boundary would extend to the center of Smith Creek even if the actual distance to that point was not exactly 100 feet.

The metes and bounds description will continue to describe a series of courses and distances, each one corresponding to a boundary of the parcel being described, until the boundary has been described all the way around back to the point of beginning. A metes and bounds description must end at the point of beginning; otherwise it does not describe a totally enclosed tract. The figure below illustrates a simple metes and bounds description.

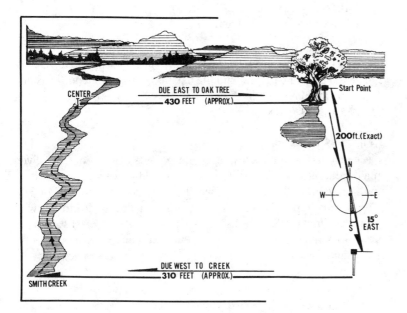

METES AND BOUNDS DESCRIPTION

A tract of land, located in Smith County and described as follows: beginning at the old oak tree, thence south 15° east, 200 feet, thence north 90° west, 310 feet more or less to the center line of Smith Creek, thence northwesterly along the center line of Smith Creek to a point directly west of the old oak tree, thence north 90° east, 430 feet more or less to the point of beginning

As you can see, metes and bounds descriptions tend to be quite lengthy, and are often confusing. Add to this the fact that monuments and reference points do not always maintain their exact locations over the years, and it becomes clear that an actual survey of the property is essential when dealing with descriptions of this type.

CONFLICTING DIRECTIONS

As noted above, discrepancies sometimes occur between the various elements of a metes and bounds description. In resolving such discrepancies the order of priority is as follows:

- natural monuments,
- then man-made monuments,
- then courses, then distances,
- then names (e.g., "Smith Farm"),
- then areas (e.g., "40 acres").

In a conflict between any two of the above elements, the one with higher priority will prevail. For example, if a land description reads "east 240 feet to the old oak tree" and the oak tree is really in a northeasterly direction, the reference to the old oak tree will take precedence over the course.

COMPASS BEARINGS

Directions or courses in metes and bounds descriptions are given in a peculiar fashion. A direction is described by reference to its deviation from either north or south, whichever is closer. Thus, NW or 315° is written as north 45° west, since it is a deviation of 45° to the west of north. Similarly, SSE or 157½° is written south 22½° east, since it is a deviation of 22½° to the east of south. East and west are both written relative to north: north 90°east, north 90° west, respectively.

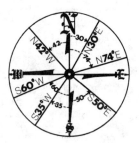
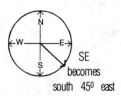

SE becomes south 45° east

COMPASS BEARINGS ARE GIVEN BY REFERENCE TO NORTH OR SOUTH

RECTANGULAR SURVEY

Rectangular survey: a method of describing land by reference to a series of grids laid out over the United States

Also called the government survey, the rectangular survey describes land by reference to a series of grids. These grids may be confusing at first and we recommend that you study the accompanying diagrams closely.

The grids are composed of two sets of lines, one set running north/south, the other east/west. Each grid is identified by a principal meridian, which is the original north/south line established in that grid, and by a base line which is the original east/west line. (See Diagram 2.1)

Grid lines run north and south at six-mile intervals from the principal meridians, and east and west parallel to and at six-mile intervals from the baseline. The east/west lines are called township lines, and divide the land into rows or tiers which are called township tiers. The north/south lines, called guide meridians or range lines, divide the land into columns which are called ranges. (See Diagram 2.2)

A particular area of land which is located at the intersection of a range and a township tier is called a township, and it is identified by its position relative to the principal meridian and base line. For example, the township which is located in the fourth tier north of the base line and the third range east of the principal meridian is called "township 4 north, range 3 east." (See Diagram 2.3)

Grid systems are identical across the country, so it is necessary to include in the description the particular principal meridian which is being used as a reference. (Since each principal meridian has its own base line, it is not necessary to refer to the latter.) It is also good practice to mention the county and state where the land is situated so as to avoid any possible confusion. Thus a complete description of a township is T4N, R3E of the "X" meridian, Smith County, State.

Each township measures 36 square miles and contains 36 sections, each 1 square mile. (See Figure 2.4) Smaller parcels of land can be identified by reference to sections and partial sections, as illustrated. (See Diagram 2.5)

GOVERNMENT LOTS

A government lot is a parcel of land of irregular shape or size which is referred to by a number. Because of the curvature of the earth, the convergence of range lines, and errors, it is impossible to keep all sections exactly one mile square. The sections along the north and west boundaries of each township are irregular in size. The quarter sections along the north and east boundaries of these sections are used to take up the excess or shortage. The quarter quarters, then, along the north and west boundaries of a township are given lot numbers.

Government lots may also result when a body of water or other obstacle prevents surveying an accurate square-mile section.

Principal meridian: the major north/south line in a rectangular survey grid

Base line: the major east/west line in a rectangular survey grid

Township tiers: rows of land (running east/west) in a rectangular survey

Ranges: columns of land (running north/south) in a rectangular survey

Township: the parcel of land located at the intersection of a range and township tier that measures 36 miles by 36 miles

Government lot: an irregularly shaped lot referred to by number in a rectangular survey

FIGURE 2.1

There are three principal meridians (original north/south lines) in California. Each principal meridian has its own base line (original east/west line).

UNITS OF MEASUREMENT FOR LAND	
UNITS OF AREA	1 Tract = 24 mi. × 24 mi. (576 sq. mi.) = 16 townships 1 Township = 6 mi. × 6 mi. (36 sq. mi.) = 36 sections 1 Section* = 1 mi. × 1 mi. (1 sq. mi.) = 640 acres 1 Acre = 43,560 sq. ft. = 160 sq. rods 1 Square Acre = 208.71 ft × 208.71 ft.
UNITS OF LENGTH	1 Mile = 5,280 ft. = 320 rods = 80 chains 1 Rod = 16½ ft. 1 Chain = 66 ft. = 4 rods

* Note: To determine the area of partial sections, simply multiply the fraction of the section by 640. For example,

    1 half-section = ½ × 640 = 320 acres
    1 quarter-section = ¼ × 640 = 160 acres
    1 quarter-quarter section = ¼ × ¼ × 640 = 40 acres

FIGURE 2.2

Range Lines
Township Lines
Mt. Diablo Meridian
Base Line

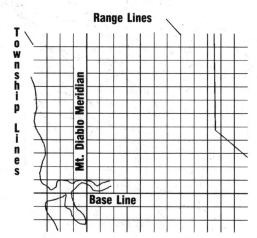

East/west lines are "Township lines," north/south lines are "Range lines."

FIGURE 2.3

Mt. Diablo Meridian
Base Line

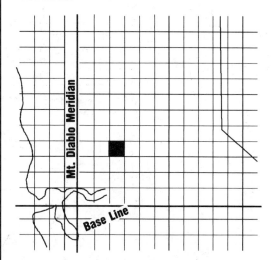

Township 4 North, Range 3 East

FIGURE 2.4

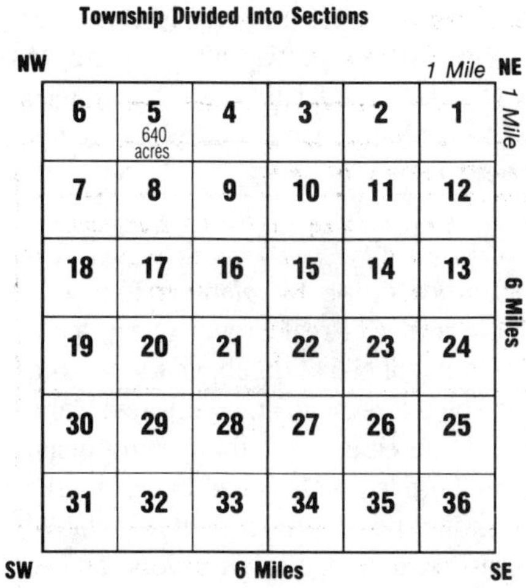

Township Divided Into Sections
NW
1 Mile
NE
1 Mile
6 5 4 3 2 1
640 acres
7 8 9 10 11 12
18 17 16 15 14 13
19 20 21 22 23 24
30 29 28 27 26 25
31 32 33 34 35 36
6 Miles
SW
6 Miles
SE

A Township contains 36 Sections.

FIGURE 2.5

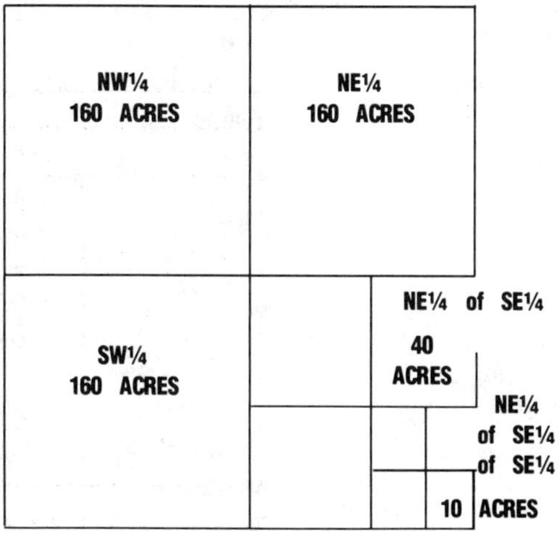

NW¼ 160 ACRES
NE¼ 160 ACRES
SW¼ 160 ACRES
NE¼ of SE¼
40 ACRES
NE¼ of SE¼ of SE¼
10 ACRES

A Section can be divided up into smaller parcels.

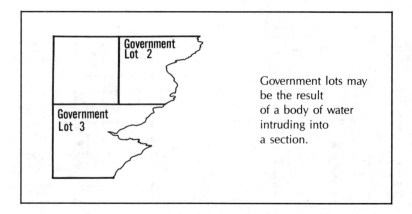

Government lots may be the result of a body of water intruding into a section.

OTHER METHODS OF DESCRIPTION

There are other methods of describing land besides the three major systems discussed above. Any time an adequate description of property is already a matter of record, e.g., contained in a recorded deed, then a simple reference to the instrument containing the description is adequate to describe the land. Also, generalized descriptions such as "all my lands" or "Smith Farm" or "123 A St." can be sufficient if they enable an unambiguous determination of what property is being described. However, a cautious dealer in real estate will always prefer to use the least ambiguous description possible, since to do so is insurance against future problems. It should be noted that street addresses are not acceptable descriptions in many states.

AIR LOTS

Datum: an established plane of elevation used in describing a particular elevation above the ground

Bench mark: a subsidiary reference point to a datum

Not all real property can be described simply by reference to a position on the face of the earth. Some forms of real property, e.g., condominiums, require description in terms of elevation above the ground as well. These descriptions are made by reference to an established plane of elevation, called a datum. Most large cities have their own official datum, and frequently subsidiary reference points called bench marks are also established. A bench mark is a point whose position relative to a datum has been accurately measured. Thereafter, surveyors can use the bench mark as a reference when it is more convenient than the datum.

CHAPTER SUMMARY

1. All valid deeds must contain an adequate description of the land being conveyed. An adequate description is one that allows a precise determination of the property being referred to. To be sure the description used is adequate, it is best to use the property's legal description. There are three major types of legal description: lot and block, metes and bounds, and government survey.

2. The lot and block method describes land by referring to a lot number on a plat map that has been filed with the county recorder. Because the plat map contains a detailed description of the land, simple reference to the plat map is sufficient.

3. The metes and bounds method describes land by a series of courses and distances. It starts at a defined "point of beginning" and then describes the boundaries of the parcel until an enclosed tract of land has been described. A metes and bounds description is usually quite lengthy and is often confusing. Particular care must be used to refer to monuments (e.g., the old oak tree) that will maintain their location over time.

4. The government survey (or rectangular survey) describes land by reference to a series of grids. The original north/south lines of the grid are called "principal meridians," the original east/west lines of the grid are called "base lines." The overlapping lines create 36 square mile parcels called "townships." Each township is in turn made up of 36 sections. Each section is one square mile. Smaller parcels of land can be described by referring to portions of sections, e.g., the NW ¼ of the SW ¼ of Section 17.

CHAPTER 2—QUIZ
LAND DESCRIPTION

1. A section of a township contains the following number of acres:

   a) 360
   b) 580
   c) 640
   d) 560

2. If a quarter section faced a road, how many square, one acre lots could be sold along one side of the section?

   a) 20
   b) 13
   c) 12
   d) 24

3. What percentage of a section would equal 1/60 of a township?

   a) 60%
   b) 70%
   c) 80%
   d) 90%

4. What part of a section measures ¼ of a mile by ¼ of a mile?

   a) 1/4 of a section
   b) 1/8 of a section
   c) 1/16 of a section
   d) 1/36 of a section

5. Choose the correct legal description.

   a) Section 6, T. 6S, R. 6N
   b) Section 10, T. 8S, R. 4W
   c) Section 16, T. 6S, R. 2N, H. B & M
   d) Section 20, T. 18N, R. 8E, H. B & M

6. How far is it between the boundary lines of a township?

   a) 6 miles
   b) 60 miles
   c) 1 mile
   d) 2 miles

7. Sections in a township are numbered consecutively 1 through 36. The first section in the township would be located in the:

   a) southeast corner
   b) southwest corner
   c) northeast corner
   d) northwest corner

8. Which of the following is the largest area:

   a) 10% of a township
   b) three sections
   c) two miles square
   d) 5,280' x 5,280'

9. How many 50' by 110' lots could be obtained from an acre of land?

   a) 6
   b) 10
   c) 9
   d) 7

10. How wide is a four-acre easement that runs along the western edge of a section?

    a) 33 feet
    b) 55 feet
    c) 66 feet
    d) 88 feet

11. If you combined the E½ of the W½ of the NE¼ of Section 8 and the S½ of the N½ of the NW¼ of Section 10, how many acres would you have?

    a) 20
    b) 40
    c) 60
    d) 80

12. Section 6 in a township is:

    a) next to section 22 in the adjacent township
    b) due south of section 23 in the same township
    c) an inside section of the same township
    d) part of the west boundary of the same township

13. How many acres in an area of land which measures 330 by 660 feet?

    a) 2
    b) 25
    c) 16
    d) 5

14. What is the distance around the boundaries of a section?

    a) 21,220 ft.
    b) 10,560 ft.
    c) 21,120 ft.
    d) None of the above

15. An area of 1 square mile is equal to a:

    a) township
    b) tract
    c) section
    d) quarter section

16. Lot 17 of Benton Addition, City of Topanga would be part of what type of legal description?

    a) Township survey
    b) Metes and bounds
    c) Plat map
    d) Condominium

17. The government survey system utilizes a grid of:

    a) North and south lines called meridians
    b) East and west lines called parallels
    c) Both a) and b)
    d) Neither a) nor b)

18. When describing a compass direction in a metes and bounds description, it is customary to:

    a) measure the number of degrees the angle deviates from north or south
    b) measure the deviation of the angle from east or west
    c) use magnetic north as a basis for measurement
    d) describe degrees as a bearing from 0 degrees through 180 degrees

19. How many miles separate section 2 from section 35 in township 6 south, range 2 east, Humboldt Meridian?

    a) Two
    b) Four
    c) Seven
    d) Three

20. In a recorded plat, the lots are described by:

    a) distances and courses
    b) reference to townships
    c) lot and block number
    d) None of the above

21. A column of townships running north and south is called:

    a) a tier
    b) a range
    c) a section
    d) None of the above

22. Land description by measurement and direction is called description by:

    a) metes and bounds
    b) recorded plat
    c) government survey
    d) None of the above

1. c) A section of a township contains 640 acres.

2. c) A quarter section measures ½ mile on each side, which is equal to 2640 feet. A square acre measures 208.71 feet on each side for a total area of 43,560 sq. ft. 208.71 divided into 2640 goes slightly more than 12 times.

3. a) There are 36 sections in a township, so one section equals 1/36 of a township.
   % × 1/36 = 1/60
   % = 36/60
   % = 60%

4. c) A section is one mile on each side. A quarter section is ½ mile on each side. A quarter-quarter section measures ¼ mile on each side and is equal to 1/16 of the area of the section. (¼ × ¼ = 1/16)

5. d) A government survey description must refer to the principal meridian that is being used. Townships are counted to the north and south of the baseline; ranges are counted to the ease and west of the principal meridian.

6. a) A township measures 6 miles on each side.

7. c) Township sections are numbered across and down in snake-like fashion, starting from the NE corner of the township.

8. c) 10% of a township is 3.6 square miles. 3 sections is 3 square miles. 2 miles square is 4 square miles. 5,280' × 5,280' is 1 square mile.

9. d) A 50' × 110' lot contains 5500 square feet. An acre contains 43,560 square feet. 5500 divided into 43,560 goes more than 7 but not quite 8 times.

10. a) Four acres equals 4 × 43,560 square feet, a total of 174,240 square feet. A section is one mile (5,280 feet) on each side. Area equals length times width, so 174,240 = 5,280 × width. Dividing 174,240 by 5,280 gives the answer 33 feet.

11. d) A section is 640 acres; a quarter section is 160 acres. Half of half of a quarter section is ½ × ½ × 160 = 40 acres. Twice that amount is 80 acres.

12. d) Section six is in the northwest corner of the township.

13. d) 330 × 660 = 217,800 square feet. An acre is 43,560 square feet. 217,800 divided by 43,560 equals 5.

14. c) A section is one mile (5,280 feet) on each side. 4 × 5,280 = 21,120.

15. c) A section is one square mile.

16. c) Subdivision descriptions refer to lot numbers on a recorded plat.

17. c) In the government survey, land is described by reference to north/south meridians (also called range lines) and east/west parallels (also called township lines).

18. a) Compass bearings in metes and bounds descriptions are given relative to north or south, whichever is closer.

19. b) Section 2 is on the north boundary of the township. Section 35 is below it on the south boundary. Four one-mile wide sections lie in between.

20. b) Lot and block numbers are used to identify lots on a subdivision plat.

21. b) A range is a north/south column of townships that is between two consecutive range lines.

22. a) Metes and bounds descriptions describe boundaries by course (direction) and distance.

Chapter 3

ALIENATION

OUTLINE

  I. Wills
    A. Types of wills
    B. Terminology
    C. Probate procedures
 II. Intestate Succession and Escheat
III. Accession
    A. Accretion
    B. Reliction
    C. Avulsion
    D. Fixtures
 IV. Adverse Possession
    A. Requirements
        1. actual, open and notorious
        2. hostile
        3. claim of right or color of title
        4. continuous
        5. property taxes
    B. Perfecting title
  V. Transfer
    A. The patent
    B. Dedication
    C. Decisions of the court
    D. Condemnation
    E. Deeds
        1. requisites of a valid deed
        2. types of deeds
        3. recording

KEY TERMS

alienation	will
probate	intestate succession
escheat	accession
accretion	reliction
avulsion	fixtures
adverse possession	patent
dedication	quiet title action
partition action	foreclosure action
condemnation	inverse condemnation
grant deed	warranty deed
special warranty deed	quitclaim deed
recording	indexing
constructive notice	

CHAPTER OVERVIEW

A property owner may choose to transfer property by any one of several different methods, such as selling to an arm's length buyer or leaving it to heirs in a will. However, property may also be transferred involuntarily, as in a sheriff's foreclosure sale or when the property has been condemned. This chapter describes the various types of transfer and what is required for each.

INTRODUCTION

Alienation: the process of transferring title of property from one person to another

The process of transferring ownership of real property from one party to another is called **alienation**. California statutes provide for five methods of alienation:

- will
- succession
- accession
- occupancy
- transfer

Alienation may be either **voluntary** or **involuntary**. Voluntary alienation includes transferring property by will or deed. Involuntary alienation (a transfer of property without any action by the owner) can be the result of rules of law, accession or occupancy (the process of adverse possession).

WILLS

The will (or testament) is a common form of voluntary alienation. California recognizes two basic types of wills:

- the formal witnessed will,
- the will written and signed in the maker's own handwriting (holographic will).

A witnessed will must be signed by the person making the will in the presence of at least two witnesses. The witnesses must also sign an acknowledgement that the maker declared the document to be his or her will. A holographic will is only valid if the main provisions are in the maker's own handwriting. Provisions that are typewritten or pre-printed will be disregarded when a court interprets a holographic will.

TERMINOLOGY

The person making the will is called the **testator** (male) or **testatrix** (female). A testator **bequeaths** personal property to legatees and **devises** real property to devisees. An amendment to a will is called a **codicil**. The directions contained in the will are carried out by an **executor** (or **executrix**) who is named in the will, under the supervision of the **probate** court. Probate is the procedure by which a will is proved valid and its directions carried out.

WILL TERMINOLOGY

**Testator/
Testatrix:** one who makes a will

Bequeath: transfering personal property by will

Devise: transfering real property by will

Codicil: amendment to a will

**Executor/
Executrix:** carries out directions in a will

Probate: procedure to prove a will's validity

PROBATE PROCEDURES

Probate: the process of administering a will

A transfer of real property by will (to the beneficiaries or to a third party) must have the approval of the probate court. In California, these courts are the superior courts. If property in the estate is sold, the sale is usually in the form of a public auction. Note that all commissions involved with the sale of real property from an estate are subject to approval of the superior court.

INTESTATE SUCCESSION AND ESCHEAT

Intestate succession: when a person dies without a will, his or her estate is distributed according to a statutory schedule

When a person dies without leaving a will (intestate), the law provides for the division of his or her property by a process called intestate succession. In general, separate property passes first to the surviving spouse, and children, then to various other relatives. Community property passes to the surviving spouse. Persons who take property by intestate succession are called **heirs**. Intestate succession is supervised by the probate court (superior court). The probate court appoints an administrator to carry out the statutory distribution of the property.

Escheat: if a person dies without heirs, his or her property goes to the state

If a person dies intestate and no heirs can be found, the property of the decedent reverts to the state by the process of **escheat**. Two years after the decedent's death, the Attorney General may bring a court action and have the property sold. Since the state is the ultimate source of title to property, it is also the ultimate heir when no intervening interested parties exist.

ACCESSION

Accession: additions to property by natural or human means

Accession is any addition to real property resulting from natural or artificial causes. "Accession" includes:

- accretion,
- reliction,
- avulsion, and
- the addition of fixtures.

ACCRETION

When riparian or littoral land is enlarged by waterborne soil deposits (called alluvion or alluvium), the riparian or littoral owner acquires title to the new land. A key feature of accretion is that the build-up of soil must be gradual and imperceptible.

RELICTION

When riparian or littoral land is enlarged by the retreat of the body of water, the riparian or littoral owner acquires title to the newly exposed land. Like accretion, the retreat of the waterline must be gradual and imperceptible. Reliction is also called dereliction.

AVULSION

Avulsion is the violent tearing away of land by flowing water or waves, or as a result of a sudden change in a watercourse. Avulsion does not transfer title; the severed land still belongs to its original owner. Erosion, by contrast, refers to the gradual wearing away of soil due to the action of wind or water.

FIXTURES

Articles of personal property may be converted to real property if they are affixed to land so as to indicate an intent to make them part of the realty. An exception is the case of an improvement made in error. If a person makes an improvement on the land of another in the mistaken but good faith belief that he or she has a right to do so, then the improver may remove the improvement upon payment of damages to the true owner or other interested party.

ADVERSE POSSESSION

Adverse possession is the process by which the possession and use of property matures into title. The law of adverse possession recognizes that the use of land is important. It encourages land use by providing that a property user may eventually attain an interest in the property paramount to that of an owner who does not use the property. The precise requirements for obtaining title by adverse possession vary from state to state and are usually described in state statutes. These requirements are often highly technical and they must be followed exactly in order to obtain title. Legal counsel should be obtained in transactions where title may be affected by adverse possession.

Adverse possession: obtaining title through open and continuous possession

REQUIREMENTS

There are five basic requirements for adverse possession in California. Possession of the land must be:

1) actual, open and notorious;
2) hostile to the owner's interest;

3) under claim of right or color of title;

4) continuous for five years.

5) The claimant must pay the property taxes during the 5 years.

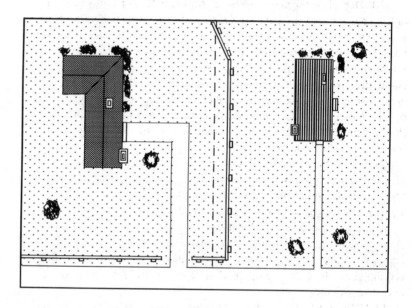

USE OF PROPERTY CAN MATURE
INTO TITLE BY THE PROCESS OF
ADVERSE POSSESSION

ACTUAL, OPEN AND NOTORIOUS. Actual possession means occupation and use of the property in a manner appropriate to the type of property. It does not require residence on the property unless residence is an appropriate use. Thus actual possession of farmland may be achieved by fencing the land and planting crops, while actual possession of urban property would require a residential or commercial use of the property. The requirement of "open and notorious" possession means that the possession must be such as to put the actual owner on notice that his or her interest in the property is being threatened. In essence, this requirement is the same as the actual possession requirement. Actual possession may be defined as a use constituting reasonable notice to the world that the adverse possessor claims ownership of the property.

HOSTILE. The adverse possessor must intend to claim ownership of the property and defend that claim against all parties. Hostile intent is proven by the adverse possessor's actions. If the adverse possessor uses the property in the same fashion as an owner would use it, then hostile intent exists. Hostile intent is also proven by **color of title**, which is the adverse possessor's good faith but mistaken belief that he or she is the owner of the land. An example of an adverse possessor with color of title is one who takes possession under an invalid deed. Note that the hostility requirement cannot be satisfied if the possession is with the permission of the actual owner.

CLAIM OF RIGHT OR COLOR OF TITLE. This requirement is virtually identical to the "hostility" requirement. The adverse possessor must claim title to the property as his or her right, based on either the fact of possession or a defective written instrument (color of title).

An adverse possessor with color of title may acquire title to all the property described in the defective instrument, even if he or she occupies only part of the property. A claimant without color of title can acquire good title only to property that he or she actually occupies, e.g., encloses, cultivates, etc.

CONTINUOUS. Continuous possession is that degree of occupancy and use of property which would be expected of an average owner. Intermittent use of land may be continuous if appropriate to the type of property, for example, seasonal farmland or summer resort property. However, if possession is interrupted by the true owner for the purpose of regaining possession, the continuity is broken. Continuous possession must be maintained for 5 years before the adverse possessor gets an ownership interest.

PROPERTY TAXES. The adverse claimant must pay all taxes levied and assessed during the 5 year period of occupation. Payment of taxes by the true owner may prevent acquisition of title by adverse possession.

PERFECTING TITLE

Since the adverse possessor's interest is not of record, he or she must take additional steps to acquire marketable title. Marketable title can be acquired by a quitclaim deed from the true owner, but the more common procedure is to bring a quiet title action. Note that title to government property can never be acquired by adverse possession.

TRANSFER

Property can be acquired by transfer by one of several means. The most common method is by deed. Other methods include patents, dedication, court decisions and condemnation.

THE PATENT

Title to all real property originates with the sovereign government. The government holds absolute title to all lands within its boundaries, except for what it grants to various other entities or persons. The process whereby title to land is first passed from the government to a private party is known as a patent. The patent is the ultimate source of title for all lands under private ownership.

DEDICATION

Dedication: giving private property to the public

Dedication is the transfer of real estate from private ownership to public use. Although dedication is commonly accomplished by a voluntary act of the grantor, in many cases the conveyance is made under the constraint of law. While a dedication may be the result of purely philanthropic motives, more often it is done in exchange for a benefit from the public entity which is the grantee.

> **Example:** the dedication of land for streets and utility easements in exchange for permission to subdivide a tract.

Such dedications are called **statutory dedications** because they are prescribed by statute and must be accomplished in compliance with the relevant statutory procedure, found in the Subdivision Map Act.

A second type of dedication is that which arises by common law, called **common law dedication**. The usual requirement for such a dedication is the grantor's acquiescence in the public use of his or her property for a prolonged period of time. Common law dedication may also occur if a public entity passes an ordinance accepting an implied dedication. Common law dedications need not be in writing because they are a result of the grantor's actions.

DECISIONS OF THE COURTS

Title to property can be conveyed by court order in accordance with state statutes and the precedents of the common law. The most common forms of court action are the quiet title action, the suit for partition, and foreclosure.

QUIET TITLE ACTION. The quiet title action is used to remove a cloud on the title when the title cannot be cleared by the more peaceable means of a quitclaim deed. The court makes a binding determination of the various parties' interests in a particular piece of real estate.

SUIT FOR PARTITION. A suit for partition is a means of dividing property held by more than one person when the owners cannot agree among themselves how to divide the property. The decision of the court is conclusive as to the parties involved. Frequently the court will order the property sold and the proceeds divided among the co-owners.

FORECLOSURE ACTIONS. Persons holding liens against real property may force the sale of the property if the debt secured by the lien is not paid. Foreclosure is available for any type of lien that attaches to real property, including mortgages, deeds of trust, mechanics' liens and judgment liens. The court will order the sheriff to seize the debtor's property and sell it at auction (sheriff's sale, tax sale, execution sale). The buyer at the auction receives a certificate of sale which ripens into title if the debtor does not redeem the property within a specific time period, usually one year.

EXECUTION SALE. When a property is sold to satisfy a court judgment, the court issues a writ of execution authorizing the seizure and sale of the debtor's property.

CONDEMNATION

Under the Constitution, the government has the power to take private property for public use. However, the government must give just compensation to the owner of the condemned property. The government's power to condemn (take) property is called the power of eminent domain. The two essentials for exercise of this power are:

- the use must be a public use, and
- the condemning entity must pay just compensation.

Public use is considered to be roughly equivalent to public benefit. In cases of mixed public and private benefit the question is more difficult, but it may be safely said that there is no authority for the government to take one person's land for the sole purpose of turning it over to another person.

Just compensation means that the condemning agency must pay the fair market value of the property. The power of eminent domain may be exercised by any government and also by some semi-public entities such as public utility companies.

INVERSE CONDEMNATION. If a property owner feels that his or her property has been taken or damaged by a public entity, he or she may

Inverse condemnation: an action brought by a private citizen to get the government to pay just compensation for damaged or taken property

bring a suit called an inverse condemnation action. The purpose of this action is to force the government to pay the fair market value of the taken or damaged property.

THE DEED

The most common form of voluntary alienation is by deed. A deed is a document whereby the owner of real property, called the **grantor**, conveys all or part of his or her interest in the property to another party, the **grantee**. The process of alienating real property by deed is known as conveyancing. Thus a grantor conveys real property to a grantee by means of a deed.

REQUISITES OF A VALID DEED. To be valid, a deed must:

- be in writing,
- describe the parties,
- be signed by a competent grantor,
- contain words of conveyance (the granting clause), and
- contain an adequate description of the property.

A deed must be **in writing** and be **signed by the grantor** in order to satisfy the requirements of the Statute of Frauds. The Statute of Frauds requires any transfer of an interest in real property (with a few minor exceptions) to be in writing and signed by the party to be bound by the transfer.

The deed must also **identify the grantee**. The grantee need not be a competent party, he or she need only be alive (or legally in existence in the case of a corporation). The name of the grantee is not required so long as an adequate description of the grantee is given, for example, 'John Smith's only sister'.

If there is more than one grantor, all of the grantors must sign the deed. Thus, if a prior deed named several grantees, all of them must sign as grantors of a new deed. The signature of the grantor's spouse is often required in order to release statutory marital interests in real property (e.g., community property rights). For this reason, it is a good idea (although not required) to state the grantor's marital status in the deed and to obtain the spouse's signature if the grantor is married.

A grantor must be **legally competent** in order to execute a valid deed. Competency means that the grantor is legally an adult and is sane. Any deed signed by an incompetent grantor is void. (Note: the grantee need not be legally competent to obtain title under a deed.)

The requirement of **words of conveyance**, the granting clause, is easily satisfied. One word—"grant"—or something of similar meaning is sufficient in this regard. Additional technical language usually does more harm than good and should be avoided since it adds nothing to the validity of the deed. Note that a quitclaim deed should not use the word grant; a term such as quitclaim or release should be employed to preclude the implication of warranties.

A valid deed must contain an **adequate description of the property** to be conveyed. A legal description is not required. Generally, a description is adequate if it enables a surveyor to locate the property. Ambiguous descriptions are not sufficient, but they may be clarified by the parties.

Although not essential to the validity of the deed, there are certain terms which should be included when they are applicable. The deed should state the nature of the interest the grantor is conveying (for example, fee simple or life estate). Where not specified, the grantor's entire interest is presumed to pass to the grantee. The nature of the respective interests of multiple grantees should also be specified (for example, tenants in common or joint tenants). The nature of the multiple interests is usually stated in a separate clause called an habendum clause.

A VALID DEED

I hereby grant	. . . . words of conveyance
Greenacres Farm	. . . . description of property
to Enos Palmer.	. . . . identifiable grantee
(signed) Sam Smith	. . . . signature of competent grantor
	. . . . in writing

ACKNOWLEDGMENT, DELIVERY AND ACCEPTANCE. In addition to the requirements for a valid deed, there are further requirements in order to effect a proper conveyance. Conveyance requires a valid deed, plus acknowledgment,* delivery and acceptance.

Acknowledgment is the process by which the grantor attests to witnesses that his or her signature is genuine and made voluntarily. The witness is normally a notary public, but may not be a person who has an interest in the transfer.

---

* While not strictly required, acknowledgment is a practical necessity since it is often the only way to prove the validity of the grantor's signature.

A deed becomes effective and title passes to the grantee when the deed is **delivered**. Delivery is more than mere physical transfer of a document; it is words or conduct manifesting the grantor's intent to make an immediately effective transfer of an interest in land. The grantor's intent is the controlling issue, not the method of delivery. Because of the complexity of legal doctrines employed in this area, advice of counsel should always be sought when there is a question as to the sufficiency of delivery. Conveyance is completed when the grantee accepts delivery of the deed.

NON-ESSENTIAL TERMS. A recital of the purchase price (consideration) is not essential to a valid deed, but it is helpful because it results in a presumption that the transaction was a purchase rather than a gift. The grantee of a gift deed is vulnerable to certain claims of the grantor's creditors and does not receive the same protection from recording statutes that is accorded to a purchaser. A recital of consideration is usually phrased as 'for $1.00 and other valuable consideration'.

Other items which are not essential to the validity of a deed are the date of conveyance, the grantee's signature, the grantor's seal (in most cases), warranties and technical terminology. 'I hereby grant Greenacres Farm to Enos Palmer. (signed) Sam Smith' is a valid deed, assuming that Sam Smith is legally competent.

TYPES OF DEEDS. There are many different types of deeds, but the ones which are used most often are the grant deed, quitclaim deed, trustee's deed and deed executed under court order.

The **grant deed** is the most commonly used deed in California. A grant deed uses the term 'grant' in its words of conveyance and contains two warranties:

Grant deed: a deed that warrants that the grantor has not already conveyed title to the property and has not caused encumbrances to attach to the property; the most commonly used deed in California

- the grantor has not previously conveyed title to anyone else, and
- the grantor has not caused any encumbrances to attach to the property other than those already disclosed.

Additional warranties and covenants may be stated in the deed if the parties so desire. The grant deed also conveys to the grantee all after-acquired title of the grantor.

Example: The grantor, Smith, conveyed title to Blackacre to White. In truth, Smith did not own the title to Blackacre, but then obtained title after the purported conveyance to White. The interest later acquired by Smith (title to Blackacre) passes automatically to White under the original deed.

The deed which provides the greatest protection to a purchaser of real estate is the **warranty deed**, also known as the general warranty deed. The grantor in a warranty deed makes five basic covenants (promises). These covenants have the effect of warranting against defects in the title which arose either before or during the grantor's tenure (period of ownership). Warranty deeds are seldom used in California, since even greater protection is available through the use of title insurance.

The **special warranty deed** also contains the five covenants found in the general warranty deed, but the scope of the covenants is limited to defects which arose during the grantor's tenure. The grantor makes no assurance regarding defects which existed before his or her tenure. The grantor only warrants that he or she has not caused any defects in the title. This type of deed is employed most often by entities which do not have the power or authority to make further warranties (e.g., corporations).

WHEN RECORDED MAIL TO: FOR RECORDER'S USE ONLY:

John and Mary Investor
123 Center Street
Berkeley, California 94705

Grant Deed

FOR VALUE RECEIVED, *SYNDICATION ASSOCIATES* (hereinafter called "Grantor"), *a California corporation*, **grants to** *JOHN INVESTOR* **and** *MARY INVESTOR* **(hereinafter collectively called "Grantee"), as** *joint tenants*, **all that certain real property located in the City of** *Berkeley*, **County of** *Alameda*, **State of California (hereinafter called the "Property"), more particularly described** *in Exhibit A, attached hereto and incorporated herein by reference thereto.*

IN WITNESS WHEREOF, Grantor has executed this Grant Deed this   *3*   day of   *November*   , 1982.

"Grantor"
SYNDICATION ASSOCIATES
By_____   Its   *President*
By_____   Its   *Secretary*

MAIL ALL TAX STATEMENTS TO GRANTEE AT:
123 Center Street, Berkeley, California 94705

Quitclaim Deed

GRANTING CLAUSE:
Quitclaims, Releases, Remises

ADEQUATE DESCRIPTION:
Legal description preferred but not necessary

CAPABLE GRANTEE:
Live person (natural or artificial)

WARRANTIES:
None. Will convey whatever interest grantor has, which may be none.

_____
Grantor

* Quitclaim Deed is designed primarily to remove clouds from title.

Quitclaim deed: a deed without warranties most often used to cure technical defects in the title

The **quitclaim deed** contains no warranties of any sort and gives the grantee protection only against claims made by the grantor. A quitclaim deed conveys only the interest the grantor has when the deed is delivered. Thus, it may convey nothing at all if the grantor has no interest at that time. But if the grantor does have an interest in the property, the quitclaim deed will convey that interest equally as well as any other type of deed. The usual reason for using a quitclaim deed is to **cure clouds on the title**. These are defects which normally result from technical flaws in an earlier conveyance, such as a misspelling of one of the parties' names or an error in the description of the estate. A quitclaim deed is also used when the grantor is unsure of the validity of his or her title and wishes to avoid any warranties in that regard.

Example: a grantor who holds title by virtue of an inheritance which is being challenged in probate court. If the grantor wants to transfer the property, he or she will probably use a quitclaim deed.

Care should be taken in the preparation of such deeds because using such terms as 'grant' or 'convey' may imply that the grantor has warranted the title. A quitclaim deed should employ only terms such as 'release', 'remise' or 'quitclaim' to describe the transfer of the estate.

When a trustee conveys property, he or she uses a **trustee's deed** which contains a provision stating that the conveyance is in accordance with the trustee's powers and responsibilities under the trust.

Court-ordered deeds take a variety of forms, depending on the laws of the state where the property is located. These deeds are only executed after a court-ordered sale of property; therefore they should state the exact amount of the purchase price (consideration) which was approved by the court. A common example of a deed executed under court order is the sheriff's deed.

RECORDING

Recording is a procedure designed to protect purchasers of real property from the secret claims of other parties. State statutes provide that an interest which is recorded is superior to one which is not recorded. Thus a purchaser can discover the nature and extent of all interests in the property simply by examining the records. The purchaser can then protect his or her own interest by recording it and thereby giving notice of his or her claim to the world.

> Recording: filing an instrument affecting real property with the county recorder in the county where the property is located; protects the interest of the party filing

The California recording system is of the race/notice type. If a seller sells land to one buyer and then sells it again to a second buyer, the second buyer can get good title to the property if he or she records his or her interest first. The second buyer must not have any knowledge (notice) of the first buyer's interest. If the first buyer is the first to record or if the second buyer has actual or constructive notice of the first sale, then the first buyer will get the property.

INDEXING. Recording is accomplished by filing a copy of the deed at the office of the county recorder in the county where the property is located. Documents pertaining to certain federal land may be recorded at the Bureau of Land Management. The recorder indexes the deed according to grantor and grantee, and in some cases according to tract as well. These indices serve as the basis for title searches. A purchaser can search the grantor index to determine if the seller has already conveyed the interest to another party. The purchaser will also search the grantee index to discover the source of the grantor's title, and trace the title back through a chain of title (successive grantors and grantees) that is long enough to ensure the validity of the grantor's title.

> Indexing: listing recorded documents according to grantee, grantor, or tract

GRANTEE-GRANTOR INDEX

WINGET   **G 07**

GENERAL INDEX · INDIRECT · COUNTY, STATE

6,741   01/04/88 · 06/30/88

DATE & NO.	GRANTEES	GRANTORS	RECORDED INSTRUMENT	REMARKS	LOT	BLOCK	LEGAL DESCRIPTION ADDITION
88-01-12-0409	WINGET Charles & Agnes B	Driscoll, Frank Etux	W Deed	MF			27 26 27
88-04-26-1006	Ralph Eugene & Kathleen Mary	Shockley,FrederickEtux	W Deed	MF	03		Short Plat 107701412
88-06-21-0881	WINGROVE Philip C. & Ida D. Etal	Seattle First Natl. Bank	F Reconvy	MF			SEE 850327-0261
88-01-29-0022	WINIECKI Robert D. & Katherine L. Etal	Mason McDuffie Mtg. Corp.	F Reconvy	MF			SEE 830802-0833
88-01-19-0801	WINING Vernon K. & Glenna E. Etal	Household Finance Industrial LN CO, III	F Reconvy	MF			SEE 860519-0072
88-06-30-0964	WINKEL David J. & Sharon A.	Harrington, David Etux	W Deed	MF E100858	TRS 22, 39-43 PT		
88-04-20-1164	Mearl A. & Mary C.	Elmer, Gary Etux	W Deed	MF E995787			22 25 05
00-04-12-0365	WINKELMANN German J. & Zlato B.	Mears, Annabelle M.	W Deed	MF	03	04	Lake Hills No. 23

GRANTOR-GRANTEE INDEX

DOUTHIT   **B 12**

GENERAL INDEX · DIRECT · COUNTY, STATE

6,741   01/04/88 · 06/30/88

DATE & NO.	GRANTORS	GRANTEES	RECORDED INSTRUMENT	REMARKS	LOT	BLOCK	LEGAL DESCRIPTION ADDITION
86-05-08-0572	DOUTHIT David T. & Norma A.	Pioneer Federal Savings Bank Etal	D of TR	MF			SEE DOCUMENT
85-05-08-0572	David V. Etal		Agreement	MF			In Sec. 10 24 05
85-11-27-0479	David V. Etal	Bankers Life Co. Etal	DT with asgn	MF			SEE DOCUMENT
85-11-27-0480	David V. Etal	Bankers Life Co.	ASN RNT & LE	MF			SEE DOCUMENT
85-12-04-0571	David V. Etal	Eastgate Sewer District	Bill of Sale	MF			SEE DOCUMENT
85-12-04-0572	David V. Etal	Eastgate Sewer District	Bill of Sale	MF			SEE DOCUMENT
85-12-04-0573	David V. Etal	Eastgate Sewer District	Easement	MF	01PT		Lincoln Executive Cntr
86-01-17-0851	David V. Etal		Easement Agr	MF	TR A		80-12R
86-04-10-0207	David V. Etal	First National Bank Menneapolis Etal	DT with Asgn	MF			SEE DOCUMENT
86-06-12-0705	Maury E. Jr. & Pamela P. Etal	Citicorp Homeowners Inc Etal	D of TR	MF			SEE DOCUMENT
85-05-29-0147	Maury & Pamela	Sanderson, C. Bevitt Etal	D of TR	MF			SEE DOCUMENT
86-06-12-0705	Maury & Pamela Etal	Citicorp Homeowners Inc Etal	D of TR	MF			SEE DOCUMENT
86-07-16-1536	DOUTHITT Robert H. & Dianne L. Etal	Hedeen, Richard Etux	F Reconvy	MT			SEE 820728-0647
85-04-09-0673	DOUTHWAITE John Etal	Washington Natural Gas Co.	UCC Filing	MF	12	09	Eastgate Add Div K
86-07-22-0538	DOUTLICK Deborah J.	Rainier Financial Services Co. Etal	D of TR	MF	09-10	17	Overland Park Add

Because of the grantor/grantee system of indexing, it is possible that a deed could be recorded in such a way that a title search would not discover it.

> **Example:** Suppose Smith gives a deed to Jones, who does not record his interest. Jones then conveys to Baker, who promptly records. If Smith then makes another conveyance of the same property to Walker, Walker will not be able to discover Baker's interest because Baker is not in Smith's chain of title. There is a break in the chain of title between Smith and Baker because the connecting interest was not recorded.

The general rule in these situations is that the subsequent purchaser (Walker) is not charged with constructive notice of deeds (called wild deeds) which are not in the chain of title.

Almost any document which affects title to land may be recorded, including deeds, mortgages, contracts, judgments or notices of legal proceedings against property (called lis pendens). A deed must be acknowledged before it can be recorded (primarily in order to protect against forgeries) and it must include an address where property tax bills can be sent. Also, the Federal Fair Housing Act prohibits the recording of any deed which contains a racially restrictive covenant.

EFFECT OF RECORDING. Recording has two significant consequences. Most importantly, it gives constructive notice of the recorded interest to all subsequent purchasers, and thereby prevents such purchasers from becoming bona fide purchasers. Constructive notice is notice which would have been discovered had it been looked for.

Recording also creates a presumption that the recorded instrument is valid and effective. Recording will not serve to validate an otherwise invalid deed, nor will it protect against interests which arise by operation of law, such as adverse possession.

Constructive notice: "notice to the world"; everyone is assumed to have knowledge of recorded documents, regardless of whether they actually do

---

CHAPTER SUMMARY

1. A property owner transfers ownership of property to another person through a process called alienation. Alienation may be either voluntary or involuntary. California recognizes five methods of alienation: by will, succession, accession, occupancy and transfer.

2. When a person dies, his or her real property transfers to others under a will or by the rules of intestate succession. When a person dies without a will, they are said to have died intestate. Property from an estate is transferred under a will through the probate process. The property is distributed according to the terms of the will under the jurisdiction of the probate court. Property of an intestate person is distributed to his or her heirs according to state statute, also under the jurisdiction of the probate court. If a person leaves no heirs, the property escheats to the state. (Voluntary and involuntary alienation)

3. Ownership of property may be transferred by accession (involuntary alienation). Accession actually refers to the addition to real property by various natural or artificial means. These means include accretion, reliction, avulsion, and fixtures.

4. Adverse possession is another way of acquiring title to property (involuntary alienation). Adverse possession is a means by which a person may acquire title to property by using it openly and continuously for five years.

5. Property may be alienated by transfer—by dedication, court decision, condemnation, or deed. By deed is the common way of voluntarily transferring property. To be valid a deed must be in writing, describe the parties, be signed by a competent grantor, contain words of conveyance, and contain an adequate description of the property. The most common type of deed in California is the grant deed. For property to be conveyed, there must be a delivery and acceptance as well as a valid deed. Once the deed is delivered and accepted, it should be recorded to protect the interest of the new owner.

CHAPTER 3—QUIZ
ALIENATION

1. Which of the following is NOT capable of receiving title by means of a deed?

   a) Incompetent
   b) 17 year old
   c) Infant
   d) None of these

2. Which of the following is essential to a valid deed?
   a) Must be in writing
   b) Parties must be competent to convey and capable of receiving grant of property
   c) There must be a granting clause
   d) All of these

3. Which of these is NOT essential to the validity of a deed?
   a) Consideration
   b) Competent grantor
   c) Description
   d) Capable grantee

4. Of the following, which would cause a deed to be void?
   a) Grantee is fictitious person
   b) It was signed by a mark
   c) Grantee used an assumed name
   d) None of these

5. After Carson dies, a will and deed are found in his safe; the deed is made out to his church; the will does not mention his house. Therefore, the church should be concerned with:

   a) acknowledgement
   b) delivery
   c) statute of frauds
   d) statute of limitation

6. Mr. Brown and Mrs. Brown owned some land as community property. Mrs. Brown wanted a niece to inherit her share of the property when she died, but did not want to tell her husband. So she made out a proper grant deed conveying her interest to her niece, with her signature duly acknowledged, and gave it to a close friend who agreed to hand it over to the niece after Mrs. Brown's death. Mrs. Brown died and the friend carried out the instructions. The deed was:

   a) invalid for lack of proper delivery
   b) invalid, since she could not deed her interest in community property
   c) valid because the friend could testify to Mrs. Brown's intent
   d) valid, since the deed was delivered to a close relative after the grantor's demise

7. A quitclaim deed is most commonly used to:

   a) cure title defects
   b) give notice to the world
   c) give after-acquired title
   d) None of the above

8. There are implied warranties by the grantor in a grant deed. One of the following is NOT among them.

   a) Property has not been encumbered by grantor except as disclosed
   b) The interest being conveyed has not previously been conveyed to others
   c) The interest held by grantor is being transferred
   d) The grantor holds a certificate of title

9. Bequeath is to personal property as devise is to:

   a) bill of sale
   b) real property
   c) transfer of title
   d) deed

10. A will entirely written in the testator's own hand-writing is called a:

    a) holographic will
    b) nuncupative will
    c) intestate will
    d) witnessed will

11. Probate means an action to:

    a) cure a defect by a quitclaim deed
    b) prove title by adverse possession
    c) process a will to establish its validity
    d) obtain access to a safe deposit box

12. Broker Green sold real property belonging to an estate being probated. The amount of her commission was determined by:

    a) her exclusive listing
    b) the court
    c) the executor
    d) the probate code

13. Recording of instruments which transfer or encumber real property does NOT:

    a) give constructive notice of an instrument's contents
    b) create a presumption of delivery
    c) give actual notice of an instrument's contents
    d) give priority over subsequently recorded instruments

14. The purpose of recording a real estate contract is to:

    a) establish responsibility for payment of property tax
    b) assure payment of excise tax
    c) serve notice to the world of buyer's interest
    d) establish priorities of subsequent liens

15. The most commonly used deed in California is the:

    a) quitclaim deed
    b) warranty deed
    c) grant deed
    d) trust deed

16. Involuntary alienation of an estate means:

    a) no person can be compelled to transfer title without his consent
    b) aliens are forbidden to own estates in fee simple
    c) ownership of estates may be transferred by operation of law
    d) None of the foregoing

17. If Matthews dies intestate, his property would:

    a) be distributed according to his will
    b) be distributed to his heirs
    c) escheat to the county where the property is located
    d) go to his church

18. When a person dies intestate and no heirs can be found for intestate succession, his real property will revert to the state through a process known as:

    a) reconveyance
    b) reversion
    c) escheat
    d) succession

19. Possession under a claim of adverse possession must be:

    a) open and notorious
    b) hostile
    c) continuous
    d) All of these

20. George Crow, owner of a tract of land, occupied ten feet over on Delbert's land because he was mistaken about the true boundary. During this adverse occupation, Delbert notified Crow that he was a trespasser. The period for adverse possession passed and Delbert now sues Crow.

    a) Crow now owns the subject ten feet
    b) Delbert continues to own the land since he gave effective notice to Crow
    c) Crow must pay Delbert the reasonable value of the ten feet
    d) Crow can occupy only one-half of the ten feet, or five feet

1. d) Grantors must be sane and at least 18 years old to give up their title, but a person need only be alive in order to be capable of receiving title.

2. d) A valid deed must have: written form, granting clause, capable grantee, adequate description, and competent grantor.

3. a) There must be a competent grantor, description, and a capable (alive) grantee. No consideration need be stated in the deed.

4. a) The grantee in a deed must be a living person; a fictitious person is not living.

5. b) Since the deed was not delivered during Carson's lifetime, no valid delivery was made.

6. a) A deed cannot be delivered after the death of the grantor. There was no proper delivery.

7. a) While a quitclaim deed may convey title, should the person conveying the land have title, these deeds are generally used to cure title defects, such as to correct a faulty legal description.

8. d) These "implied warranties" or guarantees are considered by law to be a part of the deed, even though they are not stated.

9. b) Personal property is bequeathed and real property is devised by will.

10. a) A holographic will is one whose main provisions are in the testator's own handwriting, rather than typewritten or preprinted. It is valid even though it is unwitnessed.

11. c) Probate is an action by the superior court to establish the validity of a will.

12. b) The court determines the compensation but usually will allow the customary rate. The executor or administrator cannot bind the estate, or give an exclusive listing.

13. c) Actual notice is notice that has really (actually) come to the awareness of someone else.

14. c) One of the effects of recording may be the establishment of priority over subsequent liens, but the purpose of recording is to give notice to the world (constructive notice) of the buyer's interest.

15. c) Most California conveyances are in the form of a grant deed.

16. c) Involuntary alienation of an estate means the transfer of ownership by operation of law. Examples include eminent domain and foreclosure procedures.

17. b) When one dies intestate, his or her property is distributed to the heirs; if there are no known heirs, the property escheats to the state.

18. c) The transfer to the state of real property of a person who died intestate and had no heirs is known as escheat.

19. d) The requirements for title by adverse possession are open and notorious use; use hostile to the will of the owner; continuous use for five years; the adverse possessor must also pay the taxes during this period and be in possession of the property under claim of right or color of title.

20. a) Crow owns the land because his possession was open, notorious and hostile to the will of the owner. Delbert should have taken legal action to have Crow removed before the statute of limitations expired.

ESTATES IN LAND

OUTLINE

I. Estates
   A. Freehold estates
      1. fee simple estates
      2. defeasible fee
      3. life estates
   B. Less-than-freehold estates
      1. estate for years
      2. periodic tenancy
      3. tenancy at will
      4. tenancy at sufferance
II. Methods of Holding Title
   A. In severalty
   B. Concurrently
      1. joint tenancy
      2. tenancy in common
      3. community property
      4. other methods

KEY TERMS

estate
less-than-freehold estate
defeasible fee
leasehold estate
periodic tenancy
tenancy at sufferance
concurrent ownership
tenancy in common

freehold estate
fee simple absolute
life estate
estate for years
tenancy at will
severalty
joint tenancy
community property

tenants in partnership   corporations
syndicates   real estate investment trusts

CHAPTER OVERVIEW

There are many different types of interests in and methods of owning property. Property may be owned solely by one individual or jointly by more than one. The owner or owners may hold all rights and title to the property, or only own certain specified and limited rights. The type of ownership or the nature of an interest in property affects how the property may be used, encumbered, and transferred. This chapter explains the various types of ownership interests and their accompanying rights or obligations.

Real estate law, especially in the area of estates in land, is full of unusual and often strange-sounding terminology. Terms that were used hundreds of years ago are still firmly entrenched in today's real estate language. While these words may sound foreign and be a little difficult to grasp at first, don't be discouraged. The concepts are fairly easy to understand and, with a little practice, you'll be able to use these ancient legal terms with ease.

ESTATES

Estate: an ownership interest in real property

The term "estate" generally refers to an ownership interest in real property. An interest in land may vary in degree, quantity, nature, duration or extent and there are different types of estates for each different type of ownership interest.

An estate (or ownership interest) is measured in terms of duration and whether the interest is possessory now or will become possessory in the future. "Possessory" means the holder of the estate has a right to use and possess the property now or sometime in the future.

All estates are interests in land, but not every interest in land is an estate.

> **Example:** A mortgage gives a lender a financial interest in the property, a lien, but such an interest is not an estate. The lien is not an ownership interest because it is not possessory.

Estates fall into two categories:

- freehold estates, and
- less-than-freehold estates

A freehold estate is an interest in real property that has an indeterminable (not fixed or certain) duration. The holder of such an estate is usually referred to as an owner. All other possessory interests are leasehold (less-than-freehold) estates. A leasehold estate has a limited duration, such as a lease for one year. The owner of a leasehold estate is referred to as a tenant; the owner of the leasehold has possession of the property but not title.

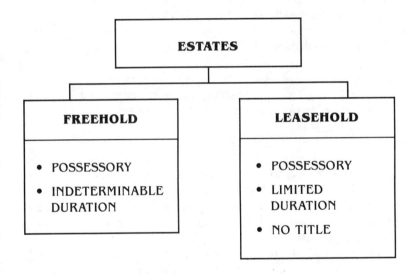

FREEHOLD ESTATES

The freehold estate got its name back in the Middle Ages. It originally referred to the holdings of a freeman under the English feudal system during the reign of William the Conqueror. Freehold estates can be subdivided into fee simple estates and life estates.

FEE SIMPLE ESTATES. The fee simple estate, also called the "fee," the "fee simple," or the "fee simple absolute" is referred to as the **estate of inheritance**. It is the largest estate that can exist in land. It is the highest and most complete form of ownership. It is of potentially infinite duration and represents the whole "bundle of rights."

Freehold estate: an interest in property of indeterminable duration; a possessory interest

Fee simple absolute: the largest ownership interest possible; of potentially infinite duration and freely transferable

- A fee simple gives the owner the right to create lesser estates.
- It is freely transferable and inheritable.
- The estate has no prescribed termination date, and theoretically can be owned in perpetuity by the titleholder and his or her heirs.

In contrast, another freehold estate is the life estate, the duration of which is measured by the life of one or more persons. The life estate terminates upon the death of the measuring life, while the fee simple absolute estate is perpetual.

When a fee simple owner passes title by deed, will, or otherwise, it is presumed that the grantee (new owner) receives a fee simple absolute interest unless there is language incorporated into the deed which indicates the intent of the grantor to confer a lesser estate.

DEFEASIBLE FEE OR FEE SIMPLE QUALIFIED. Estates may be qualified by their grantors. For example, a grantor may, in transferring an estate, specify that it will continue only until the happening of a particular event.

> **Example:** Able conveys Blackacre to "Barney and his heirs so long as it is used for church purposes and when it is no longer used for church purposes it shall revert back to Able or his heirs."

A qualification like this creates what is called a qualified fee estate. The owner of the qualified fee holds the same interests as the owner of the fee simple estate, but the qualified fee holder's interest may be terminated on the occurrence of a specified event. A qualified fee may be referred to as a base fee, fee simple subject to a condition subsequent, or conditional fee.

LIFE ESTATES. An estate for life is a freehold estate that is limited in duration to the life of a specified person or persons.

> **Example:** Noel gives Blackacre to Beatrice for her lifetime, calling for a reversion of title to Noel on her death. Beatrice is the life tenant (holder of the life estate), and the duration of the life estate is measured by her lifetime.

The measuring life may be that of the grantee—in this instance Beatrice—or the life of another. Suppose, for example, Angie gives Blackacre to Howard for the life of Charlie. Howard has a life estate which will end with the death of Charlie.

Defeasible fee: a freehold estate that may terminate on the happening of certain stated conditions

Life estate: a freehold estate that is measured by the life of one or more persons

The fee simple estate is a perpetual estate; the life estate is a lesser estate because it is limited in duration, i.e., it will terminate with the death of the measuring life. Since the fee simple owner, in giving the life estate, only gives an estate of limited duration, there must necessarily be a portion of the estate which remains after the life estate terminates. This remaining portion is called the estate in reversion or the estate in remainder.

Estate in Reversion. If the grantor stipulates that the property will revert to him or her at the end of the measuring life, the grantor holds an estate in reversion. The grantor has a future possessory interest in the property. On the death of the person whose life the estate is dependent upon, the estate will revert to the grantor or his or her heirs.

Estate in Remainder. If the grantor stipulates the property should go to a person other than him or herself on the death of the life tenant, that other person has an estate in remainder and is called the remainderman. The only difference between reversion and remainder estates is that the former is held by the grantor (or the grantor's heirs) and the latter by a third party.

The remainderman has a future possessory interest in the remainder which is transferable and inheritable. The interest that will pass to the designated party on the death of the life tenant is a fee simple estate.

The life tenant has the same rights as the fee simple absolute owner, including the right to profits or rents, and the right to lease or mortgage the property. Similarly, the life tenant has the same duties as the fee simple owner: to pay taxes, assessments and liens. But the life tenant also has certain additional duties which are created by the fact that there is someone with a future possessory interest in the property:

- The life tenant must not commit waste, which means that the life tenant must not engage in acts which will permanently damage the property, and harm the interests of the reversionary or remainder estate.
- The life tenant must also allow for the reasonable inspection of the property by the remainderman, who is permitted to check for possible waste or destruction of the property.

The life tenant may transfer or lease his interest in the property, but it should be noted that the life tenant can only give, sell, or lease that which he or she has. In other words, a lease given by a life tenant will terminate upon the death of the person designated as the measuring life. It need not be honored by a remainderman. Similarly, a mortgage on a life estate loses its status as a valid lien upon the death of the person named as the measuring life.

LESS-THAN-FREEHOLD ESTATES

Less-than-freehold estate: a leasehold estate; the holder has the exclusive right to possession

Less-than-freehold estates are more commonly known as leasehold estates. The holder of the leasehold estate is the tenant, who does not own the property, but rather has a right to exclusive possession of the property for a specified period of time.

The leasehold is created by a contract called a lease. The parties to a lease are the landlord (lessor), who is the owner of the property, and the tenant (lessee), the party with the right of possession. The lease creates the relationship of landlord and tenant. It grants the right of exclusive possession for a specified period of time to the tenant, with a reversion of the possessory rights to the owner at the end of the rental period. The lease is a contract and its provisions will be interpreted under contract law.

TYPES OF LEASEHOLD ESTATES. The four most important leasehold estates are:

- estate for years
- periodic tenancy
- tenancy at will, and
- tenancy at sufferance.

Estate for years: a leasehold estate of a fixed duration

Estate for Years. The estate for years is a tenancy for a fixed term. Its name is misleading in the sense that the duration need not be for a year or a period of years; it must only be for a <u>fixed term</u>.

> **Example:** Bob rents a cabin in the mountains from Clark for a period from June first through September fifteenth. Bob has an estate for years because the rental term is fixed. Since the rental term is fixed, the lease will terminate automatically on the expiration of the rental period.

Neither party is required to give notice to terminate the lease agreement. As with most contracts, the lease is assignable by the tenant. If either party wants to terminate the lease before the end of the lease period, they may do so but only by mutual consent. The termination of a lease by mutual consent is called **surrender**.

Periodic tenancy: a leasehold estate that continues for a period of time, continually renewing itself for similar periods of time until terminated by proper notice

Periodic Tenancy. A periodic tenancy, also known as an estate from year to year, is an estate which continues for one year or a fraction of a year (quarter, month, week, or day), and for successive similar periods, until terminated by either party by proper notice. The required notice is often the same as one of the successive periods, e.g., one month for a month-to-month tenancy. The periodic tenancy continues for an indefinite length of time and is without a specific expiration date.

The periodic tenancy is often created by a tenant taking possession of property without agreeing to a definite termination date. The most important characteristic of a periodic tenancy is that it automatically renews itself. Unlike the estate for years, which automatically terminates, the periodic tenancy continues automatically until one of the parties gives notice to terminate. Failure to give proper notice will result in the automatic extension of the lease for an additional period. The periodic tenancy is also assignable unless prohibited by the terms of the lease agreement.

Tenancy at Will. The tenancy at will is usually created after a periodic tenancy or estate for years has terminated. This tenancy is created with the agreement of both parties and can be terminated at the will of either. A tenancy at will is often used when a lease has expired and the parties are in the process of negotiating the terms of a new lease.

Tenancy at will: a leasehold estate that exists indefinitely until notice to terminate is given

The term of the lease is indefinite and will continue until either party gives proper notice to terminate. Thirty days' notice of termination is required in California. Note, however, that unlike the estate for years or periodic tenancy, which are not affected by the death of the landlord or tenant, the tenancy at will automatically expires upon the death of either the landlord or tenant. Also, the estate is not assignable.

Tenancy at Sufferance. The tenancy at sufferance is not really an estate in land. "Tenancy at sufferance" is a term used to describe a situation where a tenant lawfully comes into possession of the property under a valid lease, but holds over after the tenancy has expired. The tenant continues in possession of the premises, but without the consent of the landlord.

Tenancy at sufferance: not an estate; a situation where the "tenant" originally takes possession of the property lawfully but stays on without the owner's consent

> **Example:** Joe has a one-year lease with Landlord Sam. At the end of the term, Joe refuses to move out. Joe initially obtained possession of the property legally (under a valid lease), but is remaining on the property without the consent of Sam.

The tenancy at sufferance is simply a way to distinguish between a tenant who lawfully entered into possession of real property and who holds over without consent and a trespasser who never had permission to enter the land. Because the tenant has no possessory right in the land, this form of possession does not rise to the level of an estate and there is no need to give notice to terminate. However, the landlord still cannot forcibly evict the tenant; the proper legal procedures for eviction (serving notice, a court hearing, and removal by a legal authority) must be followed.

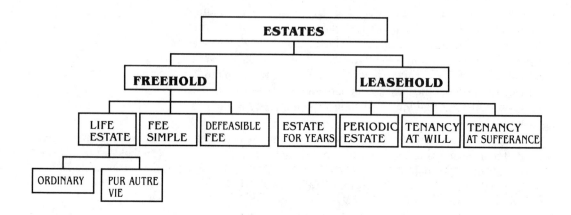

METHODS OF HOLDING TITLE

Title to real property may be held by one person, called ownership in severalty, or it may be held by two or more persons at the same time, called concurrent ownership.

SEVERALTY

Severalty: when title to property is held by one entity

If a person holds the title to property individually, the property is owned in severalty. The term is derived from the word "sever," which means to keep separate or apart. A sole owner is free to dispose of the property at will. Real property may be owned in severalty by natural persons (human beings) or artificial persons (including corporations and cities and states).

CONCURRENT

Concurrent ownership: when title to property is held by more than one entity

Concurrent ownership (also called co-ownership) exists where two or more people simultaneously share title to a piece of property. There are several forms of concurrent ownership, each with distinctive legal characteristics. The most common forms of concurrent ownership are:

- joint tenancy
- tenancy in common
- tenancy in partnership, and
- community property.

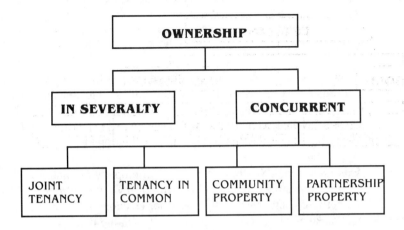

JOINT TENANCY. A joint tenancy exists where two or more persons are joint and equal owners in certain real property. Only one title exists and it is vested in two or more persons. The most distinguishing feature is the **right of survivorship**, which means that on the death of one of the joint tenants, his or her interest passes by operation of law to the other joint tenant(s). To create a joint tenancy, the "four unities of title" must exist. These unities are the:

- unity of interest
- unity of title
- unity of time, and
- unity of possession.

These four unities signify that each joint tenant has an equal interest in the property (unity of interest), that each received the title through the same deed or will (unity of title), which was executed and delivered at one time (unity of time), and that each holds undivided possession of the property (unity of possession). If any one of these unities does not exist when the tenancy is created or if one is broken during the tenancy, the joint tenancy either is not established or will cease to exist.

Each joint tenant has an equal interest in the property and an equal right to possess (occupy) the entire property. Therefore, use by a particular joint tenant cannot be confined to any specific part of the property.

Joint tenancy: co-ownership created with unities of interest, title, time and possession; most important characteristic is right of survivorship

Example: Two joint tenants own the property fifty-fifty; each has the right to possess and use the whole property at any time. One joint tenant cannot exclude the other from any part of the property.

The most distinctive feature of the joint tenancy is the right of survivorship. Since the title passes directly to the other joint tenant(s) upon the death of one joint tenant, the deceased's interest may not be devised (to devise is to give real property by will). That is, the heirs of the deceased joint tenant have no interest in the joint tenancy property.

Example: Jones, Smith, and Brown own property as joint tenants. Jones dies. Smith and Brown now own the entire property fifty-fifty. Neither the heirs nor creditors of Jones can make any legal claim to the property. On her death, it ceased to be a part of her estate. Accordingly, the property is not subject to probate and could not have been willed by Jones.

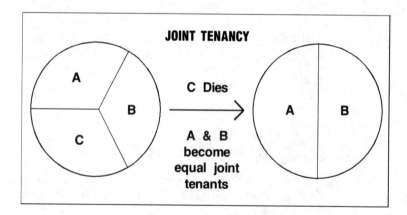

Termination of Joint Tenancy. A joint tenancy is terminated when any one of the four unities is destroyed. A joint tenant is not prevented from conveying his or her interest in the joint tenancy and may freely do so. However, the conveyance would destroy the unity of time and/or interest and terminate the joint tenancy with respect to the ownership of the conveying joint tenant.

Example: Bob and Jack own real property as joint tenants. If Bob conveys all of his interest to Mary, the joint tenancy between Bob and Jack will terminate. Since Mary and Jack did not receive their title through the same instrument or at the same time, they cannot be joint tenants. In fact, Mary will receive an undivided one-half interest as a tenant in common.

The advantage to holding property as joint tenants is that the title passes directly to the other joint tenant(s) upon the death of one joint tenant. In this way, the normal delays and costs caused by probate proceedings are avoided. Also, the survivors hold the property free from the debts of the deceased tenant and also from the liens against his or her interest. However, there are disadvantages, such as the fact that the joint tenant gives up the right to dispose of his or her property by will.

TENANCY IN COMMON. In contrast to the joint tenancy, there is but one unity to the tenancy in common: the right of possession. Each tenant in common owns an interest which may be unequal, but which is undivided. That is, there could be a 60/40 division of ownership between two tenants in common, but each would have an equal right to possess all the property. Regardless of the percentage of ownership, a tenant in common cannot be prevented from possessing the entire property and cannot be confined to any specific portion of the property. No tenant in common can be charged rent for the use of the land in possession.

Tenancy in common: co-ownership that is undivided but that can be unequal—only unity is unity of possession; no right of survivorship

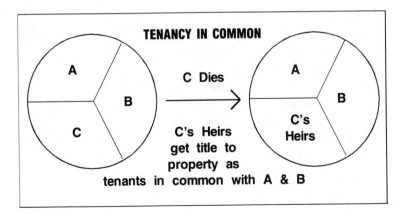

TENANCY IN COMMON

C Dies

C's Heirs get title to property as tenants in common with A & B

No right of survivorship attaches to the tenancy in common. Each tenant in common may transfer his or her title by will or deed. He or she may also mortgage his or her interest without the consent of the other owners. Such a transfer does not terminate the tenancy in common.

Termination of the Tenancy in Common. A tenancy in common may be terminated by a partition suit, a legal action that divides the interests in the property and destroys the unity of possession. If possible, a court will actually divide the land into separate parts. Often it is not possible to divide the property fairly, so the court orders the estate to be sold and the proceeds to be divided among the tenants in accordance with their fractional interests.

COMMUNITY PROPERTY. California is a community property state. The community property laws of California trace back to Spanish and Mexican origin, unlike the common law real property concepts followed by most states, which trace back to England. Basically, community property states recognize two types of property ownership: separate and community property. Community property is all property acquired during a valid marriage that is not separate property. Separate property is primarily property that is acquired before marriage, but also includes other property which will be discussed below.

Property acquired during marriage, other than separate property, is community property. Each spouse has a one-half interest in community property. This one-half interest is deemed to be the separate property of each spouse and thus may be devised by that spouse.

Separate property is defined by the Civil Code of California and includes the following:

- all property owned by either husband or wife before marriage.
- all property acquired by gift or inheritance during the marriage.
- the profits, rents, or proceeds acquired from the sale of separate property and any property purchased with such separate funds.
- earnings and accumulations of either spouse (and of minor children in his or her custody) while living apart from the other spouse.
- money damages awarded to either spouse in a civil action for personal injuries, if the action arose after an interlocutory decree of dissolution or decree of legal separation, or while living separately from the other spouse.

Example: The money in a husband's account deposited there before marriage is his separate property. If he does not deposit any funds in the account after marriage and then

Community property: property acquired and owned equally by husband and wife during marriage uses the money to buy stock, the stock is his separate property. He uses separate funds to buy the stock; thus, the stock is his separate property. The separate property money does not automatically convert to community property upon marriage.

Example: If the husband above deposited community funds, such as his paycheck, in the checking account after marriage, the account may be deemed to be community property. The husband has commingled community and separate property and if he uses money from the account, he will have the burden to show that separate funds were used. Similarly, if the husband transferred funds from his separate checking account into a joint or community account, such transfer would be deemed a gift to the community. Thus, all the transferred funds would be community property; the separate property identity would be lost by the transfer.

Management and Liability. The interest of the husband and wife in community property during marriage may be described as present, existing and equal, and the community property is under the equal control and management of both the husband and wife. Since both husband and wife control and manage equally, certain restrictions are placed on how they may treat community property, both real and personal.

The conveying, encumbering, or giving of community personal property is restricted by statute. Neither spouse may give away community personal property without the consent of the other spouse. Neither spouse may sell, convey or encumber furniture, furnishings or fittings of the home, or clothing or wearing apparel of the other spouse or minor children, without the written consent of the other spouse. Also, the selling, conveying, encumbering or leasing for a period over one year of any community real property or interests therein requires both the husband and the wife to join in the execution of the instrument.

The community property is subject to the debts of either spouse.

Disposition. When community property is conveyed, both the husband and wife must enter into the conveyance and both must sign the deed. If either spouse fails to sign, then the conveying spouse can only convey that which he or she owns (i.e., a one-half interest in the property). Thus, such a conveyance is not of the entire property and the conveyance may be set aside later. If a spouse is conveying separate property or his or her one-half interest in the community property to the other spouse, the conveying instrument should contain a recital that the property is intended to be the separate property of that other spouse.

The one-half interest each spouse has in community property may be disposed of by will. Upon the death of either spouse, a one-half interest in the community property automatically passes to the surviving spouse. If the deceased dies with a will (testate), his or her one-half interest will pass according to the terms of the will. However, if the deceased dies without a will (intestate), the surviving spouse will receive the decedent's one-half of the community property; that is, the surviving spouse will take all of the community property. The separate property of each spouse will pass either by the terms of the will or, if no will exists, by the rules of intestate succession.

Dissolution and Community Property. California is not a "divorce on grounds" state; a spouse need not prove such elements as cruelty or adultery in order to dissolve a marriage. California is a dissolution state and the only bases for a dissolution are "irreconcilable differences" or "incurable insanity." When a marriage is dissolved the general rule that courts follow is to divide the community property equally. This equality in division does not occur in every situation and there are a number of exceptions. The court has discretionary power to make unequal distributions if justice so requires.

> **Example:** One spouse is operating an on-going business. The court, in its discretion, may award the business to the spouse who runs it and award a cash interest in the business to the other spouse, or award the other spouse a greater share of other community property, or offset the difference in a variety of other ways.

OTHER FORMS OF JOINT OWNERSHIP. The law also recognizes other types of joint ownership in the form of a variety of legal entities, such as:

- partnerships
- corporations
- joint ventures
- syndicates
- real estate investment trusts
- condominiums, and
- cooperatives.

Syndicates. A syndicate generally consists of numerous individuals who pool their financial resources together to acquire real estate for income production, resale at a profit, or both. The syndicate, as such, is not a recognized legal entity. The underlying ownership is usually in the form of a limited partnership, although a syndicate's property may be held in a variety of ways, such as by a corporation, a general partnership, or in trust. The form of ownership is usually based on tax considerations and the consequences for the parties involved.

Syndicates are generally interested in large and expensive pieces of property to be used for development, investment or speculation. The participants range from individuals to other legal entities such as corporations. The interest of each member is usually limited to a fixed share or a percentage, depending upon the particular arrangements that are made.

Partnership. A partnership is generally defined as an association of two or more persons, to carry on, as co-owners, a business for profit. There are two types of partnerships:

- general, and
- limited.

The duties and liabilities of a general partnership are controlled by the Uniform Partnership Act, as adopted by California. Similarly, limited partnerships are controlled by the Uniform Limited Partnership Act.

A partnership is contractual. Although the agreement need not be in writing, it is wise to spell out the terms in a written agreement. If the agreement is not in writing, the partnership will be governed by the terms of the Uniform Partnership Act. However, if the agreement is in writing, the terms of the written agreement will govern rather than the terms of the Uniform Act.

The partners in a **general partnership** all share in the profits, debts and management of the partnership as tenants in partnership. Each partner has an equal interest in and right to equal possession of the partnership property for partnership purposes. The partners' interests in the profits and losses are also equal unless otherwise agreed to in the partnership agreement. Also, each partner is both a principal for and an agent of the partnership for business purposes. Thus, most of the acts of a partner, including the execution of legal documents and instruments, will be binding on the partnership. Needless to say, the partners are fiduciaries of one another; they have duties of utmost good faith in their dealings with one another.

The partnership may acquire property in the partnership's name, which subsequently must be conveyed in that name. In general, all

Syndicates: numerous individuals who pool their resources to engage in a profitable real estate transaction.

Tenants in partnership: partnership property is owned equally by the partners property brought into the partnership or acquired by or on account of the partnership is partnership property, and therefore subject to partnership obligations. The partnership property is not open to the claims of the creditors of the individual partners, but only to the creditors of the partnership. However, each partner is personally liable for the partnership's debts; a creditor of the partnership can make a claim against an individual partner's property.

A **limited partnership** is a partnership with one or more general partners, who have unlimited partnership liability and an exclusive right to manage the partnership, and one or more limited partners. Limited partnerships are strictly statutory creations under the Uniform Limited Partnership Act.

The limited partner has personal liability only to the amount of the limited partner's capital contribution. The limited partner has no voice in management. In fact, if a limited partner does take part in the day-to-day control of the business, he or she will be managing the business and may be held liable to the same extent as a general partner. Thus, the limited partner should be cautious about his or her participation in the business.

Corporate property: owned by the corporation itself, not by the stockholders of the corporation

Corporations. Corporations are in almost every sense creatures of the state. They are artificial, legal persons composed of individuals who are empowered to conduct business as one person, the corporation. The corporation is a separate entity from its stockholders; it is capable of perpetual existence and the death of stockholders does not affect its operation. The corporation, not the stockholders, owns the corporate property and controls the daily management functions. The stockholders' liability is limited and the stockholders own only an intangible and transferable right to share in the profits and surplus of the corporation.

Joint Venture. A joint venture is similar to a partnership except it is created for a single business transaction or for a series of individual transactions. It is not intended to be a continuous business of indefinite duration. Joint ventures are generally governed by the same rules as partnerships. An example of a joint venture would be a property owner, an architect and a building contractor joining together to design and construct a particular building.

Real Estate Investment Trusts (REIT's). Real estate investment trusts are authorized by the Internal Revenue Code of 1960 and are supervised by the Corporations Commissioner. The investment trust invests in real estate and real estate mortgages exclusively. Since the trust is unincorporated, it avoids corporate taxation. The trust is only taxed on its retained earnings, provided that 90% or more of its income is distributed to the shareholders; thus, large distribution of its income to its shareholders avoids any significant taxation to the trust. The trust is advantageous because small investors can take advantage of big investment opportunities by pooling resources, and because it provides potentially higher returns from diversified investments.

COMMON FORMS OF JOINT OWNERSHIP

	Joint Tenancy	Tenancy in Common	Community Property
Creation Presumed:	no	yes	yes
Equal possession:	yes	yes	yes
Equal interest:	yes	no	yes
Right of survivorship	yes	no	no
Ability to convey own interest:	yes	yes	no

CHAPTER SUMMARY

1. An estate is an ownership interest in real property. There are two major types of estates: freehold and less-than-freehold. A freehold estate is a possessory estate that also transfers title to the property; a less-than-freehold estate transfers possession, but no title (e.g., a month-to-month lease).

2. An estate can be held in different ways, namely, in severalty and concurrently. Ownership in severalty is ownership by one person or entity. Joint or concurrent ownership is ownership by two or more persons or entities.

3. The major types of concurrent ownership are joint tenancy (with the right of survivorship), tenancy in common (no right of survivorship), community property (ownership between spouses), and tenancy in partnership.

CHAPTER 4—QUIZ
ESTATES IN LAND

1. The right to possess real property and have exclusive use of that property is best defined as:

   a) equity
   b) an estate
   c) sole proprietorship
   d) ownership

2. An estate of inheritance is known as:

   a) a freehold
   b) less than a freehold
   c) greater than a freehold
   d) None of these

3. Which of these is a freehold estate?

   a) Estate at will
   b) Life estate
   c) Estate for years
   d) Leasehold

4. Which of the following is not a characteristic of a fee simple estate?

   a) Freely transferable
   b) Freely inheritable
   c) Definite duration
   d) Unlimited duration

5. Which of the following is true?

   a) A fee simple estate is a freehold estate
   b) An estate for years is not considered a freehold estate
   c) A life estate is a freehold estate
   d) All of the foregoing are true

6. A qualified fee is:

   a) a sale of land with a number of easements
   b) a sale for a particular use or purpose (school or church) and where such use is ended, the property reverts to grantor
   c) tenure by adverse use until real owner brings court action to reclaim title
   d) a term in description of land acquired by patent

7. A conveyance of title with the condition that the land shall not be used for the sale of intoxicating beverages creates:

   a) a less-than-freehold estate
   b) a defeasible estate
   c) an estate on condition precedent
   d) reservation

8. Bates conveys a fee simple title to the Avon Baptist Church, so long as it is used for church purposes. In 1974, the church abandons the property, due to environmental changes. Title to the property will:

   a) remain in the church
   b) escheat to the state
   c) revert to Bates
   d) be owned by the church and Bates, as joint tenants

9. "C" grants an estate to "B" for the life of "X". "B" dies. The estate:

   a) ceases to exist
   b) reverts to the original owner
   c) vests in "X" in trust until "C's" death
   d) passes to heirs of "B"

10. By will, Calhoun devises his property to his daughter, Mary Calhoun, for life, and at her death to "her children." At Calhoun's death, Mary, 30 years of age and unmarried, deeds a fee simple estate to Davis. The title is:

    a) valid
    b) invalid
    c) Davis obtains a fee tail estate
    d) Davis is a tenant

11. Mrs. Black inherited a life estate in the family home from her mother, with the provision that it go to the grandson in fee simple after her death. Which of the following is false?

    a) Mrs. Black can rent the home from month to month
    b) She can convey fee simple title to the lot but not the house
    c) She can mortgage her interest
    d) She can sell an interest in the title she holds

12. A wife signs a lease which leases community property for 9 months without the signature of her husband. The lease probably is:

    a) invalid
    b) unenforceable
    c) valid
    d) valid only if lessee did not know of the marriage

13. Community property is owned by:

    a) churches
    b) husband and wife
    c) the municipality
    d) the community council

14. A limited partner:

    a) is limited in his liability for debts of the partnership
    b) has unlimited liability for debts of the partnership
    c) is personally liable for the portion of partnership debts caused by actions of the general partner(s)
    d) is limited to a $5,000 investment in the business

15. Sole ownership by an individual is ownership:

    a) in common interest
    b) in gross
    c) in severalty
    d) in joint tenancy

16. Real property owned by a city or county, such as parks, school buildings, city hall, etc., is owned as:

    a) joint tenancy
    b) community property
    c) severalty
    d) tenants in common

17. Joint tenancy ownership to be effective must have:

    a) ownership of community interest
    b) unity of severalty, possession, occupancy and state
    c) mutual interest as tenants in common
    d) unities of interest, possession, time and title

18. One of the following is wrong or doesn't make sense. Joint tenants always have:

    a) equal right to use of the property
    b) the right to bequeath good title to heirs
    c) their interests during the same period of time
    d) exactly the same title to the property

19. Two brothers, John and Bill, owned valuable property left to them by their father as joint tenants. Both married later, and then Bill died intestate. His widow would acquire:

    a) no interest in the property
    b) half interest as joint tenant with John
    c) half interest as tenant in common
    d) one-quarter interest in the property

20. Mary and Tom Smith were joint tenants. Mary deeded her interest to Jack Jones. Jack Jones and Tom Smith are now:

    a) tenants in severalty
    b) partners
    c) survivorship tenants
    d) tenants in common

21. Which of the following would create a tenancy in common?

    a) One of three joint tenants dies
    b) A joint tenant wills property to a third person
    c) A joint tenant gives his interest to a third person
    d) None of the above

22. A co-owner's undivided interest without the right of survivorship is a:

   a) joint tenancy
   b) tenancy in common
   c) tenancy in severalty
   d) tenancy by the entirety

23. You own property as a tenant in common. You always have the unity of:

   a) time
   b) title
   c) interest
   d) possession

24. Concerning tenancy in common, which of the following is correct?

   a) Each party's interest must be equal
   b) Each tenant must acquire title at the same time
   c) Any party may sell without the consent of the others
   d) All of the above

25. A lease for a definite period of time is:

   a) a lease at will
   b) a fee simple
   c) an estate for years
   d) a tenancy at sufferance

1. b) An estate in real property is defined as the right to possess property and have exclusive use.

2. a) An estate of inheritance is a freehold estate; it is the largest type of estate possible.

3. b) There are two classifications of estates: freehold and leasehold. An estate at will and estate for years are leasehold estates, not of indeterminate duration like a freehold estate.

4. c) An estate that has a definite or limited duration cannot be a fee simple estate. For an estate to be a fee, it must be freely transferable, freely inheritable and of unlimited duration.

5. d) All of the foregoing are true.

6. b) A qualified or defeasible fee is a fee simple estate that will revert to the grantor when a condition is breached.

7. b) A defeasible estate is one that will be defeated upon the happening of a certain event.

8. c) As a conditional, defeasible estate, it will terminate when the condition is broken, and title will revert to the grantor.

9. d) Since the life estate is based upon the life of "X" it is not terminated by the death of "B". "B's" interest still exists and it would be transferred to his heirs.

10. b) Mary can only convey a life estate measured by the duration of her life. A fee simple estate is of indeterminate duration.

11. b) She holds no fee simple in the property to convey. She could sell the property to another for her lifetime. She holds a life estate and could only convey the same.

12. c) Both spouses need not sign the lease if it is for a term less than one year.

13. b) Community property is all property acquired during marriage that is not separate property.

14. a) Limited partners are liable for partnership debts only to the extent of their investment.

15. c) The legal term "severalty" means "sole, separate, and exclusive possession, dominion or ownership." An estate in severalty indicates sole ownership — by one person only.

16. c) Severalty is ownership by a single person or legal entity, including a city, county, or state.

17. d) We have mixed these up a little to confuse you, but the essentials are "time, title, interest and possession."

18. b) As the surviving joint tenant receives the interest of the deceased joint tenant, there is nothing for the latter to leave by will.

19. a) John would acquire full title to the property as he was joint tenant and Bill's interest was his separate property.

20. d) Because the unities of time and title are no longer present, Tom and Jack are tenants in common with an equal right to possession.

21. c) If a joint tenant transfers his or her interest to a third party, the unity of time and title will be broken. Unless otherwise provided, the new interest held would be a tenancy in common. A joint tenant cannot will his or her interest, as it goes to the surviving joint tenant(s) on his or her death.

22. b) Tenants in common have no right of survivorship; they may will their interest.

23. d) Tenancy in common is ownership by two or more persons who hold an undivided interest without the right of survivorship. Their interests need not be equal nor need they take title at the same time, but they always have an equal right to possession of the whole property.

24. c) In a tenancy in common, any party may sell without the consent of the others. He or she may also will his or her share without consent.

25. c) Any lease that is negotiated for a set period of time is known as an estate for years. This would include a lease for one week, two months, one year or ten years, etc.

ENCUMBRANCES ON LAND

OUTLINE

I. Encumbrances Defined
II. Financial Encumbrances (Liens)
   A. Types of liens
      1. mortgages
      2. deeds of trust
      3. mechanics' liens
      4. tax liens
      5. special assessments
      6. attachments
      7. judgment liens
   B. Lien priority
III. Non-Financial Encumbrances
   A. Easements
      1. easements appurtenant
      2. easements in gross
      3. creating an easement
      4. terminating an easement
   B. Private restrictions
      1. covenants
      2. conditions
IV. Encroachments
V. Homestead Law

KEY TERMS

encumbrance   voluntary lien
involuntary lien   general lien
specific lien   C, C, and Rs

materialman's lien   encroachment
attachment lien   mechanic's lien
easement appurtenant   easement in gross
dominant tenement   dominant tenant
servient tenement   servient tenant
easement by necessity   prescriptive easement
license   profit
homestead

CHAPTER OVERVIEW

After reading the preceding chapter, you are now aware that parties may own property or an interest in property without owning all rights to the property. An interest in property held by someone other than the property owner is called an encumbrance. Encumbrances may be purely financial, such as mortgages or tax liens, or they may affect the use of the property, such as easements and private restrictions. Difficulties may arise when an owner attempts to sell or transfer property which is encumbered. This chapter describes the various types of encumbrances and the effect they have on property.

ENCUMBRANCES DEFINED

Encumbrance: a right or interest in property held by someone other than the property owner

An encumbrance is a right or interest in real property held by someone other than the property owner. The interest can be financial or non-financial in nature. A financial interest affects title, a non-financial interest affects the use or physical condition of the property.

FINANCIAL ENCUMBRANCES (LIENS)

Voluntary lien: a lien arising with the consent of the landowner

A lien is a security interest in property. It is a charge against property giving a creditor the right to sell the property and use the proceeds to pay the debt if the debtor fails to pay it. The most common example is a mortgage lien.

Liens may be voluntary or involuntary. A **voluntary lien** is one which arises through the consent of the property owner. Examples of voluntary liens would be mortgages or trust deeds, where the landowner voluntarily places a lien against his or her property as security for a loan. **Involuntary liens** (sometimes called **statutory liens**) arise through operation of law without the owner's consent. An example of an involuntary lien would be a property tax lien.

Involuntary lien: a lien arising by operation of law; consent of the landowner is not required

---

ENCUMBRANCES

FINANCIAL	NON-FINANCIAL
• mortgages	• easements
• deeds of trust	• private restrictions
• mechanics' and materialmen's liens	• profits
• judgments	
• attachments	
• property tax liens	
• special assessments	
• other tax liens	

Liens may also be general or specific. A **general lien** is a lien which attaches to all of the debtor's property, such as a judgment lien. A **specific lien** attaches only to a particular piece of property. A mortgage is an example of a specific lien. It is a lien only against the particular parcel(s) of land offered as security for the loan.

General lien: a lien which attaches to all the property of the debtor

Specific lien: a lien which attaches only to the secured property

The right which a lien creates in favor of the creditor, that is, the right to have the property sold to satisfy the debt, is called a **security interest**. A creditor who has a lien against the debtor's property is called a **secured creditor**.

A lien does not prevent the owner from transferring the property, but the new owner takes the property subject to the existing lien.

TYPES OF LIENS

The following are some of the more common liens against real estate.

MORTGAGES. A mortgage is a specific, voluntary lien created by a contract between the landowner (the **mortgagor**) and the creditor (the **mortgagee**) in which the property owner gives the creditor a lien against property to secure payment of a debt. The essence of a mortgage is that the mortgagee can force the sale of the property if the mortgagor fails to pay the debt. This process is called **foreclosure**.

DEEDS OF TRUST. A deed of trust, or trust deed (also a voluntary, specific lien) is used for the same purpose as a mortgage. There are three parties rather than the two found in a mortgage transaction. The borrower is called a **trustor** or **grantor**; the lender or creditor is called

Mechanic's lien: a lien filed by one supplying either labor or materials in the construction of improvements

the **beneficiary**; and there is an independent third party (often an attorney or title insurance company) called the **trustee**. The deed of trust is the most commonly used security device in California.

MECHANICS' LIENS. These liens (involuntary and specific) are authorized by California statute. They are allowed in favor of persons who provide labor or materials that are used to improve real property. A common example would be a contractor who builds a house or other structure on a vacant lot. If the person who supplies labor or materials is not paid, he or she may put a lien on the property and, if necessary, force the sale of the property to have the debt paid. Any worker (including contractors, subcontractors, laborers and materialmen) can obtain a lien against real property by filing a notice of the claim at the office of the recorder in the county where the property is located.

The claim for the lien must be placed within a short period of time after the worker stops working. If a notice of completion or notice of cessation is properly filed by the owner, then mechanics' liens must be filed within **30 days** of the time the notice is recorded, except that an original or general contractor is given **60 days** to file. A **notice of completion** can only be filed within 10 days after a project is completed. A **notice of cessation** can only be filed at least 30 days after work on a project has stopped, for whatever reason. If neither notice is recorded, then all workers have **90 days** from the time work ceased on the project in which to file their lien claims.

If a mechanic's claim is properly filed, it creates a lien on the property which takes precedence over all other liens which attached to the property after the work was begun. The lien must be foreclosed within 90 days of the time it is recorded, or else it is lost forever.

When a tenant orders work to be done on leased property, the landlord can protect the property from mechanics' liens by posting a **notice of non-responsibility** at the premises and filing one at the office of the county recorder, stating that the property may not be made security for the payment of the tenant's debts. The notice must be posted within 10 days of the time the owner discovers the unauthorized work.

PROPERTY TAX LIENS. Local property taxes create involuntary, specific liens against real property. Property is assessed (appraised for tax purposes) and taxed according to value (ad valorem). Real property taxes become a lien on March 1 of the year prior to the year in which they are due.

SPECIAL ASSESSMENTS. Special assessments result from local improvements such as road paving or sewer lines that benefit some property owners, but not all property within the county; they are involuntary, specific liens. The properties that have benefited from the improvement are assessed for their share of the cost of the improvement.

OTHER TAX LIENS. Many other taxes, such as state and federal income taxes, can result in liens against property.

ATTACHMENTS. When a party files a lawsuit, there is a very real danger that by the time a judgment is entered, the party sued will have converted his or her property to liquid assets and left the jurisdiction, leaving the other party with little more than a piece of paper. To prevent such an occurrence, the **plaintiff** (the person who starts the lawsuit) can ask the court to issue a **writ of attachment** directing the sheriff to seize enough of the **defendant's** (the person defending the suit) property to satisfy the judgment the plaintiff is seeking. While this may be an actual physical seizure in the case of personal property, in the case of real estate the attachment is normally made by filing a writ of attachment or by some other official proceeding.

Attachment lien: a lien placed on property by a party to a suit in anticipation of a favorable judgment

JUDGMENT LIENS. Judgment liens are involuntary, general liens. If a lawsuit results in a money judgment against the loser, the winner (the **judgment creditor**) may obtain a lien against the loser's (the **judgment debtor's**) property. The lien attaches to all property owned by the debtor in the county where the judgment was entered and also attaches to any property acquired by the debtor during the **lien period** (length of time the judgment creditor has to take action on the lien). The judgment may also be filed in other counties in the state.

	VOLUNTARY	**INVOLUNTARY**
SPECIFIC	MORTGAGES DEEDS OF TRUST	PROPERTY TAXES SPECIAL ASSESSMENTS MECHANICS' LIENS
GENERAL		JUDGMENTS IRS LIENS

LIEN PRIORITY

It is not unusual for a piece of property to have liens against it totalling more than the amount the property will bring at a forced sale. In such a situation, the court must determine how the proceeds of the sale are to be distributed. Rather than allocating the money among the lienholders in a pro rata fashion, the normal rule is to pay the liens according to their priority. This means that the lien having highest priority is paid first. If any money is left over, the lien having second highest priority is paid, and so forth.

The most common way of determining lien priority is by date of recordation. The lien which is recorded first will be paid first, even though another lien may have been created first.

> **Example:** Suppose a property owner borrows money from two banks, $5,000 from National Bank on March 17 and $5,000 from State Bank on May 5 of the same year, giving mortgages to both banks when the loan funds are received. If National Bank does not record its mortgage until July 14, but State Bank records its mortgage promptly on May 5, State Bank's lien will be paid before National Bank's if the loans are not repaid and the property is foreclosed.

While the general rule is "first in time (to record), first in right," there are exceptions to the rule. For example, some types of liens are given special priorty. Real property tax liens are always paid first, regardless of their priority in time. The priority of a mechanic's lien is determined by the date work first started on the project, rather than the date the lien was recorded.

NON-FINANCIAL ENCUMBRANCES

While financial encumbrances affect title to property, non-financial encumbrances affect the physical use or condition of the property itself. Thus, a property owner can find the use of his or her land encumbered by a right or interest held by someone else. Some of the more common forms of non-financial encumbrances are discussed below.

EASEMENTS

An easement is a right acquired by someone to use another person's land for a particular purpose. It is a non-possessory interest in land, meaning it gives the easement holder a right to use the land, but no title or right of possession. An easement is not an estate.

> **Example:** If a landowner had an easement across his neighbor's lot to provide access to the public road, he would

have a right to make a reasonable use of that easement to get to and from his property. However, he would not have the right to build a shed or other structure on the land covered by the easement or make any use of the easement other than as a driveway.

The two types of easements are **easements appurtenant** and **easements in gross**.

EASEMENTS APPURTENANT. An easement appurtenant is one which benefits one parcel of land and burdens another parcel of land. The parcel with the benefit is called the dominant tenement; the one with the burden is called the servient tenement. The owner of the dominant tenement is called the dominant tenant; the owner of the servient tenement is known as the servient tenant. Do not confuse the terms "tenement," which is the land, and "tenant," which is the landowner. Probably the most common example of an easement appurtenant is a driveway easement providing access across one parcel of land to another. In the accompanying diagram, Lots B and C have easements appurtenant crossing Lot A which provide access to a public highway. Lots B and C are dominant tenements and Lot A is the servient tenement.

Easement appurtenant: an easement that burdens one parcel of property and benefits another

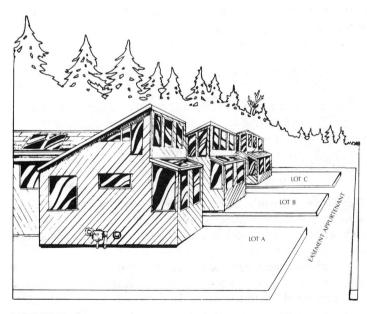

EASEMENT

An easement appurtenant passes with or "runs" with the land. This means that if either the dominant or servient tenement is transferred to a new owner, the new owner also acquires the benefit or the burden of the easement.

EASEMENTS IN GROSS. An easement in gross benefits a person (a dominant tenant) rather than a parcel of land. Where there is an easement in gross there is no dominant tenement, only a servient tenement or tenements.

Easement in gross: an easement that benefits only a person or entity, not another parcel of property

> **Example:** If Wilson has the right to enter Abernathy's land and fish in Abernathy's stream, Wilson is a dominant tenant with an easement in gross over Abernathy's land (the servient tenement). The easement serves Wilson and not a parcel of land.

Since the easement in gross belongs to an individual and not a dominant tenement, it is a personal right that will extinguish on the death of the dominant tenant—in the instance above, Wilson. A personal easement in gross may not be assigned by its owner to a third party.

Most easements in gross are commercial easements. The most common example is the easement right held by utility companies to install and service their lines. Commercial easements in gross are considered more substantial interests than personal easements and can be assigned from one utility company to another.

CREATING AN EASEMENT. Easements can be created by several methods:

- express grant
- express reservation
- implication
- dedication
- condemnation
- prescription, or
- reference to a recorded plat

An **express grant** is a conveyance or agreement giving someone an easement in or across another's land. It should be in writing and comply with all other requirements of a document conveying an interest in land.

An **express reservation** or exception is similar to an express grant in that it is created by a written document. A landowner, when conveying a parcel of land, may reserve to him or herself an easement in the land being conveyed.

Example: Suppose Carmichael owns 100 acres abutting on a state highway and sells 50 acres containing all the highway frontage. In the sale agreement and subsequent deed she may reserve to herself an easement across the 50 acres sold to provide access to the remaining 50 acres.

An easement by **implication** can be either an implied grant or an implied reservation. For an easement to be created by implication, the easement must be reasonably necessary for the enjoyment of the property and the easement's prior use must be apparent. If Carmichael in the example above had kept the 50 acres on the highway and sold the other 50 acres, an easement would probably have been created by implication if there was an existing driveway that had been used frequently in the past. An easement by **necessity** is a special type of easement by implication, established if there is absolutely no other way of access to a landlocked parcel. Apparent prior use is not required in this case.

A private landowner may grant an easement to the public to use some portion of his or her property for a public purpose, such as for a sidewalk. This is called **dedication**. The dedication may be express or implied.

The government may exercise its power of eminent domain and **condemn** private property for a public purpose, such as for a road. This power may also be granted to and exercised by private companies providing services to the public, such as railroads and power companies.

An easement by **prescription** is created through long and continued use without the permission of the landowner. Acquiring an easement by prescription is similar to acquiring ownership through adverse possession. The necessary elements of an easement by prescription are:

- use is open and notorious (apparent to the landowner)
- use is hostile (without the permission of the landowner)
- use is reasonably continuous for 5 years
- use is under a claim of right

If a landowner subdivides and sells his or her land according to a **recorded plat**, the purchasers acquire easements to use the roads and alleys shown on the plat.

Easement by implication: an easement established by apparent prior use that is reasonably necessary for the enjoyment of the property.

Prescriptive easement: an easement created by continuous use

TERMINATING AN EASEMENT. An easement can be terminated by:

- release
- merger
- abandonment
- prescription
- destruction of the servient tenement, or
- failure of purpose

The holder of the easement may **release** his or her rights in the servient tenement. This would be done by a written document, usually a quitclaim deed to the owner of the land subject to the easement.

Since an easement is by definition the right to make some use of another person's land, if the owner of the easement acquires ownership of the servient tenement the need for the easement will no longer exist and it will be terminated through **merger**.

An easement may be terminated if the owner of the easement **abandons** it. Termination by abandonment requires proof that the owner intended to abandon it. This normally requires acts by the owner indicating an intent to abandon the easement. Mere non-use is not abandonment. One exception: if a *prescriptive* easement is not used for five years, a court may rule that it has terminated, even though there was no intent to abandon it.

An easement may be extinguished by **prescription**—if the owner of the servient tenement prevents the dominant tenant from using the easement.

> **Example:** If the servient tenant were to build a substantial fence around his property with no gate to allow the dominant tenant access to his easement for 5 years, and the dominant tenant did nothing about the fence, the easement would terminate.

When an easement exists in a building rather than in land (for example, the right to use a stairway), the involuntary **destruction** of the building, such as by fire or earthquake, will terminate the easement, even if the building is rebuilt.

If the purpose for which the easement was created ceases, then the easement terminates by **failure of purpose**. This might occur if an easement were created for the particular purpose of a railroad or power line right of way and the company removed the rails or lines and discontinued use.

SOME COMMON TYPES OF EASEMENTS

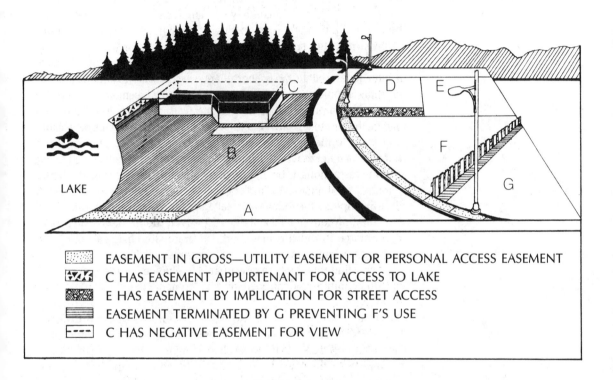

EASEMENT IN GROSS—UTILITY EASEMENT OR PERSONAL ACCESS EASEMENT
C HAS EASEMENT APPURTENANT FOR ACCESS TO LAKE
E HAS EASEMENT BY IMPLICATION FOR STREET ACCESS
EASEMENT TERMINATED BY G PREVENTING F'S USE
C HAS NEGATIVE EASEMENT FOR VIEW

EASEMENT—
RIGHT ACQUIRED BY SOMEONE TO USE
ANOTHER'S LAND

EASEMENT APPURTENANT—
EASEMENT BENEFITS A PARCEL OF LAND

EASEMENT IN GROSS—
EASEMENT BENEFITS A PERSON

PRIVATE RESTRICTIONS

C C and Rs: "conditions, covenants and restrictions" often placed on lots by a subdivider

Private restrictions, or deed restrictions, are restrictions placed on a landowner's use of his or her property by some previous owner of the property. Probably the most common example of private restrictions is the list of restrictions placed by a subdivider on lots within a subdivision. Called a declaration of restrictions or **"C, C, and Rs"** (conditions, covenants, and restrictions), they contain such items as limitations on the use of the property (e.g., to single-family housing) and restrictions on parking in the street at night.

As long as the restrictions are not unconstitutional or in violation of some federal, state, or local ordinance, or contrary to a judicial determination of some public policy, they will normally be enforced by a court. A typical example of an unenforceable restriction would be one prohibiting the sale of a property to someone because of their race or religion.

It is up to the property owners to enforce the C, C, and Rs. If the character of a neighborhood changes because the residents failed to enforce the restrictions, they may be prevented from ever enforcing them.

> **Example:** A subdivision plat contains a restriction prohibiting commercial activities. However, the residents don't enforce it and the neighborhood gradually changes from completely residential to mostly commercial. The residents may find that they are now unable to enforce the restriction to prohibit new commercial development.

Private restrictions are of two types: **covenants** and **conditions**.

COVENANTS. A covenant is a promise to do or not do something. The violation of a covenant can result in an injunction ordering the owner to comply with the covenant or an award of money damages for failure to comply with the covenant.

CONDITIONS. A condition can have more serious consequences. A condition in a deed places a condition on the nature of the owner's title, and a breach of the condition can result in forfeiture of the title. This would most often result in a reversion of ownership to the grantor or the grantor's heirs.

Since the law abhors a forfeiture, a court will usually construe a restriction to be a covenant, rather than a condition, if there is any ambiguity.

ENCROACHMENTS

An encroachment is a physical item which is wholly or partially on someone else's property. An example might be a fence or garage which was built partially over the property line onto the neighbor's land. Most encroachments are unintentional, the product of miscalculation or poor planning. The encroachment may be a **trespass** if it violates the owner's right to possession. A court can order an encroachment's removal, or if the cost of the removal would be too high, it can award money damages instead.

Encroachment: a structure overhanging or intruding onto another's property

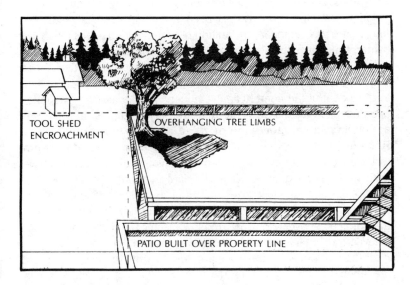

TOOL SHED ENCROACHMENT

OVERHANGING TREE LIMBS

PATIO BUILT OVER PROPERTY LINE

SOME COMMON CAUSES OF ENCROACHMENTS

Enroachments are not revealed by a title search. Accordingly, they are not covered by a standard title policy. If it is an obvious encroachment, a physical inspection of the property would reveal it. If its presence is not so apparent, such as an outbuilding that is only inches over the property line, a survey may be necessary. In any event, an extended coverage title policy will usually insure against encroachments.

Technically, an encroachment is not an encumbrance because it is not a right or interest held by the encroacher. However, if ignored for the five-year prescriptive period, the encroachment could ripen into a prescriptive easement or even title by adverse possession.

HOMESTEAD LAW

California's homestead law provides a limited amount of protection for a debtor's home against judgment lien creditors. The protection applies to the dwelling where the person resides. The dwelling may be virtually any type of building, as long as it is used as the homestead claimant's principal residence: a single-family residence, condominium, cooperative apartment, mobile home or other building, along with any outbuildings.

Homestead: limited protection from the execution of judgment liens on residential property

The homestead exemption may be claimed by filing a **declaration of homestead** at the county recorder's office or by claiming the exemption after the property has been levied on in a judgment lien foreclosure proceeding. A declaration of homestead may be filed by the owner, the owner's spouse or by a guardian, attorney-in-fact or other person authorized to act on behalf of the owner. When a declaration of homestead has been filed, the property is exempt from judgment liens to the extent of the homestead exemption. The homestead exemption is a protection against **judgment liens** only; it affords no protection against **tax liens, mortgage or deed of trust liens, mechanics' liens** or attachments for **child support payments.** Nor does it protect the owner's equity in excess of the amount of the exemption set forth in the homestead law. The standard exemption is $30,000. The exemption for a member of a family unit is $45,000. The exemption is $75,000 if the debtor is over 65, over 55 and low income (no more than $15,000 per year), married and low income (no more than $20,000 per year), or unable to work because of a disability.

If the homestead claimant's equity in the property does not exceed the amount of the exemption, the property may not be sold to satisfy a judgment. However, if the judgment debtor's equity does exceed the exemption amount, a judgment lien may attach to the value of the property above the exemption amount, and the property may be sold to satisfy the debt. If a homestead property is sold to satisfy a valid lien, the sale proceeds are applied in this order: first, to pay all liens and encumbrances not subject to the homestead exemption (a deed of trust, for example); second, to the homestead claimant for the applicable amount of the exemption ($30,000, $45,000 or $75,000); third, to pay the costs of sale; fourth, to the judgment creditor to satisfy the debt; and, finally, if any surplus is left, the remaining amount goes to the judgment debtor. Any proceeds the debtor receives from a forced or voluntary sale are exempt (up to the appropriate exemption amount) for up to six months, during which time the funds may be reinvested in another homestead property.

A homestead is terminated when the property is sold, when the homesteader files a **declaration of abandonment**, or files a declaration of homestead on another property. The homestead exemption does not automatically terminate on the death of the claimant, however. It continues for the benefit of the spouse, children or other family members living on the property.

CHAPTER SUMMARY

1. An encumbrance is a right or interest in real property held by someone other than the property owner. Encumbrances may be financial (liens) or non-financial (easements, private restrictions).

2. A financial encumbrance (lien) affects the title to the property. It gives a creditor the right to sell the property and use the proceeds to pay off a debt if the debtor fails to pay it. A lien may be voluntary or involuntary, general or specific. The most common types of liens include mortgages, deeds of trust, mechanics' liens, tax liens, attachments and judgment liens.

3. A non-financial encumbrance affects use or possession of the property. For example, an easement gives the easement holder the right to use portions of the property for certain purposes. Private restrictions affect the use an owner may make of his or her property.

4. An encroachment (not really an encumbrance) describes a physical item which is wholly or partly on someone else's property. If an encroachment is ignored for the statutory prescriptive period, it may ripen into a prescriptive easement or title by adverse possession.

CHAPTER 5—QUIZ
ENCUMBRANCES ON LAND

1. Encumbrances can:

   a) affect or relate to the title
   b) affect or relate to the actual physical conditions upon realty
   c) Both A and B
   d) Neither A nor B

2. In real estate, we speak of general and specific liens. Examples of specific liens would be:

   a) mortgages
   b) real property taxes
   c) mechanics' liens or laborers' liens
   d) All of the foregoing

3. An option is a contract by which the owner of property gives another person the right to purchase his or her property for a stated sum within a given period of time. An option of this type is a(n):

   a) voluntary lien
   b) involuntary encumbrance
   c) voluntary encumbrance
   d) None of these

4. Real estate property taxes are:

   a) general—involuntary liens
   b) general—voluntary liens
   c) specific—voluntary liens
   d) specific—involuntary liens

5. A homestead may be considered abandoned when:

   a) a final decree of dissolution is entered
   b) both husband and wife leave the homestead premises for six months
   c) a husband abandons his wife
   d) a declaration of abandonment is recorded

6. An instrument which must be recorded to be legally effective is a(n):

   a) mechanic's lien
   b) agreement to sell real estate
   c) will
   d) deed

7. After selling on a conditional sales contract, a builder discovered that the buyer was having the home painted another color. In order to protect himself against possible liens, the builder could:

   a) warn the painters he would not be responsible
   b) file a lis pendens
   c) file a notice of completion
   d) post a notice of non-responsibility and record it

8. Johnson helped dig a sewage ditch for property owner Smith on February 21st and 22nd. On March 9th, a mortgage was recorded against the property. On March 11th, still unpaid, Johnson filed a mechanic's lien of record. Which of the following is true?

   a) The bank's mortgage lien was recorded first and has priority over the mechanic's lien
   b) The mechanic's lien could have priority over the mortgage lien if the owner had failed to record a notice of non-responsibility
   c) The mechanic's second lien status precludes a foreclosure action by Johnson
   d) the mechanic's lien has priority over the mortgage lien

9. Lewis entered a judgment of $12,800 on January 7 against Brown, who owns a tract of land. Brown gave a mortgage for $22,500 to Carlson on January 23. The mortgage is in default by August 2, and Brown agrees to deed the property to Carlson in satisfaction of the mortgage debt. Which of the following is true?

   a) The deed is void
   b) Carlson will take the property subject to the judgment of Lewis
   c) Both of the above
   d) Neither of the above

10. When at the commencement of a legal action, a plaintiff asks the court to confiscate certain property belonging to the defendant, to act as security for the satisfaction of the judgment she's seeking, the plaintiff is asking the court to issue a:

    a) garnishment
    b) writ of possession
    c) writ of attachment
    d) None of these

11. Certain documents must be acknowledged before they can be recorded. To acknowledge means:

    a) to admit or declare that you signed a document
    b) to make an affidavit
    c) to authenticate the contents of a document
    d) None of the above

12. Among purchasers for value and without notice, the first to record is the first in right. Of the following, which would not be classified as a bona fide purchaser without notice?

    a) A person buying unoccupied land from the last recorded owner
    b) A person buying a residence occupied by the grantor who is also the present owner of record
    c) A person buying a residence without inspection of the premises
    d) A person buying a vacant store building from the recorded owner

13. If two trust deeds were in existence on the same property and you wished to find out which one was the first trust deed and which was the second trust deed, you could secure this information at the county recorder's office. The priority is usually established by:

    a) the printed trust deed forms which have the words "first trust deed" or "second trust deed" on the face
    b) the date and time of recordation
    c) the county recorder's stamp "first trust deed"
    d) the execution date of each trust deed

14. The acquired legal interest, short of an estate, for use or enjoyment of property owned by another is known as:

    a) an easement
    b) a lease
    c) a deed
    d) riparian rights

15. Jones and Smith owned adjoining tracts of land. There was a 30-foot access easement running the full length of Smith's property on the contiguous side. Smith allowed Jones to use it anytime he wished. The burdened owner was:

    a) Smith, the servient tenant
    b) Jones, the dominant tenant
    c) Smith, the dominant tenant
    d) Jones, the servient tenant

16. An easement in gross benefits:

    a) the dominant tenant
    b) the dominant tenement
    c) Both of the above
    d) Neither of the above

17. One morning at breakfast, the family saw a telephone pole being placed in the rear of their yard. On calling the telephone company, they were informed that the original subdivider had recorded an easement for the company's benefit along the rear of all lots. On checking the deed, the father found no reference to the telephone company, but it recited, 'subject to easements and rights of way of record.' The easement was:

    a) ineffective as it was over ten years old
    b) valid because the area needed telephones
    c) invalid because the deed did not specifically mention it
    d) valid because an easement of record gives sufficient notice to purchasers

18. Which of the following is not a method of acquiring an easement?

    a) Prescription
    b) Grant deed
    c) Statutory dedication
    d) Trust deed

19. The creation of an easement by prescription is similar to acquiring ownership of property by:

    a) adverse possession
    b) assessed value
    c) alluvium
    d) succession

20. An easement that has been acquired by prescription may be terminated or extinguished by:

    a) merger
    b) written agreement
    c) non-use
    d) All of these

21. A man bought a house in a hurry and, after escrow closed, discovered that two years before, a neighbor had built a fence that was three feet over the property line on his side. The broker was unaware of this. If the two neighbors were unable to reach an amicable settlement, the:

    a) sale would be invalid
    b) buyer could sue the neighbor for trespass based on encroachment
    c) neighbor would acquire title by adverse possession
    d) buyer could sue the broker

22. The penalty for violations of covenants and conditions is:

    a) the same for covenants as for conditions under most circumstances
    b) more severe regarding the condition
    c) more severe regarding the covenant
    d) the same under all circumstances

23. A deed restriction in a subdivision is normally put into effect by the:

    a) FHA
    b) developer
    c) local building inspector
    d) planning commission

24. As contained in a deed, a covenant:

    a) binds all subsequent grantees
    b) can be classified as subsequent or precedent to vesting of the estate
    c) is the same as an easement
    d) can require title reversion to grantor on grantee's violation of the covenant

25. Bates developed a subdivision in 1940. Each deed contained a restriction that "no building except a private dwelling house shall be erected on said lot." Curtis, a purchaser of two lots, sold them to Bacon in 1977. On February 21, 1978, Bacon started to excavate for the erection of a four-story garden-type apartment building. Since 1940, the street has been widened to a four-lane artery, and a pony league baseball park has been built across the street, flanked by several business establishments. Under these circumstances:

a) the apartment building will be permitted
b) the apartment building will be permitted upon payment of damages to the protesting property owners
c) Both a) and b)
d) Neither a) nor b)

1. c) All encumbrances can affect or relate to the title of an owner's property in the sense that, although the owner is able to sell his or her property when encumbered, the purchaser takes the property subject to each and every encumbrance. Encumbrances such as easements or restrictive covenants affect the physical use of the property.

2. d) A specific lien affects one parcel of property only. A general lien can affect all property owned by a debtor. In the event the owner fails to meet his or her financial obligations (as evidenced by the lien), a forced sale of the property can be provoked to satisfy the debt. If the lien was specific, such as mortgages, mechanics' liens, special assessments and property taxes, only the specific property acting as security for the debt may be sold; any other property the debtor owns remains unaffected. If the lien was general, like I.R.S and judgment liens, any or all of the debtor's property is subject to a forced sale.

3. c) The property owner voluntarily contracts with a prospective purchaser and receives consideration for the option contract. An option contract is an encumbrance since any transaction involving the property is "burdened" by the right of the holder of the option to purchase the property within the time and price specifications of the option contract.

4. d) If a property tax is unpaid, the tax can be satisfied only from the sale of the specific property upon which the tax was levied. The only voluntary liens are mortgages and deeds of trust.

5. d) Homestead protection terminates when the property is sold or when a declaration of abandonment is recorded.

6. a) A mechanic's lien does not exist unless it is recorded within the time specified by law. The mechanic's lien is one of the few documents that must be recorded to be legally effective. Some others include a homestead declaration of abandonment, limited partnership agreement, satisfaction of mortgage and deed of reconveyance.

7. d) The notice should be posted on the site (actual notice) and recorded (constructive notice).

8. d) The labor was provided before the mortgage lien was filed of record. It is the date of the labor, not the date the mechanic's lien was recorded, that determines priority.

9. b) There is no law against transferring an interest in property encumbered by a judgment. However, the new owner, Carlson, takes the property subject to Lewis's judgment lien.

10. c) The writ of attachment is sought to encumber the property of the defendant pending the outcome of the lawsuit. A writ of attachment is a lien.

11. a) An acknowledgment is a declaration, witnessed by a notary public, that the declarant did sign a document.

12. c) The purchaser is not "bona fide" when he has not inspected the premises; after all, a party in possession imparts constructive notice to the world of some claim to the possession or ownership of the premises.

13. b) The priority of trust deeds is set by the date of recording. The trust deed recorded first will be the first trust deed and any subsequent recorded trust deeds would be junior trust deeds.

14. a) This is a common definition of the term. An estate is the right to possess and have exclusive use of land. An easement interest is not as great an interest in the land as an estate interest, because the easement right is limited to some specific use, such as ingress and egress, while an estate brings with it the right to exclusive possession and use. The key words in the question are "short of an estate." A leasehold interest is an estate.

15. a) Jones was benefited by the easement, Smith was burdened by Jones's use of it.

16. a) A dominant tenant has the right to use the servient tenant's land. It doesn't matter whether it is an easement appurtenant or easement in gross. Remember, there is no dominant tenement with an easement in gross.

17. d) The family was put on notice by the reference in the deed and the easement was good. It is customary not to specifically recite all of the easements in the deed. It is up to the family to check the records if they are interested.

18. d) A deed of trust, like a mortgage, is a financial lien and does not create an easement.

19. a) An easement gained by prescription resembles adverse possession except that under adverse possession, one may gain title to real property and not merely an easement. All of the essential requisites are the same in both cases, except the adverse possessor must also pay the taxes for the statutory period and, in most cases, have "color of title."

20. d) Any easement can be terminated by merger or a written agreement. "Merger" means the dominant and servient tenements fall under one ownership. A prescriptive easement may be terminated by non-use.

21. b) The fence is an encroachment. The encroachment could ripen into an easement, or even title, if the requisites for a prescriptive easement or adverse possession are met by the party guilty of encroachment. That would take five years, however, and here the fence was built only two years before.

22. b) A covenant is a promise within an agreement and, if broken, the remedy is money damages. A condition, in the strict legal sense, usually means a loss of title when violated.

23. b) The developer is the seller—the grantor. The developer will usually draft a set of restrictions—called C, C, and Rs—to assure uniformity of property use in the subdivision. This is done to satisfy prospective purchasers that there will be ongoing homogeneity and continuity of land use in the development throughout their period of ownership.

24. a) But note: only the grantor or other grantees can enforce the covenant.

25. a) In situations like these, the court will exercise some judicial discretion. Where the purpose of the original restriction is no longer achievable, the courts will not enforce the restrictions. In this instance, the residential character of the neighborhood has been destroyed and the restriction no longer serves a useful purpose.

Chapter 6

AGENCY

OUTLINE

I. Creating an Agency Relationship
  A. Creation
    1. express agreement
    2. ratification
    3. estoppel
  B. Subagents
II. Terminating the Agency
  A. Acts of the parties
    1. mutual agreement
    2. principal revokes
    3. agent renounces
    4. expiration of agency term
  B. Operation of law
    1. fulfillment of purpose
    2. death or incapacity
    3. extinction of subject matter
    4. bankruptcy
III. Parties in the Agency Relationship
  A. Agent
  B. Principal
  C. Employee v. independent contractor
  D. The agent's authority
    1. actual
    2. apparent (ostensible)
IV. Duties of the Parties
  A. The agent's responsibilities
    1. disclosure of material facts
    2. loyalty
    3. obedience and utmost good faith
    4. reasonable care and skill
    5. accounting

B. Agent's duties to third parties
   1. liabilities of the agent
C. Duties of the principal
   1. the commission
V. Unauthorized Practice of Law

KEY TERMS

agent	principal
third party	subagent
fiduciary	ratification
estoppel	actual agency
apparent agency	dual agent
misrepresentation	procuring cause
secret profit	unauthorized practice of law

CHAPTER OVERVIEW

In a typical real estate transaction, the real estate agent represents the seller's interest and tries to find a potential purchaser for the property. An agency relationship exists between the seller and the real estate broker/agent. There are specific rules which govern agency relationships, and certain duties an agent owes to the principal. This chapter defines the parties in an agency relationship, describes how an agency relationship is created and terminated, and explains the duties of the various parties.

CREATING AN AGENCY RELATIONSHIP

Agent: a person authorized to represent another

Principal: a person who authorizes another to represent and act for him or herself

An agency is a relationship resulting from an agreement in which a principal authorizes an agent to represent, act for and be subject to the control of the principal in dealings with third parties. The parties in the agency relationship are: the **agent**, the person authorized to represent another; the **principal**, the party who authorizes and controls the actions of the agent; and **third parties** who seek to deal with the principal through the agent.

In the typical real estate transaction, the principal is the landowner. The principal wants to sell or lease his or her property and so employs the services of a broker, who is the agent. The broker/agent represents the principal/seller's interest and tries to procure a potential purchaser, the third party.

The agency relationship creates many duties and responsibilities on the part of both the agent and the principal; it also defines the liabilities of each party. These duties, responsibilities, and liabilities will be discussed in detail below.

CREATION

No particular formalities are required to create an agency relationship. Formation of an agency merely requires the consent of both parties and may be formed expressly, by ratification, or by estoppel.

EXPRESSLY. Most real estate agencies are created expressly through listing agreements (discussed in Chapter 7, *Contract Law*). An express agreement need not be in writing to create a valid agency. However, as a practical matter, it is advisable to put the agreement in writing to avoid misunderstandings. Also, consideration is not essential to create an agency. This means that no promise of compensation has to be made for the rights, responsibilities and liabilities of an agency to be imposed.

> **Real Estate Agency.** An agreement to employ an agent to sell or purchase real estate for compensation must be in writing and must be signed by the principal, the party to be charged. Since the agency requires a written contract to be enforceable, it must have all the essential elements of a contract, including an offer and acceptance, a legal objective, competent parties, and consideration.

> **Power of Attorney.** A power of attorney to convey real estate, where the agent is given the power to transfer title and enter into sales contracts on behalf of the principal, must be in writing and recorded.

RATIFICATION. An agency is created by ratification when the principal approves of acts performed by:

(a) a person who is without authority to act for the principal, or
(b) an agent who acts in excess of his or her authority.

Ratification occurs when the principal accepts the benefits of the person's acts, such as performing a contract negotiated by the "agent". The ratification must be done with full knowledge of the agent's actions in

Ratification: when a principal accepts the benefits of the acts of an unauthorized agent, an agency is created by ratification

100 CALIFORNIA PRINCIPLES

negotiating the contract or it may be rescinded. However, if the principal fails to investigate the agent's actions when such an investigation would reveal pertinent information about ratification of the agency, there can be no rescission. A principal is not protected from liability because of self-imposed ignorance of the facts.

ESTOPPEL. Estoppel means that because of the principal's acts or behavior, he or she is prohibited (estopped) from denying the agent's authority.

Estoppel: a principal may not deny the existence of an agency when he or she, by acts or words, led a third party to believe that the agency existed

> **Example:** In the past, Son has frequently been known to handle business affairs for Father and appears to be his general agent; actually, no agency exists. With Father's knowledge, Son gives Broker an exclusive listing for one of Father's properties. Father does nothing to dissuade Broker from believing an agency exists, such as protesting when the "for sale" sign is placed on the property. Broker negotiates a sale, but at closing Father refuses to pay Broker's commission, claiming Son never had the authority to commit him to paying a commission. Broker sues Father for the commission. The court would probably estop (prevent) Father from denying authority since he had negligently or deliberately caused Broker to believe, and rely on, Son's apparent authority. The legal doctrine of estoppel bars someone from using as a defense (in court) an argument that contradicts a previously held position.

TERMINATING THE AGENCY

An agency may be terminated either by acts of the parties or by operation of law.

ACTS OF THE PARTIES

There are several ways the parties can terminate an agency agreement. These include:

- mutual agreement
- principal revokes
- agent renounces
- agency term expires

MUTUAL AGREEMENT. The parties may, of course, terminate the agency by mutual agreement at any time.

PRINCIPAL REVOKES. The principal may revoke the agency by firing the agent whenever he or she wishes (remember, an agency relationship requires the consent of both parties). However, if revoking the agency breaches a contractual agreement, the principal may be liable for any damages suffered by the agent because of the breach. For example, the principal may be held liable for the expenses incurred by the agent in pursuit of a buyer prior to the revocation; or, if the broker produces a purchaser before the listing term would have expired, the principal may be liable for the agent's commission.

> **Exception:** If the agent's authority is "coupled with an interest", it may not be revoked by the principal. An agency coupled with an interest is one where the agent has an interest in the property that is the subject of the agency. For example, a broker and two others own a 20-acre parcel. They decide to subdivide it and sell one-acre homesites. The broker is given the exclusive right to sell the individual lots. Since she has an ownership interest, her authority as agent cannot be revoked.

AGENT RENOUNCES. The agent may also renounce the agency at any time. As discussed above, if there is a contract the agent may be liable for the principal's damages resulting from the breach. However, since the agent has entered into a personal services contract (he or she has agreed to provide personal, professional skills to the principal), the principal would not be able to demand specific performance as a remedy. The courts will not force a person to perform personal services as this could violate the constitutional prohibition against involuntary servitude.

EXPIRATION OF AGENCY TERM. The agency will automatically terminate when the agency term expires, if it has not terminated sooner by some other method. If the listing agreement has no specific termination date, it is deemed to expire within a reasonable time. Note that if there is no specified expiration date, either party may revoke the agency without liability for any damages caused by the revocation. In California, failure to include an expiration date in an exclusive listing agreement (see Chapter 7) is grounds for revocation or suspension of a broker's license.

OPERATION OF LAW

Several occurrences terminate the agency relationship automatically; neither party has to take any action. These occurrences include:

- fulfillment of the purpose of the agency
- death or incapacity of either party
- extinction of the subject matter
- bankruptcy

FULFILLMENT OF PURPOSE. If the purpose of the agency is fulfilled, the agency terminates. For example, if an agent is hired to sell the principal's property and the agent does so, the agency is terminated by fulfillment.

DEATH OR INCAPACITY. The agency is terminated prior to execution if the agent or the principal dies. Most states provide that the agency also terminates when either party becomes incompetent. Generally, the agent has no power to act after the death or incompetency of the principal, even if the agent is unaware of the principal's death or incompetency.

EXTINCTION OF SUBJECT MATTER. The subject matter of the agency is the real estate involved; if the property is in any way extinguished (e.g., sold or destroyed) the agency automatically terminates.

BANKRUPTCY. The bankruptcy of either the principal or the agent will terminate the agency.

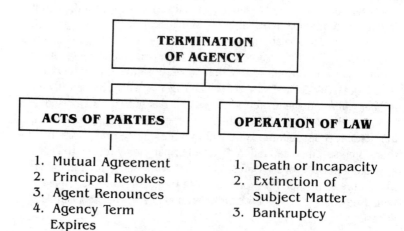

Parties in the Agency Relationship

Agents

The type of relationship that exists between the parties depends largely on the type of authority the agent has. The amount of authority granted to the agent determines what type of agent he or she is. There are three kinds of agents:

- the universal agent
- the general agent, and
- the special agent

UNIVERSAL AGENT. A universal agent is authorized by the principal to do all things that can be lawfully delegated to a representative. This agent has the greatest degree of authority.

GENERAL AGENT. A general agent is authorized to handle all the matters of the principal in one or more specified areas, such as the principal's business affairs. He or she has the authority to conduct a wide range of activities on a continuous basis on behalf of the principal. For example, a business manager who has the authority to handle personnel matters, enter into contracts, and manage the day-to-day operations of the business is a general agent.

SPECIAL AGENT. A special agent has limited authority to do a specific thing or conduct a specific transaction. For example, an attorney who is hired to litigate a specific legal matter, such as a person's divorce, is a special agent.

Typically, a broker is a special agent because he or she has only limited authority. The broker is hired for a specific purpose, to find a ready, willing and able buyer for the principal/seller. A real estate broker can be granted broader powers, but usually is not.

Principal

The principal is the person who authorizes the agent to act for and represent him or her. Although the principal is often a landowner/seller, the principal may also be a proprietor who wishes to sell his or her business, or even a buyer who is seeking a special kind of property. The principal is considered to be the broker's client.

Subagents

In many cases, an agent delegates some of his or her authority to another person. That person is then called a **subagent**. In California, an agent can only delegate power to a subagent in one of these circumstances:

1. the act to be carried out by the subagent is purely mechanical;
2. the agent can't legally perform the act and the subagent can;
3. delegating the powers in question is the standard business practice in the area; or
4. the principal has expressly authorized the delegation.

When the power has been lawfully delegated, the subagent represents the principal in the same way the agent does. The principal—not the agent—is responsible for the subagent's acts. However, if the agent's delegation of power was not authorized (and also does not fit into categories 1, 2, or 3 listed above), the agent is liable for the acts of the other person, and the principal is not. The other person is merely an agent of the agent, not a subagent of the principal.

A cooperating broker—one who cooperates with a listing broker to bring about a sale—is often a subagent of the seller. That isn't necessarily so, however: if the cooperating broker is representing the buyer, the seller has no legal responsibility for that broker's actions.

SALESPERSON, BROKER, AND PRINCIPAL

Under the terms of the California Real Estate Law (discussed in Chapter 17), a real estate salesperson cannot act directly as the agent of a seller or any other principal in a transaction (a buyer, lessor, or lessee). The salesperson must be employed by a licensed broker, who is the principal's agent. The broker is required to supervise the salesperson, and is always legally responsible for the salesperson's actions.

Since the broker is always responsible for the salesperson, a salesperson cannot be considered the principal's subagent in California. Instead, the salesperson is simply the broker's agent—an agent of the agent. That doesn't mean the principal cannot be held liable for the salesperson's acts, however. Unless the agent had no authority to employ other people in carrying out the agency, the principal may be legally responsible for the acts of the agent's agents. A real estate broker is presumed to have authority to employ a salesperson, because that's the standard practice in the industry. So *both* the seller/principal and the broker/agent can be held liable for a real estate salesperson's acts.

INDEPENDENT CONTRACTOR vs. EMPLOYEE

An agent occupies one of two roles in relation to his or her principal: **independent contractor** or **employee**. An independent contractor is generally hired to perform a particular job, and uses his or her own judgment as to how the work will be carried out. In contrast, an employee is hired to perform whatever jobs the employer (the principal) requires, and is given instructions on how to accomplish each task. An employee is supervised and controlled much more closely than an independent contractor.

The distinction is important in the real estate business primarily because of tax and employment laws. An employer is required to withhold income taxes and social security contributions from an employee's earnings. But that requirement does not apply to a principal who hires an independent contractor.

As you've seen, California law makes a real estate broker responsible for supervising his or her salesperson. In that sense, a salesperson is always the broker's employee. Even so, a real estate salesperson can be treated as an independent contractor for tax purposes. The Internal Revenue Service considers a real estate salesperson to be an independent contractor if:

1. he or she is a licensed real estate agent;
2. substantially all of his or her compensation is based on sales (commission) rather than hours worked; and,
3. the services are performed under a written contract that states that the individual will not be treated as an employee for tax purposes.

If these criteria are met, the broker is not required to withhold taxes and social security contributions from the salesperson's compensation.

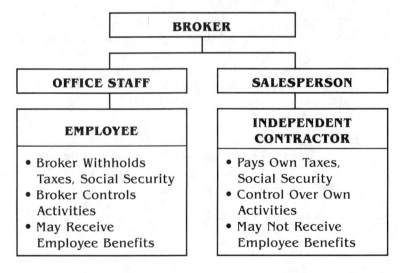

THE AGENT'S AUTHORITY

There are two types of agency authority: actual authority, and apparent or ostensible authority.

Actual authority: agency created by an express or implied grant of authority

ACTUAL. Actual authority is given by the principal either expressly or impliedly.

Express actual authority is communicated to the agent in express terms, either orally or in writing. If an agent does something that was not expressly authorized by the principal, the principal may ratify the unauthorized act by accepting the benefits of the act. Ratification is the equivalent of having authorized the agent's actions in advance.

Implied actual authority is the authority to do what is necessary to carry out acts expressly authorized.

> **Example:** Based on custom in the real estate industry, a broker has the implied actual authority to hire a salesperson and to delegate certain tasks to that person. In contrast, the authority granted to a broker to procure a purchaser does not imply the power to enter into a contract to convey title or execute a deed.

The principal will be bound by acts performed by the agent within the scope of the agent's actual authority.

Apparent authority: agency created by the acts or words of the agent or principal which lead a third party to believe the agency exists

APPARENT (OSTENSIBLE). An apparent agency is one where no actual authority has been granted to the agent but authority exists nonetheless because of the acts of the agent and/or principal. In other words, apparent authority exists when the principal's or agent's words or conduct lead another person to believe that the agent has authority. (See the example in the "Estoppel" section above.)

A principal is bound by the acts of an agent performing within the scope of apparent authority. However, declarations of the agent alone or the mere impression by a third party that a person has agency authority cannot establish apparent authority; but, if the principal is aware of such declarations or acts and makes no effort to deny any authority, then apparent authority will be established.

> **Note:** A third party has a duty, when dealing with an agent, to make a reasonable effort to discover the scope of the agent's authority. The third party will not be able to hold the principal liable where the agent acts beyond the scope of actual authority and the principal's conduct does not indicate approval of such acts. Especially when a contract with a third party limits the agent's

authority to make representations, that third party is on notice that any representations made by the agent beyond the written terms of the agreement are without authority.

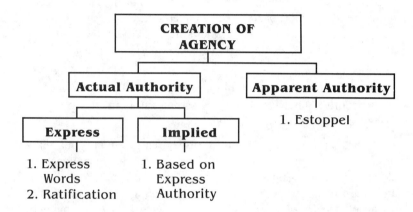

DUTIES OF THE PARTIES

THE AGENT'S RESPONSIBILITIES

The agency relationship is a **fiduciary** relationship. A fiduciary is someone who acts for the benefit of another in a relationship founded on trust and confidence. As a fiduciary, the agent must act with loyalty and good faith. The agent must always serve the best interests of the principal and thus owes the principal the following duties:

Fiduciary relationship: a legal relationship founded on trust and confidence

- disclosure of material facts
- loyalty
- obedience and utmost good faith
- reasonable care and skill
- accounting

DISCLOSURE OF MATERIAL FACTS. The agent must keep the principal fully informed of any material facts. Any fact which would influence the principal's judgment or decision should be revealed. For instance, if the broker knows the potential buyer is in dire financial straits, he or she must so inform the principal, even if it means losing a sale and the subsequent commission.

It is important for the agent to remember that communication to the agent is deemed to be communication to the principal. If a third party provides information to the agent, the law assumes that the principal also knows the information, regardless of whether, in fact, the principal was told such information. Thus, the principal may be held liable, by default, for failure to perform some required task the agent knew about but never communicated to the principal. However, the agent will in turn be liable to the principal for any loss caused by the failure to communicate information or to disclose material facts.

There are a number of areas where the broker will, often unintentionally, fail to disclose material facts. These troublesome areas include:

Dual agency: when an agent represents more than one principal party in a transaction

- failure to present all offers
- failure to inform client of property's true value
- failure to disclose agent's role as purchaser, and
- failure to reveal dual agency

An agent may fail to **present all offers**. The agent must make the principal fully aware of all existing offers, regardless of how unacceptable the offers may appear. The principal has the right to know about anything which might affect his or her decision and the principal, not the agent, decides which offer is acceptable. Also, the agent should not hesitate to relay an offer to the principal, even if its acceptance would mean a smaller commission to the agent; the agent's first loyalty is to the principal.

An agent may fail to inform the principal of the **property's true value**.

> **Example:** Seller calls broker and says he wants to list his property for $55,000. Broker inspects the property and notes it is actually worth $80,000. The broker lists it for $55,000 and subsequently buys it for himself at the listed price. The broker has violated his fiduciary duty to the principal by failing to inform the principal of the property's true value; the broker has failed to reveal all material facts and has gained a secret profit.

It is not improper for the broker to buy the principal's property for him or herself with the principal's knowledge and consent, and then resell the property for a profit. However, the broker must provide the principal with the broker's estimate of the real value of the property before the property is sold.

The agent may fail to disclose his or her **role as purchaser**. A broker cannot buy the principal's property without the knowledge and consent of the principal. If the broker attempts to do so (for example, through a straw buyer or corporation), the principal can probably avoid paying the commission or have the sales agreement set aside because the broker violated a fiduciary trust.

The agent may fail to reveal a **dual agency**. A dual agency exists where the broker is employed by both the seller and the buyer to the same transaction. In California, a dual agency is permissible as long as the broker has the full knowledge and consent of all parties. However, a conflict of interest is inherent in dual agency. A seller is looking for the highest price for his or her property, while the buyer is looking for the lowest price. It would be difficult, if not impossible, to adequately represent these two opposing interests. Thus, a dual agency should be entered into with great caution.

An agent should also be careful to avoid situations where it appears to both parties that the agent is working on his or her behalf. For instance, a broker may be the actual agent of the seller under a listing agreement, but the buyer may believe that the agent, who is showing the buyer various properties, is really acting on his behalf. A listing broker should carefully explain to each potential buyer that he or she is acting for the seller and owes the seller the utmost loyalty and good faith.

To avoid some of the confusion regarding who is representing whom, California statutes require real estate agents to provide prospective buyers and sellers with an agency disclosure form. A listing agent is to give the seller the disclosure form prior to entering into the listing agreement. A selling agent is to give the seller the form prior to presenting the seller with an offer to purchase. A selling agent is to provide the buyer with the form as soon as practicable prior to execution of the buyer's offer to purchase. An example of such a disclosure form is shown on the following pages.

In addition, an agent must give the seller and the buyer an agency confirmation statement. The agent checks a box on the confirmation statement to show which party or parties he or she is representing. The parties must sign the statement, indicating that they understand the agent's role and accept it. Many deposit receipt forms include an agency confirmation statement (see Chapter 7).

LOYALTY. The agency relationship is based on confidence, so loyalty is a must. The agent must place the principal's interests above the interests of a third party by refusing to reveal **confidential information**.

> **Example:** The agent should not reveal the principal's financial condition or the willingness of the principal to accept a lower price, unless the principal has authorized such disclosure.

DISCLOSURE REGARDING
REAL ESTATE AGENCY RELATIONSHIPS

(As required by the Civil Code)
CALIFORNIA ASSOCIATION OF REALTORS® (CAR) STANDARD FORM

When you enter into a discussion with a real estate agent regarding a real estate transaction, you should from the outset understand what type of agency relationship or representation you wish to have with the agent in the transaction.

SELLER'S AGENT

A Seller's agent under a listing agreement with Seller acts as the agent for the Seller only. A Seller's agent or a subagent of that agent has the following affirmative obligations:
To the Seller:
   (a) A Fiduciary duty of utmost care, integrity, honesty, and loyalty in dealings with the Seller.
To the Buyer & the Seller:
   (a) Diligent exercise of reasonable skill and care in performance of the agent's duties.
   (b) A duty of honest and fair dealing and good faith.
   (c) A duty to disclose all facts known to the agent materially affecting the value or desirability of property that are not known to, or within the diligent attention and observation of, the parties.

An agent is not obligated to reveal to either party any confidential information obtained from the other party which does not involve the affirmative duties set forth above.

BUYER'S AGENT

A selling agent can, with a Buyer's consent, agree to act as agent for the Buyer only. In these situations, the agent is not the Seller's agent, even if by agreement the agent may receive compensation for services rendered, either in full or in part from the Seller. An agent acting only for a Buyer has the following affirmative obligations.
To the Buyer:
   (a) A fiduciary duty of utmost care, integrity, honesty, and loyalty in dealings with the Buyer.
To the Buyer & Seller:
   (a) Diligent exercise of reasonable skill and care in performance of the agent's duties.
   (b) A duty of honest and fair dealing and good faith.
   (c) A duty to disclose all facts known to the agent materially affecting the value or desirability of the property that are not known to, or within the diligent attention and observation of, the parties.

An agent is not obligated to reveal to either party any confidential information obtained from the other party which does not involve the affirmative duties set forth above.

AGENT REPRESENTING BOTH SELLER & BUYER

A real estate agent, either acting directly or through one or more associate licensees, can legally be the agent of both the Seller and the Buyer in a transaction, but only with the knowledge and consent of both the Seller and the Buyer.

In a dual agency situation, the agent has the following affirmative obligations to both the Seller and the Buyer:
   (a) A fiduciary duty of utmost care, integrity, honesty and loyalty in the dealings with either Seller or the Buyer.
   (b) Other duties to the Seller and the Buyer as stated above in their respective sections.

In representing both Seller and Buyer, the agent may not, without the express permission of the respective party, disclose to the other party that the Seller will accept a price less than the listing price or that the Buyer will pay a price greater than the price offered.

The above duties of the agent in a real estate transaction do not relieve a Seller or a Buyer from the responsibility to protect their own interests. You should carefully read all agreements to assure that they adequately express your understanding of the transaction. A real estate agent is a person qualified to advise about real estate. If legal or tax advice is desired, consult a competent professional.

Throughout your real property transaction you may receive more than one disclosure form, depending upon the number of agents assisting in the transaction. The law requires each agent with whom you have more than a casual relationship to present you with this disclosure form. You should read its contents each time it is presented to you, considering the relationship between you and the real estate agent in your specific transaction.

This disclosure form includes the provisions of article 2.5 (commencing with Section 2373) of Chapter 2 of Title 9 of Part 4 of Division 3 of the Civil Code set forth on the reverse hereof. Read it carefully.

I/WE ACKNOWLEDGE RECEIPT OF A COPY OF THIS DISCLOSURE.

BUYER/SELLER_____ Date_____ TIME_____ AM/PM

BUYER/SELLER_____ Date_____ TIME_____ AM/PM

AGENT _____ By _____ Date_____
    (Please Print)   (Associate Licensee or Broker-Signature)

A REAL ESTATE BROKER IS QUALIFIED TO ADVISE ON REAL ESTATE. IF YOU DESIRE LEGAL ADVICE, CONSULT YOUR ATTORNEY.

This form is available for use by the entire real estate industry. The use of this form is not intended to identify the user as a REALTOR®. REALTOR® is a registered collective membership mark which may be used only by real estate licensees who are members of the NATIONAL ASSOCIATION OF REALTORS® and who subscribe to its Code of Ethics.

OFFICE USE ONLY
Reviewed by Broker or Designee _____
Date _____

EQUAL HOUSING
OPPORTUNITY

Copyright© 1987, CALIFORNIA ASSOCIATION OF REALTORS®
525 South Virgil Avenue, Los Angeles, California 90020   FORM AD-11

SF-Oct-87

Reprinted with permission, California Association of Realtors® Endorsement not implied.

Part of this loyalty is the avoidance of **secret profits**. For example, a broker cannot list a property, knowing it to be worth much more than the listing price, and secretly have his mother-in-law buy the property for him, selling it immediately for a tidy profit. California regulations prohibit real estate agents from buying an interest in property from the principal, such as through a relative or friend, without the full knowledge and consent of the principal.

Secret profit: a real estate agent must disclose all profits to be made from the transaction to his or her principal or be guilty of making secret profits from the transaction

In summary, the agent must not personally profit from the agency relationship through the use of confidential information discovered during the agency relationship, and must not have any personal interest in the transaction unless it is with the principal's knowledge and consent.

OBEDIENCE AND UTMOST GOOD FAITH. The agent must obey the instructions of the principal and carry them out in utmost good faith. The agent's acts must also be in conformity with the purpose and intent of the instructions. A broker can be held liable for any loss caused by failure to obey the principal's instructions.

REASONABLE CARE AND SKILL. The agent has a duty to use reasonable care and exercise skill in the performance of his or her duties. When an agent holds him or herself out as possessing certain skills or abilities, the agent must act as a competent person having those skills and abilities. For example, a person who holds herself out to be a real estate broker must exercise the care and ability of a competent broker. If the broker causes the principal harm due to negligence or carelessness, the broker will be liable to the principal for the injury.

Negligence: performing one's duties without exercising reasonable care and skill

ACCOUNTING. The agent must account for all funds or other valuable items received on behalf of the principal. The agent must report the status of those funds (trust funds) and must avoid mixing them with his or her personal accounts (commingling). In California, agents are required to deposit all trust funds in a special trust or escrow account; this is to prevent any improper use of the funds. (See Chapter 17, *License Law*)

AGENT RESPONSIBILITIES TO PRINCIPAL
FULL DISCLOSURE
LOYALTY
OBEDIENCE, GOOD FAITH
REASONABLE CARE AND SKILL
ACCOUNTING

DUTIES OF THE AGENT TO THIRD PARTIES

While agents owe the utmost good faith and loyalty to their principals, this doesn't mean they can treat their customers with reckless disregard. In recent years, increasing numbers of state courts have held agents to ever higher standards of honesty and fair dealing in their transactions with third parties.

GENERAL LIABILITY. Brokers must avoid inaccuracies in their statements to potential buyers. Any material misstatement, if intentional, may constitute fraud; and even an unintentional misstatement may be considered negligence. In either case, the buyer has the right to rescind the transaction and/or sue for damages. While it is not the duty of the agent to verify every statement made by the seller, if the broker has reason to suspect that a statement is false, the broker has the duty to disclose this to the buyer. The broker also has a duty to disclose any known latent material defects about the property. A latent defect is one which is not discoverable by ordinary inspection.

EASTON LIABILITY. California court decisions and statutes give the California buyer significantly greater protection and impose significantly greater disclosure burdens on the licensee than is true in most other states.

Prior to 1984, it was unlawful under the Real Estate Law for a licensee to fail to disclose to a prospective buyer or lessee any facts known to the licensee which materially affected the value or desirability of the property, when the licensee had reason to believe that such facts were not known to or readily discoverable by the prospective buyer or lessee. The agent was not required to inspect the property or to disclose defects or facts which were readily observable by the buyer, such as an obviously dilapidated exterior or broken windows.

> **Note:** Examples of facts which have been considered by California appellate courts to materially affect value or desirability include: that the home was constructed on filled land; that improvements had been made without a building permit and in violation of zoning or building codes; that the structure was condemned; that the building was termite infested; and that the amount of net income for a piece of income property was incorrect.

This basic disclosure obligation was expanded by a 1984 court decision and by a statute later passed by the state legislature in response to the court decision. Now the agent must not only disclose information known to the agent, but must also conduct an inspection in order to discover material facts for the buyer. This rule applies to one- to four-unit residential properties.

The facts of the court decision, *Easton v. Strassburger*, were as follows: In 1976, a broker listed a property which included a 3,000 square foot home, a swimming pool, a guest house and one acre of land. The home had been built on improperly compacted fill and the sellers had experienced two earth slides while they owned the property. The sellers did not inform the listing broker or the buyer of the prior soil problems. Two agents with the listing broker inspected the property. Evidence indicated that one or both of them knew the house was built on fill, saw netting on a slope which had been placed there following a previous slide, and saw that the floor in the guest house was not level. In short, there were "red flags" indicating problems associated with soil slippage and settling. Despite these "red flags," neither agent ordered soil tests, conducted any more extensive investigation, or mentioned anything to the buyer.

The buyer purchased the property for $170,000. After taking possession, more large slides on the site caused substantial damage. Later appraisals indicated the property was worth no more than $20,000 in its damaged condition and that repairs might cost over $200,000. The buyers sued the listing broker, the sellers, and the builders. The jury found all defendants liable in varying amounts.

On appeal, the court ruled against the listing broker. The court held that a real estate broker representing a seller of residential property has a duty to conduct a reasonable and diligent inspection of the property and to disclose to prospective purchasers all facts materially affecting the value or desirability of the property that would be revealed by such an inspection.

The court decision created substantial doubt among California real estate licensees and insurance companies as to exactly what was required of them. Accordingly, the state legislature passed a statute in 1985 to clarify the holding in the case.

The statute requires a licensee marketing one- to four-unit residential property to conduct a reasonably competent and diligent visual inspection of the property. The agent must disclose to prospective buyers any facts which would materially affect the value or desirability of the property which would be revealed by such an inspection. Both listing brokers and cooperating brokers have this duty. The broker's visual inspection need not include areas which are not reasonably accessible to a visual inspection. If the property is a condominium or cooperative apartment, the inspection need be of the unit only. The inspection statute generally does not apply to new subdivisions.

The standard of competence and care to be applied in the broker's inspection is that of a reasonably prudent real estate licensee and is measured by the degree of knowledge acquired through the education, experience and examination that is required to obtain a license.

The required disclosures are most often made in the appropriate section of a disclosure form (Real Estate Transfer Disclosure Statement) that sellers must present to buyers. This form provides for several disclosures required under California law, including the seller's disclosure of structural changes or alterations made without appropriate permits, seller's and broker's disclosures of facts which would materially affect the property and which are not readily discoverable by the buyer, and the broker's disclosure of material facts known or discoverable to the broker from a reasonably diligent inspection of the property. A sample form is shown on the following pages.

In summary, there are five steps an agent should follow to avoid *Easton* liability:

1. **Inquire:** ask the owner about the condition of the property
2. **Inspect:** conduct a careful visual inspection of the property
3. **Point out:** disclose any problems revealed in the inspection
4. **Recommend:** recommend the seller or buyer obtain the advice of a specialist regarding the problems discovered
5. **Disclose:** disclose all the information discovered on the required disclosure form

DUTIES OF THE PRINCIPAL TO THE AGENT

The principal has the duty to perform the agency contract or be held liable for its breach. He or she also has a duty to reimburse the agent for expenses; however, the normal real estate agency, by custom and agreement, generally provides that expenses will be paid out of the broker's commission. The principal has a duty, in certain circumstances, to indemnify the agent for losses suffered because of the agency. Perhaps the most important duty is the duty to compensate the agent for his or her services. Even if there is no explicit statement of compensation in the agency agreement, there is a presumption that payment will be made for services rendered.

Listing: an employment contract between a broker and a landowner/seller

THE COMMISSION. The usual form of payment for real estate agents is the commission, or brokerage fee. This commission is usually computed as a percentage of the total amount of money involved in the sale. The commission is not set by law and is a matter of agreement between the parties. To avoid confusion and ambiguity, the precise terms should

REAL ESTATE TRANSFER DISCLOSURE STATEMENT

(CALIFORNIA CIVIL CODE 1102, ET SEQ.)

CALIFORNIA ASSOCIATION OF REALTORS® (CAR) STANDARD FORM

THIS DISCLOSURE STATEMENT CONCERNS THE REAL PROPERTY SITUATED IN THE CITY OF_____
_____, COUNTY OF_____, STATE OF CALIFORNIA,
DESCRIBED AS _____.
THIS STATEMENT IS A DISCLOSURE OF THE CONDITION OF THE ABOVE DESCRIBED PROPERTY IN COMPLIANCE
WITH SECTION 1102 OF THE CIVIL CODE AS OF _____, 19____. IT IS NOT A WARRANTY
OF ANY KIND BY THE SELLER(S) OR ANY AGENT(S) REPRESENTING ANY PRINCIPAL(S) IN THIS TRANSACTION,
AND IS NOT A SUBSTITUTE FOR ANY INSPECTIONS OR WARRANTIES THE PRINCIPAL(S) MAY WISH TO OBTAIN.

I
COORDINATION WITH OTHER DISCLOSURE FORMS

This Real Estate Transfer Disclosure Statement is made pursuant to Section 1102 of the Civil Code. Other statutes require disclosures, depending upon the details of the particular real estate transaction (for example: special study zone and purchase-money liens on residential property).

Substituted Disclosures: The following disclosures have or will be in connection with this real estate transfer, and are intended to satisfy the disclosure obligations on this form, where the subject matter is the same: _____
_____
_____
_____

(LIST ALL SUBSTITUTED DISCLOSURE FORMS TO BE USED IN CONNECTION WITH THIS TRANSACTION)

II
SELLER'S INFORMATION

The Seller discloses the following information with the knowledge that even though this is not a warranty, prospective Buyers may rely on this information in deciding whether and on what terms to purchase the subject property. Seller hereby authorizes any agent(s) representing any principal(s) in this transaction to provide a copy of this statement to any person or entity in connection with any actual or anticipated sale of the property.

THE FOLLOWING ARE REPRESENTATIONS MADE BY THE SELLER(S) AND ARE NOT THE REPRESENTATIONS OF THE AGENT(S), IF ANY. THIS INFORMATION IS A DISCLOSURE AND IS NOT INTENDED TO BE PART OF ANY CONTRACT BETWEEN THE BUYER AND SELLER.

Seller ☐ is ☐ is not occupying the property.

A. The subject property has the items checked below (read across):

☐ Range	☐ Oven	☐ Microwave
☐ Dishwasher	☐ Trash Compactor	☐ Garbage Disposal
☐ Washer/Dryer Hookups	☐ Window Screens	☐ Rain Gutters
☐ Burglar Alarms	☐ Smoke Detector(s)	☐ Fire Alarm
☐ T.V. Antenna	☐ Satellite Dish	☐ Intercom
☐ Central Heating	☐ Central Air Conditioning	☐ Evaporator Cooler(s)
☐ Wall/Window Air Conditioning	☐ Sprinklers	☐ Public Sewer System
☐ Septic Tank	☐ Sump Pump	☐ Water Softener
☐ Patio/Decking	☐ Built-in Barbeque	☐ Gazebo
☐ Sauna	☐ Pool	☐ Spa ☐ Hot Tub
☐ Security Gate(s)	☐ Garage Door Opener(s)	☐ Number of Remote Controls _____
Garage: ☐ Attached	☐ Not Attached	☐ Carport
Pool/Spa Heater: ☐ Gas	☐ Solar	☐ Electric
Water Heater: ☐ Gas	☐ Solar	☐ Electric
Water Supply: ☐ City	☐ Well	☐ Private Utility ☐ Other_____
Gas Supply: ☐ Utility	☐ Bottled	

Exhaust Fan(s) in _____ 220 Volt Wiring in _____
Fireplace(s) in _____ ☐ Gas Starter
☐ Roof(s): Type: _____ Age: _____ (approx.)
☐ Other: _____
Are there, to the best of your (Seller's) knowledge, any of the above that are not in operating condition? ☐ Yes ☐ No If yes, then describe. (Attach additional sheets if necessary.): _____
_____
_____

B. Are you (Seller) aware of any significant defects/malfunctions in any of the following? ☐ Yes ☐ No If yes, check appropriate space(s) below.
☐ Interior Walls ☐ Ceilings ☐ Floors ☐ Exterior Walls ☐ Insulation ☐ Roof(s) ☐ Windows ☐ Doors ☐ Foundation ☐ Slab(s)
☐ Driveways ☐ Sidewalks ☐ Walls/Fences ☐ Electrical Systems ☐ Plumbing/Sewers/Septics ☐ Other Structural Components
(Describe: _____
_____
_____)
If any of the above is checked, explain. (Attach additional sheets if necessary): _____
_____
_____

Buyer and Seller acknowledge receipt of copy of this page, which constitutes Page 1 of 2 Pages.
Buyer's Initials (_____) (_____) Seller's Initials (_____) (_____)

— OFFICE USE ONLY —
Reviewed by Broker or Designee _____
Date _____

REAL ESTATE TRANSFER DISCLOSURE STATEMENT (TDS-14 PAGE 1 OF 2)

Reprinted with permission, California Association of Realtors® Endorsement not implied.

C. Are you (Seller) aware of any of the following:

1. Substances, materials, or products which may be an environmental hazard such as, but not limited to, asbestos, formaldehyde, radon gas, lead-based paint, fuel or chemical storage tanks, and contaminated soil or water on the subject property. . . . . □ Yes □ No
2. Features of the property shared in common with adjoining landowners, such as walls, fences, and driveways, whose use or responsibility for maintenance may have an effect on the subject property. . . . . □ Yes □ No
3. Any encroachments, easements or similar matters that may affect your interest in the subject property. . . . . □ Yes □ No
4. Room additions, structural modifications, or other alterations or repairs made without necessary permits. . . . . □ Yes □ No
5. Room additions, structural modifications, or other alterations or repairs not in compliance with building codes. . . . . □ Yes □ No
6. Landfill (compacted or otherwise) on the property or any portion thereof. . . . . □ Yes □ No
7. Any settling from any cause, or slippage, sliding, or other soil problems. . . . . □ Yes □ No
8. Flooding, drainage or grading problems. . . . . □ Yes □ No
9. Major damage to the property or any of the structures from fire, earthquake, floods, or landslides. . . . . □ Yes □ No
10. Any zoning violations, nonconforming uses, violations of "setback" requirements. . . . . □ Yes □ No
11. Neighborhood noise problems or other nuisances. . . . . □ Yes □ No
12. CC&R's or other deed restrictions or obligations. . . . . □ Yes □ No
13. Homeowners' Association which has any authority over the subject property. . . . . □ Yes □ No
14. Any "common area" (facilities such as pools, tennis courts, walkways, or other areas co-owned in undivided interest with others). . . . . □ Yes □ No
15. Any notices of abatement or citations against the property. . . . . □ Yes □ No
16. Any lawsuits against the seller threatening to or affecting this real property. . . . . □ Yes □ No

If the answer to any of these is yes, explain. (Attach additional sheets if necessary.): _____

_____

_____

Seller certifies that the information herein is true and correct to the best of the Seller's knowledge as of the date signed by the Seller.

Seller_____ Date _____

Seller_____ Date _____

III
AGENT'S INSPECTION DISCLOSURE

(To be completed only if the seller is represented by an agent in this transaction.)
THE UNDERSIGNED, BASED ON THE ABOVE INQUIRY OF THE SELLER(S) AS TO THE CONDITION OF THE PROPERTY AND BASED ON A REASONABLY COMPETENT AND DILIGENT VISUAL INSPECTION OF THE ACCESSIBLE AREAS OF THE PROPERTY IN CONJUNCTION WITH THAT INQUIRY, STATES THE FOLLOWING:

_____

_____

Agent (Broker
Representing Seller)_____ By_____ Date _____
                          (PLEASE PRINT)   (ASSOCIATE LICENSEE OR BROKER-SIGNATURE)

IV
AGENT'S INSPECTION DISCLOSURE

(To be completed only if the agent who has obtained the offer is other than the agent above.)
THE UNDERSIGNED, BASED ON A REASONABLY COMPETENT AND DILIGENT VISUAL INSPECTION OF THE ACCESSIBLE AREAS OF THE PROPERTY, STATES THE FOLLOWING:

_____

_____

Agent (Broker
obtaining the Offer)_____ By_____ Date _____
                          (PLEASE PRINT)   (ASSOCIATE LICENSEE OR BROKER-SIGNATURE)

V

BUYER(S) AND SELLER(S) MAY WISH TO OBTAIN PROFESSIONAL ADVICE AND/OR INSPECTIONS OF THE PROPERTY AND TO PROVIDE FOR APPROPRIATE PROVISIONS IN A CONTRACT BETWEEN BUYER AND SELLER(S) WITH RESPECT TO ANY ADVICE/INSPECTIONS/DEFECTS.

I/WE ACKNOWLEDGE RECEIPT OF A COPY OF THIS STATEMENT.

Seller_____ Date _____   Buyer_____ Date _____

Seller_____ Date _____   Buyer_____ Date _____

Agent (Broker
Representing Seller)_____ By_____ Date _____
                          (PLEASE PRINT)   (ASSOCIATE LICENSEE OR BROKER-SIGNATURE)

Agent (Broker
obtaining the Offer)_____ By_____ Date _____
                          (PLEASE PRINT)   (ASSOCIATE LICENSEE OR BROKER-SIGNATURE)

A REAL ESTATE BROKER IS QUALIFIED TO ADVISE ON REAL ESTATE. IF YOU DESIRE LEGAL ADVICE, CONSULT YOUR ATTORNEY.

Page 2 of _____ Pages.

OFFICE USE ONLY
Reviewed by Broker or Designee _____
Date _____

REAL ESTATE TRANSFER DISCLOSURE STATEMENT (TDS-14 PAGE 2 OF 2) be spelled out in the listing agreement. The commission percentage is usually based on the sales price rather than the list price, and the broker's commission may be reduced if the actual sales price is lower than the list price.

The amount of the commission must be negotiable because it is a violation of federal antitrust laws for brokers to set uniform commission rates. Any discussion of commission rates among members of competing firms could give rise to a charge of price-fixing.

EARNING THE COMMISSION. Depending upon the purpose of the agency agreement, the agent is generally employed to find a purchaser who is ready, willing and able to meet the principal's terms of sale. A ready, willing and able purchaser is a buyer who is not only willing to enter into a binding contract on the seller's terms and conditions, but is also financially and contractually able to do so.

The parties to the transaction need not enter into a written agreement for the broker to be entitled to a commission. It is enough if the parties are in agreement as to the essential terms of the sales transaction. These essential terms include:

1) price;
2) amount of cash downpayment;
3) mortgage term;
4) interest rate; and
5) amortization.

However, merely introducing the purchaser to the seller does not entitle the broker to the commission. For instance, if the transaction was subsequently negotiated by another broker, the second broker might earn a commission instead. See the discussion of "procuring cause," below.

Once the agent has procured a ready, willing and able purchaser, the commission is earned, even if the sales agreement is never consummated. Many factors may prevent the sale from being completed, such as:

- the owner changing his or her mind about selling
- defects in the owner's title
- the inability of the owner to deliver possession
- the mutual agreement of the owner and the buyer to cancel the sales agreement.

These factors will not prevent the broker from earning the commission.

Sometimes there is controversy over whether a buyer was in fact ready, willing and able. In most states (including California), if a written agreement has been entered into, courts will automatically assume the buyer was ready, willing and able. It is thought that since the seller accepted the purchaser by entering into the written agreement, the seller has waived his or her right to later claim the buyer was unacceptable. This is true even if the buyer immediately defaults because of financial inability to perform. However, if no written contract has been signed and the agreement is still at a verbal stage when the deal falls through, the broker must then prove that the prospective buyer was financially able to perform the contract.

REQUISITES FOR COLLECTING A COMMISSION. In order to collect a commission, the broker must:

Procuring cause: prerequisite to earning a commission under an open listing; producing a ready, willing and able buyer

- be properly licensed at the time the service was provided,
- have a valid contract of employment (listing agreement), and
- (when it's an open listing) be the procuring cause of the sale.

The broker who was primarily responsible for the parties' agreement or whose actions caused a chain of events resulting in the parties' agreement is the **"procuring cause;"** that is, he or she was responsible for procuring a ready, willing and able buyer on the seller's terms. Remember, there is no need for the parties to actually sign the agreement before the broker is entitled to a commission. It is enough if there is a "meeting of the minds" on the important elements of the sales transaction, whether it be written or verbal. Most conflicts as to whether a broker is a procuring cause arise in the open listing situation. (With an exclusive listing, a broker may be entitled to a commission even if he or she was not the procuring cause of the sale.)

> **Example:** Principal gives five open listings to as many different brokers. Two of these brokers showed the property to the same buyer, and one of them successfully negotiated an offer. With a nonexclusive listing (open listing), it is the agent who effected the sale (the procuring cause) who is entitled to the commission.

SALE COMPLETED AFTER LISTING EXPIRES. If a sales agreement is signed before the listing expires, the broker has earned the commission, even if the transaction does not close until after the listing's expiration date. Additionally, a prudent broker will incorporate what is known as an **extender** or **safety clause** into his or her exclusive listing. This clause provides that the broker is entitled to a commission if the seller sells the property to any person the broker negotiated with during the listing term. This is to protect the broker against parties conspiring to deprive him or her of a commission by waiting until the listing has expired. The broker usually has to provide the seller with a list of all those he or she negotiated with in connection with the property, and the list must be delivered to the seller on or before the expiration of the listing. This way the seller knows whom he or she can sell the property to without being liable for a commission.

CONDITIONS. The payment of a commission can be made dependent on any lawful condition. For instance, a common condition is the inclusion of a "no deal, no commission" provision in the listing agreement. This condition makes the commission contingent upon the deal closing and the seller receiving the full purchase price. If this condition is not met (for example, because the buyer could not get financing), the commission need not be paid. However, if the condition is prevented by the bad faith or fraud of the principal, the broker may still collect his or her commission.

Conditions: contract parties sometimes make their performance contingent on the happening of a certain event; for example, the principal may not be liable for the agent's commission unless the transaction closes

UNAUTHORIZED PRACTICE OF LAW

In recent years, conflicts have arisen between state bar associations and real estate boards concerning when a real estate agent's acts amount to an unauthorized practice of law. While real estate brokers and salespersons bring buyers and sellers together, they must realize that they cannot give legal advice; only a licensed attorney may give legal advice.

For the most part, where a broker merely fills in a preprinted form contract of sale incidental to earning his or her commission, the broker's acts will not be unlawful. However, if the broker fills in the form as a separate and distinct act, not in conjunction with a sale, and charges the client separately for this service, the broker will be guilty of the unauthorized practice of law. The broker should be warned against providing advice or services that are of a legal nature and that are not incidental to procuring a purchaser for the seller.

If the broker prepares a will or deed, for example, to create a joint tenancy in land, such acts are beyond the scope of the broker's powers and are the unauthorized practice of law. The wise broker will carefully check with his or her state or local real estate board to ascertain what acts may properly be performed.

Unauthorized practice of law: a real estate agent cannot give legal advice or draft complicated clauses in contracts without engaging in unauthorized practice of law

Even when filling out standard forms in the ordinary course of business, brokers must remember that inserting complicated clauses that require legal expertise will subject them to the penalties of unauthorized practice of law. Brokers should confine themselves to general property descriptions, the price to be paid and the finance terms.

CHAPTER SUMMARY

1. An agency relationship can be created by express agreement (the most common method), ratification or estoppel.

2. Agency relationships may be terminated by an act of either party, because an agency relationship requires the consent of both parties. Acts of the parties include mutual agreement, revocation by the principal, renunciation by the agent, or expiration of the agency term without renewal. Operations of the law may also terminate the agency relationship: fulfillment of the purpose of the agency, death or incapacity of either party, extinction of the subject matter, or bankruptcy.

3. The agent has five important duties to the principal: disclosure of material facts, loyalty, obedience and utmost good faith, reasonable care and skill, and a full accounting of funds involved.

4. The real estate agent also has duties towards third parties, most importantly those imposed as a result of the *Easton* case. Under the statute that followed *Easton*, the agent must perform a careful visual inspection of the property, report to the third party any problems revealed by the inspection, recommend the third party obtain expert advice, and disclose all the information discovered during the inspection in the required disclosure form.

5. The major duty the principal owes the agent is payment of the commission upon completion of the agency agreement.

CHAPTER 6—QUIZ
AGENCY

1. Real estate brokerage is governed by the law of:

   a) the Statute of Frauds
   b) agency
   c) the Uniform Commercial Code
   d) retribution

2. An agency relationship can be created by all of the following EXCEPT:

   a) express agreement
   b) ratification
   c) estoppel
   d) revocation

3. All of the following are necessary to the creation of an agency relationship EXCEPT:

   a) consideration
   b) agreement of both parties
   c) principal with capacity
   d) mutuality

4. Hanson owns a five-acre tract of commercial property that Allison wants to purchase. During negotiations, Hanson allows Allison to assume that Broker Timmons is his agent. Allison discusses the property with Timmons and can rely on representations the broker makes because:

   a) an express agency has been created
   b) Timmons is Hanson's general agent
   c) Timmons is an ostensible agent of Hanson
   d) any information obtained from a licensed broker may be relied on by prospective buyers

5. Maria Garcia acted on behalf of Tom Hilton without his authority, or even the appearance of authority. At a later date, Tom approved of her actions. This would be an example of:

   a) express agreement
   b) ratification
   c) estoppel
   d) assumption of authority

6. An agency relationship can be terminated by which of the following?

   a) Mutual rescission
   b) Incapacity of either party
   c) Extinction of the subject matter
   d) All of the above

7. All of the following might legally terminate a listing with a broker EXCEPT:

   a) bankruptcy of the client
   b) inability of the broker to find a buyer within a reasonable amount of time
   c) a fire which destroys the listed property
   d) an economic depression

8. An agency coupled with an interest is one:

   a) that cannot be revoked before its expiration date
   b) where the broker makes a secret profit at the expense of his or her principal
   c) where the broker receives an interest-bearing note in payment of his or her commission
   d) where a suit is filed for the commission, which constitutes a lien on the real estate

9. An agent warrants:

   a) his or her authority to act on his client's behalf
   b) his or her client's capacity to perform
   c) Both of the above
   d) None of the above

10. A real estate broker is liable to the buyer if he or she:

    a) executes a contract in the seller's name after proper power of attorney authorization
    b) acts in excess of the authority given him or her by the principal
    c) makes statements based on misrepresentations by the seller
    d) gives the buyer's deposit money to the seller and the sale later fails through no fault of the agent

11. A seller listed his home with a broker at $140,000; he asked for a quick sale. The broker showed it to a buyer, saying that the seller was financially insolvent and would take $130,000. The buyer offered $130,000 and the seller accepted. Regarding the broker's action, which of the following is correct?

    a) He did not violate his fiduciary obligation to the seller because the seller accepted the offer
    b) He did not violate his fiduciary obligation because the seller hired him to sell the property, which he did
    c) He violated his fiduciary obligation to the seller because he acted in excess of his authority by offering the property for sale at less than the listed price
    d) He was unethical and violated his obligations to the seller, but as the seller accepted the offer, no harm was done and the broker has no liability to the seller

12. Mrs. Campbell owned a home worth $130,000 and had $45,000 cash to invest. She was interested in acquiring income property and engaged Broker Brown as her agent to find it for her, agreeing to pay him a standard commission for his services. Broker Brown showed her an apartment building which she considered to be worth $175,000. Brown then purchased an option to buy this building for $160,000, and assigned the option to an officer of a corporation he controlled. The officer exercised the option and purchased the building in the name of the corporation. Broker Brown then arranged for Mrs. Campbell to acquire the apartment building in exchange for her home and the $45,000 cash. Which of the following is true?

    a) Broker Brown violated his agency obligations and could be liable to Mrs. Campbell
    b) Brown did not violate any duties to Mrs. Campbell because she was able to acquire the property for what she considered it to be worth
    c) A broker is never permitted to take an option on property
    d) An agent may never acquire his principal's property

13. A broker is engaged by a client to buy property for a specified sum. The broker locates a suitable property and purchases it for himself at a lower price. The broker then offers it to his client for the higher price without revealing the price he paid for it. This is an example of:

    a) secret profit
    b) divided agency
    c) revocation
    d) false promise

14. Commingling is a violation of both agency law and the real estate license law. Which one of the following would NOT be considered commingling?

    a) Depositing a buyer's deposit money check in the broker's commercial account
    b) Cashing a buyer's deposit money check and placing it in the broker's safe
    c) Holding an uncashed deposit check at the direction of the buyer and seller
    d) Depositing a buyer's deposit check in the broker's personal checking account

15. Broker Green has an exclusive listing for a four-family residence at $225,000, with a $50,000 downpayment. She found a buyer who signed an offer of $200,000 with a $55,000 cash downpayment, which she submitted to the owner. The owner said he would think it over and let Green know. In the meantime, a broker with whom Green had agreed to cooperate on the listing brought a signed offer of $210,000 with a $45,000 down payment. Green refused to present this offer to the owner until she had advised the owner what to do about the first offer. Green was:

    a) right, as she would have to split the commission on the other broker's offer if accepted
    b) right, because the second offer had a smaller downpayment
    c) wrong, as the second offer was for more money
    d) wrong, because the agent must submit all offers promptly

16. A broker has several salespersons working for her. One of the salespersons receives a written offer accompanied by a deposit on property listed by the broker. Later the same day, one of the other salespersons in the office obtains an offer, also with a deposit, on the same property. Pursuant to the salespersons' agreement, it is decided to submit only the first offer until it is accepted or rejected. The broker's action is:

a) permissible because only the first offer must be submitted, if the second offeror is notified in writing that there already is a full price offer
b) permissible only if the first offer is substantially higher than the second offer
c) not permissible because all offers must be submitted to the seller
d) not permissible because the broker has a fiduciary responsibility to both buyer and seller

17. If a broker holds an option as well as the listing and decides to exercise his option, he must:

a) reveal in writing to the owner the amount of his expected profit
b) obtain the written consent of the owner
c) disclose to his buyer that he is dealing as a principal, not as an agent
d) All of the above are correct

18. A broker obtained an exclusive listing on a property for thirty days at $120,000. On the last day of the listing the broker brought the seller an offer to purchase the property signed by E. Gilligan. When asked who E. Gilligan was, the broker replied, "A client of our firm." The deal was closed. Actually the buyer was the mother-in-law of the broker and was a member of his household. Later the seller brought action to rescind the transaction.

a) The transaction will be rescinded
b) It will not be rescinded since the property was sold at the listing price
c) The transaction will not be rescinded, but the broker will have to forfeit his commission
d) The buyer will own the property as trustee for the seller

19. Broker Brown has a listing on a property and she and the seller know the plumbing is leaking. Which of the following is true?

a) The broker need not mention this to the prospective buyer if the seller tells the broker in writing not to mention it
b) The broker need not mention this to the buyer if he offers to purchase "as is"
c) The broker must disclose the leak to all prospective buyers
d) The broker need disclose the leak to the buyer only if the buyer asks

20. When an agent does not have the authority to appoint subagents but proceeds to use the help of cooperating brokers, these brokers become:

a) agents of the principal
b) agents of the buyer
c) agents of the listing agent
d) None of the above

1. b) The law of agency is the body of law most relevant to the field of real estate brokerage.

2. d) Revocation terminates an agency.

3. a) Consideration is necessary for the formation of an enforceable contract, but is not necessary for the creation of an agency.

4. c) Timmons is an ostensible agent of the seller.

5. b) The subsequent approval of Garcia's earlier, unauthorized, acts would be ratification.

6. d) All three alternatives would terminate an agency.

7. d) Bankruptcy of the principal, an agent's failure to perform, and destruction of the subject matter would all terminate an agency; changing economic conditions alone would not.

8. a) An agency coupled with an interest cannot be revoked by the principal prior to the agreed-upon expiration date.

9. a) An agent generally warrants only his or her authority to act for the principal, not the principal's capacity to perform.

10. b) An agent who acts in excess of his or her authority is liable for any resulting damages.

11. c) The broker violated duties of loyalty, trust and confidence by divulging confidential information (that the seller would accept a low offer) to the buyer, and would be liable to the seller for any damages caused by the breach of fiduciary duties.

12. a) Brown violated his duties to Campbell by acting as a principal in the transaction, and making a profit, without disclosing that to her.

13. a) This is an example of a secret profit.

14. c) Holding an uncashed check at the direction of both parties to the transaction would not be commingling.

15. d) An agent is obligated to present all offers to the seller promptly.

16. c) All offers must be submitted to the seller.

17. d) An agent who acquires an interest in property listed with him/her should disclose all material facts to the seller and obtain the seller's consent. When selling property in which the agent has an interest, that must be disclosed to the buyer.

18. a) It is likely that the agent's failure to properly disclose his relationship with the buyer will give the seller the right to rescind the transaction.

19. c) A broker has an obligation to disclose latent defects which are known to the broker. An "as is" clause in the purchase contract is usually no defense for failure to make a disclosure required by law.

20. c) If an agent employs cooperating agents without the consent of the principal, they are agents of the listing agent but are not subagents of the seller.

Chapter 7

CONTRACT LAW

OUTLINE

I. Legal Classifications of Contracts
   A. Express vs. implied
   B. Unilateral vs. bilateral
   C. Executory vs. executed
II. Ingredients for a Valid Contract
   A. Capacity
   B. Mutual consent
      1. offer
         a. terminating an offer
         b. counteroffer
      2. acceptance
         a. fraud
         b. undue influence
         c. duress and menace
   C. Lawful objective
   D. Consideration
   E. Writing
III. Legal Status of Contracts
   A. Valid
   B. Voidable
   C. Unenforceable
   D. Void
IV. Terminating a Contract
   A. Full performance
   B. Agreement between the parties
      1. rescission
      2. cancellation
   C. Assignment
   D. Novation
   E. Accord and satisfaction

KEY TERMS

contract	capacity
mutual consent	offer
counteroffer	acceptance
fraud	undue influence
duress	lawful objective
consideration	valid
void	voidable
unenforceable	rescission
cancellation	novation
accord and satisfaction	liquidated damages
specific performance	tender
anticipatory repudiation	statute of frauds
option agreement	equitable title
forfeiture	

CHAPTER OVERVIEW

Contracts are a significant and inescapable part of the real estate business. Almost everyone has a basic understanding of what a contract is. However, there are certain specific requirements which must be met for a contract to be valid and binding. It is important for real estate brokers and agents to be able to recognize and understand the various types of real estate contracts. This chapter describes these contracts and explains: what legally constitutes a contract, how a contract can be terminated, what is considered a breach of contract, and what remedies are available when a breach occurs.

DEFINITION OF A CONTRACT

A real estate licensee deals with contracts on a daily basis: listing agreements, deposit receipts, option agreements and lease agreements are all contracts. Thus, it is important for the licensee to understand the legal requirements and effects of contracts.

Simply stated, a contract is "an agreement between two or more competent persons to do or not to do certain things for consideration." An agreement to sell a car, deliver lumber or lease real property is a contract. If it meets minimum legal requirements, it can be enforced in court.

Contract: an agreement between competent parties to do or not to do certain things for consideration

LEGAL CLASSIFICATIONS OF CONTRACTS

Every contract will be express or implied, unilateral or bilateral, and executory or executed.

EXPRESS v. IMPLIED. An express contract is one that has been put into words. It can be written or oral. Each party to the contract has stated what he or she is willing to do and knows what is due from the other party. Most contracts are express agreements. An implied contract, or contract by implication, is created by the acts of the parties, not by express agreement.

> **Example:** If a written lease agreement expires, but the tenant continues to make payments and the landlord continues to accept them, both parties have implied their consent to a new lease contract.

UNILATERAL v. BILATERAL. A unilateral contract exists where only one of the contract parties is legally obligated to perform. The most common unilateral real estate contract is the option agreement, discussed later in this chapter. A bilateral contract is formed when there has been an exchange of promises and all parties are legally committed to perform. Most contracts are bilateral.

EXECUTORY v. EXECUTED. An executory contract is one that is in the process of being performed. An executed contract has been fully performed. With respect to contracts, the terms "executed" and "performed" are synonymous.

INGREDIENTS FOR A VALID CONTRACT

A valid and binding contract must have four ingredients:

1) parties who have the legal capacity to contract;

2) mutual consent;

3) a lawful objective; and

4) consideration.

CAPACITY

Capacity: in order to enter a valid contract, the party must be 18 years old or older and mentally competent

An individual must be at least 18 years old to enter into a valid contract. He or she must also be competent.

AGE EIGHTEEN. Eighteen years old is sometimes referred to as the **age of majority**. Those under the age of 18 (minors) do not have contractual capability. Generally, if a minor signs a contract, it is voidable by the minor; that is, it cannot be enforced against him or her.

> **Example:** A 16-year-old signs a contract to buy a motorcycle. The seller cannot enforce the contract against the minor, but the minor can compel the seller to honor the agreement.

When a minor makes an agreement concerning real property, however, the agreement is *void*. Neither the minor nor the other party can sue to enforce it.

COMPETENT. If an individual has been declared incompetent by a court, he or she may not legally enter a contract and any agreement he or she signs is void. If an individual is judicially determined to be incompetent after signing a contract, but it is felt that he or she was probably incompetent when the agreement was signed, the contract is voidable at the discretion of the court-appointed guardian.

Contracts entered into by a person who is temporarily incompetent (under the influence of alcohol or drugs, for example) may be voidable if action is taken within a reasonable time after regaining mental competency.

MUTUAL CONSENT

Mutual consent: for a valid contract, each party must agree to the terms; this is done through offer and acceptance

Each party must consent to the agreement. Consent is presumed if a party signs the agreement, unless it can be established that the signature was improperly obtained. There must be no evidence of fraud, duress, undue influence, menace or mistake.

A person can't use failure or inability to read an agreement as an excuse for nonperformance. No contract should be signed until its contents are fully understood. An illiterate person should have a contract explained thoroughly by someone who is concerned with his or her welfare.

Mutual consent is alternatively referred to as mutual assent, mutuality or meeting of the minds. No matter what it's called, it is achieved through the process of **offer and acceptance**.

OFFER. An offer shows the willingness of the person making it to enter into the contract under the stated terms. To be valid, an offer must:

1) be communicated,
2) express a willingness to contract, and
3) be definite and certain in its terms.

The person making the offer (the offeror) must communicate the offer to the individual receiving the offer (the offeree). If the offer proposes a real estate contract, it must be in writing.

Whatever words make up the offer, they must clearly indicate that the offeror intends to enter a contract.

An offer that does not clearly state what the offeror is proposing is said to be illusory—vague—and any agreement reached as a result is unenforceable.

TERMINATING AN OFFER. There are many ways an offer can be terminated, including:

1) revocation by the offeror
2) time lapse
3) death or insanity of the offeror
4) rejection of the offer, or
5) qualified acceptance

The offeror can **revoke** the offer any time up until he or she is notified that the offer has been accepted. Before a contract can be formed, the offeree must not only accept the offer, he or she must also communicate that acceptance to the offeror before the offer is revoked.

Every offer should set a deadline for acceptance. If it does and the acceptance is not communicated to the offeror within the time allocated, the offer **terminates automatically**. If a time limit is not contained in the offer, a reasonable amount of time is allowed. What is reasonable will be determined by the court if a dispute arises.

If the offeror **dies** or is declared **insane** prior to acceptance of the offer, it is terminated.

A **rejection** terminates the offer. The offeree cannot change his or her mind later and bind the offeror to the offer.

> **Example:** John offers to purchase Harry's house for $135,000. Harry rejects the offer the next day. Later on in the day, Harry rethinks the transaction and decides to accept John's offer. He can't, because the offer terminated with his rejection.

Offer: shows the offeror's willingness to enter into a contract on the stated terms; it must be communicated, express a willingness to contract, and be definite in its terms

Counteroffer: a qualified acceptance; a counteroffer terminates the original offer and ripens into a contract on acceptance by the original offeror

A qualified acceptance (sometimes called a **counteroffer**) is actually a rejection of the offer and a tender of a new offer. Instead of accepting all the terms of the offer or rejecting it outright, the offeree "accepts" with certain modifications. This will happen when some, but not all, of the terms of the original offer are unacceptable to the offeree. When there is a qualified acceptance, the roles are reversed; the offeror becomes the offeree and can accept or reject the revised offer. If he or she chooses to accept the counteroffer, the acceptance must be communicated to the person who made it—the original offeree. If the original offeror rejects the new offer, the offeree cannot go back and accept the original offer. The original offer was terminated by rejection.

> **Example:** Jones offers to buy Smith's property under the following conditions: the purchase price is $215,000, the closing date is January 3, and the downpayment is $35,000. Smith agrees to all the terms but the closing date, which she wants to be February 3. By changing one of the terms, Smith has rejected Jones's initial offer and made a counteroffer. Now it is up to Jones to either accept or reject Smith's offer.

Acceptance: shows the offeree's willingness to enter into the contract on the terms stated in the offer; it must be communicated to the offeror

ACCEPTING THE OFFER. To bind the offeror, the offeree must communicate acceptance to the offeror in the agreed-upon manner within the agreed-upon time (or before the offer is revoked). If no time or manner of acceptance is stated in the offer, a reasonable time and manner will be implied. The offeree's acceptance must also be free of any negative influences, such as fraud, undue influence, duress or menace. If a buyer's offer or a seller's acceptance is influenced by any of these negative forces, the contract is voidable by the damaged party.

Fraud: a misrepresentation of a material fact to one who relies on the statement as truth

Fraud is a misrepresentation of a material fact to someone who relies on the misrepresentation as truth.

Undue influence is using one's influence to pressure a person or taking advantage of another's distress or weakness of mind to induce him or her to enter a contract.

Duress is compelling someone to do something—like enter a contract—against his or her will with the use of force or constraint.

Menace is the threat of duress.

LAWFUL OBJECTIVE

Lawful objective: both the consideration and purpose of the contract must be lawful for the contract to be valid

For a contract to be valid and enforceable, both the consideration and the purpose of the contract must be lawful. Examples of contracts with unlawful objectives are contracts to pay interest rates in excess of the state's usury limit or contracts relating to unlawful gambling. If a contract does not have a lawful objective, it is void.

It should be noted that sometimes contracts contain some lawful provisions and some unlawful provisions. In these situations, it may be possible to sever the unlawful portions of the contract and enforce the lawful portions.

> **Example:** Smith and Jones enter into a contract to buy and sell an apartment house. A clause in the contract prohibits the buyer from renting any of the apartments to persons of a certain race. The contract to buy and sell the property would probably be enforceable, but the clause prohibiting rentals to members of a certain race would be void as against public policy.

POSSIBILITY OF PERFORMANCE. As well as being lawful, the objectives of a contract must be possible. This does not mean possible for the person who promised to do it; it means possible for anyone.

> **Example:** Able enters a contract to sell a house to Brown that he doesn't own. The contract is not void for impossibility of performance. While it may be impossible for Able to perform (since he does not own the house), it is not impossible for anyone to perform (the true owner could sell the house). Able may be required to buy the house and sell it to Brown or to pay Brown damages for breach of the contract.

CONSIDERATION

Consideration is something of value, such as money, goods, services, or promises to provide money, goods or services; it must be either a benefit or a detriment to one of the parties; it can be a promise not to do a particular act. The typical real estate sales contract contains a promise by the purchaser to pay a certain amount of money to the seller at a certain time and in a certain manner (such as cash at closing or in monthly installments), and a promise by the seller to convey title to the purchaser when the price has been paid. Both parties have given and received consideration.

Consideration: anything of value, such as money, goods, services, promises; anything of legal detriment or benefit to one of the parties

As a general rule, the contract will be enforceable as long as the consideration has value, even though the consideration exchanged is not equal. A contract to sell a piece of property that has a value of $120,000 for a price of $105,000 would be enforceable. However, in cases where the disparity in value is quite large (such as a contract to sell a piece of property that has a value of $185,000 for $65,000), a court may refuse to grant specific performance, particularly if the parties have unequal bargaining power (such as where the buyer is a well-informed real estate developer and the seller is elderly, uneducated, and inexperienced in business).

IN WRITING

Real estate contracts have a fifth requirement: they must be in writing under the Statute of Frauds.

Statute of Frauds: requires certain contracts to be in writing

STATUTE OF FRAUDS. The Statute of Frauds is a law requiring certain types of contracts to be in writing and signed by the parties in order to be enforceable. The particular contracts covered vary slightly from state to state. Only those types of contracts covered by the Statute of Frauds must be in writing to be enforceable. Other contracts may be oral.

In California, contracts which relate to real estate transactions and are required to be in writing include:

1) any agreement which by its terms cannot be performed within one year of execution (such as a five-year lease);
2) any agreement to convey real property (such as a deposit receipt);
3) any agreement to assume the debts of another (such as assumption of a mortgage);
4) any agreement to employ an agent for compensation to sell, buy, lease for longer than one year, or exchange real property (a listing agreement);
5) employment agreements between real estate brokers and their salespersons;
6) contracts for the sale of goods if the sales price is $500 or more (UCC Statute of Frauds); and,
7) limited partnership agreements.

Note that a lease for one year or less may be required to be in writing if it is not completed within one year of the **date of agreement**. If the parties agree to a one-year lease on June 30, but the lease term doesn't begin until July 1, the lease must be in writing.

The "writing" required by the Statute of Frauds does not have to be in any particular form, nor does it have to be contained entirely in one document. A note or memorandum of the agreement or a series of letters will suffice as long as the writing identifies the subject matter of the contract, indicates an agreement between the parties and its essential terms, and is signed by the parties to be bound or their agents.

VERBAL CONTRACTS. Occasionally a court will enforce a verbal contract that should have been in writing. This might occur if there is evidence that the contract exists and of its terms, and if one party has completely or substantially performed his or her obligations under the contract. This is a relatively rare occurrence. The safest course is to put it in writing.

A VALID CONTRACT
CONSIDERATION
CAPACITY
MUTUAL CONSENT
LAWFUL OBJECTIVE
WRITING (for real estate contracts)

LEGAL STATUS OF CONTRACTS

A contract's legal status will fall into one of four categories:

1) valid
2) voidable
3) unenforceable, or
4) void

VALID

If the contract contains all the essentials, the contents can be proven in court, and it is free of any negative influences, it is a valid agreement and can be enforced.

VOIDABLE

A voidable contract is a contract which on its face appears to be valid, but which has a defect giving one or more of the parties the power to avoid performance or rescind the agreement. Contracts entered by minors or temporarily incompetent persons or contracts entered as a result of fraud are normally voidable by the injured party (the minor, the temporarily incompetent individual, or the one defrauded).

It is important to note that action must be taken to rescind a voidable contract. Unlike a contract which is void from the outset, a voidable contract cannot simply be ignored. Failure to take action within a reasonable time may result in a court declaring the contract impliedly ratified. Alternatively, the injured party may decide that he or she would rather continue with the agreement and expressly ratify it.

UNENFORCEABLE

An unenforceable contract cannot be enforced in court for one of the following reasons:

1) its contents cannot be proved
2) it is a verbal contract that was supposed to be in writing
3) the other party has been damaged and has a voidable contract, or
4) the statute of limitations has expired.

CONTENTS CANNOT BE PROVED. This is most often a problem associated with verbal agreements. Even if the law does not require a certain kind of contract to be written, it is a good idea to put it in writing because it avoids confusion and misunderstanding. Furthermore, the written agreement must clearly state all that has been agreed upon. Vaguely worded contracts are illusory and unenforceable.

VERBAL CONTRACT. As explained above, some contracts are required to be in writing before they can be enforced. Real estate sales contracts are among them. A verbal real estate agreement can be performed if the parties are willing, but if one party elects not to complete the deal, the other party could not enforce the agreement in court.

ONE PARTY HAS VOIDABLE CONTRACT. If one party has a voidable contract, the other is left with an unenforceable contract.

STATUTE OF LIMITATIONS EXPIRED. The statute of limitations limits how many years after a contract is breached the injured party may sue to enforce the contract. Once the specified number of years has elapsed since the breach, a court may no longer enforce the contract.

VOID

A void contract is no contract at all; it is a legal nullity without force or effect. This most often occurs because one of the essential elements, such as mutual consent or consideration, is completely lacking.

Example: One of the parties to a contract was declared mentally incompetent by a court prior to entering the contract. Since the party had no capacity to enter into a contract, it is void.

A void contract may be disregarded without the necessity of taking action to rescind.

TYPE OF CONTRACT	LEGAL EFFECT	EXAMPLE
VOID	No contract at all	An agreement for which there is no consideration
VOIDABLE	Valid until rescinded by one party	A contract with a minor
UNENFORCEABLE	Party may not sue for performance	A contract where the statute of limitations has expired
VALID	Binding and enforceable	An agreement with all the requirements for a valid contract

TERMINATING A CONTRACT

An existing contract can be terminated by 1) full performance; or 2) agreement between the parties.

FULL PERFORMANCE
Full performance means all that has been agreed upon has been done—the contract is executed.

AGREEMENT BETWEEN THE PARTIES
The parties to the contract can agree to terminate it by one of two methods:

1) rescission, or
2) cancellation.

Rescission: the parties
agree to terminate their
agreement and place
themselves as nearly as
possible in the positions
they were in prior to
entering the contract.

Cancellation: the parties
agree to terminate their
agreement, but previous
acts are unaffected

Assignment: the contract
rights or obligations of
one party are assigned to
another person, but the
original party still retains
secondary liability.

Novation: one contract is
replaced by another
contract or one party to
the contract is replaced
by another party

RESCISSION. A rescission is occasionally referred to as a "contract to destroy a contract." The buyer and seller sign an agreement that terminates their previous agreement and puts them as nearly as possible back in the positions they were in prior to entering the agreement. If any money or rights exchanged hands (such as a downpayment), they would be returned. If just one of the parties wants to rescind and circumstances justify such a unilateral rescission, a court might order the rescission. So, a rescission can be by agreement or by court order.

CANCELLATION. A cancellation is different from a rescission in that it does not go as far. The parties agree to terminate the contract, but previous acts are unaffected. For example, money paid prior to cancellation is not returned.

When agreeing to purchase real property, a buyer generally makes a good faith deposit, called an **earnest money deposit**, which the seller is entitled to keep if the buyer defaults on the agreement. If buyer and seller agree to terminate the contract and the earnest money deposit is refunded to the purchaser, the contract has been rescinded. If the deposit is kept by the seller, the contract has been cancelled.

ASSIGNMENT OR NOVATION

If the contract is not to be terminated, but one or more of the parties wants to withdraw, this can be accomplished by:

1) assignment, or
2) novation.

ASSIGNMENT. Any contract, other than a personal services contract, can be assigned from one person to another, unless a clause in the contract prohibits such an assignment.

> **Example:** A buyer is purchasing a home on a land contract over a period of 15 years. In the absence of any prohibitive language, he can sell the home, accept a cash downpayment, and assign his contract rights and liabilities to the new purchaser. The new owner would assume primary liability for the contract debt, but the original buyer would retain a secondary liability.

NOVATION. The term "novation" has two generally accepted meanings. One type of novation is the substitution of a new party into an existing obligation. If a buyer under a real estate contract is released by the seller in favor of a new purchaser under the same contract, the first purchaser has novated—she is relieved of all liability connected with the contract.

Novation may also be the substitution of a new obligation for an old one. If a landlord and tenant agree to tear up a three-year lease in favor of a new ten-year lease, the old agreement is replaced with the new one.

ASSIGNMENT vs. NOVATION. The difference between assignment and novation is one of liability. Where a contract is assigned, there is continuing liability on the part of the assignor (the original contract party). The novator, on the other hand, is released from liability, either because he or she was replaced with an individual who was approved by the other contract party, or the contract was replaced with another that was acceptable to the other contract party.

ACCORD AND SATISFACTION. An accord and satisfaction occurs when someone who has a contractual right against another agrees to accept something different (usually less) than what was called for in the original agreement.

> Accord and satisfaction: one party agrees to accept something other than the originally promised performance in full satisfaction of the contract

> **Example:** Able is obligated to pay Baker $1000 on July 4. He offers to pay $800 on July 1 instead, explaining that he simply does not have and will not be able to get any more money than that. If Baker agrees to accept $800 on July 1 as satisfaction of the $1000 owed on the fourth, Able pays it, and Baker accepts it, there has been an accord (the agreement) and satisfaction (performance of the agreement) which would relieve Able of the original obligation.

BREACH OF CONTRACT

A breach of contract occurs when a party fails, without legal excuse, to perform any promise contained in the agreement. When a breach occurs, there are four possible remedies for the damaged party:

1) rescission
2) liquidated damages
3) damages, or
4) specific performance

RESCISSION

As previously explained, a rescission is a termination of the contract by returning all the parties to their original positions. The seller refunds the buyer's earnest money deposit and the buyer gives up his or her equitable interest in the property. The rescission can be mutual or unilateral.

LIQUIDATED DAMAGES

The parties to a contract sometimes agree in advance what amount will serve as full compensation to be paid should one of the parties default.

> **Example:** Able agrees to buy 25,000 widgets from Baker. They agree that if Baker cannot deliver the widgets to Able on time, Baker will pay Able $5,000 as full compensation. If Baker failed to deliver the widgets on time, Able could only receive the $5,000 from Baker; she could not sue for an additional amount, even if her actual damages were greater than $5,000.

In a real estate transaction, the amount of liquidated damages (if any) is generally the buyer's earnest money deposit. If the seller keeps the deposit and releases the buyer from the contract, the agreement is cancelled. For residential transactions (one to four units), California law limits liquidated damages to 3% of the purchase price. So if the deposit was more than 3%, the seller will have to return the excess to the buyer.

DAMAGES

This is the amount of money that can be recovered through a court action by a person who has been damaged by the default of another. If a seller breaches a contract, the buyer has no good faith deposit to keep as liquidated damages, and the buyer may elect to sue for money to compensate for the damage the breach caused.

SPECIFIC PERFORMANCE

Specific performance: as a remedy for breach of contract, the court can order the breaching party to perform as promised

Specific performance is a legal action designed to compel a defaulting party to perform under the terms of the contract. A court can order a seller to sign and deliver a deed or a buyer to complete a purchase.

TENDERING AN OFFER

A tender is an unconditional offer by one of the contract parties to perform his or her part of the agreement. Frequently it is referred to as "an offer to make an offer good." A tender is usually made in contemplation of the other party's default and is necessary before legal action can be taken on the breach.

>   **Example:** If a seller suspects the buyer does not plan to complete the purchase (and he intends to sue the buyer if this happens), the seller must attempt to deliver the deed to the buyer as promised in the real estate sales contract. If the tender is made, and the buyer refuses to pay the agreed price and accept the deed, the buyer is placed in default and the seller may then undertake the appropriate legal action.

Of course, if a buyer has reason to believe the seller does not plan to complete the sale, he or she tenders the offer by attempting to deliver the full amount promised in the purchase and sale agreement to the seller. When the seller refuses to accept the money and deliver the deed, he or she is in default.

Sometimes there is an **anticipatory repudiation** by one of the parties. An anticipatory repudiation is a positive statement by the defaulting party indicating he or she will not or cannot perform according to the terms of the agreement. When this happens, no tender is necessary as a basis for a legal action.

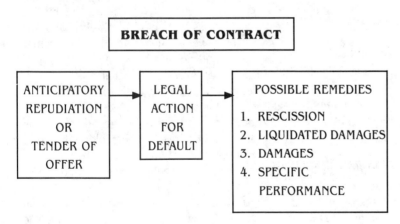

TYPES OF REAL ESTATE CONTRACTS

There are several contracts the real estate agent should be familiar with. These include the listing agreement, the deposit receipt, the option and the installment sales contract.

LISTING AGREEMENT

The listing agreement is a written employment contract between a property owner and a broker, employing the broker to find a buyer or tenant who is ready, willing and able to buy or lease on the owner's terms. Entering into a written listing agreement is a prerequisite to a broker collecting a commission.

There are three types of listing agreements. The primary distinctions between them are:

- the conditions under which a seller is obligated to pay a commission
- whether the seller has a right to list the property with more than one broker
- whether the seller can sell the property him or herself without liability for a commission.

The three types of listing agreements are:

- open listings
- exclusive agency listings
- exclusive right to sell listings

OPEN LISTINGS. In an open (non-exclusive) listing, the principal may contract with many brokers to procure ready, willing and able buyers. The principal is liable for a commission only to the broker who first procures a ready, willing and able buyer. Furthermore, the principal may sell the property him or herself and not pay a commission to any of the brokers. The sale of the property cancels all other open listings.

There are obvious disadvantages for the broker in this type of arrangement. Since the listing automatically terminates once the property is sold, a broker without notice of the sale may continue to look for a purchaser after the property has, in fact, been sold and receive no compensation for such work. Also, this type of arrangement is likely to produce quarrels between brokers as to who procured the buyer or who procured a buyer first.

EXCLUSIVE AGENCY. In the exclusive agency situation, the principal appoints one broker as the exclusive agent to procure a purchaser. The seller is then obligated to pay the broker a commission if the property is sold by that broker or any other person; the listing broker is the exclusive broker.

However, the principal still has the right to sell the property him or herself, without the assistance of any other broker, and without any obligation to pay the exclusive broker a commission. Once the property is sold, the exclusive agency automatically terminates, regardless of the agency period in the listing agreement. The exclusive agency must have a definite termination date; otherwise, the broker may be subject to discipline or loss of license.

EXCLUSIVE RIGHT TO SELL. Under an exclusive right to sell listing, the principal must pay the broker a commission, regardless of who procures the purchaser, including the principal. This type of listing is the listing most often used in the real estate industry because of the protection it affords the broker. As with the exclusive agency, a definite termination date is required.

To summarize, the exclusive right to sell listing is the only one which obligates the seller to pay a commission when the seller is the one who finds the buyer. Under open and exclusive agency listing agreements, the seller is free to market the property on his or her own and, if successful, to sell the property without liability for a commission. There is, of course, enormous potential in these situations for disputes between the seller and broker as to who was the procuring cause of the sale. The exclusive right to sell listing eliminates this problem because the seller is obligated to pay the commission regardless of who finds the buyer.

The Code of Ethics of the National Association of REALTORS® encourages the use of exclusive listings whenever possible. This would include both exclusive agency and exclusive right to sell listing agreements. Theoretically, exclusive listings result in better service to the seller. Since the broker has a more secure claim for a commission if the property is sold, the broker is more likely to work harder to sell the property. With exclusive listings, there is also less potential for disputes among competing brokers.

MULTIPLE LISTING. A multiple listing is not a particular type of listing; it is simply a listing (of whatever type) submitted to a multiple listing service. A multiple listing service is an association of brokers who have agreed to share information and listings to maximize their exposure to the public and facilitate more and faster sales. On sale of a property, the listing broker shares the commission with the selling broker, based on a percentage split negotiated between the two brokers.

NET LISTING. A net listing is also not a type of listing, but refers to the manner in which a broker's commission is determined. Under this type of arrangement, the seller stipulates a net amount of money he or she wants to derive from the sale of the property. The broker may then offer to sell the property at a price higher than the listing price. If the property is sold, the broker's commission is the amount over the net amount.

Example: Seller insists on $145,000 net to her from the sale. Broker sells the property for $158,000. Broker's commission is $13,000. The listing could have been open, exclusive agency, or exclusive right to sell, each providing for a specific "net" to the seller.

A common problem with the net listing is that it lends itself readily to fraud, because of the uncertainty over the sales price set or received by the broker.

In a net listing, the broker must reveal the amount of his or her commission to the principal before the principal commits him or herself to the transaction for which the commission is due. Failure to do so may result in loss of the broker's license.

DEPOSIT RECEIPT

In California, the deposit receipt (also known as the purchase contract and receipt for deposit), is the most commonly used document in the sale of real property.

The deposit receipt serves four functions:

- First, it is a receipt for the buyer's earnest money deposit made in conjunction with the buyer's firm offer to purchase.
- Second, it becomes the contract of sale after it is properly signed by the buyer and seller.
- Third, it protects the broker because the acceptance section of the document (wherein the seller accepts the contract) provides for the payment of a specified brokerage fee by the seller; the seller cannot accept the contract without also making a written promise to pay the broker's commission.
- Fourth, it includes the agency confirmation statement required by law in residential transactions.

Once the agreement has been signed by all parties it becomes a binding contract (assuming that all the elements of a valid contract which were discussed earlier have been included), and the terms cannot be modified without agreement by all parties. In California an agent is required to give all parties to the contract a copy at the time they sign.

Prior to the execution of a deposit receipt, real estate agents are required to submit all offers received to the principal and must also disclose to prospective buyers all property defects. (See Chapter 6, *Agency*)

EXCLUSIVE AUTHORIZATION AND RIGHT TO SELL
MULTIPLE LISTING AUTHORIZATION
THIS IS INTENDED TO BE A LEGALLY BINDING AGREEMENT — READ IT CAREFULLY.
CALIFORNIA ASSOCIATION OF REALTORS® (CAR) STANDARD FORM

1. **EXCLUSIVE RIGHT TO SELL:** I hereby employ and grant _____ hereinafter called "Broker," the exclusive and irrevocable right commencing on _____ , 19____ , and expiring at midnight on _____ , 19____ , to sell or exchange the real property situated in the City of _____ , County of _____ , California described as follows: _____

2. **TERMS OF SALE:** The purchase price shall be _____ ($_____), to be paid as follows _____

   The following items of personal property are included in the above stated price: _____

3. **MULTIPLE LISTING SERVICE (MLS):** Broker is a Participant of _____ ASSOCIATION/BOARD OF REALTORS® Multiple Listing Service (MLS) and this listing information will be provided to the MLS to be published and disseminated to its Participants in accordance with its Rules and Regulations. Broker is authorized to cooperate with other real estate brokers, to appoint subagents and to report the sale, its price, terms and financing for the publication, dissemination, information and use by authorized Association/Board members, MLS Participants and Subscribers.

4. **TITLE INSURANCE:** Evidence of title shall be a California Land Title Association policy of title insurance in the amount of the selling price.

Notice: The amount or rate of real estate commissions is not fixed by law. They are set by each Broker individually and may be negotiable between the Seller and Broker.

5. **COMPENSATION TO BROKER:** I hereby agree to compensate Broker, irrespective of agency relationship(s), as follows:
   (a) _____ percent of the selling price, or $_____ , if the property is sold during the term hereof, or any extension thereof, by Broker or through any other person, or by me on the terms herein set forth, or any other price and terms I may accept, or _____ percent of the price shown in 2. or $_____ , if said property is withdrawn from sale, transferred, conveyed, leased, or rented without the consent of Broker, or made unmarketable by my voluntary act during the term hereof or any extension thereof.
   (b) The compensation provided for in subparagraph (a) above if property is sold, conveyed or otherwise transferred within _____ calendar days after the termination of this authority or any extension thereof to anyone with whom Broker has had negotiations prior to final termination, provided I have received notice in writing, including the names of the prospective purchasers, before or upon termination of this agreement or any extension hereof. However, I shall not be obligated to pay the compensation provided for in subparagraph (a) if a valid listing agreement is entered into during the term of said protection period with another licensed real estate broker and a sale, lease or exchange of the property is made during the term of said valid listing agreement.
   (c) I authorize Broker to cooperate with other brokers, to appoint subagents, and to divide with other brokers such compensation in any manner acceptable to brokers.
   (d) In the event of an exchange, permission is hereby given Broker to represent all parties and collect compensation or commissions from them, provided there is full disclosure to all principals of such agency. Broker is authorized to divide with other brokers such compensation or commissions in any manner acceptable to brokers.
   (e) Seller shall execute and deliver an escrow instruction irrevocably assigning Broker's compensation in an amount equal to the compensation provided in subparagraph (a) (above) from the Seller's proceeds.

6. **DEPOSIT:** Broker is authorized to accept and hold on Seller's behalf a deposit to be applied toward purchase price.

7. **HOME PROTECTION PLAN:** Seller is informed that home protection plans are available. Such plans may provide additional protection and benefit to a Seller and Buyer. Cost and coverage may vary.

* 8. **KEYBOX:** I authorize Broker to install a KEYBOX: (Initial) YES (____/____) NO (____/____)
   Refer to reverse side for important keybox information.

9. **SIGN:** Authorization to install a FOR SALE/SOLD sign on the property: (Initial) YES (____/____) NO (____/____)

10. **PEST CONTROL:** Seller shall furnish a current Structural Pest Control Report of the main building and all structures of the property, except _____ . (Initial) YES (____/____) NO (____/____)

11. **DISCLOSURE:** Unless exempt, Seller shall provide a Real Estate Transfer Disclosure Statement concerning the condition of the property. I agree to save and hold Broker harmless from all claims, disputes, litigation, and/or judgments arising from any incorrect information supplied by me, or from any material fact known by me which I fail to disclose. (Initial) (____/____)

* 12. **TAX WITHHOLDING:** Seller agrees to perform any act reasonably necessary to carry out the provisions of FIRPTA (Internal Revenue Code §1445) and California Revenue and Taxation Code §§18805 and 26131, and regulations promulgated thereunder. Refer to the reverse side for withholding provisions and exemptions.

13. **EQUAL HOUSING OPPORTUNITY:** This property is offered in compliance with federal, state, and local anti-discrimination laws.

* 14. **ARBITRATION OF DISPUTES:** Any dispute or claim in law or equity arising out of this contract or any resulting transaction shall be decided by neutral binding arbitration in accordance with the rules of the American Arbitration Association, and not by court action except as provided by California law for judicial review of arbitration proceedings. Judgment upon the award rendered by the arbitrator(s) may be entered in any court having jurisdiction thereof. The parties shall have the right to discovery in accordance with Code of Civil Procedure §1283.05. The following matters are excluded from arbitration hereunder: (a) a judicial or non-judicial foreclosure or other action or proceeding to enforce a deed of trust, mortgage, or real property sales contract as defined in Civil Code §2985, (b) an unlawful detainer action, (c) the filing or enforcement of a mechanic's lien, (d) any matter which is within the jurisdiction of a probate court, or (e) an action for bodily injury or wrongful death, or for latent or patent defects to which Code of Civil Procedure §337.1 or §337.15 applies. The filing of a judicial action to enable the recording of a notice of pending action, for order of attachment, receivership, injunction, or other provisional remedies, shall not constitute a waiver of the right to arbitrate under this provision.
   "NOTICE: BY INITIALLING IN THE SPACE BELOW YOU ARE AGREEING TO HAVE ANY DISPUTE ARISING OUT OF THE MATTERS INCLUDED IN THE 'ARBITRATION OF DISPUTES' PROVISION DECIDED BY NEUTRAL ARBITRATION AS PROVIDED BY CALIFORNIA LAW AND YOU ARE GIVING UP ANY RIGHTS YOU MIGHT POSSESS TO HAVE THE DISPUTE LITIGATED IN A COURT OR JURY TRIAL. BY INITIALLING IN THE SPACE BELOW YOU ARE GIVING UP YOUR JUDICIAL RIGHTS TO DISCOVERY AND APPEAL, UNLESS THOSE RIGHTS ARE SPECIFICALLY INCLUDED IN THE 'ARBITRATION OF DISPUTES' PROVISION. IF YOU REFUSE TO SUBMIT TO ARBITRATION AFTER AGREEING TO THIS PROVISION, YOU MAY BE COMPELLED TO ARBITRATE UNDER THE AUTHORITY OF THE CALIFORNIA CODE OF CIVIL PROCEDURE. YOUR AGREEMENT TO THIS ARBITRATION PROVISION IS VOLUNTARY."
   "WE HAVE READ AND UNDERSTAND THE FOREGOING AND AGREE TO SUBMIT DISPUTES ARISING OUT OF THE MATTERS INCLUDED IN THE 'ARBITRATION OF DISPUTES' PROVISION TO NEUTRAL ARBITRATION."
   (Initial) BROKER (_____) SELLER (____/____)

15. **ATTORNEY'S FEES:** In any action, proceeding or arbitration arising out of this agreement, the prevailing party shall be entitled to reasonable attorney's fees and costs.

16. **ADDITIONAL TERMS:** _____

17. **ENTIRE AGREEMENT:** I, the Seller, warrant that I am the owner of the property or have the authority to execute this agreement. The Seller and Broker further intend that this agreement constitutes the complete and exclusive statement of its terms and that no extrinsic evidence whatsoever may be introduced in any judicial or arbitration proceeding, if any, involving this agreement.

   I acknowledge that I have read and understand this agreement, including the information on the reverse side, and have received a copy.

   Date _____ , 19____   _____ , California
   Seller _____   Address _____
   Seller _____   City _____ State _____ Zip _____
   In consideration of the above, Broker agrees to use diligence in procuring a purchaser.   Phone _____
   Real Estate Broker _____   By _____
   Address _____   City _____ Date _____

OFFICE USE ONLY
Reviewed by Broker or Designee _____
Date _____

* REFER TO REVERSE SIDE FOR ADDITIONAL INFORMATION

FORM A-14

REAL ESTATE PURCHASE CONTRACT AND RECEIPT FOR DEPOSIT
THIS IS MORE THAN A RECEIPT FOR MONEY. IT IS INTENDED TO BE A LEGALLY BINDING CONTRACT. READ IT CAREFULLY.
CALIFORNIA ASSOCIATION OF REALTORS' (CAR) STANDARD FORM

_____ , California, _____ , 19 ____

Received from _____

herein called Buyer, the sum of _____ Dollars $ _____

evidenced by ☐ cash, ☐ cashier's check, ☐ personal check or ☐ _____ , payable to _____

_____ , to be held uncashed until acceptance of this offer as deposit on account of purchase price of

_____ Dollars $ _____

for the purchase of property, situated in _____ , County of _____ California,

described as follows: _____

1. **FINANCING:** The obtaining of Buyer's financing is a contingency of this agreement.

    A. DEPOSIT upon acceptance, to be deposited into _____ $ _____

    B. INCREASED DEPOSIT within _____ days of acceptance to be deposited into _____ $ _____

    C. BALANCE OF DOWN PAYMENT to be deposited into _____ on or before _____ $ _____

    D. Buyer to apply, qualify for and obtain a NEW FIRST LOAN in the amount of _____ $ _____

        payable monthly at approximately $ _____ including interest at origination not to exceed _____ %,

        ☐ fixed rate, ☐ other _____ all due _____ years from date of origination. Loan fee not to

        exceed _____ . Seller agrees to pay a maximum of _____ FHA/VA discount points.

        Additional terms _____

    E. Buyer ☐ to assume, ☐ to take title subject to an EXISTING FIRST LOAN with an approximate balance of _____ $ _____

        in favor of _____ payable monthly at $ _____ including interest at _____ % ☐ fixed rate.

        ☐ other _____ . Fees not to exceed _____ .

        Disposition of impound account _____

        Additional terms _____

    F. Buyer to execute a NOTE SECURED BY a ☐ first, ☐ second, ☐ third DEED OF TRUST in the amount of _____ $ _____

        IN FAVOR OF SELLER payable monthly at $ _____ ☐ or more, including interest at _____ % all due

        _____ years from date of origination, ☐ or upon sale or transfer of subject property. A late charge of _____

        _____ shall be due on any installment not paid within _____ days of the due date.

        ☐ Deed of Trust to contain a request for notice of default or sale for the benefit of Seller. Buyer ☐ will, ☐ will not execute a request

        for notice of delinquency. Additional terms _____

    G. Buyer ☐ to assume, ☐ to take title subject to an EXISTING SECOND LOAN with an approximate balance of _____ $ _____

        in favor of _____ payable monthly at $ _____ including interest at _____ %

        ☐ fixed rate, ☐ other _____ . Buyer fees not to exceed _____ .

        Additional terms _____

    H. Buyer to apply, qualify for and obtain a NEW SECOND LOAN in the amount of _____ $ _____

        payable monthly at approximately $ _____ including interest at origination not to exceed _____ % ☐ fixed rate.

        ☐ other _____ , all due _____ years from date of origination.

        Buyer's loan fee not to exceed _____ . Additional terms _____

    I. In the event Buyer assumes or takes title subject to an existing loan, Seller shall provide Buyer with copies of applicable notes and Deeds

        of Trust. A loan may contain a number of features which affect the loan, such as interest rate changes, monthly payment changes, balloon

        payments, etc. Buyer shall be allowed _____ calendar days after receipt of such copies to notify Seller in writing of disapproval.

        FAILURE TO NOTIFY SELLER IN WRITING SHALL CONCLUSIVELY BE CONSIDERED APPROVAL. Buyer's approval shall not be

        unreasonably withheld. Difference in existing loan balances shall be adjusted in ☐ Cash, ☐ Other _____

    J. Buyer agrees to act diligently and in good faith to obtain all applicable financing. _____

    K. ADDITIONAL FINANCING TERMS: _____

        _____

        _____

    L. TOTAL PURCHASE PRICE _____ $ _____

2. **OCCUPANCY:** Buyer ☐ does, ☐ does not intend to occupy subject property as Buyer's primary residence.

3. **SUPPLEMENTS:** The ATTACHED supplements are incorporated herein:

        ☐ Interim Occupancy Agreement (CAR FORM IOA-11)　　　☐ _____

        ☐ Residential Lease Agreement after Sale (CAR FORM RLAS-11)　☐ _____

        ☐ VA and FHA Amendments (CAR FORM VA/FHA-11)　　☐ _____

4. **ESCROW:** Buyer and Seller shall deliver signed instructions to _____ the escrow holder, within _____ calendar days

    of acceptance of the offer which shall provide for closing within _____ calendar days of acceptance. Escrow fees to be paid as follows: _____

    _____

Buyer and Seller acknowledge receipt of copy of this page, which constitutes Page 1 of _____ Pages.

Buyer's Initials (_____) (_____)　　Seller's Initials (_____) (_____)

THIS STANDARDIZED DOCUMENT FOR USE IN SIMPLE TRANSACTIONS HAS BEEN APPROVED BY THE CALIFORNIA ASSOCIATION OF REALTORS' IN FORM ONLY. NO REPRESENTATION IS MADE AS TO THE APPROVAL OF THE FORM OF ANY SUPPLEMENTS NOT CURRENTLY PUBLISHED BY THE CALIFORNIA ASSOCIATION OF REALTORS' OR THE LEGAL VALIDITY OR ADEQUACY OF ANY PROVISION IN ANY SPECIFIC TRANSACTION. IT SHOULD NOT BE USED IN COMPLEX TRANSACTIONS OR WITH EXTENSIVE RIDERS OR ADDITIONS.

A REAL ESTATE BROKER IS THE PERSON QUALIFIED TO ADVISE ON REAL ESTATE TRANSACTIONS. IF YOU DESIRE LEGAL OR TAX ADVICE, CONSULT AN APPROPRIATE PROFESSIONAL.

OFFICE USE ONLY
Reviewed by Broker or Designee _____
Date _____

REAL ESTATE PURCHASE CONTRACT AND RECEIPT FOR DEPOSIT (DLF-14 PAGE 1 OF 4)

Reprinted with permission, California Association of Realtors® Endorsement not implied.

Subject Property Address: _____

5. **TITLE:** Title is to be free of liens, encumbrances, easements, restrictions, rights and conditions of record or known to Seller, other than the following: (a) Current property taxes, (b) covenants, conditions, restrictions, and public utility easements of record, if any, provided the same do not adversely affect the continued use of the property for the purposes for which it is presently being used, unless reasonably disapproved by Buyer in writing within _____ calendar days of receipt of a current preliminary report furnished at _____ expense, and (c) _____
_____
Seller shall furnish Buyer at _____ expense a California Land Title Association policy issued by _____
_____ Company, showing title vested in Buyer subject only to the above. If Seller is unwilling or unable to eliminate any title matter disapproved by Buyer as above, Buyer may terminate this agreement. If Seller fails to deliver title as above, Buyer may terminate this agreement; in either case, the deposit shall be returned to Buyer.

6. **VESTING:** Unless otherwise designated in the escrow instructions of Buyer, title shall vest as follows: _____

(The manner of taking title may have significant legal and tax consequences. Therefore, give this matter serious consideration.)

7. **PRORATIONS:** Property taxes, payments on bonds and assessments assumed by Buyer, interest, rents, association dues, premiums on insurance acceptable to Buyer, and _____ shall be paid current and prorated as of ☐ the day of recordation of the deed; or ☐ _____ . Bonds or assessments now a lien shall be ☐ paid current by Seller, payments not yet due to be assumed by Buyer; or ☐ paid in full by Seller, including payments not yet due; or ☐ _____ . County Transfer tax shall be paid by _____ . The _____ transfer tax or transfer fee shall be paid by _____ . PROPERTY WILL BE REASSESSED UPON CHANGE OF OWNERSHIP. THIS WILL AFFECT THE TAXES TO BE PAID. A Supplemental tax bill will be issued, which shall be paid as follows: (a) for periods after close of escrow, by Buyer (or by final acquiring party if part of an exchange), and (b) for periods prior to close of escrow, by Seller. TAX BILLS ISSUED AFTER CLOSE OF ESCROW SHALL BE HANDLED DIRECTLY BETWEEN BUYER AND SELLER.

8. **POSSESSION:** Possession and occupancy shall be delivered to Buyer, ☐ on close of escrow, or ☐ not later than _____ days after close of escrow, or ☐ _____

9. **KEYS:** Seller shall, when possession is available to Buyer, provide keys and/or means to operate all property locks, and alarms, if any.

10. **PERSONAL PROPERTY:** The following items of personal property, free of liens and without warranty of condition, are included: _____
_____

11. **FIXTURES:** All permanently installed fixtures and fittings that are attached to the property or for which special openings have been made are included in the purchase price, including electrical, light, plumbing and heating fixtures, built-in appliances, screens, awnings, shutters, all window coverings, attached floor coverings, TV antennas, air cooler or conditioner, garage door openers and controls, attached fireplace equipment, mailbox, trees and shrubs, and _____ except _____

12. **SMOKE DETECTOR(S):** State law requires that residences be equipped with an operable smoke detector(s). Local law may have additional requirements. Seller shall deliver to Buyer a written statement of compliance in accordance with applicable state and local law prior to close of escrow.

13. **TRANSFER DISCLOSURE:** Unless exempt, Transferor (Seller), shall comply with Civil Code §§1102 et seq., by providing Transferee (Buyer) with a Real Estate Transfer Disclosure Statement: (a) ☐ Buyer has received and read a Real Estate Transfer Disclosure Statement; or (b) ☐ Seller shall provide Buyer with a Real Estate Transfer Disclosure Statement within _____ calendar days of acceptance of the offer after which Buyer shall have three (3) days after delivery to Buyer, in person, or five (5) days after delivery by deposit in the mail, to terminate this agreement by delivery of a written notice of termination to Seller or Seller's Agent.

14. **TAX WITHHOLDING:** Under the Foreign Investment in Real Property Tax Act (FIRPTA), IRC §1445, every Buyer of U.S. real property *must*, unless an exemption applies, deduct and withhold from Seller's proceeds 10% of the gross sales price. Under California Revenue and Taxation Code §§18805 and 26131, the Buyer must deduct and withhold an additional one-third of the amount required to be withheld under federal law. The primary FIRPTA exemptions are: No withholding is required if (a) Seller provides Buyer with an affidavit under penalty of perjury, that Seller is not a "foreign person," or (b) Seller provides Buyer with a "qualifying statement" issued by the Internal Revenue Service, or (c) Buyer purchases real property for use as a residence and the purchase price is $300,000 or less and Buyer or a member of Buyer's family has definite plans to reside at the property for at least 50% of the number of days it is in use during each of the first two twelve-month periods after transfer. Seller and Buyer agree to execute and deliver as directed any instrument, affidavit, or statement reasonably necessary to carry out those statutes and regulations promulgated thereunder.

15. **MULTIPLE LISTING SERVICE:** If Broker is a Participant of an Association/Board multiple listing service ("MLS"), the Broker is authorized to report the sale, its price, terms, and financing for the publication, dissemination, information, and use of the authorized Board members, MLS Participants and Subscribers.

16. **ADDITIONAL TERMS AND CONDITIONS:**
ONLY THE FOLLOWING PARAGRAPHS 'A' THROUGH 'K' *WHEN INITIALLED BY BOTH BUYER AND SELLER* ARE INCORPORATED IN THIS AGREEMENT.
Buyer's Initials   Seller's Initials
_____ / _____   A. **PHYSICAL AND GEOLOGICAL INSPECTION:** Buyer shall have the right, at Buyer's expense, to select a licensed contractor and/or other qualified professional(s), to make "Inspections" (including tests, surveys, other studies, inspections, and investigations) of the subject property, including but not limited to structural, plumbing, sewer/septic system, well, heating, electrical, built-in appliances, roof, soils, foundation, mechanical systems, pool, pool heater, pool filter, air conditioner, if any, possible environmental hazards such as asbestos, formaldehyde, radon gas and other substances/products, and geologic conditions. Buyer shall keep the subject property free and clear of any liens, indemnify and hold Seller harmless from all liability, claims, demands, damages, or costs, and repair all damages to the property arising from the "Inspections." All claimed defects concerning the condition of the property that adversely affect the continued use of the property for the purposes for which it is presently being used (☐ or as _____) shall be in writing, supported by written reports, if any, and delivered to Seller within _____ calendar days FOR "INSPECTIONS" OTHER THAN GEOLOGICAL, and/or within _____ calendar days FOR GEOLOGICAL "INSPECTIONS," of acceptance of the offer. Buyer shall furnish Seller copies, at no cost, of all reports concerning the property obtained by Buyer. When such reports disclose conditions or information unsatisfactory to the Buyer, which the Seller is unwilling or unable to correct, Buyer may cancel this agreement. Seller shall make the premises available for all Inspections. BUYER'S FAILURE TO NOTIFY SELLER IN WRITING SHALL CONCLUSIVELY BE CONSIDERED APPROVAL.
Buyer's Initials   Seller's Initials
_____ / _____   B. **CONDITION OF PROPERTY:** Seller warrants, through the date possession is available to Buyer: (1) property and improvements, including landscaping, grounds and pool/spa, if any, shall be maintained in the same condition as upon the date of acceptance of the offer, and (2) the roof is free of all known leaks, and (3) built-in appliances, and water, sewer/septic, plumbing, heating, electrical, air conditioning, pool/spa systems, if any, are operative, and (4) Seller shall replace all broken and/or cracked glass; (5) _____
Buyer's Initials   Seller's Initials
_____ / _____   C. **SELLER REPRESENTATION:** Seller warrants that Seller has no knowledge of any notice of violations of City, County, State, Federal, Building, Zoning, Fire, Health Codes or ordinances, or other governmental regulation filed or issued against the property. This warranty shall be effective until the date of close of escrow.

Buyer and Seller acknowledge receipt of copy of this page, which constitutes Page 2 of _____ Pages.
Buyer's Initials (_____) (_____)   Seller's Initials (_____) (_____)

OFFICE USE ONLY
Reviewed by Broker or Designee _____
Date _____

REAL ESTATE PURCHASE CONTRACT AND RECEIPT FOR DEPOSIT (DLF-14 PAGE 2 OF 4)

Subject Property Address _____

Buyer's Initials   Seller's Initials

_____/_____   _____/_____   **D. PEST CONTROL:** (1) Within _____ calendar days of acceptance of the offer, Seller shall furnish Buyer at the expense of ☐ Buyer, ☐ Seller, a current written report of an inspection by _____ a licensed Structural Pest Control Operator, of the main building, ☐ detached garage(s) or carport(s), if any, and ☐ the following other structures on the property _____

(2) If requested by either Buyer or Seller, the report shall separately identify each recommendation for corrective measures as follows:
   "Section 1": Infestation or infection which is evident.
   "Section 2": Conditions that are present which are deemed likely to lead to infestation or infection.
(3) If no infestation or infection by wood destroying pests or organisms is found, the report shall include a written Certification as provided in Business and Professions Code § 8519(a) that on the date of inspection "no evidence of active infestation or infection was found."
(4) All work recommended to correct conditions described in "Section 1" shall be at the expense of ☐ Buyer, ☐ Seller.
(5) All work recommended to correct conditions described in "Section 2," if requested by Buyer, shall be at the expense of ☐ Buyer, ☐ Seller.
(6) The repairs shall be performed with good workmanship and materials of comparable quality and shall include repairs of leaking showers, replacement of tiles and other materials removed for repairs. It is understood that exact restoration of appearance or cosmetic items following all such repairs is not included.
(7) Funds for work agreed to be performed after close of escrow, shall be held in escrow and disbursed upon receipt of a written Certification as provided in Business and Professions Code § 8519(b) that the inspected property "is now free of evidence of active infestation or infection."
(8) Work to be performed at Seller's expense may be performed by Seller or through others, provided that (a) all required permits and final inspections are obtained, and (b) upon completion of repairs a written Certification is issued by a licensed Structural Pest Control Operator showing that the inspected property "is now free of evidence of active infestation or infection."
(9) If inspection of inaccessible areas is recommended by the report, Buyer has the option to accept and approve the report, or within _____ calendar days from receipt of the report to request in writing further inspection be made. BUYER'S FAILURE TO NOTIFY SELLER IN WRITING OF SUCH REQUEST SHALL CONCLUSIVELY BE CONSIDERED APPROVAL OF THE REPORT. If further inspection recommends "Section 1" and/or "Section 2" corrective measures, such work shall be at the expense of the party designated in subparagraph (4) and/or (5), respectively. If no infestation or infection is found, the cost of inspection, entry and closing of the inaccessible areas shall be at the expense of the Buyer.
(10) Other _____
_____

Buyer's Initials   Seller's Initials

_____/_____   _____/_____   **E. FLOOD HAZARD AREA DISCLOSURE:** Buyer is informed that subject property is situated in a "Special Flood Hazard Area" as set forth on a Federal Emergency Management Agency (FEMA) "Flood Insurance Rate Map" (FIRM), or "Flood Hazard Boundary Map" (FHBM). The law provides that, as a condition of obtaining financing on most structures located in a "Special Flood Hazard Area," lenders require flood insurance where the property or its attachments are security for a loan.
   The extent of coverage and the cost may vary. For further information consult the lender or insurance carrier. No representation or recommendation is made by the Seller and the Broker(s) in this transaction as to the legal effect or economic consequences of the National Flood Insurance Program and related legislation.

Buyer's Initials   Seller's Initials

_____/_____   _____/_____   **F. SPECIAL STUDIES ZONE DISCLOSURE:** Buyer is informed that subject property is situated in a Special Studies Zone as designated under §§ 2621-2625, inclusive, of the California Public Resources Code; and, as such, the construction or development on this property of any structure for human occupancy may be subject to the findings of a geologic report prepared by a geologist registered in the State of California, unless such a report is waived by the City or County under the terms of that act.
   Buyer is allowed _____ calendar days from acceptance of the offer to make further inquiries at appropriate governmental agencies concerning the use of the subject property under the terms of the Special Studies Zone Act and local building, zoning, fire, health, and safety codes. When such inquiries disclose conditions or information unsatisfactory to the Buyer, which the Seller is unwilling or unable to correct, Buyer may cancel this agreement. BUYER'S FAILURE TO NOTIFY SELLER IN WRITING SHALL CONCLUSIVELY BE CONSIDERED APPROVAL.

Buyer's Initials   Seller's Initials

_____/_____   _____/_____   **G. ENERGY CONSERVATION RETROFIT:** If local ordinance requires that the property be brought in compliance with minimum energy Conservation Standards as a condition of sale or transfer, ☐ Buyer, ☐ Seller shall comply with and pay for these requirements. Where permitted by law, Seller may, if obligated hereunder, satisfy the obligation by authorizing escrow to credit Buyer with sufficient funds to cover the cost of such retrofit.

Buyer's Initials   Seller's Initials

_____/_____   _____/_____   **H. HOME PROTECTION PLAN:** Buyer and Seller have been informed that Home Protection Plans are available. Such plans may provide additional protection and benefit to a Seller or Buyer. The CALIFORNIA ASSOCIATION OF REALTORS® and the Broker(s) in this transaction do not endorse or approve any particular company or program:
a) ☐ A Buyer's coverage Home Protection Plan to be issued by _____
   Company, at a cost not to exceed $_____ , to be paid by ☐ Buyer, ☐ Seller; or
b) ☐ Buyer and Seller elect not to purchase a Home Protection Plan.

Buyer's Initials   Seller's Initials

_____/_____   _____/_____   **I. CONDOMINIUM/P.U.D.:** The subject of this transaction is a condominium/planned unit development (P.U.D.) designated as unit _____ and _____ parking space(s) and an undivided interest in community areas, and _____ _____ . The current monthly assessment charge by the homeowner's association or other governing body(s) is $_____ . As soon as practicable, Seller shall provide Buyer with copies of covenants, conditions and restrictions, articles of incorporation, by-laws, current rules and regulations, most current financial statements, and any other documents as required by law. Seller shall disclose in writing any known pending special assessment, claims, or litigation to Buyer. Buyer shall be allowed _____ calendar days from receipt to review these documents. If such documents disclose conditions or information unsatisfactory to Buyer, Buyer may cancel this agreement. BUYER'S FAILURE TO NOTIFY SELLER IN WRITING SHALL CONCLUSIVELY BE CONSIDERED APPROVAL.

Buyer's Initials   Seller's Initials

_____/_____   _____/_____   **J. LIQUIDATED DAMAGES: If Buyer fails to complete said purchase as herein provided by reason of any default of Buyer, Seller shall be released from obligation to sell the property to Buyer and may proceed against Buyer upon any claim or remedy which he/she may have in law or equity; provided, however, that by initialling this paragraph Buyer and Seller agree that Seller shall retain the deposit as liquidated damages. If the described property is a dwelling with no more than four units, one of which the Buyer intends to occupy as his/her residence, Seller shall retain as liquidated damages the deposit actually paid, or an amount therefrom, not more than 3% of the purchase price and promptly return any excess to Buyer. Buyer and Seller agree to execute a similar liquidated damages provision, such as CALIFORNIA ASSOCIATION OF REALTORS® Receipt for Increased Deposit (RID-11), for any increased deposits. (Funds deposited in trust accounts or in escrow are not released automatically in the event of a dispute. Release of funds requires written agreement of the parties, judicial decision or arbitration.)**

Buyer and Seller acknowledge receipt of copy of this page, which constitutes Page 3 of _____ Pages.
Buyer's Initials (_____) (_____)   Seller's Initials (_____) (_____)

┌─────── OFFICE USE ONLY ───────┐
│ Reviewed by Broker or Designee _____
│ Date _____
└───────────────────────────────┘

REAL ESTATE PURCHASE CONTRACT AND RECEIPT FOR DEPOSIT (DLF-14 PAGE 3 OF 4)

Subject Property Address _____

K. ARBITRATION OF DISPUTES: Any dispute or claim in law or equity arising out of this contract or any resulting transaction shall be decided by neutral binding arbitration in accordance with the rules of the American Arbitration Association, and not by court action except as provided by California law for judicial review of arbitration proceedings. Judgment upon the award rendered by the arbitrator(s) may be entered in any court having jurisdiction thereof. The parties shall have the right to discovery in accordance with Code of Civil Procedure § 1283.05. The following matters are excluded from arbitration hereunder: (a) a judicial or non-judicial foreclosure or other action or proceeding to enforce a deed of trust, mortgage, or real property sales contract as defined in Civil Code § 2985, (b) an unlawful detainer action, (c) the filing or enforcement of a mechanic's lien, (d) any matter which is within the jurisdiction of a probate court, or (e) an action for bodily injury or wrongful death, or for latent or patent defects to which Code of Civil Procedure § 337.1 or § 337.15 applies. The filing of a judicial action to enable the recording of a notice of pending action, for order of attachment, receivership, injunction, or other provisional remedies, shall not constitute a waiver of the right to arbitrate under this provision.

Any dispute or claim by or against broker(s) and/or associate licensee(s) participating in this transaction shall be submitted to arbitration consistent with the provision above only if the broker(s) and/or associate licensee(s) making the claim or against whom the claim is made shall have agreed to submit it to arbitration consistent with this provision.

"NOTICE: BY INITIALLING IN THE SPACE BELOW YOU ARE AGREEING TO HAVE ANY DISPUTE ARISING OUT OF THE MATTERS INCLUDED IN THE 'ARBITRATION OF DISPUTES' PROVISION DECIDED BY NEUTRAL ARBITRATION AS PROVIDED BY CALIFORNIA LAW AND YOU ARE GIVING UP ANY RIGHTS YOU MIGHT POSSESS TO HAVE THE DISPUTE LITIGATED IN A COURT OR JURY TRIAL. BY INITIALLING IN THE SPACE BELOW YOU ARE GIVING UP YOUR JUDICIAL RIGHTS TO DISCOVERY AND APPEAL, UNLESS THOSE RIGHTS ARE SPECIFICALLY INCLUDED IN THE 'ARBITRATION OF DISPUTES' PROVISION. IF YOU REFUSE TO SUBMIT TO ARBITRATION AFTER AGREEING TO THIS PROVISION, YOU MAY BE COMPELLED TO ARBITRATE UNDER THE AUTHORITY OF THE CALIFORNIA CODE OF CIVIL PROCEDURE. YOUR AGREEMENT TO THIS ARBITRATION PROVISION IS VOLUNTARY."

"WE HAVE READ AND UNDERSTAND THE FOREGOING AND AGREE TO SUBMIT DISPUTES ARISING OUT OF THE MATTERS INCLUDED IN THE 'ARBITRATION OF DISPUTES' PROVISION TO NEUTRAL ARBITRATION."

Buyer's Initials   Seller's Initials

____ / ____   ____ / ____

17. **OTHER TERMS AND CONDITIONS:** _____
_____
_____
_____

18. **ATTORNEY'S FEES:** In any action, proceeding or arbitration arising out of this agreement, the prevailing party shall be entitled to reasonable attorney's fees and costs.

19. **ENTIRE CONTRACT:** Time is of the essence. All prior agreements between the parties are incorporated in this agreement which constitutes the entire contract. Its terms are intended by the parties as a final expression of their agreement with respect to such terms as are included herein and may not be contradicted by evidence of any prior agreement or contemporaneous oral agreement. The parties further intend that this agreement constitutes the complete and exclusive statement of its terms and that no extrinsic evidence whatsoever may be introduced in any judicial or arbitration proceeding, if any, involving this agreement.

20. **CAPTIONS:** The captions in this agreement are for convenience of reference only and are not intended as part of this agreement.

21. **AGENCY CONFIRMATION:** The following agency relationship(s) are hereby confirmed for this transaction:

LISTING AGENT: _____ is the agent of (check one):
(Print Firm Name)

☐ the Seller exclusively; or ☐ both the Buyer and Seller

SELLING AGENT: _____ (if not the same as Listing Agent) is the agent of (check one):
(Print Firm Name)

☐ the Buyer exclusively; or ☐ the Seller exclusively; or ☐ both the Buyer and Seller.

22. **AMENDMENTS:** This agreement may not be amended, modified, altered or changed in any respect whatsoever except by a further agreement in writing executed by Buyer and Seller.

23. **OFFER:** This constitutes an offer to purchase the described property. Unless acceptance is signed by Seller and a signed copy delivered in person, by mail, or facsimile, and received by Buyer at the address below, or by _____ who is authorized to receive it, on behalf of Buyer, within _____ calendar days of the date hereof, this offer shall be deemed revoked and the deposit shall be returned. Buyer has read and acknowledges receipt of a copy of this offer. This agreement and any supplement, addendum or modification relating hereto, including any photocopy or facsimile thereof, may be executed in two or more counterparts, all of which shall constitute one and the same writing.

REAL ESTATE BROKER _____   BUYER _____
By _____   BUYER _____
Address _____   Address _____
_____   _____
Telephone _____   Telephone _____

ACCEPTANCE

The undersigned Seller accepts and agrees to sell the property on the above terms and conditions and agrees to the above confirmation of agency relationships (☐ subject to attached counter offer).

Seller agrees to pay to Broker(s) _____
compensation for services as follows: _____

Payable: (a) On recordation of the deed or other evidence of title, or (b) if completion of sale is prevented by default of Seller, upon Seller's default, or (c) if completion of sale is prevented by default of Buyer, only if and when Seller collects damages from Buyer, by suit or otherwise, and then in an amount not less than one-half of the damages recovered, but not to exceed the above fee, after first deducting title and escrow expenses and the expenses of collection, if any. Seller shall execute and deliver an escrow instruction irrevocably assigning the compensation for service in an amount equal to the compensation agreed to above. In any action, proceeding, or arbitration between Broker(s) and Seller arising out of this agreement, the prevailing party shall be entitled to reasonable attorney's fees and costs. The undersigned has read and acknowledges receipt of a copy of this agreement and authorizes Broker(s) to deliver a signed copy to Buyer.

Date _____ Telephone _____   SELLER _____
Address _____   SELLER _____

Real Estate Broker(s) agree to the foregoing.
Broker _____ By _____ Date _____
Broker _____ By _____ Date _____

This form is available for use by the entire real estate industry. The use of this form is not intended to identify the user as a REALTOR®. REALTOR® is a registered collective membership mark which may be used only by real estate licensees who are members of the NATIONAL ASSOCIATION OF REALTORS® and who subscribe to its Code of Ethics.

Page 4 of _____ Pages.

OFFICE USE ONLY
Reviewed by Broker or Designee _____
Date _____

REAL ESTATE PURCHASE CONTRACT AND RECEIPT FOR DEPOSIT (DLF-14 PAGE 4 OF 4)

TYPICAL CLAUSES. Reference should be made to the sample deposit receipt for examples of typical clauses normally found in a contract to purchase and sell real estate.

OPTION AGREEMENT

Option: a unilateral contract; an agreement to keep an offer open.

An option agreement is essentially a contract to make a contract; it is an agreement which creates a right to buy, sell, or lease property for a fixed price over a set period of time. Because the agreement is a contract, it must have all the necessary elements of a contract: offer, acceptance, and consideration. The parties to an option agreement are the **optionor** (generally the seller) and the **optionee** (generally the buyer).

UNILATERAL CONTRACT. The option agreement is a unilateral contract, an instrument which binds only one party and is accepted by performance.

> **Example:** Bob wants $100,000 for his home and tells Mike that he will keep the offer open for two weeks if Mike pays Bob $500 for the option. Mike may accept the offer by tendering $500 to Bob; he has then accepted by performance. Upon performance by Mike, Bob is the only person bound by the agreement. That is, Bob must keep the option open for two weeks or he breaches the contract.

In contrast, a bilateral contract contains mutual promises to perform: a promise by the seller to sell and a promise by the buyer to buy. Both parties are bound by their promises to perform, and these mutual promises create the consideration for the contract.

Once the optionee accepts the option, the optionor is bound to keep the option open for the specified period of time. The optionee is not required to exercise his or her right to buy or lease the property; he or she may exercise the option at his or her discretion. However, if the optionee decides to buy or lease, he or she should give written notice of acceptance to the optionor according to the terms of the agreement. If the optionee fails to exercise the option right within the specified time, the option will automatically expire.

Consideration. The option agreement must be supported by valuable consideration, which may take the form of cash, property, or a promissory note. The consideration may be nominal in nature and no minimum amount is required. But the consideration must, in fact, pass between the parties; a mere recitation of the consideration in the agreement will not be sufficient. The only exception is in a lease-option agreement—the provisions of the lease themselves will be sufficient consideration to support the option.

The option contract must be in writing; oral agreements are unenforceable. Furthermore, since the option anticipates that a sale may take place, the underlying terms of the sale (price, legal description, terms of sale, etc.) should be correct and specified in detail in the option agreement.

Contract Right. The executed option creates a contract right; it is not an interest in real property. Therefore, an option cannot be used as security for a mortgage or a deed of trust. In an option agreement, the title does not pass and the optionee has no monetary rights against the title. The death of the optionor will not affect the rights of the optionee, who may still exercise the right to purchase or lease; the option contract is binding on the heirs and assignees of the optionor.

The option agreement can be assigned, unless there is language in the contract which prohibits assignment. The exception is when the consideration paid by the optionee is in the form of an unsecured promissory note. In this case, the written permission of the owner must be obtained before the option may be assigned.

Recording. The option agreement may also be recorded. If it is recorded, the rights of the optionee will relate back to the date of the option and therefore take priority over the rights of intervening third parties with notice of the option. However, if the option is recorded and is not exercised, a release should also be recorded to avoid a possible cloud upon the title.

LAND CONTRACT

Under a land contract, or installment contract, the purchaser buys the property on an installment basis. The parties to the contract are the vendor (seller) and the vendee (buyer). Periodic payments towards the purchase price are made over a period of years, and during that time the vendor retains legal title to the property. The deed is not delivered to the vendee until the full purchase price is paid. The vendee has equitable title to the property, which is the right to possess and enjoy the property while paying off the purchase price.

Both parties to the contract, the vendor and the vendee, can assign their interests in the contract, unless there is an agreement prohibiting assignment.

A land contract is made up of three elements:

1) a contract,
2) the immediate transfer of possession from seller to buyer, and

Equitable title: the right in property a vendee obtains under a land contract; the right to possess the property even though the vendee does not have legal title

3) the seller's promise to transfer legal title upon full payment of the contract.

Example: Smith agrees to buy Jones's farm for $250,000, to be paid at the rate of $25,000 per year for ten years. Jones allows Smith to take possession of the farm, and promises to convey legal title to the farm to Smith when Smith has paid the full purchase price. Smith and Jones have entered into a land contract.

REASONS FOR USING A LAND CONTRACT. The land contract is used when the seller is financing the buyer's purchase. It is essentially a security device: the seller extends credit to the buyer and holds title to the property as security for repayment of the debt. Usually the deed to the property is placed in escrow, to be delivered if and when the buyer executes the contract. The land contract is used when more conventional financing is unavailable due to scarcity of loan funds or a buyer's inability to qualify for a conventional loan.

By using the land contract, the parties obtain the same advantages of any type of seller financing. The buyer avoids the need to make a large downpayment and can often obtain terms more favorable than those available from lending institutions. The seller offering a land contract can attract a wider range of potential buyers and thereby obtain a higher price for the property than would be possible with conventional financing. The seller may also prefer to sell under a land contract to avoid the lengthy mortgage foreclosure proceedings in the event of default. A land contract can be recorded, and should be recorded to protect the buyer's rights. The seller (vendor) cannot prohibit recording by the buyer (vendee) as a condition of the contract.

CHAPTER SUMMARY

1. A contract is "an agreement between two or more competent persons to do or not to do certain things for consideration."

2. In order for a contract to be valid and binding, the parties must have the legal capacity to contract, and there must be mutual consent, a lawful objective, and consideration. Real estate contracts must be in writing under the Statute of Frauds.

3. A contract may be either valid, voidable, unenforceable, or void.

4. An existing contract can be terminated by full performance or by agreement between parties. The parties can agree to terminate the contract by rescission or cancellation.

5. A breach of contract occurs when a party fails, without legal excuse, to perform any promise contained in the agreement. When a breach occurs, the four possible remedies for the damaged party are rescission, liquidated damages, damages, or specific performance.

6. The types of contracts a real estate agent should be familiar with are the listing agreement, the deposit receipt, the option, and the installment sales or land contract.

CHAPTER 7—QUIZ
CONTRACT LAW

1. In a listing agreement, the seller of real estate agrees to pay the broker a commission if the broker procures a buyer "ready, willing and able" to buy. In the agreement, the broker agrees to use due diligence in procuring a buyer. This agreement is a(n):

    a) bilateral contract
    b) unilateral contract
    c) agreement of sale
    d) deposit receipt

2. Persons who lack capacity may:

    a) appoint a guardian on their behalf
    b) appoint a guardian who cannot contract on their behalf but is limited only to supervising their activities
    c) contract, provided any agreement they enter into is ratified by the appointed guardian
    d) None of these

3. In order for a contract to be valid and binding, there must be:

    a) mutuality
    b) mutual assent
    c) offer and acceptance
    d) All of the above

4. Taylor signs an offer to purchase real property, but suddenly dies before the listing agent notifies him of the unqualified acceptance of his offer by the seller.

    a) Taylor's death constitutes a revocation of the offer
    b) The contract is binding on the heirs provided they are to be found financially capable
    c) The contract is binding if the administrator is notified of the seller's acceptance prior to revoking the offer
    d) Both a) and c)

5. Which of the following is the definition of fraud?

    a) Failure to disclose information which you have a duty to disclose
    b) Making a promise with no intent to fulfill it
    c) Devious practices in business
    d) All of the above

6. Where one party to a contract was induced to sign under physical threat to his person, the contract is:

    a) void
    b) voidable
    c) illegal
    d) Any of these

7. A void contract is one that is:

    a) not in writing
    b) not enforceable by either party
    c) rescindable by agreement
    d) amortized

8. A voidable contract becomes enforceable by:

    a) ratification
    b) novation
    c) estoppel
    d) None of the above

9. An oral contract for the exchange of real estate is:

    a) enforceable
    b) unlawful
    c) unenforceable
    d) enforceable under specific provisions of the real estate law

10. The term "rescinded" in real estate most nearly means:

    a) rewritten
    b) rejected
    c) reworded
    d) terminated

11. The mutual agreement to substitute a new obligation for an old one is:

    a) a mutual rescission
    b) a novation
    c) accord and satisfaction
    d) an assignment

12. A sum that is to be full damages if a breach of contract occurs is called:

    a) just compensation
    b) deficiency judgment
    c) consideration
    d) liquidated damages

13. An offer by one of the parties to the contract to carry out her part of the agreement is called:

    a) estoppel
    b) performance
    c) tender
    d) All of these

14. An oral agreement of sale may be enforced where:

    a) the consideration price is less than $2,500
    b) there is a downpayment of 20% of the consideration
    c) the purchaser has gone into possession, paid part of the purchase price, and made improvements
    d) the broker guarantees performance

15. Until the end of July, Mark Wong has the right to buy Sylvia Cartwright's land for $22,000. This is::

    a) a purchase contract
    b) an option
    c) a land contract
    d) a tender

16. An owner signed a listing with a broker where it was understood that if the property was sold through the efforts of any other broker, or the owner, the listing broker would not be entitled to a commission. This kind of contract is called:

    a) a net listing
    b) an exclusive agency listing
    c) an exclusive right to sell listing
    d) an open listing

17. A broker is authorized to show property under an open listing agreement. According to the terms of most open listing agreements, he should:

    a) write a memo to the seller giving the names of the prospects to whom he has shown the property
    b) phone the seller and notify him of the prospects' names
    c) introduce the parties
    d) write a memo to the office

18. Mary Pearl listed her home with Broker Smith. She subsequently sold her home without any assistance from Smith. Nonetheless, a court ruled that Mary owed Smith a full commission. The logical explanation for the court's action must be that:

    a) Smith had an option on the house
    b) Smith had an exclusive listing
    c) Smith had an open listing
    d) Smith had an exclusive right to sell listing

19. A vendor sells property to a vendee using a:

    a) land contract
    b) deposit receipt
    c) net listing
    d) specific performance agreement

20. An installment purchase contract does NOT give the buyer:

    a) possession
    b) the right to lease the property
    c) legal title to the property
    d) the right to demise the property

1. a) Broker and seller have exchanged promises. This creates a bilateral contract.

2. d) Guardians are appointed by the court and supervised by the court. They can contract on behalf of the individual they represent, but must answer to the court. Persons lacking capacity cannot contract under any circumstances.

3. d) All three of the choices represent different ways of saying the same thing.

4. a) Death of the offeror revokes the offer. His heirs will not be forced to enter into the contract.

5. d) Legally, fraud requires a knowing misrepresentation or suppression of a material fact with the intent that the other party rely upon that deceit.

6. b) This would be a contract signed under menace or duress, which would be voidable.

7. b) If a contract is void, it cannot be enforced by the courts.

8. a) If the party who has the right to void a contract ratifies it instead, the contract becomes valid and enforceable.

9. c) The Statute of Frauds requires all contracts for the sale or exchange of real property to be in writing.

10. d) To rescind a contract means to terminate the contract and place both parties back in their original positions.

11. b) Novation is the substitution of a new contract for an existing one; it must contain all four contract essentials.

12. d) The sum agreed upon in advance as payment for a breach of contract is liquidated damages.

13. c) A party to a contract will 'tender' (make good) the offer, usually when he or she anticipates the other party to the agreement does not intend to perform.

14. c) When one party has partially performed by taking possession and making improvements, the oral agreement becomes enforceable against the non-performing party. This partial performance removes the contract from the requirements of the Statute of Frauds.

15. b) Wong has an option to purchase.

16. d) An open listing permits the seller to list with any number of brokers and be obligated to pay a commission only to the first broker to produce an offer from a ready, willing and able buyer at the listing price or other price acceptable to the seller.

17. a) This would be the best way for the broker to prove that he was the procuring cause of a subsequent sale to one of the prospects.

18. d) Under an exclusive right to sell listing, the owner is obligated to pay the commission to the broker, regardless of who sells the property.

19. a) The parties to a land contract are the vendor (seller) and the vendee (buyer).

20. c) Title remains with the seller until the contract is fully performed. The buyer receives possession and the right to use the property, which is an equitable interest.

REAL ESTATE MATH

OUTLINE

KEY TERMS

area	base
height	interest
principal	square feet
fraction	decimal
numerator	denominator
square	rectangle
per annum	net income
capitalization	value after

value before   gross income
prorations   per diem
parallelogram   triangle
percentage   commission
profit and loss

CHAPTER OVERVIEW

Math is a fundamental tool used by real estate licensees in all aspects of their profession. A real estate licensee uses math to compute loan amounts, closing costs, commissions and the square footage of property and homes. Because math is such a vital part of the real estate profession, we have included a thorough discussion of both the best approach to solving math problems and the various formulas you will need for most of the basic mathematical computations.

APPROACH TO SOLVING MATH PROBLEMS

The following step-by-step approach is suggested to simplify solving the types of math problems you are most likely to encounter on a real estate exam. It is the approach that will be followed in the examples given in the following pages.

READ THE QUESTION. The most important step is to thoroughly read and understand the question. You must know what you are being asked before you can successfully work any math problem. Once you have determined what it is you are to find (for example, area, amount of commission, total profit or percentage of profit) you will know what formula to use.

WRITE DOWN THE FORMULA. Write down the correct formula. For example, the area formula is: area equals base times height, $A = B \times H$. The formulas are all listed at the end of this chapter.

SUBSTITUTE. Substitute the numbers you have been given in the problem into the formula. You may find that there are numbers in the problem that you do not need. It is not unusual for a math problem to contain information that is unnecessary to solve the problem. That's why it's so important to read the question first and determine what you're looking for. Then the formula will guide you in deciding what information is necessary.

While in many problems you'll be able to substitute numbers into the formula without taking any additional steps, in other problems it may be necessary to take one or more preliminary steps. For instance, you may find it necessary to convert fractions to decimals before you can carry out your computations.

CALCULATE. Once the numbers are substituted into the formula, you must do some computations to find the unknown. Most of the formulas have the same basic form ($A = B \times C$). The problem will give you two of the three numbers (or information to enable you to find two of the numbers) and then you will either have to divide or multiply to find the third number, the one you are looking for to solve the problem.

Whether you must multiply or divide is determined by the element in the formula you are trying to discover. For example, the formula $A = B \times C$ may be converted into three different formulas, depending upon the element you wish to discover:

- If the quantity A is unknown, then the following formula is used: $A = B \times C$. The number B is multiplied by C; the product of B times C is A.

- If the quantity B is unknown, the following formula is used: $B = A \div C$. The number A is divided by C; the quotient of A divided by C is B.

- If the quantity C is unknown, the following formula is used: $C = A \div B$. The number A is divided by B; the quotient of A divided by B is C.

Thus, the formula, $A = B \times C$, may be used three different ways depending upon which quantity is unknown:

$A = B \times C$

or

$B = A \div C$

or

$C = A \div B$

Example: A room is 10 feet wide and 15 feet long. How many square feet does it contain?

Read the Question. This problem asks you to find the area of a room. You will need the area formula, area = base $\times$ height, $A = B \times H$.

Write Down the Formula. $A = B \times H$

Substitute. Substitute the numbers given in the problem into the formula: $A = 10 \times 15$

Calculate. Multiply the B and H numbers together to get the answer.

$A = B \times H$

$A = 10 \times 15$

$A = 150$ The room has 150 square feet.

Suppose the problem had given you the area of 150 square feet and the dimensions of one side, 10 feet, and asked for the length of the remaining side. First, the given numbers would be substituted into the basic formula.

$A = B \times H$

$150 = 10 \times H$

The height or the remaining side is what the problem asks for. Thus, the basic formula would be converted to find the quantity H: $H = A \div B$ or $H = 150 \div 10$. The quantity A is divided by B: $150 \div 10 = 15$. The quotient of 150 divided by 10 is 15. The remaining side, the height, is therefore 15 feet.

CONVERTING FRACTIONS TO DECIMALS

Most people find it much easier to work with decimals than fractions. Also, hand calculators can multiply and divide by decimals. Therefore, in most instances it is advisable to change fractions into decimals. In order to do so, divide the top number of the fraction (called the numerator) by the bottom number of the fraction (called the denominator).

Example: To change ¾ into a decimal, divide the top number, 3, by the bottom number, 4.

$3 \div 4 = .75$

Example: to change ⅔ into a decimal, divide the top number, 2, by the bottom number, 3.

$2 \div 3 = .66667$

Of course, if you are using a hand calculator, it will make the conversion for you. Divide 2 by 3 and your calculator will give you the answer with the decimal point in the right place.

To add by decimals or subtract by decimals, line the decimals up by decimal point.

> **Example:** To add 3.75, 14.62, 1.245, 679.0, 1412.8, and 1.9, put the numbers in a column with the decimals lined up and add.
>
> $$\begin{array}{r} 3.75 \\ 14.62 \\ 1.245 \\ 679.0 \\ 1412.8 \\ +1.9 \\ \hline 2113.315 \end{array}$$

To multiply by decimals, do the multiplication, ignoring the decimal points. Then give the answer as many decimal places as the total number of decimal places in the multiplying numbers.

> **Example:** Multiply 24.625 times 16.15. The two numbers contain a total of five decimal places (three in 24.625 and two in 16.15).
>
> $$\begin{array}{r} 24.625 \\ \times16.15 \\ \hline 397.69375 \end{array}$$

Just add up the decimal places in the numbers you are multiplying and put the decimal point the same number of places to the left.

> **Example:** Multiply .2 × .4. There is a total of two decimal places.
>
> $$\begin{array}{r} .2 \\ \times.4 \\ \hline .08 \end{array}$$

Note that in this case a zero must be added to move the decimal point two places left.

To divide by decimals, move the decimal point in the outside number all the way to the right, and then move the decimal point in the inside number the same number of places to the right.

Example: Divide 26.145 by 1.5.

$$1.5\overline{)26.145}$$

Move the decimal in 1.5 all the way to the right (one place) and move the decimal in the inside number the same number of places to the right.

$$1.5.\overline{)26.1.45}$$
$$\rightarrow \qquad \rightarrow$$
$$\begin{array}{r} 17.43 \\ 15\overline{)261.45} \end{array}$$

Just as with addition and multiplication, the above steps are unnecessary if you use a hand calculator. If the numbers are punched in correctly, the calculator will automatically give you an answer with the decimal in the right place.

AREA PROBLEMS

SQUARES, RECTANGLES AND PARALLELOGRAMS

The formula for finding the area of squares, rectangles and parallelograms is: area equals base times height.

$$A = B \times H$$

Square   Rectangle   Parallelogram

Example: If a room measures 15 feet along one wall and 12 feet along the adjoining wall, how many square feet of carpet would be required to cover the floor?

Write Down the Formula. $A = B \times H$
Substitute. $A = 15 \times 12$
Calculate. Since the quantity A is unknown, multiply B times H for the answer.

$B \times H = A$

$15 \times 12 = 180$

180 square feet of carpet is needed to cover the floor.

Example: If carpet is on sale for $12 per square yard, how much would it cost to carpet the room in the above example?

In this problem, you must first determine how many square feet there are in a square yard, and then determine how many square yards there are in 180 square feet. A square yard is a square that is one yard on each side. There are three feet in a yard.

Write Down the Formula. $A = B \times H$
Substitute. $A = 3 \times 3$
Calculate. The quantity A is the unknown; thus, multiply B times H.

$B \times H = A$

$3 \times 3 = 9$

There are 9 square feet in a square yard.

Now we'll divide 9 into 180 to see how many square yards there are in 180 square feet.

$180 \div 9 = 20$

There are 20 square yards in the room. If carpet is selling for $12 per square yard, it will cost 12×20, or $240 to carpet the room.

TRIANGLES

The formula for finding the area of a triangle is: area equals ½ base times height.

$$A = \tfrac{1}{2} B \times H$$

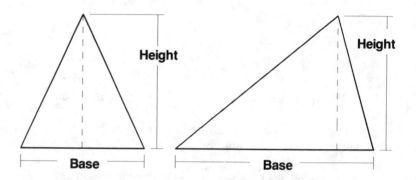

Example: If commercial building lots in a certain neighborhood are selling for approximately five dollars per square foot, for about how much should the pictured lot sell?

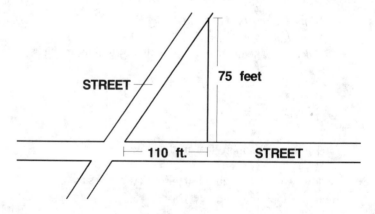

Write Down the Formula. $A = \tfrac{1}{2} B \times H$

Substitute. $A = \tfrac{1}{2} \times 110 \times 75$

Calculate. The quantity A is unknown; thus, multiply ½ B times H, or $\tfrac{1}{2} \times 110 \times 75$. The order of multiplication is not important. You can multiply 110 times 75 and then multiply that product by ½, or you can multiply ½ times 75 and then multiply the result by 110. The answer will be the same:

a) *110 × 75 = 8250*
    ½ × 8250 = 4125

b) *½ × 110 = 55*
    55 × 75 = 4125

c) *½ × 75 = 37.5*
    37.5 × 110 = 4125

The lot contains 4125 square feet. If similar lots are selling for about five dollars per square foot, this lot should sell for about five times 4125, or *$5 × 4125 = $20,625.*

ODD SHAPES

The best approach to finding the area of an odd-shaped figure is to divide it up into squares, rectangles and triangles. Find the areas of those figures and add them all up to reach the area of the odd-shaped lot, room, building or whatever else the problem requires.

Example: If the pictured lot is leased on a 66-year lease for $3.00 per square foot per year, with rental payments made monthly, how much would the monthly rent be?

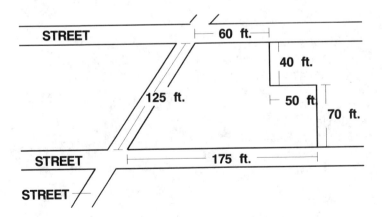

First, divide the lot up into rectangles and triangles.

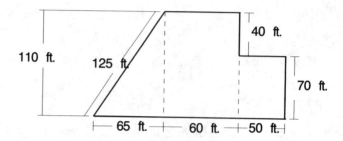

The next step is to find the areas of the following figures and add them together.

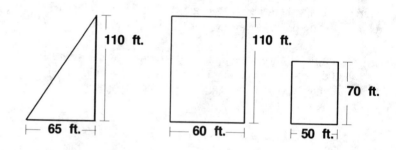

Triangle
   Write Down the Formula. $A = \frac{1}{2} B \times H$
   Substitute. $A = \frac{1}{2} \times 65 \times 110$
   Calculate. $\frac{1}{2} \times 65 \times 110 = 3575$

Rectangle
   Write Down the Formula. $A = B \times H$
   Substitute. $A = 110 \times 60$
   Calculate. $110 \times 60 = 6600$

Rectangle
   Write Down the Formula. $A = B \times H$
   Substitute. $A = 50 \times 70$
   Calculate. $50 \times 70 = 3500$

Add the three areas:

$$3,575$$
$$6,600$$
$$+\ 3,500$$
$$\overline{13,675}$$

The lot contains 13,675 square feet. The annual rental at $3.00 per square foot per year would be:

$3 \times 13,675 = \$41,025$ per year

The monthly rent payment would be one-twelfth of the annual rent:

$41,025 \div 12 = 3,418.75$

Thus, the monthly rental payment for this odd-shaped lot is $3,418.75.

PERCENTAGE PROBLEMS

It is necessary to convert percentages to decimals and vice versa, so that the arithmetic in a percentage problem can be done in decimals.

To convert a percentage to a decimal, remove the percentage sign and move the decimal point two places to the left. This may require adding one or more zeros.

Example: *98% becomes .98*
5% becomes .05
32.5% becomes .325
17½% becomes .175

To convert a decimal to a percentage, do just the opposite. Move the decimal two places to the right and add a percentage sign.

Example: *.15 becomes 15%*
.08 becomes 8%
.095 becomes 9.5%

The conversion of percentages to and from decimals is necessary to work a wide variety of real estate math problems, including commission, interest, capitalization, and profit and loss problems.

Whenever something is expressed as a percentage of something else, it means you should multiply. The word "of" means "times" or multiply.

Example: What is seventy-five percent of $40,000?

First convert the percentage to a decimal: 75% becomes .75; "of" $40,000 means "times" $40,000.

$.75 \times 40,000 = 30,000$

Seventy-five percent of $40,000 is $30,000.

Percentage problems are usually of the type shown in the above example. You have to find a part of something or a percentage of the total. A general formula might be: a percentage of the total equals the part, or percentage times total equals part.

$\% \times T = P$, or
$P = \% \times T$

Example: A house is listed for sale with a broker at a price of $72,000, with an agreement to pay a commission of 6% of the sales price. It sells for $70,000. How much is the commission?

Write Down the Formula. $P = \% \times T$

Substitute. Change the percentage to a decimal. *6% becomes .06*

$P = \% \times T$

$P = .06 \times 70,000$

Calculate. The unknown quantity is P; thus, the total is multiplied by the percentage.

$.06 \times 70,000 = 4200$

The commission is $4,200.

PROFIT AND LOSS PROBLEMS

Profit and loss problems can be solved in the same way as percentage problems. The formula for profit and loss problems is a variation of the percentage formula: value after equals percentage times value before.

$$VA = \% \times VB$$

The "value after" is the value of the property after the profit or loss is taken. The "value before" is the value of the property before the profit or loss is taken. The "percent" is 100% plus the percentage of profit or minus the percentage of loss. The idea is to express the value of the property after a profit or loss as a percentage of the property's value before the profit or loss. If there is no profit or loss, the value after is exactly 100% of the value before, because the value has not changed. If there is a profit, the value after will be greater than 100% of the value before, since the value has increased. If there is a loss, the value after the loss is less than the value before the loss, so the value after will be less than 100% of the value before. Remember, a percent "of" something means that percent "times" something.

Example: Ms. Brown bought a house 5 years ago for $50,000 and sold it this year for 30% more than she paid for it. What did she sell it for?

Write Down the Formula. $VA = \% \times VB$
Substitute. In order to get the percent you must add the percentage of profit or subtract the percentage of loss from 100%. In this case there is a profit, so you add 30% to 100% and convert it to a decimal.

$$100\% + 30\% = 130\%$$

$$130\% = 1.30$$

$$VA = 130\% \times (of) \; VB$$

$$VA = 1.30 \times 50,000$$

Calculate. $VA = 1.30 \times 50,000$
$VA = 65,000$

Ms. Brown sold the house for $65,000.

Example: Mr. Panza sold his house this year for $40,000. He paid $60,000 for it two years ago. What was the percentage of loss?

Write Down the Formula. VA = % × VB
Substitute. 40,000 = % × 60,000
Calculate. The percentage is the unknown; thus, the value after is divided by the value before.

$$\% = \frac{VA}{VB}$$

$$\% = \frac{40,000}{60,000}$$

Divide the bottom number into the top:

40,000 ÷ 60,000 = .67

The value after the sale is approximately 67% of the value before. Subtract 67% from 100% to find the percentage of loss:

$$\begin{array}{r} 1.00 \\ -\ .67 \\ \hline .33\ \ loss \end{array}$$

Example: A house sold for 18% more than the owner paid for it. The owner received $62,000 from escrow after paying a commission of 7% of the sales price and other closing costs totaling $589. What did the owner originally pay for the house?

Write Down the Formula. VA = % × VB
Substitute. VA = 1.18(100% + 18%) × VB

A separate calculation must be made here in order to determine the value after. The value after is the total of the seller's net ($62,000), the closing costs ($589) and the broker's commission (7% of the total). In mathematical form,

T(total) = 62,000 + 589 + (7% × T), or

T − (7% × T) = 62,000 + 589

Since T is equal to 100% of (times) the total, we can rewrite the equation as:

(100% × T) − (7% × T) = 62,000 + 589, or

$(100\% - 7\%) \times T = 62,589$

$93\% \times T = 62,589$

$.93 \times T = 62,589$

$T = 62,589 \div .93$

$62,589.00 \div .93 = 67,300$

The sales price is $67,300, which can now be substituted into the profit and loss formula as the value after.

$VA = 1.18 \times VB$

$67,300 = 1.18 \times VB$

Calculate: Isolate the unknown.

$$VB = \frac{67,300}{1.18}$$

Divide the bottom number into the top number.

$$1.18.\overline{\smash{)}67300.00.00} \quad \overset{57,033.90}{}$$

The owner paid $57,033.90 for the house.

CAPITALIZATION (INVESTMENT) PROBLEMS

Capitalization problems involve the capitalization approach to value, an appraisal technique used to arrive at a determination of value. Capitalization problems are another form of percentage problem. The formula is: income = rate × value.

$I = R \times V$

The "income" is the annual net income produced by the investment property. Frequently it is necessary to deduct bad debt plus vacancy factors and expenses from gross income to arrive at the net income before substituting. The "rate" is the percentage of return the investor desires on the investment. The rate of return varies according to many factors. A requirement for a higher rate of return will mean a higher capitalization rate and a lower value for the same income. The "value" is the value or purchase price of the investment.

You can see that this formula is very similar to the basic percentage formula, part = % × total.

> **Example:** A property produces an annual net income of $26,000. If an investor desires an 11% rate of return, what should he pay for the property?
>
> *Write Down the Formula.* $I = R \times V$
> *Substitute.* $\$26,000 = .11 \times V$
> *Calculate.* Isolate the unknown quantity.
>
> $V = 26,000 \div .11$

Divide the top number by the bottom number.

$$
\begin{array}{r}
236{,}363.64 \\
.11\overline{\smash{)}\ 2600.00.00} \\
\rightarrow \qquad \rightarrow
\end{array}
$$

The investor should be willing to pay $236,363.64 for the property.

> **Example:** If a property is valued at $100,000 using an 8% capitalization rate, what would it be valued at using a 10% capitalization rate?
>
> *Write Down the Formula.* $I = R \times V$
> *Substitute.* $I = .10 \times V$

Here it is necessary to work a preliminary problem to find the income. Use the same formula and the value at an 8% capitalization rate:

$I = R \times V$

$I = .08 \times 100,000$

$I = 8,000$

The net income is $8,000 annually. It is the same property, so we can use the same income to find the value at a 10% capitalization rate.

$I = R \times V$

$8,000 = .10 \times V$

Calculate. Isolate the unknown quantity.

$V = \dfrac{8,000}{.10}$

Divide the top number by the bottom number.

$$.10. \overline{\smash{\big)}\,8000.00.}$$
$$\quad \xrightarrow{\hspace{0.5cm}} \qquad \xrightarrow{\hspace{0.5cm}}$$

The value of the same property using a 10% capitalization is $80,000. This problem demonstrates that a higher capitalization rate applied to the same net income will result in a lower value.

Example: A ten-unit apartment building has six units that rent for $300 per month and four units that rent for $350 per month. Allow 5% for vacancies and uncollected rent. Expenses include: annual property taxes of $4,800, monthly utilities of $475, maintenance expenses of approximately $1,600 per year. The owner has an outstanding mortgage balance of $21,000 at 8% interest, with monthly payments of $312. If an investor requires a 13% rate of return what should she offer for the property?

Write Down the Formula. $I = R \times V$

Substitute. It is necessary to calculate the annual net income before substituting. First, calculate the annual gross income.

$300/mo. $\times$ 12 mo. = 3,600/year $\times$ 6 units = $21,600

$350/mo. $\times$ 12 mo. = 4,200/year $\times$ 4 units = $16,800
$$\underline{}$$
$$\$38,400$$

The gross income is $38,400 per year.

Next find the bad debt/vacancy factor and deduct it from the gross income to find the effective gross income. The bad debt/vacancy factor is 5% of the gross income.

bad debts + vacancies = .05 × 38,400

bad debts + vacancies = $1,920

The loss to be expected from bad debts and vacancies is $1,920 per year.

$$
\begin{array}{rl}
38,400 & \textit{(gross income)} \\
-\ 1,920 & \textit{(bad debts and vacancies)} \\
\hline
36,480 & \textit{(effective gross income)}
\end{array}
$$

Next deduct the expenses from the effective gross income to arrive at the net income. Remember, since you are trying to find annual net income, all the expenses must be annual also. The expenses are as follows:

Property taxes $4,800 per year	4,800
Utilities $475 per month × 12	5,700
Maintenance $1,600 per year	1,600
	12,100

The annual expenses are $12,100.

$$
\begin{array}{rl}
36,480 & \textit{(effective gross income)} \\
-\ 12,100 & \textit{(annual expenses)} \\
\hline
24,380 & \textit{(annual net income)}
\end{array}
$$

Now, substitute the net income and the rate into the formula *I = R × V:*

24,380 = .13 × V

Calculate. Isolate the unknown quantity.

$$V = \frac{24,380}{.13}$$

Divide the top number by the bottom number to find the unknown, the value.

$$
\begin{array}{r}
187,538.46 \\
.13\,\overline{\smash{\big)}\ 24380.00.00} \\
\end{array}
$$

→   →

The investor should be willing to pay approximately $187,538 for the property.

Example: Assume a property with the same income and expenses as in the preceding problem. If an investor paid $250,000 for the apartment house, what capitalization rate was used?

Write Down the Formula. I = R × V
Substitute: We already know the net income from working the preceding problem: *24,380 = R × 250,000*
Calculate. Isolate the unknown quantity.

$$R = \frac{24,380}{250,000}$$

Divide the top number by the bottom number.

$$250,000\overline{)24,380.0000} \quad .0975$$

The investor used a capitalization rate of approximately 9.75%

TAX PROBLEMS

Real estate tax problems are worked in basically the same manner as percentage problems. The formula is: taxes = rate × value.

$$T = R × V$$

As you can see, this is quite similar to the general percentage formula, part = rate × total.

Here, the amount of taxes is the "part," the tax rate is the "rate," and the value of the property (as determined by sales price) is the "total."

Example: A property recently sold for $174,670. How much transfer tax will be assessed on the transfer?

Write down the Formula. T = R × V
Substitute. The transfer tax rate for most counties is $1.10 per each $1,000 of value transfered, or $.55 for every $500 or fraction thereof.

In order to substitute a figure for V, we must first determine how many $500 of value (or fractions thereof) there are in the total transfered value: $174,670. To do that, we must divide $174,670 by $500.

$$\frac{349.34}{500 \overline{) \$174,670}}$$

From the above equation, we see that there are 350 increments of $500 or portions thereof (the .34 is a portion of 500, so 349 is rounded up to 350).

Now we can substitute the figures into the formula.

$T = .55 \times 350$

Calculate. $T = .55 \times 350$

$T = \$192.50$

There will be a transfer tax of $192.50 imposed on the transaction.

INTEREST PROBLEMS

Interest problems are worked in basically the same manner as percentage problems. The formula is: interest equals principal times rate times time.

$I = P \times R \times T$

As you can see, this is quite similar to the general percentage formula, part = rate $\times$ total.

Here, the amount of interest is the "part," the interest rate is the "rate," and the principal (the amount of the loan or sales price) is the "total." Interest rates are expressed as annual rates, that is, a certain percent per year. Therefore, it is necessary to account for the time in years or parts of years.

Example: If a $2,000 note bears interest at the rate of 13% per annum and matures in one year, how much interest will be paid?

Write Down the Formula. $I = P \times R \times T$
Substitute. $I = 2000 \times .13 \times 1$

Calculate. I = $260
The interest is $260.

Example: If $450 in interest at the annual rate of 12½ %
accrues on a loan in six months, how much is the amount
of the loan?

Write Down the Formula. I = P × R × T
Substitute. 450 = P × .125 × 6/12

The time is expressed as a fraction of a year. It is more
convenient to convert the fraction to a decimal.

450 = P × .125 × .5

Calculate. Isolate the unknown quantity P.

$$P = \frac{I}{R \times T}$$

$$P = \frac{450}{.125 \times .5}$$

First multiply the two bottom numbers together, and then
divide that product into the top number.

$$P = \frac{450}{.0625}$$

$$\begin{array}{r} 7200 \\ .0625\overline{)\ 450.0000.} \\ \rightarrow \end{array}$$

The amount of the loan, or the principal, is $7200.

Example: A home loan has monthly payments of $625,
which include principal and 9% interest (paid in arrears) and
$47.50 per month for tax and insurance reserves. If $27.75
of the June 1 payment was applied to principal, what was
the outstanding principal during the month of May?

Write Down the Formula. I = P × R × T
Substitute. I = P × .09 × 1/12

The interest portion of the payment can be found by deducting the parts of the payment allocated to reserves and principal.

$$
\begin{array}{rl}
625.00 & \textit{(total payment)} \\
-\ 47.50 & \textit{(reserves)} \\
\hline
577.50 & \\
-\ 27.75 & \textit{(principal payment)} \\
\hline
549.75 & \textit{(interest portion of June payment)}
\end{array}
$$

$$\$549.75 = P \times .09 \times 1/12$$

Calculate.

$$P = \frac{I}{R \times T}$$

$$P = \frac{549.75}{.09 \times 1/12}$$

$$P = \frac{549.75}{.0075}$$

$$.0075\overline{)\ 549.7500.} \quad = 73,300$$

The outstanding principal is $73,300.

PRORATIONS

Proration is the allocation of one expense among two or more parties. Prorations are usually required at real estate closings, where the cost of such items as taxes and insurance are allocated between the buyer and the seller. The formula for proration is: share = daily rate × number of days.

$$S = R \times D$$

To work on a proration problem:

1) Find the annual or monthly amount of the expense.
2) Then find the daily rate of the expense (per diem). For real estate exams, it is usually sufficient to use 30-day months and 360-day years when converting monthly or annual rates to per diem rates. Thus, the daily rate equals 1/30th of the monthly rate or 1/360th of the annual rate.
3) Next determine the number of days for which the person is responsible for the expense.
4) Finally, substitute the daily rate and number of days into the formula and calculate.

Example: As part of the closing costs, the buyer of a house is required to pay interest on the purchase loan from the date of closing to the end of the month. The loan has a principal amount of $72,000. The interest rate is 16%. The transaction closes on June 22.

Write Down the Formula. $S = R \times D$

1) Find the annual or monthly amount of the expense. For this problem, use the interest formula to calculate the amount of the expense.

$$I = P \times R \times T$$
$$I = 72,000 \times .16 \times 1$$
$$I = 11,520$$

The interest is $11,520 per year.

2) Then find the daily rate of the expense. Divide the annual rate by 360.

$$\begin{array}{r} 32 \\ \hline 360 \overline{)\,11,520} \end{array}$$

The daily rate is $32.

3) Next find the number of days. On interest and tax prorations, the buyer pays for the day of closing. There are nine days: June 22, 23, 24, 25, 26, 27, 28, 29, and 30.

4) Finally, substitute the daily rate and number of days into the formula and calculate.

Substitute. S = 32 × 9
Calculate. 32 × 9 = 288

The buyer's prorated interest charge would be $288.

Example: The sale of a house closes on August 10. The annual property taxes of $1440 have not yet been paid. How much does the seller owe the buyer at closing?

The seller owes the buyer the taxes for the period July 1 through August 9, the period of time the seller owned and occupied the house. The buyer will owe the taxes from August 10 on.

Write Down the Formula. S = R × D

1) First find the annual amount. Here the annual amount is given, $1440.
2) Next find the daily rate.

$$360 \overline{)\ 1440\ }^{\ 4}$$

3) Count the number of days.

30 days − July (30-day months)
* 9 days − August*
39 days total

4) Multiply the number of days times the daily rate.

Substitute. S = 4 × 39
Calculate. 4 × 39 = 156

The seller will owe $156 for taxes at closing.

COMMISSION PROBLEMS

Most commission problems can be solved with the general percentage formula, part = percentage × total.

$$P = \% \times T$$

The "percentage" is the commission rate or percentage and the "total" is the amount that the commission is based on. This is most often the sales price of a piece of property, but could also be lease payments. The "part" is the amount of the commission.

Example: A listing agreement provides for a commission of 7% of the sales price to be paid to the broker. If the salesperson is entitled to ⅔ of the commission, how much should the salesperson receive if the property sells for $65,000?

Write Down the Formula. P = % × T
Substitute. Change the percent to a decimal.

7% becomes .07
P = .07 × 65,000

Calculate. The part is the unknown quantity; thus, the percentage is multiplied by the total.

.07 × 65,000 = 4550

The commission is $4550. The salesperson is entitled to ⅔ of that amount. Convert the fraction to a decimal:

2 ÷ 3 = .6667

The salesperson is entitled to approximately 67% of the total commission.

Write Down the Formula. P = % × T
Substitute. Change the percent to a decimal.

67% becomes .67

P = .67 × 4550

Calculate. .67 × 4550 = 3048.5

The salesperson is entitled to $3048.50.

Example: A listing agreement provides for a commission of 7% of the first $100,000 and 5% of any amount over $100,000. If the commission was $8250, what was the sales price?

Write Down the Formula. $P = \% \times T$

First find out how much of the commission is attributable to the first $100,000.

Substitute. $P = .07 \times 100,000$
Calculate. $P = 7,000$

$7000 of the commission is from the first $100,000. Next, determine how much commission remains:

$8,250 *(total)*
− 7,000 *(commission for first $100,000)*
$1,250 *(attributable to sales price in excess of $100,000)*

Write Down the Formula. $P = \% \times T$
Substitute. $1250 = .05 \times T$
Calculate. The quantity of T is unknown. The basic formula should be converted to isolate the unknown, T.

$T = P \div \%$

$T = 1250 \div .05$

Divide the bottom number into the top to find the unknown.

$$.05 \overline{)\ \begin{array}{l} 25,000. \\ 1250.00. \end{array}}$$
→   →

The sales price in excess of $100,000 is $25,000; thus, the total sales price is:

$100,000 + $25,000 = $125,000.

CHAPTER SUMMARY

1. The step-by-step approach is suggested in solving real estate math problems. First read the question, then write down the formula, substitute the numbers you have been given into the formula, and finally calculate to find the unknown.

2. The best way to find the area of an odd-shaped figure is to divide it up into squares, rectangles and triangles, find the areas of those figures and then add them all up.

3. When converting percentages to decimals, move the decimal point two places to the left.

FORMULAS

Converting Fractions to Decimals: divide numerator (top number) by denominator (bottom number).

Converting Percentages to Decimals: move decimal point two places to the left.

Area Formula: area = base × height, $A = B \times H$

Area Formula for Triangles: area = ½ base × height, $A = ½ B \times H$

Percentage Formula: part = percentage × total, $P = \% \times T$; convert percentage to decimal and multiply total times the decimal.

Value After Formula: value after = percentage × value before, $VA = \% \times VB$

Capitalization Formula: net income = value × rate, $NI = V \times R$

Tax formula: taxes = rate × value, $T = R \times V$

Interest Formula: interest = principal × rate × time, $I = P \times R \times T$

Proration Formula: share = daily rate × number of days, $S = R \times D$

1) find annual or monthly amount
2) find daily amount
3) determine number of days; and
4) substitute and calculate.

CHAPTER 8—QUIZ
REAL ESTATE MATH

. An owner sold a lot with a front footage of 90 feet and a depth of 250 feet for $2.25 a square foot. What was the selling price?

a) $347.50
b) $607.50
c) $24,300
d) $50,625

A building used for storage measures 100 feet by 220 feet. It rents for $0.32 per square foot per year. What is the rent over a year's time?

a) $7,040
b) $7,400
c) $50,880
d) $48,080

Which of the following is smaller than an acre?

a) 4,860 square yards
b) 180 square rods
c) 180 feet by 240 feet
d) 0.16% square mile

A rectangular property with 8,690 square yards has 318 front feet. What is the depth of the property?

a) 245.94 feet
b) 27.32 feet
c) 27.32 yards
d) 81.98 feet

The third quarter interest on a $7,600 loan at 8% interest is:

a) $608
b) $76
c) $152
d) None of the above

6. A client wants $63,000 for his property after he pays a 7% commission and 4 1/2% other sales and closing costs. The sales price will have to be:

a) $71,186
b) $70,245
c) $65,968.59
d) $67,742

7. In order to earn $60 per month on a 9.5% investment, how much do you need to invest?

a) $632
b) $7,200
c) $7,579
d) $758

8. Mr. Smith sold three lots for a total of $39,000. He sold lot A for $1,000 more than lot C, and lot B for $4,000 more than lot A. Mr. Brown sold lot C for:

a) $10,000
b) $11,000
c) $12,000
d) $13,000

9. The assessed value is $48,700. The tax rate is $1.02 per $100 of assessed valuation. The tax is:

a) $496.74
b) $489.60
c) $584.40
d) $594.14

10. The outside dimensions of a two-story house measure 32.5 feet by 45.8 feet. The cost of construction of the first story was $31 per square foot and the cost of the second story was $22 per square foot. A detached garage measuring 21.6 feet by 20.8 feet cost $16 per square foot. What was the total cost of construction?

a) $86,079
b) $78,890
c) $53,332
d) $99,475

11. Mr. Jones borrows $6,000 for two years at 8% interest per year. If the interest is prepaid and discoounted from the loan proceeds, he will receive:

   a) $6,000
   b) $5,520
   c) $5,040
   d) $6,960

12. A property earns a net income of $210 per month. The capitalization rate is 7%. The value of the property is:

   a) $17,640
   b) $3,000
   c) $40,000
   d) $36,000

. d) The area of the lot is 90 × 250 = 22,500 square feet. The sales price is 22,500 × 2.25 = $50,625.

. a) The area of the building is 100 × 220 = 22,000 square feet. The annual rent is .32 × 22,000 = $7,040.00.

. c) An acre is 43,560 square feet, which is equal to 4840 square yards, 160 square rods, or 1/640 (.156%) of a square mile. 180 × 240 = 43,200 square feet.

. a) 8,690 square yards equals 78,210 square feet (9 × 8,690 = 78,210). The area of a rectangle divided by its length gives the depth, so 78,210 divided by 318 = 245.94 feet, the depth of the lot.

. c) 8% of $7,600 is $608.00 (.08 × 7600 = 608). One quarter of $608.00 is $152.00 (.25 × 608 = 152).

. a) 63,000 = 100% of sales price − 11 1/2% of sales price.

63,000 = (100% − 11 1/2%) of sales price

63,000 = .885% × sales price

Rearrange the equation to isolate the unknown:

63,000 divided by .885 = $71,186.44 (sales price)

. c) I = P × R × T

60 = P × 9.5% × 1/12

60 = P × .095 × 1/12

P = 60 divided by (.095 × 1/12) = $7,578.95.

8. b) A = 1000 + C; B = 4000 + A; A + B + C = 39,000.

Rearrange the first equations: C = A − 1,000; then substitute into the third equation:

A + (4,000 + A) + (A − 1000) = 39,000

3A + 4,000 − 1,000 = 39,000

3A = 39,000 − 3,000

3A = 36,000

A = 12,000

Substitute A = 1000 + C, so C must equal $11,000

9. a) (48,700 divided by 100) × 1.02 = 487 × 1.02 = $496.74.

10. a) Each floor of the house has an area equal to 32.5 × 45.8 or 1488.5 square feet. The cost of the first floor is 1488.5 × 31 = $46,143.50. The cost of the second floor is 1488.5 × 22 = $32,747.00. The area of the garage is 21.6 × 20.8 = 449.28 square feet, so its cost is 449.28 × 16 = $7188.48. The total cost is therefore 46,143.50 + 32,747.00 + 7,188.48 = $86,078.98.

11. c) 8% of $6,000 is .08 × 6,000 = $480.00. Interest for two years is 2 × 480 = 960.00. Mr. Jones receives $6,000 minus $960.00, or $5,040.00.

12. d) First convert monthly to annual income: $210/month times 12 equals $2,520/year. Then use the capitalization formula: net income equals value times rate, or 2520 = V × 7%. Rearrange the equation to isolate the unknown, and convert the percentage to a decimal: 2520 divided by .07 = V. The value is therefore $36,000.

REAL ESTATE FINANCE

OUTLINE

I. Real Estate Finance
II. Government's Role in Real Estate Finance
  A. U.S. Treasury
  B. Federal Reserve
    1. reserve requirement
    2. discount rate
    3. open market operations
  C. Office of Thrift Supervision
  D. FDIC
III. Instruments of Finance
  A. Promissory note
  B. Security devices
    1. mortgage
    2. deed of trust
    3. special provisions in finance instruments
    4. variable payment plans
    5. land contract
    6. wraparound loan
IV. Finance Disclosure Requirements
  A. Truth in Lending Act
  B. Purchase money loan disclosure law
  C. Mortgage Loan Broker Law

KEY TERMS

U.S. Treasury	Federal Reserve System
reserve requirement	discount rate

FDIC   Office of Thrift Supervision
promissory note   negotiable instrument
mortgage   deficiency judgment
deed of trust   junior lienholder
adjustable-rate mortgage   graduated payment mortgage
growing equity mortgage   land contract
wraparound   Truth in Lending Act
Mortgage Loan Broker Law

CHAPTER OVERVIEW

No matter what the property is, or how great the sales agent, the buyer can't buy unless he or she can afford the purchase. This usually means finding the right kind of financing at the lowest possible rates. It is important to understand the types of financing available and the factors which affect the availability and cost of money.

REAL ESTATE FINANCE

For most people, there is no single transaction that involves more money than the purchase of a home. Because most buyers are financially unable to pay cash for their property, finance is the lifeblood of the real estate industry. Without financing, few people in the United States would be able to own their own home.

Also, most buyers want to take advantage of "leveraging." Leveraging is an investment concept that means that a homeowner can, with a small downpayment, receive a future profit based on the full purchase price, not just the actual money paid out.

Homebuyers are able to finance their purchases only when there is a ready supply of affordable money. This supply of money depends on the state of the "money market," on which the government has a significant effect.

THE GOVERNMENT'S ROLE IN REAL ESTATE FINANCE

Economic stability is directly tied to the balance of the supply of and demand for money. It has long been known, for example, that increased economic activity follows an increase in the number of dollars in circulation. Conversely, if funds are withdrawn from circulation, an economic slowdown will result.

Certainly prevailing interest levels will affect the demand for money. High interest rates discourage demand and keep money out of circulation. Lower interest rates encourage demand and stimulate economic activity.

Thus, responsible manipulations of the availability and cost of money can do much to achieve economic balance, and there are certain federal agencies which are empowered to exercise this kind of control over our economy. The most prominent include the **United States Treasury**, the **Federal Reserve System** and the **Office of Thrift Supervision**.

UNITED STATES TREASURY

The United States Treasury is this nation's fiscal manager. It has financial responsibility for the federal government's day-to-day activities, including keeping federal agencies operating and managing the staggering federal debt.

U.S. Treasury: has financial responsibility for government activities

Treasury funds come from federal income tax payments, social security deposits and a variety of lesser sources.

DEFICIT FINANCING. When federal income falls short of federal spending, a deficit results, and it is the Treasury's responsibility to locate money to cover the deficit. It does this by issuing interest-bearing securities to investors, and these securities are backed by the U.S. Government. This amounts to borrowing money from the private sector. Private investors invest in government securities instead of other investments because of their low risk, and thus private funds are siphoned away from other investment areas, such as real estate.

Heavy government borrowing puts a drain on the number of dollars in circulation, and the result is an economic slowdown. Thus the greater the federal deficit, the more money the government has to borrow and the more taxing the effect on our economy.

On the other hand, a small federal deficit translates into limited government borrowing and a more substantial supply of investment funds for private industry.

FEDERAL RESERVE SYSTEM

The Federal Reserve System was established in 1913 under the Federal Reserve Act. Frequently referred to as the "Fed," its original purpose was to provide this nation with a means of selling or discounting commercial paper and to upgrade the quality of supervision over banking activities. Its responsibilities have broadened considerably since its inception.

Federal Reserve System: the nation's central banking system; supervises growth of money and credit

The Fed is the nation's central banking system. It is responsible for monetary policy and the regulation of commercial banks.

The Fed's principal function is to supervise the growth of money and credit so as to ensure a continued rise in the standard of living for this country's citizens. It is empowered to establish policies that will effectively resist deflationary and inflationary pressures.

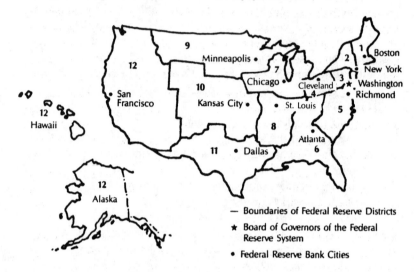

THERE ARE TWELVE FEDERAL RESERVE DISTRICTS.

The Federal Reserve System consists of twelve **Federal Reserve Banks** and their twenty-four branches, which are situated in twelve federal reserve districts throughout the United States.

The entire system is regulated by a seven-member board of governors (the **Federal Reserve Board**) appointed by the president of the United States and approved by the Senate. The Federal Reserve Board is based in Washington, D.C. All federally chartered banks are members of the system. (A charter is a document issued by a state or federal agency, authorizing a bank or savings and loan to do business.)

There are **three tools** relied upon by the Fed for implementing monetary policy:

- reserve requirements
- federal discount rates, and
- open market operations

Reserve requirement: a certain amount of funds banks must keep on reserve with the Fed

Of these, open market transactions in government securities are the most important.

RESERVE REQUIREMENT. The reserve requirement is the percentage of deposits that commercial banks are required to maintain on deposit. The reserve requirement protects depositors by ensuring the bank will have adequate reserves to meet unusual customer demand. However, changes in the minimum reserve requirement can have a secondary effect. By increasing the reserve requirement, the Fed can reduce the amount of money that banks have available to lend. On the other hand, a reduction in reserve requirements frees more money for investment or lending by banks. An increase in the reserve requirement, then, tends to decrease available loan funds and increase interest rates. Conversely, a decrease in the reserve requirement tends to increase funds available for lending and to decrease interest rates.

DISCOUNT RATE. The federal discount rate is the interest rate charged by Federal Reserve Banks on loans to commercial banks. Increasing the discount rate usually results in the banks charging higher interest rates to their customers, since they will have to charge more interest on money they lend if they have to pay more interest on the money they borrow.

Discount rate: interest rate at which the Fed loans funds to banks

OPEN MARKET OPERATIONS. Open market operations are transactions by the Fed in buying and selling government securities. Open market transactions are the primary method relied upon by the Fed in its efforts to control the money supply, and with the money supply, inflation and interest rates. Only money in circulation is considered part of the money supply, so actions by the Fed which tend to increase or decrease money in circulation increase or decrease the money supply.

Open Market Operations: purchase and sale of government securities by the Fed

A purchase of government securities increases the money supply. The Fed may pay for the securities by cash, check or, if purchasing from a bank, simply by crediting the bank's reserves with the Fed. Any of those actions would increase the amount of money in circulation.

Sales of government securities decrease the money supply. If the Fed sells securities, the money used to pay for the securities is taken out of circulation (whether payment is by cash, check or, if the purchaser is a bank, by reducing the bank's reserves with the Fed).

Other things being equal (which they seldom are), interest rates tend to fall with increases in the money supply and to rise with decreases in the money supply.

OFFICE OF THRIFT SUPERVISION

The Federal Home Loan Bank System was organized in 1932 to help stabilize the savings and loan industry. It served a parallel function to the Federal Reserve System. It was organized in a similar fashion and

OTS: regulates S&Ls in same manner that Fed regulates commercial banks and regulated savings and loan associations in the same manner that the Fed regulates commercial banks.

In the late 1980's, a crisis developed in the savings and loan industry as many S&Ls across the country became insolvent. In response to this crisis, the Financial Institutions Reform, Recovery, and Enforcement Act (FIRREA) was enacted in 1989. This act reorganized the Federal Home Loan Bank System. The Federal Home Loan Bank Board was eliminated and replaced by the Office of Thrift Supervision (OTS).

The OTS now acts as the regulator of the thrift industry. A new board called the Federal Housing Finance Board (FHFB) has taken over the duties of the Federal Home Loan Bank Board. The FHFB now acts as the overseer of mortgage lending by Federal Home Loan Banks.

The OTS has regulatory powers similar to the Federal Reserve. However, the policies of the OTS have less impact on the national economy, since commercial banks control a much greater volume of deposits than do savings and loans.

FEDERAL DEPOSIT INSURANCE CORPORATION (FDIC). When banks failed during the Great Depression, thousands of people lost the money they had deposited. To prevent that kind of disaster from happening again, the federal government began insuring deposits in certain institutions: now if a bank became insolvent, the government would reimburse its depositors. The Federal Deposit Insurance Corporation (FDIC) was established to insure deposits in commercial banks and savings banks, and the Federal Savings and Loan Insurance corporation (FSLIC) insured deposits in S&Ls.

FDIC: insures deposits in banks and S&Ls

As a result of the savings and loan crisis in the 1980's, when hundreds of S&Ls failed, the FSLIC itself became insolvent. So the FDIC was reorganized to insure S&L deposits as well as bank deposits. Its insurance program is now known as the Deposit Insurance Fund (DIF). The DIF has two separate branches: the Bank Insurance Fund (BIF) and the Savings Association Insurance Fund (SAIF). The FDIC (which is an arm of the Treasury Department) also supervises the operations of banks and S&Ls, including their lending policies.

INSTRUMENTS OF FINANCE

An instrument is a tool or device used to perform a task or accomplish a goal. In business it is a document, such as a contract, mortgage or deed, that describes an agreement or objective. Very often an instrument acts as proof of an agreement and is used to enforce that agreement in court.

The documents most often used in real estate finance are the **promissory note** and a security instrument, which will either be a **mortgage** or a **deed of trust**.

PROMISSORY NOTE

The promissory note is a written promise to pay money. Notes are usually negotiable, meaning the creditor (the holder of the note) can assign the debt to another.

Promissory note: a written promise to pay money

Though the note is a contract by itself and could be enforced in a court of law, it is always accompanied by a mortgage or trust deed when used for real estate loans. If the borrower's promise to repay is not kept, the lender can either sue on the note in court or, more probably, foreclose according to the terms of the mortgage or deed of trust. To foreclose a real estate lien is to institute legal procedures necessary to have a property sold to satisfy a debt. So the property serves as security for repayment of the debt. Accordingly, a real estate loan is called a **secured loan**.

PARTIES TO A PROMISSORY NOTE. The promissory note is referred to as "two-party paper." The debtor is called the **maker** and the creditor is the **payee**.

NEGOTIABLE INSTRUMENTS. A negotiable instrument is a written promise or written order to pay money. The promissory note is an example of a negotiable instrument. Drafts and bank checks are three-party negotiable instruments.

Negotiable instrument: a promise to pay money which can be transferred from one party to another like money

A negotiable instrument is freely transferable. When properly prepared, it is accepted as the equivalent of cash. To be considered a negotiable instrument, a promissory note must contain each of the following elements. It must be:

1. An unconditional promise
2. In writing
3. Signed by the maker(s)
4. Promising to pay a sum certain in money
5. Definite as to the terms of repayment
6. Payable "to order" or "to bearer"

A promissory note's principal purpose is to document a borrower's promise to repay money. Some of its more important ingredients are highlighted above. If a lender wants a note to be clearly negotiable, he or she should include language in it that allows for the eventuality that it will be transferred to someone else, such as showing the debt payable to order. If the words "or more" are inserted after the stated installments, the borrower can pay the debt sooner than agreed.

Promissory Note

FOR VALUE RECEIVED, maker will pay to
ORDER or BEARER

THE SUM OF $_____at____% interest

PAID AS FOLLOWS: $_____ a week,
month, year OR MORE, starting_____.

ACCELERATION: In the event of default,
payee or bearer can declare all sums due
and payable at once.

_____   _____
MAKER/BORROWER   DATE

SIGNING THE NOTE. Though many copies of the note may be prepared, just one is signed, and it is signed only by the borrower. This is a measure designed to protect the borrower. Since a promissory note is a negotiable instrument, the borrower does not want more than one signed copy in circulation at any given time. When the debt is paid, the signed copy is returned to the borrower marked "paid."

ENDORSEMENT. If a note is made payable "to bearer," transfer from the original payee to another can be made by simple delivery. If the note is made payable "to the order" of a specific person, that person must "order" the maker to pay the transferee by endorsement, or signature.

TYPES OF NOTES. There are three types of promissory notes:

- Straight note: the note calls for payments of "interest only"; the entire principal is due on the due date.
- Amortized note: the note calls for payments of "principal and interest"; the principal is fully paid off with the last payment.
- Partially amortized: the note calls for "principal and interest," but instead of being paid off at the due date, there is a balloon payment due.

Amortization, the gradual liquidation of a debt through regular principal and interest payments, was introduced to the real estate lending industry by the savings and loan industry in the late 1930's. Long-term (15 to 30 years), fully amortized residential real estate loans are the rule today rather than the exception.

SECURITY DEVICES
(VOLUNTARY LIENS)

The process of placing property under a lien as security for the payment of a debt is called **hypothecation**. There are two basic types of real property security devices: the **mortgage** and the **deed of trust**. (The **land contract** is an alternative type of security.) The deed of trust is by far the most commonly used in California, primarily because it is favored by lenders.

LIEN THEORY VS. TITLE THEORY

There was a time when lenders took actual possession of land used to secure their loans. In a literal sense they held the properties that were acting as collateral until the debts were repaid. During the period of indebtedness, the lender was the owner of the land. When a debt was retired, title and possession were returned to the borrower.

As the real estate lending business developed and expanded, it became impractical for lenders to physically possess the lands that served as collateral. Custom gradually changed to permit borrowers to retain possession of their properties. Title was still transferred to the lender for the term of the loan. By this method the lender secured title to the collateral and the borrower kept the full complement of property rights— the right to use, lease, sell, enjoy, etc. Title unaccompanied by the "bundle of rights" is called "bare title." Rights to the benefits of property, in the absence of legal title, are referred to as "equitable rights." This concept of the lender holding title to the secured property is called title theory. Title theory is embraced by only a handful of states.

Most states, including California, endorse the **lien theory**, which holds that the borrower retains title throughout the term of the loan, and that the mortgage acts as a lien securing the debt.

MORTGAGE

When the security instrument selected is a mortgage, the borrower is called a **mortgagor**, and the lender is a **mortgagee**.

Mortgage: a two-party security instrument that must be foreclosed judicially

While the purpose of the promissory note is to create a personal liability on the part of the mortgagor, the mortgage is designed to create a lien on the collateral property. The borrower continues to use the property during the term of the debt, and when the obligation is fully extinguished, the lien is released. The mortgage does not have to be recorded to act as a lien on real property, but without recordation only the lender and borrower would know the lien exists.

ACCELERATION CLAUSE. Every mortgage contains an acceleration clause, giving the lender the option of declaring the entire balance immediately due and payable if the borrower defaults on the promissory note or mortgage. Sometimes this is referred to as "calling the note." If the borrower fails to pay the balance, as demanded, the lender can sue on the note or foreclose.

SATISFACTION OF MORTGAGE. When a mortgage debt is paid in full, a "satisfaction piece" is used to release the mortgage lien. The lender must deliver the satisfaction piece to the borrower when full payment has been made. The mortgage will not be released as a lien of record until the satisfaction piece is recorded. The satisfaction piece is formally referred to as a certificate of discharge.

MORTGAGE FORECLOSURE. Mortgage foreclosures are sometimes called **judicial foreclosures** because they involve the use of the courts. On default, a complaint is filed by the lender against the borrower with the court in the county where the collateral property is located. Any **junior lienholders** are also made parties to the lawsuit, so they have an opportunity to defend their interests in the property.

When the complaint has been heard in court, in the absence of unusual circumstances the judge issues a **decree of foreclosure**, ordering the sale of the property to satisfy the debt. The judge appoints a receiver to conduct the sale. The sale, which takes the form of a public auction, is frequently referred to as a **sheriff's sale**.

Between the date the decree of foreclosure is issued and the date the sheriff's sale is held, the borrower is entitled to redeem the property by paying off the debt in full. This is often called the **period of equitable redemption**. After the sale, under certain circumstances the borrower will have an additional year to redeem the property, known as the **period of statutory redemption**. When the property is sold subject to the right of statutory redemption, the successful bidder at the sheriff's sale receives a **certificate of sale** instead of a deed. Only at the end of the redemption period is the bidder given a **sheriff's deed** that transfers title to the property.

It is the one-year redemption period that makes a mortgage very unappealing to many investors; understandably, they do not want to wait so long to gain title to the property. For this reason, bidders at sheriff's sales are uncommon, and often the lender acquires the property by bidding the amount owed.

The mortgagor (borrower) is entitled to keep possession of the property during the one-year redemption period, provided he or she pays reasonable rent to the holder of the certificate of sale. If the proceeds from the sale exceed the amount necessary to satisfy all valid liens against the property, the surplus belongs to the borrower.

REQUIRED NOTICE. The lender's attorney normally records a **lis pendens** (notice of pending legal action), which will make the judgment of the court binding on all persons who acquire interests or liens in the property while the foreclosure action is pending. After the decree of foreclosure has been issued, a **notice of sale** must be published and posted.

Mortgage

MORTGAGING CLAUSE
Sometimes called a granting clause

ADEQUATE DESCRIPTION
Legal description preferred but not necessary

ACCELERATION CLAUSE
Lender can demand full payment upon default

MORTGAGE AMOUNT
The amount of the debt and maturity date must be stated

DEFICIENCY JUDGMENTS. If the proceeds of a judicial foreclosure are insufficient to satisfy the mortgage debt, the mortgagee may obtain a deficiency judgment against the mortgagor unless the transaction is exempted by the **anti-deficiency rules**. The anti-deficiency rules

Deficiency judgment: when foreclosure sale is not enough to pay the debt, creditor may be able to get a personal judgment against debtor for the deficiency

prohibit deficiency judgments under the following circumstances:

1) when the foreclosure is by trustee's sale (non-judicial foreclosure);
2) when the security agreement is a purchase money mortgage given to the seller for all or part of the purchase price;
3) when the security agreement is a purchase money mortgage given to a third-party lender to finance the purchase of an owner-occupied residential dwelling of four or fewer units;
4) when the fair market value of the property exceeds the amount of the debt.

DEED OF TRUST

Deed of trust: a three-party security instrument that can be foreclosed non-judicially

The deed of trust, also called a **trust deed**, is the most popular type of security device. Though its purpose is the same as that of a mortgage—to secure the promissory note—it is quite different in certain important respects, the most significant being the foreclosure method.

The deed of trust is a three-party device. The parties to a trust deed are **trustor** (borrower), **beneficiary** (lender) and **trustee** (neutral third party). When the debt is paid in full, the beneficiary directs the trustee to release the lien of the trust deed by signing and recording a **deed of reconveyance** (reconveyance deed). Where a beneficiary fails to release a trustor in a timely manner, the beneficiary is liable in an action for damages and subject to a statutory penalty of $300. (The terms "deed of trust" and "deed of reconveyance" are based on title theory. In California, however, these instruments do not actually transfer title to the property. Like a mortgage, a deed of trust merely creates a lien.)

FORECLOSURE. A **power of sale** clause is found in every deed of trust. It is a statement authorizing the trustee to sell the property upon default by the trustor. This is called non-judicial foreclosure, because the power of sale makes it unnecessary to file a lawsuit to foreclose. In the event of default, at the direction of the beneficiary, the trustee conducts an out-of-court auction (called a **trustee's sale**) and uses the proceeds from the sale to pay off the debt. If the trustee's sale results in a surplus, the excess amount belongs to the trustor.

On default, the lender first notifies the trustee of the default, who in turn sends a **notice of default** to the borrower. In addition, the trustee notifies anyone who has subsequently recorded a deed of trust or mortgage and anyone else who has recorded a request for notice of default and sale. The trustee is required to provide notices to all lienholders.

The trustor may reinstate the loan at any time from the notice of default until five business days before the sale by curing all delinquencies. If the borrower pays all past-due installments and penalties, the loan is reinstated and the trustee cannot sell the property.

If the trustor has not reinstated the loan within three months of the notice of default, the trustee publishes a **notice of sale** of the property in a newspaper of general circulation. The notice of sale must appear weekly and the sale cannot take place until at least **20 days** have elapsed since the first date of publication (the sale could take place on the twenty-first day after publication). Additionally, a notice of sale must be posted on the security property and sent to everyone who received a notice of default.

During the five days before the scheduled sale date the borrower cannot reinstate the loan. However, the borrower can still redeem the property by paying off the full balance of the loan at any time prior to the actual sale. If the borrower is unable to reinstate the loan or pay off the entire debt, a third way to escape foreclosure is to give the beneficiary a **deed in lieu of foreclosure**, which can help protect the borrower's credit and prevent the costs of foreclosure. The lender must be willing to accept the deed.

Once the sale takes place, the borrower loses all rights to the property and the trustee issues a deed, called a **trustee's deed**, to the successful bidder at the sale. The lender may bid at the sale, and is entitled to apply the amount due on the loan towards the bid (called credit bidding).

DEFICIENCY JUDGMENTS. If a lender forecloses on a deed of trust by means of a trustee's sale, its recovery is limited to the proceeds of the sale. The lender cannot bring any further action against the borrower, even if the sale proceeds do not cover the amount owing on the loan. A suit to recover such a deficiency is barred by the anti-deficiency rules.

JUNIOR LIENHOLDERS. A trustee's sale under a deed of trust destroys not only the borrower's interest in the property, but also the interests of any junior lienholders (those with subordinate liens). To protect junior lienholders, the senior lienholder must send notices of the default and sale to all junior lienholders who have recorded interests in the property. If the notices are not sent to a lienholder of record, that lienholder is not bound by the sale.

A junior lienholder can protect his or her interest by paying the delinquencies on the senior lien (curing the default) and adding the amount of these payments to the balance due on the junior loan, or by purchasing the property at the trustee's sale. The junior lienholder may then

Junior lienholder: one who holds a lien that is subordinate to another in lien priority (if necessary) foreclose his or her own lien. A purchaser at a junior lienholder's sale takes title to the property subject to any senior liens which may exist.

> **Example:** Smith borrows $10,000 from 1st Bank, secured by a first deed of trust. Later, Smith borrows an additional $20,000 from 2nd Bank and gives 2nd Bank another deed of trust (second deed of trust). 1st Bank is the senior lienholder, and 2nd Bank is the junior lienholder. If Smith defaults on 1st Bank's loan, 2nd Bank can pay off the amounts due (up until five days before the date scheduled for the trustee's sale) and thus prevent 1st Bank from selling the property. The payment is added to the balance owed by Smith on the 2nd loan. If Smith defaults on 2nd Bank's loan, 1st Bank need not take any actions to protect its lien because a buyer of the property at 2nd Bank's trustee's sale will take title to the property subject to 1st Bank's lien.

Trust Deed

GRANTING CLAUSE

ADEQUATE DESCRIPTION
Legal description preferred but not necessary

LOAN AMOUNT AND MATURITY DATE
The amount of the debt and the maturity date must be stated

POWER OF SALE
A provision permitting trustee to sell property in the event of default

_____
                    TRUSTOR

ADVANTAGES/DISADVANTAGES. Three significant benefits of the deed of trust to the lender should be apparent:

1) the lender can recover the property within four months of default, as opposed to one or two years for foreclosure of a mortgage;
2) there is no post-sale redemption period during which the borrower can recover the property;
3) there is no need to go to court in order to recover the property (although a deed of trust can be foreclosed by court action if so desired).

The only disadvantage of a deed of trust to the lender is minor. He or she is not entitled to a deficiency judgment if the trustee's sale fails to raise enough money to pay off the loan.

FORECLOSURE ALTERNATIVES. The beneficiary under a trust deed has the option of foreclosing non-judicially (trustee's sale) or judicially, by converting the trust deed to a mortgage. Though lenders seldom convert trust deeds to mortgages, it is done occasionally when a substantial deficiency is inevitable and the enforcement of a deficiency judgment appears to be possible (e.g., if the borrower owns other real estate or assets that can be reached). Mortgages cannot be converted to trust deeds.

SPECIAL PROVISIONS IN FINANCE INSTRUMENTS

The following are typical provisions found in mortgages and trust deeds.

ACCELERATION. A clause giving the lender the right to "call the note"—demand immediate payment of the entire loan amount—upon the default of the borrower.

ALIENATION. Also called a due-on-sale clause, an alienation provision is one that calls for the entire loan balance to be paid immediately if the property is transferred. Alienation clauses are not allowed in FHA or VA loans, but they are routinely included in conventional loan agreements as a means of preventing sales by loan assumption or land contract.

In every real estate loan agreement written in California since July 1972 where the collateral property contains four or fewer residential units, any alienation clause must be recited in both the promissory note and the security agreement.

PREPAYMENT PROVISION. A "lock-in clause" is a clause prohibiting early payment of the loan. Sometimes lenders allow partial prepayments up to a certain percentage of the loan without penalty.

Example: The deed of trust may state, "the borrower may pay up to fifteen percent of the original loan amount in any twelve-month period without penalty."

This is called the prepayment privilege. If a fee is charged for prepayment, the fee is called a prepayment penalty. All FHA and VA loans can be prepaid without penalty. California law prohibits conventional lenders from imposing prepayment penalties after five years on one- to four-unit owner-occupied dwellings. The law also limits the amount of prepayment penalties that can be imposed during the first five years of a residential loan.

ASSUMPTION. In the absence of an alienation clause, any real estate loan can be assumed. If a borrower sells the property to another who agrees to "assume and pay the mortgage (or trust deed) according to its terms," the new borrower becomes **primarily liable**, and the original borrower retains a **secondary liability** in the event of default.

If the original borrower wishes to be relieved of any liability whatsoever, the lender may permit a substitution of liability, called **novation**, on approval of the new borrower's credit and financial status. Normally, the lender will expect to be compensated for the substitution in the form of an assumption fee or an upward adjustment in the existing interest rate, or both.

If a buyer purchases a property with an existing loan, but takes title **"subject to"** the loan instead of assuming it, he or she has no liability for payment to the lender. The seller remains primarily liable for the loan. The buyer is liable to the seller for payment, of course.

VARIABLE PAYMENT PLANS

Up until the early 1980's, the traditional long-term, fixed-rate amortized real estate loan was the only type of loan readily available. The interest rate was fixed over the life of the loan and the mortgage payments remained the same month after month. However, the high interest rates and expensive housing of the last decade made the traditional loan too expensive for a large portion of potential homeowners. To make home financing more widely available, lenders began offering variable rate/payment loans.

The three most common variable rate/payment programs were the adjustable-rate mortgage (ARM), the graduated payment mortgage (GPM), and the growing equity mortgage (GEM). In today's more stable economy, the ARM is the only type of variable-rate financing that remains popular.

ADJUSTABLE-RATE MORTGAGE. The interest rate on an ARM is tied to a particular index (e.g., costs of funds or one-year Treasury security). As the index changes periodically to reflect the change in market interest rates, so does the loan interest rate. When the interest rate changes, the loan payments also change to reflect a new amortization schedule. ARM rates and payments change at specified periods, usually six months or one year. There are also limits to the amount of rate and payment increases that can be imposed over the life of the loan. A big advantage to the borrower is that, because he or she is assuming part of the risk of rising interest rates, lenders offer ARMs at lower interest rates than fixed-rate loans.

Adjustable-rate mortgage: a loan where the interest rate (and payments) fluctuate according to the market cost of money

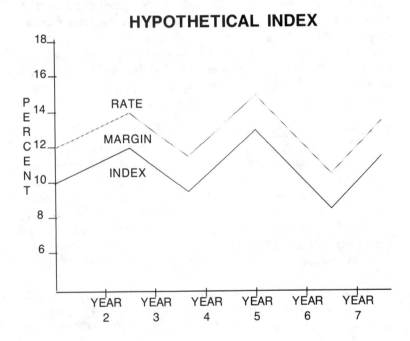

HYPOTHETICAL INDEX

GRADUATED PAYMENT MORTGAGE. To help borrowers qualify for a loan, graduated payment plans call for lower payments in the early years of the loan. The loan payments gradually increase over the years as the borrower's income is expected to increase. (Most graduated payment programs were discontinued because of problems with high rates of default.)

Graduated payment mortgage: a loan where the payments gradually increase over the term of the loan to allow a borrower to qualify for a larger loan

Growing equity mortgage: a loan where the payments gradually increase over the term of the loan so the loan will be paid off earlier

GROWING EQUITY MORTGAGES. The major benefit of a GEM is that the loan principal is paid off much sooner than with the traditional 30-year loan. Payments increase every year, but the increase is applied directly to the remaining principal balance. GEMs are less common today because borrowers' incomes seldom rise as fast as the GEM payments.

LAND CONTRACT

Land contract: security for a debt where the seller retains title to the property and the buyer obtains possession

An alternative security instrument is the **land contract**, also called an **installment sale agreement** or **contract of sale**. By any name, it is a purchase and sale agreement that calls for installment payments to the seller over a period of time. The seller under a land contract is a **vendor** and the buyer is a **vendee**.

When the contract is used, the seller retains title for the contract period. The buyer takes possession of the property and holds an equitable interest. If the buyer defaults, the seller may terminate the contract and retake possession of the property. On the other hand, if the buyer pays the contract debt in full, the seller completes the sale by delivering a deed to the buyer. The land contract is not widely used in California, except by the Cal-Vet program (see Chapter 10).

WRAPAROUND LOAN

Wraparound loan: a loan where the payments encompass the payments on an already existing loan as well as the new loan

A wraparound mortgage or deed of trust includes the balance due on an existing mortgage or trust deed, called an **underlying loan**, and an additional amount advanced by the wraparound lender. The total debt (wraparound plus underlying loan) is treated as a single obligation as far as the buyer is concerned. This means he or she makes one payment on the entire debt, and the payment is generally based on an interest rate that is higher than the rate accompanying the underlying loan. The wraparound lender (seller or third party) makes the underlying payment.

Wraparounds are most popular in periods of tight money when interest rates on other types of loans are too high and the underlying loan balance is low, requiring too large a downpayment for an assumption.

FINANCE DISCLOSURE REQUIREMENTS

TRUTH IN LENDING ACT

Truth in Lending Act: federal law that requires lenders to make certain disclosures to borrowers on application for a loan

The Truth in Lending Act is federal legislation which is implemented by the Federal Reserve Board's **Regulation Z**. The purpose of the act and of Regulation Z is to require lenders and credit arrangers to disclose to borrowers the complete cost of credit on consumer loans. For most

Comparison

TRUST DEED		MORTGAGE
Trustor—borrower Beneficiary—lender Trustee—third party	**Parties**	Mortgagor—borrower Mortgagee—lender
Deed of reconveyance	**Lien Released**	Satisfaction of mortgage or certificate of discharge
Trustee's sale or judicial foreclosure	**Foreclosure Process**	Judicial foreclosure (lawsuit)
Notice of default; notice of sale	**Notice**	Lis pendens; notice of sale
Trustor can **reinstate** up to five days before sale; **redeem** until sale	**Borrower Rights After Default**	Mortgagor can **reinstate** until decree of foreclosure; may be allowed to **redeem** up to one year after sale
Not permitted with non-judicial foreclosure	**Deficiency Judgment**	Permitted unless: 1) purchase money mortgage given to seller; 2) purchase money mortgage given to lender to finance purchase of owner-occupied dwelling with 4 units or less; 3) fair market value exceeds debt

loans covered by the act, disclosure must be made both of the **total finance charges** and of the finance charges expressed as an **annual percentage rate (APR)**. Advertising in connection with consumer loans is also regulated.

APPLICATION. The following kinds of loans (made to natural persons) are covered by the act if the loan is to be repaid in more than **four installments** or if a **finance charge** is made:

1) real estate loans for personal, family or household purposes;
2) consumer loans (loans for personal, family or household purposes) for $25,000 or less.

Lenders and persons who arrange for credit in the ordinary course of their business must comply with the requirements of the act and Regulation Z if they make or arrange for the types of loans listed above.

EXEMPTIONS. The act applies only to loans made to natural persons, so loans made to corporations or organizations are not covered. Loans made for **business, commercial** or **agricultural** purposes and loans **in excess of $25,000** (other than real estate loans, which are covered regardless of amount if made for personal or household purposes) are also exempt.

REQUIREMENTS. The primary disclosures that the lender or credit arranger must make to the borrower are the total finance charge and the annual percentage rate (APR). The **total finance charge** is the sum of all charges imposed by the lender in order for the borrower to obtain credit. In addition to the interest on the loan, some costs which would be included as finance charges would be:

- loan fees,
- finders' fees,
- service fees,
- credit life insurance premiums, and
- points paid by the borrower

(One "point" is one percent of the loan amount, paid to the lender at the outset as a fee for making the loan on the agreed terms.) Some examples of costs which would not be considered finance charges in connection with a home loan include the title search fee and the title insurance premium, credit report charges, the appraisal fee, and points paid by the seller.

The **annual percentage rate** (APR) is the relationship of the total finance charge to the amount of the loan, expressed as an annual percentage. It must be computed accurately to one-fourth of one percent.

A **disclosure statement** must be given to the borrower. The disclosure statement does not have to be on a particular form, but it must be clear and understandable and must include all the disclosures required by Regulation Z. In addition to the total finance charge and annual percentage rate, the form must disclose the total amount financed, the payment schedule, the total number of payments, the total amount of payments, late fees or prepayment charges, and a statement concerning whether the loan may be assumed by a subsequent purchaser of the property.

Additional disclosures are required for adjustable-rate home loans. The lender must give the borrower a general informational brochure on ARM loans, the *Consumer Handbook on Adjustable Rate Mortgages,* written by the Federal Reserve Board and Federal Housing Finance Board. The lender must also provide specific information regarding the particular

ARM loan program being applied for, such as the index, the initial rate, any interest rate or payment caps, and an explanation of how the interest rate and payment will be determined.

The Truth in Lending Act has some special rules for home equity loans. (A home equity loan is a loan secured by the borrower's existing residence, as opposed to a loan financing the purchase or construction of a residence.) When the security property is the borrower's principal residence, the act gives a home equity borrower a right of rescission. The borrower has the right to rescind the loan agreement up until three business days after signing the agreement, receiving the disclosure statement, or receiving notice of the right of rescission, whichever comes latest. If the borrower never receives the statement or notice, the right of rescission does not expire for three years. (It's important to remember that this right only applies to home equity loans. There is no right of rescission for a loan financing the purchase or construction of the borrower's principal residence.) The Truth in Lending Act also requires certain disclosures for home equity plans that involve repeated extensions of credit, as opposed to a single loan.

It is important to remember that the Truth in Lending Act and Regulation Z do not limit the maximum amount of finance charges; they just require disclosure of what the charges are.

ADVERTISING. Advertising of credit terms is strictly controlled by the act. The advertising regulations apply to all those who use commercial advertising of consumer credit, not only to creditors and arrangers of credit. For example, a real estate broker advertising financing terms for a listed home has to comply with Regulation Z.

In general, the cash price or the annual percentage rate may be advertised. If any other particulars are advertised, then all the particulars must be advertised. If terms such as:

- the downpayment,
- the amount of any finance charge,
- the amount of any payment,
- the number of payments, or
- the term of the loan

are advertised, then the:

- downpayment,
- terms of repayment, and
- the annual percentage rate

must be included. For instance, an advertisement that reads, "Assume 11% VA loan" would violate the Truth in Lending Act requirements if it did not go on to reveal all of the loan's particulars as just explained. Advertising of a general rather than a specific nature is permitted, such as "low down," "easy terms," "low interest rates."

RESIDENTIAL PURCHASE MONEY LOAN DISCLOSURE LAW

California law requires that certain disclosures be made to both parties when there is purchase money credit extended by the seller and there is an "arranger of credit." An arranger of credit, for the purposes of the law, is either:

1) a person who is not a principal party to the transaction who is involved in negotiating the terms of the credit agreement, who participates in preparing the documents, or who is directly or indirectly compensated for arranging for credit or for assisting in arranging the sales transaction (except for lawyers), or
2) an attorney or real estate licensee who is a principal party to the transaction, if neither party is represented by a real estate licensee.

The law applies if the transaction involves:

1) credit for all or part of the purchase price extended to the purchaser by the seller of a one- to four-unit residential property; and,
2) the credit arrangements involve a finance charge or provide for four or more payments, not including the downpayment; and,
3) there is an arranger of credit.

Certain transactions are **exempt**, such as those in which RESPA or Truth in Lending disclosures are required.

DISCLOSURES. If this purchase money disclosure law applies to the transaction, certain written disclosures must be made before the purchaser executes any note or security instrument. The disclosures are:

1) to the purchaser, by the arranger of credit and the vendor with respect to information in the knowledge of the vendor; and,
2) to the vendor, by the arranger of credit and the purchaser with respect to information in the knowledge of the purchaser.

Here are some, but not all, of the disclosures that this law requires:

1) a description of the terms of the note and security documents and the property involved;
2) a description of the terms and conditions of senior encumbrances (such as a first trust deed which the buyer will be taking subject to or assuming);

3) a warning that, if refinancing is contemplated due to a credit arrangement that is not fully amortized, such refinancing may be
   difficult or impossible to obtain in the conventional mortgage
   marketplace;
4) a disclosure of any potential for negative amortization and the
   effect negative amortization would have;
5) if the financing involves a wraparound or all-inclusive trust deed,
   information regarding the person responsible for making payments
   to the prior lienholders, and information relating to balloon
   payments or prepayment penalties on any prior encumbrances;
6) employment, income and credit information about the prospective purchaser, or a statement that the arranger of credit has made
   no representation regarding the creditworthiness of the purchaser.

MORTGAGE LOAN BROKER LAW

Real estate agents often help purchasers obtain financing. This
assistance may go beyond simply helping the buyer apply to one institutional lender. In some cases, it's necessary to get loans from two
or more lenders to raise enough cash to close the transaction.

California's Mortgage Loan Broker Law (also known as the Necessitous
Borrowers Act or the Real Property Loan Law) regulates real estate agents
who act as loan brokers. The law requires a loan broker to give the borrower a disclosure statement. And for some loans secured by residential property, the law places restrictions on the fees and commissions
paid by the borrower or received by the loan broker, and regulates other
aspects of the loan terms. Only an overview of a few of the law's key
provisions is presented here.

Disclosure Statement. The disclosure statement required by the
Mortgage Loan Broker law must be on a form approved by the Real Estate
commissioner. It discloses all the costs involved in obtaining the loan,
and the actual amount the borrower will receive after all costs and fees
are deducted. The borrower must receive the statement before signing
the note and security agreement.

A disclosure statement is generally required whenever a real estate
agent negotiates a loan or performs services for borrowers or lenders
in connection with a loan. There is an important exception, however:
the disclosure statement is not required if the lender is an institutional
lender and the commission paid to the loan broker by the borrower is
2% of the loan amount or less.

Mortgage Loan Broker
Law: state law which
places certain
requirements on real
estate agents who arrange
financing

Commissions, Costs, and Terms. For certain loans secured by residential property with one to four units, the Mortgage Loan Broker Law limits the commissions and costs that a real estate agent may charge the borrower for arranging the loan. Specifically, these restrictions apply when the loan involves a first deed of trust for less than $20,000 or a junior deed of trust for less than $10,000.

for these loans, the maximum commissions the loan broker can charge are:

- for a first deed of trust,
  - —5% of the principal if the loan term is less than three years, and
  - —10% of the principal if the loan term is three years or more.

- for a junior deed of trust,
  - —5% of the principal if the term is less than two years,
  - —10% of the principal if the term is at least two years, but less than three years, and
  - —15% of the principal if the term is three years or more.

Also, the costs of making these loans (such as the appraisal and escrow fees) cannot exceed 5% of the loan amount, or $195, whichever is greater. In any case, the costs charged to the borrower must never exceed $350, and must not exceed the actual costs.

The Mortgage Loan Broker Law also prohibits balloon payments in these loans if the loan term is short. When the security property is an owner-occupied home, balloon payments are prohibited if the term is less than six years. Otherwise, balloon payments are prohibited if the term is less than three years. (These rules don't apply to seller financing, however.) For the purposes of this law, a balloon payment is one that is more than twice as large as the smallest payment required by the loan agreement.

MORTGAGE LOAN DISCLOSURE STATEMENT (BORROWER)
CALIFORNIA ASSOCIATION OF REALTORS® (CAR) STANDARD FORM
(As required by the Business and Professions Code Section 10240 and Title 10, California Administrative Code, Section 2840)

_____
(Name of Broker/Arranger of Credit)

_____
(Business Address of Broker)

I. SUMMARY OF LOAN TERMS

A. PRINCIPAL AMOUNT OF LOAN . . . . $ _____

B. ESTIMATED DEDUCTIONS FROM PRINCIPAL AMOUNT

   1. Costs and Expenses (See Paragraph III-A) . . . . $ _____

  * 2. Commission/Loan Origination Fee (See Paragraph III-B) . . . . $ _____

   3. Liens and Other Amounts to be Paid on Authorization of Borrower
      (See Paragraph III-C) . . . . $ _____

C. ESTIMATED CASH PAYABLE TO BORROWER (A less B) . . . . $ _____

II. GENERAL INFORMATION ABOUT LOAN

A. If this loan is made, you will be required to pay the principal and interest at _____% per year, payable as

   follows: _____   _____ payments of $_____

           (number of payments)   (monthly/quarterly/annually)

   and a FINAL/BALLOON payment of $_____ to pay off the loan in full.

     "NOTICE TO BORROWER: If you do not have the funds to pay the balloon payment when it comes due, you may have to obtain a new loan against your property to make the balloon payment. In that case, you may again have to pay commissions, fees, and expenses for the arranging of the new loan.

     In addition, if you are unable to make the monthly payments or the balloon payment, you may lose the property and all of your equity through foreclosure. Keep this in mind in deciding upon the amount and terms of this loan."

B. This loan will be evidenced by a promissory note and secured by a deed of trust in favor of lender/creditor on property located at (street address or legal description):

_____
_____

C. 1. Liens presently against this property (do not include loan being applied for):

Nature of Lien	Priority	Lienholder's Name	Amount Owing

   2. Liens that will remain against this property after the loan being applied for is made or arranged (include loan being applied for):

Nature of Lien	Priority	Lienholder's Name	Amount Owing

     NOTICE TO BORROWER: Be sure that the amount of all liens is stated as accurately as possible. If you contract with the broker for this loan, but it cannot be made or arranged because you did not state these lien amounts correctly, you may be liable to pay commissions, fees, and expenses even though you did not obtain the loan.

D. If you wish to pay more than the scheduled payment at any time before it is due, you may have to pay a PREPAYMENT PENALTY computed as follows:

_____
_____
_____
_____

E. The purchase of credit life or credit disability insurance is not required of the borrower as a condition of making this loan.

F. The real property which will secure the requested loan is an "owner-occupied dwelling."   YES _____   NO _____
                                                                 (Borrower initial opposite YES or NO)

   "For purposes of restrictions on scheduled balloon payments and unequal payments, an "owner-occupied dwelling" means a single dwelling unit in a condominium or cooperative or a residential building of less than three separate dwelling units, one of which will be owned and occupied by a signatory to the mortgage or deed of trust within 90 days of the signing of the mortgage or deed of trust. For certain other purposes relating to this loan, "dwelling" means a single dwelling unit in a condominium or cooperative, or any parcel containing only residential buildings if the total number of units on the parcel is four or less, which is owned by a signatory to the mortgage or deed of trust."

     Borrower hereby acknowledges the receipt of a copy of this page, which constitutes page 1 of 2 pages.

                Borrower's Initials (_____) (_____)

                                     ——— OFFICE USE ONLY ———
                                       Reviewed by Broker or Designee _____
                                       Date _____

MORTGAGE LOAN DISCLOSURE STATEMENT (BORROWER) (MS-14 PAGE 1 OF 2)

Reprinted with permission, California Association of Realtors®. Endorsement not implied.

III. DEDUCTIONS FROM LOAN PROCEEDS

A. ESTIMATED MAXIMUM COSTS AND EXPENSES to be paid by borrower out of the principal amount of the loan are:

PAYABLE TO

	Broker	Others
1. Appraisal		
2. Credit investigation		
3. Delivery		
4. Drawing/Document preparation		
5. Escrow		
6. Notary:		
7. Notice of delinquency:		
8. Processing:		
9. Recording:		
10. Tax service:		
11. Title insurance:		
12. Other costs and expenses		

TOTAL COSTS AND EXPENSES .... $ _____

*B. LOAN BROKERAGE COMMISSION/LOAN ORIGINATION FEE .... $ _____

C. LIENS AND OTHER AMOUNTS to be paid out of the principal amount of the loan on authorization of the borrower are estimated to be as follows:

PAYABLE TO

	Broker	Others
1. Fire or other hazard insurance premiums		
2. Credit life or disability insurance premium (see Paragraph II-E)		
3. Beneficiary statement fees		
4. Reconveyance and similar fees		
5. Discharge of existing liens against property:		
6. Other:		

TOTAL TO BE PAID ON AUTHORIZATION OF BORROWER $ _____

If the loan to which this disclosure statement applies is a loan secured by a first deed of trust in a principal amount of less than $20,000 or a loan secured by a junior lien in a principal amount of less than $10,000, the undersigned licensee certifies that the loan will be made in compliance with Article 7 of Chapter 3 of the Real Estate Law.

*This loan ☐ may / ☐ will / ☐ will NOT (check one) be made wholly or in part from broker-controlled funds as defined in Section 10241(j) of the Business and Professions Code.

NOTICE: This disclosure statement may be used if the broker is acting as an agent in arranging the loan by a third person or if the loan will be made with funds owned or controlled by the broker. If the broker indicates in the above statement that the loan "may" be made out of broker-controlled funds, the broker must notify the borrower prior to the close of escrow if the funds to be received by the borrower are in fact broker-controlled funds.

_____   _____
(Name of Broker)   (Name of Designated Representative)

_____   _____
(License Number)   (License Number)

_____ OR _____
(Signature of Broker)   (Signature)

NOTICE TO BORROWER

DO NOT SIGN THIS STATEMENT UNTIL YOU HAVE READ AND UNDERSTOOD ALL OF THE INFORMATION IN IT. ALL PARTS OF THE FORM MUST BE COMPLETED BEFORE YOU SIGN.

Borrower hereby acknowledges the receipt of a copy of this page which constitutes page 2 of 2 pages.

DATE: _____   _____
                                              (Borrower)

                                    _____
                                              (Borrower)

D.R.E. Ref.: MLDS-423 12-7-89

MORTGAGE LOAN DISCLOSURE STATEMENT (BORROWER) (MS-14 PAGE 2 OF 2)

CHAPTER SUMMARY

1. The most prominent federal agencies empowered to exercise control over the availability and cost of money are the United States Treasury, the Federal Reserve System and the Office of Thrift Supervision.

2. A negotiable instrument is a written promise or written order to pay money and is freely transferable. For a promissory note to be considered a negotiable instrument, it must be an unconditional promise, in writing, signed by the maker, stating a sum certain in money, definite as to terms of repayment, and be made payable "to order" or "to bearer."

3. California follows the lien theory, which holds that when property is used as security for the payment of a debt, the borrower retains title to the property, and the mortgage acts as a lien against the property, securing the debt.

4. A deed of trust or trust deed acts the same way as a mortgage in securing the promissory note. The main difference between a mortgage and a deed of trust is the method of foreclosure.

5. The three most common variable rate/payment programs are the adjustable-rate mortgage (ARM), the graduated payment mortgage (GPM), and the growing equity mortgage (GEM). In today's economy, the only type of variable rate financing that is still popular is the ARM.

6. The Truth in Lending Act requires lenders and credit arrangers to disclose to borrowers the complete cost of credit on consumer loans.

CHAPTER 9—QUIZ
REAL ESTATE FINANCE

1. Rates on mortgages are influenced by:

   a) the supply of housing
   b) the supply and demand for money
   c) Both a) and b)
   d) Neither a) nor b)

2. A decrease in the number of dollars in circulation generally causes interest rates to:

   a) decrease
   b) increase
   c) remain the same
   d) None of the above

3. The FDIC:

   a) insures deposits in banks and S&Ls
   b) has replaced the Federal Reserve Board
   c) is better known as "the Fed"
   d) was abolished under FIRREA

4. Mr. Smith purchased a duplex for $200,000, paying $40,000 down. Two years later he sold it for $280,000, and realized a two hundred percent increase on his original investment. This is an example of:

   a) escalation
   b) leverage
   c) plottage
   d) highest and best use

5. The maximum amount (other than commissions) of all costs and expenses that a broker can charge for negotiating a two-year loan of $8,000 secured by a 1st trust deed on real property is:

   a) 4% of the loan
   b) $195
   c) $350
   d) $400

6. Which of the following is not a true statement regarding the Federal Reserve System?

   a) The United States is divided into twelve districts, with a reserve bank in each district
   b) The system is administered by state governors
   c) All federally chartered banks must be members
   d) The Federal Reserve Board regulates the flow of money and credit

7. The entity that has responsibility for this country's fiscal management is the:

   a) Federal Reserve System
   b) Office of Thrift Supervision
   c) FHFB
   d) U.S. Treasury

8. Under the Mortgage Loan Broker Law, the maximum commission allowed on a $7,000 first trust deed for three years is:

   a) $350
   b) $700
   c) $70
   d) $1,000

9. The Mortgage Loan Broker Law applies to residential first trust deeds of:

   a) $20,000
   b) $30,000
   c) $35,000
   d) None of the above

10. A promissory note calling for payment of interest only during its term is called a/an:

   a) amortized note
   b) installment note
   c) negotiable note
   d) straight note

11. Promissory notes often include an "or more" provision. These important words:

    a) allow for an accelerated pay-off
    b) make it possible to borrow additional funds on the same note
    c) provide for a loan moratorium in the event of a disaster
    d) indicate the note has several makers

12. When a buyer assumes an existing loan, the:

    a) seller is released from obligation by the lender
    b) seller becomes secondarily liable for the loan
    c) seller remains primarily liable for the loan
    d) buyer is liable only to the seller for the loan

13. A note in which the principal amount is systematically reduced through regular payments of both principal and interest is known as a/an:

    a) junior loan
    b) straight note
    c) amortized note
    d) None of the above

14. The clause in a deed of trust, mortgage or promissory note which permits the lender to declare the entire unpaid balance due and payable at once, upon default of the borrower, is a/an:

    a) acceleration clause
    b) escalator clause
    c) forfeiture clause
    d) default clause

15. A clause in a deed of trust, mortgage or promissory note which permits the lender to call the outstanding balance due and payable should the property be sold by the borrower is a/an:

    a) forfeiture clause
    b) balloon payment clause
    c) exculpatory clause
    d) alienation clause

16. A land contract is a method of financing sometimes substituted for mortgage or trust deed financing. Consequently, a land contract is:

    a) the same as a mortgage
    b) a security device
    c) similar to a lease
    d) a lease with an option to buy

17. California is a lien theory state. This means:

    a) the first to record is the first in right
    b) liens recorded against a property can be foreclosed through the courts
    c) mortgages and trust deeds are liens and do not give the lender title to the property
    d) All of the above

18. The trustor in connection with a trust deed is the party who:

    a) lends the money
    b) receives the payments
    c) signs the note
    d) releases the lien

19. Under a mortgage, the mortgagor is the party who:

    a) lends the money
    b) receives the payments on the note
    c) holds the mortgage
    d) signs the note and gives the mortgage

20. Which of the following documents accompanies the deed of trust?

    a) A deed
    b) An abstract of title
    c) A contract of sale
    d) A promissory note

21. To be a valid and enforceable instrument, a deed of trust must contain a clause requiring the trustor to:

    a) keep the property insured against fire
    b) keep the property in good condition
    c) pay taxes and assessments before delinquent
    d) None of these

22. In order to foreclose a mortgage, a mortgagee would:

    a) notify the trustee of default
    b) file an attachment in the amount of the debt
    c) notify the mortgagor of default, wait ninety days, and publish a notice of default in a local paper
    d) file a lawsuit

1. b) Interest rates are determined by the availability of money and the demand for it.

2. b) Interest rates usually increase when the money supply decreases.

3. a) The FDIC insures bank and S&L deposits.

4. b) Using borrowed funds to turn a profit is called "leverage."

5. c) The Mortgage Loan Brokers Law limits expense charges to a maximum of $350.00.

6. b) The Fed is governed by the seven-member Federal Reserve Board.

7. d) The Treasury Department is fiscal manager for the United States.

8. b) Ten percent is the limit on commissions for loans of 3 years or more secured by a 1st deed of trust.

9. d) The Mortgage Loan Broker's Law applies to residential first trust deeds of less than $20,000.

10. d) A straight note calls for interest payments only during the term of the loan, with a balloon payment at the end.

11. a) The words "or more" allow a prepayment. Without them the borrower could be forced to pay the loan over its entire term, with no prepayment privilege.

12. b) The seller would become secondarily liable if the note were assumed by the buyer.

13. c) This is the definition of an amortized loan. Amortization is sometimes referred to as "liquidation" of a debt.

14. a) An acceleration clause gives the lender the right to "accelerate" the loan's due date to the present, because of nonpayment or some other form of default.

15. d) This is the definition of an "alienation clause."

16. b) The land contract secures the debt for the seller (vendor).

17. c) In California mortgages and trust deeds act as liens; they do not give a lender any form of title. This is the meaning of "lien theory."

18. c) The trustor is the borrower under a deed of trust.

19. d) The borrower is the mortgagor; the lender is the mortgagee.

20. d) The promissory note is secured by a deed of trust or mortgage.

21. d) The deed of trust doesn't have to have provisions regarding these matters, but it should, and it usually does.

22. d) Mortgages are foreclosed by suing the borrower for default in a court of law.

Real estate lenders and government-backed programs

Outline

I. Types of Lenders
  A. Commercial banks
  B. Savings and loans
  C. Life insurance companies
  D. Mutual savings banks
  E. Mortgage companies
  F. REITs
  G. Pension plans
  H. Private individuals
II. Government-Backed Programs
  A. FHA
    1. FHA insurance
    2. characteristics
    3. loan programs
  B. VA
    1. characteristics
    2. eligibility
    3. guaranty amount
    4. loan amounts
  C. Cal-Vet
    1. eligibility
    2. characteristics
III. National Mortgage Market
  A. FNMA
  B. GNMA
  C. FHLMC

KEY TERMS

primary market	secondary market
mortgage broker	real estate investment
mortgage banker	trusts (REITs)
FHA	VA
MIP	FNMA
Cal-Vet	GNMA
mortgage-backed	FHLMC
securities	

CHAPTER OVERVIEW

In the last chapter, you learned about real estate finance. Now it is time to learn where finance money comes from and how to get the necessary financing. There are many types of real estate lenders, and each has different characteristics and investment guidelines. There are also several government agencies that sponsor financing programs. Knowledge of the real estate financing markets will help you understand what types of financing are available and which option would be best for a particular transaction.

REAL ESTATE MARKETS

There are two markets for real estate loans:

1) the local market, and
2) the national market

LOCAL MARKET

Primary market: the local real estate finance market where lenders lend money to borrowers

The local market is sometimes called the primary market. It is the "ground level" money market and the one that is most familiar to the public. It is in the local market that personal, automobile, business and mortgage loans are arranged between the borrower and the lender.

The source of most funds used for loans of any kind is individual savings or investments—primarily savings. Banks and savings and loans reinvest for profit the savings entrusted to them by their depositors. How much money they have to reinvest (the amount of individual savings) is dependent to a large extent on political and economic activities in the immediate area. Local wage levels, interest rates, and employment trends influence individual savings habits.

TYPES OF REAL ESTATE LENDERS

There are many types of real estate lenders in the primary market. The most significant among them are listed below, along with a summary of the lending characteristics of each.

COMMERCIAL BANKS. Commercial banks are the largest source of investment funds in the U.S. As their name implies, they are oriented towards commercial lending activities, supplying capital for business ventures and construction. Important lending criteria for commercial banks include established relationships with customers and the quality of the collateral.

Most of a commercial bank's assets are in the form of demand deposits (better known as checking accounts), which the depositor can withdraw at any time. Because their deposits are subject to immediate withdrawal, traditionally commercial banks did not get too involved in real estate lending. Instead they preferred short-term investments, such as personal and business loans. For the most part, their real estate lending activities were limited to construction and home improvement loans, with repayment periods ranging from three months to five years (in contrast to residential loans, which generally have repayment periods from 15 to 30 years). In the 1980s, however, residential lending by commercial banks increased, and they now account for approximately 30% of residential loans.

SAVINGS AND LOAN ASSOCIATIONS. The savings and loan association is an institution organized under state or federal charter to encourage thrift and to make investment capital available for home loans. The majority of funds entrusted to savings and loan associations are savings deposits made by individuals. Of the deposits reinvested, most are placed in real estate loans. Over 75% of these loans are for single-family dwellings. As a rule, savings and loan associations prefer to make conventional loans (loans without government insurance or guaranty), but will make FHA and VA loans under certain circumstances.

Other characteristics of savings and loan associations include a preference for medium to long-term loans (15-30 years) and a greater concern for the quality of the property used as security than other types of lenders.

LIFE INSURANCE COMPANIES. Insurance companies control vast amounts of capital in the form of insurance policy premiums. Money invested in life insurance policies is generally not subject to sudden withdrawal (as are bank deposits) and does not earn the high returns that are now common for other forms of investment. For these reasons, insurance companies are able to safely invest large sums in long-term real estate loans.

Insurance companies generally prefer loans for large-scale commercial projects as opposed to residential mortgages. The companies rarely make loans directly to borrowers; instead, they select **loan correspondents,** such as local mortgage companies, to invest their money for them.

MUTUAL SAVINGS BANKS. Although there are some mutual savings banks in the northwestern states of Alaska, Oregon and Washington, most are located in the northeastern part of the United States. These banks are mutual companies that distribute profits to their depositors/owners in the form of interest or dividends on savings accounts.

Mutual savings banks have always been among the most conservative of lenders. Their activities were oriented towards the communities they served, allowing close supervision of their loans. Although their conservative lending stance has not altered, mutual savings banks have begun investing outside their own communities, seeking the safety of diversification.

MORTGAGE COMPANIES. When a bank, savings and loan association or mutual savings bank accumulates more deposits than necessary to meet local demand, it will frequently seek the services of a competent mortgage company to invest the excess funds in a selected regional or national market. The mortgage company will be one of two types: a mortgage broker or a mortgage banker.

Mortgage broker: an intermediary who brings borrowers and lenders together for a fee

A **mortgage broker** brings together borrowers and lenders in certain loan transactions. As a rule, the mortgage broker acts only as a go-between (locating lenders for borrowers) and seldom loans money or services the loan after it has been made.

The mortgage broker operates on a fee basis, usually charging a one-time fee for the services, and the fee is invariably a percentage of the loan amount—two or three percent or more.

Since the mortgage broker's compensation is proportionate to the size of any loan he or she helps negotiate, most mortgage brokers prefer to work with large commercial loans.

The principal distinction between a mortgage broker and a **mortgage banker** is that the latter not only helps arrange loans for lenders and borrowers, he or she usually services the loan after it has been made as well. Servicing a loan involves collecting payments, inspecting the properties that serve as collateral and handling foreclosures, where necessary.

With the advantage of servicing income, which endures for the life of a loan, the mortgage banker can profitably place residential real estate loans. In fact, most mortgage bankers are known primarily as residential lenders, and they traditionally make more FHA and VA loans than all other lenders combined.

As a rule, mortgage bankers do not lend their own money; they usually borrow from their banks on a short-term basis to make their real estate loans. Then they sell the loans to investors, such as savings and loans, banks and insurance companies, while retaining the right to service the loans for a fee.

REAL ESTATE TRUSTS. A trust is an unincorporated association of investors managed by a trustee (or trustees). The trust is created by a written instrument and vests the entire trust estate in the trustee. The trust beneficiaries have no legal interest in the property owned by the trust; they have only the right to compel the performance of the trust according to the terms of the trust instrument.

Real estate investment trust (REIT): a group of at least 100 investors who enjoy the benefits of a corporate-like structure without the tax disadvantages

In 1960, by means of the Real Estate Investment Trust Act, Congress made it possible for investors to enjoy the flow-through tax advantages of a partnership while retaining some of the more important qualities of a corporate operation. The act allows investors who prefer real estate as an investment to receive tax benefits similar to those granted to mutual funds and other regulated investment companies. Unlike ordinary corporations, whose earnings are subject to double taxation (first at the corporate level and again as personal income when distributed to stockholders), the real estate trust earnings are taxed only once, after they have been distributed to their investors. An REIT must have at least 100 investors.

PENSION PLANS. Savings in pension plans represent almost one-third of all consumer savings. As such, they are a major source of investment money and could become a major contributor to the real estate market. To date, however, pension fund managers have been inclined to direct their funds into other forms of investment, and the role they will play in real estate finance in the future is unclear.

PRIVATE INDIVIDUALS. Private individuals have always been a force in the world of real estate finance. The majority of private lenders are sellers who extend credit to their purchasers. This is referred to as "taking back" or "carrying back" part of the sales price.

When interest rates are high or money is in short supply, buyers are more inclined to ask owners to sell their properties on installment terms. Accordingly, private financing becomes much more prevalent when funds from traditional sources are scarce or too expensive, or both.

If an owner's property is free and clear of any mortgage debt, the purchaser can make a downpayment that is large enough to be mutually agreeable, and pay the balance of the purchase price to the seller on agreed-upon installment terms. The purchaser gives the seller, at the time of closing, a mortgage or trust deed that secures the debt and stipulates that the property shall act as collateral in the event of default.

GOVERNMENT FINANCING PROGRAMS

There are several government agencies (both federal and state) that sponsor financing programs. These programs are generally geared towards the middle- to low-income borrowers or special groups of people (e.g., veterans). The three types of government-sponsored financing we will discuss here are:

- FHA-insured loans
- VA-guaranteed loans, and
- Cal-Vet loans

(NOTE: loans which are not backed by a government agency are called "conventional" loans.)

FHA-INSURED LOANS

FHA: the Federal Housing Administration; it insures residential loans

The Federal Housing Administration, or the FHA, was created by Congress in 1934 as part of the National Housing Act. The purpose of the Act, and of the FHA, was to generate new jobs through increased construction activity, to exert a stabilizing influence on the mortgage market and to promote the financing, repair, improvement and sale of real estate nationwide.

Today, the FHA is part of the Department of Housing and Urban Development (HUD); its primary function is to insure loans. Approved lenders are insured against losses caused by borrower defaults on FHA-insured loans. The FHA does not build homes or make loans.

FHA INSURANCE. The FHA is a giant federal insurance agency. Its insurance program is called the **mutual mortgage insurance plan**. Under the plan, lenders who have been approved by the FHA to make insured loans either submit applications from prospective borrowers to the local FHA office for approval or, if authorized by the FHA to do so, perform the underwriting functions themselves (review of appraisal, credit examination, etc.). Lenders who are authorized by the FHA to fully underwrite their own FHA loan applications are called direct endorsers.

As the insurer, the FHA incurs full liability for losses resulting from default and property foreclosure. In turn, the FHA regulates many of the conditions of the loan. FHA regulations have the force and effect of law; these regulations and FHA procedures and practices have done much to shape the face of the real estate lending industry today.

FHA LOANS VS. CONVENTIONAL LOANS. FHA loans have a number of features which distinguish them from conventional loans. The most significant differences are:

1) **No secondary financing for the downpayment.** The FHA minimum downpayment for a particular loan must be paid by the borrower in cash. The buyer may not resort to secondary financing from the seller or another lender to borrow any portion of the minimum downpayment or other closing costs.

2) **Buyer must pay own impounds (reserves).** The prepayable reserves on FHA loans for property taxes and homeowner's insurance must be paid by the borrower. With VA loans and many conventional loans, the seller is permitted to pay all of the buyer's settlement costs, including the prepaid reserves, if the seller is willing to do so. (Tax and insurance reserves are referred to by several different terms, including impounds, prepaid items, and prepayable expenses.)

3) **Mortgage insurance (MIP) is required on all loans.** Regardless of the size of the downpayment, mortgage insurance is required on all FHA loans. Conventional loans do not usually call for mortgage insurance unless the loan-to-value ratio exceeds 80%.

4) **All FHA loans are assumable.** Many conventional mortgages and deeds of trust contain an alienation clause or due-on-sale clause, which allows the lender to demand that the loan be paid in full in the event of sale. FHA and VA loans do not contain due-on-sale clauses. Therefore, FHA loans are assumable. But a credit check on the new borrower is required for assumption of any FHA loan originated after January 15, 1990.

5) **No prepayment charges.** Many conventional loans contain prepayment provisions which impose charges if the borrower pays off the loan within the first few years. These charges can be quite substantial. FHA and VA loans do not contain prepayment clauses; they may be paid off at any time without additional charges.

One primary advantage of an FHA loan over a conventional loan is that downpayment requirements are substantially smaller. The downpayment for an FHA loan is often as low as 5%, compared to the 10% to 20% usually required for a conventional loan. However, because FHA programs are aimed at the low- or middle-income homebuyer, there are limits on loan amounts. The maximum amounts vary from one community to another. The basic maximum for single-family homes is $67,500; the maximum in the highest-cost areas is $124,875.

INTEREST RATES AND POINTS. The FHA does not set maximum interest rates for insured loans. Interest rates on FHA-insured loans are freely negotiable, determined by market trends in the financing industry. FHA rates tend to be somewhat lower than conventional rates, due to the perceived lower risks of a government-insured loan.

At one time, borrowers were prohibited from paying discount points on FHA-insured loans; any points had to be paid by the seller. That restriction has been eliminated, and borrowers are now allowed to pay some or all of the points.

THE MIP. The feature which distinguishes FHA mortgage payments from conventional and VA mortgage payments is inclusion of the mutual mortgage insurance premium, more popularly referred to as the MMI or the mortgage insurance premium (MIP).

MIP: the insurance premium paid to the FHA on taking out an FHA-insured loan

The MIP is a **one-time premium**. It may be paid in cash at closing or financed over the term of the loan. The amount of the premium varies depending upon both the term of the loan and whether the premium is to be paid in cash at closing or financed. Premiums are smaller for shorter-term loans and for premiums paid in cash. If paid in cash at closing, the premium for a 30-year loan is equal to 3.661% of the loan amount; if financed, the premium would be 3.8% for a 30-year loan. Beginning in 1991, new FHA borrowers will also be required to pay an **annual premium** of 0.5% during the first several years of their loan term.

FHA LOAN PROGRAMS. The FHA has several programs; the ones of most interest to the average homebuyer include:

- **Section 203b**—For fixed-rate loans on single-family homes and residential duplexes, triplexes, and fourplexes. This is the standard FHA-insured loan, accounting for about 70% of all FHA loans. It can be used for an initial purchase loan or for refinancing.
- **Section 203b(2)**—For loans on single-family homes purchased by veterans. (Not the same as a VA-guaranteed loan.)
- **Section 234(c)**—For loans on condominium units.
- **Section 251**—For adjustable-rate mortgages (available for the same types of property covered by the 203(b) program). The ARM must have a 30-year term.

Until 1989, the FHA was willing to insure loans on investment property—property the borrower did not intend to occupy. Nearly all FHA programs no longer cover investment property. For all of the programs listed above, the borrower must occupy the property.

VA-GUARANTEED LOANS

The Veterans Administration guarantees repayment of certain residential loans made to eligible veterans. VA loans are available to purchase single-family homes or multiple-family residences containing up to four units. There are no investor loans guaranteed by the VA. If the property is a single-family dwelling, the veteran must intend to occupy it as his or her residence; if the property is a multiple-family dwelling, the veteran must occupy one of the units.

VA: the Veterans Administration; it guarantees loans made to eligible veterans

Several characteristics of VA-guaranteed loans are highly attractive to borrowers:

- Unlike most loans, a typical VA loan may be obtained with no downpayment.
- VA loans contain no prepayment penalties and no due-on-sale clauses. Although VA loans are assumable, a complete credit check of the assumptor is required prior to the assumption of any VA loan made after March 1, 1988.
- The interest rate on VA loans may not exceed the maximum allowable rate determined by the Veterans Administration. The maximum VA rate is normally below the prevailing market rate for conventional loans.
- VA loans have no mortgage insurance (neither private mortgage insurance nor FHA-style mutual mortgage insurance). However, a funding fee of up to 1.875% is charged.
- Discount points are paid by the seller. The borrower may be charged a loan fee of up to one percent by the lender.
- Finally, secondary financing is permitted in conjunction with most VA loans.

ELIGIBILITY. Eligibility for VA loans is based on the length of continuous active service in the U.S. armed forces. The minimum requirement varies depending upon when the veteran served.

90 days continuous active duty, any part of which occurred:

1. September 16, 1940 through July 25, 1947 (WWII)
2. June 27, 1950 through January 31, 1955 (Korea)
3. August 5, 1964 through May 7, 1975 (Vietnam)

181 days continuous active duty, any part of which occurred:

1. July 26, 1947 through June 26, 1950
2. February 1, 1955 through August 4, 1964
3. May 8, 1975 through September 7, 1980

24 months continuous active duty for veterans who enlisted after September 7, 1980, except:

1. individuals discharged for disability;
2. individuals discharged for hardship;
3. any case in which it is established that the person is suffering from a service-connected disability not the result of willful misconduct and not incurred during a period of unauthorized absence.

Veterans who are discharged for hardship or for a nonservice-connected disability are eligible only if they have served a minimum of 181 days. There is no minimum active duty service requirement for veterans discharged for a service-connected disability.

Persons who have served six months active duty training only are not eligible. There is also no eligibility for persons who received a dishonorable discharge.

AMOUNT OF GUARANTY. VA loan amounts are determined by the VA appraisal, called a Certificate of Reasonable Value (CRV). Only a portion of the loan will be guaranteed by the VA. The maximum guaranty has been increased over the years as follows:

- WWII guaranty was $4,000;
- increased on September 1, 1951, to $7,500;
- increased on May 7, 1968, to $12,500;
- increased on December 31, 1974, to $17,500;
- increased on October 1, 1978, to $25,000;
- increased on October 1, 1980, to $27,500;
- increased on February 1, 1988, to $36,000;
- increased on January 1, 1990, with a sliding scale formula as follows:

Loan Amount	Guaranty Amount
up to $45,000	50% of loan amount
$45,000—$56,250	$22,500
$56,251—$90,000	40% of loan amount
$90,001—$144,000	$36,000
over $144,000	$36,000 plus 25% of the amount above $144,000, up to a maximum of $46,000

The current sliding scale formula means that the guaranty amount will vary according to the loan amount. For example:

Loan Amount: $110,000
Guaranty Amount: $36,000

Loan Amount: $150,000
Guaranty Amount: $37,500

VA LOAN AMOUNTS. There is no maximum VA loan amount, except for the requirement that the loan may not exceed the appraised value of the property as determined by the CRV or the sales price, whichever is less. However, most (though not all) lenders require that the VA guaranty cover at least 25% of the loan amount for a zero-down loan. Thus as a practical matter, a vet will find it difficult to obtain a VA loan greater than $184,000 ($184,000 × .25 = $46,000).

If a downpayment is used in connection with a VA loan, VA regulations permit a buyer to finance part or all of the downpayment (secondary financing) if the following conditions are met:

1) the total of all financing does not exceed the reasonable value of the property;
2) the buyer's income is sufficient to qualify based on the payments required for both loans;
3) the interest rate on the second does not exceed the current VA rate of interest; and
4) there are no more stringent conditions connected with the second mortgage than apply to the VA first mortgage (such as a late payment penalty). Exception: the second mortgage may contain a due-on-sale clause.

CALIFORNIA VETERANS FARM AND HOME PURCHASE PROGRAM (CAL-VET)

The California Veterans Farm and Home Purchase Program makes low-interest real estate loans (commonly referred to as Cal-Vet loans) available to qualified veterans for the purchase of farms or homes, including mobile homes and condominiums. The State Department of Veterans Affairs processes, originates and services the loans until they are paid in full.

Cal-Vet: a loan program for California veterans

The state sells bonds to raise funds to purchase and take title to the homes or farms sought by eligible veterans. In turn, the state sells the properties to the veterans under land contracts. The state retains title throughout the contract term. During this period the veteran has an equitable interest in the property. The contract debt is repaid by the veteran at a very low rate of interest, through monthly payments over a period of years.

The normal contract term on homes and farms is 30 years, though occasionally repayment periods are for as long as the maximum 40 years. An exception is the mobile home loan, which usually has a term of 15 to 20 years, depending on the age and condition of the mobile unit when the contract is made. The maximum mobile home contract term is 25 years.

The vet must pay an appraisal charge (usually between $100 and $350) and there is a loan origination fee of $425, $25 of which must be paid at the time of application.

ELIGIBILITY. To be eligible for Cal-Vet financing, a veteran must be a native of California or have been a bona fide California resident upon entry into the armed forces. Furthermore, the veteran must have served at least 90 days on active duty, a portion of which was during a wartime period. California veterans discharged before 90 days because of service connected disability are still eligible. In lieu of wartime service, a veteran can have served in certain U.S. military campaigns or expeditions. An eligible veteran must apply for the Cal-Vet financing **within 30 years of discharge** from active duty, unless the veteran was wounded in action, was a prisoner of war or is a disabled veteran. The veteran must have received an **honorable discharge** or have been released under honorable conditions.

MAXIMUM LOAN AMOUNTS. Cal-Vet loan ceilings vary depending on the type of property being financed. Presently they are as follows.

a) single-family home or condominium $125,000
b) mobile home on veteran's own lot $90,000
c) mobile home in mobile home park $70,000
d) farm $200,000

LOAN-TO-VALUE RATIOS. The maximum Cal-Vet loan-to-value is 97% (3% downpayment) on purchase prices of $35,000 or less, and 95% (5% down) on purchase prices of more than $35,000.

SECONDARY FINANCING IS ALLOWED. Secondary financing at the time of purchase is allowed, provided the sum of the Cal-Vet contract and the secondary loan amount do not exceed 90% of the appraised value, set by the Department of Veterans Affairs.

Additionally, the combined average interest rate of the Cal-Vet and second loans cannot exceed the current rate allowed for a VA-guaranteed home loan.

CAL-VET LOAN HAS VARIABLE INTEREST RATE. The contract payments are subject to change over the contract term because the Cal-Vet land contract bears a variable interest rate.

VETERAN MUST OCCUPY. Approved veterans or their immediate families must occupy their properties within **60 days** after signing a Cal-Vet contract. The transfer, encumbering or leasing of property under a Cal-Vet contract is prohibited without the written permission of the Department of Veterans Affairs. Temporary permission to lease the property will be granted if the need to do so is compelling, but the **maximum rental term is 4 years**.

SINGLE-FAMILY DWELLING. If the Cal-Vet loan is for a home, it must be a single-family dwelling (including condominiums and mobile homes).

PREPAYMENT PENALTY. If the contract is prepaid in whole or in part within the first five years, the borrower must pay an amount equal to six months' interest on the amount paid in excess of 20% of the loan amount.

NATIONAL MARKET

The availability of funds in the primary market (the ability of a particular lender to lend out money to prospective borrowers) depends a great deal on the existence of the **national**, or secondary, market. An individual lender may have either an excess or a shortage of funds to loan out, depending on the conditions of the local economy. It is the national market which balances out that excess or shortage by transferring funds from areas where there is an excess to areas where there is a shortage.

Secondary market: the national real estate finance market where investors buy and sell real estate loans

The national secondary market consists of private investors and government agencies that buy and sell real estate mortgages. A real estate loan is essentially an investment, just like stocks or bonds. The lender commits its funds to making a loan in the expectation that the money will generate a return in the form of interest payments. Real estate loans can be bought and sold just like other investments. The value of the loan is influenced by the rate of return on the loan compared to the market rate of return as well as the degree of risk associated with the loan (the likelihood of default).

The national market serves two vital functions: it promotes investments in real estate by making funds available for real estate loans and it provides a measure of stability in the primary market by moderating the adverse effects of real estate cycles. The effect the national market has on the primary market can be seen by taking a brief

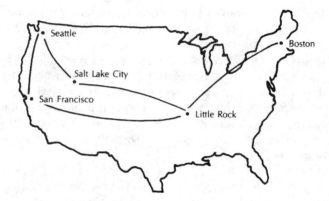

A shortage of money in one region of the country can be offset by transferring surplus monies from other regions.

look at the flow of mortgage funds: first, mortgage funds are given to the homebuyer by a lending institution; that mortgage is then sold by the lender to a secondary agency, which may in turn sell it to other investors in the form of mortgage-backed securities (a debt obligation with mortgages as collateral). As mortgage-backed securities are sold by the secondary agency, more funds become available to that agency for the purchase of new mortgages from the primary market. As more mortgages are purchased from the primary market, more funds become available for lenders to pass on to borrowers. Were it not for the national market, a scarcity of money at the local level would be crippling; real estate activity would slow drastically and the entire community would suffer.

The secondary market is able to function as it does because of standardized underwriting criteria. Underwriting standards are used to qualify the borrower and the property; they include such items as loan-to-value ratios and income-to-expense ratios. Each mortgage issued by each individual lender must conform to the secondary market's underwriting standards or it will not be purchased on the secondary market. These standards assure a uniform quality control that inspires confidence in the purchasers of the mortgage-backed securities. The purchasers know that the mortgages backing the securities must be of a minimum quality, which lessens the risk of investing in properties they cannot view or assess for themselves.

The existence of a secondary market has a stabilizing effect on local mortgage markets. It represents a medium for the exchange of funds and mortgages between investors from money surplus areas and those from money shortage areas. Because of the secondary market, investors are assured that even in times of inadequate funds, they can commit themselves to long-term real estate loans and still be able to liquidate them when necessary through the secondary market.

The federal government has helped to create a permanent secondary mortgage market. While private investors (e.g., insurance companies and pension plans) make up a portion of the secondary market, the agencies created by the government are the major forces in the secondary market. These agencies are the:

- Federal National Mortgage Association (FNMA)
- Government National Mortgage Association (GNMA), and
- Federal Home Loan Mortgage Corporation (FHLMC).

FEDERAL NATIONAL MORTGAGE ASSOCIATION (FNMA)

The Federal National Mortgage Association, often referred to as "Fannie Mae," began as a federal agency in 1938, and its original purpose was to provide real estate lenders an element of liquidity by acting as a secondary market for their existing mortgage loans. This function is especially vital in tight money periods because by purchasing existing loans from real estate lenders, FNMA frees their money for reinvestment in the primary money market. The lenders continue to service the loans for a fee, which involves billing, collections, property tax follow-up work and foreclosure services, when necessary.

FNMA: the Federal National Mortgage Association; a leading secondary market agency that purchases loans from commercial banks

Originally, FNMA purchased only FHA and VA loans; today it buys conventional loans as well.

In 1968, legislation was enacted which reorganized FNMA into a private corporation, and common stock for FNMA was offered over-the-counter for purchase by the general public. At the same time a new federal agency was created, the Government National Mortgage Association (GNMA), which assumed FNMA's governmental responsibilities, while FNMA ventured on as a private member of the free enterprise system.

GOVERNMENT NATIONAL MORTGAGE ASSOCIATION (GNMA)

GNMA, usually called "Ginnie Mae," was established in 1968, and is one of many federal agencies that are part of the Department of Housing and Urban Development (HUD).

GNMA's responsibilities include the management and liquidation of certain older FNMA loans and the purchase at the secondary market level of many types of loans that are socially significant but are not necessarily attractive to private secondary market investors. These

GNMA: the Government National Mortgage Association; a leading secondary market agency that purchases VA and FHA loans purchases include loans for urban renewal projects, housing for the elderly, and other special assistance programs.

GNMA's most prominent role is played through its **mortgage-backed securities program**, which is a comprehensive plan that enables qualified lenders to obtain additional funds for lending purposes by pledging blocks of their existing loans as collateral for securities issues. The mechanics of the program are beyond the scope of this text, but in essence it is government support for lenders who use the real estate loans they have made as collateral to raise money through the issuance of securities.

FEDERAL HOME LOAN MORTGAGE CORPORATION (FHLMC)

FHLMC: the Federal Home Loan Mortgage Corporation; a leading secondary market agency that purchases loans from savings and loans

Created through the Emergency Home Finance Act of 1970, the Federal Home Loan Mortgage Corporation, generally referred to as "Freddie Mac," buys mortgages in the secondary mortgage market primarily from savings and loan associations.

The "credit crunch" of the late 1960's resulted in an outflow of funds from traditional savings and loans that was so severe that these institutions were barely earning enough to cover operating costs. There was no money available for real estate lending purposes. The formation of the FHLMC created a reliable secondary market for savings and loans, enabling them to liquidate portions of their real estate loan holdings and to free money to make new real estate loans.

While FNMA emphasizes the purchase of mortgage loans, the FHLMC also actively sells the loans from its portfolio, acting as a conduit for mortgage investments. The funds generated by the sale of the mortgages are then used to purchase more mortgages.

CHAPTER SUMMARY

1. There are several types of real estate lenders in the local market. These include commercial banks, savings and loans, life insurance companies, mortgage brokers, pension plans, REITs, and private individuals. Each lender has different characteristics and each focuses on a different type of real estate loan.

2. Various government agencies are involved in residential financing. Typically, they are focused on low- to middle-income borrowers or a special class of borrowers. Each has its own requirements for loans

and loan applicants. Federally-backed financing includes FHA-insured loans and VA-guaranteed loans. State financing includes Cal-Vet loans.

3. Lenders in the primary market depend on investors in the secondary market for mortgage funds. The secondary market, by buying and selling loans, encourages investment in real estate, frees funds to make yet more real estate loans, and provides stability to an otherwise volatile finance market. The three main secondary market agencies are the Federal National Mortgage Association (FNMA), the Government National Mortgage Association (GNMA), and the Federal Home Loan Mortgage Corporation (FHLMC).

CHAPTER 10—QUIZ
REAL ESTATE LENDERS AND GOVERNMENT-BACKED PROGRAMS

1. The lender that specializes in real estate home loans, deals in conventional loans, services its own loans, and makes many medium- to long-term loans is a/an:

   a) savings and loan association
   b) commercial bank
   c) insurance company
   d) mutual savings bank

2. The largest source of single-family home financing on a conventional basis is:

   a) commercial banks
   b) savings and loan associations
   c) mortgage brokers
   d) mutual savings banks

3. The lender that invests a major portion of its assets in long-term real estate loans, does not make loans directly to borrowers and likes large loans on commercial properties is a/an:

   a) commercial bank
   b) savings and loan
   c) insurance company
   d) mutual mortgage company

4. Jones bought a farm for $9,000 twenty-five years ago. It is now free and clear and valued at $130,000. He asks a real estate broker to get him a $100,000 loan against the property. The broker would be least likely to apply to which of the following for the loan?

   a) Commercial bank
   b) Mutual savings bank
   c) Savings and loan association
   d) Insurance company

5. Which lending institution prefers to make local loans, considers the previous relationship with the customer to be of great importance, and prefers short-term loans?

   a) Savings and loan association
   b) Commercial bank
   c) Mortgage company
   d) Life insurance company

6. An agent who arranges loans between lenders and borrowers and then services the loans is most likely to be a:

   a) loan processor
   b) mortgage banker
   c) mortgage broker
   d) mutual correspondent

7. A prospective homebuyer desiring an FHA-insured loan would apply to:

   a) the FHA only
   b) an approved mortgagee
   c) Both a) and b)
   d) Neither a) nor b)

8. If a borrower defaults on an FHA-insured loan, any losses sustained by the lender as a result of the foreclosure are made up through:

   a) an attachment lien against the borrower
   b) an assessment against the lender
   c) the mutual mortgage insurance plan
   d) the U.S. Treasury

9. According to VA regulations, what is the maximum fee a borrower can pay a lender for obtaining a VA loan?

   a) One percent
   b) Two percent
   c) Seven percent
   d) No maximum

10. A requirement for a borrower under an FHA-insured single-family residence loan is that he or she:

    a) pay the downpayment in cash
    b) take out a loan of $124,875 or less
    c) Both a) and b)
    d) Neither a) nor b)

11. One of the advantages of buying a home with FHA-insured financing, as opposed to a conventional loan, is that:

    a) the FHA sets a limit on interest rates
    b) FHA-insured loans are quicker to close and easier to obtain
    c) an FHA-insured loan does not require mortgage insurance
    d) the interest rate is likely to be lower with an FHA-insured loan

12. The penalty for prepaying an FHA-insured loan is:

    a) 2% of the loan balance at the time of prepayment
    b) 1% of the loan balance at the time of prepayment
    c) 1% of the original loan amount
    d) None of the above

13. Which of these programs will cover a loan made to an investor who does not intend to occupy the property he or she is purchasing?

    a) FHA 203b
    b) VA
    c) Cal-Vet
    d) None of the above

14. In the case of a VA-guaranteed loan the borrower may:

    a) sell the property "subject to" the loan
    b) not repay the loan ahead of schedule
    c) Both a) and b)
    d) Neither a) nor b)

15. VA-guaranteed loans:

    a) are limited by the VA to $100,000
    b) require private mortgage insurance
    c) require a ten percent downpayment if the sales price is above $100,000
    d) None of the above

16. A Certificate of Reasonable Value is issued by the:

    a) Federal National Mortgage Association
    b) Veterans Administration
    c) Federal Housing Administration
    d) All of the above

17. The buyer may use a second mortgage loan for part of the financing in connection with a VA-guaranteed first mortgage loan:

    a) only if both the husband and wife are entitled to veterans' benefits
    b) only if the purchase price exceeds $144,000
    c) only if the total financing of first and second loans does not exceed the CRV
    d) under no circumstances

18. The amount a qualified lending institution may loan to a qualified veteran on a VA-guaranteed loan is limited by the VA to:

    a) the assessed value of the property
    b) $100,000
    c) the amount of the veteran's entitlement
    d) the amount shown on the Certificate of Reasonable Value

19. If a non-veteran purchases a property encumbered by a VA-guaranteed loan, the debt:

    a) must be repaid immediately
    b) can be assumed by the new purchaser
    c) Both a) and b)
    d) Neither a) nor b)

20. With respect to conventional, FHA-insured and VA-guaranteed loans, which of the following is correct?

   a) All three are insured or guaranteed, but VA-guaranteed loans have higher interest rates than either FHA or conventional loans
   b) FHA-insured loans are at a higher loan-to-value ratio than VA-guaranteed loans, but lower loan-to-value ratio than most conventional loans
   c) Conventional loan interest rates are lower, but these loans are not insured or guaranteed
   d) Conventional loans are usually at a lower loan-to-value ratio, and the interest charged on FHA-insured or VA-guaranteed loans tends to be lower

21. Which of these is a secondary marketing agency?

   a) The Federal National Mortgage Association
   b) The Government National Mortgage Association
   c) The Federal Home Loan Mortgage Corporation
   d) All of the above

22. Under the Cal-Vet program:

   a) the buyer receives title immediately upon close of escrow
   b) the buyer receives title by making payments on time for two years
   c) the buyer receives title after completely paying off the loan
   d) the buyer never receives title

1. a) These are the characteristics of a savings and loan.

2. b) Savings and loan associations.

3. c) These are the characteristics of insurance companies that invest in real estate.

4. d) Insurance companies prefer to invest their money through loan correspondents and do not usually make loans at the primary market level.

5. b) These are the characteristics of a commercial bank.

6. b) Mortgage bankers arrange loans. They will usually service the loans as well. Mortgage brokers also arrange loans, but usually do not service them.

7. b) The FHA insures loans made by approved mortgagees, that is, lenders who have met the FHA's requirements for approval to make FHA loans. The FHA does not make loans.

8. c) Under the mutual mortgage insurance plan, private lenders are protected against losses when they foreclose properties acting as security for FHA-insured loans.

9. a) This charge is normally called a loan fee, origination fee or service charge, and is limited to 1%.

10. c) The FHA requires the borrower to pay the downpayment in cash and places a limit on the maximum loan amount.

11. d) Historically FHA loans have interest rates below conventional rates.

12. d) Neither the FHA nor the VA permits lenders to assess a prepayment penalty.

13. d) For all of these programs, the borrower must intend to occupy the property.

14. a) Any VA loan can be prepaid, and the VA does not allow an alienation clause.

15. d) There is no maximum loan amount, but the guaranty amount is limited.

16. b) The CRV is a VA appraisal.

17. c) Among other restrictions placed on secondary financing in connection with VA loans, the total financing may not exceed the reasonable value of the property.

18. d) While there is no maximum VA loan amount, the loan cannot exceed the appraised value.

19. b) All VA loans can be assumed.

20. d) Conventional loan-to-value ratios are lower than those set by the FHA or VA, and the conventional interest rates are usually higher.

21. d) FNMA, GNMA, and the FHLMC are the key secondary marketing agencies in the U.S.

22. c) Under Cal-Vet, the state buys property and resells it to the veteran on a land contract. Title passes when the contract is fully paid.

REAL ESTATE APPRAISAL

OUTLINE

I. Appraisal Defined
II. Value Defined
   A. How value is created
   B. How value in exchange is created
III. Principles of Value
IV. The Appraisal Process
V. Market Data Approach to Value
   A. Elements of comparison
   B. Comparable sale must have been at arm's length
VI. Cost Approach to Value
   A. Replacement cost methods
   B. Depreciation
VII. Income Approach to Value
   A. Contract rent vs. economic rent
   B. Operating expenses
   C. Capitalization
   D. Gross income multipliers
VIII. Correlation and Final Estimate of Value

KEY TERMS

utility value
arm's length transaction
highest and best use
principle of change
cost approach
unit-in-place method
depreciation
equilibrium

value in exchange
principle of substitution
supply and demand
integration
square foot method
quantity survey method
deferred maintenance
disintegration

principle of contribution
regression
principle of anticipation
functional obsolescence
economic life
effective gross income
gross income multiplier
principle of conformity
progression
correlation
economic obsolescence
contract rent
capitalization

CHAPTER OVERVIEW

In a real estate transaction, the buyer and the seller often disagree as to what the property is worth. And before committing to financing the transaction, a lender will want to know the true value of the property. It is therefore necessary to find out what the property is worth, as for an arm's length transaction, aside from any emotional or subjective values placed on it by the buyer or seller. An estimation of value is called an appraisal. This chapter describes what is meant by the term "value," and explains the various methods of appraisal used in estimating value.

APPRAISAL DEFINED

An appraisal is an estimate or an opinion of value. The term "appraisal" also refers to the act of estimating value. An appraisal usually takes the form of a written statement, called an **appraisal report**, setting forth the appraiser's opinion of the value of a piece of property as of a given date. A synonym for appraisal is **valuation**.

An appraiser may be asked to help a seller decide on a fair asking price, or a buyer may seek an opinion on how much to pay for the property. Whoever employs the appraiser is the client. The appraiser is the agent. A principal/agent relationship exists and the laws of agency apply.

In addition to helping determine a fair asking or purchase price for a property, an appraiser's services are regularly required for any one of the following reasons:

- to estimate the relative values of properties being exchanged;
- to assist a lender in establishing the maximum loan amount;
- to provide an expert opinion of value for properties involved in the liquidation of estates, corporate mergers, corporate acquisitions or bankruptcies;
- to establish rental rates;

- to determine the amount of hazard insurance coverage necessary;
- to estimate remodeling costs;
- to identify raw land's highest and best use;
- to estimate market value for taxation purposes;
- to help establish value in a condemnation proceeding.

THE ROLE OF THE APPRAISER

VALUE DEFINED

Value is a term with many meanings. The most common definition of value is "the present worth of future benefits." The degree of value is usually measured in terms of money.

For appraisal purposes, value falls into two general classifications: **value in use** and **value in exchange**. A property might be worth one thing to its owner (use value) and quite another to a would-be purchaser (exchange value). Use value is often measured subjectively, whereas exchange value is determined more objectively.

Utility value: value to the owner/user

Value in use is also called utility, subjective value or emotional value. It is the commodity's value to its owner/user.

> **Example:** A large, expensive, one-bedroom home, designed, built and occupied by its owner would undoubtedly be worth more to the owner than to the buyer, who would look at the property objectively and expect more than one bedroom for the price.

Value in exchange: market value, the price the property would bring in a sale conducted under ideal market conditions.

Exchange value, more commonly called **market value**, is the more significant of the two value classifications. Identifying the estimated market value of a property is the purpose of most appraisals. As a matter of fact, market value will be the purpose in every instance, except where no market exists.

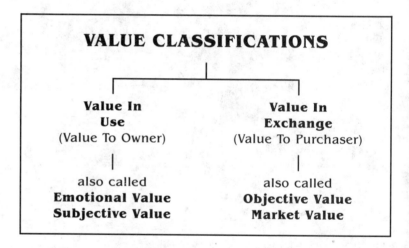

VALUE CLASSIFICATIONS

Value In Use
(Value To Owner)

also called
Emotional Value
Subjective Value

Value In Exchange
(Value To Purchaser)

also called
Objective Value
Market Value

Market value is the highest price a property would bring if the sale were to take place under conditions ideal to both buyer and seller. These conditions include:

- an absence of abnormal pressure to act,
- exposure of the property on the open market for a reasonable period, and
- full knowledge of the property's merits and shortcomings.

The Federal Housing Administration offers a succinct explanation of market value: "The price which typical buyers would be warranted in paying for the property for long-term use or investment, if they were well informed, acted intelligently, voluntarily, and without necessity."

HOW VALUE IS CREATED

For an object to have value, it must contain two ingredients: **utility** and **scarcity**.

Utility refers to the ability to arouse desire for possession, and the power to give satisfaction. While this usually means an object must be useful, the terms utility and usefulness in this context are not the same. Utility is dependent on individual desires. Warm clothing, for example, is useful but lacks utility for the individual in a tropical climate who seeks relief from the heat.

There must also be an element of scarcity. An object in excessive supply will lose value, regardless of its degree of utility. Food has a vital utility, but if more food is produced than can be consumed, the excess has no value.

HOW VALUE IN EXCHANGE IS CREATED

For an object to have a market value, the desire stimulated by its utility must be joined with the ability to buy it—purchasing power. Desire, coupled with purchasing power, translates into demand. But even with demand, there is no market value if the property is not freely transferable. Publicly owned properties, like libraries, universities and courthouses, are not transferable and have no market value.

MARKET VALUE VS. MARKET PRICE. Both the courts and the FHA distinguish between market value and market price. Market price is the price paid for a property, regardless of whether the parties to the transaction were informed and acting free of pressures. Market value is what should be paid if a property is purchased and sold under the ideal circumstances previously described. A sale made under ideal conditions is called an arm's length transaction.

Many forces influence our attitudes and behavior. Three of them interact to create, support, or erode property values:

- social ideals and standards,
- economic fluctuations, and
- government regulations.

FORCES AFFECTING VALUE

1. Social ideals and standards
2. Economic fluctuations
3. Government regulations

Obsolete architectural styles, a change in attitude regarding family size, and the emergence of the two-car family are examples of social forces that affect (unfavorably) the value of homes with outmoded designs, too many bedrooms or one-car garages. Economic forces include employment levels, availability of money, interest rates, business trends or any other factors that affect the community's purchasing power. Government regulations, such as zoning ordinances, building restrictions or fire regulations, help shape the utility of land and serve to promote, stabilize or discourage demand for it.

PRINCIPLES OF VALUE

Over the years, by observing the actions of buyers, sellers and investors in the marketplace, appraisers have been able to develop a reliable body of principles, referred to as the **principles of land utilization**. Appraisers depend on the constancy of these principles to guide them when making decisions in the valuation process.

Highest and Best Use
(Alternate Use Considerations)

Present Use	Alternate Use 1	Alternate Use 2	Alternate Use 3
Warehouse	Parking Lot	Service Station	Triplex
Annual Net Income $19,280	**Estimated Annual Income** $16,800	**Estimated Annual Income** $20,500	**Estimated Annual Income** $14,300
Estimated Value $175,000	**Estimated Value** $151,000	**Estimated Value** $184,000	**Estimated Value** $132,000

The appraiser should consider potential uses for the land as though it were vacant, and for the land with its existing buildings, if any. By estimating the value of the land when put to alternate uses, the appraiser can decide whether the land is presently serving its highest and best use or if it could be put to a loftier use that would substantially increase its value.

Highest and best use: the use which would produce the greatest net return over time

PRINCIPLE OF HIGHEST AND BEST USE. Highest and best use is among the most important of all considerations when trying to estimate the value of real property. Highest and best use refers to the most profitable use: the use that will provide the greatest net return over a period of time. Net return usually refers to gross income minus expenses, but it cannot always be measured in terms of money. With residential properties, net return might manifest itself in the form of amenities—the pleasure and satisfaction derived from living on the property.

Estimating the highest and best use may be a simple matter of confirming that deed restrictions or an existing zoning ordinance limit the property to its present use. Usually, the present use of a property is its highest and best use. But change is constant and a warehouse site that was once profitable might now generate a greater net return as a parking lot.

PRINCIPLE OF CHANGE. The appraiser must look at all property with the understanding that it is in a constant state of change. It is the future, not the past, that is the primary consideration when estimating value. What is happening to the property? What is its future? How do prospective buyers view its potential? The appraiser's conclusions are dependent on his or her judgment, experience, astuteness and perceptiveness.

Principle of change: property is in a constant state of change, through phases of integration, equilibrium, and disintegration

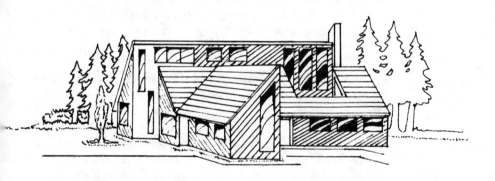

Equillibrium: a period of stability and little change.

Related to the principle of change is the theory that property has a three-phase life cycle: **integration, equilibrium,** and **disintegration**.

Integration is also referred to as development and represents the early stages of the cycle, when the property is being developed. Equilibrium is the period of stability, when the property undergoes little, if any change. Finally, disintegration is that declining period when the property's present economic usefulness is near an end and constant upkeep is necessary.

Integration: period of development

Equilibrium: period of stability

Disintegration: period of decline

Economic life: period
during which property
may be profitably utilized

Supply and demand:
values rise with increased
demand and decreased
supply; values fall with
decreased demand and
increased supply

Principle of substitution:
a buyer will not pay
more for a property than
it would cost to acquire
an equally desirable
substitute

Principle of conformity:
maximum value is
achieved with reasonable
consistency in size and
quality of structures, and
socio-economic
conformity

Regression: loss in value
caused by surroundings

Progression: increase in
value from surroundings

Principle of contribution:
value added by a
particular improvement.

Every property has both a physical and an economic life and it is invariably the economic life—that period during which land and its improvements may be profitably utilized—that ends first. The appraiser must recognize and take into account the stage of the property's life cycle when estimating its present worth.

PRINCIPLE OF SUPPLY AND DEMAND. Supply and demand affects all marketable commodities. Values rise as demand increases and supply decreases, and diminish when the reverse is true.

Land supply, or lack of it, refers to the availability of land in a certain area which can serve a specific purpose. Land scarcity, by itself, does not create demand. The availability of financing, interest rates, wage levels, property tax levels and population growth or shifts are all factors which influence the demand for real estate. People who want real estate must also be able to afford it. The strongest desire must be coupled with purchasing power—the financial ability to buy the land.

PRINCIPLE OF SUBSTITUTION. This principle states that no one will pay more for a piece of property than they would have to pay for an equally desirable substitute property, provided there would be no unreasonable or costly delay in acquiring that substitute property. Explained another way, the principle of substitution holds: if two properties that are for sale or for lease are alike in every respect, the least expensive one will be in greater demand.

PRINCIPLE OF CONFORMITY. The maximum value of land is achieved when there is an acceptable degree of social and economic conformity in the area. Conformity should be reasonable, but not carried to an extreme.

From the standpoint of an appraiser, conformity takes several forms. With residences, it can mean similarities in the size and general structural quality of the homes in the area. Where there is inconsistency in this regard, there is value instability. A home of noticeably lower quality than those around it will have a regressive effect on the value of those homes (**principle of regression**). Conversely, its association with the higher quality homes will have a progressive effect on its own value (**principle of progression**).

Retail stores grouped closely together, provided the use-density is in balance, is another example of conformity. Customers like to frequent shopping districts and are reluctant to shop at stores isolated from others. Being situated in a shopping district is desirable for a retailer as long as the competition does not become excessive.

PRINCIPLE OF CONTRIBUTION. Contribution refers to the value an improvement adds to the overall value of the property. Some improvements will add more value than the expense of making them; others will cost more than they contribute to value.

A remodeled basement ordinarily will not contribute its cost to the value of the home. On the other hand, the addition of a second bathroom, because of its functional worth, may increase a home's value by more than the cost of installing it.

The undesirable property will have a regressive effect on the value of the more appealing property alongside it.

PRINCIPLE OF ANTICIPATION. Value is created by the anticipated benefits of owning a property in the future. It is not past benefits, but future benefits that arouse a desire to own.

Anticipation can help or hurt value, depending on what informed buyers and sellers expect to happen to the property in the future. Normally, they expect property values to increase, because the supply is fixed and the demand continues to rise. However, in certain instances, buyers and sellers anticipate that values will decline, as when a large chunk of important retail property is to be condemned by the city for a street widening project.

Principal of anticipation: present value is affected by expected future benefits or disadvantages of ownership

THE APPRAISAL PROCESS

Properly done, the appraisal process is orderly and systematic. The appraiser is charged with a large responsibility, that of forming an opinion of value on which the client—buyer, seller, or lender—will undoubtedly base one or more important decisions. While there is no officially standardized procedure, appraisers generally carry out the appraisal process in the following manner.

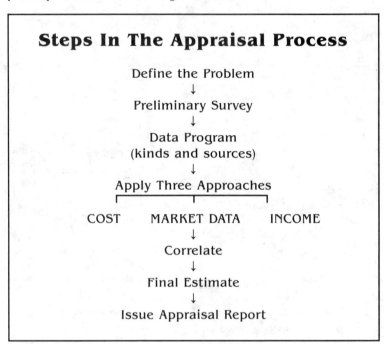

1. **Identify the Problem.** When the appraiser is hired, he or she is asked to solve a problem, namely that of clarifying the value of something. Since appraisals can be made for different purposes and serve any number of separate functions, the first step in the appraisal process is to identify the nature and extent of the problem to be solved. Among other things, this involves identifying the property and establishing the purpose and function of the appraisal.

2. **Determine What Data Is Needed and Where It Can Be Found.** The data on which the value estimate will be based is divided into two categories: **general** and **specific**.

   General data has to do with matters external to the property being appraised. It includes population trends, prevailing economic circumstances, zoning, proximity of amenities (shopping, schools and public transportation), as well as the condition and quality of the neighborhood itself.

Specific data relates to the property being appraised. The appraiser will want to gather information about the title, the buildings and the site.

3. **Gather and Verify the General Data.**

4. **Gather and Verify the Specific Data.**

5. **Select and Apply the Valuation Method(s).** In many cases, the appraiser will approach the problem of estimating value three different ways: the cost approach, the market data approach and the income approach. In other instances, he or she will use only the method that seems most appropriate. Whether one, two or three approaches are used is a matter of judgment.

   Sometimes, a particular method cannot be used. Raw land, for example, cannot be appraised by the cost approach. A public library, on the other hand, must be appraised by the cost method because it does not generate income and no market exists for it.

6. **Correlate Value Indicators for Final Value Estimate.** The figures yielded by each of the three approaches are called value indicators, meaning they give indications of what the property is worth but are not final estimates themselves.

   The appraiser will take into consideration the purpose of the appraisal, the type of property being appraised and the reliability of the data gathered for each of the three approaches. He or she will place the greatest emphasis on the approach which seems to be the most reliable indication of value.

7. **Issue Appraisal Report.** The formal presentation of the value estimate and an explanation of what went into its determination are made in the form of an appraisal report.

MARKET DATA APPROACH TO VALUE

The market data approach is the comparison of information on properties of a certain kind and class with characteristics of the property being appraised.

Appraisers use this method whenever possible because intelligently selected market information is an excellent way to measure the actions of informed buyers and sellers in the marketplace. Where there is an adequate number of recent sales of similar properties, the value indicated by the market data technique can be very reliable.

In the application of this technique, it is the appraiser's task to gather pertinent information about comparable sales, making feature-by-feature

Market approach: value is estimated by comparison with recently sold similar properties

comparisons against the property under appraisal. The appraiser then translates his or her findings into an estimate of the market value of the subject property.

Occasionally, the appraiser's job is made easier by an ample number of recent sales involving properties similar to the subject property. However, sometimes usable comparable properties are in short supply. The market data method is the most popular method for appraising single-family residences because there is usually an abundance of comparable data. Single-family residential sales account for a vast majority of real estate transactions nationwide.

The alternative appraisal methods—replacement cost and capitalization—will be used when there are not enough comparable sales to use the market data method. When appraising residences, an appraiser needs at least three reliable comparables to have enough data to form and support an opinion of value. Certain properties like publicly-owned buildings and churches have no market (or income) and must be appraised by the replacement cost method.

ELEMENTS OF COMPARISON

The appraiser gathers pertinent data on three or more properties that are comparable to the subject property. The test for whether a property is comparable or not involves checking the primary elements of comparison:

- time of sale
- location of the property, and
- physical characteristics of the property

TIME. Generally, very recent sales are more reliable indications of market values than sales from the distant past. Economic conditions change, and if the changes have been significant in the months or years since a comparable sale occurred, the appraiser may have to reject the comparable sale altogether. If the change has been a steady, but measurable, increase in property values in the area, the appraisal may be a simple matter of making adjustments for the appreciation that has generally affected values.

A rule of thumb is that the sale should have occurred within the previous year.

LOCATION. Prices for identical structures can vary from one neighborhood to the next. Usually, the closer in location the comparable property is to the subject property, the more likely its price will provide a meaningful guide to value. It is best if the comparable property and the subject property are in the same neighborhood.

PHYSICAL CHARACTERISTICS. A comparison of physical characteristics includes the site and its buildings. Important site comparisons are frontage, depth, area, landscaping and contour. Building characteristics consist of number of rooms, square footage, quality of construction, age and functional utilities.

COMPARABLE SALES MUST HAVE BEEN AT ARM'S LENGTH

Regardless of any other consideration such as time of sale or degree of structural similarity, if a comparable sale was not an arm's length transaction, the appraiser cannot rely on it as an indication of value. To qualify as an arm's length transaction, both seller and buyer must have been informed of the property's merits and flaws, neither can have been acting under unusual pressures or duress, and the property must have been tested in the marketplace for a reasonable period.

Arm's length transaction: a sale where buyer and seller are informed, neither are under undue pressure, and the property is on the market for a reasonable length of time

The appraiser must also consider seller and buyer motives when deciding whether to include or reject a comparable transaction. An owner might deliberately sell property for less than it is worth if there are tax advantages to be gained from doing so. An individual might pay more than market value for a lot adjoining her business property because she must have it for parking. Or a sale between relatives might be influenced more by love than a concern for market value. Many of the circumstances which would make a sale ineligible as an arm's length transaction would be revealed by interviews with the principals to the transaction or the agent of record.

The terms of the sale also do much to influence value today. More and more buyers have demonstrated a willingness to pay more for a property if the financing terms are attractive.

Where there is a scarcity of comparable sales, the appraiser can refer to properties presently listed for sale. The appraiser must keep in mind, however, that asking prices tend to be high and frequently represent the ceiling of the market value range. The appraiser can also use offers from buyers, though they are difficult to confirm because records of offers are usually not kept. Offers are consistently at the low end of the market value range. Actual market value typically is somewhere between offers and listed prices.

COST APPROACH TO VALUE

Cost approach: value is estimated by estimating cost to replace improvements, less depreciation, plus value of site

The cost approach to value involves estimating the cost to reproduce or replace existing buildings, then adding to that the estimated value of the site on which they rest. Because the cost approach involves estimating the value of land and buildings separately, then adding them together, it is sometimes called the **summation method**.

One rationale for the use of the cost method is that it tends to identify the ceiling of the market value because buyers will not pay more for property than it would cost to replace it, provided there would be no costly delay in finding the replacement (principle of substitution).

REPLACEMENT COST METHODS

There are three ways to estimate the replacement cost of a building: the square foot method, the unit-in-place method and the quantity survey method.

SQUARE FOOT. The square foot method involves multiplying the cost per square foot of a recently built comparable structure by the number of square feet in the subject property. Because it involves comparing costs, it is sometimes called the **comparative cost method**. It is the replacement cost method appraisers use most often.

The comparable building is unlikely to be exactly the same as the building being appraised because there will be variations in design, shape and grade of construction that will moderately or substantially affect the square foot costs. The appraiser must make refinements in his or her estimates to reflect the cost variations. When a comparable new building is not available, the appraiser relies on current manuals for basic construction costs.

The number of square feet in a building is determined by calculating outside measurements, and multiplying width by depth.

UNIT-IN-PLACE. The unit-in-place method involves a series of estimates of the cost to replace specific component parts of the building such as floors, roof, plumbing, foundation and the like. The estimates use cost measurements such as the square foot and cubic foot when defining replacement costs of the various components. For example, one of the estimates might be a certain number of dollars per one hundred square feet of roofing. Another component estimate would be a certain amount per cubic foot or cubic yard of concrete for an installed foundation. By this method, the appraiser estimates separately the cost to replace all of the structure's component parts, adding them together in the end to find the replacement cost of the structure itself. All estimates include the cost of materials, labor and profit.

The unit-in-place method is more detailed and likely to be more accurate than the square foot method. Like the square foot method, it relies on cost manuals for component cost figures.

QUANTITY SURVEY. Sometimes referred to as the price take-off method, a quantity survey involves a detailed estimate of the quantities

---

Square foot method: replacement cost estimate based on cost per square foot to build comparable structure

Unit-in-place method: replacement cost estimate based on cost of components in building

Quantity survey method: replacement cost estimate based on detailed cost of material, labor and indirect costs and prices of construction materials as well as the costs of installation (labor), which are added to the indirect costs (building permit, survey, builder's overhead and profit) for what is generally regarded as the most accurate replacement cost estimate. Because it is time-consuming and very complex, the method is generally used by experienced contractors and price estimators. Appraisers seldom use this method.

DEPRECIATION

Depreciation is the difference between the value of the existing improvements and the cost of replacing them. It represents a loss in value due to age, neglect, undesirable features within the property or negative influences from without.

Land value plus replacement cost of its buildings is usually the maximum a property can be worth, because no one will pay more for something than it would cost to replace it (principle of substitution). When appraising a used property, the value is determined by estimating the replacement cost, deducting the depreciation and adding the value of the land. In the absence of extraordinary circumstances, a used building is not worth as much as a new one. The difference is the depreciation.

Depreciation takes three forms: physical deterioration, functional obsolescence and economic obsolescence.

PHYSICAL DETERIORATION. Also called **deferred maintenance**, this form of value loss is evidenced by wear and tear, decay, cracks and structural defects. It is usually the most obvious form of depreciation. The extent of physical deterioration is measured by the cost to correct it. Accordingly, it is the simplest kind of depreciation to spot and estimate. Physical deterioration is curable or incurable (see below).

FUNCTIONAL OBSOLESCENCE. This is a loss in value due to functional inadequacies such as poor floor plan, unappealing design, outdated fixtures, or too many bedrooms in relation to the number of bathrooms.

Like physical deterioration, functional obsolescence is either curable or incurable. **Curable depreciation** is not so extensive that the cost of correcting it cannot be recovered in the sales price. **Incurable depreciation** is either impossible to correct or so expensive that it is not practical. It would make little sense, for example, to install an elevator in a three-story apartment house at a cost of $75,000 if, in the opinion of the appraiser, it would not add at least that amount to the value of the property. If it would not, the functional obsolescence caused by the absence of an elevator would be seen as incurable.

Depreciation: loss in value from any cause

Deferred maintenance: loss in value from physical deterioration

Functional obsolescence: loss in value from functional inadequacies on the property itself

A house with four bedrooms and just one bath loses value due to functional obsolescence.

Economic obsolescence: loss in value from causes occurring outside the property itself

ECONOMIC OBSOLESCENCE. This represents value losses from causes outside the property. It is a kind of depreciation resulting from the action of forces beyond a property owner's control. As a result, it is virtually always incurable. Zoning changes, neighborhood deterioration, adverse changes in traffic patterns (such as a new freeway rerouting traffic away from a motel) or exposure to nuisances (like the noise from airplanes as they land and take off near a home) are examples of factors that can create economic obsolescence.

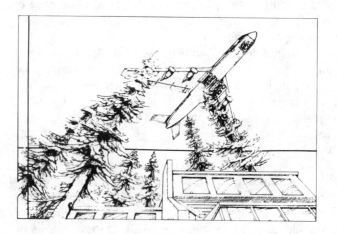

Properties near an airport may lose value to economic obsolescence, a negative external force in the form of low-flying aircraft.

Estimating depreciation accurately is the most difficult phase of the replacement cost valuation technique. In many cases, the depreciation estimates are highly subjective, and they are never any more reliable than the judgment and skill of the appraiser making them.

INCOME APPROACH TO VALUE

The income method of appraising is based on the idea that there is a relationship between an income property's earnings potential and its market value to an investor.

CONTRACT RENT VS. ECONOMIC RENT

When appraising by the income method, also called the **capitalization** or **investment approach** to value, the appraiser tries to find the property's net income. He or she does this by estimating the rent the property would bring if it were presently available for lease on the open market. What it would earn is called **economic** rent, to be distinguished from what it is earning, which is referred to as **contract rent**.

Capitalization: converting estimated future net income into an estimate of present value by use of capitalization rate

The income approach is based on the theory that an investment property's value is the price an informed investor will pay today for the net income produced over the balance of the property's economic life. So the appraiser, like the investor, is concerned with the property's earnings potential (economic rent), as opposed to its actual earnings (contract rent). Contract rent paid in the past is termed **historical rent**. Historical rent can be a reliable indication of the direction a property's earnings potential is headed. Steady rent increases or decreases in the past are strong statements on whether contract rent is above or below the economic rent.

Economic rent: rent which could be obtained if property were currently available for lease

Contract rent: rent being paid under current lease

From the economic rent, the appraiser will make certain deductions to arrive at a property's net income. It would be unrealistic, for example, to expect a rental property to be fully occupied throughout its productive life. Vacancies must be expected. Also, there will inevitably be tenants who do not pay their rent. So the appraiser must allow for occasional vacancies and unpaid rents. Called a **bad debt/vacancy factor**, the expense is expressed as a percentage of the potential gross income and is deducted from that figure to arrive at a more realistic gross income figure, called the **effective gross income**.

The appraiser, when evaluating the effective gross income, is concerned with its three most significant characteristics: **quantity, quality** and **durability**.

Effective gross income: potential gross income, less allowance for bad debts and vacancies

QUANTITY. What is presently being earned? What are the potential earnings?

QUALITY. A strong tenant, like a government agency or blue chip corporation, makes the property's income more reliable and enhances the value of the property.

DURABILITY. This refers to the expected duration of the property's income-producing ability. Durable income is visible in a long-term lease. The rental paid in connection with a lease is the contract rent. If it is well below the economic rent and the duration is long-term, the value of the property will suffer. If the contract rent is reasonably close to the economic rent and the lease agreement contains a provision for periodic rent hikes, such as cost-of-living increases, the durability of the contract rent is an asset.

OPERATING EXPENSES

From the effective gross income, the appraiser will deduct expenses connected with operating the building. They fall into three classifications: **fixed expenses, maintenance expenses** and **reserves for replacement**.

FIXED EXPENSES. These include real estate taxes and hazard insurance.

MAINTENANCE EXPENSES. Services for tenants, like utilities, supplies, cleaning, administration costs, building employee wages and repairs.

RESERVES FOR REPLACEMENT. These are regular allowances set aside to replace building and equipment items that are expected to wear out in a short period, such as roofs, heating equipment, air conditioners and kitchen ranges.

10-UNIT APARTMENT

Potential Annual Gross Income	$66,000
Less	
Bad Debt/Vacancy Factor (5%)	3,300
Effective Gross Income	62,700
Less	
Fixed Expenses	12,200
Maintenance Expenses	17,200
Reserves for Replacement	7,200
NET INCOME	$26,100

There are other expenses such as the owner's income taxes, depreciation reserves and mortgage principal and interest payments—called **debt service**—which are not deducted from the effective gross income to arrive at net earnings. These are not considered operating expenses from an appraisal standpoint.

When the fixed expenses, maintenance expenses and replacement reserves have been deducted, the result is net income. It is this figure which is capitalized to determine the property's value.

CAPITALIZATION

The process of converting income produced by an investment property into a meaningful value is called capitalization. The mathematical procedure is expressed as follows:

Annual Net Income ÷ Capitalization Rate = Value.

Example:

$$\frac{Net\ income:\ \$26,100}{Capitalization\ rate:\ 0.11} = \$237,273\ Value$$

The **capitalization rate** is the rate of return an investor receives or requires in connection with income-producing property.

Ordinarily, income-producing property is purchased for investment purposes. The investor seeks a certain rate of return on the capital invested in the property. When the desired return is selected, the equation shown above is used to determine how much an investor can pay for a property which is generating a known income and still realize the desired return.

Example:

1) property's annual net income = $10,000
2) investor's desired return = 12%
3) *$10,000 ÷ 12% = $83,333*

In the example, the investor can pay up to $83,333 for a property earning $10,000 net and realize the desired yield of 12%.

SELECTING A CAPITALIZATION RATE. In order to estimate an income-producing property's value to a typical investor, the appraiser must be familiar with the yield requirements of investors in the marketplace for similar properties.

There are a number of ways the appraiser can find a property's capitalization rate. For instance, he or she can analyze recent sales of comparable properties and assume their capitalization rates would be about the same as the one to be selected for the subject property. This is called the **direct comparison** method.

Regardless of the capitalization rate selection technique used, two very important considerations when settling on a rate are the quality and durability of the investment property's income. Quality and durability influence the risk factor. The greater the risk, the higher the capitalization rate and the lower the property's value. On the other hand, the smaller the risk, the lower the capitalization rate and the higher the value.

GROSS INCOME MULTIPLIERS

Whenever possible, the appraiser will apply all three approaches to value—market data, replacement cost and capitalization—then analyze the results and decide which of them should carry the most weight when preparing the final value estimate.

Some properties, such as single-family dwellings, are not generally thought of as income producing. In these instances, the capitalization method is not used. In its place, appraisers like to use the **gross income multiplier** method. Since income from residential property takes the form of rent, this method is also called the **gross rent multiplier** method.

Gross income multiplier: a number which, when multiplied times the gross rent, gives a rough estimate of value

Rental income represents a percentage of the price paid for a rental property. What that percentage is will vary from one real estate market to the next.

Example:

1) Sales price = $60,000
2) Monthly rent = $600
3) Monthly rent = one percent of sales price

Monthly rents may run about one percent of selling prices in one market and more or less in another. A market exists where specific rental properties compete with each other for tenants. How much tenants are willing to pay for rental housing in a given area depends on the many factors, previously discussed, that interact to form value. Certainly, supply and demand and employment and wage levels play important roles. In any event, rental prices for similar properties within the same market tend to be much alike for competitive reasons. The result is that if one rental property has a monthly income that is one percent of its sales price, comparable properties will have similar income-to-selling price ratios.

A monthly gross income multiplier is established by dividing the sales price by the monthly rental income. An annual gross income multiplier is achieved by dividing the sales price by the annual rental income.

Example:

    1) *$60,000 ÷ $600 = 100 monthly multiplier*
    2) *$60,000 ÷ $7,200 = 8.33 annual multiplier*

When appraising a residential rental property, armed with monthly or annual gross income multipliers for an area, an appraiser can get an indication of a property's value by multiplying its monthly or annual rent by the appropriate figure.

Example: For Annual Multiplier

    1) Annual multiplier for comparable rentals
       is 8.33
    2) Subject property rents for $8,000 a year
    3) *8.33 × $8,000 = $66,640* value

Example: For Monthly Multiplier

    1) Monthly multiplier = 100
    2) Subject property rents for $500 a month
    3) *100 × $500 = $50,000* value

To arrive at a reliable gross income multiplier, an appraiser should have no fewer than four comparable properties that are presently rented within the same market.

The gross income multiplier method can be used with other types of properties, but ordinarily it is not. It is applied almost exclusively to residential rental units. Its principal weakness is that it is based on gross income figures and does not take into account vacancies or operating expenses. If two three-bedroom homes have the same income, the gross multiplier method would indicate they are worth the same. But if one is old and has higher maintenance costs, its value is actually less. At best, gross rent multipliers provide the appraiser with a rough approximation of value.

CORRELATION AND FINAL ESTIMATE OF VALUE

Correlation: assembly and interpretation of factors affecting value to reach final estimate of value

Throughout the appraisal process, the appraiser is searching for facts on which he or she will base the ultimate conclusions. In many cases, the facts are self-evident and require nothing beyond simple verification. In other instances, they are unclear, barely discernible as facts, and require expert interpretation.

In appraisal terms, **correlation** refers to assembly and interpretation of numerous factors which operate independently, or merge, to influence values. Nowhere in the appraisal process does the appraiser's experience and judgment play a more critical role.

The final value estimate is not the average of the indications of value delivered by the three appraisal methods—cost, income and market data. Rather, it is the figure which represents the appraiser's expert opinion of value after all tangible and intangible criteria have been identified, analyzed, and measured for the impact they will have individually and collectively on a property's value.

Once the final estimate of value is determined, it is put into the form of an appraisal report. The two most common types are:

- **Narrative.** A thorough, detailed, written presentation of the facts and reasoning behind an appraiser's estimate of value.
- **Form.** Brief standard form used by agencies, such as the FHA, and by lending institutions, such as banks and savings and loans. This is the most common type of appraisal report.

CHAPTER SUMMARY

1. An appraisal is an estimate or opinion of value. The most common definition of value is "the present worth of future benefits." For appraisal purposes, value is generally measured in terms of money. To be valuable, an item must have utility, scarcity, demand and transferability.

2. Appraisers have developed several "principles of value" which guide them in the valuation process. These include the principle of highest and best use, the principle of change, the principle of supply and

UNIFORM RESIDENTIAL APPRAISAL REPORT

Property Description & Analysis   **UNIFORM RESIDENTIAL APPRAISAL REPORT**   File No. _____

SUBJECT

Property Address	Census Tract _____
City _____ County _____ State _____ Zip Code _____	
Legal Description	
Owner/Occupant _____ Map Reference _____	
Sale Price $ _____ Date of Sale _____	PROPERTY RIGHTS APPRAISED
Loan charges/concessions to be paid by seller $ _____	☐ Fee Simple
R.E. Taxes $ _____ Tax Year _____ HOA $/Mo _____	☐ Leasehold
Lender/Client _____	☐ Condominium (HUD/VA)
	☐ De Minimis PUD

LENDER DISCRETIONARY USE

Sale Price	$ _____
Date	_____
Mortgage Amount	$ _____
Mortgage Type	_____
Discount Points and Other Concessions	
Paid by Seller	$ _____
Source	_____

NEIGHBORHOOD

	Urban	Suburban	Rural
LOCATION	☐	☐	☐
BUILT UP	☐ Over 75%	☐ 25-75%	☐ Under 25%
GROWTH RATE	☐ Rapid	☐ Stable	☐ Slow
PROPERTY VALUES	☐ Increasing	☐ Stable	☐ Declining
DEMAND/SUPPLY	☐ Shortage	☐ In Balance	☐ Over Supply
MARKETING TIME	☐ Under 3 Mos.	☐ 3-6 Mos.	☐ Over 6 Mos

PRESENT LAND USE	%	LAND USE CHANGE	PREDOMINANT OCCUPANCY	SINGLE FAMILY HOUSING PRICE $ (000)	AGE (yrs)
Single Family		Not Likely	☐ Owner		
2-4 Family		Likely	☐ Tenant		
Multi-family		In process	☐ Vacant (0-5%)	Low	
Commercial		To _____	☐ Vacant (over 5%)	High	
Industrial				Predominant	
Vacant					

NEIGHBORHOOD ANALYSIS

	Good	Avg	Fair	Poor
Employment Stability	☐	☐	☐	☐
Convenience to Employment	☐	☐	☐	☐
Convenience to Shopping	☐	☐	☐	☐
Convenience to Schools	☐	☐	☐	☐
Adequacy of Public Transportation	☐	☐	☐	☐
Recreation Facilities	☐	☐	☐	☐
Adequacy of Utilities	☐	☐	☐	☐
Property Compatibility	☐	☐	☐	☐
Protection from Detrimental Cond.	☐	☐	☐	☐
Police & Fire Protection	☐	☐	☐	☐
General Appearance of Properties	☐	☐	☐	☐
Appeal to Market	☐	☐	☐	☐

Note: Race or the racial composition of the neighborhood are not considered reliable appraisal factors.
COMMENTS: _____

SITE

Dimensions _____	Topography _____	
Site Area _____	Size _____	
Zoning Classification _____ Corner Lot _____	Shape _____	
HIGHEST & BEST USE Present Use _____ Zoning Compliance _____	Drainage _____	
	Other Use _____	View _____

UTILITIES	Public	Other	SITE IMPROVEMENTS	Type	Public	Private
Electricity	☐		Street		☐	☐
Gas	☐		Curb/Gutter		☐	☐
Water	☐		Sidewalk		☐	☐
Sanitary Sewer	☐		Street Lights		☐	☐
Storm Sewer	☐		Alley		☐	☐

Landscaping	_____	
Driveway	_____	
Apparent Easements	_____	
FEMA Flood Hazard	Yes ☐	No ☐
FEMA Map/Zone	_____	

COMMENTS (Apparent adverse easements, encroachments, special assessments, slide areas, etc.) _____

IMPROVEMENTS

GENERAL DESCRIPTION	EXTERIOR DESCRIPTION	FOUNDATION	BASEMENT	INSULATION
Units _____	Foundation _____	Slab _____	Area Sq. Ft. _____	Roof ☐
Stories _____	Exterior Walls _____	Crawl Space _____	% Finished _____	Ceiling ☐
Type (Det./Att.) _____	Roof Surface _____	Basement _____	Ceiling _____	Walls ☐
Design (Style) _____	Gutters & Dwnspts. _____	Sump Pump _____	Walls _____	Floor ☐
Existing _____	Window Type _____	Dampness _____	Floor _____	None ☐
Proposed _____	Storm Sash _____	Settlement _____	Outside Entry _____	Adequacy _____
Under Construction _____	Screens _____	Infestation _____		Energy Efficient Items _____
Age (Yrs.) _____	Manufactured House _____			
Effective Age (Yrs.) _____				

ROOM LIST

ROOMS	Foyer	Living	Dining	Kitchen	Den	Family Rm	Rec. Rm	Bedrooms	# Baths	Laundry	Other	Area Sq. Ft
Basement												
Level 1												
Level 2												

Finished area above grade contains _____ Rooms _____ Bedroom(s) _____ Bath(s) _____ Square Feet of Gross Living Area

INTERIOR

SURFACES	Materials/Condition
Floors	_____
Walls	_____
Trim/Finish	_____
Bath Floor	_____
Bath Wainscot	_____
Doors	_____
Fireplace(s) # _____	

HEATING	
Type	_____
Fuel	_____
Condition	_____
Adequacy	_____
COOLING	
Central	_____
Other	_____
Condition	_____
Adequacy	_____

KITCHEN EQUIP	
Refrigerator	☐
Range/Oven	☐
Disposal	☐
Dishwasher	☐
Fan/Hood	☐
Compactor	☐
Washer/Dryer	☐
Microwave	☐
Intercom	☐

ATTIC	
None	☐
Stairs	☐
Drop Stair	☐
Scuttle	☐
Floor	☐
Heated	☐
Finished	☐

IMPROVEMENT ANALYSIS

	Good	Avg	Fair	Poor
Quality of Construction	☐	☐	☐	☐
Condition of Improvements	☐	☐	☐	☐
Room Sizes/Layout	☐	☐	☐	☐
Closets and Storage	☐	☐	☐	☐
Energy Efficiency	☐	☐	☐	☐
Plumbing-Adequacy & Condition	☐	☐	☐	☐
Electrical-Adequacy & Condition	☐	☐	☐	☐
Kitchen Cabinets-Adequacy & Cond.	☐	☐	☐	☐
Compatibility to Neighborhood	☐	☐	☐	☐
Appeal & Marketability	☐	☐	☐	☐
Estimated Remaining Economic Life	_____ Yrs
Estimated Remaining Physical Life	_____ Yrs

CAR STORAGE:			House Entry ☐
No. Cars _____	Garage ☐	Attached ☐ Adequate ☐	Outside Entry ☐
Condition _____	Carport ☐	Detached ☐ Inadequate ☐	Basement Entry ☐
	None ☐	Built-In ☐ Electric Door ☐	

COMMENTS

Additional features: _____

Depreciation (Physical, functional and external inadequacies, repairs needed, modernization, etc.) _____

General market conditions and prevalence and impact in subject/market area regarding loan discounts, interest buydowns and concessions _____

This is a typical form report, in this instance the Uniform Residential Appraisal
Report used by FNMA, FHLMC, FHA and VA.

demand, the principle of substitution, the principle of conformity, the principle of contribution and the principle of anticipation.

3. The appraisal process has several steps. The first step is to identify the problem. The appraiser then must determine what data is needed and where to find it (this includes general and specific data). Next the data must be gathered and verified. Valuation methods are then applied. The three methods are market data, cost, and income. The value indicators derived from using one or more of the three valuation methods are correlated into a final estimate which is written up in the appraisal report.

4. The market data method (the method most often used for appraising residential property) is based on comparing the values of similar properties. The cost method takes into account the cost of building a similar property. The income method uses the net income produced by a property to estimate its value.

CHAPTER 11—QUIZ
REAL ESTATE APPRAISAL

1. The real estate appraisal is an estimate of value:

    a) based on appraisal tables
    b) based on analysis of facts as of a specific date
    c) derived from data covering the preceding six months
    d) derived from tax assessments covering the past five years

2. The conditions of sale will affect the:

    a) price of the subject property
    b) cost of the subject property
    c) value of the subject property
    d) utility of the subject property

3. The sum of money at which a property is offered for sale is the:

    a) value
    b) book value
    c) price
    d) market value

4. The prime requisites of value are:

    a) demand, transferability, cost, scarcity
    b) demand, scarcity, utility, transferability
    c) demand, cost, transferability, age
    d) demand, cost, transferability, utility

5. The highest and best use to which a lot could be put is determined by:

    a) what use would presently produce the largest net income
    b) what use would produce the greatest net income in future years
    c) how tall a building the neighborhood would warrant
    d) what similar vacant lots are being leased for

6. The concept holding that it's the future, not the past, which is of prime importance in estimating value is called the:

    a) principle of substitution
    b) principle of change
    c) principle of supply and demand
    d) principle of competition

7. Plans have been announced for a multimillion dollar shopping center to be built next door to a vacant lot you own. Property values in the area of the proposed site will tend to increase as a result of this announcement. This is an example of the principle of:

    a) anticipation
    b) highest and best use
    c) supply and demand
    d) substitution

8. An appraiser wants to determine if it is economically feasible for the owner of an apartment building to put in a swimming pool for his tenants' use. The appraiser would be most concerned with the principal of:

    a) regression
    b) substitution
    c) conformity
    d) contribution

9. The value of single-family homes is least protected in a neighborhood where there is:

    a) a similarity of homeowners' income
    b) an increase in the mixture of average quality homes with good quality homes
    c) a minimum of violations of existing restrictions
    d) a predominance of individuals from one ethnic group or religious affiliation

10. In the event a person integrated a high quality home costing $350,000 into a neighborhood where other homes were valued at $145,000, he or she would suffer a loss in value by economic obsolescence due to:

a) regression
b) supply and demand
c) progression
d) aversion

11. There are three approaches to valuation and all three should be used. Depending on the type of property being appraised, however, one approach will have more weight and authority. The comparison approach is given greatest weight in the appraisal of:

a) investment property
b) service property
c) single-family dwellings
d) industrial property

12. One of the chief advantages of the market data approach in the appraisal of real property is that:

a) it is very reliable when there is an adequate number of comparables
b) it takes very little time
c) it can be used for any type of property
d) None of the above

13. In which of the following situations would the comparative method of appraisal be least reliable?

a) When all comparables are in the same price range
b) In a real estate market that is inactive
c) When the comparables are located in another neighborhood
d) When all the comparables were arm's length transactions

14. An appraiser who is using the comparison method to appraise a single-family residence would never use the selling price of which of the following?

a) A similar home that sold over six months age
b) A similar home that sold recently but is located in another neighborhood
c) A similar home that was sold by owners who were forced to sell at any price because of financial difficulties
d) A home of similar size but situated on a corner lot

15. When appraising property, which of the following would be least important when using the replacement cost approach?

a) Current construction cost per square foot
b) Rental cost per square foot
c) Depreciated expense
d) Estimated land value

16. It cost $45 per square foot to build a home of 2,500 square feet. The cost per square foot to build a home of the same quality that has 1,500 square feet should be:

a) less
b) more
c) the same
d) None of the above

17. The most expensive and time-consuming method of estimating the cost of construction is:

a) unit-in-place
b) quantity survey
c) comparison method
d) income approach

18. The replacement cost method of appraising real property:

a) tends to set the upper limits of value
b) would be the method used in appraising special purpose properties
c) is good as to new improvements
d) All of the above

19. The market value of an improved property may:

    a) exceed or be less than replacement cost of the improvements added to the market value of the land
    b) be greater than the cost of land and improvements but never less than their cost
    c) never be greater or less than the cost of the land and improvements
    d) equal but at no time exceed the value of the land and current reproduction costs of the improvements

20. An appraiser was hired to estimate the value of City Hall, a very beautiful and unique structure with Roman architecture. Which approach to value did she use?

    a) Capitalization
    b) Reproduction
    c) Comparison
    d) Any of the above

21. Which of these forms of depreciation is associated with deferred maintenance?

    a) Functional obsolescence
    b) Economic obsolescence
    c) Physical deterioration
    d) All of the above

22. Functional utility in a dwelling is dependent upon:

    a) the desires of its occupants
    b) the floor plan and equipment
    c) zoning in the area
    d) the condition of the heating system

1. b) An appraiser's estimate of value is considered to be valid only for that point in time for which the estimate was made.

2. a) The conditions of a sale, such as a forced sale, may affect the market price of the property (the amount paid) but would have no affect on its cost, value or utility.

3. c) According to the American Institute of Real Estate Appraisers, price is "the amount of money paid, asked or offered where a sale is contemplated." Market price, specifically, is the amount paid for the property.

4. b) The four essentials of value are scarcity, transferability, utility, and demand.

5. a) The highest and best use is the use which at the time of the appraisal would produce the greatest net return.

6. b) This is the definition of the principle of change.

7. a) This would be an example of the principle of anticipation, which holds that value is created by the expectation of benefits to be derived in the future.

8. d) Will the proposed improvement — the swimming pool — contribute enough value in the form of higher rents from tenants, and, ultimately, net income to the owner, to justify the expense of installing it?

9. b) A mixture of average and good quality homes in the same neighborhood would violate the principle of conformity.

10. a) A loss in value is caused by association with many lesser valued houses in close proximity.

11. c) The comparison approach would be the most reliable method regardless of the type of property being appraised, because recent sales prices of similar properties reflect the attitudes of buyers and sellers on the open market — an invaluable guide for any appraiser. However, when appraising something other than a residence, the appraiser very often is not able to find enough sales of similar properties to serve as reliable value indicators and he or she must then apply other techniques.

12. a) When there are enough recent sales of similar properties, the value indicated by the market data approach is quite reliable. The expense in time to gather the data may prove to be quite high, however.

13. b) There is no available data in an inactive market. If, however, the appraiser has had some recent sales and can determine the rate of appreciation, he or she can update sales that occurred six months ago or more.

14. c) The price of a forced sale is never used in making comparisons of selling prices for appraisal purposes. The selling price of a home that was sold one year ago can be adjusted to reflect any inflationary trend, and selling prices of homes in other neighborhoods can also be used by allowing for differences in the neighborhoods.

15. b) The cost method involves estimating the current cost of construction, less the amount of accrued depreciation, then adding back in the value of the land.

16. b) The larger the home, the less it should cost per square foot. There are certain fixed costs, such as kitchens and bathrooms, which must be included in every home, regardless of size. Furthermore, the cost of grading the lot and installing plumbing and sewage systems exists no matter how small the home.

17. b) The quantity survey is the most time-consuming of the methods employed in the cost approach to estimate replacement cost.

18. d) The cost approach method is frequently used to set a ceiling upon the value established by the other two methods. It is particularly appropriate for appraising newly built improvements where the construction represents the highest and best use of the land. It is also the most appropriate method for appraising special purpose properties such as public schools, city halls, libraries, etc.

19. a) While the replacement cost normally sets the upper limit of value, in time of unusual demand, market value may exceed replacement cost. Examples of such occasions would be the World War II years (when there was a moratorium on building) and, more recently, the Alaskan oil boom (when demand far outstripped the ability of builders to create the supply).

20. b) Reproduction is the only approach available. There is no income for capitalization and there are no comparable sales.

21. c) Physical deterioration is the type of depreciation that results from wear and tear, deferred maintenance, etc.

22. b) Good planning and design result in functional utility.

Chapter 12

ESCROW AND TITLE INSURANCE

OUTLINE

I. Real Estate Escrows and Closing
  A. Definition of escrow
  B. Escrowees
  C. Opening and closing an escrow
  D. Double-entry bookkeeping
  E. Typical closing costs
  F. Prorations
  G. RESPA
II. Title Insurance
  A. Abstract of title
  B. Title insurance
    1. obtaining title insurance
    2. limits on coverage

KEY TERMS

escrow
escrow instructions
settlement statement
credits
RESPA
abstract of title
extended coverage policy

escrowee
double-entry bookkeeping
debits
prorations
title insurance
standard coverage policy

CHAPTER OVERVIEW

The real estate agent's job does not end when the parties sign the purchase and sale agreement. Many matters must be taken care of before the sale can be finalized and a commission paid to the agent. The service provided by the agent during the closing process is every bit as important as the agent's marketing efforts prior to the sale. Careful shepherding of the parties through closing will prevent unnecessary delays and gain the agent a reputation for professionalism. An agent must be familiar with escrow, title insurance, and the requirements for closing and closing costs.

REAL ESTATE ESCROW AND CLOSING STATEMENTS

DEFINITION OF ESCROW

The state of California defines escrow as "any transaction wherein one person, for the purpose of effecting the sale, transfer, encumbering, or leasing of real property to another person, delivers any written instrument, money, evidence of title to real or personal property, or other thing of value to a third person to be held by such third person until the happening of a specified event or the performance of a prescribed condition, when it is then delivered by such third person to a grantee, grantor, promisee, promisor, obligee, obligor, bailee, bailor, or any agent or employee of any of the latter."

Escrow: when a neutral third party holds funds/documents for the parties to the transaction, to be disbursed on the happening of specified events

There are two essential requirements for the creation of a valid escrow:

- There must be a legally binding and enforceable contract between the parties (e.g., a purchase and sale agreement, escrow instructions signed by the buyer and seller, or a combination of the two).
- There must also be a "conditional delivery with relinquishment of control" — the parties must deposit funds or documents with the third party along with instructions to disburse the funds or deliver the documents only upon the happening of a specified event. If the parties retain any control over the deposited items, there is no valid escrow.

ESCROWEES

An escrowee is the neutral third party who holds the items deposited by the parties and disburses them after the conditions of the escrow are satisfied. The escrowee also performs additional services such as preparing documents, calculating settlement costs and recording.

Escrowee: the neutral third party who holds the documents/funds for the parties to the transaction for later disbursal

Title companies are the most common escrowees in northern California. In the southern part of the state, independent escrow companies also close a large number of transactions. Many institutional lenders (banks, savings & loan associations and insurance companies) have their own escrow departments which are used as closing agents for transactions they finance. Under certain circumstances, attorneys and real estate brokers may also act as escrowees.

Escrow companies are required to be licensed by the state Department of Corporations under the Escrow Law; only corporations may be licensed as escrow companies, individuals are not eligible. Exempted from this licensing requirement are banks, S&Ls, insurance companies, attorneys and real estate brokers, all of whom are regulated by other agencies.

EXEMPT FROM ESCROW LICENSING LAW

BANKS
SAVINGS AND LOANS
INSURANCE COMPANIES
ATTORNEYS
REAL ESTATE BROKERS

Real estate brokers are exempt from the Escrow Law "while performing acts in the course of or incidental to a real estate transaction in which the broker is an agent or a party to the transaction and in which the broker is performing an act for which a real estate license is required." This exemption allows brokers to provide certain services to their clients without becoming subject to regulation by another agency. It does not permit brokers to operate as escrow agents when they have no bona fide interest other than that of providing escrow services.

Brokers who want to perform escrow services should be aware that the Corporations Commissioner and the Attorney General take a dim view of arrangements that attempt to circumvent the intent of the Escrow Law. (Independent escrow companies are subject to much more stringent regulations than are brokers under the Real Estate Law.) Schemes such as "broker-escrow cooperatives" — where brokers operate a joint branch location that performs escrow services, and accept a nominal commission split in exchange for performance of escrow services — may subject the errant broker to civil and criminal penalties, as well as loss of license. The simple fact that a referral fee is paid to a real estate broker in exchange for referral of escrow business is evidence that the one receiving the referral is subject to the license requirements of the Escrow Law.

It should also be noted in this context that acceptance of "kickbacks" or similar compensation for referring customers to an escrow business is grounds for suspension or revocation of a real estate license under the Real Estate Law.

OPENING AND CLOSING AN ESCROW

Escrow instructions: instructions signed by the buyer and seller telling the escrow agent how to proceed with the closing

The first step in the escrow procedure is to open the escrow. This is done by giving the escrowee the information needed to prepare preliminary escrow instructions. Once the instructions are signed and returned to the escrowee, he or she orders a preliminary title report showing the condition of title to the property. This information is forwarded to the buyer's lender, along with a copy of the escrow instructions. Note that the escrow instructions must correspond to the terms of the loan the lender is willing to make. Any discrepancy in the loan amount or terms (such as interest rate, repayment period or discount points) will require amended escrow instructions. The lender will not disburse any loan funds into the escrow (or even approve the loan) until the instructions correspond to the terms of the loan.

Early in the escrow process, the escrowee also contacts the seller's lender to obtain a payoff figure for the seller's loan. This is done by sending a 'demand for payoff' or 'request for beneficiary's statement' to the lender, who then returns copies of the completed form to the escrowee and the title company. Structural pest inspections are also ordered as soon as possible to avoid delays in closing which may be caused by the need for repairs to the property.

When the buyer's loan is approved, the lender forwards the loan documents (note, deed of trust and Truth-in-Lending statement) to the escrowee. At this point, the buyer completes his or her part of the transaction by depositing the necessary funds into escrow and signing the loan documents, which are then forwarded to the lender.

The seller is ready to close when the escrowee receives the payoff figures from the seller's lender and the pest control inspection detailing any needed repairs. This information allows a reasonably accurate determination of the seller's proceeds from the sale. The pest control inspection, along with notices of completion of any required repairs, are forwarded to the buyer's lender if necessary.

Hazard insurance is another item common to most escrows. The new hazard insurance policy for the buyer, or an assignment of the seller's existing policy, is forwarded to the new lender prior to disbursal of the loan funds. Before escrow can close, any other contingencies of the sale, such as sale of the buyer's existing home, must be satisfied or waived.

Once all contingencies are satisfied, the lender disburses the loan funds to the title company. The escrowee also sends the seller's grant deed to the title company for recording. The title company records the deed, deed of trust, reconveyance deed and other documents, and then provides the escrowee with the information (final payoff of the seller's loan, title and recording fees, etc.) necessary to prepare the final closing statements. The escrowee prepares the statements and makes the necessary disbursements of funds to the seller, broker and other entities. The title insurance policy is issued and the buyer receives copies of the completed loan documents, insurance policies and inspection reports.

DOUBLE-ENTRY BOOKKEEPING

The accounting technique applied to most settlements is a simple form of double-entry bookkeeping. The escrow holder can prepare separate statements for the buyer and seller, or can combine them, showing the allocation of debits and credits for both parties side by side. License examinations use the latter format, and so will we.

Double-entry bookkeeping: an accounting technique that applies credits and debits to the appropriate party

Settlement statement: written interpretation of the financial elements of the contract

SETTLEMENT STATEMENT

	BUYER'S STATEMENT		SELLER'S STATEMENT	
	Debit	Credit	Debit	Credit
Sales Price	52,000.00			52,000.00
Deposit		1,500.00		
Commission — 7%			3,640.00	
Mortgage Balance			35,822.24	
Prepaid Interest	261.00		156.70	
New Loan		45,000.00		
Taxes — Prorated		327.10	327.10	
Loan Origination Fee · 1%	450.00			
Fire Insurance	192.00			
Title Insurance — standard			238.10	
Title Insurance — extended	135.00			
Tax Reserve — 2 months	183.00			
Appraisal Fee	75.00			
Credit Report	50.00			
Survey Fee	255.00			
Discount Points			2,850.00	
Documentary Stamps			57.20	
Balance Due From Buyer		6,773.90		
Balance Due To Seller			8,908.66	
TOTALS	$53,601.00	$53,601.00	$52,000.00	$52,000.00

Settlement statements are written interpretations of the financial elements of the contract.

Preparing a settlement statement involves little more than determining what charges and credits apply to a given transaction and seeing that they are allocated to the right parties. When allocating expenses, the escrow holder is guided largely by the terms stated in the purchase and sale agreement or the escrow instructions, if any. The proper distribution of expenses can also be influenced by local custom, provided the custom does not conflict with the terms of the purchase and sale agreement.

> **Example:** A buyer usually pays the cost of appraisal, and that cost is ordinarily charged to him or her at the time of settlement. However, if the seller contractually agreed to pay the appraisal fee, local custom would be disregarded and the expense would show as a debit to the seller.

Of course, both local custom and agreements between the parties must not run contrary to local, state or federal law.

The real estate agent should know what settlement costs are applicable to every kind of real estate transaction and be in a position to inform buyers and sellers accordingly. The principals to a transaction are entitled to know the full extent of their costs before signing a contract, rather than having to discover them at the time of the settlement.

TYPICAL CLOSING COSTS

The following is a real estate transaction settlement guide. It explains how the various charges and credits are usually allocated.

Debits: a charge against a party

Credits: an item paid to a party

1. On the settlement statement, **debits** are expenses owed and **credits** are items receivable.
2. Both principal parties have debit and credit columns on their settlement statements. The sum of the buyer's credits must equal the sum of the debits. This is also true with the seller's statement.
3. Where an item is payable by one party to the other, it will show as a debit to the former and a credit to the latter.
4. An item payable by one of the parties, but not to the other, shows as a debit to the former and does not show on the other's statement at all. For instance, if the buyer orders an extended policy of title insurance, the cost would be debited to the buyer but would not affect the seller.
5. Certain items will show as a credit to one, but not a debit to the other. For example, if the terms of the sale call for a pay-off of the seller's existing loan, property tax and insurance reserves held

by the seller's lender will be refunded and will show as a credit to the seller, but not a debit to the buyer.

6. The sequence in which the financial items are listed in the settlement statements is a matter of choice, though the purchase price is almost always the first figure entered and the last figures noted reveal the balance due from the buyer and the balance due to the seller.

Items most frequently appearing in settlement statements are listed below.

PURCHASE PRICE. Paid by the buyer to the seller, it is listed as a debit to the buyer and a credit to the seller.

DEPOSIT. Called an **earnest money** or **good faith deposit**, it is the money the buyer put up as a show of good faith, usually at the time the purchase and sale agreement was signed. It is a credit to the buyer at settlement, as it has already been paid. Since the entire purchase price has already been debited to the buyer and credited to the seller, no entry regarding this item is made on the seller's statement.

SALES COMMISSION. Normally a seller's expense, the real estate broker's commission is entered as a debit to the seller.

NEW FIRST MORTGAGE (DEED OF TRUST). If the buyer secures a new loan to finance part or all of the sale, the loan amount is listed as a credit to the purchaser. Like the deposit, it is part of the purchase price already credited to the seller. No entry is made on the seller's statement.

ASSUMED MORTGAGE (DEED OF TRUST). The mortgage amount assumed by the buyer is part of the money used to finance the transaction and, like a new loan, is credited to the buyer. The loan balance is then subtracted from the purchase price, along with all other items charged (debited) to the seller, to establish how much the seller will net at closing. The assumed loan balance is a debit to the seller.

PURCHASE MONEY MORTGAGE (DEED OF TRUST). If the seller carries a portion of the purchase price and secures the debt with a mortgage or deed of trust, it is called a **purchase money mortgage** or **deed of trust**. Like a new or assumed loan, it shows up in the buyer's credit column. At the same time, it reduces the amount of cash the seller will receive at closing and is listed as a debit to the seller.

PAY-OFF EXISTING MORTGAGE (DEED OF TRUST). If the seller pays off the existing loan, his or her net is reduced by that amount. It is a debit to the seller. No entry is made on the buyer's statement.

REAL ESTATE CONTRACT (LAND CONTRACT). If the seller sells the property under a land contract, it is credit extended by the seller which reduces his or her net at closing. Debit the seller and credit the buyer.

STANDARD TITLE INSURANCE POLICY. In northern California, the buyer usually pays; in southern California, the seller usually pays.

EXTENDED TITLE INSURANCE POLICY. Sometimes called the **lender's policy** or the **mortgagee's policy**, it is the extended coverage policy the purchaser agrees to provide the lender as consideration for obtaining the loan. Debit the buyer.

APPRAISAL FEE. A debit to whoever requests the appraisal. This is usually the buyer.

CREDIT REPORT. The lending institution charges the buyer for the cost of the credit investigation. Debit the buyer.

SURVEY. Usually a charge to the buyer. Sometimes lenders will require a survey as a condition of making the loan. Unless otherwise instructed, debit the buyer.

ESCROW FEE. Also called a settlement fee or closing fee, it is the escrow holder's charge for services rendered. The expense can be paid exclusively by one of the parties or shared by agreement.

LOAN FEE. Alternatively called a **loan fee, loan origination fee** or **loan service fee**, it is a lender's one-time charge to the borrower for setting up the loan. The FHA and VA limit the loan fee to one percent of the loan amount, while conventional lenders usually charge more—one and one-half to three percent or more. Debit the buyer.

LOAN ASSUMPTION FEE. A fee charged the buyer when assuming an existing loan. Debit the buyer.

FIRE INSURANCE POLICY (NEW). The buyer will ordinarily pay for insurance coverage one to three years in advance. Debit the buyer.

LOAN DISCOUNT (POINTS). The VA prohibits borrowers from paying any portion of a loan discount in connection with their guaranteed loans. Debit the seller. If a conventional or FHA lender discounts a loan, responsibility for the expense can be negotiated.

REVENUE STAMPS. Also referred to as **documentary tax stamps**, they must be affixed to any deed, instrument or writing that grants, conveys or assigns title to real estate. Debit the seller.

TITLE SEARCH. Also called a title examination, it is an expense normally charged to the buyer for the opinion of a title company or attorney as to the condition of a property's title. Debit the buyer.

PREPAYMENT PENALTY. Not allowed in connection with FHA and VA loans, this is a charge to the seller for paying off the loan sooner than agreed. Conventional loans do assess prepayment penalties and sometimes they are quite substantial. Confirm the amounts with the lenders. Debit the seller.

IMPOUND ACCOUNT (ESCROW ACCOUNT). If the seller has money deposited with the existing lender to pay property taxes and insurance premiums as they fall due, when the loan is paid off, the unused portion of the impound account is returned to the seller. Credit the seller. If the buyer is assuming the loan and the reserve account, credit the seller and debit the buyer.

RECORDING FEES. Certain documents such as deeds, real estate contracts, leases, options, mortgages, deeds of trust, satisfaction pieces, and reconveyance and fulfillment deeds will be recorded as a means of serving notice to the world that a buyer or seller has acquired a right or interest or satisfied a debt in connection with a piece of property. Fees are charged for recording the documents. As a rule, they are quite minimal and are charged to the party who benefits by the recordation. Buyers, for example, pay to have their deeds recorded. Sellers pay the cost of recording lien releases, like the satisfaction piece or deed of reconveyance. Debit the appropriate party.

ATTORNEY'S FEES. Debit the party who incurs legal fees related to the transaction.

SALE OF CHATTELS. If the seller is including some personal property items in the sale, credit the seller and debit the buyer for the agreed amount. A **bill of sale** must be signed by the seller and delivered to the buyer at settlement.

PRORATIONS

To prorate is to divide and allocate an expense equally or proportionately according to time or use.

Certain real estate expenses recur, such as hazard insurance, property taxes and interest payments on a mortgage. At settlement, it must be determined whether or not the property owner is current, in arrears or ahead with these payments. If in arrears, the amount must be confirmed and entered as a debit on the closing statement. If in advance, the seller is entitled to a credit. When figuring prorations, a 360-day year and 30-day months are sometimes used to simplify the calculations. However, now that calculators are available in almost every office, there is a trend toward using a 365-day year and the actual number of days in each month.

> Prorations: dividing and allocating expenses proportionately according to time or use

INSURANCE. Insurance is usually paid well in advance. At closing, the seller is entitled to a credit for the unused portion of the policy. If the buyer is going to assume the policy, debit the buyer, credit the seller.

INTEREST ON A MORTGAGE (DEED OF TRUST). Interest is almost always paid in arrears. If a principal and interest payment is made for March, the principal portion of the payment is applied to March, but the interest part of the payment covers February. Should the property be sold on March 15 (settlement date), the seller would owe interest to March 15. Debit the seller. If the buyer assumes the loan, the first payment will be April 1, which would pay interest for March. Debit the seller to March 15; credit the buyer the same amount.

PROPERTY TAXES. If the seller has paid the property taxes for the year, he or she is entitled to a prorated refund based on the closing date. The seller is responsible for taxes to the date of closing, the buyer is responsible for the date of closing and thereafter.

> **Example:** If the annual taxes are $1,080 ($3.00 per diem) and the deal closes on January 2, the seller is responsible for taxes through January 1, or 181 days ($3.00 $\times$ 181 = $543); and the buyer is liable for the balance of the year's taxes (179 days $\times$ $3.00 = $537).

PREPAID INTEREST. When a new loan is obtained, the lender usually sets the first payment due date ahead to the first of not the following month, but the month thereafter. The purpose of this practice is to allow the buyer time to recover financially from the strain of the sale. The buyer can then make the next mortgage installment payment without undue hardship. A loan made on June 20 will ordinarily have a first payment date of August 1. As explained earlier, the August payment will cover interest for the month of July. However, the loan was made on June 20 and the lender must collect interest for the interim period— from June 20 to the first of July. In this instance, the lender simply debits the buyer eleven days interest (June 20 through June 30) at settlement. It is called **prepaid** or **interim interest**.

RENT. If the property generates rental income that has been paid for some period beyond the settlement date, the seller is debited and the buyer is credited by that amount. If the rent is paid in arrears, credit the seller the amount due, and debit the buyer an equal amount.

BALANCES DUE. Subtract the buyer credits from the buyer debits for the "balance due" amount. Enter this amount as a credit. The seller's balance is the amount owed the seller after all debits have been subtracted from the sum of all credits. Enter as a debit if credits exceed debits. Enter as a credit if debits exceed credits.

RESPA

RESPA: Real Estate Settlement Procedures Act; requires a Uniform Settlement Statement to be drawn up prior to closing and allows parties to inspect it before closing

The Real Estate Settlement Procedures Act, commonly known as RESPA, applies to most sales of one- to four-unit residential property (including condominiums, coops and mobile homes) involving

	BUYER'S STATEMENT		SELLER'S STATEMENT	
	DEBIT	CREDIT	DEBIT	CREDIT
Purchase Price	X			X
Deposit		X		
Documentary Transfer Tax			X	
Sales Commission			X	
Pay-Off Existing Loan			X	
Assume Existing Loan		X	X	
New Loan		X		
Purchase Money Loan		X	X	
Title Search	X			
Standard Title Insurance	VARIES ACCORDING TO LOCAL CUSTOM			
Extended Title Insurance	X			
Loan Discount (Points)	BY AGREEMENT, EXCEPT VA (DEBIT SELLER)			
Loan Fee	X			
Property Taxes				
Arrears		X	X	
Current/Not Due		X	X	
Prepaid	X			X
Insurance				
Assume Policy	X			X
New Policy	X			
Interest				
Pay-off Existing Loan			X	
Assume Existing Loan		X	X	
New Loan	X			
Impound Accounts				
Pay-off Existing Loan				X
Assumption	X			X
New Loan	X			
Credit Report	X			
Survey, Inspection	BY AGREEMENT			
Appraisal	X			
Escrow Fee	BY AGREEMENT			
Sale of Chattels	X			X
Misc. Recording Fees	X		X	
Balance Due From Buyer		X		
Balance Due Seller			X	
TOTALS	X	X	X	X

An Equal Housing
Lender

MEMBER F.D.I.C.

GOOD FAITH ESTIMATE OF SETTLEMENT CHARGES
AND
ITEMIZATION OF AMOUNT FINANCED

Listed below is the Good Faith Estimate of Settlement Charges made pursuant to the requirements of the Real Estate Settlement Procedures Act (RESPA). Loan types: ☐ CONV ☐ Fixed Rate ☐ ARM ☐ GEM ☐ FHA ☐ VA ☐ Assumption ☐ Substitution of Liability.

This Good Faith Estimate is provided, based upon your application for a loan of $ _____ for _____ years, with a requested interest rate of _____ %. (_____ % of Loan to Value). This Loan has a _____ year call option.

Branch _____ Number _____   Purchaser _____

Prepared by _____ Date _____

Application # _____   Prop. Address _____

_____

Mailing Address _____

ESTIMATED SETTLEMENT CHARGES*

Estimate Closing Date _____

		Loan Amount	$ _____
Amount Paid to You Directly	$ _____	Prepaid Finance Charges	
Amount Paid to Your Account	$ _____	Loan Fee	$ _____
Amount Paid to Others on Your Behalf		Loan Discount (Paid by Borrower)	$ _____
Credit Reporting Agency	$ _____	Buy Down Fee (Paid by Borrower)	$ _____
Appraisal	$ _____	Tax registration	$ _____
Title Company _____	$ _____	Private Mtge. Insur. Prem.	$ _____
Reconveyance _____	$ _____	Insurance Reserve PMI/FHA	$ _____
Public Officials	$ _____	Interim Interest $ _____ per Day $ _____++	
Settlement Fee to Lender	$ _____	Review Fee	$ _____
Inspection Fee _____	$ _____		
Attorney Review Fee _____	$ _____	Total Prepaid Finance Charges	$ _____ (2)
Real Estate Taxes _____	$ _____		
Real Estate Tax Reserve to Lender	$ _____	Total Amount Financed	$ _____
Hazard Insurance Reserve to Lender	$ _____	(Loan Amount - Prepaid Finance Charges)	
_____	$ _____		

This is a notice to you as required by the Right to Financial Privacy Act of 1978 that the Veterans Administration Loan Guaranty Service or Division/Federal Housing Administration has right of access to financial records held by a financial institution in connection with the consideration or administration of assistance to you. Financial records involving your transaction will be available to the Veterans Administration Loan Guaranty Service or Division/Federal Housing Administration without further notice or authorization but will not be disclosed or released to another Government agency or department without your consent except as required or permitted by law.

Total Amount Paid to Others $ _____ (1)

*"THIS FORM DOES NOT COVER ALL ITEMS YOU WILL BE REQUIRED TO PAY IN CASH AT SETTLEMENT. FOR EXAMPLE, DEPOSIT IN ESCROW FOR REAL ESTATE TAXES AND INSURANCE. YOU MAY WISH TO INQUIRE AS TO THE AMOUNTS OF SUCH OTHER ITEMS. YOU MAY BE REQUIRED TO PAY OTHER ADDITIONAL AMOUNTS AT SETTLEMENT," (FOR FURTHER EXPLANATION OF THESE CHARGES CONSULT YOUR BOOKLET ON SETTLE-MENT COSTS.)

++This interest calculation represents the greatest amount of interest you could be required to pay at settlement. The actual amount will be determined by the day of the month on which your settlement is concluded.

Principal & Interest .... $ _____ **	Purchase Price	$ _____	Total to Close	$ _____
Mtg. Ins. Prem. .... $ _____	Less Loan Amount	$ _____	Less Monies Paid	$ _____
1/12 Annual R/E Taxes ..... $ _____	Down Payment	$ _____	Est. Funds	
1/12 Hazard Ins. .... $ _____	Plus:	$ _____	to CLOSE	$ _____
Homeowner's Dues .... $ _____	C/C Etc. (1&2 Above)	$ _____	Source of Funds to CLOSE:	
Other .... $ _____				
EST. MONTHLY PMT. ...... $ _____			_____

**Principal and Interest Amounts for GPM's, GEM's and Buydown (years)

Annual percentage increase in payment _____%.

1st	$ _____	2nd $ _____	3rd $ _____
4th	$ _____	5th $ _____	6th $ _____
7th	$ _____	8th $ _____	9th $ _____
10th	$ _____	11th $ _____	12th $ _____

☐ Adjustable Rate Mortgage: Payment Rate _____% Index _____ Chg. Rate: Pmt. _____ mos. Int. _____ mos.

The undersigned hereby acknowledges receipt of a photocopy of this page and a HUD Guide to Settlement Costs booklet.

_____   _____
(Borrower)   (Co-Borrower)

RL-040 8-89

institutional financing where the purchase loan is secured by a first mortgage on the property. The Act does not apply to loans used to finance the purchase of 25 acres or more, loans for the purchase of vacant land, or transactions where the buyer assumes or takes subject to an existing first lien loan.

In transactions subject to RESPA, the lender must give the borrower a good faith estimate of the closing costs at the time of the loan application (see form). The lender is also required to give the borrower a booklet published by the Department of Housing and Urban Development which describes closing costs, settlement procedures and the borrower's rights.

The entity handling the closing must prepare the settlement statement on a HUD form called a Uniform Settlement Statement, and the buyer must be allowed to inspect the statement on the day before closing if requested. (There is an exception to the inspection requirement when the buyer or his or her agent does not attend the settlement or when the escrowee does not require a meeting of the parties. Thus the inspection provision does not apply to most escrows in California. In these circumstances, the escrowee is required to mail the statement to the borrower as soon as possible after closing.)

RESPA also prohibits kickbacks and unearned fees in connection with covered transactions, and provides for criminal penalties and triple damages in the event of a violation. This provision does not apply to referral fees paid between real estate brokers, but will apply to any other fees received by a broker other than the commission; such fees must be earned.

TITLE INSURANCE

Given the complexity of real property law and the high cost of real estate, it is reasonable to expect that a landowner will want to take all necessary steps to ensure that his or her interests are protected. One means of accomplishing this is to obtain warranties of title from the grantor of the interest, but warranties are of little value if the grantor is financially unable to back them up.

ABSTRACT OF TITLE

The owner could also obtain a complete history of all the recorded interests in the property (called a chain of title) or a condensed history of those interests (called an abstract of title), and then have the history examined by an attorney who could render an opinion of the condition

Abstract of title: a condensed history of all the recorded interests in the property of the title. But the owner will still have no protection against latent or undiscovered defects in the title. Thus as a practical matter most landowners will protect their interests by procuring a policy of title insurance.

TITLE INSURANCE

Title insurance: a contract under which the insurer agrees to reimburse the policy holder for losses from covered defects in the property title

Title insurance is a contract whereby the title insurance company agrees to indemnify the policy holder against any losses caused by defects in the title, except for defects specifically excluded from the policy. That means the company will reimburse the policy holder for the losses. The title company will also handle the legal defense of any claims based on defects which are covered by the policy. Title insurance may be purchased by either the seller or the buyer of real property; the responsibility for procurement of the policy is usually defined in the contract of sale.

OBTAINING TITLE INSURANCE. The procedure for obtaining title insurance involves two steps. First the owner (or buyer) pays a fee to the title company to cover the cost of a title search. Most title companies have their own sets of records (called title plants) so they do not have to bother with searching the files in the recorder's office.

After the title search is completed, the title company issues a report (preliminary title report) on the condition of the title. The report lists all defects and encumbrances of record; these items will be excluded from the policy coverage. If the owner is satisfied with the report, he or she will purchase a policy of insurance by paying the required premium; one payment covers the entire life of the policy.

LIMITS ON COVERAGE. Title insurance policies may be limited in effect by a number of factors. As mentioned above, all defects and encumbrances of record are listed in the policy and excluded from coverage. In addition, the liability of the title company cannot exceed the face value of the policy.

Standard coverage policy: protects against latent defects in the chain of title

The extent of protection also varies according to the nature of the policy. Under a **standard coverage policy**, the policy holder is protected against latent defects in the chain of title, such as forged deeds, incompetent grantors, and improperly delivered deeds. The standard policy in California is known as the **CLTA** policy and was established and standardized by the California Land Title Association, the trade organization for title companies in this state. This policy covers risks which are a matter of public record, forgery, impersonation and incapacity of any person who was a party to a transaction involving title to the property, the possibility that a deed of record was not delivered with intent to convey title, any loss which might arise from a federal estate tax lien which is valid without notice on death, and any expenses incurred in defending title.

The **extended coverage policy** provides standard coverage plus protection against risks which can be discovered through actual survey; examples of such risks are encroachments and adverse possessors. The landowner may obtain coverage of specific items which are not included in the regular policies by purchasing an endorsement to cover the particular item. Title insurance will not protect a landowner from losses due to governmental action such as condemnation or changes in zoning.

Extended coverage policy: protects against latent defects in the chain of title as well as defects which can be discovered by visual inspection and a survey of the property

TITLE INSURANCE COVERAGE

STANDARD COVERAGE	EXTENDED COVERAGE
Latent defect in title	Latent defect in title
• forged deeds	• forged deeds
• incompetent grantors	• incompetent grantors
Undiscovered encumbrances of record	Undiscovered encumbrances of record
Marketability of title	Marketability of title
Right of street access	Right of street access
	Defects apparent from inspection:
	• adverse possessors
	• encroachments
	Unrecorded encumbrances
	Unrecorded tax liens

The coverage of a title policy is also limited to damage caused by defects in the particular interest covered. Thus an owner's policy covers only defects in title, a mortgagee's policy only insures the lienholder's priority and a leaseholder's policy only insures the validity of a lease.

ALTA

Title insurance policies have been standardized to some extent through the efforts of the American Land Title Association (ALTA). ALTA is a nationwide organization of title companies which promulgates a series of uniform title policies and also promotes professional standards and ethics within the industry. The most commonly used ALTA policies are the ALTA Owner's policy which provides standard coverage for owners, and the ALTA Loan policy, which provides extended coverage for lenders.

ALTA: the American Land Title Association, an organization dedicated to standardizing title insurance policies

CHAPTER SUMMARY

1. There are two requirements for a valid escrow: 1) a legally binding contract between the parties, and 2) a conditional delivery of the transaction documents and funds with relinquishment of control.

2. The escrowee is the neutral third party who holds the items deposited by the parties and distributes them after the conditions of escrow have been met. Escrow agents must be licensed under the Escrow Law and are supervised by the state Department of Corporations. Real estate brokers are exempted from the licensing requirement.

3. An escrow is opened by giving the escrow agent enough information to prepare preliminary escrow instructions. These instructions are signed by the parties and the escrow agent then begins gathering and preparing the necessary documents for closing. The escrow agent will need proof from the parties that all the necessary conditions to the sale have been fulfilled or waived. Once all the conditions have been met or waived, the lender disburses the loan funds to the escrow agent, who prepares a settlement statement and records the deed. The funds and transaction documents are then distributed to the parties.

4. Certain expenses will be charged to the buyer and seller and certain credits will be allowed the buyer and seller. A real estate agent should be apprised of these various debits and credits. He or she must be able to inform the parties with reasonable certainty what they can expect to pay and/or receive when the transaction closes.

5. To protect the title transferred, most purchasers buy a title insurance policy. The title insurance company agrees to reimburse the policy holder for losses caused by defects in the title and also agrees to handle the legal defense of claims based on covered defects. A title policy may have standard coverage or extended coverage.

CHAPTER 12—QUIZ
ESCROW AND TITLE INSURANCE

1. Which of the following is (are) essential to the creation of a valid escrow?

   a) A binding contract between the parties
   b) Conditional delivery of funds and/or documents
   c) Both of the above
   d) Neither of the above

2. Licensed escrow companies are regulated by:

   a) the Department of Corporations
   b) the Department of Real Estate
   c) the Secretary of State
   d) the Attorney General

3. Which of the following may be licensed as an escrow company?

   a) A private individual
   b) A real estate broker
   c) A corporation
   d) A partnership

4. The fee for recording the deed of trust securing the buyer's loan would ordinarily be paid by:

   a) the buyer
   b) the seller
   c) the lender
   d) the broker

5. The escrowee is the:

   a) broker who refers the parties to the escrow company
   b) buyer, who often acts as escrow agent
   c) neutral third party who keeps the parties' funds and documents
   d) Department of Corporations officer who regulates escrow companies

6. Because real estate brokers are exempted from the escrow licensing requirements:

   a) they can accept referral fees for sending customers to escrow companies
   b) they may act as escrow agents in any circumstances
   c) they are not required to act in good faith in the escrow transaction
   d) None of the above

7. A property is sold for $135,000. If the lender charges a 1% loan fee for an 80% loan, what is the amount of the fee?

   a) $1,350
   b) $800
   c) $1,080
   d) None of the above

8. A 'demand for payoff' or 'request for beneficiary's statement' would be sent by the escrowee to:

   a) the buyer
   b) the buyer's lender
   c) the seller
   d) the seller's lender

9. If the seller carries back a purchase money note and deed of trust in a sale of real estate, the amount of the loan would be listed on the settlement statement as a:

   a) credit to the buyer
   b) debit to the seller
   c) Both of the above
   d) Neither of the above

10. What title insurance policy guarantees against every threat?

   a) Standard policy
   b) Extended coverage
   c) ALTA
   d) None of the above

11. A document setting forth a brief synopsis of all matters of record affecting the title to the real estate in question is referred to as:

    a) a title insurance policy
    b) an abstract of title
    c) a closing statement
    d) None of the above

12. The title company is least likely to make an on-site inspection if the policy is:

    a) an extended policy on a downtown vacant lot
    b) an extended coverage policy on a residence
    c) an extended coverage policy on rural property
    d) a standard policy on a residence

13. The standard title policy covers all of the following except:

    a) transferability of title
    b) risks of deed
    c) rights of others in possession
    d) conveyance by incompetents

14. The extended coverage policy covers all of the following except:

    a) unrecorded easements
    b) forged deeds
    c) rights of parties in possession
    d) losses resulting from government restrictions

15. In order for a title insurance company to examine a title rapidly and economically, it is essential that it has a:

    a) data processing plant
    b) notary public
    c) title plant
    d) large accounting staff

1. c) Both a binding contract and a conditional delivery of documents/funds are essential to a valid escrow.

2. a) The Department of Corporations regulates escrow companies.

3. c) Only corporations may be licensed as escrow companies. Real estate brokers are exempt from the licensing requirements.

4. a) It is the buyer's responsibility to record the deed of trust.

5. c) The escrowee is the neutral third party who holds the funds and documents for the parties.

6. d) None of the listed options are true: accepting kickbacks is a ground for disciplinary action, brokers can only act as escrow agents in transactions where they are acting as real estate licensees, and they must still act in good faith.

7. c) The loan fee is based on the loan amount, not the sales price. The 80% loan would equal $108,000. One percent of $108,000 is $1,080.

8. d) The demand for payoff goes to the seller's lender; the escrow agent needs to know how much the seller owes on the original loan so it can be paid off.

9. c) Seller financing is a credit to the buyer and a debit to the seller.

10. d) No policy of title insurance will insure against governmental regulations such as zoning changes.

11. b) An abstract is a condensed history of conveyances and encumbrances affecting one's title to real property.

12. d) A standard policy insures items disclosed by the record; it has no coverage against defects discoverable only by physical inspection.

13. c) Rights of others in possession would require a physical inspection. The standard title insurance covers only the defects of record.

14. d) An extended coverage policy covers everything the standard policy covers and more, including matters that will not be disclosed by search of the public records. Nothing, however, protects against government actions.

15. c) A title plant is a collection of records maintained by the title company.

Chapter 13

LANDLORD AND TENANT LAW

OUTLINE

I. Leasehold Estates
   A. Estate for years
   B. Periodic tenancy
   C. Tenancy at will
   D. Tenancy at sufferance
II. Elements of a Valid Lease
   A. Required terms
   B. Other lease terms
III. Transferring Leasehold Estates
   A. Assignment
   B. Sublease
IV. Methods of Paying Rent
V. Responsibilities of the Parties
VI. Terminating Leases
   A. Covenant of quiet enjoyment
   B. Eviction
   C. Implied warranty of habitability
   D. Failure to pay rent
   E. Illegal use
   F. Destruction of premises
   G. Unlawful detainer action
VII. Mobile Home Park Landlord-Tenant Law
   A. Rental agreement
   B. Lease requirements
   C. Removal of home upon sale
VIII. Rent Control
IX. Property Management

KEY TERMS

leasehold estate

periodic tenancy

tenancy at sufferance

assignment

fixed lease

percentage lease

ground lease

covenant of quiet
   enjoyment

unlawful detainer action

property management

estate for years

tenancy at will

security deposit

sublease

graduated lease

net lease

surrender

warranty of habitability

eviction

rent control

CHAPTER OVERVIEW

Agreements concerning property are not always related to buying and selling. A large percentage of people do not own their own property, but merely rent or lease certain rights in the property from the owner. In this type of situation, the owner of the property is called the landlord, and the party who rents or leases the property is called the tenant. A basic understanding of landlord-tenant law and the various types of tenancies is essential in the modern world of real estate.

LEASEHOLD ESTATES

The lease creates the relationship of landlord (the lessor) and tenant (the lessee). It grants the right of exclusive possession for a specified period of time to the tenant, with a reversion of the possessory rights to the landlord at the end of the rental period. Since the lease is a contract, it is interpreted under contract law.

The lease creates what is known as a leasehold estate in favor of the tenant. The four most important leasehold estates are the:

- estate for years
- periodic tenancy
- tenancy at will, and
- tenancy at sufferance

ESTATE FOR YEARS. The estate for years is a tenancy for a fixed term. Its name is misleading in the sense that the duration does not have to be for a year or a period of years; it must only be for a fixed term.

Example: Bob rents a cabin in the mountains from Clark for a period from June 1 through September 15. Bob has an estate for years because the rental term is fixed. Since the rental term is fixed, the lease will terminate automatically on the expiration of the rental period.

PERIODIC TENANCY. A periodic tenancy, also known as an estate from period to period, is an estate that continues for a year or a fraction of a year (quarter, month, week, or day), and for successive similar periods, until terminated by either party by proper notice. The required notice is often the same as one of the successive periods, e.g., one month for a month-to-month tenancy. The most important characteristic of a periodic tenancy is that it automatically renews itself. The periodic tenancy continues for an indefinite length of time and is without a specific expiration date. The most common example of a periodic tenancy is the month-to-month apartment rental.

TENANCY AT WILL. The tenancy at will is usually created after a periodic tenancy or estate for years has terminated. This tenancy is created with the agreement of both parties and can be terminated at the will of either. A tenancy at will is often used when a lease has expired and the parties are in the process of negotiating the terms of a new lease.

TENANCY AT SUFFERANCE. The tenancy at sufferance is not really an estate in land. "Tenancy at sufferance" is a term used to describe a situation where a tenant lawfully comes into possession of the property under a valid lease, but holds over after the tenancy has expired. The tenant continues in possession of the premises, but without the consent of the landlord.

Example: Joe has a one-year lease with Landlord Sam. At the end of the term, Joe refuses to move out. Joe initially obtained possession of the property legally (under a valid lease), but is remaining on the property without the consent of Sam.

The tenancy at sufferance is simply a way to distinguish between a tenant who lawfully entered into possession of real property and who holds over without consent and a trespasser who never had permission to enter the land.

ELEMENTS OF A VALID LEASE

A lease is a contract; therefore, it must contain all the essential elements of a contract to be valid. For the most part, the landlord and tenant will only be bound by the provisions of their agreement. It should be noted, however, that the courts imply certain covenants and terms in all leases, whether or not they are written in the lease. These implied covenants are discussed in detail below.

REQUIRED TERMS

WRITING REQUIREMENT. The question of whether a lease must be in writing is governed by the terms of the Statute of Frauds. Leases which will be fully performed within a year or less from the time they are executed need not be in writing; leases for over a year must be in writing or they will be unenforceable.

OFFER AND ACCEPTANCE. As with all contracts, there must be an offer and an acceptance reflecting the mutual agreement of the parties. Acceptance by the tenant may be implied from the acts of the tenant, such as the payment of rent and/or taking possession of the property.

CONSIDERATION. Every contract must be supported by consideration, and the lease is no different. The normal consideration in a lease is rent. Most leases specifically spell out when the rent is to be paid, which usually is at the beginning of the rental period. However, if the lease does not specify when the rent is to be paid, it is not due until the end of the rental period.

SIGNATURE OF THE LESSOR. The lease, to be valid, must contain the names of the lessor and lessee and be signed by the lessor. It need not be signed by the lessee—acceptance is implied by payment of rent and/or taking possession.

MAXIMUM LEASE TERMS. California law specifies the maximum duration of leases for some types of property:

- agricultural leases — 51 years;
- property within a city or town — 99 years;
- mineral, oil, gas lease — 99 years.

ADDITIONAL ELEMENTS. The parties to the contract must be legally competent and have the legal capacity to contract. The lease must have a legal purpose (courts will not enforce a contract which has an illegal purpose). Also, since this is a contract pertaining to real property, an accurate description of the property should be included.

OTHER LEASE TERMS

A lease may contain a variety of other provisions, depending on the wishes of the parties. The following are some common provisions found in many lease agreements.

SECURITY DEPOSIT. Many landlords want their tenants to provide some sort of security to insure payment of rent and to protect against property damage. The form of security varies from lease to lease, but is often an advance payment of a portion of the rent.

In California, "security deposit" is defined as any payment, fee, deposit or charge (including advance rental payments); these payments are considered security deposits regardless of what they are called by the landlord and tenant. The total security deposit in a residential lease cannot exceed twice the monthly rental payment for unfurnished rental units, or three times the monthly rent of a furnished unit. (However, if the term of the lease is six months or longer, the landlord can demand an advance payment of not less than six months' rent.) The landlord must return the deposit to the tenant within two weeks after the lease terminates along with a letter explaining the reasons for not returning any portion of the deposit. If the deposit is not returned, the landlord is liable for $200 in punitive damages plus the amount of the deposit. The fact that a payment is listed as "nonrefundable" (for example, "nonrefundable cleaning deposit") has no effect on the operation of this law; the landlord still must return the payment or written explanation within two weeks.

USE OF PREMISES. The leased property must be used for a legal purpose. Since the category of legal uses is quite broad, many landlords want to restrict the use of the property, especially in the commercial setting.

> **Example:** The landlord of a shopping center rents to a restaurant tenant with a provision in the lease requiring the landlord to allow no other competing business in the shopping center. The landlord will need to restrict the uses of other tenants in the shopping center in order to comply with the provisions of the restaurant lease.

The lessor may limit the use of the property, but the restricting language must be clear. At a minimum, the lease should state that the premises are to be used only for the specified purpose and for none other. If there is no limitation in the lease, or if the language is not clearly restrictive, the tenant may use the premises for any legal purpose. In the shopping center case, the failure to use clearly restrictive language

Security deposit: payment from tenant which ensures payment of rent and protects against property damage; governed by State law would mean that a new tenant could open another restaurant or snack bar and compete directly with the prior tenant, much to the dismay of the landlord.

INSPECTION AND ENTRY. A common term in most lease agreements is the reservation by the landlord of a right to inspect the premises. This reservation is necessary because the landlord does not have an automatic right to inspect during the leasehold term. Remember, the tenant's possession of the leasehold estate is exclusive. The landlord must specifically reserve in the lease the right to interrupt that exclusive possession by inspection or he or she will have no right to inspect the premises.

In California, entry by the landlord may be made only after reasonable notice (a minimum of 24 hours) and only for specific purposes, such as for necessary or agreed-upon repairs, showing the property to a prospective buyer/tenant, after abandonment, or by court order. Notice is not required in an emergency, when there is a threat of injury to persons or property.

OPTION TO PURCHASE OR RENEW. The lease may contain a provision which gives the tenant an option to renew or purchase the estate. Most options require the tenant to give notice of the intention to exercise the option on or before a specific date. The exact terms of the option will, of course, vary from lease to lease.

MANAGEMENT OF RENTAL PROPERTY. If a residential rental property contains more than two rental units, the name and address of the manager of the rental units must be stated in the lease. The same information must also be posted in at least two locations on the premises, including all elevators.

TRANSFERRING LEASEHOLD ESTATES

The property owner has the right to sell the property during the term of the leasehold estate. The lease will not prevent such a sale, but the sale is made subject to the lease, meaning the buyer recognizes the existence of the leasehold interest and must honor the lease for its entire term. The tenant has the right to the exclusive possession and enjoyment of the property during the term of the leasehold estate. The tenant also has the right to assign his or her lease contract, unless that right is specifically prohibited by the provisions of the lease. Thus, a tenant may, during the life of the lease, **assign** or **sublease** his or her leasehold interest.

ASSIGNMENT. An assignment of a leasehold interest is the transfer by a tenant of his or her estate for the entire balance of the unexpired term of the lease.

> **Example:** Landlord leases premises to Tenant for a period starting January 1, 1988 and ending June 30, 1989. On July 1, 1988, Tenant agrees to lease the premises to Bob for a term starting July 1, 1988 and ending June 30, 1989. This agreement between Bob and Tenant is an assignment because the transfer is for the balance of the unexpired term.

In an assignment, the assignee is primarily liable for paying rent to the landlord (the original lessor) and the tenant, or assignor, is secondarily liable for the rent. In other words, the assignee has the primary responsibility to pay the rent but the first tenant is not relieved from the duty to pay, and if the assignee fails to pay, the original tenant must.

SUBLEASE. Like an assignment, the sublease is a transfer of a leasehold estate, but for a period shorter than the unexpired term. The tenant retains an interest in a part of the lease term.

Sublease: the transfer of a leasehold estate for less than the total remaining lease term

> **Example:** Landlord leases the premises to Tenant for a period starting January 1, 1988 and ending June 30, 1989. On July 1, 1988, Tenant leases the premises to a subtenant for the period of July 1, 1988 through May 31, 1989, reserving the month of June for herself. This agreement is a sublease because Tenant has transferred less than the balance of the lease term.

In this situation, the sublessee is liable for rent to the sublessor (the tenant), rather than to the landlord/lessor of the original lease. The tenant/sublessor is still liable for the rent to the landlord.

METHODS OF PAYING RENT

There are several different rent structures that can be set up in the lease agreement. The five major types of lease payment plans are:

- fixed leases
- graduated leases
- percentage leases
- net leases, and
- ground leases

FIXED LEASE

Fixed lease: a lease which provides for a set rental amount, regardless of expenses or utilities

Sometimes called a "flat," "straight," or "gross" lease, this agreement provides for a fixed rental amount. The tenant is obligated to pay a fixed sum of money and the landlord is obligated to pay all utilities, maintenance costs, taxes and insurance. This type of lease is most commonly found in residential apartment rentals.

GRADUATED LEASE

Graduated lease: a lease which provides for periodic rental increases, usually set at specific future dates

This type of lease is similar to a fixed lease but it includes periodic increases in the rent, usually set at specific future dates and often based on the cost-of-living index. These increases are made possible by the inclusion of an **escalator clause**. This type of lease is also called a "step-up" lease.

PERCENTAGE LEASE

Percentage lease: a lease which provides for the rental to be based on a percentage of the tenant's income

This type of lease is in common usage in the commercial setting, especially in shopping centers. The rent is based on a percentage of the tenant's gross income from the tenant's business. Typically, the lease provides for a minimum rental amount plus a percentage of the tenant's business income above the stated minimum. The percentage will vary from tenant to tenant based on the type of business involved.

> **Example:** Parking lots and garages have a much higher percentage of profit on every dollar earned than other businesses, such as grocery stores or restaurants, and therefore pay a higher percentage (sometimes between 50% and 70%) of their income.

NET LEASE

Net lease: a lease which calls for a fixed rental payment plus some or all of the operating expenses

In this type of lease the tenant pays the landlord a fixed rent plus some or all of the operating expenses.

GROUND LEASE

Ground lease: a lease of the land only

This lease is a lease of the land only, where the tenant agrees to erect a building thereon. This type of lease is prevalent in metropolitan areas and is usually long-term in order to provide incentive for the construction of buildings.

> **Example:** A tenant leases a parcel of land in the downtown area and builds a 20-story office building on it. The tenant then leases office space to different tenants. In this case, a

"sandwich leasehold interest" is created. That is, the tenant who constructs the building is both a landlord (as to the building) and a tenant (as to the land).

RESPONSIBILITIES OF THE PARTIES

The tenant normally need not make any repairs to the premises, but the tenant must return the premises to the landlord in the same condition in which they were received, with allowances for normal wear and tear. The landlord, as has been shown by many court decisions, may be responsible for making necessary repairs to common areas, such as stairs, hallways, or elevators.

Neither the tenant nor the landlord has any obligation to make improvements to the leasehold property. The tenant may make improvements, which normally become the property of the landlord at the expiration of the lease; such improvements are called fixtures. If the fixtures are trade, domestic or agricultural fixtures, they can usually be removed by the tenant before the expiration of the lease. (See discussion of trade fixtures in Chapter 1, *Nature of Real Property.*)

The tenant has a right to possession of the leasehold estate and it is the landlord's responsibility to provide that possession to the tenant at the agreed-upon time. The landlord must provide actual possession rather than just the right to possession. In other words, the landlord must deliver the premises unoccupied by prior tenants or other parties. Thus, it is the responsibility of the landlord to bring a suit to evict holdover tenants and to recover possession for the new tenant.

TERMINATING LEASES

A lease may be terminated prior to the end of its term in a variety of ways. The parties may agree to terminate the lease by mutual consent (**surrender**), or termination may result from a default or breach of covenant.

COVENANT OF QUIET ENJOYMENT. In every lease there is an implied covenant of quiet enjoyment. A covenant is an agreement or promise to do or refrain from doing certain acts. The covenant of quiet enjoyment is an implied covenant; it need not be written in the lease or even consciously agreed to between the parties. The courts imply the covenant based on the fundamental nature of the lease and the rights of the parties in the leasehold estate. Under this covenant, the landlord

Surrender: mutual agreement to terminate a lease

Covenant of quiet enjoyment: an implied covenant giving the tenant the right to uninterrupted, peaceful possession of the property may not unlawfully interfere with the tenant's possession of the estate and no third party may lawfully claim the right to possess the leased property. The tenant is guaranteed, as implied in the lease, the exclusive possession and quiet enjoyment of his or her leasehold estate.

EVICTION. The covenant of quiet enjoyment is breached when the tenant is evicted from the premises. There are two types of eviction: **actual** and **constructive**.

Actual eviction is where the landlord actually expels the tenant from the premises. This expulsion would be accomplished through the legal process, as will be described later. Self-help by the landlord is unwise and will often result in severe liability on his or her part.

Constructive eviction is where the landlord causes or permits a substantial interference with the tenant's possession of the property. This interference usually results from the creation of a situation which causes the premises to become uninhabitable. For example, failure to provide heat in the wintertime, infestation of the apartment with vermin, or the failure to provide other necessities have all been found to result in constructive eviction.

IMPLIED WARRANTY OF HABITABILITY. Constructive eviction may also result from a breach of the implied warranty of habitability. In all residential leases, the landlord impliedly guarantees that the premises meet all building and housing code regulations which affect health and safety on the premises. If the premises do not meet these criteria, the tenant is not liable for the full rent until the premises are made habitable. Instead, the tenant only owes the reasonable rental value of the property in its substandard condition. If the landlord takes legal action to evict the tenant for nonpayment of rent, the tenant can use the condition of the premises as a defense. This defense is available regardless of whether there is an explicit warranty of habitability in the lease; courts will imply such a warranty in all residential leases.

TERMINATION BY DEFAULT

FAILURE TO PAY RENT. The tenant has a duty to pay rent as required by the terms of the lease. If, however, the tenant fails to pay the rent, there is no automatic termination of the leasehold estate. The landlord may have a right to terminate the lease but the landlord must first give notice to the tenant of the nonpayment. This notice is required by statute. If the tenant, after receiving notice, still fails to pay the rent, the landlord may begin the legal process to either recover the rent payments or evict the tenant.

ILLEGAL USE. If the tenant uses the premises in an illegal manner, such as in violation of the zoning code or other ordinances, the landlord

---

Actual eviction: when the landlord expels the tenant from the premises

Constructive eviction: when the tenant's possession of the property is substantially interfered with by the landlord

Warranty of habitability: an implied warranty that the rented property meets all building health and safety codes may demand that the tenant cease the illegal activity or remove him or herself from the premises. Also, if the tenant uses the premises in a manner not authorized by the lease, the tenant will have breached a provision of the lease and the landlord may be able to terminate the lease.

DESTRUCTION OF THE PREMISES. If the lease is for a part of a building, such as an office, apartment, or commercial space, the destruction of the building will frustrate the entire purpose of the lease and the tenant will be released from his or her duty to pay the rent to the end of the term. Of course, the parties may agree to handle the issue of destruction differently by so stating in their lease.

UNLAWFUL DETAINER ACTION

An action in unlawful detainer is the most common procedure used by a landlord to recover possession of property from a defaulting tenant. The landlord must give the tenant proper notice of default and allow him or her opportunity to cure the default. If the tenant fails to do so, the landlord may proceed by filing a suit for possession (unlawful detainer action) in a court of competent jurisdiction. If the court finds the tenant in default, it may issue a writ of possession which requires the tenant to leave and to remove his or her belongings peaceably from the premises or else be forcibly removed by the sheriff. Note, if the court finds that the tenant maliciously held over or failed to pay the rent, the court may award treble (triple) damages to the landlord.

Although unlawful detainer actions are given priority on the court's docket, the process of legal eviction is often slow and may take months. However, a landlord should never try to take matters into his or her own hands. A legal process exists to handle such matters, and the courts frown upon self-help by the landlord. In fact, a landlord who uses self-help may be faced with a lawsuit which could prove costly. Furthermore, if the landlord should try to force the tenant out by turning off the utilities, the landlord will be guilty of unlawful entry and detainer. The tenant may receive damages, attorney's fees, and $100 a day punitive damages.

Unlawful detainer action: court action for evicting defaulting tenants

MOBILE HOME PARK LANDLORD-TENANT LAW

Landlord-tenant law for mobile home parks is similar to that of other residential tenancies. For example, there are the same prohibitions against discrimination and similar restrictions on the landlord's right of entry. However, because of the unique nature of mobile home park tenancies (such as the cost of moving a mobile home and difficulty in finding another space), there are a number of special provisions relating to mobile home parks.

California's Mobile Home Residency Law governs the relative rights and obligations of mobile home owners and park management. For the purposes of the statute, a mobile home is defined as a structure designed for human habitation and for being moved on a street or highway under permit. This includes manufactured homes, but not recreational vehicles.

RENTAL AGREEMENTS

There are two sections in the law relating to rental agreements: one section sets out the requirements for all agreements and a second section describes provisions which, if included, will exempt the agreement from local rent control ordinances. However, all newly constructed mobile home spaces (offered for rent for the first time after January 1, 1990) are exempt from rent controls, whether or not those provisions are included in the rental agreement.

LEASE REQUIREMENTS. All mobile home park rental agreements must be written and contain the following:

1) term and rent;
2) park rules and regulations;
3) a copy of the California Mobile Home Residency Law;
4) a statement that it is management's responsibility to maintain the common facilities;
5) a description of the physical improvements to be provided to the homeowner;
6) a description of the services to be provided and any fee to be charged for the services;
7) a statement that management may charge a fee for maintaining the property on which the home is located if the homeowner fails to do so after being given 14 days' notice; and,
8) any other provisions governing the agreement.

The homeowner must be offered a rental agreement for a term of 12 months unless the homeowner desires a shorter term. The owner and management may also mutually agree to a rental term of longer than 12 months.

Agreements which meet the following criteria are **exempt from rent control** ordinances:

1) the agreement is for longer than 12 months;
2) the agreement is for actual personal residence by the homeowner;
3) the owner is given at least 30 days from the time the agreement is first offered to decide whether to accept or reject it; and,

4) the owner has 72 hours to rescind the agreement after signing it.

The owner must also be given the option of rejecting the proposed agreement for a term of longer than 12 months and accepting the agreement with the same rent and other provisions, but for a term of 12 months or less. Management may offer gifts, other than a lower rent, in order to induce owners to sign an agreement for longer than 12 months.

There are also specific provisions of the statute covering such items as notice of rent increases (60 days), installation, hook-up, maintenance and other fees and charges, pets, guests, utilities, and procedures for enforcing park rules.

GROUNDS FOR TERMINATION. Because of the high cost of moving mobile homes, California law provides special protection to mobile home owners by severely limiting the right of the landlord to terminate or refuse to renew a rental agreement. Unlike other landlords, who are free in most jurisdictions to refuse to renew a lease or rental agreement, or to terminate it on notice, with or without reason, mobile home landlords may terminate a rental agreement only for one of the following reasons:

1) failure of the owner to comply with local or state laws relating to mobile homes;
2) conduct which constitutes a substantial annoyance to other residents;
3) failure to comply with park rules and regulations;
4) failure to pay rent, utility charges or reasonable service charges;
5) condemnation of the park; or,
6) change in the use of the park.

Management or the mobile home owner must give 60 days' notice to terminate.

REMOVAL OF HOME UPON SALE

Management may require that a mobile home be removed from the park upon sale, and before the end of the lease term, only if the removal is for the purpose of upgrading the park and one of the following conditions exists:

1) the home is less than 10 feet wide;
2) if more than 20 feet wide, the home is more than 20 years old (25 years if manufactured after September 15, 1971) and does not meet applicable construction and safety standards;

3) if less than 20 feet wide, the home is more than 17 years old (25 years if manufactured after September 15, 1971) and does not meet applicable construction and safety standards; or,

4) the home is in a significantly run-down condition or disrepair, regardless of age.

RENT CONTROL

Rent control: local ordinances setting maximum limits on rental rates

Rent controls are local ordinances which set maximum limits on the rents which may be charged. The intent of such laws is to attempt to make property available for rent at reasonable rates when there is a shortage of available space. It is also believed that, without such controls, landlords might be tempted to take advantage of the shortage and charge excessive rents. In California, the power of local governments to impose rent controls is limited by state statutes regarding both commercial and residential rent controls.

Although, as will be discussed later in this section, rent control laws often have adverse economic impact and tend to be counterproductive in alleviating the underlying problem (demand exceeding supply), many California communities have rent control ordinances in effect for residential properties.

Rent controls generally fall into one of the following two categories:

1) ordinances with vacancy decontrol, and
2) ordinances without vacancy decontrol.

An ordinance with vacancy decontrol is one in which the rent controls cease when the unit becomes vacant. In effect, the ordinance protects only the current tenants. When they leave and the unit is put back on the market, the landlord may charge market rates. An ordinance without vacancy decontrol is one in which the rent controls continue whether or not the unit becomes vacant and is rented again. Many local ordinances have exemptions for new construction and/or for other properties being offered for rent for the first time.

STATE RESTRICTIONS ON RENT CONTROL

State laws restrict the power of local governments to control rent. For instance, the Costa-Keene-Seymour Commercial Property Investment Act of 1987 prohibits rent controls for most commercial property. Local governments may not enact or enforce rent controls on commercial property after January 1, 1988.

California rent controls, then, are residential rent control measures. State law prohibits local governments from compelling a property owner to continue to offer property for rent or lease. If an owner does not want to rent the property at the existing controlled rent levels, he or she may withdraw it from the market. However, if the property is later offered for rent again, it may be subject to the controls in effect at the time of withdrawal (if it is placed on the market again within one year), or those in effect at the time it is placed back on the market (if more than a year after withdrawal).

The landlord may be held liable for actual damages and punitive damages not to exceed six months' rent to any tenants who were displaced when the property was withdrawn from rental. The local government may also bring a civil action against the landlord. Local ordinances may require the landlord to first offer the units to any tenants who were displaced if the accommodations are placed back on the market up to ten years after being withdrawn. If the improvements are demolished and new ones constructed, the new accommodations may be subject to rent controls which would offer a fair and reasonable rate of return to the owner.

The general purpose of the state statute, aside from setting some limits on the powers of local governments in this area, is to eliminate "loopholes" in many local ordinances for housing which is first offered for rental or which is newly constructed.

EFFECTIVENESS OF RENT CONTROLS

Most economists believe that rent controls are not effective in accomplishing their primary goal: providing affordable housing. They argue that rents become high (maybe unreasonably high) because demand for housing far exceeds supply. In order for rents to come down, demand and supply must be brought into balance, by either reducing demand or by increasing the supply of accommodations. Rent controls usually have little positive effect toward either of these aims. The artificially low rents may in fact increase demand. In addition, controlled rent levels may provide yields to the owners that are so low that they discourage, rather than encourage, construction of new housing. Rent controls, then, often make a bad situation worse by encouraging demand and discouraging new construction when just the opposite actions are needed.

PROPERTY MANAGEMENT

Property management: the administration, maintenance and merchandising of property owned by another

The property manager is a licensed real estate broker who, for a fee, manages the operation of real property owned by another. The property manager is different from and should not be confused with a resident apartment manager who ordinarily shows available space to prospective tenants and performs other varied tasks in exchange for free rent, a salary, or both.

The primary function of a property manager is to preserve the value of the investment property while generating income for the owners. That is, the property manager should enhance the physical value and prestige of the property while generating the highest possible return.

BASIC FUNCTIONS

The property manager performs three basic functions:

1) administers the property by controlling operating expenses so as to maximize income;
2) merchandizes the property to obtain tenants and lessees; and
3) maintains the physical property by keeping it in repair and modernizing or renovating the property where needed.

The manager may fulfill these basic functions by:

- budgeting and controlling expenses
- keeping proper accounts
- securing suitable tenants
- collecting rents
- caring for the premises
- hiring and supervising employees

THE MANAGEMENT AGREEMENT

The management agreement is the contract which spells out the exact terms of employment and the purpose of the agreement; it should be in writing and should contain the following terms:

1. Description of the property to be managed.
2. Term (time period) of the management agreement.
3. Statement of the owner's purpose. The owner's purpose may be to maximize rental income, to increase the property's capital value, etc. The purpose should be clearly stated; if particular means are to be used, they should be stated as well.
4. Description of the manager's responsibilities.

5. Extent of manager's authority. The extent of the manager's authority regarding such matters as hiring, firing, supervising employees, setting rental rates, making expenditures, authorizing repairs, etc., should be expressly stated.

6. Accountability and reporting. The agreement should state how often and in what manner reports of the operation of the property should be submitted.

7. Management fee: compensation. The fee is often based on a percentage of the gross or net income of the property; it may also include a commission on new rentals, a fixed fee, or any combination of the above.

8. Allocation of costs. The property manager will incur expenses such as office rent, office help, telephone, and advertising fees. The agreement should state which of these fees will be paid by the property manager and which will be paid for by the owner as a property expense.

CHAPTER SUMMARY

1. A landlord-tenant relationship is created by a contract called a lease. A lease must be in writing if it cannot be fully performed within a year of its execution. There must be an offer and acceptance between competent parties, consideration, the signature of the lessor, a legal purpose to the lease, and an adequate property description. Other terms often included in a lease are a security deposit requirement, a limitation on the use of the premises, a clause allowing inspection and entry by the landlord, and perhaps an option to purchase and renew.

2. Leasehold estates may be transferred by assignment or sublease. Assignment is transfer of the total remaining lease term, sublease is transfer of a portion of the total remaining lease term.

3. The lease may call for one of various payment plans. The more common include: fixed lease, graduated lease, percentage lease, net lease and ground lease.

4. A lease may be terminated by surrender (mutual agreement) or because of default (failure to pay rent) or breach of covenant (of quiet enjoyment or habitability). Other causes for termination include using the premises for illegal purposes and destruction of the premises. When the landlord wants to evict the tenant for failure to pay rent or other default, he or she must institute an unlawful detainer action. Landlords should not try to evict tenants themselves.

5. Mobile home "tenants" have some special protections, including restrictions on the terms of the lease and allowable grounds for termination.

6. In California, local governments have the power to set residential rent controls, which may be one of two types: rent control with vacancy decontrol or rent control without vacancy decontrol. Many economists question the effectiveness of rent control.

7. Property management involves preserving the value of investment property while generating income for the property owners. The three major property management functions include:

   1) administering property by controlling operating expenses (to maximize income);
   2) merchandizing the property to obtain tenants; and
   3) maintaining the physical condition of the property (including modernizing or renovating).

CHAPTER 13—QUIZ
LANDLORD AND TENANT LAW

1. Which one of the following applies to a landlord-tenant relationship?

   a) Tenancy in common
   b) Tenancy at sufferance
   c) Joint tenancy
   d) Tenancy by the entireties

2. A couple's five-year lease had expired, but they continued living on the premises. If they now pay rent on a quarterly basis, this type of tenancy is:

   a) month-to-month
   b) periodic
   c) at will
   d) at sufferance

3. A lease for a definite period of time is:

   a) a lease at will
   b) a fee simple
   c) an estate for years
   d) a tenancy at sufferance

4. An estate at will is a:

   a) form of concurrent ownership
   b) tenancy of uncertain duration
   c) inheritance of property by will
   d) life estate

5. Mr. Rob leases an apartment to Ms. Hall. Mr. Rob is called the:

   a) lessee
   b) lessor
   c) vendor
   d) vendee

6. Rent may be defined as:

   a) a month-to-month tenancy
   b) the lessee's interest in real property
   c) consideration for the use and possession of real property
   d) a contract between a landlord and a lessee

7. To be binding a lease must be signed by the:

   a) broker
   b) beneficiary
   c) lessor only
   d) lessor and lessee

8. Mr. and Mrs. Brown owned a drug store on property under a twenty-year lease with ten years to go. Mr. Brown died. The lease was:

   a) valid for the ten remaining years
   b) voidable at option of the new property owner
   c) void from the beginning, as business property leases are limited to fifteen years by law
   d) void, as Mrs. Brown was not a registered pharmacist

9. When real estate under lease is sold, the lease:

   a) expires
   b) is broken
   c) must be renewed
   d) remains binding upon the new owner

10. Assume that Mr. and Mrs. Davis did not sign the one-year lease but upon taking possession of the apartment on August 1st were handed a signed copy by landlord Smith. On August 20th Mr. and Mrs. Davis move out claiming that, since they had not signed the agreement, it was a mere tenancy at will. Smith could:

    a) do nothing
    b) sue Davis immediately for the eleven months remaining unpaid rent under the lease
    c) lease the apartment to another tenant and sue Davis for the difference between what he received from the new tenant and what Davis should have paid
    d) keep only the security deposit

11. A lease may be oral and not written it if is for less than:

    a) one year
    b) two years
    c) three years
    d) four years

12. A landlord comes by every day and continually harasses the tenant. The tenant can get an injunction based on:

    a) covenant of quiet enjoyment
    b) 3-day notice
    c) unlawful detainer action
    d) tenancy at sufferance

13. You lease out your property for three years. The lease specifies the tenant will pay $850 per month the first year, $900 per month the second year, and $950 per month the third year. You have a:

    a) gross lease
    b) graduated lease
    c) triple lease
    d) straight lease

14. Under an assignment of a lease, the assignee becomes:

    a) secondarily responsible for the rent
    b) the lessor
    c) primarily responsible for the rent
    d) the subtenant

15. A lease where the lessee pays taxes and insurance is called a:

    a) graduated lease
    b) fixed lease
    c) net lease
    d) None of the above

1. b) Tenancy at sufferance is where the tenant holds over after the expiration of the lease period without the landlord's permission.

2. b) Since the lessees are paying rent, they are not tenants at sufferance. With the payment of rent on a quarterly basis, they are entitled to possess the property for the next three months. This cannot be considered month-to-month and would be classified as a periodic tenancy.

3. c) Any lease that is negotiated for a set period of time is known as an estate for years. This would include a lease for one week, two months, one year or ten years, etc.

4. b) An estate at will is one created with consent of the owner for an indefinite period.

5. b) One who rents the property is called the lessor.

6. c) One leases property and pays rent.

7. c) Though it is a good practice to have both the lessor and lessee sign a lease, only the lessor needs to sign it. If the lessee takes possession of the property and pays rent, he or she implies acceptance of the terms of the agreement and is bound by it.

8. a) Death of the lessor or lessee does not ordinarily cancel the lease. If the tenant dies, the lessor should make his or her claim for rent against the tenant's estate, as most written leases bind the heirs and administrators of the tenant's estate.

9. d) The buyer takes title "subject to" the existing lease; he or she must recognize it.

10. c) By taking possession, the Davises impliedly accepted the agreement and would be liable for any damages from breach of the lease. The landlord's damages would be the difference between what the Davises were obligated to pay and what the landlord actually received. Only the lessor needs to sign the lease.

11. a) Leases need not be written if they will be fully performed within one year after execution.

12. a) The covenant of quiet enjoyment is implied in all residential leases. It is breached if the tenant's peaceful possession of the property is disturbed.

13. b) Under a graduated lease, rent payments increase over the term of the lease.

14. c) The assignee is primarily liable for rent; the assignor retains secondary liability for the payments.

15. c) Under a net lease, the tenant pays some or all of the operating expenses, in addition to the fixed rent.

Chapter 14

GOVERNMENT CONTROL OF LAND USE

OUTLINE

I. Comprehensive Land Use Planning
   A. Planning
   B. Implementing planning
      1. zoning
      2. exceptions and alterations to zoning
      3. building codes
      4. eminent domain
II. Subdivisions
   A. Subdivision Map Act
   B. Subdivided Lands Act
   C. Types of developments
      1. condominiums
      2. planned unit developments
      3. stock cooperatives
      4. timeshare projects
      5. land projects
III. Other Laws Regulating Land Use
   A. Environmental legislation
   B. ILSFDA
IV. Fair Housing Laws
   A. State laws
      1. Unruh Civil Rights Act
      2. Fair Employment and Housing Act
      3. Housing Financial Discrimination Act
      4. License law and regulations
   B. Federal laws
      1. Civil Rights Act of 1866
      2. Federal Fair Housing Act

KEY TERMS

police power
zoning
variance
special exception
building codes
condemnation
Subdivided Lands Act
planned unit development
timeshare project
NEPA
Interstate Land Sales Full
  Disclosure Act
Civil Rights Act of 1866
Federal Fair Housing Act

comprehensive plan
nonconforming use
conditional use
rezone
eminent domain
Subdivision Map Act
condominium
stock cooperative
land project
EQA
Unruh Civil Rights Act
Housing Financial
  Discrimination Act

CHAPTER OVERVIEW

Although a property owner is said to have a "bundle of rights" in his or her property, these rights are limited by some powers of the federal, state and local governments. These powers are superior to an individual's property rights because they are necessary for the public welfare. It is important to recognize these government powers and to understand how they affect certain properties and the rights of property owners.

COMPREHENSIVE LAND USE PLANNING

Police power: the state's power to regulate activities for the public health, safety, morals, and general welfare

A government's ability to control the use of land begins with the **police power**. Police power is the power vested in a state to adopt and enforce laws and regulations necessary for the public's health, safety, morals and general welfare. A state's police power may be delegated to local governments. Police power allows state and local governments to regulate the way a person uses his or her property. Although the federal government does not have a general police power (that is, has no general power to regulate for the public health, safety, morals and general welfare), it does have authority to advance the "police power" objectives that fall within the scope of its specific powers (e.g., interstate commerce and equal protection).

Exercises of police power must meet constitutional limitations. In general, a regulation will meet constitutional requirements if the following four criteria are met:

1) it is reasonably related to the government's power to legislate for the protection of the public health, safety, morals or general welfare;
2) it applies in the same manner to all property owners who are similarly situated (it is not discriminatory);
3) it does not reduce the property value so much that the regulation amounts to confiscation; and
4) it provides a benefit to the public by preventing harm which would be caused by the prohibited use of the property.

Planning, zoning, building codes, subdivision regulations, and environmental legislation are examples of the government's authority to regulate an owner's use of private property to promote the general welfare.

PLANNING

California has many examples of the problems caused by the haphazard, unplanned growth of urban areas. To alleviate these problems and to promote more rational development in the future, the state now requires each incorporated city and county to have a **planning agency**, usually called a planning commission. The planning agency of a city may be the city council.

The planning commission is responsible for designing and adopting a comprehensive long-term **general plan** for all development within the city or county. The purpose of the general plan is to outline the development goals of the community and to design an overall physical layout to achieve those goals. Once the general plan has been adopted, all development and all land use regulations (such as zoning laws) must conform to the plan. The plan may be amended if necessary, but there must be a public hearing on the proposed change. It is worth noting that a major way to implement a general plan is through regulations adopted under the Subdivision Map Act (discussed later).

There are several state and local agencies involved in implementing the general plans of various communities. The Local Agency Formation Commission (LAFCO) has the job of insuring that all community expansions (such as annexation of new land) or mergers with other communities conform to the general plans of the communities involved. The Metropolitan Transportation Commission (MTC) coordinates transportation planning among groups of communities on a regional basis. The Association of Bay Area Governments (ABAG) attempts to coordinate the general plans of all cities and counties in the San Francisco Bay area.

Comprehensive plan: a long-range blueprint for a community's development

IMPLEMENTING PLANNING

The government uses both its police power and power of eminent domain (discussed later) to implement the comprehensive plan.

Zoning: zoning ordinances control the way land is used, generally by dividing a community into areas with specific uses

ZONING. Zoning ordinances are an important exercise of the police power. They control the ways land may be used. Zoning ordinances generally divide a community into areas (or zones) which are set aside for specific uses, e.g., agricultural, residential, commercial or industrial. The classifications may be further divided. For instance, an industrial district may be divided into a light industrial zone and a heavy industrial zone. The purpose of placing certain uses in certain zones is to ensure that only compatible uses are located in the same area.

Zoning ordinances also regulate the height, size and shapes of buildings and their locations on the lot (e.g., setback requirements prescribing the minimum distance of the building from property lines, streets or sidewalks). These regulations control population density, provide some aesthetic guidelines and ensure adequate open spaces and access to air and daylight.

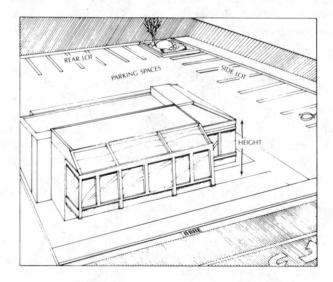

Zoning ordinances regulate a building's use, height, setback requirements, and off-street parking.

Some communities, rather than strictly prescribing the height, setback and side yard requirements for buildings, have enacted ordinances allowing the **floor area ratio (FAR)** method to be used in certain circumstances. FAR controls the ratio between the area of building floor space and the area of the lot it occupies.

Example: A floor area ratio of 2 would permit 100% of the lot to be covered by a two-story building or 50% of the lot to be covered by a four-story building. Thus, the FAR method allows flexibility in the shape and height of a building on a lot.

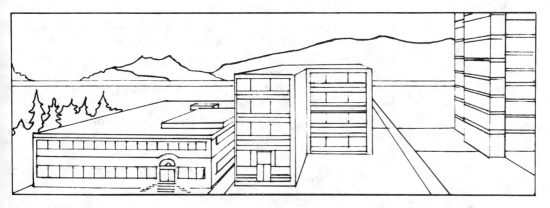

FLOOR AREA RATIO OF 2

EXCEPTIONS AND ALTERATIONS TO ZONING. Complications inevitably arise in the administration and enforcement of zoning restrictions and thus procedures (and exceptions) have been developed to cope with them, including:

- nonconforming uses
- variances
- conditional uses
- rezones

A frequent problem in the enforcement of a zoning ordinance is that of **nonconforming uses**. A nonconforming use is a use lawfully in existence at the time a zoning ordinance is adopted or amended but which does not conform with the new zoning ordinance. Such uses are permitted to remain, subject to some restrictions.

> Nonconforming use: a use in existence before a zoning change that does not comply with the new zoning ordinance

Example: If Smith is lawfully operating a bakery when the property is rezoned for single-family residential use, the bakery would be allowed to continue as a nonconforming use.

Even though nonconforming uses are allowed to remain, the general intent of the zoning laws is that all property will eventually be brought into compliance. Consequently, nonconforming uses are often subject to provisions restricting enlargement of the use, rebuilding after its destruction, and resumption of the nonconforming use after abandonment.

Variance: an exception to a zoning ordinance granted in cases of undue hardship

A **variance** is a safety valve offering administrative flexibility where private injury to the property owner far outweighs the benefit of strict enforcement of the zoning requirements. It is the authorization to build a structure or use property in a way that is prohibited by a zoning ordinance. A common example would be authorizing the construction of a house even if the topography of a lot makes it virtually impossible to comply with normal setback requirements. In most communities, the property owner applies for a variance with the local governmental zoning authority. California law prohibits local authorities from granting **use variances**—allowing a commercial use in a residential zone, for example.

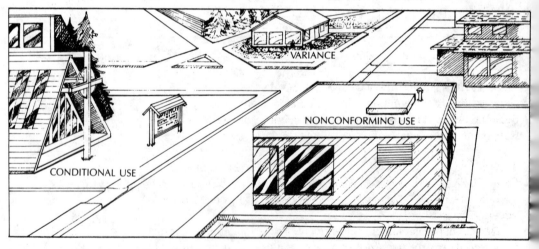

Example of nonconforming use, conditional use and variance

Factors indicating practical difficulties or undue hardship (not created by the property owner him or herself) usually must be present before a variance is granted. The undue hardship suffered must be that the owner cannot make any reasonable use of the land without the variance, not merely that he or she could make more money if the variance were granted.

Also, the proposed variance must not change the essential character of the area in which it is located.

There are situations when a special use is necessary for the community welfare but is not permitted within the applicable zone. Such a use could be a school, hospital, church, or cemetery. These uses must be located somewhere, but some control must be exercised over their location to limit adverse effects on other properties. Therefore, a common provision in zoning ordinances allows zoning authorities to issue **conditional use permits** (also called **special exception permits**) for such special purposes. Unlike the variance, evidence of unusual hardship in development of a piece of property is not required.

Conditional use: a special use (e.g., hospital, cemetery) necessary to the community that would not be permitted in the area under the normal zoning ordinances

If a property owner believes the zoning classification of his or her property is improper, he or she may petition for a **rezone** (sometimes called a **zoning amendment**) to the local appeals board. Many ordinances provide that notice must be given to surrounding landowners and that a hearing must be held before any decision is made on a petition.

Rezone: if the original zoning ordinance was improper, it will be amended with a rezone

BUILDING CODES. The enactment of building codes is another exercise of the police power. The purpose of building code regulations is to protect the public from unsafe or unworkmanlike construction. Building codes are generally divided into specialized areas, such as a fire code, electrical code and plumbing code. Codes specify construction standards as well as requirements for materials used in construction. In many cases, a structure built before a new, stricter standard is enacted may still be required to meet the new standard.

Building codes: regulate the safety/quality of construction

Enforcement of building codes is usually accomplished through **building permits** issued by the city or county. Such permits are required before a person can construct a new building or make repairs, improvements or alterations to an existing building. The permit requirement allows officials to inspect plans to verify that building codes and zoning ordinances have been complied with. Once the completed building has been inspected and found satisfactory, **a certificate of occupancy** is issued.

EMINENT DOMAIN. The power of eminent domain (not to be confused with the police power) is yet another power used to ensure compliance with a city or county's comprehensive plan. Eminent domain is the power and absolute right of a government, state or federal, to take property for a **public purpose**, such as a street, public housing or a park, upon payment of **just compensation** to the owner. A state government may delegate the power of eminent domain to local governments and to private corporations and associations, such as public utilities and railroads, that serve the public good.

Eminent domain: the power to take private property for a public purpose upon payment of just compensation

Condemnation: the
process of taking property
under the power of
eminent domain

Condemnation is the process used by the government to exercise its power of eminent domain. If the property owner and government agency disagree on the public's acquisition of a property or the price, the government can bring a condemnation action to take the property. An owner's only grounds for complaint are that the intended use of the property is not public or that the compensation is not just.

Just compensation is usually construed to mean the payment of fair market value. Fair market value is the highest price a property will bring if offered on the open market for a reasonable time period, and neither buyer nor seller is compelled to buy or sell, and both are knowledgeable as to all possible uses to which the property can be adapted.

It is important to understand the distinction between eminent domain and police power. Eminent domain is the right of the government to take private property, even against the owner's will, for a public use. Compensation must be paid to the owner when land is taken under eminent domain. Police power is the power to regulate the use of private property for the public health, safety, morals and general welfare. The government normally is not required to compensate a private owner for any proper exercise of the police power, even though the action (such as a zoning change) may result in a lower property value.

	Police Power	**Eminent Domain**
Taking property	no	yes
Public purpose	yes	yes
Compensation	no	yes

SUBDIVISIONS

Regulation of subdivisions is another method of controlling land use. The general definition of a subdivision is a "division of improved or unimproved land for the purpose of sale or lease or financing whether immediate or future." California has two basic laws which govern the subdivision of land: the Subdivision Map Act and the Subdivided Lands Act.

Subdivision Map Act:
gives cities and counties
the power to regulate
subdivisions

THE SUBDIVISION MAP ACT

This act gives cities and counties the power to regulate subdivisions and also sets out limits for this power. The purpose of the act is to ensure that subdivisions comply with the local general plan for development and to ensure that the requisite public utilities are provided for the subdivision. The act applies to all subdivisions of land of **two or more parcels**, but its most important provisions apply only to subdivisions of five or more parcels.

When land is subdivided into five or more parcels the subdivider must file a **tentative subdivision map** with the local planning agency, showing the proposed boundaries of the lots, location of utilities and access roads and provisions for the control of flooding and geologic hazards. The planning agency will approve or disapprove the tentative map, or it may approve the map conditioned on certain circumstances (e.g., dedication of easements for roads).

After the planning agency acts on the tentative map, the subdivider has 24 months in which to file a **final map** which contains details of lot surveys, streets, utility plans and dedications. No sale, lease or contract for sale or lease of any subdivided property is valid until a final map is filed. A **parcel map** may be used for a subdivision of two to four lots, condominiums or cooperatives, certain subdivisions having access to existing streets and certain subdivisions zoned commercial or industrial or with lots at least 40 acres in size. A parcel map does not have to be as detailed as a tentative subdivision map or final map.

THE SUBDIVIDED LANDS ACT

This act is a consumer protection law that requires the subdivider to disclose certain information to buyers of lots in a subdivision. The law applies to most subdivisions of a tract of **five or more parcels** and covers local sales of subdivided lots regardless of whether the lots are in the state. The lots need not be contiguous if they are part of the same project.

Such subdivided lots cannot be sold, leased or financed until the Real Estate Commissioner has investigated the subdivision and issued a **Final Subdivision Public Report** which is valid for 5 years. The report contains information about the subdivision which may affect potential buyers, such as the condition of title, provisions for utilities and improvements, terms and warranties which will apply to the transaction and obligations that buyers will incur with respect to any common financing of the lots (e.g., a prior lien which applies to the entire tract). The report must be given to all buyers, renters or financers of the subdivided lots before the transaction can be made. The person receiving the report must execute a receipt to that effect. Exception: before issuing the final report, the Real Estate Commissioner will usually issue a **preliminary report**. If the seller gives the buyer a copy of the preliminary report, then the buyer can reserve a lot in the subdivision. However, until

Subdivided Lands Act: a consumer protection law that requires certain disclosures to be made to purchasers of subdivided lots the final report is issued and received by the buyer, the buyer has the right to back out of the deal and obtain a full refund of any deposit money.

The Public Report may be used in advertising only in its entirety. Underlining, bold print, italics or other emphasis of a portion of the report is not permitted unless required by the Commissioner.

COVERAGE. The Subdivided Lands Act also applies to mobile home parks and planned unit developments with five or more lots, and to condominiums, cooperatives and community apartment projects with five or more units, residential timeshare developments containing twelve or more timeshare interests of five or more years, and to rural land projects of fifty or more vacant lots. Leases of apartments, offices and stores within a building are exempt from the law except in the case of a community apartment project. Subdivisions that are entirely within the limits of an incorporated city are also exempt.

TYPES OF DEVELOPMENTS

There are several different types of developments covered by most of the state and federal subdivision laws. Briefly, they are as follows.

TYPES OF SUBDIVISIONS REGULATED

CONDOMINIUMS
PLANNED UNIT DEVELOPMENTS
STOCK COOPERATIVES
TIMESHARE PROJECTS
LAND PROJECTS

Condominium: separate, fee simple ownership of the separate unit and tenancy in common ownership of the common areas

CONDOMINIUMS. A condominium is a development where the method of ownership is the separate, fee simple ownership of individual units with a tenancy in common ownership of common areas. The owner of a condominium unit receives a deed giving him or her absolute ownership of the unit. The occupant owns the unit, secures his or her own financing, receives an individual tax bill, and may acquire a title insurance policy on the property. Separate mortgages and other liens attach to the unit and may be foreclosed and the unit sold separately from other units in the condominium.

Normally, a governing board, elected by the condominium owner's association, performs the management function. Monthly assessments are made to cover the costs of maintenance for the common areas and these assessments may become a lien on the unit of ownership.

PLANNED UNIT DEVELOPMENTS. A planned unit development (PUD) consists of lots that are individually owned and areas that are dedicated to the community. PUDs are often a method used by some communities to provide flexibility in the size and location requirements of buildings on lots. Flexibility in zoning requirements is allowed if certain provisions are met. In order to qualify to build a PUD, a developer must submit detailed plans of his or her proposed development to a designated planning agency for approval.

Planned unit development: lots that are individually owned and common areas belonging to all the owners

STOCK COOPERATIVES. In the cooperative method of ownership, most commonly used with respect to apartment projects, the ownership of all of the units is vested in a separate entity, usually as a corporation. A corporation will put a mortgage on property to buy or to build. Other funds are raised by the sale of stock to prospective tenants. When a prospective tenant has purchased enough shares proportionate to the value of the unit he or she will occupy, the occupant receives a long-term proprietary lease. Under the lease, the tenant has the right to possession of the unit for the term of the lease and must pay rent to the corporation equal to his or her pro rata share of the amount needed to pay the mortgage, taxes, operating expenses and other debts. A governing board is usually elected by the individual owners to exercise control over the property and its maintenance and operation.

Stock cooperative: occupants buy shares of stock in the corporation which owns the building and then obtain long-term proprietary leases for the individual units

TIMESHARE PROJECTS. Timeshare interests give the owner of the interest the right to use the property (usually a condominium unit) during a fixed or variable period of time each year for a certain number of years or in perpetuity (for example, December 1-14, each year for 30 years). A development with 12 or more timeshare interests of five years or longer is a timeshare project under the Subdivided Lands Act. The buyer has a three-day right of rescission after signing the contract.

Timeshare project: the owner has the right to use the property for a specified length of time each year for a number of years

LAND PROJECTS. A land project is a subdivision of 50 or more unimproved lots offered for sale, lease or financing for residential or recreational purposes and located in an area with fewer than 1500 registered voters within 2 miles of the subdivision. In addition to the normal coverage of the Subdivided Lands Act, land projects are subject to special regulation. Provision must be made for the completion, maintenance and financing of roads, utilities and other necessary improvements, without imposing any lien or assessment against the subdivided lots. There is a 14-day rescission period from the time of sale, during which a purchaser may rescind the deal without cause. All advertising of land projects must be submitted to the Commissioner for approval.

Land project: a subdivision of 50 or more unimproved lots offered for sale or lease located in a less populated area

OTHER LAWS REGULATING LAND USE

ENVIRONMENTAL LEGISLATION

Federal, state, and local governments have enacted a number of **environmental protection laws** aimed at preserving and protecting the physical environment. This legislation can have a significant impact on the way a person uses his or her land. Some of the most significant legislation is:

NEPA: most significant federal environmental legislation

- **National Environmental Policy Act (NEPA).** NEPA is a federal law which provides that federal agencies must obtain approval for all major governmental actions significantly affecting the environment. Since a federal action has been interpreted to include a wide variety of activities, such as approval of a federal permit, NEPA can affect the way an individual uses his property.
- **Federal Air Pollution Prevention and Control Legislation.** Federal law provides that states must prepare plans for implementing clean air objectives. States are given the authority to prevent development if it would interfere with attaining or maintaining air quality standards.
- **Federal Water Pollution Prevention and Control Legislation.** Federal water pollution legislation requires that every facility discharging effluent into navigable waters or bodies of water that flow into navigable waters must obtain a permit.

EQA: California environmental legislation which requires preparation of an environmental impact report for projects affecting the environment

- **California Environmental Quality Act (EQA).** This law is similar in design to the National Environmental Policy Act. It requires the preparation of an Environmental Impact Report (EIR) for any project or development which may have a significant effect on the environment. If no EIR is prepared, the agency which regulates the development must make a finding of "no significant impact."
- **Coastal Zone Conservation Commission (CZCC).** This is a state organization which is charged with the duties of researching ways to protect the coastline and controlling development along the coast. The Commission has several regional divisions which review plans for development in the various regions of the coastal zone. No development is permitted in a coastal zone without a permit from the appropriate regional board. Development around the San Francisco Bay is controlled by the Bay Conservation & Development Commission (BCDC) as well as by the Coastal Zone Conservation Commission.

- **The Alquist-Priolo Special Studies Zones.** This act requires that a geologic report accompany any application for new development of real estate or new residential construction. The report is concerned primarily with the safety of the land with respect to earthquakes and/or landslides, two common hazards in California.

ILSFDA

The Interstate Land Sales Full Disclosure Act (ILSFDA) is a federal law designed to inform consumers about subdivisions offered for sale or lease in interstate commerce. The law generally applies to subdivisions containing 25 or more vacant lots. It is, however, a very complex statute and there are numerous exemptions based on such considerations as the number of lots, the size of the lots, whether the subdivision is subject to state or local registration and disclosure requirements, whether the purchaser has actually seen the lot, and many other factors. For subdivisions which are not exempt:

Interstate Land Sales Full Disclosure Act: federal law requiring certain disclosures to those purchasing subdivided lots

1) subdividers must file a Statement of Record with the Office of Interstate Land Sales Registration (OILSR, a division of HUD); the Statement becomes effective if not rejected within 30 days;
2) subdividers must give each prospective buyer or lessee, before signing any contract, a printed Property Report setting forth all necessary facts regarding the property that would enable the buyer to make an informed decision (e.g., description of the subdivision and lot, condition of title, liens or other encumbrances, condition of access, availability of utilities);
3) if the developer makes any representations (express or implied) to the effect that he or she will provide roads, sewers, water, gas or electric services, or recreational amenities, then the contract with the purchaser must specifically bind the developer to do so; this is known as the "anti-fraud" provision.

The buyer has a **7-day right of rescission** after signing any contract or agreement to buy or lease a lot which is covered by the ILSFDA. If the buyer has not been given the Property Report prior to signature, the right of rescission continues for 2 years following signature.

FAIR HOUSING LAWS

There are a number of laws, both state and federal, which have been enacted over the years to prohibit discriminatory behavior. Federal legislation includes the Civil Rights Act of 1866 and the Federal Fair Housing Law of 1968. State legislation includes the Unruh Civil Rights Act, the Housing Financial Discrimination Act of 1977 and the Fair Employment and Housing Act. The California License Law also prohibits real estate licensees from acting in a discriminatory manner (such acts are grounds for disciplinary action), so the real estate agent must be aware of these laws and the type of actions that are prohibited.

STATE LAWS

Unruh Civil Rights Act: state law giving all persons the right to the full use of all services provided by business establishments

UNRUH CIVIL RIGHTS ACT. This act states that all persons are entitled to the full use of any services provided by a business establishment. Of course, the act applies to real estate brokers, since a brokerage firm is considered to be a business establishment. Thus the act prohibits a broker from discriminating in the performance of his or her work.

The term "business establishment" has been interpreted in a broad sense by California courts to include apartment houses, condominium owners' associations and similar enterprises. In that context, the California Supreme Court held that the law prohibits discrimination against children by apartment owners and condominium associations. The act was subsequently amended by the legislature to permit some limited discrimination based on age (less than 45) by developments designed and operated solely for senior citizens.

FAIR EMPLOYMENT AND HOUSING ACT. This act generally prohibits all discrimination in housing in California. However, it does not apply to the refusal to rent a portion of a single-family, owner-occupied home to a boarder, or to accommodations operated by nonprofit religious, fraternal or charitable organizations.

Under the act, it is unlawful for any owner, lessee, assignee, managing agent, real estate broker or salesperson, or any business establishment to discriminate in selling or leasing any housing accommodation based on race, color, religion, sex, marital status, national origin, or ancestry. The law specifically prohibits any seller or lessor from asking about the race, color, religion, sex, marital status, national origin or ancestry of any prospective tenant or buyer or from making any statement or advertising which indicates an intent to discriminate.

The act also prohibits discrimination in the financing of housing. Under the act, it is unlawful for any person, bank, mortgage company or other financial institution to discriminate against any person or group of persons because of the race, color, religion, sex, marital status, national origin or ancestry of the person or group of persons.

THE HOUSING FINANCIAL DISCRIMINATION ACT. Under this act, financial institutions are prohibited from:

- discriminating in the provision of financial assistance to purchase, construct, rehabilitate, improve or refinance housing on the basis of the characteristics of the neighborhood surrounding the property, unless the lender can demonstrate that such consideration is required to avoid an unsound business practice;
- discriminating in the provision of financial assistance for housing on the basis of race, color, religion, sex, marital status, national origin, or ancestry;
- considering the racial, ethnic, religious or national origin composition of the neighborhood surrounding the property.

Housing Financial Discrimination Act: state law prohibiting discrimination in the financing of housing

LICENSE LAW AND COMMISSIONER REGULATIONS. California's Business and Professions Code, §125.6) prohibits discrimination by anyone holding a state business license—including real estate licensees. Three Commissioner Regulations implement this provision by addressing the duties of real estate agents with respect to discrimination based on race, color, sex, religion, ancestry, physical handicap, marital status or national origin. Regulation 2780 lists a number of actions or types of conduct which are grounds for disciplinary action. Regulation 2781 concerns panic selling or blockbusting. Regulation 2782 describes the duty of a broker to supervise agents so that they are familiar with the requirements of federal and state civil rights laws.

ANTI-DISCRIMINATION LEGISLATION	
Act	**Prohibits Discrimination**
Unruh Civil Rights Act	by any business entity
Fair Employment and Housing Act	by owners, lessees, agents, lenders
Housing Financial Discrimination Act	by lenders
License law and regulations	by licensees
Civil Rights Act of 1866	based on race
Federal Fair Housing Act	in sale, lease or financing of housing

FEDERAL LAWS

Civil Rights Act of 1866: federal law prohibiting discrimination based on race

THE CIVIL RIGHTS ACT OF 1866. This act provides that all citizens of the United States shall have the same right, in every state and territory, as enjoyed by white citizens to inherit, purchase, lease, sell, hold and convey real and personal property. The act prohibits any discrimination based on race and was upheld in 1968 by the United States Supreme Court in the landmark case of *Jones v. Mayer.* The court ruled that the 1866 federal law "prohibits all racial discrimination, private or public, in the sale and rental of property" and was constitutional based on the 13th Amendment to the U.S. Constitution, which prohibits slavery.

Federal Fair Housing Act: federal law prohibiting discrimination in housing based on race, color, religion, sex, national origin, or handicap, or against families with children

THE FEDERAL FAIR HOUSING ACT. Contained in Title VIII of the Civil Rights Act of 1968, this law makes it illegal to discriminate on the basis of **race, color, religion, sex, national origin,** or **handicap,** or against **families with children**, in the sale or lease of **residential property** or vacant land intended for the construction of residential buildings. Persons discriminated against can file a complaint with the Office of Equal Opportunity in HUD or sue in federal court. Violators may be required to pay punitive damages and compensatory damages (no limit) or penalties of up to $10,000 for a first offense (up to $50,000 for later offenses, and up to $50,000 for a first offense and $100,000 for subsequent offenses if there is a pattern of discrimination). In states with substantially equivalent legislation, such as California, complaints are referred to the state agency (the California Fair Employment and Practices Commission).

Some residential sales and leases are exempt from the provisions of the Fair Housing Law. The owner of a single-family home is exempt if three conditions are met:

1. the owner does not own more than three such homes at one time;
2. there is no real estate broker or agent involved in the transaction; and
3. there is no discriminatory advertising.

This exemption is limited to one transaction in any 24-month period, unless the owner was the most recent occupant of the home which is sold or rented.

The rental of a unit or a room in an owner-occupied dwelling which contains four units or less is exempt from the Fair Housing Law, provided rental advertisements are not discriminatory and a real estate broker is not used to locate tenants. This is called the Mrs. Murphy exemption.

Religious discrimination is permitted with respect to rentals in dwellings owned by religious organizations; lodgings in private clubs are also exempt from the law if the club is truly private and non-commercial.

The Fair Housing Law also prohibits:

- **Blockbusting:** the process by which a person induces property owners in a neighborhood to sell their property by predicting the entry of minorities into the neighborhood.
- **Steering:** the channeling of various applicants to specific areas in order to maintain or change the character of those neighborhoods.

CHAPTER SUMMARY

1. Certain restrictions are placed on a property owner's rights. It is believed that certain interests, namely the public's health, safety, morals and general welfare, override the individual's rights to his or her property. Thus the government can regulate certain aspects of real property ownership. The main power used by the government to this end is the police power. Another power is that of eminent domain.

2. A major form of control of land use is planning. General plans (adopted by cities' and counties' planning agencies) outline the development of communities. Zoning, building codes and condemnation actions are ways to implement the general plan.

3. Two acts, the Subdivision Map Act and the Subdivided Lands Act, regulate the development of subdivisions and the sale of subdivided parcels. Types of developments covered by these acts include condominiums, planned unit developments, stock cooperatives, timeshare projects and land projects.

4. Other laws regulating land use include environmental legislation (both state and federal), the Interstate Land Sales Full Disclosure Act, and fair housing laws (both state and federal). It is especially important that real estate licensees be familiar with fair housing laws as their violation is cause for disciplinary action.

CHAPTER 14—QUIZ
GOVERNMENT CONTROL OF LAND USE

1. An area of land set off by municipal authorities for a specific use is called:

   a) a cul de sac
   b) a subdivision
   c) a zone
   d) a territory

2. The primary reason for zoning is to:

   a) control the physical conditions of buildings
   b) control the number of similar businesses
   c) contribute to the public's health, safety and welfare
   d) insure the conformity of like structures in the area

3. Zoning would most likely cover:

   a) methods of financing
   b) size of buildings and architectural styles
   c) use and setbacks
   d) racial restrictions

4. In zoning, a use established after passage of a zoning ordinance, and in violation of it, is:

   a) a nonconforming use
   b) a variance
   c) illegal
   d) spot zoning

5. Where zoning precludes the intended use of the premises under contract of sale, the objection might be overcome by obtaining:

   a) an order of court
   b) a variance
   c) a non-conforming use
   d) a hardship permit

6. You list an old home on a corner in an older residential area. The home has an addition on the front which has been used as a small neighborhood grocery store, but which has been vacant for some time. Your prospect wants to re-establish the grocery business and wants to know if there is anything to prohibit it.

   a) You can assure him it is permitted, as it has recently been used as a grocery store
   b) It is permissible, as there is a similar store two blocks away
   c) You should check with the zoning authorities, as the business may have been a holdover when the area was rezoned
   d) You can assure the buyer it is O.K., as the seller would know if a business could not be started

7. An officially appointed group that studies city growth and recommends zoning policies is called a:

   a) city growth board
   b) master zoning board
   c) city policy commission
   d) planning commission

8. Some communities, rather than strictly prescribing the height, setback and side yard requirements for buildings, have enacted ordinances allowing for an alternative method, which is known as the:

   a) modified zoning plan
   b) variance system
   c) restricted ordinance method
   d) floor area ratio method

9. A land use in existence at the time a zoning ordinance is adopted or amended that does not conform to the new or amended ordinance is called a(an):

a) nonconforming use
b) ipso facto compliance
c) variance
d) none of these

10. There are situations when a special use is necessary for the community welfare but is not permitted within the applicable zone, as with some churches or schools. To put property to use in such a way, the owner must first obtain a:

a) conditional use permit
b) variance
c) nonconforming use permit
d) zoning modification

11. Jones owns some property which the city desires for the purpose of widening the street. Jones refuses to sell, so the city takes the land anyway and compensates Jones. This process is called:

a) eminent domain
b) adverse possession
c) condemnation
d) police power

12. Against his will, Farmer Malden was forced to sell his land in order that a municipal dam could be built. The principle which justifies this is known as:

a) lis pendens
b) caveat emptor
c) eminent domain
d) adverse possession

13. Mr. Marshall buys a home on the outskirts of a residential area. The city administrators approach Mr. Marshall and his neighbors to take some of their frontage for the purpose of widening the streets. Mr. Marshall refuses. The city administrators initiate condemnation proceedings. They take the property and compensate Mr. Marshall pursuant to court order. This would most properly be described as an exercise of:

a) forfeiture
b) severance
c) eminent domain
d) police power

14. If a railroad company needs to extend its property ownership beyond its present lines, it may get the needed land by:

a) eminent domain
b) injunction
c) writ of attachment
d) writ of execution

15. The authority to enact zoning ordinances comes from:

a) state supreme court
b) eminent domain
c) state's rights
d) police power

16. The difference between police power and eminent domain can best be determined by:

a) whether or not the action was by sovereign power or by statute
b) whether or not any compensation was paid to the owner
c) whether or not the improvements are to be razed
d) whether or not the owner's use was affected

17. An example of police power would be:

a) enforcement of health ordinances
b) zoning
c) building code enforcement
d) All of the above

1. c) This is the definition of a zone.

2. c) This is the reason the government becomes involved in such matters.

3. c) It is difficult for the local government to try and impose a certain architectural style; racial restrictions are against the discrimination laws; the method of financing is not a concern of the government, since the public "health, safety and welfare" is not at stake.

4. c) Unless a 'variance' is granted by the local government, the use would be illegal and could be prevented by the government, but not by private citizens.

5. b) A variance will be granted where the owner can show a reasonable need for the change, balancing his "hardship" against the needs of the local community.

6. c) Sometimes when an area is rezoned, they permit a non-conforming use to continue, but will not allow it to be revived after discontinuance

7. d) This is the definition of a planning commission. Such a group will adopt a "master plan" for the locality.

8. d) F.A.R. (floor area ratio) is a regulation of the ratio between the area of building floor space and the area of the lot it occupies.

9. a) This is a nonconforming use and is permitted to remain.

10. a) Schools and churches are common examples of conditional uses.

11. c) The process is condemnation. The right of the government to condemn is known as eminent domain.

12. c) Eminent domain refers to the government's right to take private property for public use. Eminent domain is the right, condemnation is the process.

13. c) Eminent domain is the right of the government to take private land, but unlike the exercise of the government's police power, the government must compensate the property owner when they take the property.

14. a) The right of eminent domain can be extended to private corporations whose functions serve the public good. Railroads, airports, seaports, and public utility companies are often granted the right of eminent domain for some specific purpose.

15. d) The government's right to regulate the use of private property stems from its police power. Eminent domain refers to the government's right to take private property for the public good. Police power is the government's right to regulate private property to insure the health, safety and welfare of the public.

16. b) The use of property is affected by both government powers, but only when the right of eminent domain is exercised is compensation to the property owner involved.

17. d) Police power is the right of the state to enact laws and enforce them for the order, safety, health, morals, and general welfare of the public. Another classic example of the state exercising its police power is the licensing of individuals who sell real estate.

TAXATION AND REAL ESTATE

OUTLINE

I. Real Property Taxes
    A. General real estate taxes
        1. valuation of property
        2. taxation process
        3. payment of taxes
        4. enforcement
        5. exemptions
    B. Special assessments
II. Federal Income Taxation
    A. Introduction
    B. Classifications of real property
    C. Gains and losses
    D. Nonrecognition of gain
    E. Depreciation and cost recovery deductions
    F. Deductions
III. State Personal Income Tax
IV. Other Taxes
    A. Documentary transfer tax
    B. Sales and use tax

KEY TERMS

ad valorem taxes
full cash value
tax sale
special assessments
Board of Equalization

Proposition 13
tax year
redemption period
tax deed
documentary transfer tax

sales tax	use tax
income tax	progressive tax
income	basis
nonrecognition of gain	installment sale
involuntary conversions	tax-free exchange
like kind exchange	boot
recovery deduction	

CHAPTER OVERVIEW

Tax consequences occur in almost every business transaction, and real estate is no exception. There are taxes which arise at the time of sale, general property taxes, special assessment taxes, and income tax ramifications. There are specific guidelines which are followed concerning the valuation of property and the determination of the amount of taxes owed. There are also specific rules concerning payment of taxes and enforcement procedures which are followed if taxes are not paid when due. A general knowledge of the tax burden and effects relating to real estate will help you to better evaluate the consequences and costs of real estate transactions.

PROPERTY TAXES

Real property has long been a popular way of raising revenue because land has a fixed location, is relatively indestructible and easy to assess, and is difficult to conceal. Because of these features, it is fairly certain that the taxes will be collected.

There are two types of taxes on real property: general real estate taxes (also called ad valorem taxes), and special assessments (also called special improvement taxes).

Ad valorem taxes: general property taxes assessed according to the property's value, used to pay for government services

GENERAL REAL ESTATE TAXES

General real estate taxes are levied to support the general operation and services of government, such as police and fire protection. General real estate taxes are called ad valorem (meaning according to value) because the amount of the tax is calculated according to the value of the property being taxed.

Proposition 13: law passed to limit amount of property taxes to 1% of full cash value

VALUATION OF PROPERTY. Under Proposition 13 (effective July 1, 1978), the maximum annual tax on real property is limited to 1% of its full cash value. Full cash value means fair market value. The property's full cash value cannot be increased for inflation by more than 2%

Full cash value: fair market value

per year (compounded annually) unless the property is sold, transferred or newly constructed.

If there has been no change in ownership since March 1, 1975, the 1975 value is the initial full cash value of the property. (This initial value is also called **base value**.) As previously mentioned, an inflation factor of two percent per year can be added to arrive at full cash value for the present tax year.

For any property sold or transferred since March 1, 1975, its value at the time of sale or transfer, adjusted upward at the 2% annual rate, is used. (For this purpose, a "transfer" does not include property transferred between spouses or a residence and up to $1 million worth of property transferred between parents and children.)

If property has been improved since March 1, 1975, (or since construction, sale, or transfer), it has its 1975 base value (or value from the year of construction, sale or transfer), and an additional value created by the new improvement. The total assessed value of the property may be adjusted upward up to two percent per year. Note that the land and its improvements are assessed separately, but the tax applies to the total.

If property has been newly constructed since March 1, 1975, its value is the value at the time of completion of construction, adjusted by the two percent inflation factor.

When a person who is over 55 sells his or her home and replaces it with another home in the same county, the assessed value of the old home can be used as the assessed value of the new home. In other words, the seller can carry the assessed value of the old home along in the move. For this rule to apply, the market value of the new home must not exceed the market value of the old home, and the new home must be purchased within two years after the sale of the old one. A seller over 55 who purchases a replacement home in a different county may or may not be able to transfer the assessed value of the old home to the new one. That will depend on the laws of the county where the new home is located.

Property values may be adjusted downward if appropriate due to damage or other causes. A property owner who is dissatisfied with the assessment of his or her property may appeal to a county board of equalization. The board may reduce the assessed valuation.

Board of Equalization: where taxpayers appeal their property valuations; the Board has the power to reduce the assessed valuation

The property tax is calculated by multiplying the assessed value by the tax rate.

TAXATION PROCESS. The fiscal tax year in California runs from July 1st of one year through June 30th of the next year. Property taxes become a lien on the property on March 1st of the preceding tax year. The assessment period begins on this lien date.

Tax year: July 1 through June 30

Tax rates are determined on or before September 1st of each year. The tax bill is mailed to each property owner on or before November 1st of each year. The tax bill reflects the assessor's appraised value (including the two percent inflation factor), less any exemptions to which the property owner is entitled. The taxable value is multiplied by the one percent tax limit plus any other percentage for bond indebtedness, if applicable. The result is the amount of the tax bill.

PAYMENT OF TAXES. An owner may pay taxes in two installments or may pay the total amount when the first installment is due. The first installment is due on November 1st, covers the period from July through December, and is delinquent if not paid by 5:00 p.m. on December 10th. The second installment is due February 1st, covers the period from January through June, and is delinquent if not paid by 5:00 p.m. on April 10th. A 10% penalty applies to delinquent installments.

REAL PROPERTY TAXES (Tax Year = July 1-June 30)	
TAXES BECOME LIEN	March 1
TAX RATE DETERMINED	September 1
TAX BILL MAILED	By November 1
FIRST INSTALLMENT DUE	November 1
FIRST INSTALLMENT DELINQUENT	December 10
SECOND INSTALLMENT DUE	February 1
SECOND INSTALLMENT DELINQUENT	April 10

ENFORCEMENT. If an owner fails to pay real property taxes when they are due, the county tax collector publishes a notice stating the amount due and that the amount will be in default if not paid by June 30th and the property will be sold if the taxes and penalties are not paid. If the taxes are not paid by June 30th, the property is in default and the **redemption period** begins.

Redemption period: after a default, the property owner has five years to redeem the property by paying back taxes, interest, costs, and penalties

During this five-year period, the owner can redeem the property by paying back taxes, interest, costs and other penalties. If current taxes are paid on time, then delinquent taxes can be paid in five annual installments.

After five years, if the property has not been redeemed, it is deeded to the state and the former owner loses title. The tax collector can then sell the property to someone else at a tax sale and the buyer receives a **tax deed**.

EXEMPTIONS. In California, there are a number of exemptions from property taxation, based either on ownership or use of the property. The following is a list of some of the most important.

- **Government Property.** All federal and state and most local property is totally exempt from taxation, regardless of how the property is used.
- **Property Used for Religious, Educational, Charitable or Welfare Purposes.** Property used for any of these purposes may qualify for a total tax exemption.
- **Homeowner's Exemption.** An owner-occupied property is exempt from the first $7,000 of full (taxable) value. This exemption may not be claimed if the dwelling is receiving any other property exemption.
- **Veteran's Exemption.** $4,000 of the full value of a veteran's property is exempt from taxation. In order to be eligible, a veteran's net worth cannot exceed a specified amount, which is subject to change. (The homeowner's and veteran's exemptions are not automatic. They should be applied for by April 15th of the preceding tax year.)
- **Senior Citizens.** Those 62 years or older may qualify for a deferment of property taxes on their residences if they occupy the home, have at least a 20% equity in the property, and have a yearly total household income of $24,000 or less.

SPECIAL ASSESSMENTS

Special assessments are levied for the cost of specific local improvements, such as streets and sewers. Only those pieces of property that benefit from the improvement are taxed, on the theory that the value to those properties will increase by the amount of the tax. These taxes are usually a one-time expense rather than an annual expense. The 1% tax rate limitation of Proposition 13 does not apply to special assessments.

Public improvement projects that result in special assessment liens are commonly funded by bonds issued and sold by the local agency making the improvement; once bonds have been issued, the assessment becomes a lien on the benefitted properties. Under the Street Improvement Act, a landowner can avoid a special assessment lien by

Tax sale: if the property is not redeemed by the owner, the state sells the property to a third party in a tax sale; the new owner gets a tax deed to the property

Special assessments: taxes to pay for a specific improvement levied on the property benefitted by the improvement paying his or her share of the improvement cost within 30 days of completion of construction, at which time the bonds are issued (i.e., the project "goes to bond").

California has several acts relating to special assessments and the formation of assessment districts. Some of the most important are the Vrooman Street Act, the Street Opening Act of 1903, the Street Improvement Act of 1911, and the Improvement Bond Act of 1915.

INCOME TAXATION

INTRODUCTION

Before considering the income tax consequences of real estate transactions, some basic tax concepts must be discussed.

Progressive tax: the more dollars the taxpayer earns, the higher the tax rate

PROGRESSIVE TAX. Taxes may be "proportional," "progressive" or "regressive." Our federal and state income taxes are progressive. The more dollars a **taxpayer** earns in a taxable year, the higher his or her tax rate will be. Tax rates increase in tax brackets so that an additional dollar earned by a taxpayer may be taxed at a higher rate than the dollar earned just before it, but the additional dollar earned will not increase the taxpayer's tax on dollars previously earned.

Income: any economic benefit realized that is not specifically excluded from income by the tax code

INCOME. Income may be broadly defined as any economic benefit that is realized (see below) by the taxpayer and which is not specifically excluded from income by the tax code. It includes almost anything that is received or realized and that represents an economic gain to the recipient.

Basis: an owner's investment in the property

BASIS. Basis is another vital concept in tax law. A person's basis in property is his or her investment in the property for purposes of tax treatment. The taxpayer's basis is the maximum amount that he or she can receive in payment for the asset without realizing a gain. The taxpayer's basis in the property is essential for determining profit, loss, and allowable depreciation or cost recovery deductions (discussed below) for real property.

In most cases, a person's **initial basis** is equal to the actual amount of his or her investment (that is, cost). A person who paid $120,000 for a house has an initial basis of $120,000 in the property. The initial basis may be adjusted upward or downward to arrive at an **adjusted basis**, which reflects the initial basis plus expenditures for improvements and/or minus depreciation or cost recovery deductions taken or allowable.

Example: If Shawn purchases Blackacre for $500,000 and makes $50,000 worth of improvements to the property, her adjusted basis in the property would be $550,000.

REALIZATION. A gain is not income for income tax purposes until it is realized.

Example: A person buys a house for $200,000 and over the next several years the property increases in value to $250,000. The owner has enjoyed an economic gain or benefit. The taxpayer now owns property which is worth $50,000 more than when it was acquired. However, that $50,000 is not subject to tax until it is realized.

A gain or loss is realized when a sale or exchange occurs which separates the gain from the asset. The owner derives income from the gain when the property is sold or exchanged.

RECOGNITION AND DEFERRAL. Income which is realized is subject to tax in the year it is recognized. As a general rule, any realized gain is recognized (that is, taxable) in the year realized unless there is a specific exception in the tax code. For example, a person selling a personal residence may defer taxes on the gain if the proceeds are used within two years to purchase another residence. In most cases, a nonrecognition provision in the tax laws does not completely exclude the income from taxation, but merely defers the consequences to a later year.

CLASSIFICATIONS OF REAL PROPERTY

Under the tax code, the availability of favorable tax treatment is dependent upon the class of property involved. For the purposes of determining the availability of favorable tax treatment (primarily eligibility for depreciation or cost recovery deductions or for certain tax-deferred transactions) real property may be divided into the following classes:

1) principal residence property;
2) unimproved investment property;
3) property held for the production of income;
4) property used in a trade or business; and,
5) dealer property.

PRINCIPAL RESIDENCE PROPERTY. This is the home the taxpayer occupies as his or her principal dwelling. It may be a house, duplex, condominium, cooperative, or mobile home. If the taxpayer has two homes and lives in both of them, the one in which he or she lives most of the time is the principal residence.

UNIMPROVED INVESTMENT PROPERTY. Unimproved investment property is vacant land which produces no rental income but is held for capital growth.

PROPERTY HELD FOR PRODUCTION OF INCOME. Property held for the production of income includes residential, commercial and industrial rental property used to generate rental income for the owner.

PROPERTY USED IN TRADE OR BUSINESS. Property used in a trade or business includes land and buildings, such as factories and business sites, used in the taxpayer's trade or business.

DEALER PROPERTY. This is property held primarily for sale to customers rather than for long-term investment. Subdivided property for sale to the public is usually included in this classification.

GAINS AND LOSSES

Sale or exchange of an asset normally results in either a gain or loss. Gains are normally taxable. Unless there is a provision in the tax code permitting exclusion or deferral, the gain is taxable in the year realized.

On the other hand, a loss may be recognized and deducted only if specifically authorized by the tax code. Most losses permitted recognition by the tax code are losses incurred in a trade or business or a transaction entered for profit. A business entity can deduct all its losses. An individual can deduct a loss only if it was incurred in connection with:

1) the individual's trade or business;
2) a transaction entered for profit; or,
3) a casualty loss or theft of the individual's property.

Therefore, no deduction is allowed for a loss realized on the sale of the taxpayer's principal residence.

The gain or loss realized on a transaction is the difference between the amount realized on the sale or other disposition (net sales price) and the adjusted basis of the property:

$$\begin{array}{r} \text{Amount realized} \\ - \quad \text{Adjusted basis} \\ \hline \text{Gain/loss} \end{array}$$

The amount realized consists of any money or other property received and the amount of any mortgage debt disposed of. It makes no difference whether the buyer formally assumes liability for the mortgage debt or merely takes the property subject to the mortgage. The amount realized is reduced by the selling expenses, such as commissions.

    Money received
+   Fair market value or other property received
+   Mortgage or other lien on property disposed of
−   Selling expenses
    Amount realized

CAPITAL GAINS AND LOSSES. Prior to 1987 the gain on the transfer of certain types of assets held for longer than six months (including most types of real estate other than dealer property) was eligible for **long-term capital gains** treatment. This favorable tax treatment permitted the taxpayer to exclude 60% of the gain from income. This tax benefit of real property ownership is no long available; it was eliminated by the Tax Reform Act of 1986 for dispositions of property occurring after January 1, 1987.

NONRECOGNITION AND DEFERRAL TRANSACTIONS

The Internal Revenue Code allows a taxpayer in some cases to defer recognition of gain to a later year or later transaction. Transactions in which gain may be deferred include:

- installment sales,
- the sale of a principal residence,
- involuntary conversions,
- sale of low-income housing, and
- "tax-free" exchanges.

With the exception of a limited exclusion of gain on the sale of a principal residence by an owner at least 55 years of age, these code provisions are not really "tax-free" transactions. The intent is that the realized gain will be recognized and taxed in a subsequent year.

INSTALLMENT SALES. An installment sale occurs when less than 100% of the sales price is received in the year of sale. Installment sale reporting allows the taxpayer to defer recognition of a portion of the gain to the year(s) in which the profit is received.

Installment sale reporting is permitted for all classes of property, except inventory. However, the Tax Reform Act of 1986 placed some restrictions on the deferral of gain in the installment sale of business and rental properties.

Installment sale: when less than 100% of the sales price is received in the year of sale

```
┌─────────────────────────────────────────────────────┐
│              Installment Sale Deferral                │
│                                                       │
│  1.  All classifications of real property, except     │
│      inventory, are eligible                          │
│  2.  When less than 100% of selling price is received │
│      in year of sale                                  │
└─────────────────────────────────────────────────────┘
```

SALE OF A PRINCIPAL RESIDENCE. A taxpayer who sells his or her principal residence and replaces that residence within two years may avoid paying tax on the gain in the year of sale to the extent that it is reinvested in the replacement home. This means that if the acquisition cost of the replacement home is larger than the amount realized on the sale, the entire gain is deferred. If the acquisition cost of the replacement home is less than the amount realized on the sale, the gain is deferred only to the extent of the purchase price of the replacement home.

SALE OF PRINCIPAL RESIDENCE BY TAXPAYER OVER 55. Anytime a taxpayer sells a principal residence and replaces it, he or she is entitled to the deferral of gain discussed above. Once in a lifetime a taxpayer is entitled to an exclusion of gain of up to $125,000 on the sale of a principal residence. The maximum exclusion is $62,500 for a married taxpayer filing separately. This is one of the few provisions of the tax code which permits a taxpayer to realize gain which will never be subject to tax.

To qualify for the exclusion the following conditions must be met:

1) the taxpayer must be at least 55 years of age (for a married couple only one spouse must be 55);
2) the property must have been used as the taxpayer's principal residence for at least three of the last five years.

Involuntary conversions: conversion of the real property's value to cash by means of fire, theft, etc.

INVOLUNTARY CONVERSIONS. Gain is not recognized on involuntary conversions (such as destruction of insured property by fire) if the proceeds received by the taxpayer are used to replace the property within two years of its loss. The reasoning behind this provision is that if a person is forced to "convert" property into cash which is then used to replace the "converted" property, he or she should not be burdened with large taxes on gains realized involuntarily.

SALE OF LOW-INCOME HOUSING. An owner of certain qualified low-income housing may sell such housing and reinvest the proceeds in similar housing within one year without having gain recognized. Gain which is not reinvested in similar property is recognized and taxable in the year of the sale.

"TAX-FREE" EXCHANGES. A "tax-free" exchange is really a tax deferred exchange. If investment property, income property or property used in a trade or business is exchanged for like kind property, any realized gain may be deferred to the extent that only like kind property is received. Principal residence property and dealer property are not eligible for this deferral.

Tax-free exchange: when two like kind properties are exchanged, the tax consequences of the transaction are delayed

---

Tax-Free Exchanges

1. Must be property held for production of income, for use in trade or business, or for investment

2. Must be exchanged for like kind property

3. Any boot received is taxable

In meeting the requirements for this deferral, the property received must be "like kind." This refers to the nature of the property rather than its quality. Most real estate is considered to be of like kind for the purposes of the exchange deferral without regard to whether it is improved, unimproved, residential, commercial or industrial.

If nothing other than like kind property is received, no gain or loss is recognized and the taxpayer's basis in the property received is the same as in the property transfered. However, anything received in the exchange that is not like kind property is regarded as "boot." Examples of boot would be cash, stock, or property other than like kind real estate, and differences in mortgage balances.

Like kind exchange: properties of the same nature are exchanged— most real estate is considered like kind, regardless of its use

> **Example:** If a taxpayer trades a property with an outstanding trust deed of $50,000 for a property which has an outstanding trust deed of $30,000, there would be $20,000 of boot received, regardless of whether there is a formal assumption of the loan.

If any boot is received, gain is recognized to the extent of the boot received. In the above example, the taxpayer would recognize $20,000 of gain, just as if he or she had received cash.

Tax-free exchanges can be advantageous because current tax expenses can be reduced or eliminated and property can be acquired that would be impossible to buy with the after-tax proceeds from the sale of existing property.

Boot: something other than like kind property, e.g., cash, stock, bonds

ELIGIBILITY FOR FAVORABLE INCOME TAX TREATMENT

CLASSIFICATIONS OF REAL PROPERTY AND ELIGIBILITY FOR FAVORABLE INCOME TAX TREATMENT

Real Property Classification	Installment Sales Reporting of Gain	Tax-Free Exchange	Recovery Deductions
Principal Residence	Yes	No	No
Unimproved Investment	Yes*	Yes	No
Trade or Business	Yes*	Yes	Yes
Production of Income	Yes*	Yes	Yes
Dealer	No	No	No

* Subject to IRS minimum recognition rules.

DEPRECIATION AND COST RECOVERY DEDUCTIONS

Recovery deduction: deductions from income that permit taxpayers to recover the cost of an asset used in a trade or business

Depreciation and cost recovery deductions can be deducted from income to permit a taxpayer to recover the cost of an asset used for the production of income or used in a trade or business. The deductions reduce the taxpayer's taxable income in the year taken and also decrease the cost basis of the property.

DEPRECIABLE PROPERTY. In general, only property which wears out and must be replaced is eligible for depreciation or cost recovery. Examples of such property include:

- apartment buildings
- business or plant equipment
- commercial fruit orchards

Land does not wear out and is not depreciable property. Since depreciation and cost recovery deductions are deductions from income, they are allowed only on income producing property. The following classes of property are eligible for depreciation or cost recovery deductions:

1) property held for the production of income; and
2) property used in a trade or business.

The following classes of property are not eligible for depreciation or cost recovery deductions:

1) principal residence property;
2) land (including investment property); and,
3) dealer property.

The entire expense of acquiring the asset cannot be deducted in the year the expense is incurred, as is permitted with many business expenses (such as wages, supplies, utilities). However, the expense of acquiring the asset can be deducted over a number of years (from 15 to 31½ years for most real estate). The number of years permitted is a reflection of legislative policy and has little if any relationship to actual length of time that the property may be economically useful. The whole field of depreciation and cost recovery deductions has been subject to frequent modification by Congress.

DEDUCTIONS

An allowable income tax deduction is subtracted from the taxpayer's income before taxation. A deduction reduces the taxable income and thereby reduces the income tax owed by the taxpayer. There are a number of income tax deductions permitted to real property owners. Some deductions were greatly restricted or eliminated by the Tax Reform Act of 1986. The most important deductions include:

- depreciation and cost recovery
- repairs
- real property taxes
- mortgage interest
- passive losses

DEPRECIATION AND COST RECOVERY DEDUCTIONS. Discussed above.

REPAIR DEDUCTIONS. For most properties other than personal residences, expenditures for repairs are deductible as an expense in the year paid if they are made to keep the property in ordinary, efficient operating condition and not to add to its value or prolong its life.

Repairs should be contrasted with improvements and alterations which are capital expenditures. **Capital expenditures** add to the value of the property and frequently prolong its economic life. Capital expenditures are not deductible in the year made, but are added to the property's basis. The resulting increase in the cost basis of the property will affect the gain or loss on the sale of the property and will increase the allowable cost recovery deductions (since the basis is larger) if the property is eligible for depreciation or cost recovery.

TAXES. Real property taxes are deductible. Federal income taxes are not deductible.

MORTGAGE INTEREST. Mortgage interest is deductible for home loans and for most business, income, and investment property, subject to some restrictions. For example, interest on investment property is deductible only to offset investment income. The Tax Reform Act of 1986 and subsequent amendments placed some limitations on interest deductions for personal residences (which is the only consumer interest deductible under the new law). A taxpayer may deduct interest payments on a loan of up to one million dollars used to buy or improve a residence. For other home loans (home equity loans for purposes other than acquisition or improvement), interest on loans of up to $100,000 can be deducted by a couple filing a joint return, without regard to the purpose of the loan or whether the loan exceeds the original acquisition cost of the home plus capital improvements. Taxpayers filing separate returns can deduct interest on up to $50,000 of debt.

LIMITATIONS ON DEDUCTIBILITY OF PASSIVE LOSSES. Under the Tax Reform Act of 1986, losses from passive activities, such as ownership of rental properties, can no longer be offset against income from wages, salaries, interest, dividends or royalties. Losses from passive activities can only be offset against income from other passive activities.

> **Example:** If a taxpayer had $30,000 salary income and owned one rental property, which had a net loss of $2,000 for the year, the $2,000 net loss could not be deducted from the $30,000 salary income.

However, a loss can be carried forward and used when the taxpayer does have positive income from a passive activity.

There is one **exception** in favor of individuals who actively participate in rental property activity and whose adjusted gross income does not exceed $100,000. For these taxpayers, losses from rental property of to $25,000 may be offset against their other income. The requirement for "active participation" is met if the owner actually exercises some control over the management of the rental property, for example by selecting tenants, setting rental terms or authorizing repairs and maintenance work. This exception is only available to individuals; it may not be used by an investor who is a limited partner in a limited partnership which owns the property or by an owner who owns less than a 10% interest in the property.

If the taxpayer's adjusted gross income is more than $100,000, the maximum $25,000 deduction is reduced by fifty cents for every dollar of income over the $100,000 limit. So, a taxpayer whose adjusted gross income exceeded $150,000 would not be able to take any advantage of this limited exception.

STATE PERSONAL INCOME TAX

In addition to the federal income tax, there is a California state income tax. Modifications to the California income tax law in 1983 and 1987 have brought the state law substantially into accord with the provisions of the Internal Revenue Code. For example, with limited exceptions, the California statutes simply refer to the federal law for such items as the definitions of gross income, adjusted gross income, itemized deductions and taxable income. There is a different standard deduction under state law for those who do not itemize and, of course, the tax rates on taxable income are different. As with federal law, the state income tax is a progressive tax with higher rates imposed on higher income levels. Income tax brackets and the standard deduction are adjusted for inflation by the California Franchise Tax Board each year based on the California Consumer Price Index.

OTHER TAXES

DOCUMENTARY TRANSFER TITLE TAX

California allows a county to adopt a tax on all transfers of real property located in the county. The rate is currently fixed at **.55 per $500** in value, or fraction thereof. A city within a county that has adopted a transfer tax may also adopt its own transfer tax ordinance with the tax fixed at one-half the rate charged by the county. (This simply means that the county must share half the tax with the city; the taxpayer does not pay any additional amount.)

Documentary transfer title tax: a tax on all transfers of real property imposed by the county

The tax is calculated based upon the owner's equity; outstanding loans assumed by the buyer are not considered.

SALES AND USE TAX

Sales tax is a state tax charged to retail sellers for the privilege of retailing. It applies only to retail sales of tangible personal property. This tax must be paid by the seller even if it is not charged to the buyer.

Use tax is similar to sales tax, but it is charged to buyers (and in some cases lessees) rather than to sellers. A buyer can avoid liability for this tax by obtaining a receipt for the tax from a seller who is authorized by the state to collect the tax.

A base rate of sales and use tax applies throughout the state, and additional charges are levied in some counties to pay for transit projects. Administration of the sales and use taxes (and also local transit taxes) is done by the State Board of Equalization.

Real estate licensees should be aware of the importance of paying sales and use tax in connection with sales of buildings (if severed from the land by the seller), other fixtures (not incidental to the sale of the land) and business opportunities. In the sale of a business opportunity, the purchaser may be held secondarily liable for sales tax previously owed by the seller; the cautious buyer will require that contingency funds be held in escrow until a tax clearance has been obtained. The due date of the tax is the last day of the month following the end of each quarter. There is a 10% late payment penalty and a 25% penalty for fraud or an attempt to evade payment.

CHAPTER SUMMARY

1. Property taxes are a popular way of raising revenue because the permanent nature of property increases the likelihood of the taxes being collected. There are two types of real property taxes: ad valorem (general) property taxes and special assessments. Ad valorem taxes are levied according to the value of the property, are imposed on all property in the taxing district, pay for general government services, and are generally levied once a year. Special assessments pay for specific improvements, are imposed only on property that benefits from the improvements and are generally one-time-only taxes.

2. Proposition 13 limits the amount of general property taxes to 1% of true cash value. True cash value can only be increased for inflation by 2% per year, unless the property has changed ownership or been improved. The California tax year runs from July 1 to June 30. Tax bills are sent out by November 1. The first payment is due

on November 1, the second on February 1. If a property owner fails to pay the assessed taxes, the property may be sold and the proceeds used to pay the taxes.

3. Owning real property has many income tax consequences. Real property is classified into five major types, with different tax benefits accruing to each type. Some of the tax benefits that accrue to real property owners include the nonrecognition transactions (installment sales, the sale of a principal residence, involuntary conversions, sale of low-income housing, and tax-free exchanges) and deductions (depreciation and cost recovery, repairs, real property taxes, mortgage interest, and passive losses).

4. Other taxes property owners and real estate licensees should be aware of are the documentary transfer title tax (a tax on all transfers of real property) and the sales and use tax (on the sale of buildings, fixtures and business opportunities).

CHAPTER 15—QUIZ
TAXATION AND REAL ESTATE

1. The lien priority of unpaid real property taxes is:

   a) higher than a mortgage's
   b) the same as a mortgage's
   c) lower than a mortgage's
   d) lower than that of a mortgage recorded before the tax lien attached

2. Farmer Jones is unable to pay the county taxes on his farm. The delinquent taxes would be:

   a) liens
   b) attachments
   c) easements
   d) appurtenances

3. Real estate taxes become a lien on property:

   a) on March 1st
   b) on July 1st
   c) on February 1st
   d) on November 1st

4. Which of the following liens would be given higher priority?

   a) The current real estate tax
   b) A mortgage dated last year
   c) A judgment rendered today
   d) A mechanic's lien for work started before the mortgage was made

5. Which of the following municipalities or agencies usually make levies for general real estate taxes?

   a) School districts
   b) Counties
   c) Both a) and b)
   d) Neither a) nor b)

6. A tax year runs from:

   a) January 1st to December 31st
   b) April 16th to April 15th
   c) July 1st to June 30th
   d) None of the above

7. Which of the following properties is (are) exempt from real estate taxes?

   a) The local city hall
   b) State government property
   c) Nonprofit church property
   d) All of the above

8. By what date is the first installment of general real estate taxes delinquent?

   a) February 1st
   b) April 10th
   c) November 11th
   d) December 10th

9. A charge levied by a local government to finance street paving is:

   a) an ad valorem tax
   b) a zoning charge
   c) an appurtenance
   d) an assessment

10. A property owner who is dissatisfied with assessment of his property:

    a) can sue the state in court
    b) may appeal to the County Board of Equalization
    c) is powerless to do anything about it
    d) None of the above

11. A homeowner can adjust his or her cost basis by:

    a) depreciation
    b) expenditures to keep the property in good repair
    c) foregone interest on his or her equity
    d) the cost of installing a patio

A husband and wife purchased a residence in 1985 and paid $127,000. After living in the home for one year, they sold it for $124,000. The amount of deduction that can be taken as a capital loss on their federal income tax return is:

a) $3,000
b) 50%
c) 25%
d) None of the above

Losses recognized on a limited partnership investment in rental property may be offset against:

I. the limited partner's salary or wages
II. the limited partner's income from other limited partnerships

  a) I only
  b) II only
  c) both I and II
  d) neither I nor II

Mr. Robinson, 57, has lived in his home for the past three years and is now selling it for $185,000. His purchase price was $68,500. The maximum tax Mr. Robinson will have to pay is:

a) 20% of his normal income tax rate
b) 40% of his normal income tax rate
c) 20% of $116,500
d) none

A property owner buys his residence for $100,000 and sells it for $135,000. Twenty-two months later he purchases a new residence for $138,000. What are the tax consequences?

a) No tax on the gain is paid in the year of the sale
b) The cost basis of the second home is $103,000
c) Both a) and b)
d) neither a) nor b)

Under the federal income tax code, income is subject to tax when:

a) realized
b) recognized
c) deferred
d) recovered

17. The best tax breaks are given on:

a) real property held for production of income
b) real property held for investment
c) real property held for sales
d) personal property

1. a) Regardless of the date of the recording of a mortgage, general property taxes are always the first liens to be satisfied from the forced sale of property.

2. a) County taxes, if unpaid, become a financial claim or lien upon the specific property in question. If not paid, eventually the county will sell the property at a public auction, and satisfy the tax liens from the proceeds of the sale.

3. a) Real estate taxes become a lien on property on March 1st of the year before they are due.

4. a) Taxes on real property always have the highest priority even though other liens may have been previously recorded or created.

5. c) Both school districts and counties may levy general real estate taxes.

6. c) A tax year runs from July 1st through June 30th.

7. d) All are examples of properties exempt from real estate taxes.

8. d) The first installment of taxes is due on November 1st and is delinquent if not paid by 5:00 p.m. December 10th.

9. d) A charge to finance street paving is a special assessment. Only the property benefitted by the street paving is billed for the cost of the work.

10. b) A property owner may appeal the assessment of his property to the County Board of Equalization.

11. d) The patio is a capital improvement. Depreciation claims are not allowed on personal residences.

12. d) No loss may be recognized on the sale of a personal residence.

13. b) Losses from limited partnership rental property are "passive" losses which may be offset only against other passive income.

14. d) If the taxpayer is 55 or older and has lived ɩ the property for three of the past five yeaɪ the first $125,000 of gain from the sale of h home may be excluded from income. This eɪ clusion may be elected only once in a lifetimɪ

15. c) If a new residence is purchased within tɤ years for more than the first residence's sɑ price, there is no gain reported, and the cɪ basis of the second residence is reduced by tᵇ amount of the deferred gain ($35,000).

16. b) Income is subject to tax in the year it recognized.

17. a) Property held for production of income is eliɪ ble for depreciation/cost recovery deductioɪ the other three classes of property are noɪ

RESIDENTIAL REAL ESTATE

OUTLINE

I. Construction
   A. Building codes and regulations
   B. Architectural styles
   C. Plans and specifications
   D. Wood frame construction
      1. materials
      2. termite problems
   E. The architect
   F. Glossary of construction terms
II. Buy or Rent?
   A. Advantages of renting
   B. Advantages of buying
   C. Comparison of buying versus renting
III. Condominium Ownership
   A. Advantages
   B. Disadvantages
IV. Mobile Home Ownership
   A. Advantages
   B. Disadvantages
V. Factors to Consider When Choosing a Home
   A. Neighborhood considerations
   B. The home

KEY TERMS

See glossary of construction terms within chapter.

CHAPTER OVERVIEW

In bringing a buyer and seller together, the real estate agent must be a "jack of all trades." Not only must he or she be familiar with property values, contracts, and negotiation techniques, the agent must also be familiar with the rudiments of residential construction. An agent must know the advantages of renting versus buying, and the advantages of buying different types of residences (e.g., single-family homes, mobile homes, or condominium units). It is especially important for the agent to know what factors to consider when choosing a home. If the agent can answer questions on these subjects with confidence, he or she will be viewed as a true professional by the buying public.

CONSTRUCTION

INTRODUCTION

To evaluate the quality of a building, it's necessary to have a basic understanding of the procedures and materials used in constructing the building. When dealing with large and complicated structures, such as factories or high-rise buildings, evaluation of the structure should be left to professionals such as architects and engineers. But in the case of ordinary residential buildings and small commercial structures, the real estate agent who has some knowledge of construction can make a fair evaluation of the quality of workmanship and materials that went into the building.

The agent's preliminary evaluation should be supplemented, when necessary, by the opinions of licensed professional building inspectors, especially with respect to structural soundness and the safety and suitability of plumbing and electrical components of the building.

There are several aspects of construction the real estate professional should be familiar with. These include:

- local building codes and regulations
- architectural styles
- plans and specifications, and
- construction methods and terminology

BUILDING CODES AND REGULATIONS

LOCAL CODES. Local codes and regulations prescribe the types of materials that must be used, the acceptable methods of construction, and the number and placement of such items as electrical outlets, plumbing fixtures and windows. The size and placement of a building on its lot are also governed by local regulations. The purpose of building codes and regulations is to assure the quality of buildings and also to promote a degree of uniformity in construction. Key sources of information regarding such regulations are the local planning and building departments, architects and construction contractors.

MINIMUM PROPERTY REQUIREMENTS. A second form of building regulation is the minimum property requirements (MPRs). These are standards established by certain governmental and private lending institutions with respect to the quality of buildings they finance. Buildings which do not satisfy the minimum property requirements of an organization will not be financed by that organization. MPRs are not a substitute for local building codes; they are an additional set of regulations to which the building must conform in order to qualify for financing. MPRs may or may not be more stringent than local building codes. The most commonly encountered MPRs are those established by the VA lending department.

ARCHITECTURAL STYLES

There are numerous widely recognized architectural styles, some of which are illustrated below. Of course, many buildings have their own unique style or are combinations of two or more styles. The value of a particular style is dependent mainly upon the personal preferences of the home-owner; one style is not inherently superior to another.

Colonial (or Cape Cod), Spanish, modern (or contemporary), and California ranch styles are the most popular in California.

The **Cape Cod** architectural style is usually one or two stories, with wood siding and a steep wood-shingled roof. **Spanish** style homes are one- or two-story homes with white or pastel stucco exteriors and red tile roofs. **Modern** homes usually incorporate large windows and glass doors, and are designed with an "open" interior. Because of its great flexibility, contemporary design is well suited for building on hillsides or other difficult sites. **California ranch style** homes are one-story homes with a low-pitched or flat roof. The exterior may be wood, masonry or stucco.

PLANS AND SPECIFICATIONS

Plans and specifications are drawings and text that explain in detail how a building is constructed. Plans normally include vertical and horizontal cross sections of the building that show the placement of foundations, floors, walls, roof, doors, windows, fixtures, wiring, etc. Specifications are the text that accompanies the plans. This text prescribes the type of materials to be used and the required quality of workmanship.

RANCH

MODERN

BUNGALOW

SPLIT LEVEL

SPANISH

Plans and specifications are usually prepared by an architect in the form of **blueprints**.

SOIL TEST. An important aspect of the plans and specifications is the soil test. Before commencing construction of a building, an inspection by a soil engineer is required to determine the stability of the soil and its capacity to support the weight of the proposed structure. If the site is not served by a public sewer utility, the soil engineer will also make a percolation test (**PERC test**) to determine whether the site is adequate for a septic tank and drainfield.

WOOD-FRAME CONSTRUCTION

The most common form of residential building is the wood-frame building, popular because of its low cost, ease and speed of construction and flexibility of design.

One-story, two-story and split-level homes may all be constructed with this technique. One-story homes are the simplest to construct and maintain. Because they occupy more land in relation to the living space than two-story or split-level homes, one-story homes may be uneconomical in areas where land values are high. Split-level construction is more expensive but is popular in California because it better utilizes land with varying topography and because of its attractive design. Two-story construction is the most economical per square foot of living space, since twice as much living space is provided with one foundation, one roof and the same amount of land. The inconvenience of stairs and exterior maintenance on the upper story are the primary drawbacks for two-story homes.

The construction of wood-frame buildings is illustrated in the following diagrams, and a glossary of construction terms is provided below for use in conjunction with these diagrams.

BUILDING MATERIALS. Specified building materials may be required for a particular application by the local building codes. Some materials which are commonly used in residential construction are described in the following sections.

Foundations — The basic material used in almost all modern foundations is **reinforced concrete**. Concrete has the advantages of low cost, plasticity and high compressive strength. When reinforced by steel bars or mesh embedded in the concrete, it also has good tensile strength (resistance to bending or cracking). The basic components of concrete are Portland cement, sand, gravel and water. When water is added to Portland cement, it forms the glue which holds the concrete mixture together.

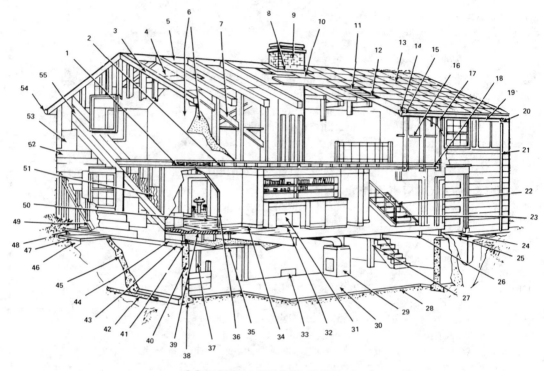

CONSTRUCTION DETAILS

1. CROSS BRIDGING
2. SECOND FLOOR JOISTS
3. ROOF RAFTERS
4. COLLAR BEAM
5. RIDGE BOARD
6. PLASTER BASE, LATH AND PLASTER WALLS
7. CROSS BRACING
8. FLASHING AND COUNTER FLASHING
9. BRICK CHIMNEY
10. TIGHT ROOF SHEATHING (ALL OTHER COVERINGS)
11. SPACED 1" x 4" SHEATHING (WOOD SHINGLES)
12. ROOFING FELT
13. FINISH ROOFING (SHINGLE)
14. SOFFIT OR CORNICE
15. FACIA OF CORNICE
16. FIRE STOPS
17. VERTICAL BOARD AND BATTEN SIDING
18. RIBBON PLATE
19. FACIA BOARD
20. LEADER HEAD OR CONDUCTOR HEAD
21. LEADER, DOWNSPOUT OR CONDUCTOR
22. STAIR STRINGER
23. MAIN STAIR TREADS AND RISERS
24. ENTRANCE DOOR SILL
25. CONCRETE STOOP
26. FIRST FLOOR JOISTS
27. BASEMENT POST
28. CINDERFILL
29. BOILER OR FURNACE
30. BASEMENT CONCRETE FLOOR
31. DAMPER CONTROL
32. ASH DUMP
33. CLEANOUT DOOR
34. BASEBOARDS
35. GIRDER
36. FRAME PARTITION
37. POST
38. FOOTING
39. SUB-FLOORING, DIAGONAL
40. FOUNDATION WALL
41. PLATE ANCHOR BOLT
42. DRAIN TILE
43. TERMITE SHIELD
44. SILL PLATE
45. GRAVEL FILL
46. GRADE LINE
47. BASEMENT AREAWAY
48. SOLE PLATE
49. CORNER BRACING
50. FINISH FLOOR
51. INSULATION, BATTS
52. WALL SIDING
53. WALL BUILDING PAPER
54. GUTTER
55. WALL SHEATHING, DIAGONAL

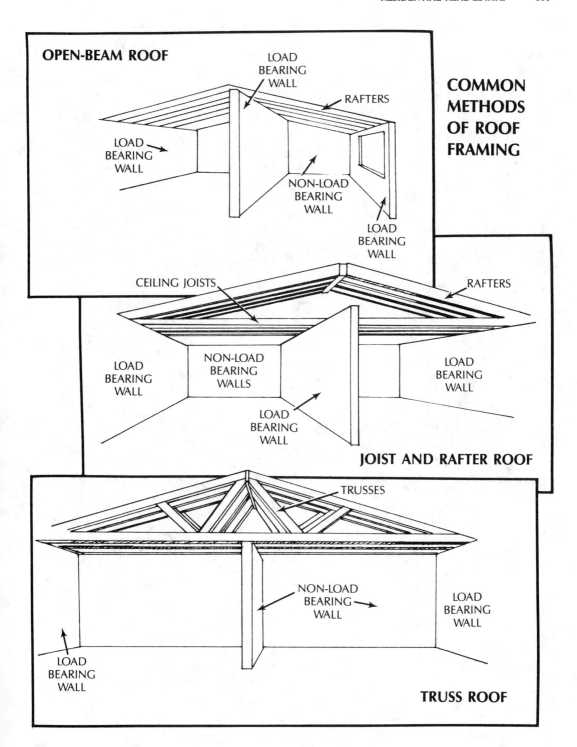

OPEN-BEAM ROOF

LOAD BEARING WALL

RAFTERS

LOAD BEARING WALL

NON-LOAD BEARING WALL

LOAD BEARING WALL

COMMON METHODS OF ROOF FRAMING

CEILING JOISTS

RAFTERS

LOAD BEARING WALL

NON-LOAD BEARING WALLS

LOAD BEARING WALL

LOAD BEARING WALL

JOIST AND RAFTER ROOF

TRUSSES

NON-LOAD BEARING WALL

LOAD BEARING WALL

LOAD BEARING WALL

TRUSS ROOF

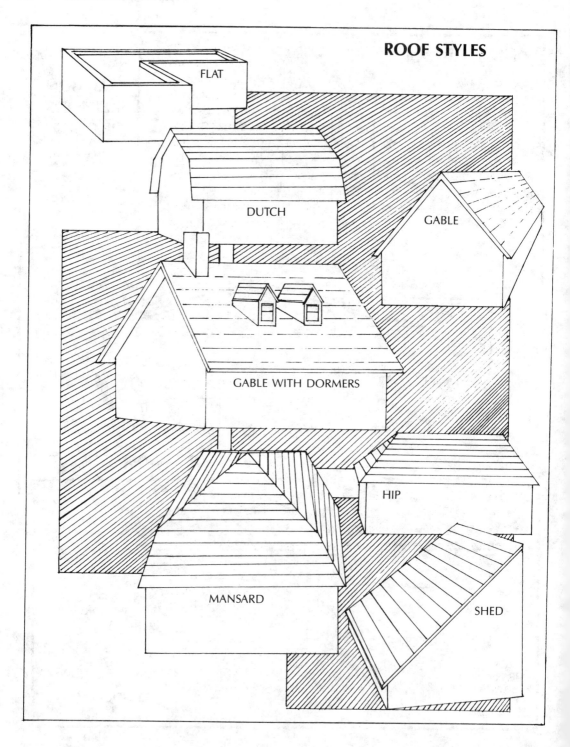

ROOF STYLES

FLAT

DUTCH

GABLE

GABLE WITH DORMERS

HIP

MANSARD

SHED

Framing — The framing is usually constructed of wooden boards and dimensional lumber, although the use of metal framing is becoming more common in some areas. The size and length of framing members may vary considerably, depending upon their particular application as girders, joists, studs, rafters, etc. Lumber is classified as either "green" or "dry," depending on its moisture content. Dry lumber is considered superior to green lumber for framing because it is less prone to warpage — the deformity in shape caused by uneven shrinking.

Exterior Sheathing and Siding — Exterior sheathing is the covering applied to the outside of the frame. It may be composed of strips of wood, approximately ¾ inch thick, which are locked together by means of a tongue-and-groove or overlapping edge. The most common form of exterior sheathing is **plywood** panels four feet wide by eight feet long, which serve an added function by providing shear strength to the walls. Shear strength is the capacity of a wall to resist sideways racking force, and is normally provided by corner bracing in the frame.

Exterior siding is the visible finish layer applied to the outside of the building. It may be plywood, boards, aluminum siding, shingles or other materials. The two most important characteristics of siding are its resistance to weathering and its aesthetic appeal.

Interior Sheathing — This is the covering applied to the inside of the frame, on the walls and ceilings. In the past, the most common form was lath and plaster, a cement-like mixture applied over a matrix of wood strips or mesh attached to the frame. Modern buildings use **drywall** construction for interior sheathing, so called because there is no need to add water to the material before application. Drywall products usually come in large sheets (like plywood) and are fastened to the frame with glue, nails or screws. Sheetrock and wallboard are two common drywall products. The joints between panels are hidden by covering them with a strip of tape imbedded in a plaster-like filler. This process is called "taping" the joints.

Roofing — The structural part of the roof is composed of plywood or boards laid perpendicular to the rafters. This sheathing is then covered with a tar-impregnated paper called **roofing felt**. The final layer of roofing may be wood shingles, tiles, composition roofing (tar-like shingles or rolls of material) or hot tar interspersed with more layers of felt (built-up roof).

Floor Covering — The strength of the floor is provided by tongue-and-groove floor boards or plywood, called sub-flooring, which are attached to the floor joists. This sub-flooring is then covered with finished flooring, which may be carpet, tile, linoleum, hardwood strips or other material.

Plumbing — Drain pipes are made of cast iron, concrete or plastic. Supply pipes are of galvanized steel, copper or plastic. Plumbing fixtures are either cast iron or pressed steel coated with enamel or fiberglass.

Electrical — Most modern wiring is in the form of **cable**, which is an insulated cord-like material containing two or more strands of copper or aluminum wire. The cable runs in circuits from a supply source (fuse box or breaker panel) to the various outlets for plugs or light fixtures. Fuse boxes have been supplanted in modern usage by **breaker panels**, which are a series of circuit breakers that automatically cut off the current in a circuit under overload conditions. Most outlets supply 110 volts of power, except for certain outlets designed for major appliances (ranges, water heaters, dryers, etc.) which supply 220 volts.

Heating, Ventilating and Air Conditioning (HVAC) — These systems are composed of heating and/or cooling appliances which serve warm, cool or fresh air to the rooms of a house through a series of galvanized sheet metal tubes called ducts. The ducts open at various places in the building, called registers, which may be closed off independently in order to direct the heat or air conditioning to areas where it is needed.

It is now common to supplement HVAC systems with insulation to reduce the cost of operating the appliances. Insulation may be in the form of batts, rolls or loose material which is resistant to the transfer of heat. It is inserted between wall studs and between the joists of floors and ceilings. Some types of insulation come in the form of sheets that are secured to the sheathing of the structure. The effectiveness of various insulating materials is called an **"R-value"**. Materials with higher "R-values" are more resistant to the transfer of heat.

TERMITE PROBLEMS. A major problem encountered with wood frame buildings is their susceptibility to damage by wood-eating insects, especially termites. Several techniques are used to minimize the possibility of termite damage:

- the ground under and around the buildings may be chemically treated with a poison that keeps termites away from the foundation;
- lumber that is in contact with the soil or the foundation, such as sills or beams, may also be treated with poison to prevent the termites from gaining access to the frame of the building; and
- metal shields may be inserted between the foundation and the superstructure to physically prevent termites from reaching the wood.

It is always a good idea, and required procedure in some instances, to have a licensed termite inspector examine a building being considered for purchase or sale. The termite inspector will provide a complete report of the structural soundness of the building, listing defects caused by moisture and fungus as well as by insects.

THE ARCHITECT

The architect is the construction industry professional with whom the real estate agent is most likely to come into contact. Most people think of an architect as a person who designs buildings, but a good architect will also provide a range of other services in the course of the construction process. Under a standard contract, an architect will first work with the owner to develop a design that fulfills the owner's needs. Next, the architect will prepare more detailed drawings, describing all the components of the building, along with an estimate of the probable cost of construction. When the design has been approved by the owner, the architect will draw up the official plans and specifications and will help the owner get bids from contractors and permits from government agencies. Finally, the architect acts as the owner's representative throughout the actual construction phase of the building, visiting the site to inspect the work, approving periodic payments to the contractor and interpreting the plans and specifications.

If the owner so desires, he or she may contract with the architect for the performance of additional services beyond the basic ones outlined above. These additional services may include financial feasibility studies, surveys, site evaluation, coordination of work by separate contractors, interior designing and alterations in the design.

SUMMARY

The real estate professional deals with buildings on a day-to-day basis. In order to effectively perform his or her job, a basic knowledge of construction industry processes and procedures is essential. The real estate professional must be familiar with the pertinent governmental and private regulations and with the more common architectural styles. He or she must also be conversant with the vernacular of construction industry professionals and be aware of the potential problems of buildings. Finally, the real estate professional must be able to recognize quality or a lack of quality in a building.

GLOSSARY OF CONSTRUCTION TERMS

Anchor Bolts — Bolts embedded in concrete, used to hold structural members in place.

Areaway — An open space around a basement window or doorway. Provides light, ventilation and access.

Beam — A principal structural member used between posts, columns or walls.

Bearing Wall/Partition — A wall/partition which supports a vertical load in addition to its own weight.

Board — Lumber that is less than two inches thick.

Bridging — Pieces fitted in pairs from the bottom of one floor joist to the top of adjacent joists, and crossed to distribute the floor load.

BTU — The British Thermal Unit, a measure of heating capacity.

Built-Up Roof — A roofing material composed of several layers of rag felt, saturated with pitch or asphalt.

Cased Opening — An interior opening without a door that is finished with jambs and trim.

Caulk — To seal and make waterproof cracks and joints.

Collar Beam — A tie beam connecting rafters at a point considerably above the wall plate.

Column — Upright supporting member, circular or rectangular in shape.

Conduit — A pipe or tube, usually metal, in which wiring is installed.

Corner Braces — Diagonal braces let into studs to reinforce corners of frame structures.

Counterflashing — Flashing used on chimneys at the roof line to cover shingle flashing and prevent moisture entry.

Crawl Space — A space between the ground and the first floor used for access.

Dimension Lumber — Lumber two to five inches thick and up to twelve inches wide.

Dormer — A projecting structure built out from a sloping roof.

Drywall — Materials used for wall covering which do not need to be mixed with water before application.

Eaves — The margin or lower part of a roof that projects over an exterior wall.

Fascia — A wooden member nailed to the ends of projecting rafters.

Fire Stop — A block or stop used in a wall between studs to prevent the spread of fire and smoke.

Flashing — Sheet metal or other material used in roof and wall construction to prevent rain or other water from entering.

Flue — The space in a chimney through which smoke, gas or fumes rise.

Footing — The spreading course or courses at the base of a foundation wall, pier or column.

Framing — The timber structure of a building which gives it shape and strength; includes the wall, floors, ceilings and roof.

Gable — That portion of a wall contained between the slopes of a roof.

Glazing — The process of installing glass into sashes and doors.

Gutter — Wooden or metal trough attached to the edge of a roof to collect and conduct water from rain and melting snow.

Header — Horizontal structural member that supports the load over an opening, such as a window or door.

Hip Roof — A roof which rises from all four sides of the building.

Interior Trim — General term for all the molding, casing, baseboard and other trim items applied inside the building.

Insulation — Any material high in resistance to heat transmission that is placed in structures to reduce the rate of heat flow.

Jamb — The top and two sides of a door or window frame which contact the door or sash.

Joist — One of a series of parallel framing members used to support floor and ceiling loads.

Lath — Material fastened to frame of building to act as a base for plaster.

Molding — Relatively narrow strip of wood used to conceal surface or angle joints, or as an ornamentation.

Partition — An interior wall that subdivides space within a building.

Party Wall — A wall used jointly by two parties under an easement agreement and erected at or upon a property line.

Pier — A column of masonry used to support other structural members.

Pilaster — A part of a wall that projects not more than one-half of its own width beyond the outside or inside face of a wall.

Pitch — Inclination or slope.

Plan — Drawing representing any one of the floors or cross sections of a building.

Plaster — A mixture of lime, cement and sand used to cover outside and inside wall surfaces.

Plate — Horizontal member of the wall frame to which the studs are attached.

Rafter — One of a series of structural members of a roof.

Reinforced Concrete — Concrete poured around steel bars or steel meshwork, in such a manner that the two materials act together to resist force.

Riser — The vertical stair member between two consecutive stair treads.

R-Value — A measure of resistance to heat transfer.

Sheathing — Structural covering; boards or prefabricated panels that are attached to the exterior studding or rafters.

Siding — The finish covering of the outside wall of a frame building.

Sill — The lowest member of the frame of a structure, usually horizontal, resting on the foundation. Also the lowest member of a window or exterior door frame.

Specification — Written document stipulating the quality of materials and workmanship required for a job.

Stud — One of a series of vertical wood or metal structural members in walls and partitions. In most modern frame buildings, the studs are set 16 inches apart.

Sub-Floor — Boards or panels laid directly on floor joists, over which a finished floor will be laid.

Timbers — Lumber five inches or larger in its least dimension.

Trim — The finish materials in a building: moldings, etc.

Trimmer — The stud into which a header is framed; adds strength to the side of the opening.

Truss — A structural unit, usually triangular in shape, which provides rigid support over wide spans.

Weephole — A small hole in the foundation wall to drain water to the outside.

BUY OR RENT?

Real estate agents are frequently placed in the position of discussing the relative advantages and disadvantages of renting versus buying a place to live. Some considerations are primarily emotional or subjective, such as security, pride of ownership, and freedom to have pets or to decorate or remodel according to personal preference. Considerations of this nature cannot be reduced to quantitative or other objective evaluation. Other elements of comparison are purely or largely financial and can be evaluated in a relatively objective manner.

ADVANTAGES OF RENTING

The advantages of renting may be briefly summarized:

- less financial commitment and risk,
- greater mobility, and
- fewer responsibilities.

INITIAL CASH REQUIREMENT. Compared to the funds necessary to buy a home, the initial cash outlay to rent is quite modest. In most cases, a security deposit and one or two months prepaid rent is sufficient. Even with a low downpayment purchase, the downpayment, loan fee and closing costs normally far exceed this amount.

MONTHLY PAYMENTS. At least for the first few years, the monthly rent is likely to be substantially less than a monthly mortgage payment. Over time, though, rents can be expected to rise (because of increasing property values and inflation) at a faster rate than the mortgage payment increases. If the mortgage is fixed-rate or if interest rates are stable, the mortgage payment is likely to increase at a relatively slow rate along with changes in property tax assessments (which are limited by California law) and homeowner's insurance premiums. It is quite possible that eventually the monthly rent would exceed the monthly mortgage payment.

ECONOMIC RISK. Renters have a small investment in the neighborhood where they live and, therefore, little economic risk. If the neighborhood and property values decline, they can simply give the required notice or wait until the end of the lease and move. On the other hand, if property values increase, the renter will receive no economic benefit from the more valuable property and rents are likely to go up as well.

MOBILITY. It is generally much easier, quicker and cheaper for a renter to move than a homeowner. The renter need only give the necessary notice or wait until the end of the lease to leave with little expense. Even if it is necessary or desirable to leave before the end of the lease or the required notice period, the forfeited deposit and/or prepaid rent is likely to be much less than the costs of selling a home and buying another one. Selling a home is often a lengthy and expensive process — taking at least a few months and costing approximately 10% of value.

MAINTENANCE AND REPAIRS. An owner must take responsibility for and pay for maintaining the property and making needed repairs. A renter, in effect, pays the cost of maintenance and repair through the rent, but has no direct responsibility for actually doing the maintenance and repairs. A renter does not face the risk of sudden and large expenditures for unexpected repairs.

AMENITIES. In many cases, renters are able to enjoy, included in their cost of shelter, the use of recreational facilities, such as swimming pools, tennis courts and other amenities that are beyond the financial abilities of most homeowners.

ADVANTAGES OF BUYING

For many people, buying instead of renting affords both subjective advantages of security and personal satisfaction and economic advantages of equity appreciation and tax deductions.

MONTHLY PAYMENTS. Mortgage payments are likely to increase slowly and slightly as the tax and insurance portions of the mortgage payment are increased. If the loan has an adjustable interest rate, payments will increase if interest rates rise. Rents are almost certain to increase more over time than will the monthly payments on fixed-rate mortgages.

INVESTMENT APPRECIATION. Although it is impossible to predict whether or how much a particular home will appreciate in value, over the last several decades home values have increased faster than the overall rate of inflation (on an average, 4% to 6% faster than the Consumer Price Index). An owner enjoys an increase in equity and net worth as the home appreciates in value. Increased equity may be used as collateral for home equity loans for home improvement or other purposes. For the renter, appreciation is likely to mean that the rents will be increased but that he or she will receive no direct advantage from increased value.

TAX ADVANTAGES. For the owner, federal income tax law allows deductions for property taxes and interest paid on a home loan. The interest on a personal residence loan is the only type of consumer interest which is still eligible for federal income tax deductions following the 1986 Tax Reform Act.

SECURITY. A homeowner enjoys a certain amount of security in knowing that he or she can continue to live in the home. A renter has no real security beyond the term of the lease. At the end of the term, or after being given appropriate notice in the case of a month-to-month rental, the tenant may be required to move and find another place to live.

PRIVACY AND FREEDOM FROM RESTRICTIONS. In most cases, an owner enjoys greater privacy than a renter and has greater freedom to use the property as desired. An owner can redecorate or remodel a home to suit his or her own personal taste, and can keep pets or engage in other activities prohibited by many rental agreements.

COMPARISON OF HOME PURCHASE VS. RENTING

Many real estate brokers have forms for comparing the net costs of renting and buying, taking into account increases in equity and tax deductions for interest payments. These forms, or worksheets, are intended to demonstrate to prospective buyers that the overall cost of buying a home may well be less than the cost of renting.

A simplified example of such a form is shown below. This worksheet has been filled in with data for a proposed purchase of a $100,000 home with the buyer to pay 10% down and obtain a $90,000 loan at a fixed annual interest rate of 11%. (These figures were chosen to keep the example simple; the $100,000 price is too low to be realistic in most of California today.) Closing costs bring the total cash requirement for purchase up to $13,000. Taxes, homeowners' insurance, the annual appreciation rate for local property values and the buyers' income tax bracket have all been estimated. The total estimated monthly payment, including principal and interest, property taxes, homeowners' insurance and the monthly renewal premium for private mortgage insurance (estimated at .35% of the outstanding loan balance per year) is approximately $1,041. The monthly cost of buying the home on those terms is compared with the cost of renting comparable housing at a monthly rental of $750.

At first impression, comparison of the monthly mortgage payment of $1,041 to the monthly rental of $750 would seem to give the advantage to renting, especially when taking into consideration the substantial initial cash investment required to purchase. However, analysis of the economic benefits from home ownership result in a lower net cost for home purchase, even taking into account the interest lost on the money spent for downpayment and closing costs.

To begin with, part of the monthly payment goes to amortize the loan. These payments to principal will likely be recovered when the home is sold. For a $90,000 loan with a 30-year term, the average monthly amortization would be $250 ($90,000 ÷ 360 months = $250). Of course, in the early years, a much smaller portion of each payment would go to principal and in the later years, a larger portion of the monthly payment would be principal amortization.

Next, some portions of the payment, the interest and the property taxes, are tax deductible. In this case, the average monthly interest is $607 (again, in the early years, a larger portion would go to interest and in the later years a smaller portion of the payment would be interest) and the average monthly payment for property taxes is $100, for a total of $707 in tax deductible items. If the buyer is in the 28% income tax bracket, that would represent a tax savings of about $198 per month ($707 × .28 = $197.96).

Finally, consideration must be given to the fact that the home is likely to appreciate in value and give the purchaser a return on his or her investment as well as a place to live. Even at the relatively modest rate of appreciation used in this example, 5% per year, the appreciation return is substantial. On $100,000, it would be $5,000 per year or about $417 per month.

After taking into account all the economic benefits of purchasing, the net effective cost of buying is only $151 per month.

COMPARISON OF ESTIMATED NET COST OF BUYING AND RENTING

BUYING

Purchase price	$100,000
Cash required (downpayment and closing)	$ 13,000
Loan amount $90,000 Term 30 years Interest rate	11 %
Estimated property taxes	$ 1,200
Estimated homeowners' insurance premium	$ 400
Estimated property appreciation rate	5 %
Estimated income tax bracket	28 %

Out-of-pocket costs:

Monthly payment:		
Principal and interest		$ 857
Property taxes		$ 100
Homeowner's insurance		$ 33
Other monthly expenses (PMI)		$ 26
Total monthly payment		$ 1,016
Less:		
Average monthly principal amortization		$ 250
Tax benefits:		
Interest portion of payment	$607	
Property tax portion of payment	$100	
Other		
Total deductible items	$707	
Monthly value of tax deduction		$ 198
Effective monthly cost of ownership		$ 568
Less: Average monthly appreciation		**$ 417**
MONTHLY NET COST OF BUYING		**$ 151**

RENTING

Out-of-pocket costs:

Monthly rent	$ 750
Less:	
Interest income from savings not invested in purchase ($13,000 @ 10%)	$ 108
MONTHLY NET COST OF RENTING	**$ 642**

The monthly rental is $750, with no federal income tax deductions and no benefit to the renter if the property appreciates in value. The renter would be able to obtain some interest or other investment yield on the $13,000 not used for downpayment and closing costs. In this example, a yield of 10% is used, giving the renter a monthly benefit of $108 and a net effective cost of renting of $642 per month.

It should be emphasized that this example is based on estimates and assumptions which may be subject to change. At higher or lower rates of interest, higher or lower property taxes, or changes in the tax law, the income tax benefits of buying could vary significantly. As previously mentioned, the average monthly principal and interest portions would be different for a buyer who intended to own the home for less than the full 30-year amortization term (say 5 years). Perhaps most importantly, higher or lower rates of value appreciation could have a great impact on the final net cost of home ownership. However, worksheets of this type serve a useful purpose in displaying the benefits of home purchase which can offset what may first appear to be the higher costs associated with buying.

CONDOMINIUM OWNERSHIP

Condominiums are often promoted as offering the benefits of both home ownership and apartment living: the tax deductions and equity appreciation of ownership coupled with the apartment renter's access to recreational facilities and freedom from maintenance responsibilities. There is, of course, some truth to these claims, but the freedom from maintenance comes at some expense, and condominium living is not for everyone.

ADVANTAGES OF CONDOMINIUM OWNERSHIP

Condominium owners enjoy many of the economic advantages of owning a single-family residence along with some of the conveniences of apartment living.

INVESTMENT APPRECIATION. A condominium owner receives the economic benefits of equity appreciation through payments to principal and through increases in the value of the unit. However, condominiums do not seem to have the same resale value as do single-family residences, so the appreciation may well be less.

TAX ADVANTAGES. Condominium owners are entitled to the same deductions for property taxes and mortgage interest as owners of detached dwellings.

SECURITY. As with single-family owners, condo owners have the security of a permanent place to live, and are not subject to termination at the end of the month or end of the lease at the landlord's whim.

FREEDOM FROM MAINTENANCE RESPONSIBILITIES. Condo owners, like apartment renters, usually have very limited exterior, yard or other maintenance responsibilities. These are generally limited to a deck, balcony, or small garden enclosure. However, even though the owner does not actually have to do the yard work, he or she has to pay for it through monthly maintenance fees paid to the owners' association.

AMENITIES. Many condominium developments have recreational facilities such as swimming pools, tennis courts and even golf courses available for the unit owners which often rival or even exceed those associated with the best apartment projects.

DISADVANTAGES OF CONDOMINIUM OWNERSHIP

As might be expected, if condo owners enjoy the advantages of both home ownership and apartment rental they must also endure some of the disadvantages of both. There are also some potential dangers that do not exist with either apartment rental or single-family ownership.

CASH INVESTMENT/MONTHLY MORTGAGE PAYMENTS. Initial investment for downpayment, loan fees, closing costs, and monthly mortgage payments are much closer to those of buying a single-family residence than for moving into an apartment.

INVESTMENT RISK. As with single-family ownership, if the neighborhood and values decline, the condo owner may suffer an economic loss.

MOBILITY. Again, as with the owner of a detached dwelling, the condo owner is faced with a lengthy and expensive process when, or if, it comes time to move.

MAINTENANCE AND REPAIRS. Although a condo owner is free from the obligation of actually performing the maintenance or repairs and, except in extraordinary circumstances, from sudden large expenses, he or she must pay for all maintenance and repairs through contributions to the owners' association. The monthly fees can be substantial in some cases and are, of course, subject to increase. Sometimes substantial increases may be imposed to cover increased labor or other maintenance costs or to cover unexpected expenses, such as painting or roofing. The monthly association fee is not voluntary; in most states (including California) failure to pay the dues can result in a lien against the unit and even foreclosure.

PRIVACY AND FREEDOM FROM RESTRICTIONS. Although condo owners probably enjoy more privacy and freedom from restrictions in the use of their units than do many apartment dwellers, their situation is much closer to that of apartment living than living in detached homes. Most condominium developments have bylaws that, among other things, may place restrictions on pets, how long guests may stay, and whether the owner has the right to rent the unit. Normally, condominium bylaws are closer to the restrictions found in apartment leases than to a single-family owner's general freedom to do anything that is not unlawful.

LEASED RECREATIONAL FACILITIES AND MANAGEMENT CONTRACTS. Two issues not faced by either apartment renters or single-family owners are potential problems associated with leased recreational facilities, parking spaces or other common areas and with long-term management agreements executed by the developer. Although certainly not frequent, there have been a number of cases where developers have retained ownership of recreational facilities and/or parking areas and leased them to the condominium, initially at reasonable rates and shortly thereafter at extremely high and unreasonable rates. In a similar fashion, some developers have entered long-term management contracts with management companies (often companies with some prior connection with the developer) at high fees. If title to the recreational facilities, parking and other similar areas does not pass to the condominium owners, a purchaser should inquire into the nature of the lease to ensure that there is no danger of steeply increasing rentals. Similarly, with management contracts, it is best if the owners' association has the power to terminate such contracts and negotiate the fees to be paid, possibly after a short initial period (such as the first year).

MOBILE HOME OWNERSHIP

Mobile homes have been the fastest-growing segment of the housing industry for a number of years. This growth has been, to some extent at least, a response to the demand for lower-priced homes. In recent years, increasing land values and construction costs, building codes and other government controls, and inflation have caused the cost of conventional on-site constructed homes to escalate dramatically. Mobile homes provide a relatively low-cost alternative for buyers, especially first-time buyers who cannot afford conventional housing.

As mobile homes have taken over a greater share of the lower-priced housing market, they have become more and more like conventional homes. A couple of decades ago, most mobile homes were single-wide homes, 10 to 12 feet wide, some as narrow as 8 feet. Most homes constructed within the last few years are at least 12 to 14 feet wide, and a large percentage of new mobile homes are double- or even triple-wide models. Although still often called mobile homes, these models are seldom really "mobile." In most cases they are not moved after being placed on site.

ADVANTAGES AND DISADVANTAGES

As with other forms of housing, mobile homes have some advantages and some disadvantages.

COST. Probably the single greatest advantage to mobile home ownership is the relatively low acquisition cost. Mobile homes offer what amounts to a complete home package, including appliances and often drapes and some other furnishings, at a much lower cost than on-site construction.

FINANCING. Availability of financing for mobile homes is generally comparable to that for conventional homes. There are FHA, VA and Cal-Vet programs for mobile home purchase. However, interest rates are frequently somewhat higher for mobile home loans.

SECURITY AND CONVENIENCE. Many mobile home parks have limited access, giving a feeling of security to the occupants. Often there are restrictions on motorcycles and other noisy equipment or activities, making mobile home parks relatively quiet places to live. In mobile home parks, the mobile home owners usually have little or no responsibility for yard work or other maintenance and upkeep aside from their own mobile homes.

DEPRECIATION IN VALUE. Conventionally constructed homes generally increase in value but the same is not true of mobile homes. Mobile homes usually decrease in value relatively rapidly. Therefore they have a much lower resale value and less equity to serve as collateral for later loans than do conventional homes.

MOBILITY. Although most newer mobile homes can hardly be considered easily movable, they can be transported if necessary. Moving a large mobile home is inconvenient and costly, but it is often less expensive than selling a conventional home and buying another one. Another factor to consider in evaluating mobility is that in many areas, there is a shortage of mobile home parks or space in existing parks. As many communities prohibit placing mobile homes anywhere other than in established mobile home parks, it may be difficult to find a spot to relocate a mobile home.

FACTORS TO CONSIDER WHEN CHOOSING A HOME

NEIGHBORHOOD CONSIDERATIONS

Since the surrounding neighborhood greatly influences the overall desirability of a home and also has a great impact on value, careful consideration should be given to neighborhood characteristics.

PERCENTAGE OF HOME OWNERSHIP. Are most of the homes owner-occupied, or is there a large percentage of rental properties? Neighborhoods that are predominantly owner-occupied are generally better maintained, less susceptible to loss in value and more likely to appreciate in value.

CONFORMITY. Values are protected if there is a reasonable degree of homogeneity in the neighborhood. This includes styles, ages, prices, sizes and quality of structures. Strictly enforced zoning ordinances and land use restrictions do much to promote conformity.

CHANGING LAND USE. Does the neighborhood land use appear stable, or are there indications of a transition from residential to some other form of land use?

STREET PATTERN. Do the neighborhood streets have good access to traffic arteries? If a property does not front on a publicly dedicated and maintained street, the buyer should ask whether there is an enforceable road maintenance agreement signed by the property owners.

AVAILABILITY OF UTILITIES. Is the home and neighborhood adequately serviced by water, electricity, gas, sewers, telephones and any other necessary or desirable services, such as television cable?

PRESTIGE. Is there a prestige factor which makes the neighborhood more desirable than another?

PROXIMITY TO EMPLOYMENT AND SHOPPING. How far is the neighborhood from important points, such as downtown, industrial (employment) regions and major shopping centers? How far is it to the nearest shopping center?

SCHOOL DISTRICT. In what primary and secondary school districts is the neighborhood located? How far away are the schools? Are they within walking distance? The quality of the local schools or school district can make a major difference in value and can be an extremely important basis of decision for many buyers with school-age children.

PUBLIC SERVICES. Is the neighborhood adequately served by public transportation, police and fire protection?

PROPERTY TAXES AND OTHER GOVERNMENT INFLUENCES. How do property taxes and special assessments compare with the levels in similar neighborhoods nearby? How is the neighborhood and surrounding area zoned? Does the zoning promote residential use and insulate the homeowner from nuisances, such as unpleasant sights, sounds and odors from industrial use areas?

SOCIAL SERVICES. Are there places of worship, hospitals or other health care facilities, and other social services nearby?

OVERALL NEIGHBORHOOD VALUES. Does it appear that the overall condition and values in the neighborhood are stable, increasing or decreasing?

THE HOME

A prospective buyer should evaluate the size, condition, amenities and other features of the lot and improvements.

SITE/VIEW. What is the size and shape of the lot? Rectangular lots are usually more desirable than odd or irregularly shaped parcels. Is the lot on the corner or in the middle of the block? Is it level, gently sloping or steep? Unusually steep lots may present a danger of soil slippage and instability. Does it appear that water runoff and drainage are good? What is the quality and extent of landscaping? In a new home, has any landscaping, such as the lawn, shrubbery and trees, already been done, or will the buyer have to put it all in? The cost of new landscaping can be quite a bit more than many first-time homebuyers realize.

Is there a view? In many areas, a view can increase value substantially and add greatly to the property's appeal and resale value.

STREET AND SIDEWALK. What is the condition of the driveway, street and sidewalks? Are there street lights and fire hydrants on the block? Are there telephone and power line poles or is there underground wiring? Are there any easements across the property which might interfere with or diminish the buyer's use and enjoyment of the property?

SEWER/SEPTIC. If the property is served by sanitary and/or storm sewers, have they already been paid for or is there a special assessment against the property? If the property is served by a septic tank and drain field, when was the last time it was cleaned and/or inspected? Has the system always functioned properly?

EXTERIOR APPEARANCE. How old is the roof and when was the house last painted? Is the present owner aware of any leaks? What is the apparent condition of the roof and flashing, gutters, downspouts, paint, siding, windows, doors and weather stripping? Thin or curled shingles, cracked, blistered or peeling paint, rusted or sagging gutters and downspouts can all be indications that costly maintenance and repairs may soon be needed. Does the foundation appear to be in good order, or are there cracks and/or other evidence of settling? If there is no basement, are there adequate vents and crawl space?

OVERALL INTERIOR LAYOUT. Is the floor plan convenient and efficient? Is it necessary to pass through the living room to reach other rooms, or through one of the bedrooms to reach another?

Does the home have bedrooms, closets and bathrooms in sufficient number and size for the family's needs? Is there a separate dining room or is the dining area part of the kitchen or living room? Is there a separate family room, children's playroom or other recreational area if needed by the family? Is there sufficient "work" space: kitchen, laundry room, and storage space for house cleaning and gardening equipment and tools?

What is the condition of the paint and/or wall paper?

Are there enough windows and natural light, especially in the kitchen and other work or recreational spaces?

LIVING ROOM/FAMILY ROOM. How large is the living room and family or recreation room, if any? Is the shape of the room and available wall space adequate for the furniture that will be placed in it?

DINING ROOM OR DINING AREA. Is the dining area convenient to the kitchen and large enough in relation to the size of the home and for the number of people who will be eating there?

KITCHEN. Is the kitchen convenient to an outside entrance and to the garage or carport? Is there adequate counter and cabinet space? What is the quality and condition of the kitchen cabinets? What is the type, quality and condition of the kitchen floor? Are any of the appliances to be included in the sale? If so, are they large enough, of good quality and in good repair?

BEDROOMS. Is the number of bedrooms and their size, especially the master bedroom, adequate for the family? Are the closets large enough? It is better for the bedrooms to be located apart from the family/living rooms, kitchen and other work or recreational spaces.

BATHROOMS. There should be at least two bathrooms if the home has more than two bedrooms. In many areas, particularly in newer homes, it is normal for there to be a bathroom with the master bedroom. What is type and condition of tile or other wall and floor coverings? Are there windows or ceiling fans to provide adequate ventilation?

PLUMBING AND ELECTRICAL SYSTEMS. If it is not a new home, what is the age of the plumbing and electrical systems? Is the plumbing copper, galvanized, plastic, or some combination of materials? Is the water pressure adequate? Do the electrical service panel and existing outlets indicate there is sufficient electrical service to the home? Do the electrical and plumbing systems, or as much of them as can be seen, appear to be in good condition? Is the present owner aware of any problems, inadequacies or defects?

HEATING, VENTILATING, AIR CONDITIONING. What type of heating system does the home have: electric, gas or oil, forced air, floor furnace, baseboard heaters? What is the type and size of the water heater? If there is air conditioning, is it a central system or window units? If it is not a new home, what is the age and apparent condition of the heating, hot water, and air conditioning systems? Is the present owner aware of any problems, inadequacies or defects?

GARAGE/CARPORT. Generally a garage is better than a carport. What is the size (single, double, triple)? Is there work or storage space in addition to automobile parking space? Is there an entrance, protected from the weather, directly from the garage or carport into the home?

ATTIC/BASEMENT. Is there a basement or attic? If so, what type of access is there from the rest of the home? Is there room for storage or work space? Would it be possible to convert all or part of it to additional bedrooms or bathrooms?

ENERGY EFFICIENT FEATURES. Escalating energy costs have resulted in an increased demand for and value in energy efficient homes. Examples of energy efficient features include clock-controlled thermostats, insulation-wrapped water heaters, insulated ducts and pipes in unheated areas, adequate insulation for floors, walls, and attic, and weather stripping for doors and windows. In some areas, solar water and space heating apparatus and design elements are popular.

CHAPTER SUMMARY

1. To accurately assess the value of a home, a real estate agent needs to be able to judge the quality of the construction. Building codes and lenders' minimum property requirements (MPRs) provide basic standards to use in an evaluation. It is important to be familiar with common construction techniques and materials, and to have some understanding of the technical systems (plumbing, wiring, heating and cooling). Knowing how to read plans and specifications can be very useful, especially when dealing with new construction.

2. A broker or salesperson is often asked to compare buying a home to renting one. The advantages of renting include less financial commitment and risk, fewer maintenance responsibilities, greater mobility, and facilities a homeowner often could not afford. The

advantages of buying include security, satisfaction in ownership, privacy, and freedom from restrictions. Although a mortgage payment is typically much larger than a rental payment, property appreciation, equity, and tax deductions make buying far less expensive than renting in the long run. Condominiums and mobile homes each have their own advantages and disadvantages for the buyer.

3. In addition to judging construction quality, a salesperson helping a customer choose a home should evaluate the neighborhood, the site, and the exterior and interior design. These affect not only the current value and resale value of the home, but what it will be like to live there.

CHAPTER 16—QUIZ
RESIDENTIAL REAL ESTATE

1. A house with many horizontal projections and vertical lines, with large areas of glass, is classified as which of the following types of architecture?

   a) Contemporary
   b) Monterey
   c) Colonial
   d) Cape Cod

2. A roof that slopes upwards from all four sides and joins is called a:

   a) gambrel roof
   b) gable roof
   c) hip roof
   d) former roof

3. In building construction, fixed standards of construction quality would be assured through:

   a) the planning commission
   b) zoning ordinances
   c) building codes
   d) None of these

4. A wall erected on the line between two adjoining properties belonging to different persons which serves as an outside wall of both buildings is a:

   a) party wall
   b) community wall
   c) line wall
   d) share wall

5. Beams which run parallel and serve the purpose of supporting floors and ceilings are called:

   a) joists
   b) collar beams
   c) stringers
   d) studs

6. In a house, a load-bearing wall:

   a) determines which way the house will face
   b) is at right angles with the door
   c) has no doors in it
   d) must be recognized when remodeling is done

7. Footing refers to what part of a newly constructed house?

   a) The timbers that support floor boards or heavy plywood with the conventional foundation
   b) Heavy masonry courses put in the ground upon which the masonry foundation rests
   c) Black top over a concrete slab
   d) The spaces between the joists (subfloor)

8. Which of the following is not drywall construction?

   a) Wallboard
   b) Plywood
   c) Plaster
   d) Sheetrock

9. Studs are attached to and rest upon a:

   a) mud sill
   b) plate
   c) subflooring
   d) sill

10. An ordinary household electrical outlet supplies:

    a) 100 watts of power
    b) 200 watts of power
    c) 110 volts of power
    d) 220 volts of power

11. BTU is a term used in reference to:

    a) a type of loan
    b) zoning classifications
    c) a government agency
    d) heating systems

p. 366

12. What is the standard spacing between the studs in a frame building?

    a) 12"
    b) 14"
    c) 16"
    d) 18"

13. In construction, the term "pier" refers to:

    a) a block of masonry that supports the building
    b) a horizontal projection of the roof line
    c) the area where the water heater is located
    d) one of the main support beams of the floor

14. The lowest part of a building is called the:

    a) sub-floor
    b) sill
    c) footing
    d) plate

15. A heavy piece of lumber used to span the opening across the top of a door or window is called a:

    a) sill
    b) stud
    c) plate
    d) header

16. Which of the following homes is least likely to appreciate in value?

    a) A two-story Cape Cod house
    b) A unit in a Spanish style condominium
    c) A double-wide mobile home
    d) A California ranch style house

17. Which of the following is an advantage of renting as opposed to owning a home?

    a) Security and stability
    b) Appreciation
    c) Federal tax deduction
    d) Mobility

18. When comparing a mortgage payment to a rental payment, all of the following should be taken into account EXCEPT:

    a) the landlord's equity in the rental property
    b) appreciation of the rental property
    c) the federal tax deduction for mortgage interest
    d) whether the mortgage interest rate is fixed or adjustable

19. All of these will go up eventually; which of them will probably increase most slowly?

    a) A rental payment
    b) A fixed-rate mortgage payment
    c) An adjustable-rate mortgage payment
    d) A convertible ARM payment

20. Over the last several decades, home values have:

    a) risen 4% faster than rents
    b) increased at the same rate as inflation
    c) appreciated 4% to 6% faster than inflation
    d) appreciated 8% to 10% faster than inflation

21. Which of the following is likely to be less of an advantage for condominium unit owners than it is for single-family home owners?

    a) Mortgage interest tax deduction
    b) Use of recreational facilities
    c) Property appreciation
    d) Security and stability

22. Phillip Nore has decided to buy a mobile home. When he looks into financing, he learns:

    a) FHA, VA and Cal-Vet programs do not cover mobile home loans
    b) there is an FHA program for mobile homes, but VA and Cal-Vet programs don't cover them
    c) interest rates are likely to be lower on mobile home loans than on loans for conventional housing
    d) interest rates are likely to be higher on mobile home loans than on loans for conventional housing

23. The value of a single-family home is enhanced if:

   a) there are rental properties as well as owner-occupied houses in the neighborhood
   b) there are retail businesses as well as houses on the block
   c) strict zoning laws have made the lots and houses in the neighborhood similar to one another
   d) All of the above

24. These lots all contain the same area. Which would generally be considered the most desirable?

   a) A rectangular lot with a gentle slope
   b) A triangular lot with a steep slope
   c) A triangular lot with a gentle slope
   d) A level T-shaped lot

25. Which of the following is considered a drawback in an interior floor plan?

   a) A door leads directly from the kitchen to the garage
   b) The front door leads directly into the living room
   c) The separate dining room is right next to the kitchen
   d) The bedrooms are isolated from the kitchen and family room

1. a) The house described is very modern in design.

2. c) This is the definition of a hip roof.

3. c) Building codes are locally adopted ordinances that set standards for construction quality.

4. a) This is the definition of party wall.

5. a) This is the definition of joists.

6. d) A load-bearing wall carries part of the weight of the structure and should not be removed during remodeling without provision for some other method of support.

7. b) Footing is a flange-like part at the base of a foundation wall which ties or locks the foundation into the ground, thus preventing shifting and settling.

8. c) Drywall construction of interior walls is where the finish material is something other than plaster.

9. b) A plate, sole or sole plate is a member, usually a two by four, on which wall and partition studs rest.

10. c) A standard outlet supplies 110 volts; outlets designed for major appliances supply 220 volts.

11. d) BTU stands for the British Thermal Unit, a measure of heating capacity.

12. c) In most modern frame buildings, the studs are set 16" apart.

13. a) A pier is an unattached piece of masonry that supports a post or beam.

14. c) The footing is the masonry base on which the rest of the building sits.

15. d) A header is the term for the structural member that spans door and window openings.

16. c) Mobile homes tend to depreciate rather than appreciate. Condominiums usually don't appreciate as quickly as single-family homes, but they do appreciate.

17. d) It is much easier and less expensive to move out of a rental than to sell a home and buy a new one. All the other answers are advantages of owning, not of renting.

18. a) The landlord's equity in the rental property is not likely to have much effect on the rental payment. (The HOMEOWNER'S increasing equity should be taken into account when evaluating the real cost of the mortgage payments.)

19. b) A fixed-rate mortgage payment will increase only very gradually, as property taxes and mortgage insurance premiums go up.

20. c) For several decades, home values have increased 4% to 6% faster than the Consumer Price Index, which is a measure of the overall inflation rate.

21. c) In general, condominium units do not seem to appreciate as much as single-family homes.

22. d) Interest rates on mobile home loans tend to be higher than the rates on loans for conventional housing. FHA, VA and Cal-Vet all have mobile home programs.

23. c) While few people would like all the houses on their street to be identical, a reasonable degree of conformity is considered desirable and enhances the value of the homes.

24. a) Rectangular lots are preferred to odd-shaped lots because more of the area can be used successfully. Steeply sloping lots are often difficult to build on and unstable, so level land or a gentle slope is preferable.

25. b) It is a disadvantage to have the front door open directly into the living room (rather than into an entry hall), since that makes it necessary to pass through the living room to get to the rest of the house. All of the other design features listed are considered advantages.

Chapter 17

CALIFORNIA REAL ESTATE LICENSE LAW

OUTLINE

I. Administration
  A. The Real Estate Commissioner
  B. The Real Estate Advisory Commission
  C. The Attorney General
II. Real Estate Licenses
  A. When license required
  B. When license not required
  C. Special licenses
  D. Qualifications for license
  E. License term
  F. License renewal
  G. License fees
  H. Continuing education requirements
III. Disciplinary Action
  A. License revocation procedure
  B. Grounds for suspension, revocation or denial of a
    license
IV. Trust Funds
  A. Definition
  B. Handling of funds
  C. Trust fund bank account
  D. Records to be maintained
V. Miscellaneous Provisions Affecting Real Estate Licensees
  A. Commissions
  B. Retention of records
  C. The Real Estate Fund

KEY TERMS

Real Estate Law
Real Estate Commissioner
State Attorney General
mineral, oil and gas
    license
trust funds
commingling
Real Estate Fund
Real Estate Recovery Account

Department of Real Estate
Real Estate Advisory
    Commission
continuing education
    requirement
trust fund account
commission
Real Estate Education
    and Research Account

CHAPTER OVERVIEW

Real Estate Law: law
governing real estate
licensing and the conduct
of real estate licensees

In California, real estate licensing is governed by what is known as
the **Real Estate Law**. The main purpose of this law is to protect the
public in real estate transactions where the services of an agent are
employed. The Real Estate Law determines who is required to have a
real estate license and sets forth the licensing requirements. Anyone who
is involved in the real estate business should be familiar with these
requirements.

ADMINISTRATION

Department of Real
Estate: implements the
Real Estate Law

The Real Estate Law is administered by the **Department of Real
Estate** of the Business and Transportation Agency, and is enforced by
the **Real Estate Commissioner**.

THE REAL ESTATE COMMISSIONER

Real Estate
Commissioner: heads the
Department of Real
Estate; responsible for
enforcing the Real Estate
Law

The California Real Estate Commissioner, the chief officer of the
Department of Real Estate, is appointed by the Governor. His or her principal responsibility is to enforce the provisions of the Real Estate Law
so as to provide the maximum protection to those who deal with real
estate licensees.

The Commissioner has the authority to investigate complaints against
licensees; regulate some aspects of the sale of subdivisions, nonexempt
franchises and real property securities; screen and qualify applicants for
a license; and investigate those alleged to be acting as real estate licensees
without a license. The Commissioner can adopt, amend or repeal rules

and regulations (which have the force of law) necessary for the enforcement of the Real Estate Law.

The Commissioner also has the power to hold formal hearings to decide issues involving a licensee, license applicant or subdivider and may, after such a hearing, suspend, revoke, or deny a license, or order a halt of sales in a subdivision. The Commissioner can bring actions for injunctions and claims for restitution on behalf of persons injured by licensees violating the Real Estate Law. He or she can also bring actions to prevent trust fund violations.

To be a Commissioner, a person must have been a real estate broker actively engaged in business for five years in California, or must have related experience associated with real estate activity in California for five of the previous ten years.

THE REAL ESTATE ADVISORY COMMISSION

The Real Estate Advisory Commission is appointed by the Commissioner. It has ten members: six real estate brokers and four members of the public. They serve without compensation at the pleasure of the Commissioner.

Real Estate Advisory Commission: advises the Commissioner regarding the functions and policies of the Department of Real Estate

The Commission meets with the Commissioner and makes policy recommendations regarding the functions and policies of the Department.

Commission meetings must be called at least four times a year by the Commissioner. Notice of the time and place of each meeting must be given at least ten days before a meeting to members and to any other person who has requested notice.

THE STATE ATTORNEY GENERAL

The **State Attorney General** is the legal advisor to the Commissioner and renders legal opinions relating to the Real Estate Law. However, it is the duty of the district attorney of each county to prosecute violations of the Real Estate Law occurring within that county.

State Attorney General: the legal advisor to the Commissioner

REAL ESTATE LICENSES

WHEN LICENSE REQUIRED

California law requires a license for all persons who are (1) engaged in the business of, (2) acting in the capacity of, (3) advertising as, or (4) assuming to act as brokers or salespersons.

BROKER. A broker is a person who does (or negotiates to do) certain acts on behalf of a client or clients for compensation (or in expectation of compensation). These acts include:

1) selling, buying, leasing, collecting rents from, and buying/selling/exchanging of leases on, real property or business opportunities (**Exception:** resident apartment manager who manages an apartment complex in which he/she lives);
2) filing applications for purchase or lease of federal land;
3) soliciting borrowers or lenders, negotiating loans, performing services in connection with loans, or buying/selling/exchanging obligations secured by real property;
4) listing, advertising or offering real property (or business opportunities) for sale/lease/exchange or financing;
5) engaging as a principal in the business of buying, selling or exchanging eight or more real property securities (sales contracts, promissory notes) within one year; and
6) collecting an advance fee to promote the sale/lease of real property or a business opportunity by advertising, listing it with a broker's association or otherwise.

SALESPERSON. A salesperson is someone who is employed by a broker to do one or more of the acts that a broker does.

WHEN LICENSE NOT REQUIRED

The following people do not require real estate licenses:

1) a person acting on his or her own behalf with respect to his or her property;
2) a person acting under a duly recorded power of attorney from the owner of the property;
3) attorneys in the performance of their duties;
4) persons acting under court order (e.g., receiver in bankruptcy, trustee, etc.);
5) a trustee under a deed of trust;
6) an appraiser making an appraisal;
7) with respect to real property securities transactions:
   a) employees of banks, savings and loan associations, insurance companies or credit unions; and
   b) licensed personal property brokers (e.g., finance companies);
8) with respect to business opportunity transactions, a licensed securities broker or dealer;
9) persons performing clerical functions and not discussing price, terms or conditions of the property.

REAL PROPERTY SECURITIES DEALER. A real property securities dealer is a person engaged in the business of selling or reinvesting funds in real property securities. A real property securities dealer must have a broker's license and also obtain an endorsement from the Commissioner. The endorsement costs $100 and is valid for the term of the license.

CORPORATION LICENSE. A corporation may designate one or more of its officers to act as brokers under a corporation license. Each officer must be individually licensed as a corporate broker, and may only act as a broker with respect to corporate brokerage business.

PARTNERSHIPS. There is no such thing as a partnership license, but a partnership may perform acts for which a broker's license is required, provided every partner through whom the partnership so acts is a licensed real estate broker.

MINERAL, OIL AND GAS LICENSE. Licensees who deal in minerals, oil and gas are required to have either a special mineral, oil and gas license, or a permit for an individual mineral, oil or gas transaction. A real estate licensee may obtain only one permit per year, allowing the licensee to participate in a maximum of ten individual transactions involving minerals, oil and gas. No special license is required for incidental sale of minerals, oil and gas along with the sale of land.

QUALIFICATIONS FOR LICENSE

BROKER QUALIFICATIONS. In order to obtain a broker's license, a person must:

1) have **two years' experience** in real estate or the equivalent
2) be at least **eighteen years old**
3) pay the license **fee**
4) be **fingerprinted**
5) meet the **education requirements**: complete **24 semester units** (eight courses) including the following five courses—real estate practice, appraisal, economics or accounting, legal aspects of real estate, and financing; the remaining three courses may be chosen from office administration, advanced legal aspects of real estate, advanced appraisal, advanced financing, real estate principles, property management, escrow, and business law
6) pass the **broker's examination**

SALESPERSON QUALIFICATIONS. In order to obtain a salesperson's license, an applicant must:

1) be at least **eighteen years of age**
2) pay the license **fee**

3) be **fingerprinted**
4) pass the **salesperson's examination**
5) meet the **education requirements:**
   a) **Nine semester units**
   b) One course, real estate principles, must be taken prior to taking the examination
   c) **Two** more courses must be completed either before issuance of the original license or within 18 months of licensure (these courses must be chosen from the following: real estate practice, appraisal, accounting, legal aspects of real estate, real estate financing, real estate economics, property management, real estate office management, escrow, and business law)
   d) If the education is not completed within 18 months, the license is suspended
   e) If all three courses are taken prior to licensure, the license fee is $120; if not, the license fee is $145
   f) Salespersons who complete the education will be able to renew their licenses the first time by completing only a three clock-hour ethics course and a three clock-hour agency course, instead of the 45 hours normally required every four years for renewal.

LICENSE TERM

An applicant who meets the requirements for a license is scheduled for the qualifying examination. Those who pass the examination apply for a license. Application for a license must be made within **one year** of passing the exam. Licenses may be renewed every four years. Brokers' and salespersons' licenses are initially issued for a four-year period.

LICENSE RENEWAL

PROCEDURE. An original four-year license may be renewed upon application to the Department of Real Estate and payment of appropriate fees, assuming continuing education requirements, discussed below, have been met. The licensee does not have to be reexamined. A renewal application must be postmarked prior to midnight of the expiration date of the current license to avoid a lapse of the license and payment of a late renewal fee. However, the application may not be filed earlier than 60 days preceding the expiration date.

DELINQUENT LICENSE RENEWAL. A license which expired within the previous two years and was not suspended or revoked may be renewed without examination, at the Commissioner's discretion, upon payment of a late renewal fee. The licensee must file an application for renewal at least 30 days prior to expiration of the two-year grace period. Two years after a license expires, all license rights are lost and in order to be licensed again, a person must meet the licensing requirements for original license applicants.

CONTINUING EDUCATION REQUIREMENT

No real estate license can be renewed unless the applicant has fulfilled his or her continuing education requirement. An applicant for license renewal must attend 45 clock hours of approved offerings within the four-year period preceding license renewal. A special form evidencing attendance must accompany the renewal application.

> **Note:** Salespersons who have completed the nine semester unit licensure requirement within the specified time limit may apply for their first renewal after completing only a three-hour ethics course and a three-hour agency course, rather than the normal 45-hour requirement.

MISCELLANEOUS LICENSE PROVISIONS

LOCATION OF LICENSES. Real estate licenses are to remain in the broker's main office. A broker working as a salesperson is to keep the license where he or she works.

CHANGE OF NAME OR ADDRESS. When a broker changes his or her office address or name, the broker must forward written notice to the Department within one business day. When the license change occurs, the certificate can be corrected by the licensee. To cancel or add a branch office, the broker must file a special form.

CHANGE OF STATUS. A broker who wishes to change his or her status and work as a salesperson may relinquish his or her license and apply for a salesperson's license, which will be issued without examination.

POSSESSION OF SALESPERSON'S LICENSE. Brokers are required to maintain possession of the licenses of salespersons employed by them.

TRANSFER OF SALESPERSON'S LICENSE. If a salesperson is transferring employment, both the former broker/employer and the new broker/employer must notify the Commissioner in writing.

CANCELLATION OF LICENSE. The death of a broker or the suspension or revocation of his or her license cancels all of his or her salespersons' licenses. The license of a salesperson who quits or is discharged is canceled, and the broker must notify the Commissioner. If a salesperson is discharged for conduct constituting grounds for disciplinary action under the Real Estate Law, the employer/broker must file a certified written statement of facts in regard to the discharge with the Commissioner.

If the employer/broker fails to file a certified written statement when required, the broker's license may be temporarily suspended or permanently revoked.

DISCIPLINARY ACTION

As previously mentioned, the Commissioner may, upon his or her own motion or upon receipt of a verified written complaint, investigate the actions of licensees. If, after the investigation, it appears that a violation of the law has occurred, a formal hearing will be held. In most circumstances, a formal hearing must be held before the Commissioner proceeds to deny, suspend or revoke any license.

LICENSE REVOCATION PROCEDURE

A formal hearing is initiated by filing an accusation (a written statement of charges) against the accused licensee (the respondent). The respondent is informed of his or her rights.

The accusation must be filed within three years of the occurrence of the alleged grounds for disciplinary action unless the act involved fraud, misrepresentation or a false promise. In this case, an action may be brought one year after discovery by the aggrieved party or three years from the occurrence, whichever is later, but in no case more than ten years from the occurrence.

The respondent may appear in the hearing with or without counsel. Testimony is taken under oath. A hearing officer hears the case and makes a proposed decision based on his or her findings. The Department or the Commissioner may accept or reject the proposed decision or reduce the proposed penalty, and will then make a formal decision. If the charges against the respondent are proven at the hearing, his or her license is suspended or revoked and he or she may not apply for reinstatement for one year. The respondent has the right to appeal the formal decision to superior court.

If a person obtained a license through fraud, misrepresentation, deceit or material misstatements of fact in the license application, the license can be suspended without a hearing. This power of the Commissioner expires ninety days after a license is issued. The suspension is only effective until the Commissioner makes a decision within thirty days after a formal hearing.

GROUNDS FOR SUSPENSION, REVOCATION OR DENIAL OF A LICENSE

The basic grounds for suspension, revocation or denial of a real estate license are as follows:

1) Misrepresentation—deliberately or negligently making a false statement of fact or failing to disclose a material fact to a principal.
2) False promise—making a false statement relating to what the promisor is going to do in the future.
3) A continued and flagrant course of misrepresentation.
4) Acting as a dual agent without the knowledge or consent of all parties involved.
5) Commingling a licensee's own money or property with property of others received or held by the licensee.
6) Failure to specify a definite termination date in an exclusive listing agreement.
7) Secret profit—the taking of any secret or undisclosed amount of compensation by a licensee.
8) Option agreement—exercising an option agreement when the licensee has a listing agreement with the principal, without revealing to the principal in writing the amount of profit and obtaining the principal's written consent.
9) Fraud—any conduct, whether included by statute or not, which constitutes fraud or dishonest dealing.
10) Send-out slip—obtaining the signature of a prospective purchaser to buy property and to pay a commission without first having obtained the written authorization of the owner of the property.
11) Obtaining a license by fraud.
12) Conviction of a felony or of a misdemeanor involving moral turpitude.
13) False advertising.
14) Using the term "Realtor" or any trade name of a real estate organization of which the licensee is not a member.
15) Negligence or incompetence.
16) Failure of a broker to exercise reasonable supervision over the activities of his or her salespersons.
17) Government trust violation—using government employment to gain access to private records and improperly disclosing their confidential contents.
18) Restricted license violation—violating the terms or restrictions in an order granting a restricted license.

19) Panic selling—using "blockbusting" tactics where business is solicited on the basis of statements regarding race, color, religion, sex, marital status, ancestry, or national origin.
20) Violations of the Corporations Code or the Franchise Investment Law.
21) Civil actions—fraud—if a final judgment in a civil suit for fraud, misrepresentation, or deceit is obtained against a licensee in regard to real estate transactions.
22) Failure to notify—employer failing to notify the Commissioner in writing of the discharge of any salesperson on the grounds of violating the license law or regulations.
23) Mobile home violations—committing fraud in the application for the registration of a mobile home, failing to provide for delivery of a properly endorsed certificate of ownership of a mobile home from seller to buyer, or participating in the sale or disposal of a stolen mobile home.
24) Blind advertising—failing to show in advertisements a licensee designation and the employing broker's name.
25) Sales price notification—a broker failing to notify the buyer and the seller in writing of the selling price within one month after the closing of the deal, unless the escrow issues a closing statement.
26) Unlicensed persons—employing or compensating an unlicensed person for any act which requires a license.
27) Failure to give a copy of any contract to the person signing at the time of signing.
28) Collection of advance rental fees—collecting of advance fees by rental agents without approval contracts and failing to provide refunds where applicable; an agent must keep accurate records and make quarterly reports to the principal.
29) Discrimination against the physically handicapped.

ADDITIONAL REGULATIONS

In addition to the statutory grounds for discipline listed above, there are certain regulations which must be followed.

REVIEW OF SALESPERSON'S AGREEMENTS. A broker must review, initial, and date all of a salesperson's contracts within five working days of preparation or signing, or before the close of escrow. The broker may delegate this authority to another broker or salesperson in writing.

BROKER-SALESPERSON AGREEMENTS. The broker must keep the written agreement between the broker and the salesperson on file at the broker's office. The broker must keep the agreement for three years from the date of termination of the agreement.

ETHICAL STANDARDS

To enhance the professionalism of the real estate industry and to protect the public, the Real Estate Commission has adopted further standards of ethics and professional conduct. These standards, set forth in Regulation 2785, are reprinted here in full:

UNLAWFUL CONDUCT

A. **Unlawful Conduct in Sale, Lease and Exchange Transactions.** Licensees when performing acts within the meaning of Section 10131(a) of the Business and Professions Code shall not engage in conduct which would subject the licensee to adverse action, penalty or discipline under Sections 10176 and 10177 of the Business and Professions Code including, but not limited to, the following acts and omissions:

1. Knowingly making a substantial misrepresentation of the likely value of real property to:
   (a) Its owner either for the purpose of securing a listing or for the purpose of acquiring an interest in the property for the licensee's own account.
   (b) A prospective buyer for the purpose of inducing the buyer to make an offer to purchase the real property.

2. Representing to an owner of real property when seeking a listing that the licensee has obtained a bona fide written offer to purchase the property, unless at the time of the representation the licensee has possession of a bona fide written offer to purchase.

3. Stating or implying to an owner of real property during listing negotiations that the licensee is precluded by law, by regulation, or by the rules of any organization, other than the broker firm seeking the listing, from charging less than the commission or fee quoted to the owner by the licensee.

4. Knowingly making substantial misrepresentations regarding the licensee's relationship with an individual broker, corporate broker, or franchised brokerage company or that entity's/person's responsibility for the licensee's activities.

5. Knowingly underestimating the probable closing costs in a communication to the prospective buyer or seller of real property in order to induce that person to make or to accept an offer to purchase the property.

6. Knowingly making a false or misleading representation to the seller of real property as to the form, amount and/or treatment of a deposit toward the purchase of the property made by an offeror.

7. Knowingly making a false or misleading representation to a seller of real property, who has agreed to finance all or part of a purchase price by carrying back a loan, about a buyer's ability to repay the loan in accordance with its terms and conditions.

8. Making an addition to or modification of the terms of an instrument previously signed or initialed by a party to a transaction without the knowledge and consent of the party.

9. A representation made as a principal or agent to a prospective purchaser of a promissory note secured by real property about the market value of the securing property without a reasonable basis for believing the truth and accuracy of the representation.

10. Knowingly making a false or misleading representation or representing, without a reasonable basis for believing its truth, the nature and/or condition of the interior or exterior features of a property when soliciting an offer.

11. Knowingly making a false or misleading representation or representing, without a reasonable basis for believing its truth, the size of a parcel, square footage of improvements or the location of the boundary lines of real property being offered for sale, lease or exchange.

12. Knowingly making a false or misleading representation or representing to a prospective buyer or lessee of real property, without a reasonable basis to believe its truth, that the property can be used for certain purposes with the intent of inducing the prospective buyer or lessee to acquire an interest in the real property.

13. When acting in the capacity of an agent in a transaction for the sale, lease or exchange of real property, failing to disclose to a prospective purchaser or lessee facts known to the licensee materially affecting the value or desirability of the property, when the licensee has reason to believe that such facts are not known to nor readily observable by a prospective purchaser or lessee.

14. Willfully failing, when acting as a listing agent, to present or cause to be presented to the owner of the property any written offer to purchase received prior to the closing of a sale, unless expressly instructed by the owner not to present such an offer, or unless the offer is patently frivolous.

15. When acting as the listing agent, presenting competing written offers to purchase real property to the owner in such a manner as to induce the owner to accept the offer which will provide the greatest compensation to the listing broker without regard to the benefits, advantages and/or disadvantages to the owner.

16. Failing to explain to the parties or prospective parties to a real estate transaction for whom the licensee is acting as an agent the meaning and probable significance of a contingency in an offer or contract that the licensee knows or reasonably believes may affect the closing date of the transaction, or the timing of the vacating of the property by the seller or its occupancy by the buyer.

17. Failing to disclose to the seller of real property in a transaction in which the licensee is an agent for the seller the nature and extent of any direct or indirect interest that the licensee expects to acquire as a result of the sale. The prospective purchase of the property by a person related to the licensee by blood or marriage, purchase by an entity in which the licensee has an ownership interest, or purchase by any other person with whom the licensee occupies a special relationship where there is a reasonable probability that the licensee could be indirectly acquiring an interest in the property shall be disclosed to the seller.

18. Failing to disclose to the buyer of real property in a transaction in which the licensee is an agent for the buyer the nature and extent of a licensee's direct or indirect ownership interest in such real property. The direct or indirect ownership interest in the property by a person related to the licensee by blood or marriage, by an entity in which the licensee has an ownership interest, or by any other person with whom the licensee occupies a special relationship shall be disclosed to the buyer.

19. Failing to disclose to a principal for whom the licensee is acting as an agent any significant interest the licensee has in a particular entity when the licensee recommends the use of the services or products of such entity.

20. The refunding by a licensee, when acting as an agent for seller, of all or part of an offeror's purchase money deposit in a real estate sales transaction after the seller has accepted the offer to purchase, unless the licensee has the express permission of the seller to make the refund.

B. Unlawful Conduct When Soliciting, Negotiating or Arranging a Loan Secured by Real Property or the Sale of a Promissory Note Secured by Real Property. Licensees when performing acts within the meaning of subdivision (d) or (e) of Section 10131 of the Business and Professions Code shall not violate any of the applicable provisions of subdivision (A), or act in a manner which would subject the licensee to adverse action, penalty or discipline under Sections 10176 and 10177 of the Business and Professions Code including, but not limited to, the following acts and omissions:

1. Knowingly misrepresenting to a prospective borrower of a loan to be secured by real property or to an assignor/endorser of a promissory note secured by real property that there is an existing lender

willing to make the loan or that there is a purchaser for the note, for the purpose of inducing the borrower or assignor/endorser to utilize the services of the licensee.

2. (a) Knowingly making a false or misleading representation to a prospective lender or purchaser of a loan secured directly or collaterally by real property about a borrower's ability to repay the loan in accordance with its terms and conditions;

   (b) Failing to disclose to a prospective lender or note purchaser information about the prospective borrower's identity, occupation, employment, income and credit data as represented to the broker by the prospective borrower;

   (c) Failing to disclose information known to the broker relative to the ability of the borrower to meet his or her potential or existing contractual obligations under the note or contract including information known about the borrower's payment history on an existing note, whether the note is in default or the borrower in bankruptcy.

3. Knowingly underestimating the probable closing costs in a communication to a prospective borrower or lender of a loan to be secured by a lien on real property for the purpose of inducing the borrower or lender to enter into the loan transaction.

4. When soliciting a prospective lender to make a loan to be secured by real property, falsely representing or representing without a reasonable basis to believe its truth, the priority of the security, as a lien against the real property securing the loan, i.e., a first, second or third deed of trust.

5. Knowingly misrepresenting in any transaction that a specific service is free when the licensee knows or has a reasonable basis to know that it is covered by a fee to be charged as part of the transaction.

6. Knowingly making a false or misleading representation to a lender or assignee/endorsee of a lender of a loan secured directly or collaterally by a lien on real property about the amount and treatment of loan payments, including loan payoffs, and the failure to account to the lender or assignee/endorsee of a lender as to the disposition of such payments.

7. When acting as a licensee in a transaction for the purpose of obtaining a loan, and in receipt of an "advance fee" from the borrower for this purpose, the failure to account to the borrower for the disposition of the "advance fee".

8. Knowingly making a false or misleading representation about the terms and conditions of a loan to be secured by a lien on real property when soliciting a borrower or negotiating the loan.

9. Knowingly making a false or misleading representation or representing, without a reasonable basis for believing its truth, when soliciting a lender or negotiating a loan to be secured by a lien on real property about the market value of the securing real property, the nature and/or condition of the interior or exterior features of the securing real property, its size or the square footage of any improvement on the securing real property.

SUGGESTIONS FOR PROFESSIONAL CONDUCT

A. **Suggestions for Professional Conduct in Sale, Lease and Exchange Transactions.** In order to maintain a high level of ethics and professionalism in their business practices, real estate licensees are encouraged to adhere to the following suggestions in conducting their business activities:

1. Aspire to give a high level of competent, ethical and quality service to buyers and sellers in real estate transactions.

2. Stay in close communication with clients or customers to ensure that questions are promptly answered and all significant events or problems in a transaction are conveyed in a timely manner.

3. Cooperate with the California Department of Real Estate's enforcement of, and report to that Department evident violations of, the Real Estate Law.

4. Use care in the preparation of any advertisement to present an accurate picture or message to the reader, viewer or listener.

5. Submit all written offers in a prompt and timely manner.

6. Keep oneself informed and current on factors affecting the real estate market in which the licensee operates as an agent.

7. Make a full, open and sincere effort to cooperate with other licensees, unless the principal has instructed the licensee to the contrary.

8. Attempt to settle disputes with other licensees through mediation or arbitration.

9. Advertise or claim to be an expert in an area of specialization in real estate brokerage activity, e.g., appraisal, property management, industrial siting, mortgage loan, etc., only if the licensee has had special training, preparation or experience in such area.

10. Strive to provide equal opportunity for quality housing and a high level of service to all persons regardless of race, color, sex, religion, ancestry, physical handicap, marital status or national origin.

11. Base opinions of value, whether for the purpose of advertising or promoting real estate brokerage business, upon documented objective data.

12. Make every attempt to comply with these Suggestions for Professional Conduct and the Code of Ethics of any organized real estate industry group of which the licensee is a member.

B. Suggestions for Professional Conduct When Negotiating or Arranging Loans Secured by Real Property or Sale of a Promissory Note Secured by Real Property. In order to maintain a high level of ethics and professionalism in their business practices when performing acts within the meaning of subdivisions (d) and (e) of Section 10131 and Sections 10131.1 and 10131.2 of the Business and Professions Code, real estate licensees are encouraged to adhere to the following suggestions, in addition to any applicable provisions of subdivision (A), in conducting their business activities:

1. Aspire to give a high level of competent, ethical and quality service to borrowers and lenders in loan transactions secured by real estate.

2. Stay in close communication with borrowers and lenders to ensure that reasonable questions are promptly answered and all significant events or problems in a loan transaction are conveyed in a timely manner.

3. Keep oneself informed and current on factors affecting the real estate loan market in which the licensee acts as an agent.

4. Advertise or claim to be an expert in an area of specialization in real estate mortgage loan transactions only if the licensee has had special training, preparation or experience in such area.

5. Strive to provide equal opportunity for quality mortgage loan services and a high level of service to all borrowers or lenders regardless of race, color, sex, religion, ancestry, physical handicap, marital status or national origin.

6. Base opinions of value in a loan transaction, whether for the purpose of advertising or promoting real estate mortgage loan brokerage business, on documented objective data.

7. Respond to reasonable inquiries of a principal as to the status or extent of efforts to negotiate the sale of an existing loan.

8. Respond to reasonable inquiries of a borrower regarding the net proceeds available from a loan arranged by the licensee.

9. Make every attempt to comply with the standards of professional conduct and the code of ethics of any organized mortgage loan industry group of which the licensee is a member.

The conduct suggestions set forth in subsections (A) and (B) are not intended as statements of duties imposed by law nor as grounds for disciplinary action by the Department of Real Estate, but as guidelines for elevating the professionalism of real estate licensees.

(**NOTE:** the Code of Ethics of the National Association of Realtors is reproduced below.)

TRUST FUNDS

A common source of confusion for the licensee is the proper handling of trust funds. It is also one of the major grounds for revocation or suspension of one's license. The fiduciary obligations of a real estate broker include the maintenance of adequate trust fund records and the proper handling of all trust funds. These responsibilities are a matter of law; they are defined by court decisions, statutes and regulations. Inability or failure to account for any trust funds, whether intentional or not, is a serious violation of the fiduciary obligation and the law.

DEFINITION

Trust funds are money or other things of value received by a licensee on behalf of a principal or any other person in the performance of any acts for which a real estate license is required, and not belonging to the broker, but being held for the benefit of others.

Trust funds: money or items received by a licensee on behalf of the principal or other party for safekeeping

HANDLING OF FUNDS

Any real estate licensee who accepts funds in connection with a real estate transaction must immediately deposit them into a neutral escrow depository, into the hands of the principal, or into a **trust fund account** maintained by the licensee in a bank or other recognized depository. "Immediately" has been interpreted to mean that the funds must be deposited no later than the next business day following receipt of such funds.

Trust fund account: a neutral account maintained by the licensee solely for trust fund deposits

The trust funds must be retained in the trust account until they are disbursed in accordance with the principal's instructions. Separate records should be maintained of all monies received, indicating their disposition. Also, the Commissioner may examine the financial records of any such trust fund account.

If the licensee receives a check from the prospective buyer prior to acceptance of the offer, the check may be held by the licensee pursuant to the following requirements: the check by its terms is not negotiable by the licensee or the buyer has given written instructions that the check shall not be deposited or cashed until acceptance of the offer, and the seller is informed (before or at the time the offer is presented) that the check is being held. Once the offer has been accepted, the broker must place the check in a neutral escrow or trust account by the next business day, unless the buyer and the seller instruct the broker in writing to deliver the check to the seller, or unless the seller authorizes the broker in writing to keep holding the check.

TRUST FUND BANK ACCOUNT

Commingling: combining a broker's own funds with trust funds

The major reason for establishing and maintaining separate trust accounts is to avoid any **commingling** of funds (that is, to keep trust monies separate from the broker's money in the broker's own general account). Should any legal action be taken against the broker, or if the broker should die, the broker's general account could be "frozen" during the course of the legal action or probate. If the client's funds were kept in the general account, they could not be reached until the conclusion of the legal action or probate. Thus, if the broker maintains a true trust account and accurate records, the client's funds are better protected from attachment and probate.

If the funds are placed in a trust fund bank account, the account should be in the name of the broker as trustee. The account may not be one which requires prior written notice to the financial institution as a condition of withdrawal.

INTEREST-BEARING ACCOUNT. A broker who receives trust funds for the payment of property taxes, assessments or insurance relating to a one- to four-unit residence may deposit and maintain those funds in an interest-bearing depository account if the account is insured by the federal government. However, none of the earned interest may inure to the broker's benefit.

WITHDRAWALS. Withdrawals from a trust fund account may not be made without the signature of the broker as trustee of the account or without the signature of at least one authorized person. The broker may authorize the following persons to withdraw trust funds:

1) a salesperson in the broker's employ;
2) a corporate officer of a corporation licensed as a broker; and
3) any unlicensed employee, provided the employee is covered by a fiduciary bond indemnifying the broker against loss of money or property by the act of such employee in an amount sufficient to cover all funds or property held in trust.

Although the broker can authorize other people to withdraw trust funds, the broker cannot delegate accountability for the funds. The broker is not relieved from compliance with the laws because of the negligence or irresponsibility of an employee.

BROKER'S FUNDS IN TRUST ACCOUNT. Although a broker should not have any of his or her own funds in the trust account, there are times when this will occur.

> **Example:** most banks have a service charge on trust accounts which the broker must pay. A broker is permitted to have up to $100 of personal funds in a trust fund to cover service charges. However, it is preferable to arrange for the bank to charge the broker's commercial account for trust account service charges.

Also, a broker may have an earned commission in a trust account. In this situation, the broker should promptly transfer the earned commission to his or her commercial account. If it is not practical to transfer it immediately, an earned commission may remain in the trust account for a period not to exceed 30 days. However, the broker's personal obligations should never be paid out of the trust account, even if the broker has an earned commission in it. The earned commission should first be transferred to the broker's general account before it is used for personal obligations.

RECORDS TO BE MAINTAINED

The broker must maintain a record of all trust funds received. The record must set out the following information in columnar form:

1) date funds were received;
2) from whom received;
3) amount received;
4) with respect to funds deposited in trust bank account, date of deposit;
5) with respect to funds previously deposited in trust bank account, check number or date of related disbursement;
6) with respect to funds not deposited in trust bank account, identity of other depository and date funds were forwarded; and,
7) daily balance of trust fund account.

If the broker maintains a formal trust cash receipts journal and a formal cash disbursements journal or other similar records, or uses an automated data processing system, in accordance with sound accounting principles, the broker is deemed to be in compliance with the records requirements.

A broker must keep a separate record for each beneficiary or transaction. These separate records must include the following information in columnar form:

1) date funds were deposited;
2) amount deposited;
3) the date of each related disbursement;
4) the check number of each related disbursement;
5) the amount of each related disbursement;
6) dates and amounts of interest credited; and
7) the balance after posting transactions.

All the records and funds are subject to inspection by the Commissioner.

A broker must retain copies of all trust records, including cancelled checks, for each transaction for three years. The retention period runs from the date of the closing of the transaction, or from the date of the listing if the transaction is not consummated.

FORM OF RECORDS. There is no particular form which must be used in recording the receipt and disbursement of trust funds. However, the broker will want to use separate forms for each type of transaction, such as for trust funds that will be deposited in a trust account, for trust funds not placed in a trust account (i.e., instruments given to the broker for delivery to a third person), and separate records for each beneficiary or transaction. The forms must include all of the required information discussed above.

MISCELLANEOUS PROVISIONS AFFECTING REAL ESTATE LICENSEES

COMMISSIONS

A **commission** is compensation paid to a broker for services rendered in connection with the sale or exchange of real property. Commissions are generally not set by law, except on certain loans, but rather are negotiated between the seller and broker. The amount or rate of a commission may not be part of a printed form or agreement for sale of four units or less of residential property, or for the sale of a mobile home. These agreements must contain a notice that commissions may be negotiated and are not set by law.

A salesperson may only receive a commission from his or her own employing broker. A broker may receive a commission from anyone (even a broker in another state) and may pay commissions to employed salespersons or to other brokers. It is unlawful for a licensed salesperson to pay a commission to any licensee except through his or her broker. Any person who pays compensation to a non-licensee for services which require a license is guilty of a misdemeanor.

A salesperson can only sue his or her broker for a commission. He or she cannot sue the broker's client. In a suit to receive a commission, the licensee must prove he or she was licensed at the time the action for which the commission is sought was performed.

RETENTION OF RECORDS

As previously discussed, a broker must keep copies of all trust records for three years. A broker must also retain for three years copies of all listings, deposit receipts, canceled checks, and other documents executed or obtained in his or her capacity as broker. These records must be made available for inspection by the Commissioner and if there is sufficient cause, these records may be audited. A broker must keep mortgage loan disclosure statements and real property security statements for four years.

THE REAL ESTATE FUND

All license fees collected by the Commissioner are placed into a **Real Estate Fund**. Eight percent of the amount of all license fees collected are placed into an **Education and Research Account**, while 12% of all fees go to a **Recovery Account**.

The Education and Research Account is designed to advance real estate education and research projects. The Recovery Account was created to provide funds from which a party injured by a real estate licensee in a real estate transaction can recover the amount of a judgment otherwise uncollectible. A person can collect a maximum of $20,000 per transaction of the amount of the unpaid judgment. Liability of the account may not exceed $100,000 for any series of transactions against any one licensee. If payment is made out of the fund on account of a licensee, his or her license is suspended until the fund is repaid.

Real Estate Education and Research Account: funded with license fees; advances real estate education and research projects

Recovery Account: funded with license fees; provides funds to compensate parties injured by licensees in real estate transactions

CHAPTER SUMMARY

1. The California Real Estate Law requires real estate licenses for those engaging in real estate activities and then regulates the action of those licensees. The purpose of the Real Estate Law is to protect members of the public who deal with real estate agents.

2. The Real Estate Commissioner enforces the provisions of the Real Estate Law by enacting regulations, investigating the activities of licensees and taking disciplinary action against those who violate the Real Estate Law. The Commissioner is advised by the Real Estate Advisory Commission and the state Attorney General.

3. The Real Estate Law determines who is required to have a real estate license and sets forth the licensing requirements. Real estate agents and soon-to-be real estate agents should be familiar with these requirements.

4. The Real Estate Law and related regulations also specify the grounds for disciplinary action and set forth recommended standards of behavior for the profession. Licensees should become intimately familiar with these standards, both those that are mandatory and those that are suggested. It is up to each individual licensee to live up to the high standards of professional conduct set by the state and professional associations.

CHAPTER 17—QUIZ
CALIFORNIA REAL ESTATE LICENSE LAW

1. A broker or salesperson license renewal applicant is required to submit proof of attendance at _____ clock hours of approved subjects/offerings within the four-year period preceding license renewal.

   a) 3
   b) 20
   c) 45
   d) 100

2. A corporation may engage in the real estate brokerage business if the officer or officers acting for the corporation:

   a) are duly licensed salespersons
   b) have authority from the Corporations Commissioner
   c) are licensed brokers
   d) is the president of the corporation

3. A real estate licensee should never advise a buyer on:

   a) the type of financing available
   b) the form in which title should be vested
   c) the length of escrow
   d) filling out credit forms

4. A broker should be familiar with standard accounting techniques in order to:

   a) correctly prepare an offer to purchase
   b) appraise residential property
   c) keep trust fund records correctly
   d) advise buyers on financing sources

5. Brokers must retain copies of all listings, deposit receipts, and trust records for:

   a) one year
   b) two years
   c) three years
   d) four years

6. Withdrawals cannot be made from a broker's trust fund by:

   a) a salesperson in the broker's employ who has been authorized by the broker
   b) the secretary of the broker who has been authorized by the broker and is covered by a fiduciary bond
   c) a corporate officer of a corporation licensed as a broker
   d) the unlicensed, unbonded spouse of a broker who has been authorized by the broker

7. The Real Estate Recovery Account will pay a maximum of _____ per transaction:

   a) $20,000
   b) $40,000
   c) $100,000
   d) no limit

8. The California Real Estate Advisory Commission consists of how many members?

   a) 7
   b) 10
   c) 12
   d) 13

9. A broker's trust fund account records must show the trust fund balance:

   a) daily
   b) weekly
   c) monthly
   d) quarterly

10. A broker may keep an earned commission in a trust fund account for no more than:

   a) one day
   b) seven days
   c) thirty days
   d) sixty days

11. Where may a broker legally place an earnest money deposit?

    a) A trust account
    b) A neutral account
    c) The hands of the broker's principal
    d) Any of the above

12. The maximum amount of a broker's own funds allowed in his or her trust account is:

    a) none
    b) $50
    c) $100
    d) $250

13. The rate of commission to be charged on a sale is determined by:

    a) the Real Estate Commissioner
    b) agreement between seller and broker
    c) agreement between buyer and broker
    d) agreement between buyer and seller

14. A broker's license:

    a) must be carried by the broker at all times
    b) should be kept in a secure place, such as a home safe or a safety deposit box
    c) must be available in the broker's main office
    d) is kept in the field office of the Department of Real Estate nearest the broker's main office

15. A salesperson may be compensated for work as an agent:

    a) by any broker
    b) only by the employing broker
    c) by any principal
    d) by any broker or principal

16. The maximum legal limit on a commission for the sale of commercial property for over $20,000,000 is:

    a) 5%
    b) 10%
    c) 15%
    d) None of the above

17. A real estate salesperson's license, if issued without any restrictions, is normally valid for:

    a) 2 years
    b) 3 years
    c) 4 years
    d) 5 years

18. Funds to support real estate education and research come from:

    a) the University of California budget
    b) a surcharge on fines from real estate criminal convictions
    c) community college budgets
    d) real estate license fees

1. c) License renewal applicants must complete 45 clock hours of continuing education during the four years prior to renewal.

2. c) Under a corporate license, officers designated to represent the corporation must also be licensed as brokers.

3. b) Matters affecting title should be referred to a licensed attorney.

4. c) Keeping accurate trust fund records is a very important aspect of real estate brokerage.

5. c) Most records must be kept for three years.

6. d) Withdrawals may not be made without the signature of the broker or an authorized person such as a salesperson, corporate officer or bonded employee.

7. a) RERA will pay up to $20,000 per transaction to satisfy unpaid judgments against licensees.

8. b) The Real Estate Advisory Commission consists of six brokers and four public members.

9. a) The record must show the daily balance of the trust account.

10. c) Earned commissions should be withdrawn as soon as possible, but may remain in the trust fund account up to thirty days if necessary.

11. d) Earnest money may be placed in trust, in a neutral escrow, or given to the principal.

12. c) A broker may keep up to $100 in a trust account to cover service charges.

13. b) Commissions are negotiated between the broker and the client/seller.

14. c) The broker's license must be displayed at the broker's main office.

15. b) Only the employing broker may compensate a salesperson.

16. d) There is no legal limit on the amount of commissions.

17. c) A salesperson's license must be renewed after 4 years.

18. d) A portion of real estate license fees is placed into the Real Estate Education and Research Account.

REALTOR®

CODE OF ETHICS
NATIONAL ASSOCIATION OF REALTORS®

Where the word **REALTOR®** is used in this Code and Preamble, it shall be deemed to include **REALTOR-ASSOCIATE®**. Pronouns shall be considered to include **REALTORS®** and **REALTOR-ASSO-CIATE®s** of both genders.

Preamble...

Under all is the land. Upon its wise utilization and widely allocated ownership depend the survival and growth of free institutions and of our civilization. The **REALTOR®** should recognize that the interests of the nation and its citizens require the highest and best use of the land and the widest distribution of land ownership. They require the creation of adequate housing, the building of functioning cities, the development of productive industries and farms, and the preservation of a healthful environment.

Such interests impose obligations beyond those of ordinary commerce. They impose grave social responsibility and a patriotic duty to which the **REALTOR®** should dedicate himself, and for which he should be diligent in preparing himself. The **REALTOR®**, therefore, is zealous to maintain and improve the standards of his calling and shares with his fellow **REALTORS®** a common responsibility for its integrity and honor. The term **REALTOR®** has come to connote competency, fairness, and high integrity resulting from adherence to a lofty ideal of moral conduct in business relations. No inducement of profit and no instruction from clients ever can justify departure from this ideal.

In the interpretation of this obligation, a **REALTOR®** can take no safer guide than that which has been handed down through the centuries, embodied in the Golden Rule, "Whatsoever ye would that men should do to you, do ye even so to them."

Accepting this standard as his own, every **REALTOR®** pledges himself to observe its spirit in all of his activities and to conduct his business in accordance with the tenets set forth below.

Articles 1 through 5 are aspirational and establish ideals the **REALTOR®** *should strive to attain.*

ARTICLE 1

The **REALTOR®** should keep himself informed on matters affecting real estate in his community, the state, and nation so that he may be able to contribute responsibly to public thinking on such matters.

ARTICLE 2

In justice to those who place their interests in his care, the **REALTOR®** should endeavor always to be informed regarding laws, proposed legislation, governmental regulations, public policies, and current market conditions in order to be in a position to advise his clients properly.

ARTICLE 3

The **REALTOR®** should endeavor to eliminate in his community any practices which could be damaging to the public or bring discredit to the real estate profession. The **REALTOR®** should assist the governmental agency charged with regulating the practices of brokers and salesmen in his state.

ARTICLE 4

To prevent dissension and misunderstanding and to assure better service to the owner, the **REALTOR®** should urge the exclusive listing of property unless contrary to the best interest of the owner.

ARTICLE 5

In the best interests of society, of his associates, and his own business, the **REALTOR®** should willingly share with other **REALTORS®** the lessons of his experience and study for the benefit of the public, and should be loyal to the Board of **REALTORS®** of his community and active in its work.

Articles 6 through 23 establish specific obligations. Failure to observe these requirements subjects the **REALTOR®** *to disciplinary action.*

ARTICLE 6

The **REALTOR®** shall seek no unfair advantage over other **REALTORS®** and shall conduct his business so as to avoid controversies with other **REALTORS®**.

ARTICLE 7

In accepting employment as an agent, the **REALTOR**® pledges himself to protect and promote the interests of the client. This obligation of absolute fidelity to the client's interests is primary, but it does not relieve the **REALTOR**® of the obligation to treat fairly all parties to the transaction.

ARTICLE 8

The **REALTOR**® shall not accept compensation from more than one party, even if permitted by law, without the full knowledge of all parties to the transaction.

ARTICLE 9

The **REALTOR**® shall avoid exaggeration, misrepresentation, or concealment of pertinent facts relating to the property or the transaction. The **REALTOR**® shall not, however, be obligated to discover latent defects in the property or to advise on matters outside the scope of his real estate license.

ARTICLE 10

The **REALTOR**® shall not deny equal professional services to any person for reasons of race, color, religion, sex, handicap, familial status, or national origin. The **REALTOR**® shall not be party to any plan or agreement to discriminate against a person or persons on the basis of race, color, religion, sex, handicap, familial status, or national orgin.

ARTICLE 11

A **REALTOR**® is expected to provide a level of competent service in keeping with the standards of practice in those fields in which the **REALTOR**® customarily engages.

The **REALTOR**® shall not undertake to provide specialized professional services concerning a type of property or service that is outside his field of competence unless he engages the assistance of one who is competent on such types of property or service, or unless the facts are fully disclosed to the client. Any person engaged to provide such assistance shall be so identified to the client and his contribution to the assignment should be set forth.

The **REALTOR**® shall refer to the Standards of Practice of the National Association as to the degree of competence that a client has a right to expect the **REALTOR**® to possess, taking into consideration the complexity of the problem, the availability of expert assistance, and the opportunities for experience available to the **REALTOR**®.

ARTICLE 12

The **REALTOR**® shall not undertake to provide professional services concerning a property or its value where he has a present or contemplated interest unless such interest is specifically disclosed to all affected parties.

ARTICLE 13

The **REALTOR**® shall not acquire an interest in or buy for himself, any member of his immediate family, his firm or any member thereof, or any entity in which he has a substantial ownership interest, property listed with him, without making the true position known to the listing owner. In selling property owned by himself, or in which he has any interest, the **REALTOR**® shall reveal the facts of his ownership or interest to the purchaser.

ARTICLE 14

In the event of a controversy between **REALTORS**® associated with different firms, arising out of their relationship as **REALTORS**®, the **REALTORS**® shall submit the dispute to arbitration in accordance with the regulations of their Board or Boards rather than litigate the matter.

ARTICLE 15

If charged with unethical practice or asked to present evidence or to cooperate in any disciplinary proceeding or investigation, the **REALTOR**® shall place all pertinent facts before the proper tribunal of the Member Board or affiliated institute, society, or council in which membership is held and shall take no action to disrupt or obstruct such processes.

ARTICLE 16

When acting as agent, the **REALTOR**® shall not accept any commission, rebate, or profit on expenditures made for his principal-owner, without the principal's knowledge and consent.

ARTICLE 17

The **REALTOR**® shall not engage in activities that constitute the unauthorized practice of law and shall recommend that legal counsel be obtained when the interest of any party to the transaction requires it.

ARTICLE 18

The **REALTOR**® shall keep in a special account in an appropriate financial institution, separated from his own funds, monies coming into his possession in trust for other persons, such as escrows, trust funds, clients' monies, and other like items.

ARTICLE 19

The **REALTOR**® shall be careful at all times to present a true picture in his advertising and representations to the public. The **REALTOR**® shall also ensure that his status as a broker or a **REALTOR**® is clearly identifiable in any such advertising.

ARTICLE 20

The **REALTOR**®, for the protection of all parties, shall see that financial obligations and commitments regarding real estate transactions are in writing, expressing the exact agreement of the parties. A copy of each agreement shall be furnished to each party upon his signing such agreement.

ARTICLE 21

The **REALTOR**® shall not engage in any practice or take any action inconsistent with the agency of another **REALTOR**®.

ARTICLE 22

In the sale of property which is exclusively listed with a **REALTOR**®, the **REALTOR**® shall utilize the services of other brokers upon mutually agreed upon terms when it is in the best interests of the client.

Negotiations concerning property which is listed exclusively shall be carried on with the listing broker, not with the owner, except with the consent of the listing broker.

ARTICLE 23

The **REALTOR**® shall not publicly disparage the business practice of a competitor nor volunteer an opinion of a competitor's transaction. If his opinion is sought and if the **REALTOR**® deems it appropriate to respond, such opinion shall be rendered with strict professional integrity and courtesy.

The Code of Ethics was adopted in 1913. Amended at the Annual Convention in 1924, 1928, 1950, 1951, 1952, 1955, 1956, 1961, 1962, 1974, 1982, 1986, 1987, and 1989.

Abandonment—Failure to occupy and use property; may result in loss of rights.

Abatement of Nuisance—The extinction, termination, removal, or destruction of a nuisance, either personally by the injured party or by a lawsuit instituted by him/her.

Absolute Fee—Fee simple absolute. Absolute or fee simple title is absolute and unqualified, unlimited in duration and unconditional. It is the highest, most complete, and best title one can have.

Abstract of Judgment—A summary of the essential provisions of a court judgment which, when recorded, creates a lien upon all the real property of the debtor within the county where recorded.

Abstract of Title—An abstract of title is a short account of what appears in the public records affecting the title of a particular parcel of real property. It should normally contain a chronological summary of all grants, conveyances, wills, transfers and judicial proceedings which in any way affected title, together with all liens and encumbrances of record, showing whether or not they have been released.

Abut—To touch, border on, end at, share a common boundary with.

Acceleration Clause—A clause in any loan agreement that calls for immediate payment of the entire debt if one or more of the provisions of the agreement is breached by the borrower.

Acceptance—Agreeing to the terms of an offer to enter into a contract, thereby making it a binding contract. Also, the act of accepting delivery of a deed.

Acceptance, Qualified—Where the offeree accepts certain provisions of an offer but rejects others. It is a counter-offer or, more accurately, a new offer.

Accession—The acquisition of title to additional real estate by its annexation to existing property. This can be caused by humans (e.g. through the addition of fixtures), or by nature (e.g. the alluvial deposits on the banks of a stream by accretion).

Accord and Satisfaction—An agreement to accept something different than, and usually less than, what was called for in the original agreement.

Accretion—The gradual increase of dry land by the forces of nature, as when water deposits sediment on waterfront property. The owner of that property becomes the owner of the new soil.

Acknowledgment—A formal declaration made before an authorized official, such as a notary public or county clerk, by a person who has signed a document, that he or she has done so as a willful act and deed. The official witnesses the signature as being the voluntary and genuine signature of the one signing. Acknowledgment is required before a document (such as a deed, mortgage, or land contract) will be accepted for recording.

Acquisition Cost—The sum required to obtain title to a piece of property. In addition to the selling price, such things as closing costs, appraisal fees, title insurance and legal fees would be included.

Acre—An area of land equal to 43,560 square feet; or 4,840 square yards or 160 square rods. There are 640 acres in a section of land and 36 sections in a township.

Actual Age—The age of the structure from a chronological standpoint—as opposed to effective age. Appraisers are concerned with effective age.

Adjacent—Nearby, bordering, or neighboring; may or may not be in actual contact.

Administrator—A person appointed by the probate court to manage and distribute the estate of a deceased person when no executor is named in the will or there is no will.

Ad Valorem—Latin phrase meaning "according to value," used in connection with property taxation.

Adverse Possession—Acquiring title to real property owned by someone else, by means of open, notorious, and continuous possession of the property, under color of title, hostile to the title of the owner of record for the statutory period and by paying all taxes assessed on the property during that period.

Affiant—The one who makes an affidavit.

Affidavit—Sworn statement made before a notary public, or other official authorized to administer an oath, and then reduced to writing.

Affirm—To confirm or ratify. Also, to make a solemn declaration instead of making a statement under oath.

Agency—A relationship of trust created when one person, the principal, delegates to another, the agent, the right to represent the principal in dealing with the third parties.

Agency, Apparent—Agency which appears to exist because of the acts of the agent and/or the principal.

Agency, Dual—Representing both parties to a transaction, such as a broker representing both buyer and seller. This can result in loss of any commission and possibly revocation of the broker's license, if both parties are not fully informed as to the existence of the dual agency.

Agency, Exclusive—A written listing agreement giving one agent (broker) the right to sell a piece of property for a specified period of time, but allowing the owner to sell the property him or herself without having to pay a commission.

Agency, Ostensible—Refers to authority an agent appears to possess that, in fact, does not exist or is in excess of that granted by the principal. If through want of ordinary care the principal allows a third party to conclude that the apparent authority exists, the principal could be liable for damages to that third party.

Agency Coupled With an Interest—An agency where the agent has an interest in the subject of the agency.

Agent—In an agency relationship, the one who is authorized to represent another (the principal).

Agent, Actual Authority of—The authority which is given to an agent by a principal, either expressly or by implication.

Agent, General—An agent authorized to handle all the matters of the principal in one area or in specified areas.

Agent, Gratuitous—An agent who does not have a valid employment contract and therefore has no right to compensation.

Agent, Implied Authority of—The authority of an agent which is implied as necessary to the performance of the express authority.

Agent, Special—An agent with limited authority to do a specific thing or conduct a specific transaction.

Agent, Universal—An agent authorized by the principal to do all things that can be lawfully delegated to a representative.

Agreement, Express—An agreement where the terms are expressed in writing.

Agreement, Mutual—An agreement where both of the parties reach a "meeting of the minds."

Air Lot—A parcel of property which does not contain any land, such as a condominium.

Air Rights—The right to undisturbed use and control of the air space over a given parcel of land. Such rights may be acquired for construction of a building above the land or building of another, or for the protection of the light and air for structures on adjoining lands.

Alienation—The transfer of title, ownership, or interest in property from one person to another.

Alienation, Involuntary—The transfer of real estate by operation of law (such as a mortgage foreclosure), natural processes or adverse possession.

Alienation, Voluntary—Voluntary transfer of real property from one person to another.

Alienation Clause—A provision in a promissory note or mortgage calling for immediate full payment of the debt if the mortgaged property is sold. Such a provision effectively prevents sales by assumption or land contract.

Alluvion—The solid material added along the bank of a river by accretion. Also called alluvium.

Alluvium—SEE: **Alluvion.**

Amenities—The intangible benefits that accompany ownership of a particular residence, such as proximity to public transportation, schools, or shopping, as well as panoramic views, architectural excellence, or the prestige that goes with living in a given community.

American Institute of Real Estate Appraisers—An association of real estate appraisers. Members are given the designation M.A.I. (Member, Appraisal Institute).

Amortization—Gradual payment of a debt in installments including principal and interest over a set period of time, where at the end of the period the entire debt has been paid.

Amortized Loan—A loan that is completely paid off, interest and principal, in equal, or nearly equal installment payments.

Annexation, Actual—Means by which personal property is converted to real property; involves a physical attachment of the property to land. SEE: **Fixtures.**

Annexation, Constructive—Conversion of personal property to real property without physical attachment to land. SEE: **Fixture.**

Annual Percentage Rate (A.P.R)—The annual percentage rate reflects all charges paid for the borrowed money, including the nominal interest rate (spelled out in the note) and all other discounts and finance charges.

Anticipation, Principle of—According to the principle of anticipation, value is created by the expectation of benefits to be received in the future.

Anticipatory Repudiation or Breach—A breach of contract committed by one party before the time for performance by informing the other party of an intention not to perform.

Anti-Deficiency Rule—A law which in some cases prohibits a deficiency judgment and limits the secured creditor to recovery of the security property in the event of a default under a deed of trust or mortgage.

Appeal—To present a case or cause for rehearing to a higher decision making body.

Appellant—The party appealing a decision or ruling.

Appellee—The party against whom a case is appealed. Also known as the respondent.

Apportionment—A division of property (as among tenants in common when the property is sold or partitioned) or liability (as between seller and buyer with closing costs) into proportionate, but not necessarily equal, parts.

Appraisal—An estimate or opinion of the value of a piece of property as of a certain date.

Appraiser—One who estimates the value of real or personal property, particularly one qualified by education, training and experience to do so.

Appreciation—Increase in value or worth. Opposite of depreciation.

Appropriation—Taking or reducing to personal possession property to the exclusion of others. Example: The doctrine of appropriation holds that the water in a natural stream belongs to the public, but an individual can take it for beneficial use, and the first one taking the water for a particular use becomes prior in right as against all others for use of the water for that purpose.

Appropriation, Prior—Doctrine of water rights, wherein priority of right is determined by priority in time of use of water. COMPARE: **Riparian Rights.**

Appropriative Right—SEE: **Appropriation, Prior.**

Appurtenance—Anything that is incident to, attached to, or pertains to the land and is transferred with it, but is not necessarily a part of it.

Appurtenances, Intangible—Rights which go with or pertain to real property and which do not involve ownership of physical objects; for example, easements or covenants.

Area—1. Locale or region. 2. The size of a surface in square units of measure, as in a house with 2,000 sq. ft. of floor, or a tract covering 10 sq. miles. 3. In residential design, the function of a spot or location, as in "work area" or "recreation area."

Arm's Length Transaction—Transaction where there are no preexisting family or business relationships, both parties have an equal bargaining position, and each protects his or her own interests.

Artificial Person—A person created by law, with legal rights and responsibilities, such as a corporation, as distinguished from a natural person, a human being.

Assessment—1. The valuation of property for taxation. 2. A non-recurring specific charge against property for a definite purpose, such as curbs or sewers.

Assessor—Official who determines the value of property for taxation.

Assets, Liquid—Cash on hand or other assets that can readily be turned into cash. Real estate holdings are not considered very liquid.

Assign—To transfer a right, title, or interest in property to another.

Assignee—The one to whom a right, title or interest in property has been transferred.

Assignment—A transfer of contract rights from one person to another.

Assignment of Contract and Deed—The substitution of a new person for the original seller in an installment sales contract.

Assignor—One who transfers a right, title or interest in property.

Assume—To take upon oneself. Example: A buyer may assume the seller's loan and mortgage when purchasing a piece of property, thereby becoming personally liable for repayment.

Assumption Fee—A sum paid to the lender, usually by the purchaser, when a mortgage is assumed.

Attachment—Seizure of real or personal property of a defendant in a lawsuit, by court order, so that it will be available to satisfy a judgment.

Attachments, Man-Made—Personal property attached to land by human effort. SEE: **Fixture.**

Attachments, Natural—Things attached to land by nature, such as trees, shrubs or crops.

Attorney-In-Fact—One who has authority to act for another under a power of attorney. The power of attorney may be limited to a particular act or purpose, or it may be general. In real estate transactions, the power of attorney must be written and recorded.

Avulsion—Sudden loss of land due to the action of water, as when a river suddenly changes course.

Balance, Principle of—The maximum value of real estate is achieved when the agents in production—labor, coordination, capital, and land—are in proper balance with each other.

Balance Sheet—A financial statement showing personal or corporate assets, liabilities and net worth (the difference between assets and liabilities) as of a specific date.

Bankrupt—1. When the liabilities of a person, firm or corporation exceed its assets. 2. One who has been determined bankrupt by a court of law.

Base and Meridian—Imaginary lines, running at right angles, used by surveyors to find and describe public or private lands. (Base lines run east to west, while meridians run north to south.)

Base Lines—East-west lines, parallel to the equator, from which township lines are established in government survey legal descriptions.

Basis—The figure on which profit from the sale of real estate is based for income tax purposes.

Basis, Adjusted—Initial basis in a property adjusted upward or downward to reflect expenditures for improvements minus any depreciation deductions taken or allowable.

Bench Mark—A mark made at a known elevation point on a permanent monument, used to calculate other elevations in a surveyed area.

Beneficiary—1. One for whom a trust is created and in whose favor the trust operates. 2. One entitled to receive the proceeds of a life insurance policy. 3. The lender on a note and deed of trust transaction. 4. One who acquires real or personal property through a will.

Bequeath—To transfer personal property to another by a will.

Bequest—Personal property that is transferred by a will.

Betterment—An improvement to real property which is more extensive than ordinary repair or replacement and which increases the value of the property.

Bill of Sale—Document used to transfer title, ownership, or interest in personal property from one person to another.

Binder—1. An agreement to consider the deposit or earnest money as evidence of the potential purchaser's good faith when he or she makes an offer to buy a piece of real estate. 2. An instrument giving immediate insurance coverage to an insured person until the regular policy is issued.

Blighted Area—An area where real property has deteriorated in value.

Block—A unit of land comprised of several lots, surrounded by streets or unimproved land.

Blockbusting—An unethical and illegal act where one person induces another to sell property, possibly at a deflated price, by stating that a change in the neighborhood with respect to race, creed, color or national origin, may occur with the result of declining property values. This practice violates both federal and state anti-discrimination laws.

Blue Laws—Statutes or ordinances restricting the transaction of business on Sundays and certain holidays.

Blue Sky Laws—Laws designed to protect the public from fraud in the promotion and sale of securities by regulating those practices.

Bona Fide—Acting in good faith, without fraud.

Bond—An instrument evidencing a debt, secured by a mortgage or deed of trust. A written obligation, normally interest bearing, to pay a certain sum at a specified time.

Bookkeeping, Double Entry—An accounting technique used in settlement statements to show debits and credits for both the buyer and seller side by side.

Boot—A term used in connection with tax-free exchanges when the properties are not equal in value to describe whatever is given (cash, services, etc.) to make up the difference in value.

Boundary—The perimeter or limit of a parcel of land; the border.

Bounds—Boundaries.

Branch Manager—An associate broker designated by the primary broker of the firm to manage the operations of a branch office.

Breach—Violation of an obligation, duty or law.

Broker—A licensed natural or artificial person who acts, for a fee, as an intermediary between parties to a real estate transaction.

Broker, Associate—One who has qualified as a real estate broker but who works for a principal broker.

Broker, Designated—A natural person, licensed as a broker, who is responsible for the brokerage activities of a partnership or corporation.

Brokerage—A broker's business. The compensation or commission charged for the broker's services is called a brokerage fee.

Building Code—Rules set up by a local government providing minimum construction standards.

Building Restrictions—Public or private limitations imposed on buildings with respect to the allowable size or type. Zoning is an example of a public restriction, while conditions or covenants in deeds are examples of private restrictions.

Bulk Transfer—This refers to the sale and transfer of all or a substantial part of the merchandise, equipment or other inventory of a business not in the ordinary course of that business.

Bulk Transfer Law—A law that requires sellers who negotiate bulk transfers (usually as a part of the sale of the business itself) to furnish buyers with a list of creditors and a schedule of the property being sold. The buyer must then give notice to the creditors of the impending sale.

Bundle of Rights—The theory that ownership of a parcel of real estate includes varied rights, such as the right to possess and use, sell, lease, and so on.

Business Opportunity—Any business which is for sale. A real estate salesperson's or broker's license authorizes its holder to engage in the sale of business opportunities, even if no real estate is involved in the transaction.

Call—In the description of real estate, where a boundary is being described or run; it is a reference to a distance, course, monument or a natural object, such as a tree or rock.

Cancellation—Termination of a contract without undoing acts which have already been performed under the contract.

Canons of Ethics—SEE: **Code of Ethics.**

Capacity—The legal ability or competency of a person to perform some act, such as enter into a contract or execute a deed or will. SEE: **Competent.**

Capital Improvement—Any improvement which is designed to become a permanent part of existing real property or any improvement which will have the effect of substantially prolonging the life of the property, such as replacement of the roof or installation of new siding.

Capitalization—A method of appraising real property by converting into present value the anticipated future net income from the property.

Capitalization Rate—A rate used in the capitalization method or income approach to appraising property. It is the rate believed to represent the proper relationship between the value of real property and the income it produces, a reasonable rate of return on an investment or the yield rate necessary to attract investment capital.

Capitalize—1. To provide with cash, or capital. 2. To determine the present value of an asset by discounting expected future income into current value.

Capture, Rule of—The person who is first to extract a mineral gets rights of ownership; applies to oil and gas.

Carry-Over Clause—A clause found in a listing agreement, providing that for some specified period following the expiration date of the listing the broker will still be entitled to the commission if someone who was shown the property while the listing agreement was in force later decides to buy.

Cash Flow—The net income after deducting from the gross income all operating and fixed expenses including both interest and principal paid on loans.

Caveat Emptor—A Latin term meaning "let the buyer beware," expressing the common law rule that a buyer purchases "as is" and at his or her own risk. The buyer is expected to examine and evaluate the property carefully before buying. This rule has lost much of its earlier strength, particularly in residential leases and sales.

C. C. & R.'s—The abbreviation for covenants, conditions, and restrictions.

Certificate of Eligibility—A certificate issued by the Veterans Administration to a veteran as evidence of eligibility for a Veterans Administration loan.

Certificate of Occupancy—A statement issued by a local government verifying that a newly constructed building is in compliance with all codes and may be occupied.

Certificate of Reasonable Value—A document issued by the Veterans Administration setting forth the property's current market value, based on a VA-approved appraisal.

Cesspool—Underground pit used to catch and temporarily hold sewage while it decomposes and leaches into the surrounding soil.

Change, Principle of—According to this principle, it is the future, not the past, that is of prime importance in estimating value, due to constant changes in social and economic forces that affect real property.

Charter—A written instrument showing a grant of power or right of a franchise.

Chattel—Personal property, such as money, livestock and automobiles.

Chattel Real—Personal property which is closely associated with real property, such as a lease.

Civil Law—The body of law concerned with the rights and liabilities of individuals in relation to one another (such as contracts), as distinguished from criminal law.

Civil Rights—Those rights guaranteed to a person by the law. The term is normally used in reference to constitutional and statutory protection against discrimination based on race, religion, color or national origin.

Civil Wrong—SEE: **Tort.**

Client—One who employs a broker, a lawyer or an appraiser. A real estate broker's client can be the seller, the buyer or both, but is usually the seller.

Closing—To close means to complete a transaction. It may mean reaching an agreement or putting the agreement into effect. In real estate, closing is the final stage in the transaction when the seller delivers the deed and the buyer delivers the purchase price.

Closing Costs—The expenses incurred in the transfer of real estate in addition to the purchase price. A typical list might include: appraisal fee, title insurance premium, real estate commission, and transfer tax.

Closing Date—Date at which the terms of a contract must be met or else the contract is terminated.

Closing Statement—A financial account given to buyer and seller at completion of a real estate transaction showing their respective credits and debits and the sums received and expended by the escrow holder.

Cloud on the Title—Any claim, encumbrance or apparent defect which affects clear title to real property.

Code of Ethics—A system of standards of accepted conduct. In the real estate profession, the Code of Ethics of the National Association of Realtors expresses the high standard of conduct expected of Realtors. Sometimes called the Canons of Ethics.

Codicil—An addition or change to a will. It must be executed with the same formalities as a will.

Collateral—Anything of value given or pledged as security for a debt or obligation.

Collusion—An agreement between two or more persons to defraud another.

Color of Title—Title that appears to be good title, but which in fact is not.

Commercial Acre—The remainder of an acre of newly subdivided land after deducting the amount of land dedicated for trees or sidewalks.

Commercial Bank—A repository for demand and savings deposits, a large percentage of which are reinvested in a variety of commercial areas.

Commercial Paper—Negotiable instruments such as promissory notes, sold normally by business corporations to meet short-term capital needs.

Commercial Property—Income-producing property zoned for business purposes, such as warehouses, restaurants, hotels and office buildings. To be distinguished from residential, industrial or agricultural property.

Commingle—To mingle or mix. In real estate circles, it means to mix personal funds with money held in trust on behalf of a client. The law is clear in this regard: trust money and personal funds must be kept separate; failure to do so will likely result in the suspension or revocation of the offender's license. SEE: **Conversion.**

Commission—1. The compensation or fee paid a broker for services in connection with a real estate transaction. 2. A group of people organized for a particular purpose or function.

Commitment—A promise to do something in the future. A finance lending institution's promise or commitment to make a loan. The commitment may be "firm" or "conditional." A conditional commitment might be contingent on something such as a satisfactory credit report on the borrower.

Common Areas—The land and improvements in a condominium, planned unit development or cooperative housing project owned and used collectively by all the residents. Common areas usually include driveways, recreational facilities, stairwells, and other areas available for common use.

Common Law—The body of law based on the decisions of judges, developed in England and incorporated into the American system of justice (in every state but Louisiana, which bases its laws on old French law).

Community Property—The property owned jointly by a married couple. Community property laws hold that any property acquired through labor or earnings of either spouse (but not through gift or inheritance) belongs to both of them equally.

Comparison Approach—The comparative analysis approach, comparative approach, market comparison or market data approach are basically synonymous terms for a method of real estate appraisal in which the recent selling prices of properties similar to the one being appraised are used as the basis for the value estimate.

Competent—Legally qualified to perform an act, such as enter into a contract; of legal age and sound mind.

Competition, Principle of—According to this principle, profits tend to encourage competition, and excess profits to encourage or result in ruinous competition.

Compliance Inspection—An inspection of a building to determine, for the benefit of a real estate lender, whether such things as building codes, specifications or conditions established by a prior inspection, have been met before a loan is made.

Condemnation—1. The taking of private property for public use through the government's power of eminent domain, such as for streets, sewers, airports or railroads. 2. Declaration that a structure is unfit and must be closed or destroyed.

Condemnation Appraisal—An estimate of the value of condemned property to determine the just compensation to be paid the parties.

Condition—A provision in an agreement or contract, limiting or modifying the rights and obligations of the parties.

Conditional Commitment—An agreement to loan a definite amount of money on a particular piece of property, subject to approval of the credit rating of some future unknown buyer.

Conditional Fee—Ownership of land which may be terminated by the previous owner if certain conditions occur.

Conditional Use Permits—Permits which allow property to be used in a manner not normally allowed under the zoning laws. May be revoked if the property is used for any purpose not specified in the permit.

Condominium—A type of ownership of real property consisting of a separate interest in an individual unit combined with an undivided interest in common areas such as hallways, stairways, the land and so forth. A condominium can be commercial or industrial, as well as residential.

Confirmation of Sale—Court approval of a sale by an executor, administrator or guardian.

Conformity, Principle of—According to this principle, the maximum value of property is realized when there is a reasonable degree of social and economic homogeneity in a neighborhood.

Consent—To agree, give permission or assent.

Conservation—1. Regarding real estate, conservation means preservation of structures or neighborhoods in a sound and favorable condition. 2. Regarding natural resources, it is preserving and/or utilizing them in such a way as to provide the greatest long-term benefit.

Conservator—A person appointed by a court to take care of the property of another who is incapable of taking care of his own property.

Consideration—Anything of value given to induce another to enter into a contract, such as money, services, goods or a promise.

Conspiracy—An agreement or plan between two or more persons to perform an unlawful act.

Consummate—To complete.

Contiguous—Physically adjoining, abutting or in close proximity, such as two parcels of real estate next to each other.

Contingency—A happening or event that is necessary before a contract becomes binding.

Contour—The surface shape or configuration of land. A contour map depicts the topography by means of lines, called contour lines, which connect points of equal elevation.

Contract—An agreement, for consideration, between competent parties to do or not do a certain thing. It is an agreement enforceable at law and as a general rule may be written or oral.

Contract, Bilateral—A contract in which each party promises to perform something in exchange for the other's promise to perform.

Contract, Broker and Salesperson—A contract between a broker and a salesperson outlining their mutual obligations.

Contract, Conditional Sale—A contract for sale of real or personal property where possession and use is delivered to the buyer at the outset, but the seller retains legal title until the conditions of the contract have been fulfilled (usually payment in full of the purchase price).

Contract, Executory—A contract in which one or both parties have not yet completed performance. An *executed* contract is one in which both parties have completely performed their obligations under the contract.

Contract, Implied—One deduced or implied by the actions of the principals; contrasted with an *express* contract, where the words forming the agreement are stated, orally or in writing.

Contract, Installment Sales—A contract for the sale of property in which the buyer receives possession of the property, but not title to it, upon signing the contract. When the full purchase price has been paid, the deed is delivered to the buyer and title is conveyed. This type of contract is also referred to as a contract of sale, conditional sales contract, or land contract.

Contract, Oral—A verbal or spoken agreement.

Contract, Sales—SEE: **Earnest Money Agreement, Deposit Receipt, Installlment Sales Contract.**

Contract, Unenforceable—One that will not be enforced through the courts because its contents can't be proven (usually an oral contract) or because it is of a type required to be in writing, like a real estate contract, but is not, or because it is voidable by the other party.

Contract, Unilateral—A contract which is accepted by performance. The offeror is not required to perform his or her part of the contract (a promise) until the offeree has performed.

Contract, Valid—A binding, legally enforceable contract.

Contract, Void—A "contract" which is really not a contract because it lacks some key element or is otherwise defective.

Contract, Voidable—An apparently valid contract which is defective in some way and may be terminated without liability by one or both of the parties.

Contractor—One who contracts to deliver labor or materials or to construct a building or to do other work for a certain price.

Contract Rent—SEE: **Rent, Economic.**

Contribution, Principle of—According to this principle, the value of real property reaches its maximum when the improvements on the property produce the highest return commensurate with the investment.

Conversion—1. Changing the use or character of a property from one thing to another. 2. Appropriating property belonging to another to one's own use.

Conveyance—The transfer of title to real property from one person to another by means of a written document, such as a deed.

Co-operative Apartment or Building—In a co-operative, the individual owner purchases shares in the corporation that owns the building. The individual receives a proprietary lease on the individual unit and the right to use the common areas.

Corner Influence—The increase in value of a piece of property due to its being on or near a corner.

Corporation—An artificial person, consisting of an association of individual natural persons, but regarded by the law as a single person, separate from the individuals.

Corporation, Foreign—A corporation doing business in one state, that was created or incorporated in another state.

Correction Lines—Adjustment lines used in the government survey system to compensate for curvature of the earth. They occur at 24 mile intervals, every fourth township line, where the distance between north and south range lines is corrected to 6 miles.

Correlation—In appraisals, correlation is the bringing together of the estimates obtained separately from three methods of appraisal (Cost, Comparison and Capitalization) to form a single final estimate of value.

Cost—The amount paid for anything in money, goods or services.

Cost Approach to Value—One of the three appraisal methods. A value estimate is arrived at by estimating the cost of replacement or reproduction of improvements on the property, then deducting from that the estimated accrued depreciation and adding the estimated market value of the land.

Cost Basis—SEE: **Basis.**

Co-tenancy—A type of ownership where two or more persons own undivided interests in the same property at the same time. SEE: **Tenancy, Joint** and **Tenancy in Common.**

Counteroffer—A new offer made by the offeree in reply to an offer to enter into a contract. It constitutes a rejection of the first offer and the roles of the two parties are now reversed. The original offeror is the offeree and can accept or reject the counteroffer. This situation commonly arises when the original offeree wants to make some change in the offer he or she has received. Any change, however slight, constitutes a rejection of the original offer.

County—A subdivision of the state created by the state and deriving all its powers from the state.

Courses—Directions in terms of compass bearings, used in metes and bounds descriptions.

Covenant—1. A written agreement or promise to do or not do something. 2. A stipulation that a property be used or not used for a particular purpose or purposes. 3. A guarantee that some state of facts exists (good title in a grantor of a deed). It occurs in such documents as leases, mortgages, land contracts and deeds.

Covenant, Restrictive—A promise not to do an act or use property for a specific purpose.

Covenant of Quiet Enjoyment—A promise that the owner will not be disturbed in the use of the land by claims of other persons to the land.

Covenant of Right to Convey—A promise that the grantor has the legal ability to make a valid conveyance.

Covenant of Seisen—A promise that the grantor has good title and right to possession of land.

Covenant of Warranty—A promise that the grantor will defend the grantee's title if it is challenged in court.

C.P.M. (Certified Property Manager)—A professional property manager who has satisfied the requirements to be designated a Certified Property Manager by the Institute of Real Estate Management of the National Association of Realtors.

C.R.E. (Counselor of Real Estate)—A member of the American Society of Real Estate Counselors.

Credit—A payment which is receivable, as opposed to a debit, which is a payment due.

Creditor, Secured—A creditor who has a lien on specific property, such as a mortgagee.

Cul-de-sac—A dead end street, normally with a circular turnaround at the end.

Customer—In real estate, a customer is usually a prospective purchaser.

Damages—The amount of money one can recover as compensation for injury to his or her person or property resulting from an act or failure to act.

Damages, Compensatory—The amount of money awarded for injury, damages or loss incurred.

Damages, Liquidated—A sum stipulated and agreed upon by the parties at the time of entering into a contract, as being payable as compensation for loss suffered in the event of a breach. The buyer's earnest money deposit is often retained by the seller as liquidated damages in the event of a breach of contract by the purchaser.

Datum—Reference point used by surveyors to determine elevation.

Dealer—One who regularly buys and sells property in the ordinary course of business.

Dealer Property—Property held for sale to customers rather than long-term investment.

Debit—A charge or a debt, listed on the left side of an accounting statement. In real estate, a debt owing at closing or settlement.

Debtor—One who owes something, normally money, to another.

Debt Service—The amount of money required to make the periodic payments of principal and interest on an amortized debt.

Decedent—A person who has died.

Declaration of Abandonment—The act of voluntarily releasing a property from homestead protection. SEE: **Homestead.**

Declaration of Homestead—The act of applying for homestead protection. SEE: **Homestead.**

Declaration of Restrictions—A statement of all the conditions, covenants and restrictions affecting a piece of property.

Dedication—An appropriation or granting of private property for public use; may be of the entire "fee simple" interest or just an easement, such as for sidewalks or streets.

Dedication, Common Law—Transfer of land from private to public ownership or use by virtue of acquiescence in public use of the land for an extended period of time.

Dedication, Statutory—Transfer of land from private to public ownership as required by law, for example as a prerequisite to subdivision approval.

Deduction—A deduction is an amount allowed to be subtracted from a person's income before taxation or from the value of a property before its value is taxed.

Deductions, Recovery—Deductions allowed businesses to enable them to recoup capital outlays for business property.

Deduction, Repair—A deduction allowed on most types of income property for expenditures made to keep the property in ordinary, efficient operating condition.

Deed—A written instrument which, when properly executed and delivered, conveys title or ownership of real property from the owner to the grantee. Deeds are of various types, the major differences between them being what covenants, if any, are made by the grantor. SEE: the various types of deeds, such as **Warranty, Grant,** or **Quitclaim.**

Deed, Administrator's—Form of deed used by an administrator of an estate to convey property owned by a deceased person.

Deed, Bargain and Sale—A deed which states the consideration and conveys the grantor's interest in the property to the grantee. It may or may not contain covenants against the grantor's acts, that is, stipulate that the grantor has done nothing to harm or cloud the title.

Deed, Correction—A deed used to correct minor mistakes in an earlier deed, such as misspellings of names or errors in description of the parcel.

Deed, General Warranty—Type of deed wherein the grantor warrants certain facts to the grantee.

Deed, Gift—A deed freely given in which the consideration is love and affection, rather than valuable consideration, such as money, goods or services.

Deed, Grant—The deed most often used in California to convey title. The grantor warrants that: 1) he or she has not conveyed title to someone else, and 2) that the estate being conveyed is free of encumbrances done, made or suffered by the grantor or those claiming under him or her.

Deed, Partial Reconveyance—The document used to release a portion of the secured property from the lien of a blanket deed of trust. SEE: **Blanket Mortgage.**

Deed, Quitclaim—A deed which operates to convey and release any interest in a piece of real property which the grantor may have. It contains no warranties of any kind, but does transfer any right, title, or interest the grantor has at the time the deed was executed.

Deed, Sheriff's—A deed delivered by the sheriff, on court order, to the holder of the **Certificate of Sale** following the period of redemption after a mortgage foreclosure.

Deed, Special Warranty—A deed in which the grantor warrants title only against defects arising during the time he or she owned the property and not against defects arising before that time; often used by executors and administrators of estates.

Deed, Statutory Warranty—A short form of the General Warranty Deed in which the covenants are implied rather than spelled out. SEE: **Warranty Deed.**

Deed, Tax—The deed given to the successful bidder when property is sold to satisfy unpaid property taxes.

Deed, Trustee's—The deed issued to a purchaser of foreclosed property at a trustee's sale.

Deed, Warranty—A deed containing warranties or guarantees of clear title and the right to convey, as well as the grantor's willingness to defend against claims that the title conveyed is not good. Also called a general warranty deed or statutory (short form) warranty deed.

Deed, Wild—Deed which cannot be located under the grantor-grantee system of indexing.

Deed Executed Under Court Order—A deed, such as a sheriff's deed or tax deed, which is the result of a court action, such as foreclosure.

Deed in Lieu of Foreclosure—Deed given by a mortgagor to the mortgagee to satisfy the debt and to avoid a foreclosure suit.

Deed of Confirmation—SEE: **Correction Deed.**

Deed of Partition—Deed used by co-owners, such as joint tenants or tenants in common, to divide up the co-owned property so that each can own a separate portion.

Deed of Release—Deed used to release property or part of it from a lien created by a land contract. Most often used when the contract covers more than one parcel of land.

Deed of Trust—A security device, similar to a mortgage, used to create a security interest in real property to secure performance of an obligation, normally a money debt. Parties to a deed of trust are trustor (borrower), beneficiary (lender), and trustee (neutral third party).

Deed Restrictions—Limitations in a deed limiting or restricting the use of the property, such as "residential only" or "no building over 35 feet in height."

Default—Failure to fulfill an obligation, duty or promise. The most common default is probably failure of a borrower or lessee to pay money when due.

Defeasance Clause—A clause in mortgages, deeds of trust and leases which cancels or defeats a certain right upon the occurrence of a certain event.

Defeasible Fee or Fee Simple Qualified—SEE: **Fee Simple Defeasible.**

Deferred Maintenance—Repair or maintenance of property that should have been done but was postponed, resulting in physical depreciation of the building.

Deficiency Judgment—A personal judgment against a debtor in the event that the proceeds from the sale of the security, after default, are not enough to pay off the loan.

Degree—In surveying, a unit of circular measurement equal to 1/360th part of one complete rotation around a point in a plane.

Delivery—The legal transfer of an instrument evidencing title or ownership. A deed must be delivered and accepted to convey title.

Demand—The desire and ability to purchase something. One of the four elements of value. SEE: **Scarcity, Transferability,** and **Utility.**

Demise—A transfer of an estate or interest in real property to another for years, for life or at will.

Density—The term refers to the number of buildings per acre or the number of occupants per unit of land, square mile, acre, etc. Zoning ordinances are designed to control not only the manner in which the land is used (residential, industrial or agricultural), but also the number of buildings situated on the land and the number of people using it.

Deposit—Money offered as an indication of good faith for the future performance of a contract to purchase. Also called earnest money.

Deposit Receipt—Written instrument used as a receipt for the earnest money and to submit an offer for the purchase of real property. Same as earnest money agreement.

Deposition—Formal out-of-court testimony of a witness in a lawsuit taken before trial, for possible use later in the trial. Testimony taken either for discovery, to determine the facts of the case, or when a witness will be unable to attend the trial, or both.

Depreciation— A loss in value. For appraisal, depreciation results from physical deterioration, such as cracks in the foundation; functional obsolescence, such as old fashioned plumbing or lighting fixtures; or economic obsolescence, such as changes in the neighborhood.

Depreciation, Curable—Physical deterioration and functional obsolescence which would ordinarily be repaired or replaced by a prudent owner.

Depreciation, Incurable—Items of physical deterioration, functional obsolescence or economic obsolescence that are physically impossible or not economically feasible to correct.

Depreciation, Straight Line—A method of calculating depreciation for appraisal purposes where an equal portion of a structure's value is deducted each year over the anticipated useful life. When the full value of the improvement has been depreciated its economic life is exhausted.

Depth Table—Mathematical table used in real estate appraisal to estimate the differences in value between lots with different depths. Front footage has the greatest value and land at the rear of the lot has the least value.

Dereliction— See **Reliction.**

Detached Residence—A home physically separated from and not connected to another by a common wall.

Developed Land—Land which has been improved by man-made additions, such as buildings, roads or sidewalks.

Developer—One who makes changes to bring land to profitable use by subdividing and/or improving it.

Devise—Gift of real property through a will. The donor is the testator and the recipient is the devisee.

Devisee—Recipient of real property under a will.

Disbursements—Term used in accounting to describe money paid out or expended.

Discount—1. An amount withheld from a loan amount at the time the loan was made. 2. To sell a note at a reduced value or less than face value.

Discount Rate—The interest rate charged by the Federal Reserve Banks on loans made to commercial banks.

Discrimination—Unequal treatment, either favorable or unfavorable, based on a class, race or group to which a person or persons belong.

Disintegration—The declining period when property's present economic usefulness is near an end and constant upkeep is necessary.

Disintermediation—Withdrawal of savings deposits from an intermediary financial institution, such as a savings and loan association or commercial bank, by its depositors, in favor of direct investment.

Documentary Tax Stamps—SEE: **Revenue Stamps.**

Domicile—The state where a person has his or her permanent home. To establish domicile, it is necessary to have both a physical presence in the state and the intent to make the state one's permanent residence.

Down Zoning—The act of rezoning land for a more limited use.

Drainage—A system which draws water off land, either artificially (as by pipes) or naturally (as by slope or natural watercourse).

Due-on-Sale Clause—A clause in a loan agreement which states that the entire amount of the loan shall be due and payable if the security property is sold.

Duplex—A single structure that contains two separate housing units, with separate entrances, living rooms, baths and kitchens.

Duress—Unlawful force, constraint, threats or actions used to compel someone to do something against his or her will.

Dwelling—A building or part of a building used or intended to be used as living quarters.

Earnest Money—A deposit or downpayment made by the prospective purchaser of real estate as evidence of good faith in completing the purchase.

Earnest Money Agreement—A contract of purchase and sale wherein the buyer deposits an amount of money as evidence of his good faith intent to purchase; called a deposit receipt in California.

Easement—A right to use some part of the property of another for a particular purpose, such as for a driveway or for installing and maintaining a water line. SEE: **Tenement, Dominant** and **Tenement, Servient**.

Easement, Implied—One created by implication.

Easement Appurtenant—An easement for the benefit of a particular piece of property. COMPARE: **Easement in Gross.**

Easement by Express Grant—Easement given to another by means of a deed.

Easement by Express Reservation—Easement created by deed in favor of a landowner who transfers part of the property.

Easement by Implication—Unwritten easement, created when a parcel of land is divided.

Easement by Necessity—An easement which is implied by law, as for example where a parcel of land is sold without any access to a road.

Easement in Gross—An easement for the benefit of a person. COMPARE: **Easement Appurtenant.**

Economic Life—The period during which improved property will yield a return over and above the rent due to the land itself.

Economic Obsolescence—Loss in value caused by factors outside the property itself, such as zoning changes or deterioration of the neighborhood.

Effective Age—The effective age of an improvement is determined by its condition, not the actual chronological age. Such things as good or poor maintenance may increase or decrease the effective age. A fifty year old home, well maintained, may have an effective age of ten or fifteen years, meaning that, in terms of remaining usefulness, it is no older than a 10- or 15-year-old home.

Egress—A passageway leading from property; a means of exiting. It is the opposite of ingress. The terms *ingress* and *egress* usually refer to easements.

Ejectment—Legal action to evict someone not legally entitled to possession of real property. SEE: **Eviction; Unlawful Detainer.**

Elements of Comparison—Elements used in the market data approach to appraisal, consisting of time, location and physical characteristics.

Emblements—Crops which are produced annually through the labor of the cultivator, such as wheat.

Emblements, Doctrine of—Right of an agricultural tenant to enter land after termination of the lease for the purpose of harvesting crops.

Eminent Domain—The power of the government to take (condemn) private property for public use, upon payment of just compensation to the owner. The power may be delegated to public corporations, such as utilities, or to public service corporations, such as railroads.

Encroachment—Unlawful physical intrusion upon the property of another, usually the result of mistake.

Encumbrance—Any right or interest in a piece of property held by someone other than the owner.

Endorsement—A method of transferring ownership of a negotiable instrument, such as a promissory note, by signing on the back of the instrument.

Endorsement, Special—An endorsement to a specific holder in due course.

Endorsement "In Blank"—An endorsement where no holder in due course is specified.

Enjoin—To prohibit by a court order, to forbid. It can also mean to command performance of an act. A court can issue an injunction enjoining an individual from doing something, like behaving in a discriminatory manner.

Equilibrium—A period of stability, during which property undergoes little, if any, change.

Equity—1. The difference between the value of a piece of property and the charges against it. 2. In law, equity is a system that overrides the common and statutory law in order to bring about a fair and just result, particularly in those areas where the remedy at law (money damages) is inadequate. Specific performance of a contract ordered by the court is an equitable remedy.

Erosion—Gradual loss of soil due to the action of water or wind.

Escalator Clause—A clause in a contract or mortgage providing for the adjustment of payments or interest in the event of certain contingencies, such as changes in taxes or the prime interest rate.

Escheat—The reversion of property to the state when a person dies without leaving a valid will and without heirs entitled to the property.

Escrow—1. The process in which something of value (such as money or documents) is held by a disinterested third party, a stakeholder called an escrow agent, until certain conditions contained in the escrow instructions have been complied with. 2. A deed or money or piece of property delivered into the keeping of an escrow agent, pending compliance by all parties to the real estate agreement.

Estate—1. The ownership interest which a person has in real property; must be an interest which is, or can become, a possessory interest. There are freehold estates (fee simple and life estates) and less-than-freehold estates (leasehold interests). 2. The property left by a decedent.

Estate, Less-Than-Freehold—A leasehold estate. An estate held by a tenant under a lease. The less-than-freehold estates include estates for years, periodic estates and estates at will.

Estate at Will—A leasehold estate for an indefinite period of time, which in most states can be terminated at any time by either landlord or tenant without notice. California requires 30 days' notice. Also called a **Tenancy at Will.**

Estate for Life, or Life Estate—A freehold estate which is held for the life of its owner or for the life of some other person (the measuring life).

Estate for Years—An estate for a definite period of time, after which the estate automatically terminates.

Estate in Fee Simple—SEE: **Fee Simple.**

Estate in Remainder—SEE: **Remainder.**

Estate in Reversion—SEE: **Reversion.**

Estate of Inheritance—An estate which may descend to heirs, such as a fee simple estate.

Estoppel—A legal doctrine that prevents a person from asserting rights or facts that are inconsistent with a previous position or representation.

Estoppel Certificate—An instrument which itself prevents individuals from later asserting facts different from those contained in the document. Often used in assignments of mortgages. The borrower signs the estoppel certificate, confirming the mortgage balance to be a given figure, and may not thereafter make any claim to the contrary. Also called a certificate of no defense or declaration of no set-off.

Ethics—A system of accepted principles or standards of moral conduct and behavior. SEE: **Code of Ethics.**

Eviction—Dispossession, expulsion or ejection of someone from property. May be either actual (a physical removal from the premises), or constructive (a violation by the landlord of the covenant of quiet enjoyment, as by shutting off the water or electricity).

Eviction, Constructive—Any act by a landlord that so impairs the tenant's quiet enjoyment of the premises or makes the property unfit for its intended use that the tenant is forced to move out.

Exchange of Real Estate—A transaction in which one piece of property is traded for another piece of like-kind property. If the property involved is held for investment or the production of income, such a transaction may result in deferral of some or all of the capital gains tax. If any consideration other than real property of like-kind is transferred, such as money, that additional consideration is known as "boot" and is taxable.

Exclusive Right to Sell—Written listing agreement giving one agent (broker) the right to sell a piece of property for a specified period of time and giving the broker the right to receive the commission if the property is sold during that time, regardless of who sells it.

Execute—To do, perform or complete, as in executing a deed by signing and acknowledging it.

Execution—Legal process whereby the court orders an official, such as a sheriff, to seize and sell property of a debtor to satisfy a judgment or other lien.

Executor—A man named in a will to carry out the provisions of the will. A woman named in a will to perform the same functions would be an **executrix.** SEE: **Administrator.**

Exemption—In the area of taxes, if persons or property are exempt from a particular tax, they are not subject to it, i.e., the persons or property are not taxed.

Express—Stated in spoken words or writing, as opposed to **implied**. An express contract is one entered into through oral or written agreement of the parties.

Extender Clause—1. A clause in a listing agreement providing for automatic renewal of the agreement after the initial period until such time as the parties agree to terminate it. 2. A clause in a listing agreement providing that the broker will still receive the commission if the property is sold during a specified period of time after the termination of the listing to someone who was a prospect of the broker during the term of the listing. Also called a "**carry-over**" **clause**, "**safety**" **clause** or **protection period clause.**

Failure of Purpose—Excuse for rescinding a contract; if the contract cannot achieve its intended purpose, the parties are released from their obligations.

"Fannie Mae"—A popular name for the Federal National Mortgage Association. Also called F.N.M.A.

Farmer's Home Administration—A federal agency of the Department of Agriculture that provides or assists in providing credit to farmers and others in rural areas, where reasonable financing from private sources is not readily available.

Feasibility Study—An analysis of the cost-benefit ratio of a proposed project, often required by lenders before giving a loan commitment.

Federal Deposit Insurance Corporation (F.D.I.C.)—A federal agency which insures deposits in state and federally chartered banks and savings and loans.

Federal Fair Housing Law—A law enacted in 1968 which makes it illegal to sell or rent residential property or vacant land that will be used for residential construction on a discriminatory basis. It does not prohibit discriminatory practices related to business or industrial real estate transactions.

Federal Home Loan Bank System (F.H.L.B.)—A federal organization consisting of twelve regional Federal Home Loan Banks, which provide reserve funds for federal savings and loan associations, performing much the same service as the Federal Reserve System does for commercial banks.

Federal Home Loan Mortgage Corporation (F.H.L.M.C.)—A federal agency that buys mortgages in the secondary market from banks and savings and loans. Also called "**Freddie Mac**".

Federal Housing Administration (F.H.A.)—Federal agency that insures residential loans. SEE: **Insurance, Mutual Mortgage.**

Federal National Mortgage Association (F.N.M.A.)—A private corporation, originally a government agency, popularly known as "Fannie Mae," which supports a secondary mortgage market by buying and selling mortgage loans.

Federal Trade Commission (F.T.C.)—A federal agency responsible for investigating and eliminating unfair and deceptive business practices. It is also the agency charged with enforcing the **Truth in Lending Law.**

Fee—An estate of inheritance in real property.

Fee, Qualified—A fee simple estate which is conveyed subject to certain conditions or limitations. For example, the grantor may deliver title with a stipulation in the deed that the property being conveyed always be used as a single family residence. If the grantee violates this condition, title reverts to the grantor. Also called a **Fee Simple Defeasible** or **Defeasible Fee.**

Fee Simple, or Fee Simple Absolute—The greatest estate one can have in real property; of indefinite duration; with no conditions or restrictions on the use of the land other than public ones, such as zoning regulations; freely transferable or inheritable. Also known as the **Fee.**

Fee Simple Defeasible—A fee estate in real property which is subject to being divested, or dispossessed, upon the happening of a certain occurrence or condition.

Fee Simple Subject to a Condition Subsequent—A defeasible fee which may be terminated by re-entry of the grantor after breach of a condition in the grant; the only form of defeasible fee currently recognized in California.

F.H.A.—Abbreviation for Federal Housing Administration.

Fiduciary Relationship—A relationship of trust and confidence, often existing where one person (the fiduciary) is allowed to represent, transact business, or hold or manage property for another.

Finance Charge—All charges assessed a borrower, directly or indirectly, in connection with the credit extended.

Financing Statement—A brief instrument which, when filed, perfects or gives notice of a creditor's security interest in an item of personal property.

Finder's Fee—A referral fee paid to someone for directing a buyer or seller to a real estate agent.

Firm Commitment—A definite agreement by a lender to make a loan to a particular borrower on a particular piece of property. Also, an agreement by the F.H.A. to insure a loan made to a specified borrower on a particular piece of property. SEE: **Conditional Commitment.**

Fiscal Year—Any twelve-month period used as a business year for accounting, tax, and other financial purposes, as opposed to the calendar year.

Fixed Disbursement Plan—A type of construction financing which calls for a series of predetermined disbursements at various stages of construction.

Fixed Term—A period of time which has a definite beginning and ending.

Fixture—Personal property which has become so affixed to real property that it is legally considered real property.

Foreclosure—Legal action instituted by a lienholder whereby property is sold to satisfy a debt following default by the debtor.

Foreclosure, Judicial—1. A sale of property by a court order to satisfy a lien. 2. A mortgage foreclosure, as contrasted with the nonjudicial deed of trust foreclosure.

Foreclosure, Nonjudicial—Where a trustee arranges the forced sale of property pursuant to the power of sale clause in a deed of trust, after default by the borrower.

Forfeiture—Loss of a right or something else of value as a result of failure to perform an obligation or condition.

4 3 2 1 Depth Rule—Appraisal method used to evaluate the different sections, from front to rear, of a parcel of land. Dividing the parcel into four equal segments, and using 100 feet depth as standard, the first segment (or front), is assigned 40% of the total value, the second 30%, the third 20%, and the rear 10%. The front of a lot has greater utility and value than does the rear.

Franchise—A right or privilege granted by a government to conduct a certain business, or a right granted by a private business to use its trade name in conducting business.

Fraud—A misrepresentation or concealment of a material fact, either known to be false or without regard as to its truthfulness or falsity, which misrepresentation is relied upon by another to his/her damage.

Fraud, Actual—Intentional deceit or misrepresentation to cheat or deceive another.

Fraud, Constructive—Action which does not reach the degree of deceit or intentional misrepresentation which is required for actual fraud but still does not meet an accepted standard of behavior at law. Often it is a result of a negligent breach of a fiduciary relationship.

Free and Clear—Title, or ownership, of real property that is completely free of any encumbrances, such as mortgages and other liens.

Freehold—An ownership estate in real property; can be either a fee simple or life estate. The holder of a freehold estate has title, as opposed to the holder of a less-than-freehold estate (leasehold estate), who is a tenant.

Frontage—The distance a piece of property extends along a street or body of water.

Front Foot—A measurement of property for sale or valuation, with each foot of frontage presumed to extend the entire depth of the lot.

Fructus Industriales—Those fruits of the land which are produced by the labor and industry of the occupant, such as crops.

Fructus Naturales—Those products which are produced by the powers of nature alone, such as uncultivated trees.

Functional Obsolescence—Loss in value of an improvement due to inadequate or outmoded equipment or as a result of either age or poor design.

Gain—That portion of the proceeds from the sale of a capital asset, such as real estate, that the I.R.S. recognizes as taxable profit.

Good Faith—SEE: **Bona Fide.**

Good Will—An intangible asset of a business resulting from a good reputation with the public and an indication of future, return business.

Government Lots—Parcels of land which, because of location (normally next to bodies of water), could not be divided into regular sections by government survey. They are given government lot numbers.

Government National Mortgage Association (G.N.M.A.)—A federal agency created when F.N.M.A. was divided into two corporations in 1968. Popularly known as "Ginnie Mae," the agency is responsible for managing and liquidating certain older FNMA loans and purchasing loans from special assistance programs (such as loans for urban renewal projects); it also has a mortgage-backed securities program.

Government Survey—A system of land description in which the land is divided into squares each approximately six miles square (containing 36 square miles), called townships, which are divided into 36 sections, each approximately one mile square and containing approximately 640 acres. Also called rectangular survey or township and range system.

Grant—To transfer or convey real property or an interest therein.

Grantee—The one who receives a grant of real property, regardless of the type of deed used.

Granting Clause—Words in a deed which indicate an intent to make a transfer of an interest in land.

Grantor—The one who conveys or transfers real property or an interest therein.

Gross Income Multiplier Method—A method of valuing residential property by reference to the rental value of the property; also called the gross rent multiplier method.

Gross Rent Multiplier—A figure which is multiplied by the gross income of a piece of property to arrive at an estimate of the property's market value. Also known as gross income multiplier. The multiplier is obtained by dividing the sales price by the rental income.

Guardian—One appointed by the court to care for or administer the affairs of another, called a ward, because of the ward's inability to conduct his or her own affairs due to age, infirmity or insanity.

Guide Meridians—North-south lines in the government survey, spaced 24 miles apart.

Habendum Clause—The clause in a deed beginning "to have and to hold" which follows the granting clause and describes how the estate will be held.

Heir—One entitled to inherit property under the laws of intestate succession.

Heirs and Assigns—Heirs are those who inherit property. Assigns are successors in interest to property, i.e., by deed.

Highest and Best Use—The use which at the time of appraisal is most likely to produce the greatest net return from the property over a given period of time.

Holder in Due Course—One who obtained a negotiable instrument in good faith and for value, before the instrument was due, and without knowledge of any defects or that the instrument had been dishonored previously.

Homeowner's Association—A non-profit association comprised of homeowners within a subdivision (including planned unit developments and condominiums), which is charged with the responsibility of enforcing the subdivision's property restrictions. The association is usually created by the developer to ensure that the neighborhood will have a means of protecting itself against future depreciation after the lots are sold.

Homestead—A limited exemption against the claims of creditors for property used as the debtor's residence. A means of protecting the debtor's home from a forced sale to satisfy a judgment lien. SEE: **Declaration of Homestead.**

H.U.D.—Abbreviation and popular name for the **Department of Housing and Urban Development.**

Hypothecate—To make real or personal property security for an obligation without giving up possession of it.

Improvements—Man-made additions to real property.

Improvements, Misplaced—Improvements on land which do not conform to the most profitable use of the site. A misplaced improvement can be an overimprovement or an underimprovement.

Income Approach to Value—A method of appraising property basing the value upon the net amount of income produced by the property. It is calculated by subtracting the expenses of the property from the total income to determine the net income. Also known as the capitalization method or investor's method.

Income, Disposable—Income remaining after payment of income taxes.

Income, Effective Gross—A measure of the income-generating capacity of rental property, defined as the economic rent less the bad debt vacancy factor.

Income, Gross—Total income before deductions for expenses, depreciation, taxes and so forth.

Income, Spendable—The money that remains after deducting operating expenses, principal and interest payments, and income tax from the gross income. Also called net spendable income or cash flow.

Incompetent—A person not legally qualified to reach proper decisions, such as a minor, insane person or one who is feeble minded.

Incorporeal Rights—Non-possessory (intangible) rights in real estate, such as a dominant tenant's right to use a servient tenant's land (easement). An easement appurtenant is an incorporeal hereditament (inheritable) and an easement in gross is an incorporeal right, but not inheritable.

Increasing and Diminishing Returns, Principle of—Holds that a point is reached where additional investments in land in the form of labor or capital will not be justified by the resulting increase in net income.

Independent Contractor—One who, exercising independence in the choice of work to be performed, contracts to do or perform certain work for another person according to the independent contractor's own means and methods, without being subject to the control of such other persons except as to the product or result of the work. Real estate brokers are usually independent contractors.

Indexing—Means of cataloging documents such as deeds in the recording office; deeds are indexed according to grantor and grantee, and sometimes according to location of the land.

Ingress—Refers to access to property by a dominant tenant while exercising his use right (easement). Sometimes refers to the access a tenant has to leased property. Opposite of egress.

Injunction—A court order prohibiting some act or compelling an act to be done.

Innocent Improver—One who makes an improvement on land in the mistaken belief that he owns the land.

Installment Sale—A sale in which less than 100% of the selling price is received in the year of sale.

Instrument—A legal document that transfers title, creates a lien, or gives a right to payment, such as a deed, deed of trust, or contract.

Insurance, Casualty—Insurance against losses on property caused by fire, flood, theft or other disaster.

Insurance, Mutual Mortgage—The insurance provided by FHA to insure lenders against loss through foreclosure. The premium is paid by the borrower to the lender, who forwards it to the FHA.

Insurance, Private Mortgage—Insurance available to conventional lenders who are willing to make real estate loans exceeding the standard 80% loan-to-value ratio. The excess amount is insured by a private mortgage insurance company.

Insurance, Title—An insurance policy under which the insured is protected against any loss suffered as a result of the title to land not being as represented in the policy.

Insurance, Title, Extended Coverage Policy—A form of title insurance that insures against defects that would be found by an inspection and survey of the insured land.

Insurance, Title, Standard Coverage—A form of title insurance usually provided to the purchaser of real property by the seller. The standard form protects against title defects appearing in the chain of title, including such things as forgeries or deeds executed by incompetents, but does not protect against defects not appearing in the chain of title, such as the rights of parties in possession (i.e., adverse possessors) or unrecorded easements.

Integration—The beginning stage of the life cycle of a property; the development stage.

Interest—1. A charge for the use of another's money, sometimes referred to as rent for the use of money. 2. A right in or share of something. Partial ownership is an interest in real property, and a mortgage is evidence of a lender's financial interest in property.

Interest, Compound—Interest computed both on the principal and its accrued interest.

Interest, Prepaid—Interest on a loan which is paid at the time of closing or settlement; sometimes called interim interest.

Interest, Simple—Interest that is computed on the principal amount of the loan only. The type of interest charged in connection with real estate loans.

Interstate Land Sales Full Disclosure Act—Federal legislation designed to provide consumers with full and accurate information in regard to property which is sold or advertised across state lines.

Intestate—The characterization of a person who has died without leaving a valid will.

Intestate Succession—Transfer of property of a decedent who has not left a will; controlled by statutes.

Invalid—Unfounded in law; not of binding force; not valid.

Inventory—A detailed list of the stock-in-trade of a business.

Inverse Condemnation Action—A court action by a private landowner against the government seeking compensation for damage to property that resulted from government action.

Investment Property—Unimproved property that produces no income, but is held for capital growth through increases in price.

Inverted Pyramid—A way to envision ownership of land; theoretically, a person owns all the earth and sky which is enclosed by an inverted pyramid with its tip at the center of the earth and its base corresponding to the boundaries of the property, extending into the sky.

Joint Venture—Two or more individuals or organizations joining together for one specific project. A joint venture is of limited duration; if the members of the venture undertake another project, the association may become a partnership.

Judgment—The final determination by a court of the rights and responsibilities of the parties in a lawsuit. If the court's finding includes an award of money as damages, the judgment can become a general lien on the debtor's property.

Judgment Creditor—A person to whom money is owed by virtue of a judgment in a lawsuit.

Judgment Debtor—A person who owes money by virtue of a judgment in a lawsuit.

Just Compensation—SEE: **Eminent Domain.**

Land—In a legal sense it is the solid part of the surface of the earth (as distinguished from water), everything affixed to it, by nature or by man, and anything on it or in it, such as minerals and water.

Landlocked—A parcel of land without access to any type of road or highway. The owner of landlocked land can obtain an easement by necessity from the court.

Landlord—A lessor. A landowner who has leased his or her property.

Landmark—A monument, natural or artificial, set up on the boundary line of two adjacent estates, to fix the boundary.

Latent Defects—Defects in property that are not visible or apparent.

Lateral Support—The right to support of soil in its natural state from land adjoining it. An owner is protected by law from excavation on neighboring property that would deny this support.

Lawful Object—The objective of a contract which is not against the law.

Lease—A contract for the possession and profits of real estate in return for rent. The property owner is the lessor, the tenant is the lessee.

Lease, Flat—Also called a straight lease, it is one with regular, equal payments; one in which the amount and the time for payment remain constant throughout the term of the lease.

Lease, Graduated—A lease in which the payments begin at one rate but increase at agreed intervals over the term of the lease.

Lease, Gross—A lease where the lessee pays a fixed amount and the lessor pays the charges incurred through ownership of the property, such as taxes and insurance. COMPARE: **Net Lease.**

Lease, Ground—A lease of the land only, normally for a long term, and sometimes secured by improvements placed on the land by the user.

Lease, Net—A lease requiring the tenant to pay all the costs of maintaining the building, such as taxes, utilities and insurance, in addition to the rental fee paid the landlord.

Lease, Percentage—A lease in which the rental is based on a percentage of the monthly or annual gross sales.

Lease, Sandwich—A leasehold interest lying between the primary lease and the operating lease, or the lease of the lessee in possession.

Lease, Straight—A lease in which the rent is paid in periodic equal payments, such as $850.00 per month. Also called a flat lease.

Leaseback—SEE: **Sale-Leaseback.**

Leasehold Estate—A tenant's right to occupy real estate during the term of the lease.

Legacy—A gift of personal property by will; a bequest. The person receiving a legacy is a legatee.

Legal Description—A method of describing a parcel of real estate that is recognized by law. Property can be legally described by (a) Lot, Block and Subdivision (also called maps and plats or recorded map); (b) Government Survey (also called Township and Range or Rectangular Survey System); or (c) Metes and Bounds.

Legal Person—A person created by law, possessing certain powers and duties of a natural person; usually this is a corporation. Also called an artificial person.

Legatee—Recipient of personal property under a will.

Lenders, Institutional—Banks, savings and loan associations and life insurance companies, that invest others' funds in mortgages and other loans; as distinguished from individual or private lenders who invest their own money.

Lessee—The party to a lease known as the tenant.

Lessor—One who has leased property to another. The party to a lease known as the landlord.

Leverage—The effective use of borrowed money to finance an investment such as real estate.

Liability, Joint and Several—A form of liability in which several persons are responsible for a debt both individually and as a group.

License—1. A special privilege, not a right common to all. The privilege conferred by a public body on a person for the doing of something which he or she otherwise would not have the right to do. 2. The personal, revocable and non-assignable permission or authority to enter upon the land of another for a particular purpose.

L.I.D.—Local Improvement District.

Lien—A charge upon property for the payment or discharge of a debt or duty. The right which the law gives to have a debt satisfied out of a particular thing. A charge or claim upon property which encumbers it until the obligation is satisfied.

Lien, Attachment—A lien on property to prevent transfer of the property pending the outcome of litigation.

Lien, Equitable—A lien arising out of fairness. It can evolve from a written contract where intent to create a lien on a particular property is clearly indicated, or by court order in an effort to apply justice and fair play.

Lien, General—A lien against all the property of a debtor.

Lien, Involuntary—A lien placed against property by operation of law without consent of the owner. Mechanic's liens, judgments and I.R.S. liens are involuntary.

Lien, Judgment—A legal claim on all of the property of a judgment debtor, making it possible for the judgment creditor to have the property sold to satisfy the debt.

Lien, Materialman's—Similar to a mechanic's lien, but it refers specifically to sums owed suppliers, as opposed to laborers, for materials provided in connection with a construction project.

Lien, Mechanic's—A statutory lien that can be placed against property by those who provide labor or materials for construction relative to that property when they have not been paid. The lien's priority is determined by the date the labor or material is furnished, not the date the document is filed of record.

Lien, Property Tax—A lien on property to secure payment of property taxes.

Lien, Specific—A lien which attaches only to a particular piece of property, as opposed to a **General Lien** which attaches to all of the debtor's property.

Lien, Statutory—A liens which is created by law, rather than by contract, such as a tax lien.

Lien, Tax—A lien on property to secure the payment of taxes.

Lien, Voluntary—A lien placed with the consent of the owner.

Lienholder, Junior—A secured creditor whose lien is lower in priority with respect to another lien.

Lien Theory—The theory holds that upon giving a mortgage or deed of trust as security for a debt, the borrower does not give up any part of his title. The lender holds a lien during the period of indebtedness but not title.

Life Estate—An estate to be held by a grantee or devisee for the term of his own life, or for that of another person, or for more lives than one. Where a life estate exists there must also be an estate in reversion or an estate in remainder.

Like-Kind Exchange—SEE: **Tax-Free Exchange.**

Lineal—Relating to line; having length only. A lineal mile is 5,280 feet in distance.

Lis Pendens—A recorded notice that a lawsuit is pending which may affect the title of the real estate of a defendant.

Listing—A written agreement or contract between a principal and an agent stipulating that the agent will be paid a commission for finding a ready, willing and able buyer to purchase the seller's property on terms acceptable to the latter. The three types are open, exclusive agency and exclusive right to sell.

Listing, Net—A listing, where the seller sets a minimum net amount for which he or she will settle and permits the agent to collect as a commission the portion of the sales price exceeding that amount. This listing is not favored by authorities and is illegal in some states because the manner in which the broker is compensated lends itself to fraud.

Listing, Open—A nonexclusive listing given by an owner to as many different brokers as desired. Only the broker who finds the buyer is entitled to a commission and a sale automatically terminates all other open listings. Under an open listing the broker must be prepared to prove he or she was the procuring cause of the sale.

Littoral Land—Land which has as a boundary a body of standing water, such as an ocean or lake.

Littoral Owner—Landowner whose land borders on a lake.

Loan, Budget—A mortgage loan where the payments are set up to cover more than the principal and interest, normally for proportionate amounts of such things as property taxes, fire insurance and special assessments.

Loan, Construction—A loan made to cover the cost of construction of buildings, usually with an agreement that the loan amount is advanced in installments as the work progresses.

Loan, Conventional—Loan without government insurance or guarantee.

Loan, Guaranteed—A loan which is guaranteed by the V.A. or any interested party, other than the borrower.

Loan, Interim—A temporary short-term loan made to finance construction; usually paid off on completion of construction with the proceeds of a take-out loan.

Loan, Participation—A loan in which the lender receives some yield in addition to the specified interest rate, such as a percentage of income or profits, or some portion of ownership of the venture. The practice is used mainly in large commercial loans, particularly by insurance company lenders.

Loan, Permanent—SEE: **Loan, Take-out.**

Loan, Rollover—A type of loan wherein the interest rate is periodically renegotiated, usually every three to five years.

Loan, Seasoned—A loan with an established record of timely payment by the debtor.

Loan, Take-out—A long-term loan used to take over or pay off a short-term or interim loan.

Loan Assumption Fee—A fee charged to the buyer by the existing lender in return for permission to assume an existing loan.

Loan Correspondent—A representative who negotiates and services loans for other lenders. Loan correspondents are usually mortgage companies who sell loans to banks, savings and loans, and insurance companies at the secondary market level, while retaining the right to service the loan for a fee.

Loan Fee—A fee charged by lenders in return for the issuance of a loan; also called a loan origination fee.

Loan-to-Value Ratio—This refers to the maximum loan the lender is willing to make in relation to the appraised value.

Lock-in Clause—A clause in a note or installment sales contract prohibiting full payment of the debt before the date set in the contract.

Lot—A parcel of land in a subdivision.

Lot, Block and Subdivision—A form of legal description; land is described by reference to a lot, block and subdivision appearing on the maps and plats recorded in the Office of the County Auditor or Recorder. Also called maps and plats description.

Love and Affection—The consideration often used when real estate is conveyed between family members with no money exchanged. The law recognizes love and affection as good consideration (as distinguished from valuable consideration, which is money, goods or services).

M.A.I.—Member of the Appraisal Institute. The initials identify a member of the American Institute of Real Estate Appraisers of the National Association of Realtors.

Majority, Age of—Age at which persons become legally competent; in California, age 18.

Maps and Plats—SEE: **Lot, Block and Subdivision.**

Market Data Approach—One of the three standard methods of appraisal; based on comparing similar properties. Also called the comparison or comparative analysis approach.

Market Price—The price actually paid for property. Not the same as market value.

Master Plan—An overall plan for the development of a city or county, which is used as a guide for the development of zoning regulations.

Material Fact—A material fact is one that the agent should realize would be likely to affect the principal's judgment in any decision relative to the subject of agency. Failure to disclose a material fact constitutes a violation of the trust.

Meeting of Minds—Another term for mutual consent.

Megalopolis—An extensive, heavily populated, continuously urban area, including any number of cities.

Merger—1. The union of two or more separate interests by the transfer of all the interests into one. 2. The acquisition by one owner of the title to adjacent parcels. If a dominant and servient tenement are merged under one ownership, the easement is no longer necessary and is terminated.

Meridians—Imaginary north-south lines which intersect base lines to form a starting point for the measurement of land in the Government Survey method of land description.

Metes—Measurements.

Metes and Bounds—A method of legal description that requires a high degree of accuracy. Metes refer to distances, while bounds refer to boundaries defined by monuments or landmarks. The description starts at an easily identifiable point of beginning, follows boundaries for precise distances and ultimately returns to the point of beginning.

Mill—One-tenth of one cent; the measure used to state the property tax rate. A tax rate of one mill on the dollar is the same as a rate of one-tenth of one percent of the assessed value of property.

Mineral Rights—Rights to subsurface lands and the profits from them. Mineral rights usually belong to the owner of the surface lands, unless reserved by a previous grantor or otherwise conveyed.

Minimum Property Requirements (MPR)—Requirements concerning the physical condition of a building; meeting the MPRs is a prerequisite to approval of financing from certain lenders.

Minor—A person who has not reached the age at which the law recognizes a general contractual capacity; in California, a person under 18.

Monument—A visible marker, natural or artificial, used to establish the lines and boundaries of a survey. Natural monuments can include boulders, marked trees, streams or rivers; artificial (man-made) monuments might take the form of stakes, wood or steel posts, or a cement slab.

Mortgage—A document that details the terms of a real estate loan agreement and serves as the lender's security for the debt. Parties to the agreement are the mortgagor (borrower) and mortgagee (lender).

Mortgage, Assumption of—Taking over the primary liability on an existing mortgage.

Mortgage, Balloon—A mortgage that provides for payments that do not fully amortize the loan by the loan's maturity date. The balance of the mortgage is then due in one lump sum (balloon payment) at the end of the term.

Mortgage, Blanket—A mortgage or trust deed which covers more than one piece of real estate.

Mortgage, Chattel—A mortgage of personal property. It has been replaced in states which have adopted the Uniform Commercial Code (including California) by the security agreement.

Mortgage, First—The mortgage or deed of trust that is superior in right to any other on a property. Without a subordination agreement, this will normally be the one that is recorded first. SEE: **Mortgage, Junior.**

Mortgage, Hard Money—A mortgage or deed of trust given to a lender in exchange for cash, as opposed to a lien given to a seller in exchange for credit.

Mortgage, Junior—A second mortgage (or third, fourth, etc.) that is subordinate to a first mortgage in terms of priority. Priority refers to the order in which the liens will be paid in the event the property is sold. With certain exceptions, priority is established by the date a lien is recorded: the first to record is first in priority.

Mortgage, Open-end—A mortgage which permits the borrower to reborrow the money paid on the principal, usually up to the original amount, without rewriting the mortgage.

Mortgage, Package—A mortgage or deed of trust used in home financing that is secured by both the real property and certain items of personal property, such as appliances, drapes, carpeting, etc.

Mortgage, Participation—A real estate loan in which the lender participates in the earnings generated by the mortgaged property.

Mortgage, Purchase Money—A mortgage or deed of trust given by the buyer as part or all of the purchase price, and executed and delivered as part of the same transaction in which the security property is acquired. Usually refers to a mortgage given by the buyer to the seller to secure an amount still owed to the latter.

Mortgage, Satisfaction of—The instrument given to the mortgagor by the mortgagee when the debt has been paid in full, acknowledging that the debt has been paid and consenting to discharge of the mortgage.

Mortgage, Senior—A mortgage or deed of trust which has a higher lien priority than other liens.

Mortgage, Wraparound—A mortgage or deed of trust which secures a loan that includes the amount of the balance due on an existing loan. Also called all inclusive trust deed or mortgage.

Mortgage Company—A loan correspondent that deals in real estate loans that are readily saleable in the secondary mortgage market.

Mortgagee—The receiver of the mortgage; the lender of the money secured by the mortgage.

Mortgaging Clause—The clause in a mortgage that describes the security interest which will be conveyed to the mortgagee.

Mortgagor—A person who mortgages his property to another; the maker of a mortgage.

Multiple Listing Service—An organization of brokers who share their listings.

Mutual Consent—When all parties approve or assent to the terms of a contract freely. One of four essential elements to any valid contract; the others include **capacity, lawful objective** and **consideration.**

Mutuality—SEE: **Mutual Consent.**

Mutual Water Company—A water company formed by property owners in a given community for the purpose of obtaining a supply of water at reasonable rates. Stock in the company is issued to individual members.

N.A.R.—National Association of Realtors.

Narrative Report—A thorough appraisal report in which the appraiser summarizes factual material, techniques and appraisal methods used, to convince the reader of the soundness of the estimate. It is a more comprehensive report than the form report or the estimate given in a simple letter or certificate.

National Environmental Policy Act (NEPA)—Federal legislation which regulates all development by governmental agencies and all private development that requires a permit or approval from a federal agency.

Natural Person—An individual, a private person, as distinguished from an artificial person, such as a corporation.

Natural Servitude—A legal doctrine which states that a property owner is liable for any damages caused by diversion or channeling of flood waters from his or her property onto someone else's.

Negotiable Instrument—An instrument containing an unconditional promise to pay a certain sum of money. It can be a check, promissory note, bond, draft or stock. SEE: **Note, Promissory.**

Nominal Interest Rate—The interest rate stated in a promissory note. SEE: **Annual Percentage Rate.**

Nonconforming Use—A property use that does not conform to current zoning requirements, but is allowed because the land was being used in that way before the present zoning ordinance was enacted.

Notary Public—An appointed officer whose primary function is to attest and certify the acknowledgment made by another when signing documents such as deeds, mortgages and land contracts.

Note—SEE: **Note, Promissory.**

Note, Demand—A note that is due whenever the holder of the note demands payment.

Note, Installment—A promissory note that calls for periodic payments of principal and interest until the debt is fully paid.

Note, Joint—A note signed by two or more persons with joint and several liability for payment; that is, each can be required to pay the full amount, not merely his or her share.

Note, Promissory—A written unconditional promise to pay a certain sum of money to order or to bearer, on demand or at a specified time in the future.

Note, Straight—A promissory note in which only interest payments are made during the term of the note, and the entire principal is due in one lump sum at maturity.

Notice, Actual—Actual knowledge acquired when given express information of a fact.

Notice, Constructive—Knowledge of a fact implied by law, based on a presumption of notice because the fact could be discovered by reasonable diligence or inspection of public records. Also called notice to the world.

Notice of Cessation—A notice of record by the owner of property where construction has ceased, though the project has not been finished; it limits the time the laborers and suppliers have to file mechanics' liens.

Notice of Completion—A notice filed of record announcing the completion of construction and limiting the period in which mechanics' liens may be filed.

Notice of Default—A notice sent by a secured creditor to a debtor, informing the debtor of a breach of the loan agreement.

Notice of Non-responsibility—A notice which, if recorded and posted on the property in a timely manner, will protect a property owner from the effect of mechanics' liens filed for work which was not requested by the owner.

Notice of Sale—A notice sent to a borrower informing him or her that property is scheduled to be sold in a foreclosure sale.

Notice to Quit—A notice to a tenant, telling him or her to vacate rented property.

Novation—The substitution of a new obligation for an old one.

Obligatory Advances—Disbursements from construction loan funds that the lender is obligated to make (by prior agreement with the builder) when the builder has completed certain phases of construction.

Obsolescence—Any loss in value due to reduced desirability and usefulness. There is **functional obsolescence** (factors within the property itself) and **economic obsolescence** (factors outside the property).

Offer, Illusory—An offer which is not a legally valid offer; an offer which requires something more than simple acceptance in order to create a contract.

Offer, Tender—An unconditional offer by one of the contract parties to perform his or her part of the agreement; made when the offeror believes the other party is breaching, it establishes the offeror's right to sue.

Offeree—One to whom an offer is made.

Offeror—One who makes an offer.

Office of Thrift Supervision—The federal agency that regulates the savings and loan industry; replaced the Federal Home Loan Bank Board.

Off-site Improvements—Improvements which add to the usefulness of a site but are not located directly on it, including streets, curbs, street lights and sidewalks.

Open Housing Law—A federal law prohibiting housing discrimination. Also called the federal fair housing law.

Option—A right, given for a valuable consideration, to purchase or lease property at a future date for a specified price and on specified terms. The right may or may not be exercised, at the option holder's discretion. If he or she does not choose to exercise the option, the consideration is forfeited. The property owner is the optionor, the potential buyer the optionee.

Optionee—The person to whom an option is given.

Optionor—The person who gives an option.

Orientation—The placement of a house on its lot with regard to its exposure to the sun and wind, privacy from the street, and protection from outside noise.

"Or More"—A provision in a promissory note which permits an early payoff of the debt.

Overimprovement—An improvement to land that is more expensive than necessary.

Ownership—The rights of an owner. Title to property, dominion over property. The right of possession and control, including the right to protect and defend such possession against intrusion or trespass.

Ownership, Concurrent—Ownership by more than one person.

Ownership in Severalty—Ownership by an individual person.

Par—The accepted standard of comparison; average; face value; equal. A mortgage sold at the secondary market level for 97% of par has been sold for 3% less than the face amount of the loan.

Parallels—Called standard parallels, they are the imaginary lines used in the Government Survey System that run east and west, parallel to the equator. Also called Latitude Lines.

Parcel—A specified lot or tract of real estate, particularly a specified part of a larger tract.

Partial Release Clause—A clause found in some mortgages and deeds of trust providing for release of part of the property from the blanket lien upon compliance with certain conditions (usually payment of a certain part of the debt); common in the financing of subdivisions. The release instrument would be a **partial satisfaction of mortgage** or **partial reconveyance deed**, depending on whether it is being used to release a mortgage or trust deed.

Partition Action—A court action to divide property between co-owners (such as joint tenants or tenants in common), normally occurring when one owner wishes to divide and the others do not, or when the co-owners cannot come to agreement as to how the division should be made. If the court cannot practically divide the property physically, as in the case of one house owned by six co-owners, the court will order a sale and divide the proceeds.

Partner, General—A partner who has the authority to manage and contract for a general or limited partnership, and who is fully and personally liable for debts of the partnership.

Partnership—According to the Uniform Partnership Act, "an association of two or more persons to carry on, as co-owners, a business for profit." Although a partnership may be operated under an assumed name or under the surnames of the partners, it is regarded as a collection of individuals and, unlike a corporation, does not have a separate legal existence.

Partnership, General—A form of business organization in which each member has an equal right to manage the business and collect profits, as well as an equal responsibility for the debts of the business.

Partnership, Limited—A business arrangement which limits certain of the partners' liability to the amount they invested. Usually a limited partner is not permitted to have a voice in managing the company; his or her role is primarily that of an investor. The limited partnership must have at least one managing partner (general partner).

Party Wall—A wall located on the boundary line between two adjoining parcels of land, which is used or intended to be used by the owners of both properties.

Patent—The instrument used to convey federal or state government land to a private individual.

Percolation Test—A test to determine the ability of the ground to absorb or drain water; used to determine the suitability of the site for construction, particularly for installation of a septic tank system.

Personal Property—Any property which is not real property; movable property not affixed to land; also called chattels or personalty.

Personalty—Personal property; the main characteristic is movability. COMPARE: **Realty.**

Physical Deterioration—Loss in value (depreciation) resulting from wear and tear, deferred maintenance, etc.

Physical Life—Estimated time a building will remain structurally sound and capable of being used.

Plaintiff—The party who brings or starts a lawsuit; the one who sues.

Planned Unit Development—A development designed for intensive use of the land, combining a high density of dwellings with maximum utilization of open space.

Planning Commission—A local governmental agency created to direct and control the use and development of the land by recommending zoning ordinances, adopting a general or master plan, etc.

Plat—A detailed map of a large tract (usually a subdivision), recorded in the county where the land is located.

Plat Book—A public book of maps of subdivided land, showing the blocks, lots and parcels.

Plot Plan—A plan showing lot dimensions and the layout of improvements (such as buildings and landscaping) on a property site.

Plottage—The consolidation of several parcels of land into one, resulting in greater utility and consequent higher value.

Point of Beginning—A landmark used as the initial reference point in a metes and bounds description.

Points—A "point" is one percent of the principal amount of a loan, paid to the lender at the time the loan is made to give the lender an additional yield above the interest rate. Because of the points paid at the outset, the lender is willing to make the loan at a lower interest rate. Also called discount points.

Police Power—The power of the state and local governments to enact and enforce laws for the general welfare of the public. Since the exercise of the police power is merely regulating and not taking private property, no compensation is paid to the owner.

Possession—The holding and peaceful enjoyment of property. In the case of a lease, the tenant is in actual possession; the owner has constructive possession by right of title.

Possessory Rights—Rights to occupy and use land; not necessarily ownership of land.

Potable Water—Water that is safe to drink.

Power of Attorney—A written instrument authorizing one person (the attorney in fact) to act as another's agent to the extent stated in the instrument. If it authorizes action in a real estate transaction (such as signing a deed on behalf of the principal), the power of attorney must be recorded.

Power of Sale Clause—A clause in a deed of trust which gives the trustee the right to sell the debtor's property without a court action, following default by the borrower.

Prepayment Penalty—The amount the debtor must pay the creditor as a penalty for paying off a debt before maturity. Not permitted in FHA or VA loans.

Prepayment Privilege—The right of a borrower to pay off a loan before it is due.

Prescription—A method of acquiring a right in real property (normally an intangible right such as an easement) by open, notorious, continuous, and uninterrupted use hostile to the will of the owner, for the prescribed period of time (in California, five years). COMPARE: **Adverse Possession**

Primary Mortgage Market—The market where loan transactions are made directly between borrowers and lenders. COMPARE: **Secondary Mortgage Market**

Prime Rate—The interest rate a bank charges its largest and most desirable customers.

Principal—1. One of the parties to a transaction, such as the buyer or seller of a home. 2. One who employs an agent in a principal-agent relationship. 3. The basic amount of a debt, as opposed to the interest.

Principal Meridian—The principal or prime meridian is the north-south line used as a reference line for numbering ranges in the Government Survey System.

Principal Residence Property—Any real estate an owner actually lives in as his or her principal dwelling. A person can only have one principal residence at any one time.

Private Deed Restrictions—Restrictions on the use of land which are contained in private deeds or contracts; the restrictions apply only to the parties to the particular agreement and their successors in interest.

Privity—A relationship between people having simultaneous or successive interests in a right or property. For example, the dominant and servient tenants in an easement agreement are in privity to one another; so are the seller and buyer of a property.

Probate—A judicial proceeding to determine the validity of a will and to distribute the assets of a decedent. An estate is still subject to a probate action to satisfy any creditor's claims and to distribute assets, even if the decedent dies without a will.

Probate Court—The court which oversees the distribution of property under a will or intestate succession.

Procuring Cause—In a real estate transaction, the broker or salesperson who produces a ready, willing, and able buyer at the agreed price and terms. A broker must be prepared to show he or she was the "procuring cause" of the sale if the listing agreement was non-exclusive.

Progression, Principle of—An appraisal principle which holds that a piece of property of lesser value tends to increase in value when placed in an area with properties of greater value. The opposite is the principle of regression.

Property—The rights of ownership in an object, such as the rights to use, possess, transfer or encumber the object. Property also refers to the object itself, the parcel of land or the automobile or whatever. Property is divided into two main classes, real and personal.

Property Held for Production of Income—Income-producing property, such as apartments and commercial buildings.

Property Manager—A person hired by a property owner to administer, merchandise, and maintain property, especially rental property.

Property Used in a Trade or Business—Property such as business sites and factories used in one's trade or business.

Proprietorship, Individual or Sole—A business owned and operated by a single person.

Proration—The process of dividing or distributing proportionately.

Public Restriction—A law or governmental regulation limiting or restricting the use of real property.

Puffing—Superlative statements about the quality of a property that do not amount to factual representations. "The best buy in town," or "it's a fabulous location" are examples of puffing. Representations of this type, however inaccurate, are not actionable; that is, the person who said them cannot be sued for fraud, because the person who heard them should have been able to evaluate the accuracy of the statements.

Purchase and Sale Agreement—A contract for the sale of real property, wherein the buyer promises to purchase and the seller promises to convey title. In California, usually referred to as the deposit receipt.

Quantity Survey Method—In appraisal, a method of estimating the replacement cost of a structure. It involves a detailed estimate of the quantities and grades of material used and their cost (e.g., 1,500 bricks at $0.12 each), the labor hours required and their cost, and overhead expenses such as insurance and contractor's profit. It is the most time-consuming of the three methods of replacement cost estimation. The other two approaches are unit in place and square foot.

Quiet Enjoyment—The right of an owner or lessee legally in possession of property to the use and possession of the property without interference.

Quiet Title Action—A lawsuit to establish clear title to a piece of property or to remove a cloud on the title.

Range—In the Government Survey System, a strip of land six miles wide, running north and south.

Range Line—One of the north-south lines located six miles apart, used by the government survey system for the location and description of townships. They are meridians or longitude lines.

Ratification—The later confirmation or affirmation of an act that was not authorized when it was performed.

Real Estate—SEE: **Realty** and **Real Property.**

Real Estate Investment Trust—An unincorporated business association, with a minimum of 100 owners, which (if it meets certain requirements) is allowed to pass profits through to investors without paying corporate tax. The investors have limited liability.

Real Property—The land and all things affixed to or appurtenant to the land, including buildings and other fixtures. COMPARE: **Personal Property.**

Realtor—A broker who is an active member of a state or local real estate board which is affiliated with the National Association of Realtors.

Realtor-Associate—A salesperson affiliated with a Realtor.

Realty—Real property; land, its attachments and appurtenances. COMPARE: **Personalty.**

Reasonable Use—A limitation of riparian water rights which states that there is no right to waste water.

Recapture—1. Recovery by the investor of money invested in real estate. 2. Recapture clauses are of two types. One type, often found in percentage leases, especially shopping center leases, allows the lessor to terminate the lease and regain the premises if a certain minimum volume of business is not maintained. The second type, found in ground leases, allows the lessee to purchase the property after a specified period of time.

Reconveyance—This form of transfer normally occurs when the debt secured by a deed of trust has been satisfied. The trustee reconveys to the trustor (owner), releasing the security from the lien of the deed of trust.

Recording—Placing a document affecting the title to real property, such as a deed or mortgage, on file in the book of public records in the Office of the County Auditor or County Recorder for the county where the property is located. Placing such an instrument on file in the public records gives constructive notice (notice to all the world) of the existence of the instrument and its contents.

Rectangular Survey—Another name for the government survey system of land description. Sometimes called the township and range system.

Redemption, Equitable Right of—The right of a borrower to redeem property from forfeiture prior to the foreclosure sale, by paying the delinquency, together with interest and costs.

Redemption, Post-sale—The right of redemption enables a defaulting mortgagor to regain property after foreclosure by paying the amount of indebtedness, plus interest, court costs, and attorney's fees within a specified time.

Redemption, Statutory Right of—The right of a mortgagor to get property back after a foreclosure sale.

Redemption Period, Statutory—The period of time, defined by law, during which the borrower can reclaim foreclosed property by paying the full amount of the loan plus costs.

Redlining—When a lender refuses to lend money on properties in certain areas, or restricts the number of loans or the loan amounts, because the area is considered undesirable. If the practice is racially motivated, it is illegal.

Regression, Principle of—A principle of appraising which holds that a property of high value surrounded by properties of lower value will tend to lose value. Opposite of the **principle of progression.**

Regulation Z—SEE: **Truth in Lending Act.**

Reinstate—To prevent a forced sale of security property by curing the default which is the basis for the foreclosure.

Release—The act or means of giving up a legal right.

Release Clause—1. A clause in a blanket mortgage or deed of trust which allows the borrower to get certain parcels of land released from the lien upon payment of a specific sum or a specific portion of the loan. 2. A clause in a real estate contract providing for a deed to a portion of the land to be delivered upon fulfillment of a certain segment of the contract. Also known as a deed release provision.

Reliction—The gradual withdrawal or recession of water, exposing land that was previously under water. The newly exposed land belongs to the riparian owner. Also called dereliction.

Remainder—An estate which takes effect immediately upon the termination of some prior estate, such as a life estate. The holder of such an estate is a remainderman.

Remise—To give up; a term used in quitclaim deeds.

Rent—Compensation paid by the tenant or occupant of real property to the owner in exchange for the use and possession of the property.

Rent, Economic—The rent which a piece of property would bring on the open market at a given time, as contrasted with the actual rent being received (contract rent).

Rent, Ground—The earnings of improved property which are credited to the land itself after allowance is made for the earnings of the improvements.

Replacement Cost—In appraisal, the amount of money that would be needed (on the basis of current prices) to replace a structure with one having the same utility, but constructed with modern materials, design, etc. COMPARE: **Reproduction Cost.**

Reproduction Cost—The amount of money that would be needed (on the basis of current prices) to duplicate the structure being appraised, using the same or similar materials, design, quality of workmanship, layout, etc. COMPARE: **Replacement Cost.**

Rescission—In contract law, the remedy of abrogating, annulling, or terminating a contract and restoring the parties, as nearly as possible, to the positions they were in before entering the contract.

Reservation—A right retained by the grantor when conveying property; for example, mineral rights, an easement, or a life estate can be reserved in the deed.

Reserve Account—Money deposited with a lender for the purpose of paying property taxes and insurance premiums on land financed by the lender; also called an impound account.

Resident Manager—A salaried manager of a single apartment building or complex. A resident manager, unlike a property manager, is not required to have a real estate license.

Residual—1. The value remaining to property after the economic life of the improvements has been exhausted. 2. Commissions in the form of delayed payments (when a part of the commission is paid with each installment on an installment sales contract, for example) are referred to as residuals.

R.E.S.P.A.—The Real Estate Settlement Procedures Act, federal law that requires disclosure of closing costs.

Respondeat Superior, Doctrine of—A master (employer) is liable for the torts (civil wrongs) committed by a servant (employee) within the scope of his/her employment.

Restriction—A limitation on the use of real property. Restrictions may be private, such as restrictive covenants dealing with setbacks, or public, such as zoning ordinances.

Restrictive Covenant—Similar to a condition imposed in a deed, the restrictive covenant is a private agreement between the grantor and all subsequent grantees restricting the use or occupancy of the property being conveyed. Violations of covenants are stopped by court injunctions, but no reversion of title occurs.

Revenue Stamps—Stamps that are required by law to be placed on instruments of conveyance, such as deeds. Also called documentary tax stamps.

Reversion—A future estate held by a grantor, or a transfer which takes effect immediately following the preceding estate.

Rezone—A change in zoning. SEE: **Zoning Amendment.**

Right of Way—A public or private easement giving the holder the right to pass over the land of another.

Riparian Rights—The water rights of a landowner resulting from owning land which borders on a stream or other surface waters, including the right to reasonable use of the water.

Running with the Land—Rights, restrictions, or covenants which affect successive owners of a parcel of land are said to run with the land.

Sale-Leaseback—A form of real estate financing in which the owner of industrial or commercial property sells the property and leases it back from the buyer, normally under a net lease in which the seller/lessee pays taxes, insurance, etc. In addition to certain tax advantages, the seller/lessee obtains more cash through the sale than would normally be possible by borrowing and mortgaging the property, since lenders will not often lend 100% of the value.

Savings and Loan Association—An institution organized under state or federal charter to encourage thrift and make investment capital available for home loans.

Scarcity—A limited or inadequate supply of something. Scarcity is one of the four elements of value. SEE: **Utility, Demand,** and **Transferability.**

Secondary Financing—1. A loan secured by a second (or third, fourth, etc.) mortgage or trust deed. Also known as a junior mortgage or trust deed. 2. A loan from any source used to make the required downpayment and/or pay closing costs in connection with a primary loan. A personal loan from a bank to pay the finance charges connected with a conventional home loan would be an example of secondary financing.

Secondary Mortgage Market—The process of buying and selling existing mortgages and trust deeds. Also known as the secondary money market.

Section—In the government survey system, a section is one mile square and contains 640 acres. There are 36 sections in a township.

Security Agreement—A document which creates a lien upon property being used to secure a loan. The loan is a **secured loan**, the lien or interest of the lender in the debtor's property is a **security interest**, the property is the **security property,** and the lender in such a transaction is a **secured party**. When the security property is real property (rather than personal property), the security agreement is a mortgage or deed of trust.

Seizin—Actual possession of real estate by one so entitled. Also called seizen and seisin.

Separate Property—property which is not community property; includes property acquired before marriage or by gift or devise after marriage.

Servant—An employee.

Setback Ordinance—A local law prohibiting improvements from being erected within a certain distance from the property line.

Settlement—The fulfillment of promises made by the buyer and seller in the purchase and sale agreement. SEE: **Closing.**

Settlement Statement—A document prepared by an escrow agent, which reflects the financial aspects of a completed transaction.

Severalty Ownership—Ownership by one person only, severed from anyone else.

Sheriff's Sale—A judicial foreclosure sale under a mortgage or deed of trust.

Soldier's and Sailor's Civil Relief Act—A federal law which protects persons in military service against foreclosure of property mortgaged before they entered the military, if their ability to repay the loan has been materially affected by their military service.

Special Assessment—A tax against certain parcels of land which have benefitted from a public improvement (such as a road, sewer, or street lights), levied to cover the cost of the improvement.

Special Exception Permits—Permits granted under special circumstances to allow property to be used for a purpose which is not normally allowed under the zoning laws. Also called conditional use permits.

Specific Performance—A legal remedy in which a party to a contract is ordered by the court to actually perform the contract as agreed, or as nearly so as possible, rather than simply paying monetary damages.

Square Foot Method—In appraisal, a method of estimating the replacement cost of a structure; it involves multiplying the cost per square foot of a recently built comparable structure by the number of square feet in the subject structure. SEE: **Appraisal, Replacement Cost, Quantity Survey Method,** and **Unit-in-Place Method.**

S.R.A.—Senior Residential Appraiser, a designation of the **Society of Real Estate Appraisers.**

S.R.E.A.—The **Society of Real Estate Appraisers.**

Statute—A written law of the federal government or of a state government.

Statute of Frauds—A law which requires certain types of contracts to be in writing in order to be enforceable.

Statute of Limitations—A law requiring certain legal actions to be brought within a specified time limit.

Subagent—Someone appointed by an agent to assist in carrying out the agency. If the appointment was authorized by the principal, then the principal (rather than the agent) can be held liable for the subagent's acts.

Subcontractor—A contractor who, at the request of the general contractor, provides a specific service, such as plumbing or drywalling, in connection with the overall construction project.

Subdivision—A piece of land divided into two or more parcels.

Subdivision Plat—SEE: **Plat.**

Subdivision Regulations—Local laws and regulations which must be complied with before land can be subdivided.

Subjacent Support—The support which the surface of land receives from the subsurface soil.

Subject to—When a purchaser takes property subject to a trust deed or mortgage, he or she is not personally liable for paying off the loan; in case of default, however, the property can still be foreclosed on.

Sublease—A lease given by a lessee where he or she retains some portion of or interest in the leasehold, as opposed to an assignment of the entire leasehold interest.

Subordination Clause—A clause in a mortgage or deed of trust which permits a subsequent mortgage or deed of trust to take priority. Often found in instruments that secure land acquisition loans, in order to make it possible to secure construction financing with a first lien position.

Subrogation—The substitution of one person in the place of another with reference to a lawful claim or right. For instance, a title company that pays a claim on behalf of its insured, the property owner, is subrogated to any claim the owner successfully undertakes against the former owner.

Substitution, Principle of—This is a principle of appraisal stating that the maximum value of a piece of property is limited by the cost required to obtain another piece of property that is equally desirable and valuable, assuming there are no lengthy delays or costly incidental expenses involved in obtaining the substitute property.

Substitution of Liability—A buyer wishing to assume an existing loan may apply for lender approval to do so. Once approved, the buyer assumes liability for repayment of the loan, and the original borrower is released from liability.

Succession—Acquiring property through descent, by will or inheritance.

Sufferance—Acquiescence, implied permission, or passive consent through a failure to act, as opposed to express permission.

Supply and Demand, Principle of—This economic principle holds that value varies directly with demand and inversely with supply; that is, the greater the demand the greater the value, and the greater the supply the smaller the value.

Support Rights—The right to the support of land that is furnished by adjacent land (lateral support) or underlying land (subjacent support).

Surplus Productivity, Principle of—According to this principle, the net income from a property which remains after paying the costs of labor, organization, and capital is credited to the land and tends to set its value.

Surrender—Yielding or giving up an estate, such as a life estate or leasehold, before its expiration.

Survey—The process of measuring the boundaries and determining the area of a parcel of land.

Survivorship, Right of—The right of surviving joint tenants to automatically acquire the interest of a deceased joint tenant. A distinguishing characteristic of a joint tenancy.

Syndicate—An association of two or more people formed to make and operate an investment. This can be a corporation, real estate investment trust, or partnership. A limited partnership is the most common type of syndicate.

Tacking—The process whereby the period of use required for adverse possession is satisfied by two or more adverse possessors.

Tax, Documentary Transfer—A method of taxing the transfer of real property, normally by requiring stamps or some other notice to be attached to the deed before it can be recorded. In California, the tax is imposed at a rate of $.55 per $500 of value, excluding existing loans assumed by the buyer.

Tax, General Real Estate—Property taxes which apply to all land on an ad valorem basis.

Tax, Improvement—SEE: **Special Assessment.**

Tax, Property—An ad valorem tax levied on real and personal property.

Tax Foreclosure—Foreclosure by a governmental agency to obtain payment of delinquent taxes.

Tax-Free Exchange—A method of deferring capital gains tax by exchanging one piece of investment or income property for another piece of like-kind property.

Tax Sale—Sale of property under a tax foreclosure.

Tenancy—Possession of land under right or title. The possessor is the tenant.

Tenancy, Joint—A form of concurrent ownership of property by two or more people with the distinctive characteristic of right of survivorship. Joint tenants each hold an equal interest.

Tenancy, Month-to-Month—SEE: **Tenancy, Periodic.**

Tenancy, Periodic—A leasehold estate that continues for successive periods of the same length, such as from week to week or month to month, until terminated by proper notice from either party.

Tenancy at Sufferance—An occupation of land which may be terminated by the owner of the land at any time, but which is not a trespass.

Tenancy at Will—A tenancy in which the tenant is in possession with the permission of the owner, but there is no definite term or duration of possession, as when a lessor allows a holdover tenant to remain on the premises until another lessee is found.

Tenancy by the Entireties—A form of joint ownership of property by a husband and wife (in states that don't recognize community property).

Tenancy in Common—A form of concurrent ownership of real property in which two or more persons each have an undivided interest in the entire property, but no right of survivorship. COMPARE: **Tenancy, Joint.**

Tenancy in Partnership—The form of concurrent ownership in which general partners own partnership property.

Tenant, Dominant—1. The owner of a dominant tenement. 2. The private individual or corporation who owns an easement in gross.

Tenant, Holdover—A lessee who remains in possession of the property after the lease term has expired.

Tenant, Life—The person who has the exclusive right to occupy and use land for the duration of a life estate.

Tenant, Servient—The owner of a servient tenement.

Tender—An unconditional offer of performance by one of the parties to a contract, as when the buyer under a purchase and sale agreement offers to pay the purchase price, usually by depositing it in escrow. Failure of the seller to accept the money and perform the contractual obligation would place the seller in default.

Tenement, Dominant—Also called a dominant estate, it is property that receives benefits from a servient tenement (estate) by means of an easement appurtenant.

Tenement, Servient—Land burdened by an easement in favor of another property, called the dominant tenement.

Tenements—All the rights of a permanent nature associated with the land which pass with the land, such as buildings or air rights.

Tenure—The period of time during which a person holds certain rights with respect to real property.

Term—A prescribed period of time. A loan that is to be paid back over thirty years has a thirty-year term.

Testament—A will.

Testate—The condition of leaving a will upon death. The person leaving the will is the testator or testatrix.

Testator—A person who makes a will (male).

Testatrix—A person who makes a will (female).

Tier—A row of townships running east-west.

Tight Money Market—A time when there is low availability of loan funds, resulting in high interest rates.

Time is of the Essence—A clause in a contract which means that performance on the exact dates specified is an essential element of the contract; failure to perform on time is a material breach.

Title—Lawful ownership of or right to land. Also, the evidence of that ownership.

Title, After-Acquired—When a grantor attempts to convey property he or she does not have title to, but later obtains title, it is called after-acquired title. If the attempted conveyance was by a grant deed or a warranty deed, the title acquired by the grantor passes automatically to the grantee.

Title, Chain of—The history of ownership, conveyances and encumbrances that have affected title to a particular parcel of real estate.

Title, Clear—A good title to property, free from encumbrances or defects; a merchantable or marketable title.

Title, Equitable—The vendee's interest in property under a real estate contract. Also called equitable interest.

Title, Imperfect—Defective or incomplete title. An adverse possessor has imperfect title until he or she obtains a quitclaim deed from the owner of the land adversely possessed, or succeeds in a quiet title action confirming that the adverse possessor has met the requirements for acquiring the title by continuous use.

Title, Marketable—Title free and clear of objectionable liens or encumbrances, so that a reasonably prudent person with full knowledge of the facts would not hesitate to purchase the property. Also called merchantable title.

Title Plant—A collection of duplicates (usually microfilmed) of all instruments of public record affecting real estate in the county, maintained by a title company in each county in which the title company operates.

Title Report—A report issued by a title company which discloses the condition of the title to a specific parcel of land.

Title Report, Preliminary—A title report issued early in the transaction for the purpose of revealing all matters that presently affect the title. It differs from an **abstract** in that the latter will show all incidents related to the title from the original grant to the present.

Title Search—An inspection of the public record to determine all rights to and encumbrances on a piece of property.

Title Theory—This theory states that the lender is considered to hold legal title to the mortgaged property while the debt is being repaid.

Topography—The contour of the surface of the land, such as level or hilly.

Torrens System—A system for the registration of land used in some states to verify title without the necessity of a title search. It is an alternative to title insurance, since title to the land is free of all encumbrances or claims not registered with the title registrar. Not currently used in California.

Tort—A civil wrong (other than breach of contract) for which there is a remedy at law; a personal injury or property damage.

Township—In the Government Survey System, a parcel of land 6 miles square containing 36 sections, each one a mile square.

Township Lines—East-west lines, spaced six miles apart, used to describe land in the Government Survey System.

Township Tiers—East-west strips of land, six miles wide and bounded on the north and south by township lines.

Tract—1. A parcel of land of undefined size. 2. In the Government Survey System, an area comprised of 16 townships; 24 miles by 24 miles.

Trade Fixtures—Articles of personal property annexed to real property by a tenant which are necessary for his trade or business and are, therefore, removable by the tenant.

Transferability—If an object is transferable, then ownership and possession of that object can be conveyed from one person to another. Transferability is one of the four elements of value. SEE: **Utility, Scarcity,** and **Demand.**

Trespass—An unlawful physical invasion of property owned by another.

Trust Deed—One of the two main security documents for financing the purchase of real estate, the other being a mortgage. Under the trust deed, power to sell the secured property in the event of default by the **trustor** (borrower) is given to an independent third party, the **trustee**, to protect the interest of the **beneficiary** (lender). A trust deed can be foreclosed at a trustee's sale. Unlike foreclosure under a mortgage, judicial intervention is not required and there is no period of redemption following the trustee's sale.

Trust Deed, All-Inclusive—SEE: **Mortgage, Wraparound.**

Trust Funds—Money or things of value received by a real estate agent on behalf of a principal or another in the performance of any acts for which a real estate license is required, and not belonging to the agent but being held for the benefit of others.

Trust Fund Account—An account, segregated from a broker's own funds, in which a broker may deposit trust funds.

Trustee—SEE: **Trust Deed.**

Trustee in Bankruptcy—An individual appointed by the court to handle the assets of a person in bankruptcy.

Trustee's Sale—A non-judicial foreclosure sale under a deed of trust.

Trustor—SEE: **Trust Deed.**

Truth in Lending Act—A federal law, implemented by the Federal Reserve Board's Regulation Z, which requires disclosures of certain information to consumer credit borrowers. The most important required disclosures are probably the finance charge and the annual percentage rate.

Underimprovement—An improvement which, because of its deficiency in cost or size, is not the most profitable use of the land and is therefore not the highest and best use. Opposite of overimprovement. Both are misplaced improvements.

Underwriting—In real estate lending, the analysis of risk by a lender to determine the probability of a borrower's repaying a loan, and matching the risk to an appropriate term and rate of return.

Undivided Interest (UDI)—The right which co-tenants have to possession of the whole property, rather than to any particular part. Their financial interests may be equal, as in a joint tenancy, or unequal, as in many tenancies in common, but they still have equal rights to possess and use the whole.

Undue Influence—Exerting excessive pressure on someone so as to overpower the person's free will and prevent him or her from acting according to rational decision. A contract entered into as a result of undue influence can be voided.

Uniform Commercial Code—A body of law adopted in slightly varying versions in most states, which attempts to standardize commercial law dealing with such things as promissory notes, sales of personal property, and chattel mortgages. Its main applications to real estate law concern promissory notes, security interests in fixtures, and bulk transfers.

Unit-In-Place Method—In appraisal, a method of computing the replacement cost of an improvement by estimating the cost of each component (foundation, chimney, roof, etc.) and then adding the costs of all components to determine the total replacement cost. The estimated cost of each component includes material, labor and overhead. SEE: **Appraisal, Replacement Cost, Square Foot Method, and Quantity Survey Method.**

Unjust Enrichment—An undeserved benefit; a court of equity will not allow a remedy (such as forfeiture of a real estate contract) if the remedy will result in unjust enrichment of one of the parties.

Unlawful Detainer—A summary legal action to regain possession of real property, normally from a tenant who is in default under the lease.

Useful Life—The period over which a property is economically useful to the owner. Also called economic life.

Usury—Charging an interest rate higher than permitted by law.

Utility—The ability of an object to satisfy some need and/or arouse a desire for possession. One of the four elements of value. SEE: **Scarcity, Demand** and **Transferability.**

V.A.—Veterans Administration.

Vacancy Factor—An allowance for anticipated vacancies in a rental project, such as an apartment house. It is usually a percentage of the gross potential income.

Valid—The legal classification of a contract that is binding and enforceable in a court of law.

Valuable Consideration—Something of value given to influence a person to enter into a contract. It need not be transferable into dollars and cents—though it usually is—but is sufficient if it consists of a promise of personal services, goods or the relinquishment of a legal right, or anything else that would have a value to the person making the promise.

Valuation—The act or process of estimating value; essentially synonymous with appraisal.

Value—The amount of goods or services offered in the marketplace in exchange for a given product.

Value, Assessed—The value placed on property by the taxing authority (County Assessor) for the purposes of taxation.

Value, Book—The amount at which an asset is carried on the owner's accounting books, equal to the cost, plus improvements and additions, less accrued depreciation. It is normally the adjusted book value or adjusted cost basis.

Value, Face—The value of an instrument, such as a bond, note or security, which is indicated on the face of the instrument itself.

Value, Fair Market—The amount of money that a piece of property would bring if placed on the open market for a reasonable period of time, with a buyer willing but not forced to buy, and a selling willing but not forced to sell, and both buyer and seller being fully informed as to the possible use of the property.

Value, Market—The price for which property can be sold on the open market if there is a willing and informed seller and a willing and informed buyer.

Value, Objective—SEE: **Value, Market.**

Value, Salvage—The estimated amount for which a structure can be sold at the end of its economic or useful life.

Value, Subjective—The value of a product in the eyes of a particular person.

Value, Utility—The value to an owner or user. SEE: **Value, Subjective.**

Variable Interest Rate Loan—A type of loan wherein the interest rate is periodically adjusted.

Variance—Permission obtained from proper authorities to use land in a manner not in compliance with existing zoning ordinances. SEE: **Nonconforming Use, Special Exception Permits.**

Vendee—The buyer or purchaser, particularly the purchaser under a land contract.

Vendor—The seller, particularly the seller of realty under a land contract.

Vested—A presently fixed right, interest or title in real property, even though the right to possession might not occur until some time in the future.

Void—Having no legal force or effect.

Voidable—That which can be nullified or adjudged void (particularly a contract) but which is valid until some action is taken to void it. A voidable contract must be rescinded by the innocent party if he or she wishes to avoid performance. Inaction can result in ratification of the contract.

Waiver—The voluntary relinquishment or surrender of a right.

Warranties, Implied—In the sale or lease of property, a warranty created by operation of law irrespective of any intention of the seller or landlord to create it.

Waste—The destruction, damage, or material alteration of property by one in possession of the land who holds less than a fee estate, such as a life tenant or lessee.

Water Rights—SEE: **Riparian Rights; Appropriation, Prior.**

Water Table—The level at which water may be found, either at the surface or below.

Will—The written declaration of an individual that stipulates how his or her estate will be disposed of after death. Also called a testament.

Will, Holographic—A will written and signed in the testator's handwriting, which was not witnessed.

Will, Nuncupative—An oral will made in contemplation of death, often by soldiers on the field of battle. Not recognized in California.

Will, Witnessed—A will which meets the statutory requirements of a valid will; must be signed in front of two witnesses.

Without Recourse—A qualified or conditional endorsement on a negotiable instrument which removes the endorser from liability on the instrument.

Writ of Execution—A court order directing a public officer, normally the sheriff, to seize and sell property to satisfy a debt.

Yield—The return of profit to an investor on an investment, stated as a percentage of the amount invested.

Zone—An area of land set off for a particular use or uses, subject to certain restrictions.

Zoning—Government regulation of the uses of property within specified areas.

Zoning Amendment—A change in the zoning law of a community, requiring the approval of the local legislative body. Also called a rezone.

Index

Waxing
Moon

Waxing Moon

H. S. Kim

WiDō Publishing

WiDō Publishing
Salt Lake City, Utah
www.widopublishing.com

Cover Design by Steven Novak

Print ISBN: 978-1-937178-38-3
Library of Congress Control Number: 2013946684

Printed in the United States of America

"For Bernd"

"Our remedies oft in ourselves do lie,
Which we ascribe to heaven."
—Shakespeare

Part One

Mrs. Wang, the only midwife in the village, had been notified at the onset of Mistress Kim's labor, but she arrived a day and a half later in a leisurely fashion.

Nani, who received Mrs. Wang, had no chance to break the news to her, because the massive midwife in her late forties began to complain as soon as she stepped into the courtyard: the road condition was miserable, her back ached, and her eyeballs burned from lack of sleep. Besides, the baby she had just delivered was the size of a calf, she added, following Nani, who led the way with a lantern in her trembling hand.

It was a moonless night and quiet except for the occasional hooting of an owl perched on an old pine tree beyond the formidable stone walls that surrounded the property. Mrs. Wang cursed as she tripped over a stone, and she spat on the ground to cast away an evil spirit lurking in a corner, which she thought she almost saw. Her stomach growled, so she slapped her belly and said, "Keep quiet."

Nani stopped in front of the quarters where two pairs of shoes were arranged neatly, as if they were being displayed for sale. One was made of straw; the other was adorned with embroidery on the front and back.

Mrs. Wang exercised her stiff neck demonstratively. The maid, having not slept in many hours, yawned and began to announce the arrival of the midwife in a habitual manner, momentarily forgetting that only a few minutes before, Mistress Kim had given birth to a girl and then died with her eyes wide open. She started out matter-of-factly, but in the middle of the sentence her voice went hoarse as she remembered her mistress's final moments. The poor woman had held her and another maid named Soonyi by their wrists for hours until suddenly she let go of her grip, leaving purplish rings, and she had tried to say something, but her immobilized tongue choked her. During the labor her cry had sounded like the howling of a beast, and it still echoed in Nani's head.

No reply came from inside the room. Mrs. Wang took off her shoes impatiently and ascended to the antechamber, made of a century-old juniper tree. Nani remained behind, arranging Mrs. Wang's shoes on the stone next to the other shoes, and then lingered there. It was eerily quiet, and yet the air felt stuffy, as though an overcrowded party had just ended.

Mrs. Wang forcefully opened the latticed door. Two candles on a low table swerved in a synchronized motion as the breeze entered the room through the open door. At first, nothing was visible except the area around the low table, but the odor that met Mrs. Wang's nostrils quickly told her what had happened.

After a few moments, Nani entered with the lantern. Soonyi was sitting in the corner, seemingly as still and lifeless as a sack of grain, her eyes glittering with profound fear.

Mrs. Wang sat to feel the pulse of the woman on a cotton mat in a pool of her own blood. She dropped the still-warm hand of the unfortunate woman. Then suddenly, she shouted, "Bring the lantern close!" A creature between the dead woman's leg's squirmed. Mrs. Wang picked it up. She slapped the bottom of the baby, who immediately cried at the top of her lungs.

"Hot water, quickly!" Mrs. Wang shouted again. Soonyi sprang up from her corner and rushed out. Still holding the lantern, Nani trembled severely. Her mistress was still looking at her.

"Put that down and go bring linens or whatever you have," Mrs. Wang said sharply.

As she set the lantern down by the low table and left the room, Nani sobbed, her shoulders jerking.

The baby stopped crying when Mrs. Wang gave her a thumb to suck on. Mrs. Wang held the baby a little higher to show the dead woman.

Mrs. Wang felt utterly miserable. She had made a mistake, she thought to herself. Most of the well-to-do people she had dealt with fussed over the smallest signs of labor, so when a male servant, Min, from this house had handed her a letter the day before about his mistress's "excruciating pain," she didn't bother to look in his direction while she tossed millet in the air for her chickens in the yard. He urged her, using his hand gestures because he was mute, to please come with him, but she simply said that she would come when it was time for her to come.

It had happened in the past that, as a less experienced and more sympathetic midwife, she had rushed to the walled households only to find the pregnant mistress resting like a beached whale, hoping for contractions to begin. Mrs. Wang would be guided into a resting area and served meals and snacks and drinks for days on end, sometimes until cabin fever attacked her violently. As a result, she dreaded being summoned by the wealthy: they were predictably unpredictable.

But now, sitting in the room with the dead woman, she felt thoroughly regretful.

There was nothing she could do now, Mrs. Wang told herself. She then said it out loud to the face of the dead woman, as if to protest: "There is nothing I can do." She closed the dead woman's eyes. The tips of her fingers felt moist. She stopped then, not knowing what to do with the moisture on her fingers. The woman's oval face showed a certain pride, even in death. Mrs. Wang tried not to look at her. She didn't want to know her more than she already did.

The baby began to cry vehemently.

"I hate it when babies cry," Mrs. Wang muttered, and then looked about, lest anyone had heard her. She was ashamed, but the only others present were the dead woman and her baby.

The baby Mrs. Wang had delivered earlier was awfully large, and his mother had impressively sized breasts, already engorged, enough to feed twins. Triplets. Maybe she would take Mistress Kim's baby girl for milk for a while. But right at the moment, Mrs. Wang was too tired to think about the logistics of the arrangement.

The two maids reappeared, carrying a bucket of warm water and linens. Mrs. Wang clucked her tongue. She realized they were hardly older than the newborn they were going to bathe. Nevertheless, she told them what to do.

While the maids performed their duties, breathing rapidly, Mrs. Wang suddenly asked, "Do your people know what has happened?"

The two maids hesitated for a moment, glancing at each other uncomfortably.

"Have you swallowed a stone?" Mrs. Wang asked impatiently. "I don't mind tales, but I mind silence. Out with it. Now!"

Nani began to explain in an unsteady voice. Mistress Kim was the first wife of Mr. O, whose fortune and prosperity knew no bounds, except that he had no heir.

"Get to the point!" Mrs. Wang thundered.

So the story was that Mr. O was with his second wife at the moment, and when he was with her, he was not to be disturbed for any reason.

"What a pig," muttered Mrs. Wang.

☽   ○   ☾

Mrs. Wang arrived home at dawn. Her shins wobbled and her back was drenched and her head felt light from lack of sleep. As she opened her wooden gate with its missing hinge, it creaked, and her surprised rooster made an unplanned interjection of the loudest *ko-ki-yo-oo*. Her heart leaped and she almost fell on her buttocks. She was beside herself. Clenching her teeth, she strode toward the cage and took down the sickle hanging loosely. It was the tool used to trim bamboos that grew too tall and obstructed her view of the canyon.

It happened not so quickly as she would have liked. She grabbed the rooster who, intuiting the murderous instinct in his owner, struggled to escape. Mrs. Wang finally managed to chop off his head, which flew into the thicket of bamboo stems. The rooster flapped his wings as if he were winding up propellers to fly. The blood began to spurt out of his severed neck, dotting the ground in a chillingly beautiful pattern.

Mrs. Wang didn't stay to observe her rooster's last moments. Instead, she hurried to the kitchen to put a pot of water on the clay stove. Because she had been gone for so long, no fire was left. Lighting kindling, she murmured impatiently, "Come on. Get going. Good fire."

While the water was heating, she cleaned herself of the animal blood and went into her room to change. A piece of petrified rice cake was on a plate in her bedroom. God only knew how old it was. Overwhelmed with hunger, she devoured it, despite the few spots of greenish white mold that resembled certain winter flowers. Then she lay down on the warm part of the floor, under which ran a heating channel that was connected to the clay stove in the kitchen. Her bones melted on the heated floor and her spirit oozed out of her. While counting with her fingers how many hours she had stayed up, she fell into a deep sleep and woke up many hours later.

Smoke filled her room and the burned smell infuriated her. Cursing life and the gods, she ran to the kitchen, only to witness an empty, blackened pot on the kitchen stove.

Standing there in front of it, she was surprised to find herself strangely relieved. The rice cake she had eaten still felt lumpy in her stomach, and she wouldn't have felt like eating the animal she had killed so impulsively anyway. She hadn't meant to do that, actually. She had never done that before. In the past, she had always made sure that her animals died in such a way that they did not know about their own end. Why had she been so crass with her rooster? Was she going to cook the bird without depluming it? She took the pot off the stove and set it on the dirt floor to let it cool down.

She stepped outside. The sun was high in the sky, and her hens were cooing and flapping their wings, ready to get out of the cage. As soon as their door was unlatched, they rushed out into her yard. She hoped none of her creatures had seen what she had done to the rooster. A sickle wasn't the right tool to use to kill an animal in the first place. But then the brains of chickens were so small. What did they know, anyway? Now she regretted that she had no soup. It would have been good to have something hot. The thought prompted her to go to her vegetable garden in the backyard. She pulled out a few white radishes and shook the dirt off them.

While chopping the radishes, she felt her arms ache. She should make two entries in her journal about the deliveries she had just performed, but she decided to stay near the pot and keep vigil.

When the radish soup was ready, there was a knock on her gate. As she walked toward it, she could see the head of a young man above the gate, as if the head had grown out of the door while she slept.

"What is it?" Unlatching the gate, she asked, annoyed by his blank face.

He made no reply but motioned with his head toward the girl behind him. She was holding a little bundle in her arms. When she saw Mrs. Wang, she smiled broadly, as if seeing an old friend after a long time.

"What is it?" Mrs. Wang inquired once more, but then she realized that the girl was one of the two maids who had assisted her the night before, and the young man was the mute servant who had come to fetch her the other day. The baby must be the unfortunate offspring of the deceased woman. Mistress Kim. Was that her name?

"What now?" Mrs. Wang opened the gate and let them in.

Nani advanced and bragged that the baby hadn't cried at all, sounding like a proud mother.

Min stood in the front yard, gazing at the mountains on the other side of the valley. Nani brought out a letter written by Mr. O, the father of the baby.

The gist of the letter, apart from his excessive apologies for the inconvenience, was that because Mrs. Wang might know a wet nurse, he would let her decide what was to be done with her. He added a postscript: Nani is delivering the fee for the nursing mother.

There were two pouches, one for Mrs. Wang's services of the night before, and the other containing compensation for a wet nurse.

Mrs. Wang took both pouches in her hands. The one for the wet nurse was heavier than the one for herself. Maybe three times heavier. But she said nothing.

"Would you like some soup?"

Nani welcomed the idea. But Min made a gesture, which only Nani understood.

"He thinks we should get going for the sake of the baby," she interpreted for Mrs. Wang.

"I need to take care of my stomach first." The rice cake, she told herself, was hardly food: it was petrified and gave her only flatulence. She had worked hard and the chicken soup was what she deserved after all that work, except that it had vanished. So at least she would have radish soup before she did anything else for other people.

She invited the visitors to sit on the outdoor bench. The maid sat holding the baby, and the young man stood awkwardly, shooing away flies with his hands.

Mrs. Wang brought out three bowls of radish soup with

cold rice and kimchi. They ate ceremoniously, without words.

The meal put Mrs. Wang in a much better mood. So she asked, smiling, "What's his background? Who are his parents?"

"He is an orphan. Was found at the gate, bundled up in a basket when he was only a few months old."

"He is a good soul," Mrs. Wang said quietly. Good looking too, she said to herself.

Nani blushed and offered another piece of information about him. "Min wants to go live in a big city. But he will have to get permission. Actually, he wants compensation from our master for all his work before he goes."

"If he gets to leave with only Mr. O's blessing, he'll be lucky."

Nani said nothing but stared at her young man. Her eyeballs moved rapidly, as if she were dreaming, and then suddenly her eyes brimmed with tears.

Mrs. Wang wasn't a sentimental woman. So she said, "Are you all right? Do you want to lie down?"

Min put down his bowl by the well, sat down next to Nani, and clumsily rubbed her shoulder.

"Don't touch me, you idiot," Nani grumbled, her voice hardly audible.

"What's the use if he can't hear you?" Mrs. Wang didn't like this outpouring of emotion in her front yard. As if there weren't enough tragedies in this world!

"Oh, he can hear better than the creatures in the wild. That's for sure," Nani said.

The young man wiped Nani's eyes with his sleeve. And he moaned and groaned in his throat in an effort to soothe her. Abruptly, Nani stopped crying and spat out, "Idiot!"

"Let's go," Mrs. Wang commanded.

She poured the leftovers into a chipped ceramic bowl for her old dog. Mrs. Wang and Nani, with the baby, and Min began to walk down the narrow, dusty winding road into the valley.

"OH, BIG SISTER! HOW COULD YOU DO THIS TO ME? HOW could you close your eyes and abandon me?" Mistress Yee, the second wife of Mr. O, cried without shedding tears, frothing around her mouth. She drank water every few minutes and ate plums so that she wouldn't lose her voice and get too exhausted.

"I will not live without you! I *cannot* live without you!" she protested, flailing her arms in the air. Then she accidentally hit her dainty table, four dragons inlaid and lacquered, where she kept her writing brushes and papers. She was sure that she had fractured a finger. Cursing under her breath, she threw a millet-hull filled cushion toward the door. Mirae came in. She had been standing in the hallway, hoping her mistress would stop this nonsensical affair of mourning for Mistress Kim, whom, everyone knew, she had abhorred more than maggots. Mirae liked her mistress best when her mistress was being herself.

Just the other day, upon receiving the news that Mistress Kim had gone into labor, Mistress Yee had ordered Mirae to sew cotton cloth into a doll. Later in the evening, Mirae took the doll to her mistress. Mistress Yee smiled, transfixed, as if she had seen someone on the ceiling. She took a needle and pierced the doll between the legs, and then she handed it to Mirae. "Go bury this in the yard of my enemy." Mirae hesitated, unsure what it all meant. Mistress Yee dropped a bolt of silk on the ground and it rolled out to Mirae's feet. "It should be enough to make an outfit for you. You would look splendid in that color." Mirae took the silk and the doll and waited in her room until the owl hooted. She walked out in the jet black night with the doll and a wooden spatula to dig the earth. The task was harder than she had thought; she had to dig the dry earth without making any noise. She sweated, imagining herself in the silk, the color of an orange azalea. Such a thing was no use to a maid, for she would never have an occasion to wear it, but because her mistress entrusted her with a task so important and private, she felt hopeful. Someday, she thought, her mistress might be able to turn her into an elegant lady. That was a good enough reason to serve her mistress, no matter what she was asked to do. She covered the hole with the dirt and smoothed out the surface. Holding her breath, she tiptoed past Mistress Kim's quarters, from which faint groaning could be heard. When Mirae reported the successful accomplishment of her task, Mistress Yee said nothing, as if it no longer mattered.

Now, Mistress Yee moaned theatrically. "I must have broken my finger. Oh, gods, help me."

"Let me see it, Mistress," Mirae said, squatting down very close to examine her lady's finger.

"Don't touch me with your filthy hand!" Mistress Yee frowned.

Mirae knew that her mistress would menstruate any day now, but still she was taken by surprise. She had thought that they had become friends, even if in secret. She had devoted herself to her mistress even when it had meant risking her own life. For the first time, her blood boiled with hostility. She despised Mistress Yee for fussing so much over a minor scratch.

"Fetch me some potato meat to apply to my finger. It's swelling. Can't you see?" Mistress Yee cried, lifting her middle finger in the air.

Mirae sprang up and went to the kitchen where a huge cast iron pot was on the stove in which mugwort was being steeped to bathe the corpse. The aroma filled the kitchen. She took a deep breath and began to peel a potato. Then she raised a stone pestle and aimed at the potato in the stone mortar. At that moment, Nani entered the kitchen, out of breath and pink in the face. She had just returned from a trip with Mrs. Wang to drop off the newborn at Jaya's house.

Ignoring Mirae, Nani sat in the middle of the kitchen and sighed. In a minute she began to sob, thinking of Mistress Kim, her kind-hearted mistress. She felt exhausted. The situation had overwhelmed the young maid. Wiping her eyes, she got up and filled a gourd with water.

Mirae, almost done with crushing the raw potato, said, "My mistress broke her finger. She is in mourning."

"That's an interesting way of mourning," Nani commented and drank the water, dripping from both sides of her mouth onto her flat chest.

"Well, she was crying so hard. Wildly lamenting the death of your mistress. She was delirious and fell on her finger," Mirae said, wondering why in the world she was making up the story for the sake of her mistress. *What is the matter with me?*

"Heaven knows your mistress hated mine. As good as my dear lady was—she didn't speak harshly of anyone, including your mistress, in spite of all her ill intentions and deeds—I know that my mistress will not rest in peace. She will watch over her little one," Nani said and walked out of the kitchen. Beyond the threshold, she turned around and pointed out, "By the way, potato meat isn't for broken bones. It's for bee stings."

Mirae looked down at the crushed potato and wondered what remedy was for broken bones, but then she realized her mistress didn't have a broken bone. She snickered to herself. Her mistress just had a swollen finger, not even really swollen, so it didn't matter what she was crushing in the mortar.

She took a gob of potato paste and put it on a piece of gauze and carried it carefully to her mistress. On the way, she saw a group of people entering the gate. One of them was a professional wailer, another was carrying a bundle of bamboo sticks for the mourners, and another held an armful of white hemp clothing. Outside the gate, there was a banner made of cloth to indicate that the house was in mourning. But, oddly, the rice offering for the soul-escorting devils was missing.

"My lady, here is the potato paste for your finger," Mirae said, sitting down in a spot not too close to her mistress.

Furrowing between her eyebrows, Mistress Yee inspected the potato paste, which was already turning slightly brown. Then she said, "Put it on my wrist."

"Didn't you want this on your finger?"

"I changed my mind," she replied, and put her right hand out to be attended to.

Confused, Mirae put it on her wrist.

"That feels awful." Mistress Yee scowled.

"Soon it will get better," Mirae comforted her mistress.

"Now, go out and tell whomever you run into that I have a broken wrist, and that I have lost my voice from crying since this morning at the news of Mistress Kim's tragic death. You can cry, too, if you want. Go. What are you looking at? Do I have something on my face?"

"No, my lady, I am going," Mirae said and left.

What was on her mistress's mind? Mirae was still confused. In the yard, she saw Mr. O watching his cousin climb up the ladder to the tile roof with Mistress Kim's silk coat. When it was properly hung from the eaves, Mr. O shouted his first wife's name three times. Then his cousin carefully brought the coat back down and gave it to Mr. O, so that he could deliver it to dress Mistress Kim.

Mr. O looked a few years older than he had the day before. No residue of tears but he certainly looked shaken up.

In Mistress Kim's quarters, two maids were helping the hired undertaker bathe the corpse in steeped mugwort water. Her clipped nails and her hair from her comb were collected and put into five silk pouches. While the undertaker bound the feet and hands of the corpse tightly, the maids tidied up

the room and waited for a male servant to bring the coat of
Mistress Kim. Instead, Mr. O entered. The maids jumped up
and stood by the sides of the corpse. He dropped Mistress
Kim's coat on the floor and cleared his throat. He looked at his
wife for a brief moment and left at once without a word.

The undertaker stuffed the mouth of the corpse with three
spoonfuls of rice and put a coin in her sleeve to ease her journey to the next world. The hired mourner began to wail a sorrowful tune. Finally, both maids covered the corpse with her
coat, dabbing at their eyes with a cotton cloth.

Walking around the yard, Mirae realized that no one was
available to hear the tale of her mistress. Everyone was preoccupied with Mistress Kim. She went back to Mistress Yee and
lied to her for the first time. She said that everyone knew how
much she was suffering.

$$\text{☽ ○ ☾}$$

To escape the sweltering afternoon heat, Mrs. Wang sat under
a weeping willow by Sunset Lake on the way to a party at the
home of the peasant family who had been taking care of Mistress Kim's infant girl.

She devoured a cucumber to quench her thirst and sang a
song, the only song she knew by heart from her childhood.

A ri rang, A ri rang, A ra ri yo-o-o-o.

Her mother had sung this song to her as a lullaby, even
though the lyrics were about unrequited love, until she was
quite old—eight or nine. When she was ten, her mother married again, a traveling actor this time, and vanished from her life.
So she was left with her grandmother, who was a midwife, not
by training but by her experiences over the years. Her grandmother taught her how to read and write. She also taught her
how to ease the pain of shrieking women and how to deliver
babies. She told her to make an entry in a journal after each

delivery. "You learn tremendously from reviewing and writing about your experiences," her grandmother emphasized.

When Mrs. Wang was sixteen, there was a flood in her village. She and her grandmother had to relocate themselves temporarily to a relative's house. On the way there, Mrs. Wang had to lift her long skirt so as not to get it wet. A young man witnessed the beautiful shape of her bare ankles from the corner of his house, and he fell instantly in love with her.

He wrote a poem about her anklebones resembling baby peaches and so on. He had his servant deliver it to Mrs. Wang, who read it and was unmoved. She tossed the poem into a chest where she kept some of her mother's things and never looked at it again. But the young man fell gravely ill, longing for her reply. He lost his appetite and developed a fever and talked to himself constantly. His parents thought he was possessed by some evil spirit, so they threw a bowlful of rock salt at him every morning and put a knife under his pillow every night. But he only grew worse. He looked out the window for hours every day and would not respond to simple questions.

His parents learned from a male servant what ailed their son. When they learned about Mrs. Wang's family background, they urged their son to forget about her. Of course, he couldn't. So his father locked him in the grain storage room and starved him from one full moon to the next. He came out unswayed and looking better than when he had entered, so the father said, "Maybe this is his fate."

The mother of the young man visited Mrs. Wang's grandmother, who eagerly agreed to the marriage proposal. Mrs. Wang, however, had no intention of marrying anyone, especially the young man who wrote the miserable poem that didn't rhyme. But her grandmother said that she wasn't going to live forever. So Mrs. Wang was forced into the marriage. But she was determined not to have a baby, for she knew what it was like to give birth. Whenever her young husband came near her, she beat him notoriously. Once, she dragged him to a young dogwood tree in the yard and tied him to it. He wrestled with the tree to free himself and finally uprooted it. Still tied to the dogwood, he walked around to find someone to untie the rope that bound his torso to the tree. The sight of this young husband made a scene, and the story had traveled all over the village by sunrise. His parents decided to lock their daughter-in-law in the grain storage room, but Mrs. Wang fled with her belongings in a sack.

She settled down in this village, where no one knew of her past. She had to pawn her mother's gold chrysanthemum hairpin to get a room. She worked hard and earned the reputation she now had. She was generous with the poor and proper with the rich. She was also a counselor for those in trouble. Fifteen years before, just once, she had made her way back to her hometown to see her grandmother. The old woman had gone mad and lost her teeth. She didn't remember her own granddaughter. Mrs. Wang asked her for forgiveness, and her grandmother said something, but without her teeth, what came out of her mouth sounded like "Go to hell." Mrs. Wang replied, "I am not afraid of hell, Granny. But I am afraid to see Mama in hell. She might very well be there for abandoning her only daughter, and I for abandoning my own grandmother." She placed her mother's gold hairpin, which she had retrieved from the pawnshop when she had earned enough money, in her grandmother's palm, and dragged her heavy feet away. That was the last time she had seen her grandmother.

Mrs. Wang felt the heat rise from the earth as the sun settled high in the sky as she remembered her grandmother. She thought she'd better get going before it got too hot. There was a good-sized carp swimming under the water. Taking a nearby stone, she threw it at the moving fish, but only water splashed on her. She laughed at her own ludicrousness. But the water cooled her down and made her feel much better.

The corn stalks on the way to the peasants' house were taller than Mrs. Wang. She could already smell food, probably fried scallion patties, as she neared the thatched-roof mud house.

"Here I am," Mrs. Wang thundered at the entrance.

"Please come in, Mrs. Wang. Thank you for coming to our humble home," said Dubak, a copper-faced farm worker with a simple smile as he bowed down.

"Ah, Mrs. Wang. You are here already and I am not half done with cooking. Please have a seat." Jaya came out into the yard from the kitchen with Mr. O's baby in her right arm and a spatula in her left hand.

"She is doing quite well, Mrs. Wang." Jaya smiled broadly, showing the baby to her. "I really thought she wouldn't make it. She was so small and weak in the beginning. But with my milk, look at her. She is thriving. Drinking more than my son. She sometimes leaves none for him. . . ." She went on and on.

"How are you doing?" Mrs. Wang asked to divert her attention.

"I am doing fine, Mrs. Wang." Jaya smiled again.

"Are you carrying another?" Mrs. Wang asked bluntly, looking at her midriff.

"Yes, I am." Jaya's cabbage face turned purple. Naturally large, people often thought that she was pregnant when she was not.

Mrs. Wang cleared her throat. No children, no trouble had been the motto of her life, but there were people with a different outlook on life. So that was that. But right now, hunger pinched her stomach.

"Smells good here. I smelled fried scallion patties from the corn field," Mrs. Wang said. She was sitting on the raised floor at the entrance to the hut. Flies were buzzing around the food, which was covered with a hemp cloth.

"That's why I married her. She makes the best scallion patties in the village," Dubak said, dropping a bundle of potatoes in the middle of their yard. "Mrs. Wang, I would like you to take this. These potatoes taste like chestnuts. So flavorful they melt in your mouth," he said proudly.

"I appreciate your gift, but my aging legs are not as agile as they once were. I can't carry that sack back home. I will take a few," Mrs. Wang said, examining the cooked potatoes peeking out from under the hemp cloth on a low table.

"I will carry it for you."

"What did I do to deserve that?"

"You brought my son out to this world. He is such a good sleeper. He is sleeping right now by the way. But I must say, and forgive me for saying this, but Mr. O's daughter keeps my wife awake all night. Every night, she cries several times. My son and I sleep through thunder. But the baby girl's a very delicate sort," Dubak said, scratching his head vigorously.

Mrs. Wang quickly understood that the invitation to their son's one-hundredth-day birthday had a flip side. They were also wondering when another money pouch might find its way to them from Mr. O.

"Tomorrow is her hundredth day. We wonder if it will be all right to celebrate hers the way we do, or do they have something else in mind? Commoners like us don't know how to imitate the nobleman's way of life. Besides, we don't have the means to do it anyway," Dubak said, pulling his hair. "My wife says we should take her home for the occasion, so that they can see how well she has been fed and taken care of. But I say no, we can't go uninvited, even though we care for their offspring."

"I get your meaning. But I thought you were paid. I mean, your wife was paid for the entire period of nursing the baby up front. Is that not true?" Mrs. Wang asked, raising her caterpillar eyebrows.

"Yes, of course," Dubak answered. "But that's not—that's not what I am wondering. It's not the-the money," he stuttered.

"Of course it's the money," his wife interrupted. "Mrs. Wang, we are commoners. And I can only speak as a commoner. I was paid for nursing their baby. It's true they paid enough money for that. But is milk all that a baby needs? She needs clothes, she needs…" She couldn't think of what else a baby needed. "Personally, I am a little concerned that no one has ever come to see how the baby is doing. What if they don't take her back when she is done nursing? Are we stuck with her? I would like to know. What if another baby comes along? I can't care for this baby long unless—" She stopped her speech there.

"I will deliver your message. I just didn't know I was here for that mission." Mrs. Wang scowled.

"No, Mrs. Wang. That's not why we invited you. Please sit down," begged Jaya.

She brought more food to the table and then sat down across from Mrs. Wang, encouraging her to please take the chopsticks. When Mrs. Wang finally succumbed to tasting the food, Jaya pulled out her large breast to give to the whimpering baby girl.

"Do you like my scallion patties?" Jaya asked, a grin spreading across her face.

"Heavenly," Mrs. Wang replied as she picked up her third one. Right now, a bowl of mud would be delicious, she thought to herself.

After devouring half a dozen scallion patties, Mrs. Wang gulped down a large bowl of milky white rice wine. She was in an excellent mood. She burped and then she wanted to take a look at the babies. Jaya brought them close and Mrs. Wang examined them. Like his mother, the boy was double-chinned, twice the size of Mr. O's daughter. She was alert and staring at Mrs. Wang as if she understood what was being said.

"She sucks blood out of me all night long, and then when my baby boy wakes up, there is hardly any milk left for him." Jaya laughed superficially.

"When the mother of the poor thing finds her way to a good place, she will remember your effort. Even though I saw her only after she was dead, I knew she had been a good soul," Mrs. Wang said.

"Oh, we knew of her excellent reputation. A few years ago my husband was hired to escort her to her grandfather's funeral in her hometown. He said that Mistress Kim was more queenly than the queen of China," Jaya said.

Mrs. Wang got up, leaving a few coins on the table.

"What is this, Mrs. Wang?"

"Buy something for your son. What's his name?"

"Sungnam is his name. Star of the South," Jaya said self-consciously.

"A good name that is," Mrs. Wang said.

Dubak got up from the yard, where he had been mending his straw shoes. He put the sack of potatoes on his shoulder and a towel around his head.

"Are you sure you want to walk back with me with that on your shoulder?" Mrs. Wang asked.

"When you bite into one of my potatoes for dinner, you will be happy you let me carry this for you." He smiled, showing his horsey, square front teeth. He was already sweating. The blazing sun was still fastened in the middle of the sky.

Mrs. Wang led the way, thinking of the name of the boy, Sungnam. Southern star or northern star, he is a peasant. And a peasant is a peasant, she said to herself.

By the time she arrived home, the sun was heading west, and her animals were not excited to see her. The heat had been too much for them. She should have left more water, she thought, looking at the bone-dry bowls in the yard.

DR. CHOI ARRIVED AT MR. O'S HOUSE TO EXAMINE MIS-
tress Yee. She was sure she was pregnant. This wasn't the first
time she had thought she was pregnant. The other two times,
Dr. Choi's diagnoses had put the household in a somber mood
for a few days.

Mr. O was in his room, tapping his thin brass pipe on the
ashtray and fidgeting a little.

In the hallway outside Mistress Yee's room, the maid stood
behind the latticed door while the doctor felt Mistress Yee's
pulse. A few seconds later, the doctor nodded.

"What do you think?" Mistress Yee asked impatiently.

"Mistress Yee, you are indeed pregnant," the doctor
announced dryly.

"Of course I am," she said. I didn't need an old frog like you
to tell me that, she thought to herself. "Now you go and tell
my husband what you've discovered," she ordered him, without looking in his direction.

The doctor was amazed by her audacity. She looked half
contemptuous, half amused, and she gazed into thin air, as if
seeing something invisible, something only *she* had the power
to see. The doctor stood up, cleared his throat, and walked
out, looking grave.

A tray of plum wine was brought in for the doctor and
Mr. O, whose face was all mouth, from one ear to the other, at
the news. He was not getting younger and felt that this was a
divine gift, finally.

"Thank you, Dr. Choi, thank you," Mr. O said, as if it had
been the work of the doctor that his wife was pregnant.

"Mistress Yee is in good spirits, and by nature she is very strong. She will have no trouble carrying this through to the end," Dr. Choi said, remembering his first wife, Mistress Kim, whose sudden death confounded him, for her constitution had been in excellent harmony despite her delicate frame.

"I was sorry to hear the news about Mistress Kim," the doctor mentioned. He knew that it wasn't the right moment for condolences, but he couldn't stop his tongue once it got started.

"Poor woman. She was good through and through," Mr. O said. There was a tinge of melancholy in his voice. "Please," he said, recommending more plum wine to the doctor.

$$\text{☽ ◯ ☾}$$

At that moment, Mrs. Wang was on her way to Mr. O's mansion. She thought her legs were going to break, the way she had recently walked miles and miles on low fuel. She sat under an old pine tree and listened to the silence of the earth. It was good to sit in the shade. She looked inside her pouch, where no more cucumbers or rice balls remained. She never carried enough food.

Out of nowhere, a deer appeared. Its innocent eyes stared at Mrs. Wang intently, making her feel rather uncomfortable. She pretended she was a statue, fearing she might frighten the little creature. She remembered she had bought deer meat from a hunter once and it was the best thing next to beef, but right now she wasn't in the mood to strangle this little creature. There was something about the deer or, perhaps in the atmosphere, that prevented her from acting hastily. She held her breath and stared back at the deer. *Those eyes.* She had seen them before. Lurid and sad and silent. A large pinecone dropped on Mrs. Wang's head, shocking her, and she jumped up. The deer ran away. Mrs. Wang sighed.

Her legs wobbled as she walked downhill toward her destination. The night before, she hadn't been able to sleep for some reason, and during those sleepless hours, she had thought of one wish: when she grew really old and it was time for her to go, she wanted to die instantaneously, in her sleep, without knowing it. That would be a blessing.

She approached Mr. O's vast land with its colossal grove of trees, and she listened to the loud and monotonous a cappella singing of summer insects. All of a sudden a young lad jumped out of a field screaming, with a leech on his leg. Mrs. Wang took a stick and removed the bloodsucking creature. She said, "Reserve your screaming for the end of the world. It's just a leech."

"I am sorry, Mrs. Wang. I was terribly scared," he apologized.

A woman shouted from the field, "Mrs. Wang, we are having some food. Why don't you join us?"

Mrs. Wang looked up into the sky to see what time it might be, and thought, people can wait but food can't. So she joined them for lunch. The farmers and Mrs. Wang passed the weathered *Jang Seung*, totem poles. Three offering bowls of rice, with incense planted among the grains, were lined up in front of the totem poles, whose grotesque expressions were varied but muted, with faded colors and chipped noses.

The farmers met up with two women carrying trays of food on their heads. Steamed barley and young pumpkin leaves and bean paste and green chilies were their lunch. The farmers ate and talked and laughed and shouted with their food in their mouths.

"Hope we will have enough rain this year," a woman said as she stuffed her mouth with steamed barley wrapped in a pumpkin leaf.

"Last year was terrible. The brittle surface of the field cracked at the end of the summer. How many lizards and snakes did the children find, all dried up on the rocks and paths? It was just awful. Do you remember?" a young lad said.

"What kind of crops the earth yields is up to the gods," said another woman.

"That's right," agreed a man.

"What brings you down here, Mrs. Wang?" the woman asked, her cheeks bulging with food.

"Some business with Mr. O," Mrs. Wang answered.

"Is Mistress Yee pregnant?" the second woman asked, grinning.

"So soon after the death of the first wife?" a voice asked.

"Who would have thought that Mistress Kim would die so young? What a pity. She was a good lady. What use are gold and silver and a nobleman's title? When the devil takes your life away, there is nothing left to boast about," another man said.

"She was not like the second mistress, for sure. But whose life does the devil take first? There is no such thing as fairness. Enjoy your life while it lasts. The dead know no pleasure," a sinewy farmer said caustically, staring intently at the woman on the opposite side.

"Mistress Kim had the eyes of an innocent doe," a woman said, pouring rice wine into the bowls.

☽ ○ ☾

It was Mistress Kim whom Mrs. Wang had seen under the pine tree. The doleful eyes even when her breath had left her. The thought chilled her bones. Uncharacteristically quiet, Mrs. Wang took one of the bowls brimming with rice wine, which was meant for the men, and drank it until the bottom of the bowl was exposed. Without thanking her hosts for the meal, she got up and walked away like a sleepwalker.

In no time, she arrived at Mr. O's southern gate, which seemed oppressively massive. She couldn't remember her impression of the place from her previous visit. Before she banged the gate with the circular brass piece that hung in the middle, she took a deep breath. But the gate was flung open suddenly. Mistress Yee was leaving with her maid in a spectacular palanquin. She was all covered up to protect herself from the harsh sunlight.

"Who is that?" Mistress Yee asked Mirae, looking directly at Mrs. Wang.

"Mrs. Wang, the midwife," Mirae answered.

"Did my husband send for you? What an impatient man! It takes a while for the baby to arrive," she said to no one in particular and laughed in a high-pitched voice. And then she left without saying another word to Mrs. Wang.

Stunned by both her striking beauty and her blunt arrogance, Mrs. Wang stood still for a moment and observed the palanquin ambling away. She mumbled to herself, "A rose has more thorns than any other flower." Before she entered through the gate, Mrs. Wang turned around suddenly to have a glimpse of the maid once more. She was dressed in orange silk, an unusual color and fabric for a maid. Perhaps she wasn't a maid. But she was treated like a maid. Mrs. Wang slipped into the gate, thinking the maid was also a thorny rose.

Mrs. Wang took another deep breath. Her left knee throbbed. Her mind was preoccupied with the thought of Mistress Yee. A gorgeous little thing, but with eyes full of malice.

"Oh, Mrs. Wang!" Nani, overexcited, greeted her.

"Here you are. I was hoping to find you. Go and let your master know I am here to see him. Tell him it is concerning his daughter," Mrs. Wang said.

"How is the baby, Mrs. Wang?" Nani asked.

"Couldn't be better," Mrs. Wang replied quickly.

"I am so glad to hear that. Your kindness will not pass unrewarded, Mrs. Wang. I know that Mistress Kim is watching over her baby," Nani said, her face suddenly turning sad, like an old apple.

"I have no time to lose. I have a long way to go back," Mrs. Wang said.

"Please follow me, Mrs. Wang. I will take you where you can sit and wait," the maid said, sniffling.

"Where is Mistress Yee going?" Mrs. Wang asked, following the maid. It was none of her business, but she couldn't stop herself from inquiring.

"She is going to the temple to pray for a healthy son. She is pregnant, Mrs. Wang," the maid whispered.

Feeling a little irritable, Mrs. Wang didn't respond.

The maid disappeared while Mrs. Wang observed the butterflies in the flower garden. Butterflies always fascinated her. The extraordinary designs on their wings seemed to have been printed with some unknown purpose. Without those black imprints, butterflies would not be quite butterflies. Quietly, she tried to catch a yellow butterfly with her two fingers. But the surprised butterfly fluttered away ever so slowly, teasing her. When she was a little girl, she had been equally fascinated but could never catch a single butterfly. She didn't know what she would do if she caught it. What does one do with butterflies anyway?

"Our master invites you to come and see him, Mrs. Wang," Nani said from behind her.

Mrs. Wang followed her, organizing her thoughts and thinking about what she was going to say.

"Mrs. Wang is here," the maid announced.

After a few moments of formal greetings and expressions of gratitude, Mrs. Wang settled down with Mr. O in his sparsely furnished salon. A painting of a phoenix on the wall with a handsome calligraphy read, *Silence Commits No Mistake.* Mr. O lit his pipe. Mrs. Wang stared at him. Something about him, the way he squinted his eyes as he sucked in the air frantically to get the pipe going, reminded her of someone else she had met recently. Tilting her head, she was recalling the manservant. Min, was that his name? Then she shook her head collecting herself.

"What should her name be?" Mrs. Wang asked in her straightforward way.

Mr. O was struck by the way Mrs. Wang spoke with such composed authority. She was surely a hen with no tamer.

"She is without a name. And she looks as though she is going to live for a long time. She needs a name to be called by," Mrs. Wang reiterated.

"Yes, I understand. I will consult the book of our genealogy and send the name by tomorrow," Mr. O said, puffing his pipe rapidly.

"One more thing before I leave," Mrs. Wang said.

"Yes?" Mr. O raised his eyebrows.

"How long would you have the peasant family take care of your daughter?"

"I shall consult my wife and get back to you."

"But she is not your daughter's mother," Mrs. Wang said boldly, looking straight into his eyes.

What Mrs. Wang pointed out seemed to be news to Mr. O, as if he had forgotten entirely about his first wife. One of his ears moved, involuntarily, and then his mouth fumed a white cloud.

Mrs. Wang watched him placidly. He reminded her of her former father-in-law, a chain-smoker. His teeth had been browner than a dog's, and he had coughed so deeply that the hollowness in his lungs resonated. She could have broken his legs, easily, when he wanted to put her in the storage room, but she preferred to run away. Her husband had cried when he learned of her plan. "I am not the only woman in the world," she had said to him to console his broken heart.

"Ah, Mrs. Wang, I know she didn't give birth to the child, but she is her mother now by law," Mr. O finally said.

"I suppose so," Mrs. Wang responded. She had no grudge against Mistress Yee, she told herself. Whatever suits them, she thought.

"The peasant woman, Jaya she is called, is hoping to be rid of any unnecessary burden before winter. But I know you will take care of the matter without my intervening further. I've come only because I arranged your daughter's stay at the peasant woman's so she could be nursed," Mrs. Wang elaborated.

"It hurts me to hear that my daughter has become a burden on the wet nurse and her family. I have rewarded them more than generously," Mr. O said, frowning. Actually, he had forgotten how he had rewarded them.

"Well, I have done my duty. I will go now," Mrs. Wang got up.

"Thank you for all your work, Mrs. Wang," Mr. O said, getting up, too, reluctantly, holding his skinny pipe.

Mrs. Wang walked out of the house, and it was already time for dinner. On the way back, Mrs. Wang sat under the old pine tree where she had seen the doe and waited for her to appear once again, but she only saw a bird defecate from a branch high above her.

AFTER MRS. WANG'S DEPARTURE, MR. O TOOK A NAP IN his bedroom, curled up on his side without a cover. He dreamed that he was watching himself as an ancient man with white hair and a long white beard. He had a cane in his hand, and he could feel the shortness of his breath as he was climbing a mountain. There seemed to be no end to his climbing. In the middle of the mountain, he stopped to look behind him, but, strangely, he was still at the foot of the mountain. He climbed again for a long time. He saw an old pine tree and decided to sit under it. But a woman was occupying the shady spot, so he hesitated to go near it. It was a young woman of bewitching beauty. He realized that it was his first wife, Mistress Kim, as young as when she had first arrived in his house after the wedding. He wanted to say something to her, but looking at his old self, he couldn't. He thought she wouldn't recognize him. He was frightened by the sheer youth of his wife, or rather by his withering self, so he walked backward away from her. But in his mind, he hoped his wife would recognize him, call him by his name tenderly. He fell, tripping over something. He couldn't make himself get up, so he screamed for help. His wife didn't come to help him, and the branches of the pine tree turned into snakes and slithered toward him. He got up quickly and yelled angrily at his wife for not helping him. His wife was nowhere to be found, but a beautiful flower bloomed under the pine tree. The snakes were coming closer and closer to him. He screamed even louder and woke himself up.

His back was drenched and his head was spinning. He was relieved to find himself in his own room. He cleared his throat and tried to say something, but he wasn't able to for a while.

It was still light outside but very quiet.

He sat up and reviewed his dream slowly. It made him angry for two reasons. His wife hadn't come to his rescue, and why had he been such an old man while his dead wife seemed intensely young? What could it possibly mean? And then he thought about the pine branches turning into snakes, the most ominous creatures one encountered in a dream. It chilled his bones just to think of them. But his wife had turned into a pretty white flower, looking magnificent under the pine tree. Mr. O slapped his knee and thought of Mrs. Wang's visit. What was it she had wanted from him? He had to think for a moment. The woman was like a man. Her voice was deeper than his, and her eyes glared like those of a general about to strike his enemy.

After a few moments, it came to his mind. She wanted a name for his late wife's daughter. His daughter. Their daughter. He couldn't recall having seen the baby.

Mistress Kim's funeral had lasted only three days, short-ened from a seven-day event, due to Mistress Yee's insuffer-able pain with her wrist or arm, he remembered now. By the time the funeral was over, the daughter of Mistress Kim had already been sent to a wet nurse.

"One ugly baby," Mistress Yee had reported to him in bed after having seen her. "Can't be a baby of a handsome man like you," she had said, squeezing him hard without warning, which paralyzed his jaw.

He cleared his throat and called out for some help. A male servant came in. Mr. O asked him to get water for his ink and to rub the black chalk onto the stone block to bleed. While waiting, Mr. O thought of the dream once again. It no longer frightened him. But he still didn't feel good that he had appeared such an old man in his dream and his dead wife so stunningly beautiful. She was not that beautiful, he said argumentatively to himself. She had been judicious, intelligent, and well-mannered to a point that was unnecessary between husband and wife.

Mr. O began to write slowly and precisely, *Meehua*, in Chinese characters. He looked at it scrupulously and let the rice paper dry. She might want her baby to be named Beautiful Flower, Meehua. That could be a name for a girl. Not very fashionable.

He smoked for a while, and there was an announcement that Mistress Yee had returned from the temple. She entered before he welcomed her, collapsed next to him, and complained about how hard it was to kowtow one hundred eight times for the health of his son. But she would be, of course, willing to cut her flesh off her body if it were for the sake of their son.

Mr. O massaged his wife's shoulder. She fit into his embrace like a spineless creature; his first wife had felt as stiff as a bamboo stick. He laughed, knowing that Mistress Yee wouldn't have kowtowed one hundred eight times for anything. But one never knew. She might have done it for her son, he thought. People changed. Yes, people did.

"Well done, my little lamb," he said.

"What is this?" She sat up. "What did you write? Is this for me?" A smile rippled around her lips.

Mr. O confessed what it was for. Mistress Yee laughed flightily, showing her white teeth. "You shouldn't do that to that creature. She was as ugly as a forgotten pumpkin in the winter field. This adds insult to injury." She laughed once again but this time indignantly.

Gently untangling himself from his wife's limbs, Mr. O tried to put his calligraphy aside. He was a bit self-conscious about his choice for the baby girl's name. It was definitely unfashionable.

"So what motivates you to do this?" Mistress Yee asked, with a strain in her voice. She would have bitten him if she could.

"The midwife came by this afternoon and demanded a name for the girl," he answered, still thinking about the dream in the back of his mind.

"So you waited until I left to do this!" she cried, raising her eyebrows suspiciously.

"Why are you so upset? I am doing my duty or else I will be mocked. The midwife criticized me already. I felt like an idiot in front of her," Mr. O grumbled.

Mistress Yee wondered if Mrs. Wang was in any way related to the dead whore. She had called Mistress Kim a whore on the nights when her husband had chosen to be with her and Mistress Yee lay alone, consumed with jealousy and a feeling of utter defeat.

"So who is this fatso called Mrs. Wang? Is someone else paying her? What does *she* gain in this game of getting a name for the ugly infant girl?" Mistress Yee asked coquettishly.

"The peasant woman wants another payment, which I will send promptly. I can't let the peasants gossip about me," Mr. O said.

"What do you mean? I sent the woman more than most peasants earn in a lifetime!"

Mr. O lit his pipe and puffed smoke with a blank expression. He wanted to send the name to Mrs. Wang as soon as possible, so that he could forget about it. He knew no other woman like Mrs. Wang. She had stared at him directly, as if he had done something wrong to her personally. In any case, he didn't want to see her again.

5

NANI WAS ON HER WAY TO SEE MRS. WANG. IT WAS after early breakfast, and the air was clean and so crisp she could almost touch it as she walked on the dirt road up the hill.

Her mother had come with Mistress Kim when she married into Mr. O's family. Nani was an infant when she arrived with her mother, who had worked as Mistress Kim's nanny since her birth. Some years before, Nani's mother had died of pneumonia, and Mistress Kim had promised that she would marry Nani off to a decent man. But unfortunately, Mistress Kim had also passed away. Nani hadn't known how lonely she would be without Mistress Kim, who had shown more gentleness and kindness than her mother sometimes; most of the time actually. Nani had been having dreams about her mistress lately, and she would wake up in the middle of the night, unable to breathe for a moment. Mistress Kim always appeared with so much blood on her face and clothes. "Mistress, why is there so much blood on you? Whatever happened? Speak, I beg you." But Mistress Kim would gaze far away without a word. Then she would collapse and sob heartrendingly, and Nani would scream and wake up. The other maids were irritated by her hysteria so early in the morning.

Birds with bright orange chests were chirping on the branches of trees as Nani passed by. She used to ask her mother how she could fly, and her mother had replied that she would fly if she was born again as a bird. Once, Nani had asked what her mother would like to be born as in her next life. Her mother thought for a moment and said that she would like to be born as Nani's mother again.

Tears bunched up in her throat as she thought of her mother. Her mother would never be born again as her mother, she thought. If she were born again now, her mother would be younger than she was. So how could her mother ever be her mother again?

Nani looked back again and again as she climbed up the hill, swallowing her tears. Then she spotted Min. He was coming, after all. She had told him the night before about her errand, and he had nodded in agreement, but in the morning he was not outside waiting for her. So she left without him. Now he was coming hurriedly, with his mouth slightly open, as if he would say something. Nani didn't look back anymore; she climbed up faster now.

Min caught up with her in no time. Now he was right behind her. She could hear him breathe. Without acknowledging each other they climbed for a while. Finally, she was out of breath. When she reached the middle point of the hill, she decided to sit under the old pine tree. Her chest was rising and falling rapidly, and the blood rushed to her cheeks and lips. Her mouth was completely dry. White flowers stood under the pine tree arrogantly, as if claiming the place as their own.

Min sat away from the tree and was looking down the hill. The sun was already blazing down on their village.

Nani observed Min, who plucked a pine needle from a branch and began to pick his teeth while looking at his dusty toe peeking out of a worn straw shoe. He watched Nani studying the flowers. He moaned, smiling stupidly, baring his front teeth. Tufts of his hair extended in all directions, manifesting how he had slept. He moaned again smiling broadly. Nani sighed involuntarily for something as small as a seed felt stuck in her chest. But her lips curled up.

He got up and Nani flushed, not knowing where to look. He came close—still smiling—picked one of the white flowers, and put it in her hair. *You look as pretty,* he groaned, waving his hand in the air. She shot a fierce glance at him and ran up the hill. Min walked, frowning pathetically with all his facial muscles.

Inseparable they had been in their childhood. But when Nani was no longer a child and Min had begun to develop strong arm muscles, Nani's mother pulled his ear, looked straight in his eyes, and said, "Stay away from my girl. I can't afford to have a son-in-law without a patch of land. You hear me?" All he wanted was to take care of Nani, but he stayed away from her until, serendipitously, her mother died in the middle of the harsh winter. For the first year after her death, Nani was in mourning, the second year she rejected him, the third year she was upset about everything, and now, in the fourth year, she seemed to be mad only at him. But once in a while, Min found a piece of meat tucked under rice or a boiled egg in his lunchbox and his raggedy shirt hemmed.

Min walked a little faster until he noticed that Nani lagged behind. There were thick bushes of mountain berries ahead of him. He picked up a fallen branch and bent the thorny bushes to make it easier for Nani to pass by. Suddenly, Nani screamed frantically. There was a cat snake in the middle of the dirt path, its head cocked but motionless. Min advanced carefully toward the venomous creature. He threw the branch at its head, but the snake was faster than him. It disappeared into the earth.

Nani burst out crying, her shoulders shuddering, but she marched forward. When her crying subsided, Min went ahead of her and opened his palm. It was full of mountain raspberries, some of which had been crushed and bled on his palm. Without meeting his eyes, she picked a few and dropped them in her mouth. They were tart. Min dropped a few in his mouth and gave the rest to Nani.

The last stretch to Mrs. Wang's house was the steepest. Min squatted in front of Nani, inviting her for a piggyback ride. He had done that so many times when she was a little girl, but this was the first time since they had gotten older. Nani hesitated for a moment but got on his back.

Min produced a hideous but familiar moan of happiness and raced up the hill.

Nani held on to his shoulders, which felt like rocks smoothed by the water on the seashore over the years. It was a hot day, but she didn't mind the extra warmth and the moisture on his back. She realized that this was the feeling she had craved for some time, but she didn't connect it with her recent unnamable frustrations. There was no one on earth she trusted more than Min. He was a parent, a brother, a friend, and a husband already, in her mind, though she knew there had to be more to it once Min really became her husband. Her mother had said, "Stay away from him. Once a servant, always a servant. He's got a good heart, but a good heart doesn't get you a roof over your head. You will understand what Mama means later. But don't you forget what Mama says." At that time, she wasn't interested in him, so what her mother said about Min didn't register in her mind. But now she vaguely understood what she might have meant. Once a maid, always a maid. After Mistress Kim's death, Nani had felt completely lost. She was demoted to kitchen maid and was doing errands of all kinds and getting orders even from that stupid maid of Mistress Yee's. She could run away and forget about everything and marry some stranger with a roof over his head, as her mother would have liked her to. But would life without Min be possible?

She slapped Min's shoulder violently and said, "Slow down. I am going to throw up if you go that fast."

Min moaned again with sheer pleasure and adjusted his pace. Nani was as light as a feather. He could run to the next village and not feel tired at all. His heart was burning with desire to do anything for Nani, and yet doing nothing seemed to be what she wanted him to do.

"I want to get down. Let me down," Nani kicked her feet in the air. Mrs. Wang's house was in sight.

Min let her down carefully and felt the chill on his back. She still had the white flower in her hair. No woman on earth could measure up to his girl's beauty.

Before they reached Mrs. Wang's gate, Nani turned around, pulling his sleeve toward her, and asked, "Do you want to run away with me?"

6

MIN LINGERED NEAR THE ENTRANCE WHILE NANI PRE-
sented a piece of paper wrapped in a cloth to Mrs. Wang. It
was the name for Mr. O's daughter.

Mrs. Wang unfolded the paper and placed it on the wooden
bench. She looked at it for a moment. She guffawed suddenly
and thundered, "Beautiful Flower! You can't live on a name
like that. It gives you no base to live on. Beautiful flowers last
only one season."

Nani sat in front of Mrs. Wang, looking at the writing upside
down, and she followed Mrs. Wang's logic and understood it.

"Well, let me put this away for now. I'll get drinks for us."
Mrs. Wang got up and went to the kitchen. Nani motioned to
Min, who was patting the dog, to come over and sit. He came
over reluctantly but didn't sit. He hadn't officially been sent to
Mrs. Wang. He had just tagged along with Nani.

Mrs. Wang brought out three bowls of a seven-grain drink.
She drank half of hers at once, and then she encouraged them
to partake of theirs.

"Was this all you brought?" Mrs. Wang asked, wondering
about the payment for Jaya.

"Oh, Mistress Yee said she would send the fee to the nursing
mother soon, Mrs. Wang. This afternoon, in fact, Mrs. Wang,"
Nani said.

For some reason, Nani liked Mrs. Wang. She was fearless
and loud and present.

"Sit down and drink," Mrs. Wang said to Min.

So he sat on the stone step where shoes were kept, and he
drank, watching Nani intently.

"Tell me something," Mrs. Wang began. "When your mistress was dying—before I arrived, of course—I was with Jaya, whose son's enormous head was stuck and wouldn't come out. Anyway, what exactly happened that night?" Mrs. Wang gulped down her drink and stared at Nani.

"What do you mean, Mrs. Wang?" Nani asked looking puzzled.

"You don't need to say my name at the end of every sentence," Mrs. Wang said emphatically.

"I understand, Mrs. Wang," Nani said. "I am sorry, Mrs. Wang."

Mrs. Wang sucked on the roof of her mouth, but she realized that she wasn't going to change the maid's habit. She drank the last drop of her drink and encouraged them again to drink up theirs too.

"When your mistress was in labor and you thought she was dying, did you just watch her?" Mrs. Wang asked, looking at Nani critically.

"I didn't know she was dying, Mrs. Wa—, I mean, I thought she was in pain because the baby was coming. But Mistress Kim asked me in the evening, a couple of hours before you arrived, Mrs. Wa—, my mistress asked me to go and tell Mr. O to fetch the doctor, but Mr. O had just entered Mistress Yee's quarters. When I went to Mistress Yee's quarters, her maid stood like a guard dog, blocking me from advancing. I told her I needed to tell Mr. O that my mistress was in need of medical attention, but she said that she would tell him herself. I waited around. And then," Nani paused, looking uncomfortable and hesitant.

"And then what?" Mrs. Wang asked.

"And then," Nani began to shed tears, "I went back to my mistress. She was delirious. I kept telling her that the doctor was coming any minute. But it didn't seem she heard me anyway."

Standing by the wooden pole that was holding the front part of the thatched roof, Min observed Nani dry her eyes and blow her nose. He wanted to comfort her but stayed still, scratching his head, stealing a glimpse of Mrs. Wang occasionally.

"And I still see her in my dreams. She always dies with so much blood all over her." Nani sobbed now.

"It wasn't your fault. It was time for her soul to leave her body." Mrs. Wang turned to Min and asked, "Why don't you do me a favor while you are here? Can you split some firewood for me?"

Min grunted briefly in agreement and began to chop a bundle of logs with a maul.

"Mrs. Wang, will you please not tell anyone what I just said to you?" Nani pleaded.

"Why, I am going to shout what you said from the top of the hill." Mrs. Wang chuckled.

"I promised I wouldn't breathe a word about this, Mrs. Wang," Nani said, looking agitated.

"To whom did you promise what?"

"Mi-Mirae," Nani stuttered. "Mistress Yee's maid. She thinks she is a friend of Mistress Yee's. And now Mirae bosses us maids around," Nani grumbled.

"So did she ask you to promise something?"

"Well, not exactly. When Mr. O heard the news of Mistress Kim's death after breakfast the next morning, he must have wanted to know why he hadn't been informed earlier, and why the doctor hadn't been called in. Mistress Yee had told me that I should say, if asked, that Mistress Kim had died suddenly, before we even had a chance to call the doctor," she said, looking uncomfortable.

Mistress Yee hadn't spoken to Nani. It was her maid, Mirae, who had brought her a pair of new shoes and told her to keep her mouth shut or else she would not live to see the last day of her destiny. Nani had rolled her eyes, flabbergasted, at the way Mirae had employed the authority of her mistress. She did inspect the new shoes as soon as Mirae had left. They were beautiful, but they didn't fit her. Out of self-respect, she had to stop herself from running after Mirae and demanding a pair of shoes that fit her. In the end, Nani didn't have to lie about anything, for Mr. O had not asked her about Mistress Kim.

Now Mrs. Wang was asking about her mistress, and Nani realized that Mistress Kim might have been saved had the doctor been called promptly.

Mrs. Wang changed the subject abruptly. "Your boy has a wart on the back of his hand."

"He's got warts everywhere," Nani snapped, and then blushed deeply. She couldn't face Mrs. Wang. Min had another wart on the heel of his right foot. She hadn't meant to say "everywhere." There was no way to prove her innocence, but Mrs. Wang did not look shocked.

"Take a dandelion by the stem, and rub the milky juice directly onto the warts for a week or so. They will go away like snow melts in the spring," Mrs. Wang advised her.

Nani kept her glance away from Min, who was now stacking up the split wood by the chicken cage. There were fourteen new bright yellow chicks in the cage. Min widened his eyes like a child. With a corner of his mouth lopsided, he drooled because he forgot to swallow his saliva. Then a grin spread across his face.

Suddenly, Nani sprang up and said, "Oh, laundry! I need to boil the laundry. I must get back."

"Don't forget the dandelion. Warts spread. Even to other people," Mrs. Wang said as Nani got up.

Nani blushed again. Min bowed down to Mrs. Wang and groaned to thank her for the drink. Nani, still blushing furiously, left with him.

BEYOND THE MAIN GATE OF THE TEMPLE THERE WERE two more gates. Between the second and third gates stood four hideous wooden guardians, two on each side, looking down on visitors with their colorfully painted, bulging eyes. One of them held an iron sword in the air as if about to strike the visitors if they were proven to be unworthy.

This was the second time that Mirae had visited the temple with her mistress. There was something eerie about the place. Now she began to dread spending an entire day there.

Mistress Yee stepped onto the temple grounds. The deafening silence sank in her heart, and she felt powerless. She wanted to feel superior at all times, but in the temple she was made to feel small. It was like stepping into a painting: she became frozen, voiceless, an unnoticeable part of the whole.

The novice monks with shaved heads walked around with their glances low, absolutely unaffected by her incontestable elegance and beauty. Mistress Yee didn't matter. She was just another lump of moving flesh.

As she approached the main hall, she could no longer hear her own footsteps on the sandy path. Instead, the daily chanting of the Heart Sutra and the sound of the wooden hand bells rumbled steadily.

Mistress Yee passed the pagoda. Mirae followed slightly behind her. Mistress Yee took off her shoes and entered the main hall, where visitors were allowed to offer incense and meditate. A colossal brass Shakyamuni was seated in the middle, gesturing with graceful hands. Mirae arranged her mistress's shoes before she took off her own shoes and followed her in.

A young monk was tidying up the cushions on the hardwood floor inside. The air, centuries old and well tamed, smelled different from the air outside. Mistress Yee didn't like the smell. This room was like a cauldron of wishes and prayers of unfortunate people.

Mistress Yee began to kowtow. After the seventh time, she whispered to Mirae, even though no one else was present, to fan her. Inside was much cooler than outside, but Mistress Yee was having a hard time because of the heat of her own pregnant body. Mirae took out a fan from her pouch and began to fan her mistress drenched in sweat. After the twentieth time of kowtowing, Mistress Yee sat back down on the cushion and didn't want to get up again.

"You do it for me," Mistress Yee whispered firmly.

"What do you mean, Mistress?" Mirae asked, sitting down close to her.

"This is too hard for me. If I keep doing this, I might have a miscarriage," Mistress Yee complained, pouting, and dragged her body toward the wall, so that she could lean against it. "Do it eighty-eight more times," she ordered. Her voice echoed in the hall. Amitabul, with his head slightly bent toward the worshipers, appeared to be smiling mysteriously. Mirae met his eyes and was glued to his benevolent countenance.

"Don't just stand there like a statue. Kowtow!" Mistress Yee shouted, disregarding the fact that she was in a sacred place.

Mirae held her palms together earnestly and went down and up, down and up. She prayed not for the son of Mistress Yee, but for her own sake. She looked up whenever she could to the smooth face of Buddha and cried out inside herself. She didn't want to be a maid; she wanted to be a lady; she wanted to have her own maid, who would fan her, who would kowtow instead of her if she got too tired. Tears and sweat mixed and dripped from her chin.

Mistress Yee, leaning against the wall, dozed off several times. Each time she awoke, she saw her faithful maid performing her duty. Some time later, at the sound of the dull gong that echoed through the valleys of the surrounding mountains, she awoke completely and found no one but Buddha himself, looking down at her sarcastically. His right hand seemed to point outside through the westerly entrance.

Making adjustments to her stiff limbs after having sat in the same position for a while, she got up slowly, furiously. The light outside was blinding. Someone was talking in a voice, deep and low and soothing. It was the head monk in his gray robe, with his wooden beads in his hand. Mistress Yee never liked any of the stupid monks, for they didn't discern her extraordinariness. Seeing her maid conversing with the head monk—with whom Mistress Kim had had a profound relationship and whom she had accused Mistress Kim of having an illegitimate relationship with (which her husband had refused to hear about, as if she had gone mad)—her blood churned. She almost fainted. Mirae was conversing with the monk as if she understood what the baldhead was saying to her. They were standing by Sari-tower, where the calcified remains of the great master from the sixteenth century were interred.

Mistress Yee walked gingerly toward them, feeling a little dizzy and nauseous under the direct sun. When she drew close, they didn't turn to acknowledge her presence. A few moments later, after Mirae bowed to the monk and he chanted a short prayer, they looked at her. Mistress Yee didn't greet them. She bit her tongue. She exhaled looking around at the five magnificent green mountains that enveloped the temple. A volcano was bubbling inside her, but it wasn't the right moment to erupt. Without the annual donation from her husband, this temple wouldn't sustain itself for very long. She could have slapped Mirae for having left her alone, but she was a little intimidated by the luminous atmosphere around the two, who behaved as if they understood a secret that was unavailable to her.

"May I inquire about the wellness of Mr. O?" the monk asked with his eyelids cast down.

Mistress Yee raised her eyebrows to stare at the monk. She could have strangled him for not asking after *her* health. The monk bowed slightly and began to walk away.

Turning crimson with internal fire, Mistress Yee decided to faint, and she fell on her maid to cushion her impact. Mirae uttered a cry of surprise. The monk turned around and didn't panic. He came over at the same pace as he had walked away, lifted Mistress Yee, and carried her easily in his two arms to the main hall. Mirae followed, realizing that her mistress was fully conscious.

The head monk, carrying Mistress Yee in his arms, was reciting something unintelligible. As he laid her on the floor, Mistress Yee felt his breath on her face. She could smell the man in the monk. She badly wanted to open her eyes and see how close this monk was to her face, but she decided not to. Mirae came in and assisted him by bringing a cushion for her mistress's head to rest on. He asked Mirae if she could bring a bowl of cold water for Mistress Yee from the water fountain.

While they were alone in the main hall, the head monk began to speak in his deep voice. But it wasn't clear whether he was speaking to Mistress Yee or to himself.

"There exist three poisons in life: desire, anger, and ignorance. One poison is the root of the other two. To attain enlightenment, you must swallow the root of your poisons, so that you die. You die many times to attain the enlightenment of Buddha."

Mistress Yee opened her eyes and looked up at the monk. He sat near her, with his eyes closed, and his palms met each other near his chest. Now, from below, she could see the packed muscle of his shoulders beneath the robes. His lips were reciting to keep his mind occupied, or unoccupied. Still lying down on the cool wooden floor, Mistress Yee said challengingly, "What is the root of *your* poisons?"

The monk opened his eyes but didn't look at Mistress Yee.

"Did you hear what I said? How many times have you had to swallow your poisons to be the way you are? And how many more times will you have to swallow them to get to where you want to be?"

For the first time, the monk met Mistress Yee's burning eyes. He saw her small feet extending out from under her long silk chiffon skirt. He clenched his teeth and began to chant something—anything—with his eyes closed.

"I wonder what you see when your eyes are closed," Mistress Yee said, getting up. She heard Mirae taking her shoes off outside.

"Please, give the water to the illustrious one. He must be so thirsty from carrying me," she ordered her maid.

Mirae carried the water carefully and placed it in front of the monk. He was still chanting with his eyes closed, his forehead beaded with perspiration.

Mistress Yee said, "Let us leave. I have learned so much from the master. I will practice dying every day, as he has set an example for me today." She bowed toward the monk in an exaggerated manner and then left the hall, smiling triumphantly.

As THEY DESCENDED THE STONE STEPS OUTSIDE THE temple gate, Mistress Yee said, "I love this place. I will have to return often."

"That's a wonderful idea, Mistress," Mirae said.

Without turning around, Mistress Yee addressed her maid. "I think the head monk is the handsomest man my eyes have ever beheld. Don't you agree, Mirae? Of course, this is just between you and me."

"Why, Mistress, he is very handsome," Mirae said. Her ears burned. Indeed, he was a handsome man.

"I saw you flirting with him," Mistress Yee stated firmly, raising her voice, still looking straight ahead of her.

Mirae stopped. "Mistress, what do you mean?" she asked, lowering her voice.

"You heard me, Mirae," Mistress Yee said cheerfully.

"No, Mistress, you must have hallucinated. The sun was so strong it must have blinded you. I was just talking with him." Mirae's voice was trembling.

"No, I saw him whisper into your ear."

"Mistress, you have misunderstood the situation," Mirae said. She passed Mistress Yee and stood in front of her, blocking her way.

"Don't panic. I can keep a secret," Mistress Yee teased, walking around her maid.

"Please! I don't mind if you think *I* am low and despicable, but the one we are speaking of possesses the purest heart," Mirae said pleadingly.

"Ha, you are in love," Mistress Yee remarked lightheartedly contemptuously.

"Mistress, I was kowtowing in the main hall, and I felt something strange. In the beginning, I found it tedious and felt tired, but I saw the smile on Buddha's lips. It was—there are no words to describe the smile. That smile was just for me. And then I heard the monks walk by after their daily chanting, so I rushed out and followed them. The head monk was the last in the group and he turned around. I bowed to him, and when the other monks disappeared into the dining hall, I asked if he could spare me his wisdom. He simply said that wisdom is within me. I raised my head and looked at him. I almost fainted because his smile was exactly the same as Buddha's smile. I told him how he resembled Buddha. He just repeated that wisdom is within me and that I should seek answers within, not outside. Mistress, I couldn't speak further. I felt light and happy. And that was when you approached us. There was nothing else," Mirae said. And she sighed noisily.

Mistress Yee turned around and shot a glance at her maid like a cat glares at a mouse in a cul-de-sac.

"Listen to me carefully, and don't you ever forget what I have to say now." Mistress Yee came a little closer and she continued, lowering her voice, "A monkey climbed trees, and hung upside down from branches, and leaped from one branch to another. She was much admired for her dexterity, although it was nothing for her. All the animals down below applauded and wished they could do what she did. Then a dog, losing her head momentarily, thought she could do what the monkey did. She began to climb the tree, despite the advice of her sensible fellow animals, and reached the top of the tree and leaped from there to another tree. Guess what happened to that bitch? She fell on the ground and crushed her head. Only the monkey felt sorry for her. When all the other animals left, murmuring about the stupidity of the poor animal, the monkey remained and buried the dog. She placed a tombstone on the dog's grave and wrote, *May this dog be born in the form of a monkey in her next life.* So in her next life, the dog was born as a monkey. The first thing she did was to climb a tree, but she couldn't because she was still a dog in the skin of a monkey. Once a dog, always a dog. So she died once again by falling from a tree, and as she died, she wished to be born as a dog. It took two lives for this dog to learn a lesson." Mistress Yee laughed and resumed descending.

Mirae followed her mistress quietly. The sun was fierce. Her legs felt tired from kowtowing repeatedly. It would take another hour to reach the point where they had left the carriage with the male servant. Mistress Yee had decided against the ride in the carriage for fear that its movements on the steep and uneven mountain road might imperil her pregnancy.

Mirae wished that her mistress had not told her the strange story. She wanted to shift her thoughts to the head monk and what he had said. *Within myself,* she said to herself again and again.

Mistress Yee stopped. "I cannot walk anymore. Carry me on your back."

Mirae squatted down in front of her mistress. Even though Mistress Yee wasn't terribly heavy, it was still a long way to go.

Once on Mirae's back, Mistress Yee pulled Mirae's hair for her own amusement. And she said a few nasty things about the odor from Mirae's sweaty back. And then suddenly, she reached down and felt Mirae's breast, which was bound tightly under her garment, as the traditional dress required its waistband to go around the upper chest of a woman.

Shocked, Mirae almost dropped her mistress.

Mistress Yee said, "My dear Mirae, if you drop me and I have a miscarriage, you know that would be the last day of your life, don't you?"

Indeed, it would be. Mirae flushed. Her disgust for her mistress's wriggling body on her back was growing by the moment.

"This is totally ready to be touched, Mirae. Next time we go to the temple, you need to bathe yourself before we go, though. Celibate or not, the head monk cares. In fact, celibates are more sensitive. When he carried me into the main hall, I felt the touch of his strong hands. They were firm and ready to be put to a better use. Just imagine what he will be thinking of tonight when he touches his hard, lifeless wooden beads!" Mistress Yee laughed. She continued, "I hope he seeks within to find some of the answers for his desire, for they are there, plain and clear."

"Mistress Yee, I must go and pee," Mirae begged.

"Let me down, you lazybones," Mistress Yee mocked her. "Now, look what you've done!" Mistress Yee cried. Her skirt was wrinkled.

Mirae went behind the bushes.

Mistress Yee walked down alone for a while. Mirae followed her soon enough. They could see Min beside the carriage, chewing on sour grass.

"That useless urchin," Mistress Yee muttered.

Min got up as the women approached and dusted the seat with his hand where Mistress Yee would sit. He tried to help Mistress Yee mount the carriage, but she dismissed him curtly with her hand.

Some time later, they could see Mr. O's land. After passing the grove of tall poplar trees, Mistress Yee ordered Min to stop.

"If I don't eat something right now, I think I will die," Mistress Yee said.

"Go and get some food for the mistress right now," Mirae ordered Min urgently.

"He can't talk. You go!" Mistress Yee shouted.

Mirae ran to the mud house by the cornfield. She was as hungry as her mistress. During their first visit, they had been nourished at the temple, even though her mistress hadn't liked the simple vegetarian food prepared by the novice monks. But today they had left abruptly, and her mistress had forgotten all about lunch.

Min pulled the carriage to the shade under a tree and observed an army of ants in single file going into a hole.

Mirae stepped into the yard and heard a woman laughing. Mrs. Wang sat with a plateful of boiled potatoes on the mud floor in front of the hut. Jaya was nursing a baby with her chest exposed.

"Listen. My lady, Mistress Yee, is outside, starving and exhausted. She is coming back from a trip to the temple. She needs nourishment," Mirae said urgently, frowning from the headache beginning to immobilize the upper right half of her head.

It took a moment for Mrs. Wang to recognize her. Mirae was out of breath. Then she sighed from her gut, mopping her forehead. Her face was a mess and under her armpit was stained with a brown half moon. She even stank a little.

Jaya, in the middle of telling a joke, was confused. "What do you mean?" she asked, inspecting Mirae from head to toe.

"Her mistress would like some potatoes," Mrs. Wang summarized.

"Oh, Mistress Yee is here? Where is she?" Jaya was excited.

"In her carriage. My mistress is exhausted from the heat and from her visit to the temple, where she kowtowed one hundred eight times. Just give me food. I will take care of the rest," Mirae said, feeling suddenly aloof. She was annoyed by the women so at ease and disheveled, one with breasts hanging out under her open shirt, and the other indulging in food with her legs stretched out, her waistband loosened. Flies buzzed round and round.

The peasant woman wrapped two potatoes and some salt on the side and handed them to Mirae.

"Give me a bowl of water too," Mirae demanded.

Jaya passed Mr. O's daughter to Mrs. Wang and went to the kitchen. She brought out a gourd of water and gave it to Mirae.

Mirae left without thanking her.

"That's the infamous maid of Mistress Yee. She thinks she can shit gold or something just because she is favored by Mistress Yee," Jaya said, rolling her eyes.

"She does look like someone who might shit gold or something." Mrs. Wang chuckled.

Mirae took the water and the potatoes with salt to her mistress. Mistress Yee drank the water hurriedly, but she examined the potatoes with suspicion. Abruptly, she shoved the food out of Mirae's hand. The potatoes fell and rolled into the ditch at the side of the road.

As the carriage moved on with dust billowing behind it, Jaya came out, her shirt still open, holding Mistress Kim's daughter in her arms, to find the potatoes in the ditch and her gourd cracked and abandoned. She spat toward the carriage, which was now turning around the potato field that she and her husband rented from Mr. O.

"Mistress Kim was nothing like that," commented Jaya as she returned and sat down on the open mud floor in front of the hut.

Mrs. Wang didn't reply. She was peeling the last potato and said, "Do you have some rice wine? Water doesn't go with these excellent potatoes."

Jaya dawdled to the kitchen and poured a bowl of rice wine. She drank a little and burped loudly. It tasted so great that she had another sip and then took the bowl to Mrs. Wang.

"Mrs. Wang, this is all we've got to spare. We're saving the rest for my husband's uncle, who will come to see his grand-nephew, he hasn't seen him yet," she said and then smiled.

Mrs. Wang looked somewhat displeased at the half-full bowl. But she drank it all at once.

"I saw Mr. O some time ago. He promised me he would send another payment for your work," Mrs. Wang said.

"Well, in fact, yesterday Nani came to deliver gifts. A sack of this, a sack of that, and some silk. But Mrs. Wang, we don't need gifts. We need a payment," Jaya said grimly.

Mrs. Wang noticed a trace of a milky rice wine mustache above Jaya's upper lip.

"My child, that's out of my hands. I can't force Mr. O to do what you would like him to do. By the way, your potatoes are sublime."

"Thank you, Mrs. Wang. Those potatoes go to Mr. O, along with the rice and corn and beans every year. We pay our share for their land. And here I am, sustaining their bloodline with my milk, sacrificing my own son. What on earth am I to do with a roll of silk anyway?" Jaya rolled her eyes.

"Sell the silk in the marketplace if you don't want to save it for your future daughter-in-law," Mrs. Wang advised her.

"Mrs. Wang, my husband's in the field the whole day. I take food three times daily to the field for the farmers, carrying Mr. O's daughter on my back, while my son takes his naps. When should I go to the marketplace to sell the silk? Who would buy the silk from me? People would think I had stolen it. And they would want a steal of a price! Last night, my husband and I were talking about how nice it would be if we got ourselves a patch of land, just enough to grow corn and potatoes. I would raise Mr. O's daughter as my social superior." Jaya's red face was covered with beads of sweat. Now that she had spilled the truth, she felt worse, because she so badly wanted a piece of land, and Mrs. Wang didn't seem interested in making her happy.

"She is your superior as long as you live on the property of the O family. About the land, as long as you live here and pay your dues, no one is taking it away from you. It is practically yours. Why does it matter to have your name written on a piece of paper? When you die, you don't take the deed with you," Mrs. Wang said weakly. She was also exhausted from the heat, and annoyed by the loud nonsense of the woman whose face was dripping sweat profusely. Most of all, she was hungry, still very hungry after three large potatoes. They were not that large, actually.

"Mrs. Wang, we are hard up these days. My mother-in-law, you know her, she's gone crazy, and my sister-in-law doesn't want to live with her any longer. She is hitting her mother sometimes, I hear. Anyway, to make a long story short, my mother-in-law might have to move in with us. When she moves in, she will be another baby to take care of, another mouth to feed. Of course, whom should I blame but myself? I was born with so few blessings. It's all my fault," Jaya said pathetically, inspecting Mrs. Wang with her apple seed eyes. But there was no reaction; actually, Mrs. Wang was dozing off.

Jaya got up, leaving the infant on the floor, and brought out the jug of rice wine and poured some into Mrs. Wang's bowl.

Mrs. Wang opened her eyes wide and sat up straight.

"His uncle doesn't drink all that much. If I keep it in the kitchen, too much will go to my husband, who shouldn't be drinking anyway. He's got this really evil habit of drinking and then wailing afterward. I can't stand it anymore," she said, forcing a smile.

Rubbing her stomach, Mrs. Wang said, "One should coat the stomach before alcohol. Don't you have a slab of fat or something?"

"Let me check. I think I have a little something here in the jar." Jaya disappeared into the kitchen and came out with a piece of pork fat and a few raw quail eggs.

Mrs. Wang ate the quail eggs and gobbled up the pork fat. She said it was very well seasoned, the pork fat. She drank the rice wine and said that she felt like a little nap, if that wasn't too much of an imposition. So the two women took a nap with their mouths open, the two babies in between them. Flies hovered about Mrs. Wang's unappeasable mouth, sometimes landing on her face, but she slept like a corpse. The afternoon slowly passed, and then the baby boy woke up and whimpered.

Jaya got up, rubbing her eyes and wiping drool off the corners of her mouth. Her hair was matted. She offered her breast to her baby boy. Mrs. Wang snored rhythmically.

Dubak entered then, filthy and sweaty and tired. The wife pointed to Mrs. Wang with her chin, but he, showing no acknowledgment, went straight to the kitchen and came out. He looked about, moving his eyes quickly. His wife said, "What are you looking for?"

He took the jug, which normally contained rice wine. Only a few drops came out.

"There is a little left in the kitchen in the cupboard," she said, lowering her voice.

He went back to the kitchen and didn't come out for a while. The wife, leaving their son on the floor, followed him in and found her husband sitting by the clay stove and drinking.

"Don't drink it all up. Your uncle's coming," Jaya pointed out.

The man pulled his wife close and tried to grab her by her thigh, but she shrilled and stiffened and pushed him away, grinning vulgarly.

"We have a guest," she said, raising her eyebrows. "She is being difficult, though."

Her husband fell into silence. She could see the concentration on his forehead. She didn't like the sudden shift of interest from her plump thigh to something else in his head. He went to a meeting every night with some of the other peasants and talked until late about silly things. "All the aristocrats, can they be aristocrats on their own? No, only because we exist as peasants are they aristocrats. There is no such thing as noble blood. Under the skin, we are all the same. Without us sweating in the field, they would not survive. There would be no rice for them. *We* are not the leeches, living off of *them,* as they would have us believe: it's *they* who live off of *our* lives."

Those were the words frequently uttered, reported Jaya's friend in the field when all the women got together to pluck the soybeans out of the pods. Her husband had hosted several of the meetings at their house.

Dubak gulped rice wine again and said, "I am going to Seoul to get a job." He furrowed his forehead.

"Oh, do shut up," Jaya snapped, snatching the jug out of his hand.

"Is this how you talk to your husband?" He went berserk, ready to throw something at his wife, except that he didn't see anything nearby to throw.

"I thought we are all the same under the skin, husband. *I* shall go to the capital city to get a job if you don't give me the credit I deserve. You should think about what would happen if I left you for the capital city!" she said and left the kitchen. Both babies were crying at the tops of their lungs.

"Heavens! Gods! What is the matter, my babies?" said Jaya theatrically. Her voice finally woke Mrs. Wang. She sat up and combed her hair with her fingers, feeling indifferent at finding herself at someone else's place.

"I need to go and check on Chilpal's wife. Her baby has breeched, and I need to turn it before it gets too late," Mrs. Wang said, standing up and looking around to make certain she wasn't forgetting anything.

"Mrs. Wang, please put in a word for us. My husband threatens to go to the capital city to look for a job," the woman said forlornly, nursing both babies.

Mrs. Wang looked at her and the babies and wondered what Jaya was talking about. She hadn't come out of her sleep completely yet. But she remembered why she had gone there in the first place.

"By the way, I want you to call the baby Mansong, Ten Thousand Pine Trees. Hopefully, with that name, she will live longer than her mother did," Mrs. Wang said.

Dubak came out of the kitchen. He opened a hemp sack and proudly showed Mrs. Wang the fat corn he had brought from the field. "Look here. These are sweeter than sweet potatoes. Take a few, please."

Mrs. Wang said, "Thank you very much, but I don't eat corn. It gets stuck between my teeth and that drives me crazy." And she left.

Without saying goodbye to Mrs. Wang, Jaya pouted and pried Mansong's mouth open to release her swelling purple nipple. The surprised baby didn't cry, but held her foot in her hand and gazed up at her wet nurse.

"I need to feed my son first," Jaya said, as if threatening her.

A patch of dark clouds was approaching rapidly. Dubak looked up to the sky, stopping his work of pulling the husks and hairs from the corncobs. He had expected another scorching summer, so he couldn't believe his eyes. A sudden gush of wind came, blowing away the pile of cornhusks and hairs. Large drops of rain hit the earth, and his wife rushed out to collect laundry from the clothesline. By the time she came in with a mountain of laundry, she was already wet on her shoulders. The rain possibly meant no uncle in the evening. This was the night she should sit with her husband and straighten out his thoughts on not wanting to farm and going to the capital city instead. These ideas only made him miserable. And if he left, the gods only knew when he would return!

MISTRESS YEE WAS IN BED, DELIRIOUS. THE TRIP TO
the temple had drained her. Mirae sat near her mistress and
fanned not her face but her feet: her mistress didn't want to
see Mirae's nostrils. Mistress Yee moaned at intervals. Nani
brought in a tray full of nourishments, including Mistress
Yee's favorites, candied lotus roots and poached pears in rice
liqueur. But Mistress Yee waved the food away.

Mr. O, after seeing off an old friend, arrived at Mistress
Yee's quarters. He cleared his throat outside the door, and
Mistress Yee began to moan more dramatically. Mirae sprang
up to open the door.

"How is everything?" Mr. O inquired, looking about the
room and at the tray of food.

Mirae just dropped her head, folding the fan she held.

"Leave us," Mr. O said. He never wanted the maids to be
around when he was with his wife. Mirae departed, leaving
the tray of food, for she knew that her mistress might ask for
food very soon. She didn't want to be summoned again.

Mr. O waited until Mirae had closed the door behind her
and scurried away before he sat near his wife.

"How is everything?" he asked again, taking a piece of snow
white rice cake. His mind was involuntarily pondering upon
the words of his friend from a neighboring village, who had
said that the peasants were out of control, some of them
demanding their share of the land. Mr. O's friend, also a landowner, had called them ungrateful bastards. They had lived off
of his land for generations but now what they wanted was to
bring him down to shame. His friend was completely wrought

up. Do any of my tenant peasants feel this way? No, impossible, Mr. O was convinced. His people would not want to see him bankrupt. That would mean their bankruptcy as well. His people weren't that stupid. They were family people, responsible people who put rice on their tables at every mealtime.

Mr. O took a bite of white rice cake, and Mistress Yee moaned louder.

Mr. O put his hand on her buttock. "How is everything?" he inquired once more, collecting himself.

"Send a messenger to my family. Let them know I am ill. I would like to say goodbye to them before I go," Mistress Yee said feebly, looking up at her husband sideways, who was still chewing on a piece of rice cake.

"Let me massage you," Mr. O said. He began to knead her thigh. But his wife pushed his hands away, sobbing.

"My little lamb, sit up and I will feed you something. I heard you haven't had dinner yet," Mr. O said, as if talking to a child.

"No one cares about me around here."

"The visitor had so much to say, and I just couldn't get rid of him quickly. He is my childhood friend. He feels quite at home here. By the way, he sends his best regards to you," he consoled her.

Mistress Yee just snorted and sat up and shot a fierce glance at her husband.

"Now, now, anger is the root of all miseries. Ease your mind," Mr. O said softly. He was tired and wanted to lie down with his wife, who often faked illness but was as strong as a horse.

"You don't understand. The head monk at the temple, he insulted me," she said resolutely.

"What do you mean?" Mr. O asked.

"When I was done with my kowtows, I realized Mirae was no longer with me. I was so preoccupied I didn't know she had left. She is such a busybody and pokes into everything. Anyhow, I went out to see where she was. And there she was, in front of Sari-tower, conversing with the head monk." Mistress Yee hesitated a few moments. "I can't tell you the rest, because if I did, you would stop the annual donation to the temple. And I don't want that to happen," she said in a saddened voice.

"Tell me, my dear. You can trust me."

"Well, it's obscene. Noble blood streams in your veins; you must not hear such talk."

"But it concerns you. I must know it," he urged with a strain in his voice.

Her eyes glared, reflecting the flame of the candle light on the low table. Mr. O felt that his wife was hiding something from him to protect him. He grabbed her small hand.

Slowly, quietly, she spoke, as if resigned, as if she were seeing the event once again: "The head monk was fumbling under Mirae's shirt. I didn't want to attract their attention because I was so ashamed to have witnessed such foul, abominable vice. I wanted to step back into the main hall so as to hide myself, but as I started walking backward, I fainted. I think the head monk picked me up and carried me because when I opened my eyes, I found myself lying on the floor in the main hall. The head monk was looking down on me, breathing hard. I was frightened, so I asked for Mirae. He assured me that I was in good hands. Mirae didn't come for a while. I didn't know where she was. I sat up, feeling sick. The head monk mentioned something about desire being one of the three poisons in life, obviously referring to his own contaminated mind, and perhaps he was pleading with me not to reveal any of the things I had seen. But you are so persistent. And I can't lie, as you know. So there you have it, the truth. But I don't want you to act upon it hastily. We all make mistakes, monk or not."

Mr. O considered the whole confession gravely.

Many years before, his father had taken him to the temple when the head monk was eleven years old. The father wanted to show his son what the unusually talented boy could do with stones. The boy was hard at work chiseling a piece of granite without looking up at the visitors. He was in the process of turning it into a statue of Buddha. He had started at the waist, which was smooth and curvaceous to perfection. It wasn't until he got older and married that Mr. O realized the sensual quality of the art. Mr. O's father praised the incontestable skill of the obvious genius, The Little Monk, as he was called then. That was the last time Mr. O had visited the temple.

At his deathbed, his father had Mr. O promise that he would make the annual tribute to the temple. So the son honored the wish of his father, and he would until his own death.

Mr. O was sure that the head monk at the temple was the same person that he was thinking of. Now that he knew what had happened to his wife and maid, he didn't quite know what to make of it. Once again he remembered the touch of the granite's cool surface. The waist of Buddha himself. If he were to pick out the single most unforgettable moment of his life, it would be that time when he had touched the unfinished statue of Buddha.

Mistress Yee sat there, holding her breath, thinking that at any moment her husband would explode, determined to murder the head monk. Then she would have to plead, she would have to visit the temple again to advise the head monk how to escape the wrath of her husband. She would have to punish Mirae properly and teach her to behave and to be loyal to her mistress forever.

"How does the head monk look?" Mr. O asked.

"Do you think I look at other men directly in the face? I fainted! I was ill. I almost died at the temple. They didn't serve me lunch when they knew well the distance I had to travel back! Can you just collect yourself and do something about it?" Mistress Yee said, baffled and irritated.

"What happened today is, if it's true, intolerable. It's an insult to me. And to my father," he said thoughtfully.

"*If* it's true?" Mistress Yee repeated. She knew very well that it was not the right moment to lose her temper. Her tale didn't seem to have disturbed him, as she had hoped.

"I don't mean it that way. I met that monk many years ago. My father revered him. He was the best sculptor alive. I saw part of his work when he was eleven. It was divine," he reminisced. "Perhaps next time you should go to the temple with another maid. You need to teach your maid—what's her name—proper behavior. If she could tempt a monk, she is unlimited in what she might do next," Mr. O said with a benign smile.

"I am not going there ever again!" she wailed.

"That's not a bad idea. As my father once said, one doesn't need a temple to see Buddha. And one doesn't need to see Buddha to learn what one already knows." He sighed, thinking of his father.

"Then, may I ask why you encouraged me to go to the temple?" Mistress Yee asked haughtily.

"My father went to the temple frequently. I asked him the same question that you are asking now. He simply replied that there are other things you learn by doing things you already know. But I encouraged you to go because you wanted to go. When an expectant mother wants to go to the temple to pray, to celebrate the future event, to practice focusing her mind— whatever it was that you intended to do—no husband would advise her not to go," he said, getting up slowly. "I am tired tonight. Mr. Chang drained me with his stories." He walked over to the inner quarters where their bed was prepared.

Mistress Yee sat there, feeling miserable and defeated. The rain subsided; only a few drops fell from the roof onto a puddle every now and then. Tears welled up in her eyes. She thought of her mother's words, *Don't ever give up on getting what you want. Life is a battle. But it's all in your mind. If you don't want to be trampled, you need to trample those who might trample you.*

She kept telling herself that there was no reason to worry. And there really was no reason to worry. But another voice, loud and persistent, kept whispering into her mind's ear.

She blew out the candle and wiped her eyes. She let her pitch-black satin hair drop from its twist and unbraided it and then slipped out of her clothes. Her husband was fast asleep. She lay next to him, awake, until deep into the night, sorting through her thoughts and calming her agitated mind. A few minutes before she fell asleep, she smiled, her eyes almost closed, remembering a scene from her childhood. A farrier had dipped a piece of metal into a furnace and a few minutes later he took it out to show how red, how hot, how powerful it was. "Don't you dare come near me, or you will be fatally hurt," he warned the children around him, smiling mischievously at the seven-year-old Mistress Yee.

By the time Nani was so itchy that she woke up, she already had six mosquito bites on her legs. They always bit her, no one else in the room. It was just before dawn. She lifted her left leg in midair and scratched until her skin bled.

She sat up. Even though it was midsummer, the heat had temporarily abated after the pounding rain.

The little maid, Soonyi, barely fourteen but appearing younger because of her small physique, lay diagonally with her limbs stretched out in four directions. She had joined the household only a year before to assist the kitchen maid. But since last spring the kitchen maid had taken time off to take care of her dying mother in the neighboring village.

In the corner was a lump of Mirae in a pathetic fetal position, bobbing up and down as she breathed rapidly. That was strange because she usually slept on her back, with her nose arrogantly tilted up and her long legs stretched straight out. Curious, Nani crawled on her knees over to Mirae. Even before she got close to her, she could feel the heat radiating from Mirae's body. She was hot. They were not on speaking terms, but Nani shook her shoulder, reluctantly. Mirae moaned and jerked.

"What's the matter?" Nani asked grimly. It was too early to start a new day.

"I think I am dying," Mirae barely managed to say.

Nani thought quickly. Her late mother had administered every domestic disaster. After she had passed away, Nani rushed to Mistress Kim with every little anomaly in the house. But now she was alone. She had to use her own head, and it wasn't always easy.

Fever. What did Mother do about a fever? What did Mistress Kim say about a fever?

Nani gaped at Mirae. She was drenched in sweat. Her hair was loose and a few strands were stuck on the side of her face. Even when she was sick, Nani thought, she was pretty.

Min never seemed to want to touch her. On the way back from Mrs. Wang's place the day before, he could have done whatever he pleased, but he hadn't. Was he simply a nincompoop? Or was she simply not attractive? Mirae moaned again, and Nani collected herself.

Her instinct told her that she needed to dry Mirae first and change her clothes. So she pulled out a new undergarment from the chest and began to undress her. It was almost impossible and she was also uncomfortable, considering the kind of relationship she had with Mirae: they were more or less enemies. But why? Nani rummaged through her memory to remember what event had turned them into hating each other. But there was really nothing. Mirae was just too pretty. She behaved like no maid. Supercilious she was. Mistress Yee's shadow. A shameless parasite. Nani began to untie the knot at her chest. She got nervous, noticing her fingers becoming clumsy.

Nudging at the little kitchen maid with her foot, Nani called out, "Soonyi!" She was sleeping with her mouth open. Nani hated to wake her up from her dream, but she needed someone else to assist her or at least witness what she was doing.

"Soonyi!" she called once again, in a louder voice.

To her surprise, Soonyi quickly sat up, gibbered for a few moments, and then rubbed the sleep from her eyes. Looking about, she whined, "What is it?"

"Light the candle, will you?" Nani asked, with annoyed urgency in her voice.

"What's going on?" Soonyi asked.

Nani didn't answer. She removed Mirae's top garment and began to pat her dry.

Soonyi rubbed her eyes, lit the candle, and gasped. "Gods! What on earth are you doing, Big Sister?"

"Get a bowl of water. She is sick. Can't you see?" Nani said, in an exaggerated tone of voice, just as her mother had used to speak to her when she was busy.

"All right. What happened?" Soonyi asked as she was leaving the room for the kitchen, knowing she wouldn't get an answer.

"Bring a spoon too," Nani commanded.

When Soonyi came back with a bowl of water, Nani held Mirae up and asked Soonyi to feed her water with the spoon.

"She is not swallowing it, Big Sister!" Soonyi cried.

Nani was sweating profusely now too. She thought hard, her teeth rattling from nervousness and her eyes focusing on the candlelight.

"Bring me a clean cloth," Nani said.

"Where is it?" Soonyi asked, moving her innocent eyes uncertainly.

"In the cupboard. In the kitchen. I don't know. Look for it!"

Soonyi frowned and sulked, pouting her lips. She went to the kitchen. The gray light from the east was emerging, and the roosters in the distance were announcing it. She looked about to find a clean cloth in the kitchen. She saw the low table on which she had served dried cuttlefish and sesame cookies to Mr. O's visitor the day before. The cookies were untouched. She ate one. It was even better than yesterday. A little less crunchy, but sweeter from the oozing honey. She ate another. She drank a little plum wine from the jug. That was the only wine she liked, because it was sweet.

Nani examined the skin of Mirae's chest. It was a whole new world. It resembled the flesh of a peeled peach. It gleamed, blinding her.

"Big Sister, is this good enough?" Soonyi came in and showed her a piece of white cloth that was used in the kitchen for making bean curd.

Nani sighed, and snatched it from Soonyi's hand. "We need to dress her in the dry clothes. You hold her from behind and I will put the clothes on," Nani said. Mirae did not put up a fight.

Nani dipped the cloth in the water and let the end of it hang in the hot mouth of Mirae, letting her suck the moisture.

"She needs to rest. Make sure she gets water constantly, even if it's one drop at a time. I am going to ask Mistress Yee what I should do about this. Stay right here," Nani ordered, pointing her finger at Soonyi.

"I am not going anywhere, Big Sister," said Soonyi, looking worried.

Nani left the room and walked up the steps to go across the yard to Mistress Yee's quarters. Her head felt light.

Min was walking toward the kitchen with split wood on his back for the stove. He was already sweating on his neck. As he disappeared into the rear entrance of the kitchen, Nani thought about Mirae's radiant skin. She walked faster and went to the outhouse, and when she came out, Min was coming toward her to go outside to do other chores. He passed Nani without acknowledging her presence. Nani picked up a pebble and hesitated for a moment, but before he went too far, she threw the pebble and hit him on his back. He turned around and shot a glance at her.

Nani sighed in frustration.

Min strode toward her and picked her up by the arms and put her back down on the ground. She slapped him hard because she felt frightened. His Adam's apple moved up and down. He stared at her for a moment, turned around reluctantly, and began to walk away. "Idiot!" Nani said to the back of his head.

Min turned around and looked down at his feet. A group of busy ants worked right by his foot. He moved carefully, so as not to step on them. He looked down once more, as if making sure the creatures were all right. He stared at Nani's skirt blankly and then his glance moved to her feet.

Her toes wiggled. Her fingers fidgeted. She wondered what Min was thinking. He came over to her slowly and grabbed her hand. His palm was moist and hot. They walked toward the storage room. She had the key to it. They entered in silence and closed the door behind them. In the dark they stood immobilized for a while, listening to each other's breathing and getting used to the dark. And then Min pulled her close to his chest and groaned like a beast. His arms compressed her organs in her rib cage so tightly that she felt they might explode. When he finally released her, the air temporarily trapped in her throat escaped violently through her mouth, producing a loud sound, the burp of a giant. He rubbed her head ever so gently and groaned again. Nani broke out sobbing, punching his chest. He groaned again. Nani said, "I hate you!" Min kept rubbing her head and groaned more loudly. His body was trembling ever so slightly. Nani stopped punching him. She relaxed in his arms for a while.

"Gods! What am I doing here? Mirae is sick as a dog. I have to go and ask Mistress Yee what I should do!" Nani sprang up and opened the door. Before she ran, she looked around and met Min's eyes. He was smiling down at her like Buddha. She pushed him away and ran like a little rabbit, looking back with a mischievous grin on her lips.

Halfway to Mistress Yee's quarters, Nani suddenly turned around and went back to the maids' quarters. She didn't think Mistress Yee would be up. Besides, she wouldn't be interested in the welfare of her household members. She would reprove her for making noise so early in the morning.

Nani slipped into the kitchen, out of breath. Her heart was still pounding violently. She drank water in the kitchen, dripping it all over her chest. She stood there, lost in thought, reviewing what had just happened in the storage room. Min's body had felt like a perfect rock by a creek, smoothed over eons, where everyone would want to sit and listen to the sound of the cascading water or to lie down and find a million flecks of golden light dancing through the branches high above which would make one's head spin as fast as the earth rotated. For as long as she could remember, Min had loved her. He cared about her as if there were nothing else in the world, but why didn't he covet her like a normal man? She sucked her cheek, puzzled, dissatisfied, but strangely happy too.

"Big Sister!" Soonyi said, coming into the kitchen.

Nani whirled around. "You startled me!"

"I am sorry, Big Sister. I was looking for you because I needed your help to get started with breakfast," Soonyi said, on the verge of tears. She was tired. While Nani was out, Mirae had woken up and screamed about the cloth she found in her mouth. "Are you trying to choke me?" she had asked.

"How is Mirae?" Nani asked.

"Oh, she is fine. After yelling at me, she fell back asleep as soon as she put her head on the pillow," Soonyi explained.

"If she has the energy to yell, she will recover in no time," Nani said.

"What do I do with the soaked mung beans?" Soonyi asked.

"Go and rub them between your hands until they are hulled. And then you know what to do. I don't need to explain how to grind the beans, do I?"

"No, Big Sister. That's always been my chore," Soonyi assured Nani.

"When you are done, go to Mistress Yee and tell her that Mirae is sick. Very sick. Tell her she is as hot as an iron on the stove," Nani said, beginning to chop vegetables.

"I can't go see Mistress Yee," Soonyi whimpered.

"Child, what is the matter with you?" Nani asked, frowning. Half of her mind was elsewhere. Min had shoulders like ... what?

"Mistress Yee doesn't like me," Soonyi said, turning pale.

"That's no news. She likes no one," Nani said, slicing summer zucchinis as thinly as she could.

"Should I talk to her when I take breakfast to her?" Soonyi asked.

"No," Nani replied, and placed her knife on the cutting board. "You don't bring up problems before breakfast. You do that when the mistress is done with breakfast, so that at least she won't have a table full of food to turn over. Besides, if she gets upset before breakfast and refuses to eat, you will be pleading with her to eat all day long."

Soonyi looked thoughtful. She definitely didn't want to spend all day begging Mistress Yee to take her meals.

"Of course, if we could get a chance to speak to the master, that would be the simplest way out of trouble. But we might have to talk to Mistress Yee. After all, Mirae is her favorite maid. And she is going to look for Mirae any minute anyway," Nani said. "Don't stand there like a scarecrow. Will you go get me some eggs? And wake up, will you?"

"Yes, Big Sister. How many?" Soonyi asked, widening her eyes.

"Please," Nani drawled. "Don't get my blood boiling so early in the morning. You go and get however many eggs you see in the basket. Don't you know that eggs are delivered every morning by the boy down by the creek?"

"Yes, of course," Soonyi said quietly and fled the kitchen.

Nani crushed garlic with the heavy wooden handle of the knife. After putting it aside in a little bowl, she began to chop onions, which made her sniffle. Suddenly, she turned around. Nani often thought that she caught a glimpse of her late mother. She sat down by the stove and cried a little, thinking of her. Sometimes at night, she would look at the door, thinking that at any moment her mother would come in and lie down next to her. And sometimes she would see her mother in her dreams; afterward, she would feel lonely and distracted all day long. Min made her feel good, but no one would ever be able to take her mother's place, she knew. She blew her nose. She tightened the string of her apron and began to cook zucchini in a pot, stirring the vegetable intermittently.

"Big Sister, here are three eggs," Soonyi said as she came in.

"Good," Nani replied.

"What is the matter?" she asked, seeing Nani's red eyes.

"Nothing. Now I want you to get a scoop of bean paste for the soup," she said.

"Sure," Soonyi replied, looking at Nani blankly.

"Get going. Don't stand around," Nani chided Soonyi.

A few minutes later, Soonyi came in with bean paste on a spatula.

"Get a strainer. And press the paste through it into the water," Nani ordered.

Soonyi did as she was told.

In the meantime, Nani broke the eggs into a bowl. She swirled them with a spoon, adding chopped scallion and gingko nuts and sea salt. She was going to poach them in a double boiler.

In an hour, there was a hot meal on a low table. Nani and Soonyi carried it to their master and mistress, who sat close to each other, smirking about something like kids. Nani was relieved to find her superiors in a good mood.

The maids wished them a very good appetite and left. On the way back to the kitchen, Nani lectured Soonyi about how she had put her face too close to the food as they took the low table in. This was what her mother had said to her some years before.

Soonyi denied having done so, just as Nani had vehemently argued against her mother's accusation.

They walked back to the kitchen. Nani was upset. She wanted Soonyi to acknowledge her own shortcoming and say that she wouldn't do it again.

In the kitchen, Soonyi took a gulp of water and dropped a piece of fried zucchini into her mouth.

"Soonyi, let me teach you something. Don't eat standing," Nani snapped. Her mother had also said this to her often. At the time, Nani hadn't understood. But now she did. It wasn't proper. It was something a maid would do. And a maid didn't have to live the life of a maid, her mother had emphasized.

Nani set the table for three in the middle of the hardwood floor in front of the maids' shared bedroom. Then she told Soonyi to go out and get the male servants for breakfast.

It was already getting hot.

Soonyi first went inside to see if Mirae was feeling any better and if she would like to eat a little.

"Big Sister!" Soonyi shouted from inside the room.

"Calm down, child," Nani said, employing her mother's tone of voice.

"Big Sister, Mirae is so sick!" Soonyi rushed out of the room.

Nani got up and hurried in. Mirae was indeed very sick. Her body was burning and her skin was erupting with a strange-looking rash. Nani thought for a moment and ran to Mistress Yee's quarters.

There was laughter from the room. Nani hesitated. No matter how serious the problem was with a maid, it seemed inappropriate to break up her superiors' happy moment.

She cleared her throat and smoothed her hair, feeling nervous, as if she had already done something wrong.

"What is it?" Mistress Yee asked, sensing movement behind the latticed door.

"It is Nani, Mistress Yee. I am here to let you know that Mirae is burning with a fever and her skin is developing a rash. She needs a doctor," Nani managed to say.

Mistress Yee rolled her eyes theatrically.

Nani stood in the hallway like a puppet with broken strings, frozen, expressionless.

"Should I buy the fish or not?" Mistress Yee asked. Obviously, she and Mr. O must have been in the middle of a conversation.

"It doesn't matter, my dear. What counts is not your deed, but your intention, your heart. If you have the intention to do good things, then you have done good things."

"You are my inspiration," Mistress Yee said brightly, laughing.

"Don't flatter me. It doesn't suit you," Mr. O replied.

"Are you still there?" Mistress Yee called out in her high-pitched voice, irritably.

"Yes, Mistress," Nani replied nervously. Her mistress might accuse her of eavesdropping.

"You should be taking care of Mirae if she is really sick," she said curtly.

"Yes, Mistress. She needs more than my care, it appears," Nani said timidly.

"If you can afford it, go get the doctor. You don't need my permission," Mistress Yee said, half amused, half tartly.

There was a pause. How long would Mistress Yee play out her little game before Mr. O stepped in to give his order?

"What are you thinking about?" Mistress Yee asked her husband.

"Oh, nothing," he replied.

"Of course, nothing. How could you think of anything else when I am in your presence?" Mistress Yee said, amused.

"Why don't you tell her to go fetch the doctor?" Mr. O grumbled.

"We can't get a doctor every time a maid gets sick. We will soon run out of money. We need to reserve some for the likes of me," Mistress Yee said in her nasal voice, laughing mischievously.

"Let her go. I need to talk to you," Mr. O said.

"Go and get that midwife, whatever her name is," Mistress Yee said sharply.

"What can a midwife do for a maid with a fever?" Mr. O complained.

"Maybe it is not just a fever," Mistress Yee muttered, giggling like a girl.

"Now, let her go and tend to the matter," Mr. O ordered gently.

"Leave us," Mistress Yee snapped.

Nani returned to the kitchen. She saw male servants leaving for their work. She stopped Min and explained the seriousness of Mirae's state. "We need to go and ask someone, a doctor, to find out what to do about the fever," she said, looking worried. "Let's go to the marketplace. I know an herbalist. He is as good as a doctor, I hear."

Min hesitated. He knew how awfully Mirae had treated his girl, and only the other day, Nani had said, "She drives me crazy." So he produced a groan of displeasure.

Nani retorted, "If we don't, we will have another funeral in this house. That would be two funerals within a year."

They hurried to the marketplace and found the herbalist perched with at least fifty huge standing hemp sacks displayed, their open mouths spilling out their contents.

Nani explained Mirae's symptoms. The herbalist said, "Sounds like chicken pox to me. If it is, it will run its course and go away. But you need something to help her with the fever." He picked a few roots and leaves from here and there. "Make sure to stay away from the sick one until the fever is reduced."

He divided the herbs into six portions, wrapped each in rice paper, and handed them to Nani. "Cook one for half a day. Divide the brew into three portions. Let her drink one with each meal. Do the same for the following five days. Remember to stay away from her while she has the fever. Especially anyone carrying a baby!" he advised her, winking at Min.

Nani blushed. Then she realized that she had to tell her mistress, not that Mistress Yee would go near Mirae while the maid was sick.

When she arrived back home, Mr. O was leaving with a part-time male servant whose hunting skill surpassed all. They would visit the gravesite of Mr. O's parents. The servant would trim the grass, and Mr. O would serve his parents rice liquor and some food and tell them his wife was pregnant.

In the kitchen, Nani emptied one packet of the herbs into a clay brew pot. She measured water and poured it into the pot and placed it on the stove.

While watching the pot simmer, she wondered if she should tell Mistress Yee what the herbalist had said about a pregnant woman needing to stay away from Mirae. She wasn't so worried about the cost of the herbs. She could take the small amount of money from the weekly grocery shopping money. But if Mirae's illness affected Mistress Yee's health in any way, then Nani would be in big trouble.

In the afternoon, while letting Soonyi tend the pot so that it wouldn't boil over, Nani went to Mistress Yee with a plate of fruit. Mistress Yee was reading a picture book and humming a familiar tune. She was in a good mood.

"Mistress Yee, Mirae is taking medicine for her fever. It looks as though she will recover in a few days, if not before," Nani said.

"Such a silly little thing. I didn't ask you a question. Didn't your mistress teach you not to speak unless you were spoken to?"

"I am sorry, Mistress Yee. Silly was my nickname by my mother, but I dare speak because Mirae suffers from chicken pox. Of course, we will keep her away from you until she is completely recovered," Nani said.

Mistress Yee dropped her book on the floor, turning pale and looking urgent, as if she had a fishbone caught in her throat. "Are you sure it's chicken pox?"

"Her skin is breaking out with blisters, and the herbalist in the marketplace thought so," Nani replied, kneeling in the far corner of the room without breathing.

"I should believe a dog? Go get the doctor!" she ordered.

"Yes, Mistress," Nani said. She got up with a tray and left. In the yard, she kicked a pebble and grumbled about Mistress Yee's temper.

Before sunset, the doctor came and took a look at Mirae. Then he reported to Mistress Yee that while it looked like chicken pox, it could very well be a combination of boils and a nasty cold. He turned around and asked Nani how Mirae had been lately. Nani said that she couldn't think of any anomaly; Mirae had behaved like her usual self. The doctor pondered for a moment and said that he couldn't rule out chicken pox entirely, but the rash was too severe for the usual case of chicken pox. And who in the world catches a cold in the summer?

Mistress Yee didn't want to hear another word from the doctor. She would stay at her father's house until Mirae was well.

Four days later, Mirae was feeling a world better. Her fever was gone, and she was eating again, but no one spoke about her dreadful skin. Her body was still covered with purplish rashes. A part-time maid simply commented, "Better to be alive than dead, though."

When Mirae took a bath after her illness, she saw herself in full view. She panicked and sobbed bitterly for the whole afternoon, and she stayed up late that evening. When she woke the next day, she refused to eat and stopped talking to all but herself. A month later, when Mistress Yee returned, larger and happier, Mirae was a different person.

Part Two

MOST OF THE VILLAGERS, INCLUDING THE CHILDREN, had bathed and came up to the hill all spiffed up in their clean and starched outfits. Soon the full moon would be in view. Some of the men and children played tug-of-war, and some of the women sat eating specialties they prepared only for Harvest Day. It wasn't a good year, they all knew, but no one complained about the drought or the bad crops or the high taxes they had to pay the government and their landlords. What everyone talked about was the news that had just come from the capital city: a foreign ship had arrived from a faraway land.

"There were nineteen people on the ship," one person said.

"No, eighteen," another voice said.

"What does it matter how many there were? They all got killed the instant they set foot on our soil," a man said.

"What did they do?" a woman asked, chewing on a rice cake.

"Nothing," another man said.

"Well, they did something. They entered our country without permission," someone said, sitting down to join the crowd.

"But that doesn't seem grave enough a crime to deserve death," said the woman with the rice cake. "And eighteen of them," she added, horrified.

"Nineteen," someone corrected her.

"Coming to our country without permission might be a crime. Who knows?" a man said.

"Well, that doesn't make any sense," a woman said. "If you come to my house uninvited, should I pull my dagger and kill you?" she asked, rolling her eyes.

"You would be behind bars," someone said and laughed.

"Surely, I would be for killing a neighbor," the woman said, nodding her head vehemently.

"Only one of them survived. When all were thought to have been killed, five of the best shamans were summoned from the southern provinces to expel the foreign spirits and the curse the ship had brought. In the meantime, soldiers inspected the contents of the vessel. They found the strangest thing. It was a piece of furniture, but neither chest nor table. As tall as a grownup, maybe even taller, it had a face, round as a pumpkin, and it ticked constantly, and once in a while it gonged all by itself. It had its own mind because sometimes it gonged once, sometimes twice, sometimes even twelve times. What was more interesting was that they found a man, the same kind as the dead, trembling for fear of death, and hiding, horribly diseased, in a barrel where they must have kept food. When he was dragged out, he saw the shamans dance in order to stop the ticking of the tall thing. So he simply touched something on the back of it and the ticking stopped. And so this man escaped his death. The king himself ordered him to stay in the palace," a man explained, excitedly, foaming around his mouth and waving his hands.

"So he lives?" a woman asked.

"So he does," someone answered.

Everyone laughed.

"So what did they come here for?" another woman asked.

"That seems unclear," a man answered.

The enormous moon was coming up from behind the hill, and the children were playing tag in the wooded area. Under the old pine tree, a few women were clicking their tongues about the poor maid at the big house whose skin had erupted in an unsightly rash.

Mrs. Wang arrived and wanted to know where the leftover food was. She was about to collapse, she warned them. The women under the pine tree quickly got up and served the midwife some of the very best food. Sitting on a mat, Mrs. Wang devoured everything. Then she wondered if there was rice wine.

After she had finished a large bowl of rice wine, she said, "Look over there at the moon. How beautiful it is! Everyone is so busy talking that no one's looking at the moon!"

Everyone turned and looked at the moon. They fell into a brief silence because the moon was so close that they felt they could reach out their hands and touch it. It was translucent, and it almost seemed that *it* had come to see *them*. Mrs. Wang felt briefly levitated. This was why she had come: to see the moon. Of course, there was the food too.

"It looks like a large pearl!" a child exclaimed.

"What is a pearl?" a younger child asked.

"It *does* look like a pearl!" another child said.

"I see a bunny up on the moon," a girl said.

"There are two of them," a boy said.

Jaya stood up and bowed to the moon several times solemnly. She was praying for Sungnam. She prayed that he would not be a peasant like his father but someone better, someone with no boss or landlord whose invisible hands would strangle him. She prayed for Dubak, that he would focus on farming and stop going to peasant meetings where they talked about their rights and high taxes and other nonsense. She prayed that she would give birth to a healthy child.

Then she collapsed near Mrs. Wang, who leaned against a tree, humming along with the people who were singing and dancing.

"Mrs. Wang, people over there are talking about the news from the capital city. Have you heard it? About the surviving yellow man, who's now a friend of the king?" Jaya asked. She held Mansong in her arms without knowing that her nipple had escaped Mansong's mouth. Mansong was staring at Mrs. Wang with curiosity. She was no longer an infant.

"It's about time for you to wean the babies. You need to reserve yourself for the coming one," Mrs. Wang advised.

"It's hard to wean Mansong. Unlike my Sungnam, she doesn't take solid food," Jaya said. In the moonlight, she looked pretty. Everyone looked pretty. It was a beautiful night.

"Look at her teeth. She is behind the schedule. Give her porridge and steamed vegetables. Or else you will not have enough milk for the next one," Mrs. Wang urged, getting up to go and listen to the group of young men and women talking about the current news from the capital city.

They were discussing the yellow man's religion and how self-sacrificing those who believed in this religion were. They shared what they owned with others, especially those in need. And they believed everyone was equal. Some of the peasants listened intently, their faces illuminated by the moonlight.

"Dream on," Mrs. Wang snapped. Everyone turned to look at her. Unintimidated, she continued: "True. We were born equal. But look around. Some are rich, some are poor, some are peasants, some are aristocrats, and some are like Mr. O with no worries about what to eat the next day for the rest of his life."

People sat, thinking hard. Somehow it seemed Mr. O was to blame for their miserable lives. The hostility toward their landlord was palpable.

"Before you become slaves of some religion, remember that you have been slaves to your landlords. You don't need another master. That's my point," Mrs. Wang said heatedly.

Everyone fell silent. What Mrs. Wang had just pointed out made sense. They were slaves, basically, to the landlords.

"They feed you lunch on Sundays, Mrs. Wang. They give you medicine when you are sick," a young man protested, licking his lips.

"Well, what was it they gave you last Sunday?" Mrs. Wang challenged him jokingly.

They all laughed and quieted down to hear the answer.

"I was late. When I got there, the food was gone," the young man said ruefully.

More laughter broke out.

Some of the women were getting ready to descend. Their children were getting fussy, and, actually, they were also getting tired. There were loads to carry, besides their sleepy children. It had been a long, exciting day.

The radiant moon seemed mounted above them, gently brightening the whole world. They collected their belongings, while some of the men drank the last drops of rice wine, babbling on about the rights of the peasants. Mrs. Wang collected leftovers for her dog.

Groups of people began to descend the hill, warning each other to mind their steps.

Mrs. Wang made a sharp turn to go up the hill to her house. She bade farewell to the villagers and they bowed to her goodbye. Her old bones ached as she climbed the steep path. Fireflies accompanied her. Despite the familiarity of the sight, she was still moved by the little creatures, glowing at intervals in midair as if they existed just to amuse her. The air was filled with the pleasant smells of tall grass and wild flowers and ripe fruits. She took the air into her lungs with deep gratitude. Suddenly, she heard footsteps. A fox? A wolf? She stopped, concentrating with every nerve. She didn't want to attract an animal's attention right then. It would be a hassle to have to deal with it. But the sounds kept coming nearer and nearer. Then she heard a human voice, singing or crying.

"Who is it?" Mrs. Wang demanded.

A young woman came into view. She was singing in a sad voice, but the words were hard to understand.

"A young woman wandering about in the night. What a pitiful sight! Where do you belong?" Mrs. Wang thundered.

"Where do I belong?" she asked herself in an undertone, nervously. "Oh, why do you ask? I belong nowhere." She tittered and then cried. Her unkempt hair partially covered her face.

Mrs. Wang grabbed the young woman's wrist and pulled her close to her. "Let me look at you. You are the maid that belongs at Mr. O's household. Aren't you?" Mrs. Wang pulled her a little closer.

"I don't belong there. I belong in the mountains, where the beasts are and where the ghouls roam about," she cried, trying to pry her hand from Mrs. Wang's grip.

"What's your problem?" Mrs. Wang asked, looking at her fiercely. Without waiting for her answer, she continued, "Do you think roaming about in the mountains, at the graveyard, will lesson your sorrow? Alter your tragedy? Change your life? You are mistaken, my child," she said and laughed exaggeratedly. "You had beauty no one could surpass before the illness struck you. But beauty is fragile, unreliable. It's seasonal, like that of an annual flower. An annual flower is pretty because of its appearance, but a perennial is worthy because of its nature. It comes back. It endures. It is persistent." Mrs. Wang stopped here and thought about what her point was. She had to admit that she was shocked to run into this young maid, whose beauty had once been stunning. Now her face, even in the moonlight, was visibly bumpy from chicken pox.

"What do you know about me? You know nothing about me. You don't know what I had. Who says I am a maid? I was about to fly. I was even prettier than my mistress. She herself said that to me. Do you understand?" Mirae shrieked and fell on her knees.

"Go back to the graveyard and dig up the corpses and find out who was the best looking when they were alive. Ask if that makes any difference in the coffin beneath the earth. You imbecile! You are not worth speaking to." Mrs. Wang passed around the maid and walked on briskly. But still, she looked back, concerned. She was relieved when she didn't see Mirae anymore.

As she pushed her squeaky gate open, she felt good and tired. There was no place like her little place. Her dog, at seeing her, went amok, jumping around and whining. She fed the creature with the leftovers from the festival. It was getting chilly. She emptied the remaining charcoal from a metal pail into the furnace and lit a fire. She should, she thought, go to the market soon to prepare for her winter hibernation. First of all, she wanted to buy a load of dried fish and some garlic. She had enough wild greens, all dried and bunched up, dangling in straw ropes from her eaves, to last the winter.

ON THE SAME DAY AT MR. O'S—EVEN BEFORE THE annual memorial service for the ancestors, which normally took place right after dawn—Min took a bundle in a basket to Nani, who was busying herself in the kitchen with Soonyi.

"What've you got there?" Nani asked, casting her glance to the dates and nuts she was arranging on wooden plates used only for the memorial service.

Before he revealed what was in the basket, the baby inside whimpered like a puppy. Nani raised her eyebrows in surprise, although this wasn't the first time that he had brought in a baby from the front gate, abandoned by some wretched soul on a day of celebration or a dead one from the field ditched by an unfortunate woman out of wedlock. Now that Nani's mother had passed away, and also Mistress Kim, there was no chance that this baby would get to stay in the house. Mistress Yee would throw a tantrum when she found out that the baby was there, and everyone in the household would be walking on eggshells for days. Nani wasn't afraid of that. She was used to Mistress Yee. But it wasn't always trouble-free to relocate the baby. Min must have felt extra sorry for these abandoned babies because he had once been a baby in a basket. Nani remember her mother talking with other maids about Min almost a decade before, summarizing in whisper the reasons why people abandoned their own children. "Scarcity of food after drought and birth out of wedlock are the common causes of such a terrible act. But sometimes, well, rarely, the master of the house planted his seed somewhere illegitimate. And doesn't one have to reap what'd been sewn one way or another?"

Min stood there like a totem pole. Without saying anything Nani sliced off the top parts of apples and pears, as was the custom when preparing offerings for the memorial service.

"What are we going to do about this?" Soonyi asked, but her concern was superficial.

Nani stripped the smoked beef as if she heard nothing. The baby moaned pitifully, with the last bit of energy left in its system. Min looked grim but still stood there, planted. Nani arranged chestnuts on a plate. They were raw. She couldn't remember whether chestnuts were supposed to be cooked or arranged raw on the table for the memorial service, and she was sure that Mistress Yee had no clue either. Her remarkable ignorance about housekeeping was advantageous to her inferiors, except that when Nani wanted to know something there was no one to learn from.

She wiped her hands on her apron, thinking intently about what to feed the infant if she should end up having to do so. Unexpectedly, Min picked up the basket and left the kitchen. Soonyi stood up and opened her mouth to say something, but she didn't, she just looked at Nani sheepishly. After a few moments, Nani ran after Min. Near the well she pulled his arm and said, "Where're you going?"

Min yanked his arm back and walked on. Nani grabbed his arm again and asked, "What are you trying to do?"

Min stared at her briefly and walked away again. Nani remained behind and muttered, "What's he going to do with the baby? Is he going to starve it to death?" She realized that she had hurt his feelings. She walked slowly back to the kitchen.

"What on earth do you think you're doing?" Nani shouted hysterically when she saw Soonyi take a bite of mugwort-flavored rice cake. "That's for the memorial service. You know very well you can't taste food before the service!" Her voice turned metallic. "Get out. You are no help. Go get Mirae. What's she up to? Wake her up!"

Soonyi sprang up and left the kitchen, pouting and stomping. She climbed up onto the raised entrance and walked gingerly toward the bedroom. Holding the ancient door-pull, she took a deep breath before she entered. She was afraid of Mirae. Her appearance scared her. She dreaded confronting her because she didn't know what to expect each time. "Don't drop your jaw and stare at her. And don't scream," Nani had advised her. When Mistress Yee first saw her own maid after she returned from her extended stay away, she did exactly that: she dropped her jaw and couldn't speak for a long moment, and then she heaved a sigh as if she were in great pain and finally said, "Get that out of my sight!" It was typical of Mistress Yee, but it was cruel nonetheless. No one called her bosom buddy, nevertheless everyone felt sorry for her when her own mistress called her "that" just because her skin was now disfigured. It was unjust, unfair, heartless, everyone had grumbled quietly, frowning.

"Are you up?" Soonyi asked feebly, knowing very well that there would be no reply either way.

Mirae's upper body was in the sunlight coming through the window, and her eyelashes fluttered as Soonyi spoke. Soonyi didn't know that Mirae had gone to bed not long before. Nowadays she disappeared in the middle of the night and slipped in quietly before dawn. And she slept like a log until after breakfast. People got used to what they thought of as temporary madness. They were expecting her to get better sooner or later. In the meantime, Nani had to take over her job as well.

"Are you still sleeping?" Soonyi made another attempt, weakly. "Nani wants you."

Mirae opened her eyes ever so slightly and then closed them again. Soonyi slid toward Mirae on her knees. Mirae's face, unlike when she was fully awake, appeared to be peaceful, expressionless, and undisturbed. Her skin didn't look too bad. Soonyi inspected her face indiscreetly, holding her breath, puckering her mouth, and narrowing her eyes.

"So what do you think?" Mirae asked, opening her eyes, looking up directly at Soonyi. Her tone was neutral.

Surprised, Soonyi pulled herself back and turned red. Mirae didn't scream, nor did she look upset.

"I have two eyes, one nose, and one mouth, just like anyone else," Mirae said calmly.

Soonyi felt mortified. Not knowing how to respond, she kept her mouth zipped.

"What does Nani want?" Mirae asked, cocking her head.

"She wants you to help out, I guess," she said, her voice weakening at the end. She couldn't remember exactly what kind of help Nani wanted of Mirae.

Mirae flung her covers aside, went to clean her teeth with sea salt, and then marched to the kitchen. Soonyi followed her. She felt tense, interested in what Mirae was up to. She hadn't been in her right mind, let alone cooperative or working, since she had recovered from her illness.

In the kitchen, there was nothing much more to be done. Nani was cleaning up and getting ready to deliver the wooden vessels for the memorial service. When she saw Mirae, however, she stopped her hands and waited for Mirae to say something. But Mirae said nothing. She simply picked up one of the trays and walked toward the master's quarters.

"What is she up to?" Nani said in an undertone, standing with her arms akimbo, just as her mother would have done. "Don't just stand there. You carry a tray too," Nani reproached Soonyi.

"What are you so mad at me about?" Soonyi sulked, furrowing her forehead.

"I'll be right back," Nani said and left the kitchen. She walked briskly to the storage room, hoping to find Min with the baby in the basket. She felt bad that she had dismissed him earlier. So compassionate and softhearted, he couldn't ignore the abandoned baby. But Nani was so busy with no extra hands to help her. The kitchen maid hadn't yet returned from her mother's. All she heard from her was that her mother would be dying any minute now. In any case, she was glad that Mirae had finally collected herself and gotten up. Hopefully, she would go back and tend to Mistress Yee.

Pausing in front of the storage room, Nani looked about before she opened the door. Min couldn't be in there, for she was the only one among the maids and the servants entrusted with the key. Her mother had given her the keys to various places before she died, and Mistress Kim had entrusted her with them. Still, she went in. The smell of the fabric and the paper and the wooden boxes made her sneeze. She looked up and down. There were bolts of silks and cottons stacked up. She took down one particular roll of silk and touched it aimlessly, thinking about something totally unrelated. Mrs. Wang's house was what stirred her mind. She would have liked to have a house—a cottage with a thatched roof—and her own animals, and her own little patch of vegetable garden, away from everyone, maybe with Min. "Crazy," she said aloud, thinking of Min and how he had run away from her with the baby earlier. "Crazy," she said once more.

"Crazy is right!" thundered a voice.

Stupefied, Nani dropped the bolt of silk, which fell on the ground and rolled, unfolding itself until it reached the shoe of Mistress Yee who seemed to have been transported into the storage room magically. Nani wanted to pick up the silk, but her body was unwilling to move as quickly as she would like. When she finally bent down, Mistress Yee barked, "Get your filthy hands off my silk!"

Nani flinched, her lips quivering. She didn't know where to fix her glance. She was supposed to be in the kitchen. What would Mistress Yee do now? Her stomach knotted.

"I didn't know I was breeding a thief under my own roof. How did you get hold of those keys?" Mistress Yee asked, narrowing her eyes. She walked on the bed of silk toward Nani, whose eyes were brimming with tears. She wanted to say that she wasn't a thief. But she felt so small, powerless, overwhelmed. The storage room seemed to have darkened. It was hard to see what expression was on Mistress Yee's face. She could only hear Mistress Yee's heavy breathing and the rustle of her dress as she approached.

Many months pregnant, Mistress Yee ballooned in the middle. So when she stepped on Nani's foot, Nani thought that it was an accident. Except she didn't remove her foot. Mistress Yee pressed until Nani cried.

"Where did you get the keys?" Mistress Yee pressed harder on Nani's foot. Her crimson lips parted, fuming fiery air, right above Nani's nose.

"Mistress Yee, I didn't take them. They were given to me. Mistress Kim gave them to me. She used to send me here to fetch papers and brushes and other things," Nani quickly said.

Mistress Yee slapped her and shrieked, "Don't you ever mention the dead woman's name. It will bring bad luck to my baby." She released her foot and said, "I am taking your wage for this month since you ruined my silk."

Nani cried all the way to the kitchen.

"What is the matter, Big Sister?" Soonyi asked.

Nani sat by the stove in the kitchen and cried more. Mirae entered and said, "We need the rice liquor. They are about to start the ceremony."

"The hell with their ceremony!" Nani shrieked. She took off her shoes and cotton footwear. The top of her left foot was bluish yellow.

"What happened to your foot? Big Sister, it's blue!" Soonyi shouted excitedly.

"Shut up," Mirae uttered quietly. "Where is the liquor?" she asked, unperturbed.

Nani ignored her and tended her foot as if it were a baby.

"Your foot will get better in a little while, but the liquor is needed right now or else she will turn your other foot blue to match," Mirae said.

Soonyi quickly got the jug of rice liquor from the cupboard. Mirae snatched it, poured a bit into a small ceramic cup, and looked at Nani. "Drink it," she said to Nani, and left the kitchen.

"Don't mind her. She is out of her mind," Soonyi comforted her. "And she shouldn't pour the liquor before the ceremony."

Unexpectedly, Nani took the ceramic cup and drank the liquor all at once. She screwed up her face as the heat of the alcohol rushed down her chest. The heat immediately spread into her shoulders and stomach.

Never having seen Nani drink, Soonyi whispered, "Big Sister."

"Don't speak to me right now," Nani said and turned her head toward the wall. Her eyes were brimming with tears.

MISTRESS YEE WAS IN HER ROOM, SCRATCHING HER enormous tummy. For some reason, she felt terribly itchy. She hated being pregnant. Things were happening to her body without her consent, it seemed, and this state of affairs often put her in a foul mood. She was waiting for Mirae to arrive. The doctor had informed Mistress Yee that her maid was no longer contagious. In truth, Mistress Yee was glad to have Mirae attend to her because she was the only maid with the ability to anticipate and accommodate her needs. The others were clueless and subservient, and they repeatedly required detailed instructions. When Mistress Yee's subordinates were stupid, she needed to be wise and careful; this tired and frustrated her.

"Here I am, Mistress Yee," Mirae announced.

"Open the door," Mistress Yee ordered from inside her room, leaning against the cushion with her legs stretched out. Her dainty feet in her white silk footwear wriggled in boredom.

"Sit down," Mistress Yee ordered cheerfully.

Mirae sat and cast her glance down. Mistress Yee examined her face, amused and surprised. Then she said, "Cheer up, Mirae. It doesn't look as bad as you might think. You are still the prettiest among all the maids." She laughed in approval of her own sarcastic phrase.

Mirae sat silently.

"You've changed," Mistress Yee suggested. She took a moment to study Mirae's reaction. "I don't just mean your appearance. Your attitude too."

"I am sorry, Mistress Yee. I don't mean to be rude to you. And I am here to serve you," Mirae confessed.

"I don't mean your attitude toward *me*. I am talking about your attitude toward *yourself*," Mistress Yee said, grinning maliciously.

Mirae said nothing.

"Do my hair, Mirae," Mistress Yee ordered, turning around to face the folding screen which she had brought as part of her dowry. Embroidered meticulously in colorful silk and gold threads, it depicted the beginning of spring with cherry blossoms, blackbirds, and a girl on a swing by a stream. "You know, Mirae, that is me." Mistress Yee pointed at the girl on the swing.

"I know, my lady," Mirae said.

"You see what I am saying? In the past, you would have said, 'Oh, my lady, you must have been the prettiest girl ever lived.' But now, you say, 'I see, my lady.' That is not you, Mirae. You've changed. That's not a good sign," Mistress Yee said, smiling.

"I am sorry, my lady," Mirae said, taking a comb and perfumed oil.

"No apologies between you and me. You've been very good to me." She laughed. Her pitch-black hair fell on her back. Mirae began to comb it. "Do you know what has changed?" Mistress Yee asked mockingly. "A maid with a pretty face thinks she can marry up. In the end, she becomes a concubine to an aristocrat and has an illegitimate child. As soon as there is another girl with a prettier face, the man leaves her and her child. And that's the end of her glory. A maid with a homely face, on the other hand, marries a servant in the household, or even better, if she brought a male servant from outside into the household she would be given a place of her own, and she would live as a wife and mother in her own place. That's the only difference between a pretty maid and a not-so-pretty maid. I had always wondered what might become of you with your pretty face. But now, it's my opinion that chicken pox might not be a villain after all," she said, observing Mirae's reaction as she gazed at the sliver-framed looking glass in her hand.

Biting her lip, Mirae kept combing her mistress's hair.

"Hurry, Mirae. I have to dine with my husband when he is done with the memorial service. I couldn't attend with my belly this large; it's impossible to kowtow to the ancestors. That reminds me of something. I need you to deliver a packet to the temple tomorrow. My due date is approaching, and your master wants to make a special offering so that I will have a smooth delivery," she said, looking intently at herself in the looking glass.

Still, Mirae said nothing.

"Look here," Mistress Yee turned around suddenly, pulling her hair away from Mirae's hands. "I don't enjoy chattering alone. I am not your entertainer. Do you understand that?"

"I do, my lady. I will try my best not to be an annoyance," Mirae said.

"You will have to." Mistress Yee turned around and faced the folding screen again. Now Mirae had to braid her hair all over again because the braid had come loose.

When her hair was done, Mistress Yee sat up, supporting her belly with her hands, and said, "I can't wait until this is over. It's so hard to move about. I feel like I have swallowed a watermelon whole. Anyway, I was thinking that you would be the perfect nanny for the baby."

"It would be my pleasure, Mistress," Mirae replied, gloomily.

"But when I come to think of it," Mistress Yee said quickly, "well, I will have to hire someone else. No offense, but it'd be cruel if the first thing my baby had to see was you with your skin condition. Don't you think?" Mistress Yee said, pouting. She lay back against the cushion with her eyes closed so that Mirae could shape her eyebrows. Mirae clenched her teeth with shame. No tears, she told herself. She took the tweezers and began to pluck Mistress Yee's eyebrows into the shape of a seagull's wing.

"Easy!" Mistress Yee shrilled irritably, her eyes still closed. A teardrop oozed out from under her eyelid.

"I will be careful, my lady," Mirae said, holding her breath.

Mistress Yee was tempted to tell the story of her own mother, who had once been a maid, a very pretty one. Mistress Yee's father, General Bin Yee, a descendent of a famous general and, later, a member of council in the government office, had two wives already and had an affair with her mother. The first wife died of tuberculosis, and the second one was accused of indecency and removed from the house and lived elsewhere in solitude. Her mother had to face opposition from General Yee's relatives and friends and the vicious accusations that she had caused the second wife's misfortune. "Is it true?" Mistress Yee had asked her mother one day. She didn't answer then. But some days later she said, "I did it for you." When all that had happened, Mistress Yee wasn't even born. As a child, Mistress Yee held a grudge against her mother. General Yee wasn't a loving man. Mistress Yee didn't get along with him, who played the role of a general even at home. As Mistress Yee grew older, she realized that, as much as she resented her mother, she was, slowly but surely, becoming her mother's daughter.

Applying a wet cotton pad to soothe Mistress Yee's raw skin, Mirae announced that her job was done. Mistress Yee opened her eyes and said, "Mirae, please don't pull your face long. Will you stay depressed forever? It's funny. What would you have done differently that you can't do now because of your skin? You were my maid, and you are my maid, and you will be my maid unless I dismiss you. It's remarkably annoying to see you act as if you'd had a different life before the chicken pox, or whatever it was."

Mirae remembered very well how Mistress Yee had promised, or seemed to have promised, something grand, although intangible, when she was in need of help. Mirae had participated in the affairs of her mistress as if they had been scheming for a shared purpose. She sighed deeply as she was tidying up the room after her mistress had left for breakfast. She was not grieving over her disfigured skin. No, her heart sank because she had wasted her life for nothing and that she had been gravely mistaken when she thought she had a friend in Mistress Yee. "How foolish," she said aloud to herself. She laughed and laughed until she sounded like a madwoman and tears trickled down her cheeks.

EVERY YEAR, BEFORE MISTRESS KIM HAD PASSED AWAY, on holidays, especially on Harvest Day, Mr. O's servants were busy delivering packages of food to the peasants on his land as a token of gratitude and friendship. But this year, there was no such order from the master. A day after Harvest Day, Nani realized that there was an abundance of leftover food. She knew that some of the peasants expected to taste the food served on the altar in memory of Mistress Kim.

Early in the morning, Nani decided to send some food to at least a few people, thinking that Mistress Kim would have liked her to do so. She was looking for Min to make the delivery, but he was nowhere to be found. She should have been more sensitive when he had brought in the baby in the basket. But then, who had the time and the means to mother an orphan even for a day?

After a while, Nani gave up looking for Min. In the end, Bok, the errand boy for Mr. O, delivered food to a few homes, including Jaya's.

Grumbling, and feeling still a little guilty for having been heartless, Nani staggered with a mountainous load of laundry to the creek. She was the only one there doing laundry. Everyone else was probably sleeping in after the gluttonous holiday. She began to beat the sheets and clothes with a wooden bat on a flat rock. She saw Bok race by like a puppy. Nani stopped her work and shouted to him, "Have you seen Min?"

"No! He didn't sleep in the room last night," the boy shouted back, still racing across the rice field.

"Where on earth has he gone?" Nani said under her breath, beating the blanket cover harder. She hadn't meant to hurt his feelings. She would tell him that. But where was he?

The tree branches on the surface of the water danced dizzily. Suddenly, Nani raised her head to look at the surrounding mountains and was amazed by the change in the colors. It was definitely fall now. Summer was the time she had to be patient with the scorching heat and the long, stubborn afternoons that didn't want to surrender. But then the fall would ambush her, and just when she was savoring the best season of the year, it would flee without warning. Nani could feel the crispness in the air. Soon it would be too cold to do laundry in the creek.

By the time she was done with the laundry, a couple of women showed up with their laundry on their heads. They exchanged greetings, but Nani didn't feel like chatting. There were things to be done. Realistically speaking, she felt that she was the only functioning maid at the moment, and the workload was getting to her. She hurried back to the house, and as she entered the gate, Mirae was leaving, all dressed up, just as she had often done before the infamous chicken pox. Widening her eyes, she surveyed Mirae from head to toe and was impressed. Whatever had happened to her? She was back to herself. This was good, but immediately the familiar hostility she had always felt toward her churned her stomach. "A lady is born," Nani said, clucking her tongue sarcastically.

"I am going to the temple," Mirae said coolly. "Mistress Yee wants you." Mirae walked away briskly.

Nani clucked her tongue again, lingering for a while to watch Mirae sashay. She was swaying her rear end just as lasciviously as before. "Good old Mirae," Nani remarked resentfully.

The first thing Nani did was to inquire after Min when she saw Soonyi. He had not been sighted since the day before, but no one seemed to think it strange. She hung the laundry behind the maids' quarters. Then she sat down by the tool shed and pensively ate an unpeeled radish, long, white, and juicy. She was thinking about Mirae; she had seemed pretty in spite of her uneven skin. When her mother was alive, she had called Mirae a mountain fox. Legend told that a mountain fox had turned into a pretty woman at night to seduce a man so that she could eat him whole in the morning. Nani was only nine years old so the story went over her head. But now that she was older, she knew vaguely what her mother might have meant. Mirae was a different sort. There was no one to compare to her.

All of a sudden, Nani sprang up, tossing the tail of the radish in the air. She ran to Mistress Yee's quarters as fast as she could. Still panting as she was taking her shoes off, she announced her arrival. There was no reply from inside. Her heart pounded. She announced herself again, more quietly.

"What's the fuss?" said Mistress Yee irritably.

"Mistress Yee, I was told that you wanted me to come," Nani said feebly.

"I am glad you are still alive," she replied. "Come in."

Nani opened the door and said, "Mistress, I was doing the laundry. I am sorry I am late."

"Come close," Mistress Yee said, smiling unexpectedly.

Anticipating calamity, Nani approached. She was sure that Mistress Yee was about to fire her, considering what she had accused her of in the storage room.

"My blood circulation is really bad, and it makes my legs fall asleep all the time. I need a good massage on my legs," Mistress Yee said as she pulled her long skirt up. Then she pulled up her long, silky white underdress and then her long white underpants, baring her legs. Nani began to massage her legs carefully, rotating her thumbs with just the right amount of pressure.

"Ah, that feels so good. You have the touch. Did you do this for the dead woman?" Mistress Yee asked, her face completely relaxed and her eyes closed.

"No. I did it for my mother," Nani replied. Her forehead was slightly sweating.

"Well, you are doing a good job," Mistress Yee said.

A little while later, just as Nani thought that Mistress Yee was asleep, she suddenly spoke: "Nani, how old are you?"

Startled, Nani quickly answered.

"I hear you are engaged to the dumb boy. What's his name? Min. Is that correct?" Mistress Yee said with a mysterious smile.

Nani, speeding up with her massaging, was at a loss. She didn't know what to say.

"Now, that is not something to be embarrassed about. Did he ever give you an assurance he would marry you?"

"We haven't really talked about it, Mistress Yee," Nani replied.

Mistress Yee opened her eyes and burst out laughing. "You couldn't have. He can't speak!" She laughed some more. "Of course, I understand that there are other ways to communicate. And I am sure that you have mastered that language by now. But I want to know if he intends to marry you."

Nani turned apple red and focused her glance on the floor.

"Do you know that he's been disappearing at night regularly?" Mistress Yee asked in an all-knowing tone of voice. "Does he come to you?"

"I beg your pardon, Mistress Yee?"

"You heard me," Mistress Yee said, her eyes closed.

Nani was speechless.

"Does your silence mean yes?" Mistress Yee asked, fixing her glance on Nani.

"Mistress Yee, my mother taught me to behave." She stopped, unsure about what else to say.

"I don't really care what you do at night," Mistress Yee said curtly, still smiling.

Nani bit her lip and lowered her glance.

"If what you say is true—if Min doesn't come to you at night—then we need to find out where he does go every night," Mistress Yee said. Her tone was uncharacteristically serious and quiet. She raised her eyebrows questioningly and stared at Nani.

Mistress Yee seemed to expect Nani to come up with a scheme to find out where Min went at night. But she didn't really believe what Mistress Yee was saying. Min had no place to go, she was convinced, except that he had disappeared the day before because they had a little argument over the abandoned baby. Should she confess the event from the day before? That would demystify his absence. But then she would need to explain why she hadn't mentioned the incident earlier, so she sat there, listening to her own breathing.

"Will you go look for him?" Mistress Yee asked.

"Yes, Mistress Yee," Nani quickly answered.

"Where will you go to look for him?" Mistress Yee asked, her eyes sparkling.

"Well, first I will go to the field and see if he is helping out the farmers with the hay or something because he's always wanted to lend a hand. He is very strong, you see, Mistress Yee. Then I will go to Dubak's house to ask if he has seen him. They are friends," Nani rattled on until she realized that Mistress Yee was not listening to her.

"No need to go look for him. We know where he is. We are going to marry him off. I just wanted to let you know that. It seems as though he hasn't done anything to be obliged to take you as his bride. We would like to arrange a marriage between him and a village girl with a baby, out of wedlock," Mistress Yee said casually.

Nani opened her mouth. But her tongue was frozen, and her limbs were dissolving into nothingness.

"Massage my feet." Mistress Yee wriggled her toes impatiently.

Nani grabbed her left foot and began to massage it. Mistress Yee giggled, pulling it away from Nani. Nani could no longer hear or feel anything. She wanted so desperately to see Min and ask him if he loved her. Mistress Yee, still giggling, stretched her legs toward Nani, suggesting that she should go on with the massage. But Nani got up slowly and walked toward the door, as if sleepwalking.

"What are you doing?" Mistress Yee cawed to the back of Nani's head. By the time she grabbed a teacup to throw at her, it was too late: Nani was out of sight.

MIRAE ARRIVED AT NOON, WHEN THE MONKS WERE having their lunch in solemn silence in a small, dark room adjacent to the kitchen.

As she made her way down the freshly swept path toward the main hall, time frozen in the air, she could hear only her own uneven steps against gravel filled ground.

In the main hall, she sat against the far end wall and beheld the Buddha. Failing to conjure up the enlightened state she had experienced the most recent time there, she sighed, wrinkling her forehead. Her heart was a hollow place. The Buddha had no smile, the air was acrid, and all the objects in the room appeared deplorably worn out and filthy. There was a huge spider in the corner of the ceiling, suspended like a lonely acrobat. She pondered what she would like to be in her next life. Maybe a lady with many maids. Or perhaps the queen of China. No, a spider in a temple. Actually, she didn't believe in future lives. Or past lives. Only stupid people did, she thought, and smiled bitterly.

Her legs felt wobbly from the long walk. Slowly, she slid down to the floor, making a Chinese character, "Big," with her body, her arms stretched out horizontally, her legs slightly parted, and her eyes closed.

The dull and sorrowful sound of the bronze gong seeped in, filling the room. Afternoon meditation. A group of monks in their heavy drapes took careful steps to the altar room, above the stairs behind the main hall. She could imagine thirty or so bald heads in their huge robes, silently mounting the stairs. In a few moments, silence was restored. Mirae opened her eyes.

The spider plunged and miraculously landed on an invisible place in midair. It knew exactly where it was going. Mirae sat up and surveyed the Buddha, whose glance, last time, had fixated on her from wherever she looked at him. Now, no matter how hard she tried, she couldn't make eye contact with him. It didn't matter. She no longer felt reverence for him.

What comforted her, though, was that she was anonymous there. That no one would pay attention to her was small serendipity. She hoped to stay there as long as she could. She suddenly felt curious to see what else was there in the temple. She knew only the main hall and the kitchen. She could explore the place without attracting anyone's attention. She got up and slipped out and walked away from the main hall. She passed the enormous stone water tub which collected water from the hill through a bamboo pipe. A child novice arrived to fetch a pot of water. He glanced at Mirae as he walked back to the kitchen. Mirae kept walking without knowing where she was going. Passing the overgrown bamboo, she stepped into a clearing where she could see the surrounding mountains and the valley. The earth seemed to be on fire with fall colors. Her heart throbbed. She lingered there for a while, soaking in the scenery, until she heard the rumbling of a nearby voice. She turned and looked about to locate the source of the voice. Involuntarily, she walked toward the original part of the temple which had not been renovated since its construction centuries before.

Listening to the soft, soothing chanting from within, she sat on the stone steps and leaned her head against the wooden pillar. She had no doubt that it was the head monk inside. What was the question she had asked him? She couldn't recall now. He had answered her with sincerity, as if she were a lady, an important person. He had treated her with respect. No one had ever treated her that way.

Down below the dirt path there was a small vegetable garden in which a few pumpkins were hiding under their leaves.

She stared at them placidly, counting them. She paused, struck by an idea. She wanted to live there, among the monks. She wasn't sure what she would do, but she wanted to live there. She could make pumpkin soup for the monks. She could garden, although she had no experience with gardening. She could do the laundry. But then, why should she wash the stinking laundry of the bald heads?

A drop of water hit her forehead. Immediately, large drops of rain began to fall, loudly, everywhere. Surprised, she looked about. The only place where she could stay dry was inside. She pulled off her shoes quickly and stood in front of the wood-frame door. She ran her fingers through her hair, feeling self-conscious about her skin. At least the scabs were gone. Slowly, she opened the door and went in. The head monk, undisturbed, sat there, as if dead.

Closing the door, she stood, not knowing if she should sit. And if she did, where? She had expected the head monk to be surprised, or at least to acknowledge her, and to inquire after Mr. O's health as a formality. But he didn't even seem to have heard her come in. She wet her lips.

The room was small. Her breathing was the only sound. The head monk seemed to have drifted into a different world, where there was no entrance on her side, only an exit on his side. He was there but he was not there. She relaxed and immediately felt bored.

Inspecting his profile, she let the time pass. The best part of his face was his nose, and then she changed her mind. It was his lips. They were expressive even when they were still.

All of a sudden, she hiccupped. Covering her mouth and clenching her teeth, she tried unsuccessfully to stop hiccupping.

The head monk opened his eyes as if he had come alive from a dream. He said something, not to Mirae, but to the world he had just left.

Clearing her throat, Mirae began to speak, only to end with a loud hiccup.

The head monk rose, clasped his palms, and bowed obliquely to Mirae. She rose, too, and said, "I am sorry to have disturbed you."

His eyelids slowly peeled back, baring his eyes. Mirae dropped her head because she didn't want to surprise him with her disfigured skin. Heat suffused her cheeks. "I have been struck by chicken pox," she confessed.

The head monk acknowledged this by dropping his eyelids briefly, and then he made his way out.

Mirae stepped in his path. She was not sure what she was doing. But she mumbled, "I need to talk to you, if that's all right."

He stopped and she sat down in front of his feet.

He sat, too, and looked at her, his eyes full of calm compassion.

"I would like to live here. I will do anything. I will cook and clean," she said rapidly.

There was silence. The monk seemed not to have heard the urgency in her voice.

Staring at his face, lean and smooth, she could feel the age of what was holding his body, the core of him, the unreachable realm. A thousand years. She thought of the house snake who was supposed to live in between a roof and a ceiling, generation after generation, looking down on the life cycles of the inhabitants. Finally, one day when it shed its skin for the millionth time, it would become human and take over the house.

"What about your duties at Mr. O's?" the head monk asked.

Mirae's eyebrows shot up. She almost laughed. She had expected him to say something different, something profound. But what he had said was mundane, boring, stupid.

"I am not a slave. My post as a maid can be terminated. I am there because I have nowhere to go, but if you let me live and work here, I will be very happy," Mirae said, imagining herself standing triumphantly in front of Mistress Yee, asking to be released forever.

"How old is this idea?" the head monk asked gently.

"I beg your pardon?" But as soon as she spoke, she understood his question. "I was sitting outside, listening to your chanting. It occurred to me that I would really like to come and live here," she confessed, lowering her head.

The head monk smiled and said, "Do you remember the rain a few minutes ago?"

Mirae, puzzled, raised her head.

"It is gone now. If you go outside and look up at the sky, you wouldn't know that it had just poured. What comes so suddenly often goes away in the same manner. Living in a temple is not difficult, but living away from the world is not easy. One must not make a quick decision, for the mind doesn't always know what is best for one," he said. He got up to leave the room.

Mirae was unhappy. He was so stubborn. She had meant what she said. It wasn't one of her whims. Couldn't he see her face? Everyone was whispering about her skin behind her back. How could she live on like that?

She pulled his robe and cried, "Please, Illustrious! I am torn inside. I am on the verge of going mad. I hate my life. I hate my mistress. I hate the way I look now!" She wanted to shake him to make him pity her and embrace her.

He stood there like a tree, planted deep, its roots gripping into the earth, strong and immovable. This wasn't the first time that a woman had come to unburden herself to him. Surprisingly many women had opened up to him, with various agonizing problems, all overwhelming to them. Mistress Kim also had spoken her mind to him. He still remembered her clearly. She had come often, once a month, to meditate, to be away from her daily life. Her demeanor, unhesitating and precise, yet gentle and feminine, had struck him. When she sat in the meditation hall, his desire to go and catch a glimpse of her was intoxicating, but instead he fidgeted in the altar room and then took a long stroll to miss her departure. One day, he entered the meditation hall like a shadow, and she heard him come in. She didn't turn around but spoke to him resolutely. She wanted to know if it was easy to live away from the world. He hesitated, his forehead perspiring with cold sweat, not knowing whether the question was directed to him or to herself. "I am glad you don't answer me," she said. "I will not trouble you again," she added. And she had never come back. That was some years before. The last thing he had heard was that she had died while giving birth. He had burned incense and prayed for her afterlife for forty-nine days, as requested by Mr. O. But the thought of her didn't leave him, even after the forty-ninth day. She would appear in his dreams. And he would say that it was not hard to live away from the world, now that she was no longer in it. He would wake up and lament his shortcomings.

The chilled air wafted in as the head monk opened the door. Mirae stood helplessly watching him leave. His feet slithered into his wet slippery shoes. She called out to him feebly, but he walked away vigorously, his wet feet squeaking. As soon as he arrived at the kitchen, he devoured a luscious and juicy persimmon. He stood in the dark kitchen and looked at the small rectangular window. The world outside was burning orange. Placing a few persimmon seeds into a vessel where the kitchen monk saved the seeds of fruits, he sighed regretfully. It wasn't Mirae or Mistress Kim who disturbed him. It was his mind that was doing the disturbing. He left the kitchen and walked back to where he had left Mirae.

Only a missive in Mr. O's handwriting awaited him. He sat on the stone steps and looked up at the sky with his eyes closed. The light penetrated his eyelids. He saw orange and black dots swarming in a vast ocean in his eyes, making him feel warm and buoyant. A pair of fluttering lips met his. He kept his eyes closed and his body still, lest everything fall apart like a puffball in the wind. But the lips didn't linger. He opened his eyes and there was no one. All he saw were fat pumpkins haphazardly spread out in the vegetable garden, scrutinizing him with their invisible eyes.

He opened the letter from Mr. O, but it was actually from Mistress Yee, asking him to pray for blessings on her future baby and her health, and she also mentioned that she would come and see him soon.

MIRAE CAME DOWN THE MOUNTAIN HURRIEDLY. HER legs wobbled by the time she reached the market place. She no longer thought about her visit at the temple or the head monk or how she begged him to allow her to live at the temple. Mistress Yee entered her mind. And Mirae realized she had no one she'd call a friend in the entire world.

A few shoppers and peddlers meandered. A blind man, dressed in rags, began to sing poignantly. A crowd of people gathered around him. Mirae joined them. She observed the daughter of the blind man, young and pretty and filthy.

From the opposite side of the crowd, a brawny man, probably a farm worker from his dark complexion, stared at Mirae intently. She blushed deeply, feeling dry in her throat. An old woman, drunk and cheerful, stepped out in the middle and danced to the tune of the blind man's song. People clapped and cheered. The dark-skinned man on the opposite side was inching toward Mirae. In a moment he was not too far from her. The crowd momentarily applauded at the end of a song. The blind man took a bow, and his daughter picked up the coins from the cloth spread in front of her father. The crowd dispersed immediately, and the man lingered, his devouring gaze still fixed on Mirae. She suddenly turned around and walked toward the restaurant district. It was too late for lunch and too early for dinner. She found herself in an alley. From behind he grabbed her shoulder. For a while they stood, facing each other with ravenous stares. Then, he pulled the knot at her bosom to untie her upper garment. She slapped the back of his hand lightly. He pressed against the mud wall. Her breathing became heavy, and his became a groan. He touched her face, and she was wondering what he was thinking. He smirked, and all of a sudden, Mirae was sure he despised her for her scarred skin, and she felt ashamed of her appearance. She pushed him away angrily. Unprepared, he flew and landed on the ground, slightly scraping one of his fingers. He grinned, licked the blood on his finger, and shot her a glance. His neck was flushed.

"Don't come near me," Mirae warned him.

"That's not what you want to say," he said, quietly.

"Stay away from me or else," Mirae squealed, extending her arm like a shield.

"Whoa," he said, and snorted. "You led me to this alley, and you let me untie your knot, and now you say, don't come near me? That's not going to make you a lady, is it?"

He was filthy, Mirae realized, and he stank too. She was disgusted. Quickly retying the knot of her upper garment, she tried to walk away from him. But he grabbed her skirt and chortled.

"Let go!" Mirae shrieked.

He scowled and pulled at her skirt, which came off easily. She stood in her long white underskirt, baffled.

"You see, you planned this. I know all about girls like you," he said, grinning broadly.

"Give that back to me!"

"I will. Only after we settle our business here," he said, looking obviously pleased to see her at a loss and worked up.

"I am going to scream. Give that back right now!" she demanded.

"Go ahead and shout. The crowd will gather and wonder how in the world you and I ended up here. I will tell them you led me here and offered your skirt. We will be bound together and dragged to the court. You know what the sentence is for a maid who seduces a decent man? You will be flogged in public, if not worse. If that's what you want, go ahead and scream. Scream away!" He approached slowly.

Retreating, Mirae tripped over a stone and fell on her buttocks. She looked up at him fiercely with the instinct of a murderer. She picked up the stone, which was really too small to kill anyone with, and she got up, holding it tightly in her palm with all her strength.

"By the way, whatever happened to your skin?" he asked derisively, coming closer, burping up the fermented smell of rice wine.

Swallowing her saliva, Mirae hurled the stone at him, which landed on his forehead, producing a sound like an acorn falling on hard ground.

He growled and covered his forehead with his hand. At seeing his palm smeared with blood he narrowed his eyes. His upper lip twitched. Then he spat. "This is a bad day for you and me," he declared, grabbing her by the wrist.

Mirae shrilled and kicked him in his groin. One of her shoes slipped off and flew away. He grabbed between his legs, groaning. She ran as fast as she could. It was dusk and there was no one in the market place.

The earth was restless, Mirae could feel, as she heard the rustling of the tall grass by the field under the immense and darkening sky. She made her way down the steps that led to the creek and sat on the flat rock where women beat their laundry. She dipped her hands into the water and splashed it on her burning face. It had been a long day. She cleaned her neck and her shoulders and wet her hair to keep it down. A large lump was settling in her chest, and it wasn't a very good feeling. Cursing the gods, she got up and walked up the steps. She realized how late it was. Mistress Yee might slap her, but then she was going to tell her that she had gotten lost, and the rain had come which had prevented her from descending the mountain promptly. She could make up some other stories, which would let Mistress Yee know that she had nearly lost her life carrying out Mistress Yee's errand.

A figure drew near her when she got up to the grassy area. It was a man, tall, broad-shouldered, and walking stealthily.

"Who's there?" she uttered, stopping, holding her breath.

It was Min, the dumb boy. Mirae sighed with relief and said, "You frightened me! Should have said something." Then she remembered that he was mute. She laughed hysterically. It was just the dumb boy. There was nothing to fear.

Min stood there, staring at her, unmoved.

"Doesn't she ever laugh at you like this? Nani, I mean. How are you?"

She observed his shoulders, and his log-like arms. Until then, she had never really noticed him, even though they had lived in the same household serving the same master. He spat and motioned with his hand that Mirae should hurry home.

"Did you come looking for me?" she asked, taking a confident step toward him. His whole body exuded a pungent odor of alcohol. Mirae frowned, holding her nose with one hand and fanning with the other in an exaggerated manner. She laughed ridiculously.

Min lowered his head, as if to examine his straw shoes. His large toe on the right side was peeking out. It wiggled in an attempt to go back inside. Abruptly, he turned around and walked toward the house where they both belonged.

Mirae sprinted after him, whispering something to herself, her white teeth glinting. When she caught up with him, she grabbed his shirt from behind and pulled him toward her. Unexpectedly, he fell backward and landed on the grass, and he didn't move. Mirae tapped him on his side with her foot to see if he was conscious. He groaned. She collapsed next to him and lay down. He didn't move. She sprang up suddenly and complained that the ground was cold. She sat on him like a horseback rider and boldly touched his chin. He felt hard.

She giggled. She examined his face, feeling amused. Nani would kill her if she found out about this, she thought. She giggled again. Just because he couldn't talk it didn't mean that *she* needed to be silent. "Hey, dumbo," she said, and then she didn't know what else to say. How did one talk with a man who couldn't talk? She tittered. Impulsively, she untied his shirt, laughing uncontrollably. She didn't know what she was really trying to do. She fell on his chest, burying her head under his chin, still laughing. He shook her and grabbed her buttocks in his hands. Sitting on top of him, she rocked like a little boat in a tempest, docked between piers. Clutching at his shoulders, she looked up at the sky, where millions of gems sparkled. The sight was fantastically entrancing. All of a sudden the stars were falling and then the field in front of her shimmered in wet silvery sequins.

Min heaved and groaned like an animal in pain. Mirae looked down and saw his face as if for the first time. Then she laughed like a mad woman and he pushed her aside and got up. He walked away without looking back. Mirae grabbed her last shoe and threw it at him, but he had already walked too far. She watched her legs, as if they weren't part of her own body. Ignoring the dripping blood on her thighs, she stood up, fixing her clothes roughly and straightening her hair. Then she realized she had cried; her cheeks were wet. She sat again on the grass and thought about what in the world she had just done. She was a little ashamed because it was Min the dumb boy she had shared this experience with. He wouldn't be able to talk about it. It made her feel slightly better. She got up and walked home.

EVERYONE WAS CAUGHT BY SURPRISE WHEN THE FIRST frost came, because it was still the middle of the fall. No one had yet started pickling.

Enough samples of kimchi from her past clientele would arrive for her, which would last until spring, Mrs. Wang knew, but she hadn't stuffed her blanket with new cotton or pasted new wallpaper to keep the draft out. She would have to order a new quilted coat this year, for her old one was unraveling at the hem. And her shoes! She definitely needed better shoes for winter.

Mrs. Wang dreaded snow. She was beginning to fear slipping on the ice when she descended to deliver babies on short notice. She was thinking about posting an announcement that one should try to have a baby only in certain seasons. It was too much for her to go around on frozen hills and fields. She was getting old.

Sitting in front of her portable stove in the middle of the room, she was waiting for the sweet potatoes to be roasted. She kept stabbing into them impatiently with her chopstick.

Suddenly, she realized that someone was kneeling, as if being punished, before the room. It was Mirae. Her eyes darted about, and she jerked at the slightest noise from the dog or the chickens.

"Come inside! It's chilly out there," Mrs. Wang advised her.

She placed two small potatoes in a bowl. Mirae came in sheepishly. Peeling a steamy sweet potato, Mrs. Wang exercised the muscles around her mouth. "These are the best kind," Mrs. Wang said to herself, smiling contentedly. She ate it with her eyes almost closed, appreciating the taste and the warmth and the comfort that it brought to her stomach. Then she asked Mirae if she would like one, stabbing a large one in the copper stove.

"I am not hungry, Mrs. Wang," Mirae said despondently.

"Did your mistress send you here? Did she yell at you? If she was able to yell at you, she is not having a baby today. Trust me," Mrs. Wang said reassuringly. "Have a sweet potato. It just melts in your mouth," she said, taking another one out of the stove.

"It's not that," Mirae said, wiping her eyes.

"Oh, oh. Don't you shed tears in *my* house. If you are worried about your mistress, you can go now and tell her that I said I would be coming for lunch," Mrs. Wang said.

"She doesn't even know I am here," Mirae began. "I am ashamed, Mrs. Wang. I don't know how to say this, but I need your help." Mirae paused, sighing from the depths of her chest. "I am pregnant," Mirae confessed, looking miserable.

Mrs. Wang peeled another sweet potato and didn't hesitate to devour it, thinking, why are women so often surprised to find out that they are pregnant? Is it that hard to remember how you get pregnant?

Aloud, she said, "All the more reason to eat something." Mrs. Wang pushed the plate with a large, hot sweet potato toward Mirae. She covered her mouth in an effort to stifle a cry.

There was nothing like steamy sweet potatoes on a chilly day, thought Mrs. Wang, taking another one, but her appetite had diminished with the two sweet potatoes in her stomach and her troubled visitor.

"What kind of help do you need from me?" Mrs. Wang asked, nonchalantly.

Finally, Mirae broke down and sobbed. She hated herself for being in a position where she had to beg for help. Above all, she abhorred the change in her body, even though only she could notice it so far.

Mrs. Wang got up and said that she was going to do the dishes. In the meantime, she hoped Mirae would decide what kind of help she needed.

Her chickens went crazy when she went out to the yard. They thought that food was forthcoming. Her dog jumped up and down, slobbering messily. Mrs. Wang sat by the well and didn't do the dishes. Instead, she washed herself up and cleaned her teeth with a spoonful of sea salt. She then fed her chickens and swept the yard and drank a huge bowl of water. She appreciated that Mirae hadn't followed her out, crying and begging for help. She was a proud girl, all right, but then why in the world was she so stupid as to get herself pregnant? Mrs. Wang was still puzzled. Normally, those who got themselves pregnant and wailed about it afterward were missing something in the head or so dreadfully naive that Mrs. Wang didn't even bother to react to them.

"Mrs. Wang, don't you have some honey?" Mirae called from behind her. She was standing on the extended entrance of her room. "I am craving something sweet."

"Not to spare. But I have rice malt you can dip your sweet potato in," Mrs. Wang replied and went to the kitchen to fetch some. "What an insolent girl," Mrs. Wang grumbled to herself.

She brought out the rice malt in a small bowl, and in a wink Mirae had eaten the sweet potato with the syrup.

"Thank you for your kindness." Mirae rattled on, ignoring Mrs. Wang's grin. "I have been repelled by any kind of food smell, but then suddenly I felt so ravenous. I guess it's normal. I saw Mistress Yee act the same way in the early phase of her pregnancy."

"So have you decided what kind of help you need from me?" Mrs. Wang asked insouciantly.

"Don't press me. I know you have no sympathy for me. But I have no one to turn to. If Mistress Yee found out about my state, she would kick me out of the house, and I have no place to go. I need to be rid of this growth in my body," Mirae articulated with composure.

Mrs. Wang disliked the supercilious maids as much as subservient ones. "That's not a good enough reason for terminating your pregnancy," she replied.

Mirae pursed her lips determinedly and then said defiantly, "Well, Mrs. Wang. Let me then tell you the truth. This is going to be the worst reason you've ever heard. But I don't care what anyone says about it. I don't want to have a baby. That's all there is to it. I don't care whether Mistress Yee would kick me out of her house or not. I just cannot imagine myself breast-feeding a baby. I know I will kill the baby." Mirae's shoulders quivered and she bowed her head. "I never wanted to be born. Never," she whispered almost inaudibly.

A black crow cawed at that moment, crossing the sky above Mrs. Wang's thatched roof, splashing its silver-gray shit directly in her yard.

Mrs. Wang suppressed her habit of laying down her principles regarding this matter.

"Your calamity is beyond my ability. What you need to do is see an herbalist or an acupuncturist. Go to the market and see Mr. Jo behind the fabric store. He might have an answer for you," Mrs. Wang said, surveying Mirae's face.

Mirae looked up distrustfully and asked, "What can he do?"

"Many things," Mrs. Wang said and chuckled. "He can concoct a brew that will erase the growth. It takes a while to bring about the result: one cycle of the moon at least. Tell him you talked with me already," Mrs. Wang advised her.

"Thank you, Mrs. Wang. I will not forget your kindness," Mirae said, tears spilling from her large eyes.

In her younger days, Mrs. Wang would interrogate the girl about the man, urge her to go and talk it over with the pig, and so on. But her experience had taught her not to waste her breath.

Mirae got up, bowed politely, and awkwardly thanked her again before she put her shoes on.

"By the way, he might have some remedy for your skin too," Mrs. Wang said. "Not that you need to correct it, but if you still feel depressed about it, I'd ask."

Struck by the power of new hope, Mirae momentarily forgot all about her pregnancy. If only she could look the way she had used to look! She would do almost anything, she thought. "Is it true?" Mirae asked half doubtfully. "I heard that chicken pox scars can't be cured."

"Those aren't chicken pox scars," said Mrs. Wang simply.

"What was it then?" Mirae asked.

"No idea. Go and ask yourself," Mrs. Wang replied. "You will have more trouble when your scars go away. Nothing comes without a price. Just keep in mind that you will not be Mistress Yee even if you serve her a hundred years."

"I don't want to be Mistress Yee. She is the nastiest woman I know," Mirae said fearlessly.

"You need to watch your mouth and stay out of trouble. Now go. I can't idle away all day," Mrs. Wang said.

"May I take another sweet potato?"

"Take the little one."

Mirae took a medium-sized one and got up. She walked down the hill, feeling much lighter than just an hour before.

After Mirae left, Mrs. Wang mixed rice flour in water and simmered it to make glue for pasting new wallpaper. She skewered persimmons with strips of bamboo and hung them to dry in the sun. She pulled out her old coat and examined it to see if she could wear it for another year.

THE RICE FIELD, LUSCIOUS AND GREEN ALL SUMMER, WAS turning frigid gray and austere. Even the wild animals had disappeared. In good years, it was a peaceful period for farmers. But in bad years, as this year was due to the drought, it was a restless period for them even though there wasn't much else to do besides making straw shoes and straw sacks, working as roofers, or hanging out around Mr. O's mansion to pick up odd jobs.

One day early in the morning, when a farmer named Jaegon was on his way to the open marketplace to sell thimbles and knickknacks, he ran into a dog, brownish white and scrawny, by the rice field. What attracted his attention was the thing it was carrying in its mouth. The lump was bloody and, to his surprise, it appeared to be a human fetus. He tried to stop the dog to have a closer look, but it walked in circles around him, distrustfully. He didn't want to investigate the matter further, for his mind was rushing to the market. He wanted to be the first one to occupy an opportune spot. So he hurried off to his destination, looking back at intervals until the dog was no longer in sight.

Later that afternoon as the merchants were discussing the meaning of life, Mrs. Wang stopped to buy a thimble. She wanted to stuff her blanket with the new cotton. She was wondering what was being talked about so intensely.

"Oh, a horrible thing I saw this morning," Jaegon began. He told her about the bloody fetus and how he regretted not having pursued the case further.

"A lot of things look like a fetus," Mrs. Wang commented. "Especially at dawn. It could have been a dead chipmunk," she suggested, raising her eyebrows.

"Oh no, Mrs. Wang, it wasn't a chipmunk for sure. I saw it with my own eyes," Jaegon retorted.

"Do you have a large needle for sewing blankets?" Mrs. Wang said, diverting his attention.

"Sure I do," Jaegon replied quickly and opened his box to show Mrs. Wang needles of all sizes.

"That one looks just right," Mrs. Wang said and pointed to the thickest one in the box.

"Ah, that's for sewing up knitted stuff. The next one down is what you want," he said confidently.

"Give that to me then," Mrs. Wang said, and paid for the thimble and the needle.

"What else?" he asked, widening his eyes and shoving the money into his sack.

"That will do for now."

"Thank you, Mrs. Wang," he said, smiling broadly. "Have you eaten?" he asked out of politeness, even though he had nothing left to offer.

"Oh, I have. But what have you got? I can always eat more," Mrs. Wang said and chuckled good-humoredly.

At that moment, someone from a distance was calling Mrs. Wang desperately. Jaegon and the other peddlers looked in the direction of the high-pitched voice, but Mrs. Wang packed her needle and her thimble carefully into her sleeve without looking around. She was used to this sort of urgent voice wanting her attention immediately, and most of the time it was a false alarm.

Soonyi from Mr. O's household wanted Mrs. Wang. Stopping behind her, Soonyi panted loudly, with her cheeks rosy and forehead beaded with perspiration. "Mrs. Wang, my lady needs you. Mr. O sent me to fetch you right away. The wagon is waiting at the entrance of the market. Please come with me quickly or else," Soonyi said without breathing until Mrs. Wang interrupted.

"Or else what?" Mrs. Wang asked, stepping away from the crowd leisurely.

Soonyi rattled on excitedly. "Mrs. Wang, my lady is in such pain. She can't even speak."

Mrs. Wang walked on toward the entrance of the market, counting how many days had passed since her most recent visit with Mistress Yee and recalling her due date. It was early, and yet this little monkey was making a scene in the marketplace as if Mrs. Wang lived only to be summoned from wherever she was and whatever she was doing. Mrs. Wang had planned to have a drink at the pub, but now it looked as though she wasn't going to.

Twin midgets were performing circus tricks at the entrance of the market. One was standing on the soles of the other, who was lying on her back, holding a bowl of water on a stick clenched between her teeth. The one on the top was bending down carefully to drink the water from the bowl through a straw. Mesmerized by the breathtaking sight, Soonyi halted and dropped her jaw.

"Well, should we stay and have some fun?" Mrs. Wang asked, chewing on a dried squid leg.

Soonyi collected herself and led the way to the wagon, where Bok was taking a nap, leaning against one of the wheels.

Soonyi hit him on the head. He got up and bowed toward the wagon. Mrs. Wang was behind him. She offered him a dried persimmon. He bowed again and took it at once.

"Never eat dried fruit in a hurry. Or rice cake. You will choke on it, and there is no remedy for choking," Mrs. Wang said, getting on the wagon with the help of the errand boy, whose cheeks were bulging with the persimmon he was about to swallow. He nodded solemnly.

Soonyi pulled his ear. "What a piglet you are! You just had lunch."

"Big Sister, I am a growing boy," he grumbled.

"Here, children. I've got some dried squid." Mrs. Wang shared her squid with them, anticipating that there would be lots of food soon at Mr. O's. She also thought that her visit would last a while.

The mule-drawn wagon began to rattle on the stony road, and Mrs. Wang wondered if she had fed her chickens that morning, if she had closed her gate properly, and if she had hung laundry out.

The sun felt good, even though the air was chilly. Mrs. Wang closed her eyes, leaning against the haystack, and Soonyi kept talking about the recent incidents and affairs in the grand house of Mr. O. Mrs. Wang was the last person to mind good gossip.

NANI RECEIVED MRS. WANG, LOOKING GRIM. SHE
lacked her usual childish lightness. Her voice low and hoarse,
she said, "Oh, Mrs. Wang, so kind of you to come promptly.
Our lady is waiting for you."

"Give me some water," Mrs. Wang demanded.

"Surely. Please follow me," Nani said and walked on.

Mrs. Wang, following behind, could see that Nani's figure
had fully matured.

"Soonyi, stay in the kitchen. Keep an eye on the fire in the oven.
When the water boils, reduce the heat and add the chopped
onions in the bowl. Mistress Yee wants beef stew for dinner. So
beef stew it is, until she changes her mind," Nani whispered the
last sentence in a strained voice.

"How old are you?" Mrs. Wang asked Nani.

"Too old for marriage, too young for the grave. I just don't
know what to do with my life, Mrs. Wang," she replied with
a sigh.

Mrs. Wang narrowed her eyes at the maid. She herself had
said so once a long time before.

Mr. O was lingering outside his wife's chamber, looking
lost and impatient. As soon as he saw Mrs. Wang, he visibly
relaxed. Skipping any formalities, he said, "What a relief to
see you, Mrs. Wang. Please, hurry in."

Nani arranged Mrs. Wang's shoes and quickly stepped ahead
of her in the anteroom and announced Mrs. Wang's arrival, but
only low groans came from inside.

Then Mirae answered from inside, "Please come in."

Nani opened the door before Mirae finished her sentence.

Stepping into the room, Mrs. Wang looked in the ceramic chamber pot with a lovely blue magnolia blossom design. Frowning slightly, she sniffed the urine. Mistress Yee was lying with her legs raised on several pillows and her eyes half closed. Mrs. Wang sat and asked Nani when Mistress Yee had most recently eaten and urinated.

"She has no appetite, Mrs. Wang," Nani said.

Mistress Yee opened her eyes, threw a bronze bowl in her maid's direction, and barked, "That wasn't the question! Why do I have to put up with a pack of stupid maids?"

Mrs. Wang advised her, "You need to calm down. The color of your urine indicates you are not well."

"I want the baby out! I have a small frame. There is too much pressure on my hip. I can no longer sit or walk. What am I to do?"

"Let me have your hand, please." Mrs. Wang put her hand out.

Taking Mistress Yee's petite hand, Mrs. Wang closed her eyes and held her breath. After a moment, she released her hand with a deep breath.

"Please undress."

"We did that the last time you were here. Why do you need to do that again? The baby isn't coming out now, is it? I am so frightened. How in the world will a baby pass through me? I will die before that happens!" Mistress Yee complained in a high and fragile voice.

Mrs. Wang didn't respond. She just motioned for the maids to help their mistress undress. Mirae was lost in thought. Mrs. Wang snapped her fingers right next to Mirae's ear. She jerked.

"What is the matter with you, Mirae?" Mistress Yee scowled.

Mrs. Wang could see that the maid was unwell. She seemed extremely fatigued.

"I think that you might be coming down with something. You'd better leave your mistress at once so that she doesn't catch anything," Mrs. Wang said firmly.

"Oh, heavens! Is that chicken pox again?" Mistress Yee shrieked.

"No, I don't believe anyone can have chicken pox twice in a lifetime," Mrs. Wang reassured her.

"Don't get near me if you are sick. This is a bad omen. And it also means you don't care what happens to me! I will have a word with you later." Mistress Yee narrowed her eyes.

Mirae got up and bowed, looking bleary-eyed and chalk-pale like a ghost.

"She looks bad," Mrs. Wang pointed out to Nani.

Mrs. Wang examined Mistress Yee with dexterous hands. There was nothing so exquisitely created in the entire world as this woman's vagina, she decided, just as she had each time she had examined Mistress Yee. Her charcoal hair against her porcelain skin was a work of art, like the calligraphy by virtuoso Han, known for his dynamic strokes and even tone. Of course, she would not reveal her thoughts to anyone; nevertheless, she thought it unfair that she was the only one besides Mr. O to have the privilege of viewing Mistress Yee's private parts.

Mistress Yee's belly was moving up and down, and Mrs. Wang gently massaged her, asking the usual but necessary questions.

Mistress Yee giggled and said, "You are tickling me."

"Turn to your side, please," Mrs. Wang requested.

"Oh, gods, Mrs. Wang, you know how hard it is for me to move," Mistress Yee complained.

Nani, perched in the corner, came over to aid her mistress. Mrs. Wang rubbed Mistress Yee's side warily.

"That hurts." Mistress Yee winced.

Ignoring her complaint, Mrs. Wang kept massaging her belly carefully.

"I had a shooting pain in my lower abdomen the other day. Mr. O's been preoccupied with the politics recently, and he doesn't realize my due date is approaching. Please tell him he will have to pay attention to me every second from now on."

Mrs. Wang said, "You must rest but move about a little. Energy begets energy. Take plenty of fluid." There was a tinge of gloom in her voice. Mrs. Wang moved toward the door.

"Mr. O won't let you leave the house," Mistress Yee said, while Nani dressed her mistress promptly. "Nani, show Mrs. Wang where she will stay."

"Yes, Mistress Yee," Nani said quickly and led Mrs. Wang out.

Standing in the yard, Mrs. Wang said, "I need to see Mr. O right away."

Nani's face was a question mark.

"No," Mrs. Wang corrected herself.

"What is the matter, Mrs. Wang?" Nani asked.

"Let me write a letter to Dr. Choi. No. Go quickly and tell Dr. Choi to come as soon as possible," Mrs. Wang said.

"What's the matter, Mrs. Wang? Is there something wrong with Mistress Yee?" Nani asked with a grave curiosity.

"Go quickly. No. Get the boy. Your boy. What's his name? Send him to fetch Dr. Choi," Mrs. Wang said.

"Mrs. Wang, Min is not here." Nani dropped her head and explained that he had disappeared again. The first time he had disappeared, the maids and servants had kept it secret, but now he'd been gone more than three days. Mr. O had found out this morning, when he was looking for him to go fetch Mrs. Wang. Soonyi had slipped and complained that Min had not been seen for many days.

"Many days!" repeated Nani, tears swelling in her eyes. "This is the third day. But Soonyi said 'many days.' Mr. O was furious. I am sure that Mr. O will have his legs maimed when he returns."

"You need to go fetch Dr. Choi. Get someone who can run fast, or you go if you can afford to be absent for a while," Mrs. Wang said.

"Yes, Mrs. Wang. I will get Bok. He moves as speedily as a mouse," Nani said, and rushed to the backyard, where Bok was probably trimming the branches of the fruit trees and sweeping.

Mrs. Wang sat by the well near the maids' quarters and pondered the news of Min with renewed interest. He was a good-looking young man, she remembered. His eyes were lively and he carried himself seriously, in spite of his lowly state. A servant with a disability was like a chipped bowl, a disposable item, but he didn't behave like one.

Feeling wretched, she paced back and forth, and then around the well. If she could, she would have liked to have a sudden attack of stomachache so that she could go home and leave everything up to Dr. Choi. The baby inside Mistress Yee didn't seem to be active. This was the last news she wanted to break to the would-be parents. The poor would blame fate, the wealthy the doctor or the midwife or the pregnant woman or all of the above.

From inside the maids' quarters, Mirae called her through a slit in the door. "Would you like to come in and have a seat?" she asked in a feeble voice.

Mrs. Wang went inside. She wanted to lie down for a short while before the doctor arrived.

"You need some red ginseng to recover," Mrs. Wang said, surveying Mirae whose eyes were encircled with dark rings.

"Thank you, Mrs. Wang, for saving me earlier. I could not sit there any longer with Mistress Yee. When I see a pregnant woman, I feel like throwing up. I don't know why," Mirae confessed, looking miserable.

"Simmer a few roots of red ginseng and a handful of dates overnight in a clay pot. Drink the brew several times a day for a while. You will feel better. You should also eat some pork," Mrs. Wang suggested.

"I can't get hold of regular ginseng, let alone red ginseng. You know that, Mrs. Wang. I am a maid. Everything good goes to Mistress Yee first. My mistress doesn't care what happens

to me anymore," Mirae said, hopelessly. She produced a cushion for Mrs. Wang.

"Even a dog needs attending when it's sick," Mrs. Wang said.
"You will not recover speedily if you don't take a remedy and,
above all, good nourishment. If you don't have an appetite,
take licorice," Mrs. Wang said, lying down and placing the
cushion under her head.

"I want to leave this house before Mistress Yee has her baby.
I can't be a nanny. I just don't want to take care of a baby after
what I've done." She bit her lip and couldn't continue, but she
didn't cry.

"Whatever happened to Min?" Mrs. Wang asked abruptly.

Mirae widened her eyes and wondered how in the world
Mrs. Wang had penetrated her thoughts. "What makes you
think I would know anything about him?" she asked awkwardly.

"I just heard that he had disappeared," Mrs. Wang said.

"Oh, that. He is involved with those crazy peasants who
meet at night. I'll bet they drink, mainly, and gamble a little
too," Mirae said.

"Where is he now?" Mrs. Wang asked, looking into Mirae's
eyes.

"The gods only know. But when he returns, he will have to
face the consequences. Mr. O said we should report to him the
moment that Min is sighted," Mirae said thoughtfully. Her mind
drifted back to the time when she had lain with him in the field,
some months earlier. It was crazy, she thought, but the more
she tried to dismiss the incident, the stronger it flashed back.
She had been possessed, she decided: otherwise, she would
never have felt anything for a handicapped man. She was now
ashamed for having been with him. And she hoped that her
secret would remain a secret until she died.

"Is he the one?" Mrs. Wang asked, her eyes barely open.

Mirae was stunned. Somehow, she managed to maintain
her cool. "The one what, Mrs. Wang?"

From outside, Nani called, "Mrs. Wang, are you there?" Nani opened the door and informed her that Bok had run to fetch Dr. Choi. She sat, panting, examining the two inside with a friendly but suspecting smile. "Is there anything wrong with Mistress Yee?" she asked matter-of-factly, although inside she was extremely curious about what might be wrong with her pregnant mistress.

"I almost fell asleep," Mrs. Wang said, sitting up, "And I would sleep if you could just leave me alone for a minute."

"Sorry, Mrs. Wang. It's just because our previous mistress, you know what happened to her, and I am worried," Nani said in a monotone.

Mirae burst out laughing until tears welled up. When she gathered herself, she said, "You are such a fake!"

"*You* are the one who is a fake, always getting sick at your convenience. How dare you call me a fake? You get sick every day just when there's much to do. You think no one notices that? A long tail will be stepped on, sooner or later. I see your scheme!" Nani said vehemently.

Mrs. Wang cleared her throat and sat up straight, frowning contemptuously. She thundered, "You two, who taught you to behave that way in front of your senior? Don't you have any manners? Take me to the visitors' quarters so I can rest."

"I am sorry, Mrs. Wang," Nani said. Then she explained sheepishly that a servant had just started a fire in the heating chamber in the visitors' quarters; it would take a while to get the floor warm.

"Prefer to be in a cold room to a coop with squabbling chicks," Mrs. Wang said.

"Please forgive me, Mrs. Wang. Dr. Choi will arrive soon. I was just going to bring sweet rice drink. May I give you a back massage?" Nani asked.

"Do you have anything to say?" Mrs. Wang turned to Mirae.

Mirae lowered her head and whispered, "Sorry."

Mrs. Wang cleared her throat.

Nani approached Mrs. Wang and began to massage her back. "My mother used to say I was the best masseuse," she said cautiously.

"Well, I will go get the rice drink." Mirae got up.

But Mrs. Wang said, "I don't feel like anything sweet right now."

"I will bring something else then," Mirae said and left. "Bitch," she muttered on the way to the kitchen.

"So I hear that Min has joined the revolutionists," Mrs. Wang said.

"He doesn't know what he is doing, Mrs. Wang. He is a loner. How could he join any group? He is passing around pamphlets without knowing what they really mean. I read the pamphlet and asked him if he really believed what it said. He just shrugged. He is so ... so naive!" Nani pressed sharply on Mrs. Wang's spine. She continued, in a hushed voice, "Do you know what it says in the pamphlets? We are all born equal, and we deserve what the aristocrats deserve. They stole not only what belongs to us but also our right to live like human beings." She continued to massage and held her breath, waiting for Mrs. Wang's response.

"There is time for everything," Mrs. Wang said quietly.

An eerie silence hung between them. Nani stopped massaging Mrs. Wang and sat down behind her. "Mrs. Wang, some of them are in jail. Have you heard the news?" Nani asked in a restrained voice.

"Don't stop. No, right under my left shoulder. There. That feels good. I have to say, your mother was right when she said you were the best masseuse," Mrs. Wang said sleepily.

"Mrs. Wang, do you support this whole thing?" Nani asked, looking at the door.

"What thing?" Mrs. Wang asked.

"You know what I am talking about, Mrs. Wang," Nani said exasperatedly.

"I never said I don't," Mrs. Wang replied.

"Mrs. Wang, I need your help. May I confide in you?" Nani asked desperately, massaging fast.

"Slow down, child," she said.

At that moment, Mirae came in with a tray holding a few dishes, one of which was leftover yam noodles sauteed with beef strips and vegetables. The nutty aroma of the sesame oil from the dish permeated the air and whetted Mrs. Wang's already aroused appetite.

"Please," Mirae set the tray in front of Mrs. Wang, who, raising her eyebrows, examined the food. "Please help yourself," Mirae encouraged her.

Mrs. Wang took a bite of yam noodles. "Don't just look at me. You have some too," Mrs. Wang suggested weakly.

After the snack, Mrs. Wang said that she would need a little rest. Mirae and Nani left the room, and once out of Mrs. Wang's earshot, Mirae lashed out, "She must breed a bear in her stomach!"

"She has a great appetite," Nani said dismissively.

"She eats more than a cow! Didn't you see how she licked the whole tray clean?" Mirae shook her head disapprovingly.

Nani didn't want to talk behind Mrs. Wang's back, especially with Mirae. As they arrived at the kitchen, Bok was running toward them. Dr. Choi, he said, had arrived.

DR. CHOI ANNOUNCED THE WORST POSSIBLE SCENARIO in a monotone. It was even worse than Mrs. Wang had anticipated. He ruled out a stillbirth, but because Mistress's description of shooting pain in her abdomen and other symptoms he didn't think the baby would be normal. He believed the longer it stayed in the womb, the worse it would get.

Heartbroken, Mr. O didn't even ask what Dr. Choi meant by normal. He simply dropped his head, as if stabbed in his heart and whispered in a choking voice that the heavens had plotted the cruelest curse against him, and that he was the most wretched soul on earth, and he should go out in the field and hang himself and let the vultures peck on him. With his shoulders dropped, he walked to his room and locked himself in, refusing to drink or eat or be spoken to.

Mistress Yee also shut herself in her room, but only after having thrown a fierce tantrum. She didn't say, though, to leave her alone, so the maids hovered near her door like bees swarming around a beehive, having to listen to her every moan and groan. She was asking herself out loud what had gone wrong, why it had to be her, and, above all, how all this would affect her health. She was frustrated that her husband wasn't making himself available to comfort and console her.

In the kitchen, Soonyi was brewing the concoction that Dr. Choi had prescribed for Mistress Yee. It would induce contractions. As it was a delicate matter, Mrs. Wang kept coming back to the kitchen to check on the consistency and the color of the brew. "Don't let it burn," Mrs. Wang warned firmly. If the brew got too concentrated, then it would work as a tumor-dissolving remedy, and it would eradicate any growth in the body, malignant or benign.

In the visitor's quarters, Dr. Choi puffed smoke as Mrs. Wang entered. "It should be done in an hour or so," she informed him.

"Thank you, Mrs. Wang. Your service to the whole community is praiseworthy," he complimented her.

"I do what I can," she said shortly.

There was silence for a brief moment while they both thought about the same thing. And Dr. Choi asked judiciously, "What is your opinion?"

"The ground is fertile, but the seed is frail," Mrs. Wang stated boldly.

His jaw dropped. Mrs. Wang shot him an inquiring glance. He blushed and puffed smoke vigorously, and then he rubbed his temple until it turned red. Finally, he managed to say, "But then the late Mistress Kim proved that he wasn't the only problem."

"She proved nothing as far as I am concerned," Mrs. Wang said, bristling. "Poor woman. It was partly my fault she died."

"How so, Mrs. Wang? You mustn't say such a thing!" he said emphatically.

"She was dead when I arrived the night she gave birth to her little girl," Mrs. Wang admitted regretfully.

"Then it wasn't your fault she died," he said.

Mrs. Wang didn't bother to respond. She was distracted. She wondered about Mansong, Mistress Kim's daughter, who must still be in Jaya's care. The most recent time she had seen Mansong was at the Harvest Day Festival, up on the hill. How could she have forgotten all about the little girl! She had told herself to keep an eye on Mansong for the sake of Mistress Kim, whose eyes glistened in the dark with immeasurable sorrows, as she had to depart the minute her daughter arrived.

"Oh, eat your own shit!" she whispered, condemning herself.

Dr. Choi's eyes widened and his skin turned white, contrasting with his tobacco-brown teeth. "I beg your pardon?" he asked, almost timidly.

"Oh, nothing," she replied, getting up. "I need some fresh air."

Outside in the yard, the air was chilly and crisp, but it felt good in her lungs. She strolled through the gate that opened to another walled yard. As soon as she stepped into the yard, she felt the tension in the air. The waxing moon was caught between the naked branches of the persimmon tree on the other side of the yard. Something moved, but Mrs. Wang didn't know what it was. She approached the stacks of roof tiles near the persimmon tree. Something moved again. She stopped, and the thing behind the roof tiles that had moved also froze. Mrs. Wang cleared her throat and said, "Who's there?" But no reply came forth. She observed. The shadow against the wall revealed the shape of a person, hunched and bunched up with something, but maybe not just one person. It was none of her business, Mrs. Wang concluded. She turned around to go back to the visitors' quarters, but a stifled sob broke out feebly. Nani came out and begged, "Please, Mrs. Wang, don't tell anyone."

Mrs. Wang at once realized that Min was there too.

"He just now arrived, all beaten up. He can hardly walk. But he won't reveal anything. Please don't tell anyone that he is here," Nani pleaded again.

"If you don't want anyone to know about it, keep your mouth tightly shut. Now, what is going on in the kitchen?" Mrs. Wang asked.

"Oh." Nani thought for a second, and then remembered what was supposed to be happening in the kitchen. "Oh yes. Soonyi is there, keeping an eye on the pot. And Mirae is attending Mistress Yee. Everything is under control."

Mrs. Wang stared thoughtfully at the moon and then walked to the kitchen. When she saw Soonyi dozing off in front of the stove, she picked up a wooden spatula to nudge her, but then she changed her mind. Instead, she silently appropriated a half-full jug of quince wine from the tray, of which Mr. O had partaken earlier, and she left the kitchen, walking back to the persimmon tree. She placed the jug by the roof tiles and said, "Let him drink this. It might help alleviate the pain. Sleep is the best remedy when you are in pain with bruises and must not be seen."

As Mrs. Wang walked away, she heard Nani whisper "Thank you, thank you, thank you!" She went back to the kitchen and bellowed, "What on earth are you doing!" Soonyi sprang up, calling out the names of people she had seen in her dream. Mrs. Wang clucked her tongue and stirred the potion in the earthenware pot on the stove. "Bring me a hemp cloth," she said.

Soonyi opened the drawer in the kitchen and produced a brown cloth. "Is this what you want?" she asked hesitantly. Without replying, Mrs. Wang snatched the cloth and placed it on top of an empty ceramic bowl to strain the potion. She poured the scalding tarlike potion onto the loosely woven cloth with the utmost care so that she wouldn't spill it. Soonyi gagged.

Mrs. Wang chuckled. "Hand me the wooden spoon," she ordered her. Soonyi sniffled. "Concentrate," Mrs. Wang said, firmly.

"Sorry," Soonyi said and handed her a wooden spoon.

"Where is Nani?" Mrs. Wang asked, wringing the cloth out with the wooden spoon.

"I think she went to the outhouse."

"Must have eaten something wrong. It's taking her a while," Mrs. Wang commented, giving a last push with the spoon. "There," she said, exhaling deeply. "Take this to Mistress Yee," she said, tasting the potion from the earthenware pot with her finger. Soonyi gagged again. "What tastes bitter is good for you," Mrs. Wang explained.

Soonyi placed the bowl on a tray and put a rainbow color quilted cover on it.

"Put the lid on the bowl," Mrs. Wang said sharply.

"Sorry," Soonyi said. She put the lid on and walked out.

Mrs. Wang followed her. "Mind your steps," Mrs. Wang grumbled from behind her.

Nani was coming toward them.

"You sure take your time in the outhouse," Mrs. Wang said. "You take the tray and go with me to Mistress Yee. And you," she said to Soonyi, "Go back to the kitchen and spread out the remains of the potion on a flat basket to air out. We might have to brew it once more if it doesn't work by tonight."

Nani took the tray. When Soonyi was gone, Nani thanked Mrs. Wang. She informed her that Min was in the storage room.

Mrs. Wang said nothing.

When they arrived at the door, Mirae announced, "Mistress Yee is sleeping."

"Wake her up," Mrs. Wang said.

Mirae went inside. A minute later, Mistress Yee screeched, "What do you want?"

The door opened.

"Mistress Yee, you will have to drink the potion before it gets cold," Mrs. Wang said.

Mirae helped her mistress sit up. "You smell, Mirae," Mistress Yee complained.

"It's probably the potion. Please drink it all at once, and let one of your girls know at the slightest sign of pain or nausea," Mrs. Wang said.

Mistress Yee held her nose as Nani neared her with the tray. "Oh, gods. Do I have to drink this?" Mistress Yee asked, screwing up her face. Mrs. Wang ignored her. "Oh, Mother, Father, this stuff stinks like a rotting corpse!" Mistress Yee cried.

Reluctantly, she drank it. Mrs. Wang left Mistress Yee's quarters with Nani. In the yard, Bok came and informed Mrs. Wang that Dr. Choi had to leave suddenly because his daughter had contracted food poisoning.

Mrs. Wang expressed her sympathy, and she told the errand boy to go and tell Mr. O that Mistress Yee had just taken her potion, and that Mrs. Wang was waiting for her contractions to begin.

"Yes, I will," the boy replied and trotted away.

Nani led Mrs. Wang to the visitors' quarters, but Mrs. Wang said, "I need to go home briefly and take care of my animals."

"Mrs. Wang," Nani began cautiously, "what if Min went to your place early in the morning to feed them. If he could hide at your place for a couple of days..."

Mrs. Wang said nothing at first. Only after they entered the visitors' quarters did she ask if Min really had a reason to hide.

"It's my hunch, Mrs. Wang, that he has done something. He's been beaten badly. I think he escaped from jail."

"Then you shouldn't wait until morning. Go tell him before dawn to leave the house. If he is being searched for, this is the first place that will be visited."

"No one dares disturb Mr. O's household, especially while the mistress is in this condition. But Min has to hide from Mr. O as well. Mistress Yee says that Min eloped with some girl, and Mr. O says that he will break his legs when he is sighted again in the house," Nani said quickly and nervously.

Mrs. Wang thought for a moment and sighed. "Listen carefully. Your boy, I think, is deeply involved with the peasant revolutionary group that talk ceaselessly. But now they are taking action, it seems. In other provinces, some of the peasants have been hanged for their unsuccessful riots. Now the peasants are acting up in the neighboring villages."

"But Mrs. Wang, that can't be. He is deaf and mute. He is ignorant. He isn't cut out to do things like that. He does only what he is told to do. He is a mule," Nani protested defensively.

"He is told to do what he's been doing. If he is a mule, he isn't going to change his mind overnight. He can go and hide at my place."

"Mrs. Wang, what are we going to do?" Nani cried.

"I don't know about you, but I need to rest my eyes for a moment," Mrs. Wang said, sitting down. Her stomach growled, but for some reason she didn't feel like eating.

"May I stay with you, Mrs. Wang?" Nani asked, looking distressed.

"I'd like to rest if you don't mind." Mrs. Wang lay on the mat and closed her eyes.

Nani dragged her feet out of the room and closed the door. When she tried to put on her shoes, her feet didn't fit. They were swollen and felt like logs when she finally forced them into her shoes. On the way to her room, she suddenly looked up at the night sky and wished for her mother.

From the kitchen, giggles leaked out. Nani stood beside the door and peeked in. Bok and Soonyi were playing pick-up-stone. Nani stepped inside the kitchen and yelled, raising her eyebrows, "What on earth are you doing? Don't you know our lady is in critical condition? And you are here giggling away, playing like a couple of children?"

"Big Sister, I was waiting for you. Bok kept me company because I was scared," Soonyi explained and rolled her eyes.

"Bok, go now. It's late. You need to go and sleep," Nani said.

Bok left, yawning. Soonyi picked up the stones and dropped them in a box. Nani and Soonyi washed up and scrubbed their teeth with salt.

Lying side by side on their mats, Nani advised Soonyi, "Among aristocrats, seven is the age you stop being alone with the other sex until marriage. Being a maid doesn't mean you can roll about like a common stone in whichever direction you get kicked. Reserve yourself until you know what you are doing." Soonyi was already fast asleep when Nani was done with her lecture. Sometime later, Nani fell asleep only to be woken up again when Mirae rushed in to look for Mrs. Wang, for Mistress Yee was having a contraction.

BEFORE SHE REACHED HOME AT NOON, MRS. WANG heard her dog howl. She stopped on the path, treaded mostly by her alone for many years. Her dog never cried like that. Mrs. Wang hurried home and pushed the gate open forcefully.

Her wimpy dog, Tiger, stood in the middle of the yard, howling worriedly as he watched the unexpected stranger on the wooden bench.

Mrs. Wang patted Tiger. Min sat there, staring at his feet.

Mrs. Wang tapped him on the shoulder, and he raised his head wearily. He looked drowned in exhaustion. "Go feed my stove with the logs behind the house." She unlatched the cage and let the chickens out as she walked to the kitchen to find some food for Tiger. In a minute, Min carried a bundle of split wood to the stove in the kitchen. Mrs. Wang left the kitchen with a day-old barley soup in a bowl. As soon as she poured it into his bowl, Tiger gulped it down noisily.

Mrs. Wang went back to the kitchen and put water in a pot. She dropped a few cornhusks into the water and let it boil. She also soaked rice in water for lunch.

"When you are done, wash your hands and come on in," Mrs. Wang said.

She went into her room and pulled her journal out of a drawer.

Twice blown by fate, Mr. O howled like a dog, she began. She wrote the details of the birth, and she finished with a sentence, *I hope I need never return to Mr. O's.*

When she put her brush down, she realized that Min was lingering behind the latticed door on the open wooden floor. Mrs. Wang clucked her tongue, pitying him for being utterly inadequate. Opening the door, she motioned to him to come in.

Min came in like a cautious, shy cat and sat near the door.

"Find a warmer spot to sit or, even better, lie down so that the heat will soothe your aching muscles," Mrs. Wang said, getting up to go back to the kitchen.

She brought in the food and the cornhusk tea on a tray. When she entered, Min was asleep. She decided that sleep was a better remedy for him than food at the moment. She covered one bowl of rice for Min, and she began to eat the other bowl of rice.

As she was eating, she couldn't help but examine Min's face, his long legs, and his ragged outfit. Something about him reminded her of someone she knew. She held her chopsticks in midair and thought for a moment. The shape of his chin, angular and awkward; there is another person who has that chin. The lips, full and shapely.

But when she was done eating, she had to go to her drawer and pull out her old journals. Once in a while, she reread them. She had to dig deeply. The pages of those books at the bottom were brownish yellow and frayed. She was thinking, eighteen years perhaps, appraising Min.

The book was bound with bamboo sticks and waxed cotton threads used for kite fighting. She had done it herself. Nowadays, there were blank books she could buy at the marketplace, but back then she had to cut the papers and starch them to give the pages stiffness and longevity. She flipped through the pages, recognizing some names. Some of the babies from that time were having their own babies now. Dubak was one of them.

She couldn't find the journal entry with Min's name at first, but then there was a record of a baby boy, born in a hut by the Snake River in the neighboring village, which she had no recollection of. But it said a woman named Hong, pregnant out of wedlock, apparently had tried to kill herself (it didn't say how), but she survived. Mrs. Wang looked closely.

She appeared to be no more than seventeen and was extremely shy. During her labor, she made no peep, enduring her pain like a cow. In fact, her eyes resembled those of a cow. A handsome baby boy was born, and I knew I wouldn't see her again. So I asked her what she intended to call her son. She didn't seem to have thought of a name for him yet. She just wrote O on my palm, which I presumed was his last name. Then I realized she couldn't talk. She was mute. How silly I was, not to have recognized that from the beginning! Had I been a little more sensitive, I wouldn't have interrogated her with all my questions. As I was leaving her hut, she tried to offer me a few copper coins, but I didn't have the heart to take them. I pulled a silver coin from my pocket and left it before the entrance. I didn't have a good feeling about this woman. She carried a smell of loneliness. In fact, no one showed up to cook kelp soup for her. But I had to tell myself that her private life was none of my business. I wish her all the best.

Mrs. Wang read the journal entry once more and sighed. Min groaned in his sleep, twitching his lips. She looked at him once again. She shook her head.

Her floor was getting warm now and it felt good. She lay down and closed her eyes, trying to recall the woman in question, but she could not remember anything about her. Her eyelids were getting heavy and her limbs were softening. The previous night she had hardly slept, and she could feel the effect of it in her joints. She fell deeply asleep and had various dreams, none of which she could recall when she awoke to her dog's wild barking.

She sat up, feeling dazed. She was also extremely thirsty. But first she had to check on why her dog was barking so fiercely. She stepped out of her room. Beyond her bamboos spread a crimson sheet of the sunset. Her lungs expanded as she breathed in the fresh air. Each time she saw the sunset, she was happy that she had settled up on the hill, remote from anyone else. Down in the valley, where the land was more expensive because of conveniences, such as the proximity to water and the market, it was now getting overpopulated. Unlike other people, Mrs. Wang often needed time alone.

Her dog was barking toward the wooden gate and jumped around happily to see Mrs. Wang. Then he went to the gate to bark again.

"What's behind the gate?" she asked Tiger, examining her wooden gate, loosely put together and the upper hinge still out of order.

He stared at her innocently.

Mrs. Wang gathered her chickens and coaxed them into the cage. Suddenly, she remembered that Min had slept in the room with her. She turned around to check for his shoes, but they were gone. She hurried to her room and realized that she had been reading her old journal before going to bed. A few books were out on the low table, and the one she was reading was placed now near the latticed door. Obviously, Min had removed it from the low table to read it by the light near the door. Mrs. Wang lit her candle and sat to check on the open book. It was the page about a baby boy of Hong being born in a hut by the Snake River. But he couldn't have deduced any-thing from that page—unless, of course, he had other relevant information about his birth.

Her stomach growled. She put her journals back into a drawer and went to the kitchen. The cornhusk brew had been removed from the stove. She had planned to give it to Min for the swelling. A few things were missing, she realized. Dried meat that had been hanging from the ceiling, along with the garlic, was gone. A bottle of ginseng wine, which she had received as a gift, was also gone. She went to her room and checked her money jar. Untouched.

MANSONG TURNED ONE. SO DID JAYA'S FIRSTBORN. BUT the winter was a bad time to celebrate a birthday because food was scarce, and the cold, dreary weather kept people inside, all bundled up. Jaya had waited for the occasion to strike a deal with Mr. O: she wanted a piece of land for being Mansong's permanent caregiver. She was practically the mother in every sense of the term, everyone professed. But the funereal atmosphere at their landlord's suspended her ingenious plan. In the meantime, she went around grumbling to her fellow peasants about how much it cost her to have another mouth—not just a mouth, but an upper-class mouth—to feed. The sheets of ice on the road, however, kept her inside because her belly began to obstruct the view of her steps when walking. Behind her back, village women gossiped about how enormous she had gotten; she seemed about to give birth to triplets. Mr. O must have provided generously for Dubak's family when everyone else was feeding on cabbage soup with barley. That was the conclusion they drew in the end, and they felt resentful.

Indeed, that winter Mr. O's household was in a somber mood. No laughter broke out; no word was spoken without restraint; everyone whispered or gestured. When the ice in the creek melted, even though the water was still flesh-cutting cold, the maids from Mr. O's household rushed to it with the laundry. They met up with two other village women, part-time employees for Mr. O from time to time. The water gushed down the creek impressively, accompanied by a pleasantly deafening sound, and they had to shout to one another to be heard, and it felt really good to shout after the long, silent, repressive winter at Mr. O's house.

"So cold!" Nani said, dipping her hands in the water cautiously.

"It is!" a woman nicknamed Quince—literally, Ugly Fruit—said.

"Hand me the sheets," the other woman, nicknamed Cliff due to her flat chest, said.

"It was the coldest winter that I can remember," Soonyi said.

"As long as you remember?" Quince guffawed.

"How many winters have you lived?" Cliff teased her.

Soonyi blushed. "I hear that this has been the coldest winter in a decade," she said, pulling back the loose strands of her hair.

"Soonyi, stomp on the laundry. This is too bulky," Nani said.

"She weighs as much as a feather. What's the point of Soonyi stomping on it?" Cliff laughed, getting up to do the job herself. She slapped Soonyi's buttocks and said, "You need to put on some meat there if you ever want to be eligible." Her plump behind swayed as she stomped rhythmically on the pile of sheets.

"There's a new maid at Mr. O's, I hear," Quince said. "Good looking, I hear," she added. And she winked at Cliff. The two village women laughed until tears squeezed out, but Nani scowled. She never understood why some of the women talked that way when marriage hadn't brought *them* a better life. In fact, the husbands of both of these women were scumbags, lazybones, good-for-nothing drunken bums. That was why they had to come out early in the morning to wash someone else's laundry: to feed their husbands, who had not earned decent wages in years!

"Tell us about the new maid," Quince said, smirking.

Nani ignored them, pretending that she couldn't hear anything, and she kept beating the laundry with a bat, splashing water in all directions.

Quince pinched Nani on her bottom from behind which made her jump. The other three burst out laughing, and Nani said, "Stop it! You are acting like children." And she shot a warning glance at Soonyi. The other two laughed, crying, panting, and sniffling.

"I am going to have you both fired," Nani threatened, but realized immediately that was not the right thing to say. She had no authority over these women.

There was a brief moment of sulking silence. Quince broke out belligerently, "What makes you think you can talk to us like that?"

Nani said nothing.

"You could be my daughter," Quince said, and Cliff nodded hard in condemning Nani for disrespect.

"Thank the gods I'm *not* your daughter. What gives you the right to pinch me on my bottom? My own mother would have never done that," Nani said sharply, surprising herself.

"Listen to you! Is that how your mother taught you to speak to your elders?" Quince roared.

"No, she didn't teach me that. She taught me to respect the elders who deserve respect!" Nani cried.

"You little smartass!" Quince got up as if to strike her.

"Calm down." Cliff also got up. "Look, Nani, you owe her an apology. Say you're sorry and that'll be the end of this," she said.

"She owes *me* an apology," Nani said.

"Listen to her. That's what happens when you eat rice from the same pot as the aristocrats. They despise their own kind. They think they are floating on the clouds, way above us," Quince said sarcastically. She was actually a little afraid that Nani might report the incident to Mr. O, and she might end up with no employment. She couldn't afford to hang around at home all day until the farming season started.

Nani did her laundry. Tears trickled down her cheeks. On the contrary, she felt she was at the bottom of a pit, not knowing how to escape. There was no way to divorce herself from her servile status: born a maid she was going to die one. Just like her mother.

"No need to cry. It's all a joke," Cliff said.

Nani wiped her eyes. She didn't want to deal with the women anymore. She beat the laundry as hard as she could.

Quince began to complain about her husband, who stayed out late at night, drinking, and the gods only knew what else he was doing. The other night, she had to carry him home when he was found passed out on the street. She found out about it because her dog barked like crazy. She went out to find him lying unconscious. Once on her back, he threw up all over her. Oh, the foul smell! She said she wasn't going to fetch him again; she was going to let him freeze and die on the road.

Only Cliff was listening with her ears pricked up, for she had spent that night with Quince's husband. He had fed her sweet words she had never heard before. He pouted, saying his wife was no fun. He would do anything, he said, to go back in time so that he could marry Cliff, not Quince. Every time he came to visit her, he flattered her not only with words but also with little gifts.

Nani's purple hands were becoming numb from cold, and the tip of her nose felt frozen. After the arrival of Buwon, Mr. O's son, the amount of laundry seemed to have quadrupled. Some days, she felt all she did was laundry. The baby produced at least twenty diapers a day, among other things, and those weren't just to be washed. She had to boil them to really clean them, and then they also needed to be ironed. Mistress Yee also produced a lot more laundry than ever before: whatever her son drooled on had to be washed immediately, be it her cushion or her skirt or her pillow.

The women wrung out, folded, and packed the cleaned laundry into four bamboo baskets to carry it back. Quince and Cliff followed Nani and Soonyi; each had a basket on her head. At the back entrance to Mr. O's, Quince wanted to know if she and Cliff should follow in and help with hanging the laundry. Nani said no, she and Soonyi could take care of it easily.

In the backyard, Nani told Soonyi to hang the laundry. She needed to go to the kitchen to prepare lunch. The kitchen maid who had been on leave because of her dying mother had finally been dismissed. After her mother's death, her father fell senile and she had eleven siblings to take care of. Naturally, Nani took over her job.

There was now another maid, even though she was only taking care of Buwon. When he was born prematurely, he could not latch onto his mother's nipple. Mistress Yee noticed part of his upper lip was missing, and she dropped him on the floor, screaming, "Take him away!" That wasn't the only thing about his appearance that scared her. He had a rather large, misshapen head, and one leg was slightly longer than the other. She and Mr. O argued about that. She insisted that one was longer and Mr. O denied it. And this argument went on for some time, until Dr. Choi confirmed Mistress Yee's view.

When Nani arrived in the kitchen, she found Chunshim drinking water like a thirsty horse. Mistress Yee had wanted Min to marry Chunshim, but he wasn't around to be married off. Chunshim greeted Nani, wiping her mouth on her sleeve. Nani ignored her and took out the chopping board and began to slice dried green peppers. Chunshim stood there thoughtfully and then she exited the kitchen. Nani lifted her head and clenched her teeth. But a second later, Chunshim poked her head into the kitchen and said, "I know you're angry at me. But it's just a misunderstanding."

Nani dropped her knife on the chopping board and got up. She didn't know what she was going to say.

"Look, I know you think I am engaged to your guy. But I am not," Chunshim said, quietly.

"I am not concerned about that at all." Nani flushed.

"Oh," Chunshim said, genuinely surprised. "That's not what I hear."

"Whatever you hear, it doesn't concern me," Nani replied sharply.

"I am grateful that Min introduced me to this household because ... after my husband died, I didn't know what to do to feed my baby," Chunshim said.

No husband was in the picture, but she fibbed on anyway.

"Look, I don't really care," Nani said.

"Well, I just don't want you to think I am going to do anything you wouldn't like. Min has helped me lots, but he is not in love with me. He's never done anything dishonorable. You can trust me on that," Chunshim said.

Nani sighed after Chunshim had left. "He is not in love with me. Huh, *he* is not in love with *me*?" she imitated Chunshim sarcastically. "But maybe *she* is in love with *him*?" Nani yowled. She sprinkled sesame seeds in a pan and put the pan on the fire to toast them. "Huh, he is not in love with me, she says. I don't give a damn if he is in love with her or with a dog!" she said and scowled.

The last time she had seen Min was the night Buwon was born. She cleaned and fed him. She drenched him with wine to ease the pain and dragged him to the storage room. In the middle of the night, when Mistress Yee screamed and awoke everyone in the house, Nani ran to Min to tell him he needed to go and hide at Mrs. Wang's, but he had already disappeared. All he left was his vomit at the entrance of the storage room, which Nani had to clean up, then and there.

"He is not in love? He's been in love with *me* all his life!" Nani said, suddenly feeling incredibly jealous.

"What are you talking about, Big Sister?" Soonyi asked, standing at the entrance of the kitchen.

Nani blushed, wondering how long she might have been standing there.

"What should I do now?" Soonyi asked.

"Once and for all, Soonyi, I want you to use your head and figure out what you should do instead of asking me constantly what you should do!" she barked.

Soonyi pouted. And then she said, "I can't."

Nani stared at Soonyi for a brief moment, and then they both burst out laughing.

"Go and find out if braised chicken sounds good to Mistress Yee," Nani said, raising her eyebrows.

25

MISTRESS YEE TOOK A LONG TIME OVER LUNCH. SHE examined the taste of each bite on her tongue suspiciously, asking what the ingredients were and sometimes spitting it out, demanding to know if everything had been thoroughly washed. Finally, Buwon was brought in. He had just taken a nap and had a bowel movement, reported Chunshim, placing him on a yellow silk mat to be viewed.

With his partially missing upper lip, he looked hideous when he smiled. Even though Chunshim was just a nanny, she felt strangely responsible for his appearance and tried to make nothing of it by smiling and clapping when Buwon stretched his mouth to smile.

Mistress Yee lowered her glance and observed her son as if an exotic fruit had been brought in from a faraway land. She showed, however, no curiosity or interest, but contempt. Buwon smiled, producing sweet baby sounds.

"What a good boy! He is such a good boy. He hardly ever cries," Chunshim complimented him.

His head was still enormous. Dr. Choi had said that it was large because it was distressed during the birth, and he had assured her that it would shrink, by and by. But that son of a bitch had lied! Mistress Yee could see plainly that Buwon's head was growing by the day; in fact, that was the only part of his body that seemed to grow. Mistress Yee winced.

"What's that on his forehead?" Mistress Yee asked, frowning.

"Ah, that, Mistress, he scratched himself with his fingernails. That happens with babies. My son scratched himself at this age all the time," Chunshim explained frantically.

"Don't you ever bring up your son in my presence!" Mistress Yee squawked.

"Forgive me, Mistress. I will never make that mistake again," Chunshim said, lowering her head.

"Out!" Mistress Yee waved her arm dismissively.

Chunshim wrapped Buwon in a silk layette and withdrew. Mirae took the silk mat and folded it away.

"Bring me the box," Mistress Yee ordered, half lying on her cushion.

Mirae brought out a lacquered box in which Mistress Yee kept her secret. Dried dark green leaves were wrapped in a parchment. Mirae knew exactly what her part was. She crushed the leaves and rolled them in a paper. She licked one side of the paper to glue it to the other. She lit it and handed it to Mistress Yee, who sucked it, deliciously, with her eyes closed. Her delicate blue veins rose on her temple. "Ah," she said and exhaled deeply, untying the ribbon on her upper garment.

Sometime later, Mistress Yee passed out, or looked passed out. Mirae collected the articles quietly and put them back in the box. She removed the remains of the rolled-up parchment from her mistress's hand and puffed just once before she discarded it. She sat there, thinking what would happen if Mr. O stepped in right then. Of course, Mistress Yee wouldn't have smoked had Mr. O been home. At the moment, he was away at the temple. He had left suddenly the other day, and only when he arrived at the temple did he send a servant to bring what he needed for a stay longer than a couple of days. Mistress Yee had told the servant to report that she was ill, very ill. So far, no message from Mr. O had come. Surprisingly, Mistress Yee hadn't shown any signs of desperation, but Mirae knew it bothered her mistress. The only thing that prevented Mistress Yee from throwing one of her fits was Buwon, a daily reminder of her downfall. Whenever she saw him right after her lunch, she felt aghast and went hurriedly out for a walk or smoked in her room and passed out. When she woke up, her wan face looking confused, she talked funny, she called out a name no one recognized, or she acted like a little girl, and it always took a few moments for her to come to grips with reality.

Something worse might happen, Mirae's intuition told her, but she didn't know what or which side she would take. Suddenly, she found herself wondering what Nani was up to. She slipped out and sprinted to the kitchen where she found Nani and Soonyi laughing about the way Quince had swayed her buttocks. They couldn't stop laughing, even when Mirae appeared at the entrance. Soonyi, covering her mouth, wiggled her tiny bottom in an effort to imitate Quince, and Nani kept laughing, ignoring Mirae.

A moment later, Mirae asked, forcing a smile, "What's so funny?"

"Oh, one of our laundresses, she shook her buttocks in front of us, and she farted loud. Then she—" Soonyi couldn't continue. She began to giggle, bobbing her head. She wetted her lips with her tongue. Nani giggled, too, as she dried the dishes with a muslin dishtowel.

"I didn't hear the fart!" Nani said, gathering herself.

"Well, I did," Soonyi said. "It was as loud as a cannonball. You-you couldn't—oh, my—you couldn't hear—oh, my tummy, oh, it hurts—you couldn't hear because of the running water," Soonyi managed to say and laughed, a teardrop oozing out of the corner of her eye.

Mirae didn't ever find their jokes or tales funny. But she smiled, sitting on the stool, taking a dried persimmon stuffed with walnut. Nani snatched the plate and said, "There are no more persimmons after this. Mr. O is going to ask for the walnut-stuffed persimmons as soon as we run out of them. He did that last year. I had to go around the village, hunting for whatever was left. I had to barter with a chunk of dried beef for a few persimmons!"

"Does Mistress Yee want something?" Nani asked.

"No," Mirae replied, chewing the persimmon.

Nani surveyed Mirae, who normally didn't come to the kitchen unless Mistress Yee sent her.

Mirae wondered if she should tell them about Mistress Yee, what a degenerate she had become. But what was in it for her if she gave away the secret?

"Is she all right?" Nani asked, looking concerned.

"She is far from being all right. I don't know what's going to become of her," Mirae said aloofly.

But neither Nani nor Soonyi asked any questions. Nani sighed, polishing the wooden trays. Soonyi was sharpening the knife on a whetstone, waiting for Nani to say something. But Nani stacked up the trays and began to fold up the dishtowels, saying that the winter seemed to take a long time to say its farewell.

"She passed out," Mirae finally said. She wanted their undivided attention.

"What do you mean?" Nani asked, alarmed.

"She passed out," Mirae repeated.

"How?" Nani asked urgently.

"She smokes the bad stuff," Mirae explained.

"What's the bad stuff?" Soonyi asked, widening her eyes.

"Mirae, you need to explain in plain language," Nani commanded her because she now saw that Mirae might be toying with them.

"Don't you breathe a word of what I have to say," Mirae began.

"Hold it!" Nani exclaimed. "If you shouldn't share what you know, you can just stop right there. We are not the only ones with ears." She was surprised to have said exactly what her mother had said once to another maid.

"What do you mean?" Mirae asked.

Nani's mom had warned her that birds and mice eavesdropped on secrets, and that they chirped and squeaked, so the whole village would know them within a day. Thinking of her mother, Nani said, "Mistress Yee would kill you if she found out what you are doing."

"So don't tell her what I am about to say. I am not trying to gossip behind my mistress's back. I am worried about her. She is smoking the leaves, and sometimes the Chinese powder. When she sees her son, her spirit sinks low and she smokes. Mr. O should know about this, so that he can do something about it," Mirae babbled. "I came in here to make some tea for her. When she wakes up after smoking, she is always so thirsty."

Nani was dismayed. Her mother had said that addiction to opium would ruin even the emperor of China.

"Well, please don't tell anyone. Although we might have to tell Dr. Choi about this when he comes to check on Buwon," Mirae said. "Or maybe it's just a phase," Mirae added authoritatively.

Nani put a pot on the stove and said, "This is not good."

"No, it's not," Mirae said.

"Is it really bad?" Soonyi asked.

"Really bad," Nani responded, sighing theatrically.

"I know," Mirae said.

Chunshim poked her head in and asked, "Can someone help me?"

"What is it?" Mirae asked.

"Don't be afraid to come in. No one's going to bite you. You always just poke your head in as if the kitchen were not worthy of your feet," Nani said sarcastically.

"No, it's not that. I want to be able to hear the boys. What are you all doing here?" she asked, smiling broadly.

"What is the help you need?" Mirae asked.

"Oh, Buwon has diaper rash, and I am going to need warm water to bathe him. Can you prepare water and bring it in?" Chunshim asked.

"At your service," Nani replied.

"Thank you. I can always rely on you," she said gratefully and ran back to the room.

"She has it real easy," Nani said, going out with a large pot to fetch water.

"Is she always this grumpy?" Mirae asked Soonyi quietly.

"What?" Soonyi asked.

"Nothing," Mirae replied, and left the kitchen, forgetting the tea, for she had never intended to make it in the first place.

26

AFTER DRIFTING MANY DAYS, SLEEPING IN BARNS, SUS-
taining himself with the dried meat he had taken from
Mrs. Wang, and stealing eggs from chicken cages, Min managed to arrive at the confluence of the Snake River and
another river whose name he didn't know. And there it was:
Sowok Island, where the lepers were now being shipped to,
for leprosy was believed to be contagious. He offered the ginseng wine as the boat fare to the rowing man in his sixties. The
old man took Min gladly. He asked Min if he would pour the
wine for him. They drank together in silence. The boat glided
on the water smoothly. Three hawks were flying around and
around in the middle of the sky that was heartbreakingly blue.
Min looked up and counted the three hawks, again and again,
until he got dizzy.

"Why are you going there? You look fine," the rowing man
inquired tactlessly. "It's not a contagious disease, as far as I can
tell, though. I have been transporting the lepers for a decade
now. Nothing has happened to me. Their limbs fall off, like
leaves in the autumn. But they don't complain. It's interesting: they are all quite content. There is a yellow man who lives
among them. Have you heard of him? He was the only survi-
vor of the ship that arrived this past summer from a faraway
land. He was in the palace for a while, but the important members of the government council voted against him influencing
the king so he has been exiled to this place."

The boat arrived at the dock. Min bowed to the chatty old
man and walked up the hill.

It was a small island. Once he climbed up the steep path to the ridge, he could see the whole island, and the silvery water on the other side blinded him as he savored the vastness of the water and the calm of the island. He descended slowly, feeling the shock of the weight of his body against the ground each time he took a step. When he reached the bottom of the hill, he saw scattered huts, and some people by the shore, fishing with their spears. He stood behind a tree, observing them from a distance. Later on, they roasted fish on a fire, and the aroma made his stomach twist with hunger. He chewed on acorns and fell asleep behind a large rock.

Min opened his eyes to find a crowd of people standing near him, looking down, examining him. They were happily surprised. One said he was mute. Another said he was also deaf. Min almost fell back at seeing the foreign man, hardly yellow actually except for his hair. He was ashen white, as if he hadn't seen the sun in years. What haunted Min even more were his large blue fish eyes, which moved just like normal eyes but seemed to conceal his feelings.

Min panicked when they took hold of him, remembering the time of his apprehension for having helped the head of the peasants' revolutionary group. He had delivered the pamphlets explaining the condition of the peasants and the unfair tax system and the minimal wages. He had posted warning announcements for the government officials to reconsider. But all had failed, and the leader had been decapitated soon after the arrest. Min was beaten up, but he had been released when they found out he was deaf and dumb. He wished to have been a martyr, too, but his disabilities prevented even that wish from coming true. The officers had assumed he knew nothing about what was going on. After his arrest, he had been dragged, just like now; many hands grabbed him and they were looking down, studying him, except that these people were not cursing and slapping him to speak. All were silent. He was taken to a hut and fed fish and boiled radish. He ate hurriedly in front of them, bearing their stares. No one made any comment.

He spent the night there in the hut with the yellow man, or white man, whichever—it didn't matter really.

In the evening, the man scribbled fiercely for a long time in his leather-bound book. It was not in any language that Min recognized. He closed his eyes and thought of Mrs. Wang's diary. Hong was her name. The other day, when he had reached the start of the Snake River, an elderly woman informed him that the woman named Hong had moved away to the island called Sowok, where lepers were quarantined. Min had never been curious about his birth or his birth mother, who had abandoned him. What had driven him all the way to the island was his curiosity about his father.

After his release from the police, he received a new assignment from the peasant revolutionary group. He was supposed to set Mr. O's house on fire. He couldn't possibly do it as long as Nani lived there, and besides, when he had snuck into the house, Mistress Yee was having a baby. He couldn't bring himself to carry out the order. Seeing Nani also affected him. She had sobbed when she saw him bruised all over.

When he read the page that Mrs. Wang had left open, he couldn't breathe. Did she know his intention to set the house on fire? Was that why she was revealing the secret of his birth?

In the early dawn, the blue-eyed man was cooking in the kitchen. He made porridge with salt and sliced a piece of fish, not cooked but marinated in salt and vinegar. He brought it in on a tray with two spoons and one pair of chopsticks. Min and he ate together. The porridge tasted bad and the fish worse, but Min was grateful that the man didn't speak. Judging by the way his eyeballs moved, he wasn't mute; he was a normal man.

When the meal was over, Min grabbed the tray, for he wanted to do the dishes.

Later in the morning, the lepers were lining up outside his hut. And the foreign man took one person at a time. He examined the person's tongue and eyes and gave the person some white powder to put on his or her wounds. Min went out the door and gagged when he saw a person missing three fingers and half of a nose. And he was wondering what that white powder did to the patients.

Sometime past noon, after the last person had been treated, the foreign man and Min sat together by the fire, roasting their hands, observing each other's faces.

There was something repugnant about the colors of the man, Min had to admit. Tinted yellow hair and the carp eyes, but the most poignant part was his bloodless skin color. It was like death itself. And it saddened Min. He was probably dying like the lepers but with a different disease.

The man went fishing. Min went up the hill, caught two snakes, and skinned them. Outside the hut, he seared them on wooden skewers and offered them to the foreign man when he came back without catching any fish. The man looked at the meat and ate it with Min, cautiously. Min missed eating rice and kimchi and hot soup.

In the evening, the foreign man scribbled again in his book. Sitting in the corner, it dawned on Min that his profession might be along the lines of Mrs. Wang's. Perhaps he was writing about his patients. A little later, the man pulled out a map and spread it on the floor. He pointed with his pen to where they were, and then he pointed to another place far away, indicating where he came from. The man's eyes immediately reddened, and Min's chest knotted with sympathy. The map of the world was a beautiful thing to look at. But the words were written in another tongue. Min hadn't known that there were so many different places all over the map. There must be people in all those places, living and dying, with stories as painful and strange as his and this man's.

Min suddenly realized that it was impossible to guess the man's age. He could be anywhere between twenty and fifty. What had made him leave his country? It was odd. With his finger, the man traced the route he had taken.

They lay next to each other, candlelight still flickering on the low table. Min saw the man cry. Min groaned to tell him that everything was going to be all right. But his unexpected groan sounded wild and must have scared the man out of his wits. He wiped his eyes and stopped crying.

27

BEFORE DAWN, THE SOUND OF THE GONG AT THE TEM-
ple rippled gently into the hollowness of one's soul.

Mr. O was sitting in front of the wall in the guest room at the
recommendation of the head monk. His mind was intensely
focused on the sound of the gong.

Let your mind be open, and let it be part of everything that
surrounds you. Don't let any of your senses exert effort to recognize one particular phenomenon, whether it is a sound or
a pain or a thought the head monk had said. Mr. O was frustrated because that was not possible. He didn't know how to
do it. The first day he had said, "Damn it, I can't!" And the
head monk, sitting next to him in the hall with the Buddha of
the Universal Light, ignored his complaint.

Now, alone in his room, Mr. O sat facing the wall, trying
to immerse himself in the low, vibrating sound of the gong,
but his attention was directed to only one thing. His stomach
was the center of the universe at the moment. Ever since he
had come to spend time at the temple, he'd been feeling his
stomach painfully shrink. Meals were served only twice a day,
and the portions were meager. He stared at the wall and tried
to let the sound of the gong seep into his mind. He was counting automatically, and then he was distracted and lost track of
his counting. He opened his eyes, stopping his counting, and
looked about. He was staying in one of the cubicles near the
old part of the temple, behind the main hall. The cold room
was minimally furnished.

When he had arrived six days earlier and announced that he
was going to stay indefinitely, the head monk had accepted his

proposal with a bow. Mr. O had expected his sudden appearance would disturb the entire schedule of life in the temple. But things went on or, rather, nothing happened.

That first day, the head monk had silently showed him the guest room and then left. Mr. O called him back, so he could blurt out the whole story.

"My son was born. But he was born disabled. The doctor thinks he won't be normal. He will be slow in learning, or he may not be able to learn anything at all. There is something wrong with his head. I felt like jumping into the well in my yard with him. There was no place I could think of to come to hide, except this place. My father used to come here with me. Do you remember? I need to stay here for a while. I need to think about things."

The head monk listened, unperturbed, with his eyes cast on his feet, his lips slightly apart, and his palms meeting tightly under his chin. When Mr. O finished pouring out his heart to him, the other man paused for a moment and then asked if he would like some tea. Mr. O was upset because he saw that the head monk was not affected by his tragedy, which was gnawing at him. Mr. O replied angrily that he hadn't come to drink tea. The head monk bowed slightly and wished a good stay for Mr. O. He chanted something from the Heart Sutra and then left.

In a few moments, breakfast would be ready. Mr. O couldn't wait. No one would bring him food, or come to fetch him, so Mr. O got himself ready while other monks rose to go to the main hall for morning chanting and whatever else they had to do before breakfast.

It was still dark outside when Mr. O stepped out the door and walked briskly to the kitchen. A group of monks were walking in single file, the head monk following at the end. Mr. O watched the bald heads from behind, amused, and suddenly felt an urge to fling a stone with a sling at their heads, one by one. And then he remembered that he had done exactly that to an elderly servant a long time before. Sitting on a branch of a pine tree, he flung a stone using a homemade sling, which hit the servant on his forehead. He fell and bled. Mr. O laughed hysterically then. Suddenly, his own laugher echoed in his head now.

Mr. O paused by the main hall and watched the monks walk into the kitchen. No one had scolded him for injuring the servant. He couldn't even recall what had happened to the servant.

Slowly, he dragged his feet to the kitchen and entered the room where all the monks sat in silence. They passed the rice bowls to the right and around the table until everyone had a bowl of rice and a bowl of clear soup with a few green leaves. There was also pickled radish on the table. Mr. O sat next to the head monk and ate, conjuring up the image of a roasted duck. When they were done with their meals, they poured hot water into the rice bowls and with their spoons they cleaned the bowls and drank the water with whatever was floating in it. Mr. O was the first to get up and leave, in order to avoid cleaning the table and doing his own dishes. He could lower himself to do many things, but doing the dishes wasn't one of them.

He went for a walk. There was a path that led to the peak of the mountain. He was climbing steadily up and when he paused to breathe, he turned around and saw the head monk following him from a distance. He waited. The head monk came close and passed him. He followed, and from behind he asked, "Don't you all kowtow at this hour in the main hall?"

"Yes, we do," the head monk replied, and he stopped. He picked a leaf from the ground and handed it to Mr. O. "Would you like to?" he asked, pointing to the ground, handing the leaf to Mr. O.

"What?" Mr. O asked.

"There is a caterpillar crossing the road. Someone might step on it," the head monk said.

Mr. O picked up the caterpillar with the leaf and asked, "Where shall I put this?"

"Wherever you think it might want to be," he replied quietly.

"How do I know where it would like to be?" Mr. O wondered, slightly annoyed.

"Well, it was going that way, and perhaps we should put it over there," the head monk suggested.

Mr. O put it down and walked on, ahead of the monk.

They climbed to the top. The valley was blanketed with thick fog, but they could see the temple, situated deep in the middle of the mountain, in the brilliant morning light.

The head monk sat on a rock, and Mr. O sat on another rock. For a while they said nothing, but finally Mr. O broke out, "I have been kowtowing one hundred and eight times a day, and meditating—at least trying to meditate—but nothing is really happening to me. I can't really forget anything. My mind is crowded with thoughts, and they all rush to me as soon as I close my eyes to meditate, facing the wall."

The head monk sat still, observing a small bug on his robe.

Mr. O looked about and cut a leaf from a plant and handed it to the head monk, saying, "Do you want a leaf for the bug?"

The head monk looked at the freshly cut leaf with regret. And he said, "No, this bug has a pair of wings. It can go wherever it wants to."

Mr. O frowned deeply.

"So what's the point of all this? Mr. O demanded. "Why do you kowtow to the Buddha? Why do you chant? Why do you meditate? Why do you eat only twice a day? Why do you not do what you want to do? What's the point?"

The head monk smiled like a baby, fluttering his eyelashes in the sunlight. And he answered, "There is no point."

"Oh." Mr. O paused, dumbfounded and slightly piqued.

"There is no point," the head monk repeated quietly. "You call yourself 'I,' and I call myself 'I.' The novice monk also calls himself 'I.' And yet, I call you 'you.' You call me 'you.' We call the novice monk 'he.' Because we think that 'you' are not 'I,' and 'he' is not 'I.' But everyone on earth is 'I.' I am borrowing this body to live this life. You are borrowing yours to live this life. The fact that you are in your body, and are called Mr. O, is a coincidence. Nothing more. All Mr. O possesses or doesn't possess is also a coincidence. But 'I' is troubled with the 'me' that wants, desires, wishes, loves, hates, feels unhappy about, and is dissatisfied with. If you let your 'I' think this way, every 'I' feels troubled."

"I don't get it," Mr. O said, shaking his head.

"Your son was born. You expected him to be a certain way. But he arrived differently, in a disabled body. You are disappointed. You feel cursed. You are suffering because you want him to be not who he is. But remember, he is also 'I.' He is you. He is 'I.' This is what I wanted to tell you. That's why I followed you up here." The head monk got up and descended.

Mr. O didn't move. He sat still and watched the head monk become smaller down on the path to the temple. His mind was in a violent state, and he could hardly breathe.

The other day, at home in bed, when his wife had whispered, "Should we get rid of him?" his spine had curled with immeasurable fear for the naive wickedness in his wife. But he couldn't enthusiastically reprimand her, for the same thought had crossed his mind. Every morning, he woke up hoping his son was just a nightmare. But he wasn't. He was there, everywhere, tainting the smell of the air in Mr. O's world. The whole village was talking about him. Even the peasants pitied him. Or so he believed. For the first time in his life, he cried in bed alone. Whenever he looked into his wife's eyes, he shrank with harrowing loneliness. And he grew wordless. His wife found him boring now. He wanted to find solace. So he had come to the temple, hoping to find a remedy for his deepening sickness. But even the head monk had proved to be of no help.

Mr. O came down to his cubicle behind the main hall. He vowed that he would not give another penny to the temple from then on. He got up and walked out. The novice monk, not older than eight, followed him, wondering where he was going. Mr. O turned around and said, "Tell the head monk that I am gone. I will send my errand boy to fetch my belongings." Mr. O stopped at the stone tub where the spring water gathered. He took a gourd to scoop it up. He turned around and asked the novice monk, "Would you like to live in my house?"

The boy raised his eyebrows.

"Do you want to be a servant in my house?" Mr. O asked. He drank some cool water.

"A migrating bird flies to the south, but in spring, it ends up here again," the boy said timidly, blinking his eyes involuntarily.

"Is that what your master told you?" Mr. O asked, throwing the gourd back into the stone tub of water.

The boy nodded.

Mr. O retorted, "Some never return from the south because they die during the winter." He walked on. He turned around a few moments later and said, "Tell the head monk I left."

"He knows," the boy replied.

"Doesn't he teach you not to fib?" Mr. O yelled and walked on.

28

RIGHT AROUND DINNERTIME, A VOICE SHRILLED LIKE A crow's caw. Several people stopped working and listened from their yards. A woman screamed and then a man shouted, "I'm going to kill you!"

Neighbors came out with wide eyes to see what was going on. For sure, the noise came from Dubak's household.

A few people hurried to his house. Dubak's wife came out in the yard and shrieked for help. With her large belly, she could not run. When she saw the group of people approaching, she shrieked, "My husband is killing me!"

Dubak was following his wife with a raised rake in his hand, about to strike her.

A neighbor man hugged Dubak from behind to prevent him from attacking his wife. Another man grabbed Dubak's arm, saying, "Give that to me."

"This woman, I am killing her today! I am killing her!" Dubak foamed around his mouth.

"Please help me! Take that rake away from him," Jaya wailed wildly. Her hair was tousled, and her face was so swollen from the pregnancy that it was hard to see her eyes.

"Shame on you," said the neighbor, shaking Dubak.

"She killed my mother!" Dubak shouted, his voice breaking. He collapsed on the ground, sobbing.

People gasped and looked at one another and then looked at Jaya.

"Jaya, what happened?" asked a neighbor woman.

"Mother!" Dubak cried.

"Where is she?" asked another voice.

A baby cried from inside.

"My son! My little boy!" Jaya got up and rushed to their one-bedroom mud house.

The crowd followed. And Dubak shouted, "Murderer!"

The elderly mother was lying on the floor in their bedroom, and Sungnam was crying and Mansong whimpering.

Jaya picked up her son and comforted him. Several women came in and examined the elderly lady, and when they realized she was really dead, they all turned to Jaya again.

"I didn't kill her!" she howled, holding her son tightly to her bosom.

"How did she die?" a neighbor man asked.

"She was eating rice cake. She was eating too fast, too much at a time. She choked on it. What could I have done? I was in the kitchen when all this was happening. She cackled, or so I thought, and I came in to find out what was going on. She fell and died before I could do anything," Jaya said, trembling.

"No! That's not true," yelled Dubak. "Jaya sent me out to get firewood. We hadn't run out of it yet, but she said I should get some more. So I went up the hill without suspecting anything. She was roasting petrified rice cake to make it soft to feed my mother."

Jaya cried, "She only has a few teeth. Of *course* I had to roast it to make it soft!"

"Why would my mother want to eat rice cake right before dinner? In recent years, she's been eating food in broth or water because she couldn't chew well. Jaya stuffed rice cake into my mother's mouth. When I left, my mother was sleeping. When I came back, the whole plate of rice cake was gone and my mother dead!" he shouted deliriously.

The neighbors stood in the room, murmuring among themselves and not knowing whom to believe. Jaya had always complained about her mother-in-law being a nuisance because, having lost her mind, the old woman wandered off to unlikely places at least once a day. Someone always brought her back home by the evening, but never once had Jaya gone out to look for her mother-in-law. Everyone suddenly remembered that. How could a daughter-in-law stay home when her elderly mother-in-law, senile and frail, had disappeared for half a day? What if she had never returned? Was that what she secretly hoped for? On the other hand, wasn't Dubak the one who said, annoyed, "Mother, if you want to get lost, get lost someplace where we can't find you!" But a son could say that because he wouldn't have really meant it. He was her own blood.

Mansong looked up with interest at the seething crowd. She had a runny nose and chapped lips and unkempt hair. But she was smiling. The pitiful sight of Mr. O's daughter, which hadn't aroused compassion in the past, provoked outrage in people's minds now.

Suddenly, Dubak came over and snatched his wife's hair. Surprised, she fell, dropping her son on the floor. Another woman picked him up and comforted him. Dubak dragged Jaya out of the room. People followed. The men tried to untangle the couple, but not forcefully enough. The women followed, telling Dubak to stop, but not so condemningly.

Jaya shouted defiantly, "Kill me, then. *Kill me!*"

"I will! You deserve to die," her husband said, glaring and spitting on her. There was a small ax nearby which he had used to split logs to make kindling.

Holding their collective breath, the villagers watched.

Suddenly, Mrs. Wang appeared in the yard and said, "Do you have something to eat?" She looked about awkwardly and said, "Oh, I thought there was a party. Everyone was rushing to this house, so I just followed to have a bite." She laughed wholeheartedly.

"Well, Mrs. Wang, Dubak's mother passed away," a man announced in a loud voice from the crowd.

"My condolences," Mrs. Wang said, looking for Dubak.

"Well, that's hardly the end of the story!" a woman screeched.

"Death is never the end of the story."

"Mrs. Wang, this woman of mine has murdered my mother," Dubak declared, his chest heaving, his saliva splattering. Some observers were sobbing already. "And I am going to kill this one to bring justice to my mother!" He picked up the ax vindictively, and the crowd gasped.

"Well, well," Mrs. Wang spoke quickly with faked cheerfulness. "Let's have a seat. Let us witness the justice done to your mother. In fact, bring your son out to the yard so that he can see how a son brings justice to his mother so someday he will bring justice to his own mother. Ah, don't strike your wife in her belly. Your other child lives there." Mrs. Wang raised her eyebrows and stared at Dubak unflinchingly.

The crowd was hushed. Mrs. Wang stood still, without blinking. Dubak clenched his teeth. Mrs. Wang said under her breath, "You fool!"

Dubak dropped the ax and wailed pitifully, kneeling on the ground. A man took the ax away. Jaya took her baby and cried. The crowd murmured, avoiding Mrs. Wang, who got up and went into the room and picked up Mansong. She carried her out and said to Jaya, "From now on, I will take care of her."

It was dark outside and Mrs. Wang really didn't have enough energy to climb the hill carrying a child.

After a while, near the old pine tree, she stopped, breathing hard. Something glinted under the tree. It was a man's embroidered blue silk coat under the radiant moonlight.

"Ah, Mrs. Wang!" the man shouted, surprised.

"What brings you here, Mr. O?" Mrs. Wang approached. In the dark she couldn't see the details of his face but only his shapely lips and his angular jaw line. She was thinking he must have been exceptionally handsome in his youth.

"I am on my way home," he said. He didn't want to admit that he was coming from the temple.

"All alone?" Mrs. Wang asked.

"Yes, yes. My business came to a close earlier than I had expected. My servant was supposed to fetch me the day after tomorrow, but I decided to return home today. I have been away for too long," he explained, still sitting. Mrs. Wang sat, too, to take a little break.

"Whose baby is that?" Mr. O asked.

"She is hardly a baby now," she replied.

"I played around here when I was little. I climbed this tree like a monkey," he reminisced.

"I need to go," Mrs. Wang said, getting up. She had no time to hear about Mr. O's childhood. She was starving.

"Yes, I need to be going too," he said and got up. But he felt strangely hesitant to get on the path to go back to his house.

Mrs. Wang abruptly asked, "Mr. O, would you mind carrying this child for me? My old body is going to collapse before I arrive at my door."

Mr. O was taken aback at this odd request. No one had ever asked him to do anything like that. And he wasn't even sure if he could do it. He had never held a baby in his life. And yet, he couldn't refuse. Mrs. Wang's arms were already extended to him, and the child was looking at him intently. He took her in his arms awkwardly and followed Mrs. Wang.

"Oh, that feels so much better. Your kindness will not be forgotten," Mrs. Wang said.

Along the way, a large doe appeared behind the shrubs. It followed them.

Near her house, Mrs. Wang suddenly said, "I adopted her today."

"Is she an orphan?" Mr. O asked.

"No. Her father lives but isn't ready to take her at the moment."

"How villainous!" he exclaimed. He honestly couldn't believe that a parent would refuse to take care of his own child, especially when the child was healthy and perfectly normal.

"Blessings are for those who embrace them," Mrs. Wang remarked meaningfully. "And I thank you a thousand times," she said, taking Mansong back from Mr. O's numbed arms. He descended and she ascended. The doe made her way hesitantly into Mrs. Wang's front yard and lingered there. When Mrs. Wang turned around to say something to her, she jumped back into the shrubs and disappeared into the night.

ALL MORNING, NANI AND MIRAE PULLED THE LOOSE threads out of the winter blanket covers and sewed up the lighter covers for spring. Now they were ironing the pillow covers. Nani sipped water, squirted it through her teeth onto the fabric, and pressed it with a hot iron.

Mirae, her skin almost recovered, blossomed again. With her naturally crimson lips and her shiny pitch-black hair, she stood out from everyone around her.

"What's your favorite work?" Nani asked.

Mirae replied, "None. Ask me what's my least favorite work."

"What's your least favorite work?"

"Emptying Mistress Yee's pisspot," Mirae said, frowning.

"What's the next?" Nani asked.

"Giving her a massage," Mirae said.

"What's the next?" Nani pestered her.

"Everything else," she replied.

"Is there really nothing you like doing here?" Nani asked.

"Nope," Mirae said with a blank expression.

Steam escaped from the cloth as the hot iron pressed on it. Nani looked at Mirae and saw how pretty she was. And she thought, not for the first time, that Mirae wasn't cut out to be a maid. "In your next life, don't be born a maid," Nani said with a tinge of sarcasm.

"So what is it that you like so much about being a maid?" Mirae asked, snickering.

"Oh, shut up," Nani said, feeling ashamed of her nonexistent ambition to rise above her lowly state. She must have been a maid for eons, one life after another. She knew no other life.

She liked ironing. When the wrinkles on a pillowcase were smoothed out, she felt happy. She liked cooking, especially sweets. Sweets arranged on a plate, such as walnut-stuffed dried persimmons or pressed honeyed puffed rice dotted with black sesame seeds, simply delighted her. Oh, and the smell of freshly dried stiff laundry just off the clothesline: such a simple thing but so precious and familiar.

"Watch out!" screamed Mirae, smelling the burn from the iron that the daydreaming Nani held.

Nani jerked and rescued the pillowcase under her iron. She examined it and found just a bit of yellow. "Oh, gods of the mountain, help me," Nani sighed as she pressed the last pillowcase.

"So tell me," Mirae urged her. "What's *your* favorite work?"

"I am not going to tell you," Nani said, sulking.

"Whatever you say," Mirae said, folding up the pressed pillowcases.

From outside, Soonyi called, "Big Sister!"

"Big *Sister!*" imitated Mirae, drawling.

"Hello?" Soonyi said, opening the door.

"Can you not shout?" Nani scolded her, venting her frustration.

"Sorry, Big Sister. The group of women has arrived," Soonyi said.

"Oh ... them," said Nani.

"Who?" asked Mirae.

"The shamans from Yellow Horn Mountain," Nani replied, getting up. "Finish folding the pillowcases and put them aside, will you?" she asked, leaving the room. A group of shamans, five of them, were carrying their paraphernalia into the yard.

"Weren't you instructed to enter from the back door?" Nani asked.

"We were. But we had to come through the front gate. From a distance, we saw the dark spirit hovering over the rooftop.

We had to announce our arrival to the spirit defiantly. If we had snuck in from the back door, the spirit would think we were cowards. We wouldn't be able to cast out the spirit then," said the oldest of the five shamans. They wore hats in the shape of cockscombs, made of brilliant orange-and-yellow paper. They brought gongs, cymbals, bow chimes, and a drum that looked like an hourglass painted blood red.

"Please follow me," Nani said. She led them to Mistress Yee's quarters.

As she stepped into Mistress Yee's courtyard with the shamans, Chunshim was leaving with Buwon in her arms.

"Is Mistress Yee in?" asked Nani, knowing very well that she was.

Chunshim nodded, looking distressed from her short visit with Mistress Yee.

Nani cleared her throat and announced the arrival of the shamans. Mistress Yee told her to come in with them. They walked in, their bulky outfits swishing and their articles clanging. The room, filled with seven women, changed its scent. Mistress Yee told Nani to go out and fetch Mirae.

When Mirae arrived, Mistress Yee told her to have Chunshim bring in Buwon. If they were to perform Kut, the shamanic ritual, Buwon had to be present so that they could unearth the source of the curse that had possessed his body. There was some discussion about where Kut should be performed. In the end, it was decided to hold it in Mistress Yee's courtyard because she was the one who wanted it.

The shamans were setting up their altar on a straw carpet in Mistress Yee's courtyard, tuning their musical instruments and trying out their voices.

Nani quietly took her shoes off and stood, holding a stack of blankets, huge against her small body, at Mistress Yee's entrance. She heard nothing from inside although she figured that Mirae must be inside with Mistress Yee.

"I brought some spring blankets," Nani announced, trying to peep around the heap of blankets.

Mirae came out and closed the door behind her. "Mistress Yee is resting at the moment. Give them to me," Mirae said.

"In the middle of Kut?" Nani whispered doubtfully.

"It hasn't even started yet," she said, taking the blankets from Nani.

"They are starting any minute," Nani said, pointing to the courtyard with her chin.

Mirae paused for a brief moment and then whispered into Nani's ear, "She's doing it again."

"It? Oh, that," she said.

"Can you open the door for me?" Mirae asked, turning around with the blankets in her arms. Nani opened the door to Mistress Yee's room. The lady was lying on her silk mat with her upper garment loosened and her eyes closed.

Mirae picked up the red lacquered box and put it aside. She came out quietly and said, "She will wake up in an hour or so. You have to see how she looks when she wakes up."

Out in the courtyard, Chunshim brought Buwon bundled up in a silk blanket. He was dressed in a blue-green jacket and a black headdress.

One of the shamans said that Buwon should be propped up to watch Kut. But he was too young to sit still for a long time, so Chunshim would either have to sit holding him up or put him in a harnessed basket and tie it on one of the pillars of the house. "Whichever," said the shaman, straightening her hat and looking at the thin air as if she were looking at a mirror and seeing her reflection.

Chunshim sat on the straw carpet and held Buwon on her lap. Four of the shamans began to play their instruments. One of them sang too. There was no prelude. From the beginning, it was climactic, loud, and harrowing. They howled and whined and hissed. And suddenly the fifth shaman jumped high and landed in the middle of the straw carpet and began to dance, whirling forcefully.

The music played like torrential waves, unrestrained and raging. The dance went on relentlessly all afternoon and all evening until the waxing moon shot up in the middle of the ominous sky. After dinner, Mistress Yee was fed up with the noise. She was getting a headache. She asked Mirae if there was any way to have Kut come to an end. "Do they know it's a fixed price? They don't get paid more just because they prolong it," she said, scowling. Mirae tried to interrupt Kut, but the shamans were in ecstasy.

The errand boy, Bok, ran into the kitchen where Nani was cooking red beans for the next day. "Don't run," Nani scolded Bok when he came in breathlessly.

"Big Sister, Master has arrived. He just stepped in the gate," he said.

"Oh no! Oh, heavens. Oh no!" Nani jumped up and ran to Mistress Yee's quarters. Mr. O hadn't been expected to arrive at that time. Or was she mistaken? But Mistress Yee wouldn't have invited the shamans to perform Kut had she known he was arriving now.

Nani grabbed Mirae. "Look, Master has arrived," she informed her.

Mirae didn't look alarmed.

"He just stepped in the house! Do you hear me? He is approaching. What are we to do?" Nani had to shout to be heard in the midst of the gongs and cymbals.

"What can *we* do? I've already tried to stop them because Mistress Yee is having a headache from the noise," she said.

Nani was confused. She saw poor Chunshim still sitting on the straw carpet, yawning from ear to ear, and Buwon was fast asleep despite the deafening noise.

At that moment, Mr. O appeared. Nani's heart sank. He neared and froze for a moment. Chunshim got up reflexively.

Nani stepped down from the ante-floor outside Mistress Yee's room and ran to Mr. O without putting her shoes on to welcome him. But her voice blended in with the noise, and Mirae just bowed from where she was.

Mr. O was tired. He hadn't sent for his horse. Instead, he had walked the whole day alone, on an empty stomach, getting lost a couple of times in the forest, and then he had to climb up the path to Mrs. Wang's house, carrying the child. It had been a long day. When he approached his own house, he only thought of going straight to bed. But the noise from behind the gate alerted him. He asked Bok what the noise was. The boy reluctantly released the information.

All of a sudden, Kut came to a halt, and silence fell heavily. Mirae announced that the master had arrived. But the shamans were oblivious to their surroundings. One of them began to speak with a spirit. Finally, it seemed they had managed to invoke the right spirit, the one that had been trapped in the household. Mistress Yee emerged, covering her forehead with her hand. Mirae stood behind her.

"Who are you?" the shaman asked the spirit.

"I live here," the dancing shaman replied in a trembling, ethereal voice.

Nani stared at her, noticing that her voice had completely changed.

"Are you dead?" the shaman asked.

"I am in between the dead and the living," the voice said.

"What makes you linger among the living?" the shaman asked.

"My body is pierced and staked to the earth. I can't move freely," the voice said, gnawing at Nani's heart.

"Is that why you are borrowing the body of the little boy here?" the shaman asked.

"Sometimes," the voice said.

Mistress Yee stepped down on a stone next to her shoes and shouted, "Who is this spirit?"

Ignoring her, the shaman asked, "What do you want?"

"Pull the needle out of my body. Bury me properly," the voice said.

Nani pronounced her late mistress's name as if sighing and collapsed near Mr. O. She recognized her mistress. It wasn't her voice, but the way she spoke; it was her.

Bok tried to pull her upright but he couldn't.

Mr. O didn't know why the maid had mentioned his first wife's name, but his hair stood on end.

"Where can we find you?" the shaman asked.

"Behind my quarters," the voice said.

"Leave the baby at once, and I will bury you properly," the shaman said.

The spirit groaned in a way that was at once terrifying and heartrending. Nani jerked, stifling her cry. Mistress Yee grabbed one of her shoes and came toward Nani. She lifted her shoe, aiming it at Nani's head. Bok let out a piercing cry, vicariously expecting the pain. Mistress Yee struck Nani's head with her shoe, and the beads from the shoe scattered on the ground, glittering under the torchlight. Mr. O turned around and went to his quarters. Bok followed him.

At that moment, Buwon began to jerk with a seizure, and Chunshim screamed. Mistress Yee watched her son with terror, and Mirae stood still, feeling the chill in her spine.

The shamans packed up their belongings and waited for Mistress Yee to produce the payment. But she said that she would send them the money when the baby's condition improved.

"That wasn't what we were promised, Mistress," the eldest shaman said calmly.

"That was what I asked for," Mistress Yee snarled.

"We unearthed the source of the calamity that has befallen your son. Mistress's job is to hear the spirit out and do what needs to be done to undo the curse, according to your judgment. Beyond that, we have no say in Mistress's business," the shaman said.

"According to my judgment? You don't think I believe the dancer's gibberish, do you? What spirit? Her body is pierced? Generations of people have died in this household. How should I know whose body was pierced with a needle? What nee—" Mistress Yee stopped abruptly. Needle. She suddenly remembered the needle. The needle. She looked at Nani, who was obviously quite affected by the ritual. Was it really Mistress Kim? She ascended the stone step and retreated to her room. A moment later, from inside, she called for Mirae who, upon hearing her name, jerked and rushed to her mistress. Then Mirae brought out an envelope for the shamans. They cleaned the courtyard and left without saying goodbye.

THE WAXING MOON WAS THINLY VEILED WITH DARK, **30**
rapidly moving clouds. An old owl in the pine tree behind
Mr. O's house stared down on the roof. Bok's cat sat on the roof,
snarling. Bok threw a stone at the cat and urged it to come down,
but the cat seemed unimpressed by either the stone or Bok's
pleading. The stone he threw up fell back down and hit his own
head. "How did you get up there?" Bok asked. The cat looked
down at him and screeched again, looking up at the moon.

Bok gave up and went to the bathing place, where Mr. O
had left a tub full of water and his clothes. He emptied the
water and cleaned the wooden tub with a straw ball, applying ashes for the scrub. When he had tidied up everything, he
picked up Mr. O's laundry and took it to the hamper behind
the kitchen. Mr. O's laundry was not to be mixed with anyone
else's. Not even with Mistress Yee's. And it was supposed to be
folded and placed in the hamper neatly. So Bok took the time
to do it. He heard whimpering from the corner of the laundry
room. Frightened, he spoke softly, "Who's there?"

Nani got up and said, "Separate the undergarments from
the outer ones."

"Big Sister, what were you doing there?" Bok asked.

"I was talking to myself," Nani answered.

"Why?"

"Why what?"

"Why were you talking to yourself?" Bok asked curiously.

"Bok, someday you will understand. Women sometimes
have conversations with themselves. Don't ask why. All right?"
Nani said. She had actually been looking at an outfit that had

belonged to Mistress Kim. After her funeral, Mistress Yee had ordered Mirae to incinerate all Mistress Kim's belongings. The part-time workers and the maids hunted madly for things to keep for themselves. Nani guarded her mistress's things fiercely, but in the end, most of them were taken, and Nani resigned herself to thinking that it was good that some of Mistress Kim's things had survived. She kept one of Mistress Kim's outfits, not to pawn or to wear, but for the sake of the memory. It was a pine-nut-colored outfit that Mistress Kim had loved. Nani had stroked it fondly tonight. Was it really she who had spoken through the dancer? Now some doubts rose in her mind.

"Why are you looking at me like that?" Nani asked.

"Were you really having a conversation with yourself, Big Sister?" Bok asked, looking innocent.

"Go to bed," Nani said.

"Big Sister," Bok began, smiling shyly.

"Don't pester me now," Nani scolded him.

"I am still hungry," Bok said, rubbing his little belly.

Nani stepped out of the laundry room, and Bok followed her to the kitchen. She scooped out a bowl of rice and poured vegetable broth over it. He began to devour it happily.

"Don't eat fast. You are going to have a stomachache," Nani advised him. She stood up and got a quail egg marinated in seasoned soy sauce. She put it in his mouth and licked her fingers. "It didn't turn out good this time," she commented.

"Well, it's the best thing I've ever had," Bok said, grinning, wanting one more.

"It's for your master's breakfast," Nani said.

Mirae came in, surprising them.

"What a piglet you are!" Mirae said, raising her eyebrows. "You eat all day long," she said.

"I am a growing boy," Bok replied, pouting, but still chewing the food.

"What is it?" Nani asked anxiously.

"Nothing. I am going to make some tea for Mistress Yee," Mirae said.

"Tea, at this hour?" Nani asked.

"Yes, tea. At this hour," Mirae said.

"She will pee all night long," Nani said contemptuously.

"I will tell her about your concern," Mirae said sarcastically.

"I was concerned about you," Nani said, thinking of the chamber pot that Mirae would have to clean the next morning.

Mirae didn't get the meaning and put the teapot on the stove and prepared the tea leaves.

"Go to bed," Nani urged Bok.

"All right, Big Sister," Bok said and left the kitchen.

"I picked up the beads," Mirae said, grinning.

It took a moment for Nani to realize what she was talking about. And she left abruptly, slamming the kitchen door behind her.

Mirae carried the tea on a tray. The moon was out, but strangely, it didn't shine where she walked. After passing through the gate that led to Mistress Yee's quarters, the ambushed cat jumped out from nowhere and shocked her. She dropped everything and broke the teapot. She cursed the cat, or was it a cat? She looked behind her but saw nothing. She picked up the broken ceramic pieces and went back to the kitchen and placed the tray by the stove for someone else to take care of. And she left again to go see Mistress Yee. She had not asked for tea. Mirae had made it as an excuse to go see her.

She announced her arrival and wondered if Mistress Yee would need anything.

"Come in, child," Mistress Yee said from inside. She hadn't called her "child" in years. Mirae stepped into her room and closed the door behind her. Mistress Yee was lying on her silk mat. She didn't open her eyes.

"Sit down. I thought you might come," Mistress Yee said, her eyes still closed.

Mirae waited impatiently for her mistress to verbally permit her to speak. Finally, Mistress Yee asked in her fuzzy, dreamy voice, "What is it? I am tired."

"Mistress, I am frightened," Mirae confessed.

"Of what?" Mistress Yee asked, opening her eyes.

"The doll. Do you remember?" Mirae said, trembling.

"What doll?" Mistress Yee asked, slightly grinning.

"The doll you asked me to make," Mirae replied.

"For what? I don't play with dolls anymore," Mistress Yee said. She snorted.

"No, Mistress. On the night when Mistress Kim was having a baby."

"Did you make a doll?" Mistress Yee asked.

"Yes, Mistress," Mirae said softly.

"What for?" Mistress Yee asked, raising her eyebrows.

"Well, Mistress, do you really not remember the doll?" Mirae asked, baffled.

"No, but if you do, fill me in," she said.

"Mistress Yee, you asked me to make a doll on the day that Mistress Kim began to have contractions," Mirae said, finding it difficult to regurgitate the details of the crime.

"You are being convoluted, Mirae," Mistress Yee pointed out, closing her eyes again.

"I brought the doll to you. And you pierced it with a needle. And I buried it by her quarters in the middle of the night," Mirae said in her unsteady voice.

"Mirae, are you sure you are not making this up?" Mistress Yee asked.

"No, Mistress," Mirae said.

"Why is it I have absolutely no recollection of this incident?" Mistress Yee asked, sitting up.

"I can take you to the place where I buried the doll," Mirae suggested. "If you saw it, you would remember it," she assured her. A certain nostalgia flooded Mirae's chest. She was having an intimate conversation with her mistress again. Once, she had adored Mistress Yee and had done whatever it was she wanted.

Mistress Yee got up and said, unexpectedly, "Take me."

Surprised, Mirae got up and led the way. This might be a chance to become friends again with her mistress. She would prove her loyalty. Mistress Yee would love her once again. A gem she was among the maids. Mistress Yee herself had said that once.

The moon was suspended in the middle of the sky, weeping. It didn't shine. Mirae went without a lantern so as not to draw attention to Mistress Yee and herself. Mistress Kim's quarters had been out of use since her death. Mirae led her mistress behind the building and looked about.

"It was around here," Mirae said.

"Think carefully," Mistress Yee said.

"Mistress, I need to get a hoe to dig. May I?"

"Sure, I will stay right here," Mistress Yee said.

After Mirae left, a voice spoke from inside Mistress Kim's quarters, giving Mistress Yee a deadly fright. The door opened from the inside and there stood Mr. O with his stern face.

"What on earth are you doing here?" Mr. O questioned her.

"Husband, I am confused and most embarrassed to be found here in the middle of the night. I know it's not proper for me to wander about like this, but I am here under dire circumstances to be shown something that would solve the mystery that baffled me this evening. I will explain everything later. Would you please close the door and listen from within? I don't think you need an explanation if you listen carefully," Mistress Yee said most sincerely.

Mirae went to the tool shed and tried to find a hoe. When she grabbed one, the same cat sprang out again so that she felt like her heart stopped momentarily. She threw the hoe after the cat, cursing. But the animal disappeared. She picked up the hoe again and ran to Mistress Yee.

"Let me see. I am sure it was here," Mirae hit several places on the ground with the hoe. She dug here and there unsuccessfully for a while.

"I don't believe you have done such a thing," Mistress Yee remarked.

"I would bet my life that I did, Mistress Yee," Mirae said.

"There seems to be nothing," Mistress Yee said.

"Ah, here, my lady," Mirae said gladly, digging rapidly. "It's right here." Mirae took it out of the hole, shaking the dirt off the doll.

"My gods, Mistress!" Mirae gasped, dropping the doll on the ground.

"What is it?" Mistress Yee asked.

"It's bleeding," Mirae said, her voice trembling.

"What is that?" Mistress Yee asked innocently.

"It's the needle-pierced doll I buried the night Mistress Kim was having a baby," Mirae exclaimed, breaking down with fear. She sobbed.

"My gods, Mirae, how could you have done this?" Mistress Yee gasped, really surprised that her own scheme to ensnare her maid was remarkably ingenious. And she fainted, falling carefully on the ground.

Clenching his teeth, Mr. O closed his eyes as he listened. When he heard his wife fall, he came out of Mistress Kim's front door quickly and hurried around the building to strangle the maid. The moon was now bright enough to see all that was going on in the backyard of the deceased Mistress Kim's quarters.

Part Three

MIN STARED AT HIS COMPANION'S TOES BETWEEN which blood and oozing puss coagulated. The soles of his shoes completely worn out, his fungus-infested feet visibly suffered. Despite that, he had kept a steady pace behind Min for the past two days, but now he began to lag. Min picked up a stick and handed it to him.

He was feeling lightheaded and fatigued, Min could tell. Sweat broke out on his forehead and he started whispering. Min just waited patiently until Blane stopped babbling. Then they would resume their journey.

His eyes bloodshot, Blane suddenly let out a mournful squall. Min put his hand on his friend's arm. Blane wanted to go home. Min understood.

The map of the world Blane had was fascinating. Min imagined a country full of people like Blane. He knew very well how hard it had to be to be singled out. For the past two days, children burst into tears at the sight of Blane or threw stones at him with such intense hostility. All his life, people had mocked Min for having a disability. It had become a part of his life. But when he saw how even children, well, especially children, reacted to Blane, he realized that it wasn't him, possibly, that was wrong. Without rhyme or reason people had tortured him all his life for being different.

Min was the supplier of their meals as they traveled together: edible roots with fresh dirt still on them or raw eggs or acorn mush. When they were lucky, they got to roast a snake or grasshoppers. Blane frowned when Min skinned a snake. Min smiled, which he did sparingly. But in the end he convinced his companion to eat.

At night they lay several yards away from each other while a bonfire crackled in between them. There was nothing Min loved more than the night sky full of stars. Behind each star lay a story so complex and yet plain as his life. Before falling asleep, Nani came to his mind. Her childlike smile, her small feet that carried her everywhere so fast, her lips so endearing especially when she pouted in an exaggerated manner. Then he would fall asleep hoping for a dream of his sweetheart.

When a rooster yodeled, Min opened his eyes and smelled the cool earth that he so loved. Fresh air tainted with faint cow dung smell from the field. Inhaling deeply, he got up and in no time he was off to look for things to eat. He moved like a reptile. In a little while he returned to his friend, ashen-faced, fearful, and a heart full of loneliness. Min handed him mountain berries, one egg, and a pair of old straw shoes. The shoes fit him snuggly. Min grinned satisfied. No longer did Blane snatch from Min's hand for he knew now he wouldn't starve as long as he was with Min. But once he tasted the berries, he ate the rest hurriedly, making a mess all over his mouth. He refused to eat the egg. The texture of raw egg in his mouth repelled him. Min cracked it and dumped the whole thing into his mouth.

When the sun on the east resembled the color of someone's throat, they got up and marched on. Min chose hilly paths, away from residential areas, to avoid people with ill feelings. Half a day later the two young travelers arrived at the belly of an ancient mountain, which was thickly dressed in luscious green and the atmosphere impregnated with unperturbed calm.

A temple was in sight. Min stopped at the entrance where the name of the temple was carved on a huge wooden board. He turned around and waited for Blane, who was at least thirty steps behind. He dried his forehead with his bare hand. He was hungry. Wan and fatigued, Blane let out a sigh as he approached.

After passing the humongous wooden statues of guardians painted in bright red, blue, white, and green, Min turned around to check on his friend. Blane's jaw dropped staring at the guardians in awe.

When Mr. O's father had passed away, Min had accompanied Mr. O and Mistress Kim seven times over forty-nine days to the ritual to send off the spirit to a good place. Min, a young lad then, played in the yard or wandered off in the mountains until the ritual was over by noon. He was there with Nani's mom to aid their master and the mistress. He carried things.

Now they were passing the pagoda and a tree and an impressively old building, from which low rumbles flowed like ripples on an enormous lake. Min led Blane to a large stone tub where fresh water gushed down through a bamboo pipe, erasing all other sounds. Both Min and Blane gulped down water, washed their hands and filthy feet, and then drank more water. Min came close to his companion and pointed at his beard, dyed purple from the berries he had eaten that morning. Using Min as his virtual mirror, he cleaned his face carefully.

Min felt comfortable in the temple. It was his second home in a way although he had visited it fewer than two dozen times. He took his friend to the kitchen. It was empty, but as soon as they sat on the floor, a few monks entered followed by the head monk. Min got up rather frantically and bowed. The monks knew Min was a servant from Mr. O's household and that he was born with numbed tongue, but who was this amazing-looking creature whose stare gave them goose bumps? His appearance shocked the monks, the head monk could see plainly, although no one gasped. He had heard about the new religion that missionaries had brought, promising salvation without effort and everlasting life in heaven, and that the most converts were peasants for it promoted equality of the classes.

As was the custom at the temples, no questions were asked, and all present were fed. Min made eye contact with Blane to make sure he didn't worry about anything.

In the middle of the meal, Blane fainted. The head monk picked him up like a feather and carried him to a room behind the main hall and laid him on a cotton mat. The head monk peeled Blane's eyes open and inspected them. Then noticing his feet, he went out with a novice monk who immediately heated the room with split wood. The head monk came back with a concoction of oil and juice from the stems of common plants to put onto Blane's feet.

Min slipped into the main hall by stealth, vaguely remembering how he had fallen asleep behind the statue of the Buddha at the age of seven or eight. Mistress Kim had kowtowed without a break all that afternoon.

The Buddha he remembered seemed to have shrunken. But the smell, he had to close his eyes to fish out the scene that it evoked. But he couldn't. He sat in the middle of the floor and observed the visage of the Buddha. His mind gradually drifted to Nani and her frown that made him think she was concerned about him. And then to Mirae and her hideous laughter. It had tortured him to say the least. She had ignored him whenever they had run into each other. Then recently she was sitting by the well. Watching her from behind, Min could tell she was crying. He went close and tapped on her shoulder. She turned around and got up. He was ready to hug her. Her eyes were brimming with tears, but then she laughed like she was mad. Suddenly she spat on him saying, "Don't you ever come near me!" Min turned around and left her. He realized he had absolutely no feelings for her. It was Nani he had loved and would always love. Would she forgive him for having been with Mirae? He wasn't entirely sure. Someday he would have to tell her about his misconduct.

Someone tapped on him. It was a novice monk. He said it was dinnertime. Wouldn't he want to come with his friend? Min was dazed. He must have dozed off. It was the sweetest sleep he'd had in months. He got up and went to see Blane who was sound asleep. Thinking that his friend needed sleep more than anything, he didn't bother to wake him. Instead he lay next to him and fell asleep so deeply that he couldn't remember anything he dreamed the next morning when he awoke.

After breakfast, the head monk gave Min a pouch full of money. On the way down he handed it to Blane who wept before he took it. The only thing he had that was worth something was his gold ring from his grandmother. And frankly he didn't know if that would pay for his fare back to his homeland.

Both young men were full of energy. They walked down fast, humming. The sun felt good on their shoulders. The world issued a new morning like a present, and the noisy chirping of the birds rendered giddiness in the young men's throbbing hearts.

It was all her fault, Mistress Yee said regretfully, blowing her nose in her handkerchief. "As the saying goes, the darkest spot resides in the shadow right under the lamp. I didn't know I was breeding an enemy in my own home," she sobbed, referring to her negligence in overseeing her maid. After Mirae had been expelled with a restraining order, Mistress Yee promised Mr. O that she would be more careful in the future.

She had interviewed a few dozen applicants for the position in the past several months. But no one so far was good enough. Young ones were too young, old women were too old, some were too ugly, some were too fat, some were too skinny, some seemed too lazy, and so on. Mistress Yee didn't realize it, but she was looking for someone like Mirae.

The rumors about Mirae varied. Some said she had died in the mountains. Some said she had married a merchant and left for the North.

Amid all the rumors about her, Mirae had gone home, if she could call it home. Her father had not been known, and her mother had died when she was little, but she had an aunt. They had lived together until the aunt placed Mirae with Mistress Yee and married a widower twice as old as she was. He was an oil presser and owned a shop in the capital city.

When Mirae found her aunt's house behind the oil shop, she collapsed on the wooden sidewalk in front of it. A shopper with her baby on her back gasped. Another shopper asked, horrified, "Is she dead?" The oil presser immediately said, "No! She is alive." And he carried Mirae inside his house behind the shop.

"Come on out!" he shouted.

Mirae's aunt, Gomsun, came out of the sliding door, frowning. "Stop yelling. The twins are sleeping!" she squealed, pulling up and tying her skirt around her chest. "What on earth is that?" she asked, looking at her husband, who was carrying a young woman on his back.

"I have no idea. She just fell in front of our shop. Do something about it," he said, unloading Mirae in the yard. Then he hurried back to the shop, where now more people gathered to hear about the woman who had collapsed and died right there, moments earlier.

Gomsun came close, unconcerned, and examined Mirae. She didn't recognize her niece. They hadn't seen each other for some years. Gomsun tapped on her and said, "Open your eyes and speak."

Feebly, Mirae said, "Aunt Gomsun." And she lost consciousness again.

"Oh, my little Mirae!" Gomsun shouted. "What has happened to you?" she wailed. She shook her niece and poured a gourd of cold water on her face. And Mirae twitched her lips, but she didn't wake. Gomsun dragged her up to the entrance floor and cried, "My little Mirae! What's happened to you?"

Her twin boys woke up and cried. Ignoring them, Gomsun rushed to the shop, turned around to come back to fetch her twins, and then ran to the local doctor.

"Oh, Dr. Chun, please. Please, you must come with me," Gomsun said noisily.

"Calm down and explain what's going on," the old doctor said, twiddling with his long white beard.

"My niece, you see, I have a niece," she said. "I haven't seen her for so long. Anyhow, she is sick. She has just arrived in the heat. She collapsed and doesn't seem to want to wake up," Gomsun cried.

Dr. Chun got up slowly and said, "Go ahead and go. I will come soon. Make her drink water."

"Please hurry," Gomsun said, reluctantly stepping out of the house.

Gomsun walked, looking back every now and then to see if the doctor was following. When she spotted the ancient doctor with his errand boy as she turned around at the East Gate Marketplace, she felt relieved. So she cursed all the way home. Business hadn't been good lately, and a funeral would mean no business for a few days. She and her husband couldn't afford that.

When she arrived home, she found Mirae still lying on the floor, but she was now conscious.

"What happened? Is this my little Mirae?" Gomsun sat down and laid her twins on the floor. She rubbed Mirae's cheeks and cried. "Why, you are a woman now!"

Mirae closed her eyes.

"Poor thing," Gomsun said. "What happened?" Gomsun asked curiously. "How's your mistress?"

Mirae opened her eyes and turned her head around to face the wall. Her eyes were burning at the mention of "your mistress."

Dr. Chun arrived with his errand boy. He closed his eyes and felt Mirae's pulse. He finally said, "She is exhausted. Her kidneys are very weak. Recently, she has experienced a stressful event. She needs rest and good food. Above all, though, she needs to feel better about things in general."

"Whatever happened to her skin?" Gomsun asked. That was the first thing she had noticed.

"Recently I suffered from a skin disease. Some said it was chicken pox. But the herbalist who concocted brew for me said it wasn't. His remedy didn't work very well, though," Mirae said.

"You had chicken pox when you were a baby!" her aunt said.

"Did I?" Mirae felt relieved. Then obviously it was nothing permanent. Her scars would go away. She closed her eyes and sighed.

"Too much heat in her system. Cold cucumber soup. Kelp soup, radish, black sesame seeds, watermelon, and berries. These are all good things for her. Apply black sesame oil to her skin. The scars will disappear gradually. I will send my boy back with some herbs. Brew them and let her take it three times a day for the next forty days," Dr. Chun said.

Gomsun converted forty days of herbal brew into currency in her mind. And she said, "Forty days! She is just exhausted from the long trip in the heat. She is young. I am sure she will recover soon."

"If she had been old like me, she would have died. Her kidneys are very weak. Her condition will affect her liver if it's not taken care of immediately," the doctor warned her. He left with his errand boy.

Gomsun ran after them to say something about the cost of the medicine. But she only ended up saying, "Thank you, Dr. Chun. Thank you for coming."

That evening, Gomsun and her husband had a fight under their blanket. How in the world are we to feed another mouth? That was her husband's point. And Gomsun was frustrated. She agreed with him, but still she felt offended. None of the visitors from his side of the family had ever caused a conflict so serious as this between them. So she turned around and stopped speaking to her husband altogether.

Mirae drank the brew and ate some rice with steamed radish. She couldn't sleep that night; she listened to her aunt argue with her husband. There were seven children in the house, aged between zero and eight, and five of them were sleeping with Mirae in the same room. Some of them snored, some of them ground their teeth, one talked in her dreams, and another sleepwalked.

"How long are you staying, my darling Mirae?" Gomsun asked the next morning at breakfast. Her husband was roasting sesame seeds in a huge cylindrical container on the stove in the preparation room.

Mirae didn't reply.

After the argument with her husband the previous night, Gomsun had thought that Mirae could work to pay for her room and board.

"It's not that you are unwelcome here. I just thought you might want to keep busy. Energy begets energy, if you know what I'm saying. And we always need helping hands here," Gomsun said, stuffing her mouth with rice.

Mirae didn't speak for a few days, which baffled Gomsun and her husband. But she did work. She got up early in the morning to help roast the seeds and nuts. Taking a gigantic wooden spatula, she stirred them occasionally, staring at the fire burning tempestuously in the stove. She also helped with packaging the various oils. She cleaned the preparation room at the end of the day. In the evening when she cleaned, she applied leftover black sesame oil to her skin and thought about what to do with her life. Surely she wouldn't be an apprentice at the oil shop for too long.

When she was finished with the herbal medicine, Mirae looked refreshed and healthy again. Gomsun sent her out to the shop to be the shop assistant, and sales doubled within a few days. Some customers came just to look at her. Gomsun was ecstatic. She and her husband counted their money under the blanket every night now, giggling and clapping instead of arguing about their unexpected long-term visitor. One day, Gomsun's husband brought home a pair of new shoes and some blue fabric for Mirae. He said, "For all your work." And he grinned self-consciously.

Stupefied, Gomsun stood there with her jawbone unfastened. She wanted to yell at someone, but she couldn't decide whom she was angry with. Her husband was the kind who didn't remember her birthday, let alone buy presents for her. But she just said, smiling, to her niece, "The blue suits you well, sweetheart." But on the way to the seamstress's, not far from the oil shop, Gomsun asked coldly what Mirae's plan was for the future.

"There is someone waiting for me back in the country," Mirae said.

Gomsun turned around and said, "Oh, really?"

"It was a joke, Auntie. Go in. I want you to get yourself measured for an outfit. Blue isn't really my color. You have it," Mirae said, smiling.

"Oh, how kind of you. But are you sure?" Gomsun said.

"I am dead sure. Your husband bought it for you, really. But then, to be polite, he offered it to me," Mirae said.

Gomsun decided to believe that. She was measured for a skirt.

On the way back, Mirae confessed, "I am thinking about leaving."

"Oh no! Why?"

"Would you like me to stay?" Mirae asked.

Gomsun didn't quite know what to say. Did she want her pretty niece to stay or to leave?

"Why, of course! You are the only blood relative I've got. I want you to live with us the rest of my life," Gomsun declared, surprising herself.

"How nice of you, Auntie. Then I need to go back and fetch my stuff at Mistress Yee's house. But I need some money for the travel," Mirae said. "I will pay you back later by working in the shop."

"I will pay for your travel expenses, naturally," Gomsun said, imagining herself in the blue outfit.

"But your husband would be angry," Mirae said cautiously.

"I won't tell him then," she assured her niece.

Back in the shop, Mirae thanked Gomsun's husband for his generosity.

"Whatever you need," he said, smiling.

"I just told Auntie I was going back to my previous employer to collect what I left there. May I borrow some money for my travels? I will come back and work harder than before," Mirae said.

"Of course I will. No need to pay it back. Just don't tell your aunt. She is obsessed with money. She loves money more than she loves me," he said and laughed.

"I won't tell her anything," Mirae said, smiling brightly.

33

Something interesting needed to happen or else Mistress Yee was going to die of the doldrums. Every day was the same. Her husband was preoccupied with the housekeeping business all of a sudden. Her maids were stupid. Mirae, she now realized, was irreplaceable. Many interviews with candidates from all over the province had convinced her of that. And the weather was gorgeous, making her extra fidgety.

She and her husband sat together, drinking tea and eating a red bean snack.

"I think I need to do a good deed so Buwon will recover speedily," Mistress Yee said.

Mr. O reluctantly accepted her proposal.

So the next day Mistress Yee set off in a carriage to the largest harbor city on the west coast of the peninsula. She was accompanied by Nani and two male armed servants. Cherry trees blossomed as far as her eye could see. She couldn't remember the last time she had traveled. It was good to be away from home and to see new places. Life at home had recently been dreadfully tedious, with one shaman ritual after another to make the trapped spirit leave for the place where it belonged, and the endless visits from renowned doctors for her disabled son.

Buwon was able to crawl now and responsive with a smile to every sound. The size of his head had shrunk, but his upper lip was still deformed, and one of his legs was now obviously shorter than the other. Mistress Yee could not bring herself to feel connected to her son. She had begun to dread the afternoon visits with him. Often she made excuses not to see him at all.

Spring was her favorite season, every living thing competing for life and showing off its colors. Against her husband's warning of possible taunting or an attack by angry peasants, she took off her veil to let the pedestrians admire her beauty. People paid respect as they passed because she was dressed exquisitely and accompanied by a maid and servants.

After seeing what had happened to Mirae, Nani tensed up around Mistress Yee. She never knew when her mistress would erupt, accusing her of something she might or might not have done. But today Mistress Yee was in a good mood. She frequently asked Nani to pluck a certain flower and bring it to her. She would smell it and toss it away on the path.

When they finally arrived in the harbor city, where a large ship from China was docked, Mistress Yee waited at the pier while one of the male servants was making a deal with a fisherman.

"Nani, look at the men over there. Look at their hats." Mistress Yee giggled. "Is it true that Chinese men don't change their clothes until they wear out?" She looked at them with a curious expression.

"Go and smell them. Come back and tell me what they smell like," she ordered Nani.

Flabbergasted, Nani blushed at her mistress's ridiculous request.

"Go and smell them, I said!" Mistress Yee snapped, fanning herself vigorously.

"Yes, Mistress," Nani said and slowly made her way toward the seamen buying their lunch at an open grill.

The vendor spoke fluent Chinese. Nani was mesmerized by the intonations of the language. One of the men asked her something, which she couldn't comprehend, and she ran back to her mistress, a little frightened. Mistress Yee watched her maid, amused.

"So?" she asked.

"They smelled like fish," Nani managed to say.

"*Everything* smells like fish here, you idiot!" Mistress Yee said. But she didn't go on scolding her, for a bearded vendor, trying to sell a pearl, distracted her.

☽ ○ ☾

"Yes, three thousand fish," the male servant said.

Shocked, the fisherman repeated, "Three thousand fish?"

"Yes, my lady wants three thousand fish to be freed," he emphasized.

"I've got ten buckets of sardines here. Could be a thousand fish altogether. I will go and catch some more," the copper-faced fisherman said. The most recent time this had happened to him it was a childless woman, but she wanted to buy only one hundred fish to free. People who believe in an afterlife should do this a little more often, he thought. Some people believed that the fish could have been people in past lives. That meant if they freed the fish, then they would receive blessing from saving lives and their own wishes would come true in return.

"Let me ask my lady if she agrees to that," the servant said and returned to Mistress Yee.

"No, we don't have time for him to go and catch more fish. Get another man with three thousand fish," Mistress Yee snapped.

The male servant went back to the crowd of fishermen. The rumor had spread now, so everyone wanted to talk to the rich lady's servant, offering his deal. Finally, three fishermen put their fish together, claiming that the total was three thousand. Mistress Yee demanded that they count them. They dutifully counted out three thousand fish.

One of the fishermen took Mistress Yee and Nani on his boat. He rowed some distance away from the pier and said, "This is a good spot, my lady."

"Let them out," Mistress Yee ordered.

The fisherman poured two buckets into the deep green water, saying, "Long live the sardines!"

The sun was brilliant and the fish were swimming around the boat in a frenzy.

"Save that one," Mistress Yee said, pointing to one of the sardines in the third and last bucket.

"What for, my lady?" the fisherman asked, puzzled.

"So I can have it for lunch," she said, grinning mischievously.

"But—" he said and stopped. Didn't she want to save the lives of these fish for her own blessing?

Suddenly, Mistress Yee looked up and saw a figure intently looking down from the ship that was about to depart. It was Blane.

The sun blinded her. She looked down to balance herself. She looked up again, but now there was no one. She looked at the sardine that she planned to eat. It flipped helplessly in the slippery tin bucket. She looked up once again and thought for a moment. And then she freed the last sardine on a nameless impulse.

"That was good, my lady," the fisherman said, pleased.

"Nani, do you see someone up there?" Mistress Yee asked.

"No, mistress," Nani said, squinting her eyes. But she saw someone else on the pier as she spoke.

The fisherman poured out the contents of the third bucket. Then he rowed Mistress Yee and Nani back to shore. The small boat docked, and Mistress Yee got off the boat with the help of the fisherman. He smelled bad.

"Take me to a good place to eat. I am starving," Mistress Yee said to her male servants, who were waiting for her at the pier. The Chinese men were boarding, and there was an announcement, accompanied by a drum, that the ship was departing in a short while.

Nani, meanwhile, had her eyes trained on Min. He was still standing on the deck, his head lowered.

The male servants took Mistress Yee and Nani to a small restaurant with a fine reputation. It was a part of a rather small but fancy inn. Mistress Yee was served poached bass, and Nani made an excuse to leave her for a moment. Outside, the male servants were having steamed mussels.

Nani knew that Min would be watching for her from some-place around there, so she walked rapidly to a less crowded area. Min caught up with her in no time. His clothes in tatters, he reeked of stale sweat and who knew what.

"What on earth are you doing here?" she asked.

Min groaned and explained briefly with hand gestures, but he had no way to describe Blane's appearance. So he skipped that part, but Nani got the gist of his message.

"You are going around helping other people when *you* are in great need of help? Do you know what happened to Mirae?" Nani frowned. "She got eighty lashes of the whip. That was some time ago, right after you disappeared. She's been kicked out of the house. All we know is that she might be dead," Nani said, without telling him about the nature of Mirae's punishment.

Tears welled up in Nani's eyes. Min looked at her, con-cerned. He thought that she feared what might happen to her in the future. But Nani was remembering something that Mirae had said. After the beating, Mirae was locked in the storage room with her wrists and feet tied up. Nani brought her ointment for her bruises and something to drink. She dug a pebble out of Mirae's mouth with her fingers. The smooth stone had been forced into it before the beating to prevent her from screaming or biting her tongue to commit suicide. She fed her the broth. Mirae drank it and then said, "I ate your boy." At first, Nani thought that Mirae was delirious. But Mirae's look of malicious glee quickly changed Nani's mind. Humiliated and most notoriously abused, Mirae wanted to pass the pain on to someone else. "Dig your own grave," Nani spat coldly. As she got up, Mirae began to laugh hysterically. She taunted Nani with details of her dalliance with Min. Even after Nani had left the storage room, Mirae went on telling the story, knowing that Nani was behind the door, listening with heart-piercing pain.

Nani wanted to say many things but couldn't say a word. Min stood there, wiggling his big toe, which peeped out of his straw shoe. His state was no better than that of a beggar. He was looking over at the man who whetted knives and tools for the fishermen. The blade he was honing on the whetstone glinted in the sun.

"I am going," Nani warned him.

Min didn't turn to look at her.

She pulled his sleeve to get his attention. "I am leaving," Nani said, placing a coin in his sleeve. But Min refused to take it. He had money left after he had paid the ship fare for Blane. He pulled out a pouch from inside his trousers and showed the money to her.

"Where did you get it?" she asked suspiciously. But she couldn't linger any longer. Mistress Yee might be looking for her.

"What are you going to do now?" Nani asked, thinking that she didn't care what he did with his life. But she choked on her words and tears rolled down her cheeks.

Min shook her shoulder and looked into her eyes. He wanted to live there with her.

"I can't stay here with you," Nani said. If only he had asked her the year before! She would have gladly gone with him to the ends of the earth. But now she felt differently.

"Don't let Mistress Yee see you. Her servants can catch you instantly. You know how she is. She's gotten worse. Go! And don't follow me," Nani said.

Min went over to a vendor who sold rice malt pumpkin candy, and bought a few candies. He offered them to Nani.

"Go," Nani said again, taking only one. If they were meant to be together, they would meet again like two rivers at a confluence. She turned toward the restaurant. Min didn't follow her.

Mistress Yee was taking a short nap in the private room where she had dined. The low table had been removed. Nani sat on the attached bench before the entrance to the private room, staring at her mistress's shoes. Suddenly, she conjured up the sharp pain that she had felt when Mistress Yee whacked her head with a shoe on the night of the first shamanic ritual. Nani had become Mistress Yee's favorite dartboard.

Thinking of Min in rags, filthy from head to toe, Nani felt a pang in the middle of her chest, but she didn't feel like chasing after him. When Mirae had revealed their frivolous affair, Nani had cursed him to hell. She realized now, though, that she didn't hate him. On the contrary, she thought that she would always love him. For the first time, she realized that she didn't have to live in the same nest with a person in order to love him.

Mistress Yee woke up with a sharp pain in her abdomen. A doctor was summoned to the inn to check on her, and a messenger on a horse was sent to deliver a message to Mr. O that his wife was staying another day in the harbor city due to her illness.

After a treatment of acupuncture and herbal medicine, Mistress Yee fell asleep rather early that evening, and the male servants snuck out to an open pub by the water where squid catchers were getting ready for night fishing.

☽　○　☾

Nani went out to see if by chance Min was still around. And there he was, standing under the eave of a large store that sold souvenirs for foreign seamen and travelers. The store still had its lights on. When he spotted Nani, Min was so glad that his face turned tragic.

"Did you have dinner?" Nani asked him.

Rubbing his tummy, he nodded. Earlier he had grilled sardines and a bowl of rice.

They strolled on the pier, but there were too many drunkards, so they walked down to the shore where mussels covered the rocks and seaweed gathered thickly around their feet.

Min pulled something from his pouch. It was a jade necklace. Nani looked at it. She had never owned such finery.

"What good is a jade necklace to a maid!" she said sarcastically, her eyes still fixed on the pretty stone.

He put it around her neck, and Nani didn't protest. They sat down on a dry spot among many empty shells.

Nani wanted to ask him whether what Mirae had said about a passionate fling was true.

Min wanted to hold Nani. When Min joined the subversive peasant group to fight against the aristocrats, he had given up his future with Nani. He had purposefully stayed away from her, but now that he had defected from the movement, he wanted her again. When he was ordered to set Mr. O's house on fire, he couldn't bring himself to do it because Nani was there. He didn't want to be a hero. His dream turned out to be small: he wanted to be happy. And he couldn't imagine happiness without Nani.

Mirae couldn't have made up the story about Min. Nani mentally reviewed all the things that Mirae had said to her. Every word had pierced her heart, and all of those words were still there. They had taken up residence in her heart.

After he had put Blane on the ship, he had been planning to return to Mr. O's house and elope with Nani. Meeting her in this harbor city had served to show him, once more, that Nani was his fate.

There was now no noise but the soothing waves, spreading their foamy blanket again and again. The air felt cool and calm. Nani was tired. Min stretched his arm around her shoulder. Nani allowed it, but she realized that she was no longer desperate for his touch.

Min groaned, pulling her closer to him. But Nani untangled herself from his arms. She said, "I am not going to be your wife."

Min stared at her, overcome with desire. When he had been with Mirae, he had felt disgusted and good at the same time. He pulled Nani close to him and tried to kiss her. Nani slapped him and said, "Idiot, it's too late!" She ran away as fast as she could, but she didn't go back to the restaurant right away. She saw squid catchers unloading their boats at the pier. Thousands of squid spilled out from the net onto a large mat. She asked one of the fishermen how many squid she could free with a silver coin. "Thirty," he said. So she freed thirty squid while making a wish.

WHEN THE MESSENGER ON HORSEBACK FROM THE WEST coast set out to Mistress Yee's house to inform her husband, Mr. O had already left for a meeting. All the landlords in the region, with several military officers from the capital city, gathered in a private house to discuss important matters over a late luncheon.

Good-looking maids brought in exquisitely arranged food and drinks and placed them on the low tables. Musicians played ancient instruments from a pavilion in the middle of a pond filled with colorful carp and lotuses bursting into full bloom. It was a closed courtyard, providing perfect acoustics, and from all four sides one could see the musicians and the other visitors. The banquet was sumptuous. Kisengs, professional entertainers who covered their faces with fans, were there to serve the drinks, to tell tales, and to get pinched by the naughty powerful men.

One of the officers gestured to the musicians to lower the volume, so only the flutist was now playing; his tune was as ethereal as the sudden blooms of flowers in the spring season.

"His Highness is concerned about the riots of the so-called peasant revolutionary group here in our region. Most of the members have been captured and beheaded, but some are still around, indoctrinating innocent people. And this is what brings us here together," the officer began.

"In the capital city, we have implemented a new rule that the immediate family of these criminal peasants be stripped of their possessions, and be ineligible for employment," another officer said.

"And how may we strip them of their possessions? Do we need to do this by ourselves or do we hire government officers?" a landlord from a neighboring village asked. It brought some laughter around the table.

"We will be providing one officer per one hundred inhabitants. This village, exceeding one thousand inhabitants, will receive ten officers before the moon begins to wax," the same officer announced.

"In the capital city, we hang the heads of the dead peasants at the entrance of the village as a deterrent," another officer said.

By this time, not many landlords were listening. Most of them were getting red in the face, and their limbs were relaxed; some of them were making clandestine eye contact with the fan-covered kisengs.

Small conversations broke out in layers while the officer talked loudly at the prominent landlords about various schemes for preventing further riots.

"Who is that girl over in the corner?" asked a landlord with a beard.

In the society of kisengs, there was a strict rule that newcomers were not permitted to engage in conversations with men at a party, unless, of course, the men they were serving initiated the conversation.

"She is a newcomer. Needs much training," a middle-aged kiseng, named Dimple, replied quickly and poured another bowl of ginseng wine to distract Lord Ahn.

"What is her name?" he persisted.

"She is called Pumpkin," replied Dimple, smiling.

It was also customary that one didn't go by one's real name in the world of kisengs. Each girl had a pseudonym, which she picked when she joined the society. The pretty girl's pseudonym wasn't Pumpkin, but Dimple was playing with the landlords. As expected, the men laughed, examining Pumpkin's hand, which held her fan, and her shoulders, which were encased in silk the color of an orange azalea.

"Exceptional looking!" Lord Ahn exclaimed.

Some kisengs giggled.

"Amuse us with a story," he suggested to no one in particular.

Dimple began quickly, "Once upon a time, there was a woman hauling water at a well. A general came her way and asked her for some water. He was returning from a battlefield, weary and spent. The woman took a gourd and filled it only half full, and then took a few leaves from a willow branch to drop on the water. The general, very thirsty and impatient, was incensed. He threw the gourd to the ground and chided the woman severely for her odd behavior. He asked once again for water. She did exactly the same, leaves afloat in a half-full gourd. She explained that there was no remedy for choking on water. So she wanted him to drink slowly, blowing the leaves away from his mouth which would slow down his gulping. The general was impressed and grateful for her wisdom. He took her to be his wife."

They all clapped.

Lord Ahn pursued his quarry: "How about you, Pumpkin?"

Pumpkin thought for a moment and said, "I heard this story quite recently."

Caught by the familiar voice, Mr. O, who sat near Lord Ahn, turned around to hear the story.

"Once there was an evil concubine whose jealousy soared up above the sky, for the mistress of the house was having a baby," Pumpkin began. The gentlemen gave her their undivided attention. "She asked her faithful maid to go and make a voodoo doll. The maid didn't know what it was for, but her mistress wanted her to make one, so she did. The concubine pierced the doll with a needle between its legs and gave it to the maid to bury behind the quarters of the mistress of the house. The maid then realized what her mistress was up to, but she did as she was told, for a maid has no choice. The mistress of the house died after she gave birth. Sometime later, a dog unearthed the doll. The master of the house wanted to know what it all meant. The concubine accused her faithful maid of the crime. But the wise master of the house said, 'She is your maid and does what you tell her to do. She might have buried the doll, but the idea must have come from you. So you are the guilty one.' The master ordered eighty lashes for the wicked concubine and sent her away." Pumpkin trembled slightly as she ended the story.

The men applauded.

"That was a great story," said Lord Ahn. "Don't you think so?" he asked Mr. O, who was unable to utter a word for his heart was pounding so loudly.

Mr. O was aghast. He was at once ashamed, and all he hoped was to leave the place as soon as the meeting was over.

"How about you, Mr. O?" said Lord Ahn. He was asking for a story.

"Oh, I will pass. I am not much of a storyteller," he replied uncomfortably, his face reddening.

"What's Pumpkin's real name?" asked Lord Ahn.

Dimple raised her eyebrows in alarm and sulked, "Master, don't you like Dimple anymore? I am going to cry if you let me down."

He laughed, pleased.

Mr. O watched Mirae behind her fan and was impressed with how similar she was to his wife. They had the same body shape and crimson lips and shiny, pitch-black hair. They both carried themselves with aloofness. But he had to say that Mirae—for now he was convinced that the woman was indeed his former maid—was even prettier. Why hadn't he noticed that while they had inhabited under the same roof?

At the end of the party, Lord Ahn got up and reluctantly walked out, turning back once or twice to see Mirae again. But Dimple took his arm and saw him off. Other kisengs were also seeing off the visitors. Mirae sat in the room while the maids came in to clear the tables.

Mr. O got up and went close to Mirae, dropped the pouch he had on his waist, and said, "I want to compensate you for my misjudgment."

Mirae looked down at the gold coins that spilled out of the blue silk pouch and then looked up without hesitation. Her eyes were fiery. She smiled suddenly and said, "If Master would like to soothe my scarred heart, he should grant me the ring on his finger for me to live by."

"The gold coins in the pouch amount to more in value than the ring," he said. But Mirae didn't reply. Mr. O was moved. This maid, who could have had Lord Ahn, the richest man in the province, was in love with him! He blushed. Mirae smiled coquettishly, taking his hand to gently wriggle the ring off his finger. At her electrifying touch, he parted his lips involuntarily. As he caressed her hair clumsily, his lungs expanded, making him feel that he was above the floor.

Dimple came in abruptly to have warning words with Mirae, but upon finding her flirting with Mr. O, she was jubilant.

"Ah, Lord O, you are one step ahead of everyone!" she exclaimed excitedly. "This is Cherry Blossom. Her beauty could melt the heart of the toughest samurai on the neighboring island," she babbled.

Mr. O stood like a broomstick, not knowing what to say. The situation was unfamiliar to him.

"Please, Lord O. Let me know what you would like. If you would like to have a meeting with Cherry Blossom, I can arrange it. Just name the time and the date," she said, twisting the end of his sleeve.

He forced an awkward laugh because he thought it was the right moment to laugh, but it did not make him feel more comfortable. He hurried out, still laughing awkwardly. As he got on his horse, he had a hunch he wasn't going to be able to sleep that night.

When he got home, the news awaited him from the west coast that his wife would be delayed by a day, due to a violent stomachache. He was relieved.

35

DUBAK'S WIFE, JAYA, CAME HOME FROM THE OPEN MAR-
ket feeling furious. A vendor had refused to sell to her, accusing her of having killed her mother-in-law. "You stuffed the old
woman with sticky rice cake," he shouted, attracting attention
from the shoppers and other venders. And it hadn't been the
first time she was humiliated in public by a stranger. She cried,
screwing up her face, when she got home. Her neighbor was
babysitting her son, but Jaya didn't feel like picking him up
right away. Instead, she sat on the floor where red peppers
were drying on a straw mat. She had been going out of her
way to make interesting dinners for Dubak after the funeral
of his mother. He hadn't really forgiven her for who knew
what, and he still had his doubts which he could use against
her should an occasion arise. But for now, his wife was feeding him well—the gods only knew how she managed to, with
their meager household budget—and she cooperated in bed
pretty much every time he was stiff before dawn. She used to
push him away, hitting him between the legs with a pillow and
complaining that it was an insane hour for such activity.

Today, Jaya had visited the market because she heard the
news of the squid arriving from the west coast. Dubak loved
seafood, but it was hard to get it, except in the spring, when
the road from the west coast was no longer frozen and the
weather was not too hot to make everything go bad immediately. Jaya had meant to stuff squid with ground-up soybeans,
greens, and chopped carrots, and steam them on the cooking
rice. She would have sliced the colorful dish and arranged it
artfully. The taste would have cheered up any sulking heart.

But now she saw her stupidity plain and clear. It didn't matter how hard she worked to make sure her husband wouldn't try to stab her again. The whole village was bloodthirsty.

"You can have my innocent blood," she said and took a rope made of straw.

She walked over to the totem poles at the entrance to the village. She lowered her head and proclaimed that she was innocent. She had fed her mother-in-law rice cake, true, but who could have predicted that the old woman would choke and die like that? Jaya cried mournfully, telling the totem poles once again that she was innocent. It was true that her senile mother-in-law, who had wanted to be served a meal every time she turned around because she had forgotten she had just eaten, was a nuisance. Whenever Dubak came home, the mother complained that Jaya starved her. And sometimes she did starve her, but just a little. Who could have withstood such a mother-in-law? She had done a decent job taking care of her. When her mother-in-law choked on the rice cake, she didn't know what to do but watch her die. She tried to pour water into her mother-in-law's mouth, but it was no use. She turned blue and ceased breathing.

Jaya wiped her eyes and said accusingly, "I am going to kill myself to teach the villagers a lesson. *They* will be the murderers!" She prayed that she would be reborn a bird, never again a woman, a poor woman. And then she turned around and walked to the twin pine trees. She threw the rope over a branch of one. She tied a knot and stuck her head in so the rope went around her neck. Holding the other end of the rope, she began to pull. She jumped and pulled the rope at the same time, and she felt it suddenly tightening on her neck. She was just slightly above the ground, but it was enough to choke anyone to death.

Mistress Yee's carriage was just passing the totem poles, and the servants stopped when they heard the sudden thud

coming from over by the twin pine trees. The branch couldn't
endure the weight of a pregnant woman: it broke and Jaya fell
on the ground. She was moaning. Nani ran over and found
what had happened.

"Have you lost your mind!" she exclaimed.

☽ ○ ☾

From the carriage, Mistress Yee inquired after the noise and
why the servants were stopping. One of them said that there
was a woman crying under the twin pine trees. The other said
it might be Dubak's wife.

"That's not a reason to stop!" Mistress Yee cried from inside.
Her legs had been cramped for so long. She wanted to get
home as soon as possible.

The male servants hollered to Nani to come back as they
were walking away.

"My water broke!" screamed Jaya.

"Oh no!" Nani didn't know what that meant, but it seemed
like an emergency.

Nani ran to the male servants and announced that she had
to look after Jaya.

Nani was frightened and asked Jaya if she should run and
get Mrs. Wang.

Jaya said that she would be dead by the time Mrs. Wang
arrived. And then she began to scream from the extraordinary
pain. Her contractions began and her labor proceeded rapidly.

Nani trembled for a minute and then calmed down as the
contraction momentarily subsided. She had witnessed two
births. And she remembered what Mrs. Wang had done with
Mistress Yee. Nani pulled a handkerchief out of her sack, folded
it into a ball, and stuffed it into Jaya's mouth.

Jaya spat it out and said, "What the hell! I am no Mrs. Kim.
I will scream as much as I want!" Tears oozed out of the

corners of her eyes. "Look, I want you to tie the other end of this rope around the pine tree, will you?"

Nani did as told, instinctively understanding what it was for. Much sooner than she had anticipated, the pain returned to torture Jaya. Nani offered Jaya her wrist to hold, as she had done for Mistress Kim, but Jaya held onto the rope and pulled it with enough strength to uproot the tree. She screamed like an animal, tormented by an invisible enemy. Nani clenched her teeth and wiped the sweat off Jaya's forehead and chest.

"Nani, here it comes! Pull!" Jaya screamed.

Jaya pushed. The baby's head emerged. Jaya pushed again. At the third push, the whole bloody boy came out, and Nani caught him. She held the squirming body in her hands. She couldn't help but shed tears as she carefully wrapped the wet, wrinkled newborn in her handkerchief.

"Nani, give me the baby and run to my home. Get a pair of scissors and bring them to me," she said.

Nani ran. Then she stopped. She didn't have to go to Jaya's house. She should just run to the closest house.

She ran into Quince's house and yelled, "Anyone home?"

Quince looked out from her kitchen, unimpressed. "What's the fuss?" She got up when she saw Nani's bloody hands and shirt.

"Jaya had her baby by the twin pine trees. I need a pair of scissors, quick!" Nani said frantically.

At the mention of Jaya's name, Quince snorted and said, "I'd be a dog if I helped her."

"A dog knows when to bark and when to whimper. If you don't help a woman who's just had a baby, you are no better than a dog. Give me a pair of scissors right now or else you won't be working for Mr. O anymore. And your husband: he just returned from the west coast, escorting Mistress Yee. I will go over now and tell Mistress Yee that he no longer wants to be employed. Should I do that?" Nani shot her an indignant glare.

Quince laughed. But there was no need to cross Nani. Her large buttocks jiggled as she stepped up on the stone step to her room to see if her sewing box was there. She pulled out a pair of scissors from a woven basket and handed them to Nani. "Calm down, child. Nothing bad is going to happen. Once the baby's out, the baby's fine."

"Give me a sheet or something to wrap the baby with," Nani demanded. "I had only a handkerchief."

"Sure." Quince pulled a dry sheet from a clothesline and folded it into a small square. "What did she have?" Quince asked. Her tone was suddenly intimate and interested.

"It's a boy," Nani said, showing mild annoyance.

Remembering what Mrs. Wang had done, Nani went to the kitchen and dipped the scissors in water briefly. Then she put them in the fire for a few moments until they stopped sizzling. And then she dashed out.

She cut the umbilical cord, feeling extremely anxious. She didn't know if it caused the baby or the mother any pain.

Jaya thanked Nani profusely and cried, remembering how she had tried to kill herself. She thought she would name her son Soseng, Rising from Death.

Nani walked home feeling proud. Her chest was wet with the sweat of exertion. But there was something that made her chest cold besides her own sweat. She touched it mindlessly and found the jade necklace. She held it in her palm for a moment and said out loud, "My dear boy, I wish you the best of luck."

36

MISTRESS YEE TOOK A LONG BATH. SOONYI SOAPED HER and washed her hair. The little maid wasn't up to her standard. She was a delicate sort for a maid, and Mistress Yee had to tell her what to do too many times. No one was like Mirae. She had given up on finding a maid like her. She was history now. But she couldn't help thinking about her now and then. Leaning back in the wooden tub, she closed her eyes and inhaled the fragrance from the dried iris petals floating in the water.

"Tell me, Soonyi, where did Master go yesterday?" she asked, her eyes still closed.

Soonyi, wondering why Mistress Yee didn't ask him herself, replied, "He went to a meeting at Lord Ryu's house. A messenger came after breakfast, and Master left when the sun was high."

"Tell me, when did he come home?" Mistress Yee asked.

"Sometime before dinner, Mistress," she replied timidly.

"You are such a bore," Mistress Yee said, opening her eyes. Mirae would have told her all that and much more without her asking. But she didn't have enough strength at the moment to whack Soonyi.

After the bath, Mistress Yee returned to her room. She was still very tired. She told Soonyi to go and tell Nani to make beef soup with mung bean sprouts and scallion. "Tell her not to make it too spicy this time," Mistress Yee said.

Soonyi lowered her head and dashed out. While walking toward the kitchen, she chanted, "Beef soup with mung bean sprouts and scallion. Don't make it too spicy." But when she arrived in the kitchen, she saw Nani in her bloody clothes. "Big Sister! What's happened to you?"

Nani smiled and said, "You silly, don't get excited about every bloody blouse you see. Some blood is a sign of a midwife. I just delivered a baby, Jaya's baby!" she announced proudly, stretching her chin up and out.

"Really?" Soonyi gasped.

"Yep," Nani said.

"How was it?"

"Scary. Interesting," Nani said. "It wasn't like the night when Mistress Kim had her baby. Jaya's baby burst out like ... chestnuts in the fire. Just like that. I even cut the umbilical cord for her," she bragged.

Soonyi stared at Nani, a little awestruck. Then she remembered Mistress Yee's message. "Oh, Big Sister, Mistress Yee wants beef soup for dinner," she said, wondering what it was that Mistress Yee had specified about the beef soup.

"I need to wash up and change," said Nani and rushed out of the kitchen.

Nani undressed in her room, and once again she touched the jade necklace. She took it off. She wrapped it in a cloth and placed it deep in a chest of drawers, among the things that had belonged to her mother. Suddenly, her legs wobbled. She collapsed on the floor and cried silently, missing Min. She couldn't swallow her own saliva, for her throat ached as if a fishbone had gotten stuck there. Finally, Min wanted her, but she didn't want him anymore. How did one change one's mind? If she could only change hers, she would do it and marry him and live happily. But she could not make herself do something she didn't want to do.

"Big Sister!" called Soonyi, opening the door. "Sorry," she said, seeing Nani still half naked and sitting on the floor.

"Close the door!" yelled Nani. She got up, washed, and got dressed quickly. She fixed her hair, looking at herself in Mistress Kim's palm-sized mirror. Mirae had taken it from Mistress Kim's room after she had passed away, and when she was kicked out of the house, she had forgotten to pack it in her bundle.

"Should I put the water on the stove?" Soonyi asked.

"No, peel a radish and cut it into small cubes. Peel a few cloves of garlic and crush them too," said Nani.

Soonyi was still chopping the radish when Nani arrived in the kitchen. She wanted to make sure that the cubes of radish were identical in size.

Rolling her eyes, Nani snatched the knife and attacked the radish. She said, "When I'm thirsty, I'm better off if I go and get water instead of lying down on the ground with my mouth open, hoping it will rain. That's how slow you are."

Soonyi peeled the garlic cloves, pouting.

Nani tasted the first cube of radish and said, "Mmm, this is so sweet. Here, taste it, child."

Soonyi opened her mouth and took the radish. "It's good."

"Soonyi, I am sorry I was harsh, but if you want to survive as a maid and be respected you have to know what you are doing. If you wait until your superiors tell you what to do, they get tired of you. My mother used to tell me that you shouldn't *ask* the mistress what she would like for dinner; you should *tell* her what is for dinner. Of course, you have to come up with a dish she will like. But you need to train your superiors to appreciate what you cook and do. Do you understand?"

Soonyi nodded miserably.

"By the way, where is Quince? She is supposed to be here by now," Nani said, frowning. Ever since Mirae had left the house, Quince came in to help with cooking in addition to the laundry she had been doing every other day.

Nani was now making soybeans in a marinade of rice malt syrup, soy sauce, and sesame seeds.

"Slice the lotus root paper thin, and when you get a chance, pierce the pine nuts with the pine needles," Nani ordered her.

"How many pine nuts?" Soonyi asked blankly.

Nani looked at Soonyi and sighed.

"All right, all right," Soonyi said.

Quince came in then, and the first thing she said was, "I heard you actually managed to deliver Jaya's baby!"

Nani was proud, remembering the moment she had caught the baby. She forgot how frightened she had felt when she first held the slimy creature in her hands.

"Boy, Jaya was telling us all about how great you were!" Quince said. "I'm late because I took soup to her, and she was raving about you."

Nani blushed.

When the dinner was ready, the three of them carried various dishes on trays to Mistress Yee's quarters and arranged the dishes on a low table.

"Soonyi, soup to the right of the rice!" Nani whispered in a restrained voice, setting seven different kinds of sauces right in front of the soup bowls.

"When are you going to learn, Soonyi? Huh?" said Quince, guffawing like a man.

"Lower your voice!" Nani admonished her.

"Nani, do you know what we call you?" Quince asked. Soonyi turned red and fidgeted because everyone, herself included, referred to Nani by her nickname behind her back.

"Mother-in-law!" Quince said and laughed again boisterously.

Nani raised her eyebrows fiercely. At any moment, Mr. O would enter with his wife. So Nani bit her lip, suppressed her anger, and focused on the arrangement of the food on the table.

As they finished arranging the dishes, Mr. O entered. Nani dismissed Quince and Soonyi, who would go back to the kitchen, tidy up, and prepare the night snack. Nani remained to pour drinks and to listen to them fuss about the food and to provide explanations about why some things tasted a certain way and so on. A few moments later, Mistress Yee also entered. She sat with her husband. Nani took the covers from the rice bowls, poured the wine, and moved to the corner where she awaited instruction.

"So how was the trip?" Mr. O asked Mistress Yee.

"It was not easy. I thought you would run to me when you got the message that I was sick and therefore delayed," Mistress Yee said sulkily.

"When I was a boy, Dr. Choi said that if you had a stomachache from meat it would take a day to recover, but with seafood, if you didn't die immediately, it would take only one burp. So I was not worried," Mr. O replied.

As Mistress Yee lifted her spoon to take a bite of rice, she noticed what was in the beef soup. She placed her spoon back down on the table, and said, "What is this?"

"What's wrong?" Mr. O asked, looking over at the dishes on his wife's side.

"Come over here, Nani," ordered Mistress Yee. Her voice was cold and metallic.

"Yes, Mistress," Nani said, her neck perspiring.

"I asked for beef soup with scallion and mung bean sprouts!" Mistress Yee shouted.

"Mistress, we made a mistake. May I go and make beef soup with scallion and mung bean sprouts now?"

"And what am I supposed to do in the meantime?" Mistress Yee said scornfully. "One is a buffoon and the other a mental case. I really need a new maid," Mistress Yee complained. "Mirae always did exactly what I told her to do. She never failed to carry out my orders. What is the matter with all three of you? Not one of you girls has a head on her shoulders. I am going to start interviewing some more girls again and pick out a maid myself in a few days," Mistress Yee said.

For a while it had seemed taboo to mention Mirae's name in the house. But lately, Mistress Yee seemed to have forgotten all about why she had let Mirae go. She brought her up occasionally, as though what Mirae had done was not worth holding a grudge about.

"Leave us alone," Mr. O ordered Nani.

Nani got up gladly and left the room, closing the door behind her. But she stayed in the hallway between the room and the anteroom, in case she got called in again. She thought about what Quince had called her. That had come out of nowhere, considering that Nani was very kind and helpful to the other maids and the male servants. She frowned, thinking of Soonyi's lapse of memory about the beef soup. She was going to pinch Soonyi as soon as she saw her.

Mr. O rubbed his chin and said, "I am curious. You say that your previous maid always carried out your orders."

"She did. She even knew what I was thinking before I opened my mouth," Mistress Yee said and immediately flushed. "What are you trying to say?" she challenged Mr. O.

"If she did everything you asked her to do, she must have committed the evil deed according to your will," Mr. O said calmly, as if he had rehearsed his speech.

"What do you mean?" A blue river rose on one side of Mistress Yee's temple.

"I am just-just asking," Mr. O said awkwardly. He hadn't meant to argue with her about Mirae the maid. His mind raced to Mirae the kiseng. His heart quivered and his mouth dried up at the thought of her touch. The memory was so strong that it felt as though it had just happened.

"I see what you are getting at." Mistress Yee snorted. "I didn't mean to tell you this, but Mirae was in love with you. She wanted to get rid of Mistress Kim, and then me so that she could have you. I tried to awaken her from this impossible dream and lead her to goodness, but she was not made of honest material. She was already knee-deep in the swamp of her vanity. You saw what she had done with your own eyes the night when you were hiding in the room of your beloved first wife! By the way, I've been meaning to ask, why were you there in the dead woman's room?" Mistress Yee asked.

Mr. O didn't hear anything but "Mirae was in love with you."

"What are you thinking about?" Mistress Yee asked, frustrated at seeing her husband lost in his own thoughts while she was talking.

"No, no," he said distractedly.

"I asked why you were in her room," she said.

"Oh," he said, remembering. "Whatever the shaman said that evening made no sense to me, but I heard her voice. I heard her. Or at least I thought so. And my feet carried me there. I went inside. I sat where she used to sit. I felt the air curdle around my body. Soon I felt suffocated. I thought it was the old, moldy air in the room. But I know it was her. I was scared. I thought she was going to strangle me. I wanted to leave, but then I heard you talking with a maid. I wanted to know why you were there at that hour with a maid," he said.

"But you heard everything," Mistress Yee said.

"I did," he said.

"So what is it? What are you trying to say?" Her voice broke and her face turned miserable and furious.

"I don't suspect you. But when your maid was being beaten in the yard, tied up to a bench on her belly, water poured on her buttocks so that the clothing wouldn't protect against the sting of the cane, she said nothing," Mr. O pointed out.

"You think she is innocent? Is that what you are trying to say?" Mistress Yee cackled.

"The normal reaction from a maid would be to protest that she is not guilty or to beg and plead for forgiveness. She did nothing. She only glared at you without crying. Her eyes cursed you, which I found beyond insolent. An evil maid who took an attitude while being punished! But if she had been guilty, would she have acted the way she did?" Mr. O asked, realizing that he wasn't saying much. He knew his wife. The price he would have to pay for speaking his mind out loud might be much more than he was willing to pay. And what was the point of his talking anyway? He believed Mirae's version of the story just because she was divinely beautiful. Mr. O was a little ashamed when he thought about the ring he had given away on an impulse. It had belonged to his late father who had received it from the governor of the province for having been the largest donor for some project. Mr. O couldn't remember which project it was now.

It would take a barrel of grease to make her husband's head spin properly, Mistress Yee thought. She laughed and said, "My dear husband, you heard a little while ago how I valued Mirae as a maid. She was my right arm, and it was detrimental to lose her. I knew her absence would inconvenience *me*. But I had to let her go to set an example for the other maids and servants. Besides, if she had done me wrong, I would have let it pass, but it was Mistress Kim who suffered because of her. Not that I am trying to say I adored Mistress Kim, mind you, the woman was unkind to me. But I had to show that what Mirae did was evil and unforgivable. It pained me to see her go. She was part of my dowry. Her aunt had put her in my father's house. She became my handmaid at an early age. We were friends." Mistress Yee's eyes glistened and turned red.

Mr. O felt bad. His wife was fastidious and fussy, maybe, but did not possess an evil bone in her body. She was an honest soul.

"Don't let the food get cold. Let's eat," Mr. O suggested.

"I've lost my appetite," she muttered.

"Oh no. Mistress Yee, please, open your mouth," he asked, picking up a slice of pressed pork with his chopsticks. "Ah," he said, leaning closer to her.

She took the food and said, "You hurt my feelings."

"Forgive me, Mistress Yee. I am a foolish old man," he said, smiling pathetically.

When Nani heard her master and mistress laugh, she left and went to the kitchen and found Soonyi dozing in front of the stove. Nani pulled her hair from behind and said, "Where is Quince?"

"She left, Big Sister," Soonyi said.

"Left already? She is supposed to stay until we are done with the dinner dishes!" Nani shrieked.

"She said she would come back real soon," Soonyi said.

"So what's calling her this time?" Soonyi asked.

"Her husband was whistling from over the wall behind the well. Quince talked to him through a crack in the rocks in the wall. Then she just darted out, giggling. She said she was going to come back real soon," Soonyi said.

"Did you pour water into the rice pot?" Nani asked, lifting the lid of the cast iron pot on the stove.

"I-I am not sure," Soonyi stammered.

"This is too much water. It will take forever to boil," Nani complained, using a long wooden spoon to remove the rice stuck to the bottom of the cast iron pot.

"Get the table ready for us," Nani said, stirring the rice in the water. The aroma of browned rice was nutty and flavorful.

While Nani and Soonyi readied their low table, Quince showed up again. Her appearance was comically messy, with her hair flying in all directions and her shirt ribbon loose, but her cheeks were rosy and her lips cherry red. There were also a few strands of straw in her hair.

"What did you do?" Soonyi asked curiously.

Nani snorted, disgusted.

"What?" Quince asked, smirking.

"Go home," Nani said.

"I am hired to work here," Quince said.

"Then why did you leave in the middle of work?" Nani asked, sitting down by the low table.

"I was waiting for you to return so you could tell us what to do," said Quince sarcastically in her high-pitched voice which didn't seem to suit the size of her body.

"By the way, I tell you what to do because I am supposed to," Nani shrilled, remembering her nickname.

"I know. I know," Quince drawled grudgingly.

"Go to Mistress Yee's quarters and wait until she tells you to remove the table," Nani said.

"And what about you?" Quince asked.

"I am going to have dinner," she said.

"I need to have dinner too," Quince said.

"Strictly speaking, you are not supposed to eat here. You are not part of the family. You are a part-time employee," Nani said.

Quince sat her huge bottom by the table and picked up a pickled cucumber with her fingers. "Mmm, that's too sour," she said, puckering her lips.

Soonyi offered her a pair of chopsticks, surveying Nani's face.

"Thank you, child," Quince said, grinning. "Give me a bowl of rice. I am so hungry."

Her eyes cast down, Nani snickered.

"Don't sulk, Nani. My husband was delayed coming home from the west coast. He just arrived and hadn't seen me for more than a day. You will understand when you get married. Sometimes men get antsy when they don't see their women-folk for a while," Quince blabbered.

With a look of contemptuous horror, Nani got up and left. She was headed for Mistress Yee's quarters.

"It's all her mother's fault," Quince said, stuffing her mouth with a large amount of rice and the marinated sweet potato stems.

"What do you mean?" Soonyi asked.

"Her mother taught her to believe that she deserved a better life than the one of a maid. With that in her head, she thinks she can boss us around. But a maid is a maid," Quince said, grinning at Soonyi, who looked puzzled.

At that moment, Chunshim came in and said that Buwon had just fallen asleep. She was hungry. Indeed, as she spoke, her stomach growled.

Quince said, "Sit down."

Ignoring Quince, Chunshim asked Soonyi to bring a tray of food to her room.

Quince rolled her eyes as Chunshim left the kitchen and said, "She doesn't see me, huh?"

Soonyi arranged the tray with rice and a few dishes. As she was about to take it out, Quince snatched the dish of fried squash patties and put it on her low table.

"Please, Aunt Quince, put it back. She doesn't have much here," Soonyi said.

"She is *another* one who is bossing you around," Quince pointed out. "You need to make sure you don't become the maid for a pack of maids."

Soonyi left, feeling bad. "A maid for a pack of maids," she whispered to herself.

Nani was walking back and said, "What are you mumbling about?"

"Nothing."

In the kitchen, Quince burped loudly. Nani frowned and said, "You may go now. Master and Mistress have blown their candles out."

Quince grinned and said, narrowing her eyes, "Just as I said. Men get antsy."

Nani frowned and went out to wash herself. She was tired. Catching Soonyi coming from Chunshim's room, she said, "You need to finish tidying up the kitchen. I am going to bed now. I think I am coming down with something."

"Do you want ginger tea?" Soonyi asked.

"What I might have isn't what ginger tea can soothe," she replied.

In her room, without lighting the candle, Nani undressed and lay on the floor. She reviewed what Mistress Yee and Mr. O were talking about at their dinner table. With her eyes closed, she conjured up the image of Mirae again, drenched, tied down on a bench. A large, smooth tree branch swung down to hit Mirae on her bottom, and it bounced up slowly, only to go down again. The hired beater counted loudly: *twenty, twenty-one, twenty-two*. That was when Nani had come in the yard. All the maids and servants were supposed to witness the beating

242   H. S. Kimfor a lesson in what would happen to wicked servants, but
Nani had not finished cooking dinner in time. So she arrived
later. Mirae was glaring at Mistress Yee."Big Sister, are you sleeping?" Soonyi said as she came in.

Nani didn't answer. She wasn't in the mood to talk. She
now thought about Min. He had changed a lot. He looked
older, with a thinner body. How filthy he was! His hair was
unkempt, and his skin was red and leathery from the sun. She
thought about the shore where she had sat with Min. It was
the second time she had visited the west coast. The first time
there had been with Mistress Kim when she freed fish because
she wished to be pregnant. That was almost a decade ago now.
Her mother had sent her to the shore to play with shells while
she escorted Mistress Kim to the boat. She still remembered
her mother looking back again and again with a warning eye,
silently telling her not to go near the water.

Soonyi lay down on her cotton mat and immediately fell
asleep. Nani could hear her breathe evenly.

Nani yawned and looked over to the other side, where
Mirae had once slept, away from them. She yawned again and
fell asleep.

In her dream, she was back on the west coast with Min. They
were on the beach, chasing each other, barefoot, laughing
like kids. In her dreams Min was always able to laugh and talk.
Water splashed on her. Suddenly, a wave engulfed Min. Nani's
heart sank, but when the wave pulled back to the ocean, he still
stood there. Nani rushed to him, and they hugged. They ran
again by the shore. Sometime later, Min made a bonfire. Nani
sat there, warming up her cold body. Min kept throwing on
more branches to keep the fire going. Nani was feeling warm
and cozy. The world burned bright orange, and the bonfire
crackled louder and louder, and that was when she woke up.

NANI WOKE UP FROM HER DREAM. IT WAS THE MIDDLE of the night, but the brightness outside was like the early afternoon.

"Min!" she cried in a whisper. Like a dream, he was standing on the threshold, and the bright light was coming from the kitchen. It was on fire. Nani got up, and Min left quickly. "Oh no!" Nani ran out and saw what was happening to the house. The fire was not just in the kitchen, but here and there, and she could see the storage room afire too. She was about to run to check on Mr. O's quarters, but then she remembered that her master was at Mistress Yee's quarters. Suddenly, she turned and ran back to her room and shook Soonyi violently. The room was getting warm, and the crackling sound was getting alarmingly loud.

Soonyi woke up and cried like a baby. Nani couldn't take care of her. She ran out, and Soonyi followed her, begging Nani not to leave her alone. Something collapsed in the kitchen.

She ran to Mistress Yee's quarters. She turned back and told Soonyi to go and tell Chunshim to get out with Buwon and her own son. Soonyi didn't want to. She cried, trembling.

"Soonyi, go and get Buwon!" Nani shrieked. Soonyi jerked but still didn't move. Nani clouted her on the head and repeated, "Go and get Buwon!" Nani ran toward Mistress Yee's quarters without looking back. Soonyi reluctantly trotted to the building behind the guests' quarters.

Mistress Yee's quarters hadn't caught fire. Nani stood in the yard, ready to shout, but then she suddenly remembered that Min had emerged from nowhere in the middle of the night in her room. Why in the world had he showed up? Had she dreamed it all? He had stood on her threshold as if he had come to rescue her. But how could he have known that the house was on fire?

"Mistress Yee, Nani is here," she said. No reply. "Mistress Yee, please wake up!" she shouted. "Fire!" she finally cried.

Mr. O came out. And then he rushed back to get his wife. They both came out. Mr. O looked about from the raised entrance, waving his hand in the air helplessly. Bright orange light everywhere felt like a sizzling summer day. He stepped down on the ground, and a sound emerged from his mouth, but it was incomprehensible. He looked lost. He ran to his quarters, which were completely engulfed. Then he ran, passing the guests' quarters, toward the building where Buwon was supposedly asleep. At that moment, Chunshim escaped the building with a baby in her arms. Soonyi stood in the yard, crying. Bok ran to the yard. Nani arrived, panting.

"Is that Buwon?" Nani asked.

Chunshim realized that she had left Buwon behind. Shrieking, she handed her baby to Soonyi and hastened back to the building. Buwon was shrilling from inside. Nani ran after Chunshim. Bok ran after Nani. Dubak and a few other peasants who had seen the bright light coming from Mr. O's mansion came hurriedly. Mr. O arrived and heard his son cry from inside the burning building. He attempted to go in, but the three men grabbed him by his arms. Another man went in instead. A few moments later, he came out carrying Chunshim. Nani followed out carrying Buwon. Bok came out coughing hysterically.

Mr. O stood there, holding his son, and he wept, even though the servants were urging him to leave the place at once. Finally, they had to pull his son away from him so that he would follow them. Outside the house Mistress Yee, watched the house burn, standing among the peasants who had come to lend a hand. Servants went into the mansion to pour buckets of water on the flames, but their efforts were in vain. By dawn, every building had burned down, except Mistress Yee's quarters and the guests' quarters.

Mr. O stood motionless in front of the main entrance for a long time. Then he left to find Mistress Yee and his son at the guesthouse by the village hall that was meant to accommodate government officers. His servants remained to salvage whatever was left, but all was charred or partially damaged. There was nothing much even to steal. Local government officers came in the morning to examine the site and come up with a possible scenario, but they just stood for a while, awed, for the house had marked one of the most impressive sights in the village for many generations.

One of the officers found a torch that must have been used as a lighter. There was only one torch, so the officers concluded that the fire was set by one person, possibly one who knew the place quite well. But almost everyone in the village knew the house quite well. Even children drew pictures of it with chalk without consulting a grownup. The officers interrogated the village women to determine if their husbands had stayed out the night of the fire, but they all said their husbands had gone to bed early with them. When the officers asked if anyone had seen a suspicious person that evening around Mr. O's mansion, everyone shook their heads, looking blank. And that was the end of the investigation. One officer wrote a report on the case and submitted it to the local government office.

Mistress Yee was ill from the shock of the fire. She whined because she was disgusted by her temporary living quarters.

"I am going to build the same house on the same spot," Mr. O consoled her.

"It will take forever to build a house like that," Mistress Yee said, frowning.

"No, it will take one season," he said. He said it confidently to convince his invisible father in the atmosphere. He could feel how angry his father must be to see that he had ruined the house, four generations old. He could almost hear his father's stern voice: "I wish I had another son." That was what he had said sometimes when he was drinking with his guests. He didn't seem to want two sons. He seemed to want to replace his only son with another. At his deathbed, his father asked, "Will you be able to carry on my name?" Before Mr. O could muster up the courage to say that he would, his father had passed away. After the funeral, alone at his father's grave, he had cried like a child, telling him that he was not the coward his father had always assumed him to be. He wanted to have twelve sons, but as of now he only had Buwon, hardly a son.

"It will take only one season," he emphasized again, realizing that it would take more because the rice-farming season had begun and there weren't many free hands left.

"I can't live here more than a season," Mistress Yee said determinedly.

"I think we can do it in a season," Mr. O said.

"Well, we will see," Mistress Yee said skeptically.

"We will build the house in a season!" Mr. O shouted.

"Are you mad at me? Did I set the house on fire?" Mistress Yee asked, furrowing her forehead. Tears brimmed in her eyes.

"Of course not. Why should I be mad at you?" Mr. O asked regretfully.

"I don't know. You've changed. Just yesterday you suggested that Mirae had been mistreated and wrongly accused. I don't know what is going on in your mind anymore." Mistress Yee broke down and sobbed. She was tired and frustrated. The breakfast was not up to her standard. Besides, it was spring. She had planned to host an elaborate party at her house. That, of course, would have to be canceled. Also, she wanted to go and enjoy cherry blossoms by the Snake River, but that wasn't going to happen either. She had hired a seamstress to make a new dress for the occasion.

Mr. O took his wife's hand and said, "I will take care of everything."

Mr. O was not used to taking care of everything. His father, even after his marriage, hadn't entrusted him with the important matters in the house. After his death, Mistress Kim took charge of them with the excellent assistance of her maid Hosoon, Nani's mother, and so he never had to pay attention to the details of the housekeeping. All he needed to do was enjoy his life and not complain too much. Only today, when he was forced to relocate, had he realized that a couple of young girls had been running his household, and where were the menservants besides Bok? What was he thinking? There was no one who would have rescued him or his wife had they stayed in his quarters the night before. What was he really thinking? When he was little, more than a dozen servants and maids had served his family. Where had they all gone? He realized that morning he had only four, and two were bloody children. His forehead was throbbing. He didn't enjoy self-criticism. He got up. He wanted to go see the local government officers to ask about the latest findings on the fire, and he also wanted to find out how much land he would have to sell to build a new house.

Nani and Chunshim were taking care of Buwon in the rear room at the guesthouse. Luckily, he had escaped the fire unscathed except for singed hair. The hair would grow again.

"You were lucky," Nani said to Chunshim.

"I know!" Chunshim said. She still couldn't believe that she had forgotten Buwon when she ran from her burning room in the middle of the night.

"How is your baby?" Nani asked, taking Chunshim's hand.

"He is fine," Chunshim said, her eyes brimming with tears. The stress had been too great for her. She had almost let Buwon die. The thought still chilled her to the bone.

"No one's hurt," Nani said.

"That's true," Chunshim said. "Thank you for not telling Mistress Yee about what happened," she whispered, to make sure that Nani wouldn't tell their mistress.

"Not in a million years," Nani replied stoutly.

"Do you know where your Min is?" Chunshim asked.

Nani didn't reply.

"I want you to know that I never had anything to do with him," Chunshim emphasized.

Nani nodded.

"I haven't told you this, but I was never married," Chunshim said abruptly.

"Like I didn't know?" Nani said, grinning.

"I was a concubine to a wealthy man," Chunshim began. She hadn't intended to tell her story to anyone, but here she was, blurting it out. "He used to beat me!" Chunshim cried suddenly.

Nani shook her head sympathetically and squeezed the other woman's hand. "It's all right. You are not with him now."

"I ran away from that house one night. I didn't know I was pregnant. When my son was born, I didn't want him. I thought he would remind me of that man for the rest of my life. But he doesn't. He is just a darling," Chunshim said.

Nani wanted to hear more about Min, but Chunshim could talk only about her son. His sweet face so like her younger brother's. His chubby knees. His precociousness.

"I need to go and see if Quince is ever coming back with the groceries," said Nani, getting up.

"I should help you," Chunshim said.

"No, that's not your job," Nani said.

As Nani walked away, she realized that Chunshim didn't bother her anymore. For a long time, Chunshim's status had confused Nani. She wasn't a maid and she wasn't an aristocrat. She was a pain in the neck. She seemed to have it easy, just taking care of the baby. But now Nani felt sorry. What she did was not easy. When she pictured Chunshim running out with her own baby in her arms and forgetting Buwon, Nani was strangely moved. Her mother would have done exactly the opposite. She would have carried out the baby of her master, not Nani, even though she loved Nani more. For some reason, Nani was convinced about that. So she walked to the kitchen, admiring Chunshim.

Quince was waiting for Nani in the kitchen. When Nani entered the room, Quince whispered loudly, "Who set the house on fire?"

"No idea," Nani said, studying Quince's face carefully while she pretended to be checking the cabbage in the basket.

"Are you sure you don't know?"

"I am sure, Sister," said Nani, taking out the rest of the groceries clumsily. She was thinking of Min again. "He'll be damned if he has done something bad," she said. She had spoken aloud without meaning to.

"What did you say?" Quince asked, grabbing a cucumber from the grocery basket. She took an enormous bite out of it, screwing up her freckled face.

"Nothing," Nani said, snatching the cucumber back from Quince.

Quince chewed loudly, showing her crooked teeth and laughing. She now eyed the carrots in the basket.

"Go get water!" Nani said and slapped Quince's thigh, chasing her out of the kitchen as if shooing away a fly.

"All right, Mother-in-law," Quince said and ran out, giggling.

Nani sat by the stove thinking about Min again. She tried to convince herself that she had dreamed that Min was standing on her threshold. In fact, she *had* dreamed of him. She remembered it now. She and Min were on the shore. He made a bonfire. And she woke up when she heard the crackling sound of the wood in the fire.

MIRAE WAS DRESSED UP IN A BEAUTIFUL JADE-AND-RED outfit. She was having a cup of tea with Dimple, whom she called Big Sister, even though she could have easily been her mother. Dimple was flattered, and Mirae knew that.

"SO WHAT DID YOU THINK OF MR. O?" ASKED DIMPLE.

Mirae lowered her eyelids and smiled coquettishly.

"Well, the man is gold," Dimple said, smiling shrewdly and taking a sip of tea.

"Lord Ahn couldn't keep his eyes off of you, Big Sister," Mirae lied.

"He was my first," Dimple confessed. "When I joined the society, he had just returned from China, where he had studied. When he saw me, he said, 'You make my return worthwhile.' He was such a handsome man," Dimple reminisced.

"You must have been the most beautiful girl here. Of course, you still are. A real knockout," Mirae said, picking up a pumpkin-date rice cake with a bamboo pick. "Please, Big Sister, taste it. It is still warm." Mirae handed it over to Dimple, who was pleased to be so intimately treated. It made her feel young again. Most of the new kisengs froze when they saw Dimple and treated her like a lioness. She had enjoyed that role for a long time, but when she saw Lord Ahn showing a great interest in Mirae, she found herself boiling with jealousy. She no longer wanted to play the role of an old lioness, she wanted to be vulnerable again. Mirae wasn't the first girl that Lord Ahn had showed an interest in, but Dimple had never worried about it for she was sure she didn't have to. But Mirae was a different story. She reminded Dimple of herself.

"I thank you, Big Sister, for helping me with Mr. O. I was so clumsy with him," Mirae said, smiling and blushing.

"You handled him superbly," Dimple said, amused. "You haven't told me what you think of him. Tell me," Dimple urged.

"Shall I tell you the truth?" Mirae asked, smiling mysteriously, a little sadly.

"Always."

"Well, then," she began. "He is the most charming man I've ever laid eyes on."

Dimple let out a laugh of relief. Her left cheek still dimpled beautifully.

"Ah, Big Sister, look at you. You should live in a room made of mirrors so that you could look at yourself at all times. It's a pity you can't see your dimple every time it puckers. It's simply divine," Mirae said.

"You flatter me, Cherry Blossom," Dimple said.

"I am just telling the truth," Mirae replied, straight-faced.

"So what do I get if I arrange a rendezvous between you and Mr. O?" Dimple asked.

"My unwavering loyalty," Mirae answered, smiling playfully.

"You are the cleverest girl I know. I said exactly that to my boss, whom we called Fox, when she introduced me to Lord Ahn. You are my replica," Dimple said, pleased.

"You are much too kind."

"First of all, you should read romantic poetry. Mr. O loves poetry," Dimple said.

Mirae almost laughed. She didn't need to work on him any further.

"He loves the Chinese poet named Li Po. Get a book of his poetry," Dimple suggested.

"Tomorrow I will go to the marketplace and do some research," Mirae said, pouring more tea for Dimple.

"The first time Lord Ahn sat with me, he asked if I could recite a poem. I thought quickly and recited a poem from

China. 'Sharp sword too close will wound a hand/Woman's beauty too close will wound a life.'" Dimple said it with her eyes closed, as if she could see herself again in her heyday. "I warned him. But he jumped into the fire," Dimple said. And both women burst out laughing.

"But you must remember one thing. Mr. O loves his wife. He has never spent a night away from home. When he was with his previous wife, it was different. She was unable to produce an heir, and Mr. O spent a lot more time outside, but he always went home before the evening got too late. The current wife did produce an heir, but rumor has it that he is deformed. The baby is never outside the house, and Mr. O doesn't talk about him. Poor man. He is a good man, though. Everyone owes him a favor. Anyway, he is depressed. He doesn't come out of his house often enough," Dimple said.

Mirae listened with a broad smile. She was bored.

"But what attracts you to him?" Dimple asked.

Mirae knew what Dimple was thinking. Mirae was the prettiest, and she could get anyone she wanted, but why Mr. O? He wasn't the handsomest, he wasn't the youngest, and he wasn't the richest in the province.

"I've got a history with him," Mirae confessed, blushing, looking just a little gloomy.

"Oh!" Dimple clasped her hands together with the fingers interlaced.

Mirae's eyes reddened. "I am in love with him," Mirae said. "I would give my life if I could be with him," she added boldly.

Now Dimple's eyes reddened, and she extended her hand to Mirae's.

Dimple said, "You poor thing. Trust me. I will do what I can. We may not have husbands, but we sure deserve love now and then."

Mirae said nothing.

"There will be a gathering at General Hong's house at the end of this month. I will have a talk with Mr. O. I don't think it will have to be a long one, considering the way he looked at you. He was trembling! Did you see his hand?" Dimple laughed.

Tears welled up in Mirae's eyes.

"I thank you so much, Big Sister," Mirae said.

"Well, well, I think you and I make a fine team, don't we?" Dimple asked.

"Indeed, we do," Mirae said. "May I give you a little massage?"

"What an offer! I won't say no to that," Dimple said.

"If I could do half as well as you have, I would be satisfied," Mirae mumbled, anticipating a headache in between her eyebrows. She frowned. She could really use a nap.

"Oh, you will do well," Dimple said sleepily.

"Thank you for inviting me to tea."

"My pleasure," Dimple said, and clapped to summon her waiting maid.

A girl came in and removed the tea table. Mirae bowed and left. She strolled outside, thinking how awful it was to age as a kiseng. What would Dimple be like in ten years? Still talking about her good old days and how Lord Ahn had seduced her. Well, it wasn't her concern. She wasn't going to rot like that. She looked at the mountain, behind which Mr. O's mansion lay. She clenched her teeth and was about to cry. But then she burst out laughing, thinking about Mr. O's trembling hand. The passers-by turned around to look at the unusual sight of a woman laughing out loud on a street in public. But Mirae kept laughing uncontrollably. Later, in her room, she broke down and cried bitterly for a long time.

MANSONG CRIED AT NIGHT WHEN SHE FIRST ARRIVED
at Mrs. Wang's house. She woke up twelve times at night and
slept the whole day. Mrs. Wang wondered why anyone would
want to have kids. Obviously, she had made a mistake by
declaring in public that she would take care of the child. What
had possessed her to come up with such an idea?

For several days, Mrs. Wang woke up every time Mansong
cried. And she felt she was going to turn into a ghost if she
went on like that. Her head felt light and her bones were sore.
Finally, even when Mansong wasn't crying, Mrs. Wang could
hear a cry in her head. She realized that childrearing was not
her fate. In any case, she needed some help. She couldn't go
on like that. But it was against her principles to hire a maid.
Besides, she wasn't used to living with another person. Mansong was already one too many in the house.

One afternoon while Mansong slept, snoring, Mrs. Wang
sat in her room and closed her eyes, breathing in and out
slowly. The first thing she was going to do was somehow put
an end to Mansong's nighttime crying. She had tried various
herbal teas, but none of them worked. So she hired a shaman
to perform Kut to soothe the sad spirit. Actually, Mrs. Wang
despised the spirits that lingered between life and death. They
were pathetic, she thought. And petty. She was getting ready
to scold the spirit that possessed Mansong.

Lacking the funds, Mrs. Wang hired only one shaman and
she arrived with no props, colorful outfits, or instruments.

She was a different type of shaman, the woman pointed out
in a man's voice. All she needed was a bowl of uncooked rice

and a spoon on a low table and a straw mat. And she wanted Mansong to sit on the mat too.

Mrs. Wang prepared everything for the shaman in a few moments.

The shaman knelt in front of the table and mumbled something for a while. The spoon that was standing in the rice bowl began to move. She talked louder. The spoon moved a little faster, dancing. She grabbed the spoon tightly, strangling it. As perspiration dripped down her nose, she mumbled again.

The whole time, Mansong watched the shaman expressionlessly, but toward the end, she cried fearfully.

Indignant and impatient, Mrs. Wang thundered while the shaman still mumbled something unintelligible. "Get out of that child! What business do you have to possess an innocent child? You damned pathetic spirit! Go where you belong, and let the living go on with their lives without you interfering. If I could see you, I would strike you! How petty can you be to linger among the living and pester people you have a grudge against! Move on!"

"Mrs. Wang, it's Mansong's mother. She wants to be heard," the shaman said.

Mrs. Wang rolled her eyes. She was fed up.

"She wants her daughter to be acknowledged as Mr. O's. She wants her to be at her father's house," the shaman interpreted.

"You see how ignorant the spirits are? The house burned down yesterday. If Mansong hadn't been here with me, she would have turned into ash."

Addressing the spirit, she shouted, "Is that what you would have liked?" She continued, "*I* don't know what it's like to be dead, but *you* know what it's like to be alive. Sometimes the living don't know what will happen the next day. What seems to be good may turn out to be bad. You want your daughter to be in Mr. O's household because she is his daughter. But that's how we think because we can't predict the future. I thought the dead knew better! But apparently you don't. So leave life up to us, and go find your way to sink into the world of the dead," Mrs. Wang scoffed, her spittle flying.

"She will go," the shaman said. "She wants to have your word that you will watch over Mansong."

"I've promised that already. Now go! Leave the child alone!" Mrs. Wang shouted menacingly.

Mansong stopped crying. She played with the rice in the bowl.

Mrs. Wang snatched the bowl away and pulled out the spoon and said, "Let her go."

So that was the end of that Kut. Mrs. Wang served the shaman lunch. They sat at the table and the shaman said, "Mrs. Wang, you can't mess with the spirits. Sometimes they enter your body and drag you around by the hair. A woman in another village used to cut herself with a knife because she had ridiculed a spirit."

Mrs. Wang guffawed and said, "It's all in your mind. If you let the spirit bully you, it will."

"Do you think it left?" the shaman asked, looking about as if she could see the spirit.

"There is no room for it here at my house," Mrs. Wang assured her loudly, as if to make sure the spirit heard her.

"So what are you going to do with the child?" the shaman asked, taking a large spoonful of fluffy rice.

"I will see. The woman was a good sort. She can't leave because she loves her child so. But all I am saying is that she is mistaken. The child would *not* be better off with her family. And I am not better off with the child. If I were clever, I would drop her off at her father's house and make the spirit and me happy while the rest, including the child, are miserable. Maybe I should leave the matter with the gods and forget about it," Mrs. Wang said, drinking water from a large bowl.

"Oh, by the way, did you hear? The criminal has been captured," the shaman informed Mrs. Wang.

Mrs. Wang raised her eyebrows apprehensively.

"It's the dumb boy," the shaman said.

"Really?" Mrs. Wang said nonchalantly.

"He pleaded guilty before the beating," the shaman said.

"That's smart. Why go through the beating if he was going to confess anyway?" Mrs. Wang said.

"All that's needed to get him hanged now is an official letter from Mr. O, relinquishing his contract with the servant. While he belongs to Mr. O, maybe the local government can't go ahead and punish him," the shaman said. "Well, on that note, Mrs. Wang, I need to go." The shaman got up.

Mrs. Wang got up at the same time and said, "Wait a moment. Let me pay you."

"Oh, please, Mrs. Wang. Don't pay me. You expelled the spirit," the shaman said sheepishly.

"I am going to pay you, so if the spirit comes back I can complain about my expense," Mrs. Wang chuckled.

"Ah, Mrs. Wang. You should," the shaman said.

Mrs. Wang entered her room to fetch the money. As soon as she was alone, her heart sank, picturing Min hanged in public. She went out and gave a generous amount to the shaman.

Her eyes bulging, the shaman hesitated to take the money, feeling awkwardly glad.

"Oh, take it. It was worth it," Mrs. Wang said.

"The spirit was stubborn, Mrs. Wang," the shaman said.

Mansong was putting her finger into the chicken cage. Mrs. Wang went over and told Mansong that the chickens would peck on her fingers. "No, no, no," Mrs. Wang emphasized.

"Well, then, Mrs. Wang, I will see you at the spring festival," the shaman said.

"Will there *be* a spring festival?" Mrs. Wang inquired doubtfully.

"Why not?" The shaman turned around.

"Who would fund the festival if Mr. O didn't? Surely he is not in the mood for a spring festival."

"Well, he is already recruiting builders and contractors," the shaman said. "In fact, today, the master of geomancy visited Mr. O's burned house and advised him to make a slight change to the new building. The earth breathes right onto the house, and its qi has been too strong, he said. Guess what, Mrs. Wang? He also predicted that Mr. O would have a blessing of a healthy son if he made that change," the shaman rattled on.

After the shaman had left, Mrs. Wang realized that she had always found the mountain behind Mr. O's house to be oppressively overwhelming. The house was situated at the mouth of the mountain, ready to be devoured.

AFTER DINNER, MANSONG FELL ASLEEP. IT WAS A MIR-
acle. Mrs. Wang placed a bowl of clear water on her altar, outside by the bamboo garden, and thanked all the gods of the
universe, known and unknown, for taking care of the matter.
She said, "I knew it would be fine, sooner or later. But I must
thank you for helping it happen so quickly."

The moon was waning, but it still brightened her yard
enough for her to sit out on the wooden bench and enjoy her
new life with a sleeping child.

At that moment, her dog, Tiger, barked, wagging his tail.
Instinctively, Mrs. Wang turned around toward her tired-
looking gate; it really was coming to the end of its life. She
silenced Tiger and listened.

"Mrs. Wang, it's me, Nani."

Mrs. Wang got up and went to unlatch the gate to let the
unexpected visitor in.

"What is it?" Mrs. Wang asked, turning around to go back
to her bench.

Nani bit her lip.

"Take a seat," Mrs. Wang said.

As she sat, she immediately burst out crying, her small
torso shaking.

"The crying demon must have entered you," Mrs. Wang
muttered. But Nani didn't hear, for she was crying too loudly.

Nani had begun to cry the moment she heard about Min's
arrest. Her eyes were puffy, her nose was red, and her head
was now splitting with the ache of too many thoughts and the
loss of too many tears.

"Life is never fair," Mrs. Wang said, grinning. She had just gotten rid of the crying spirit, but here came another one. Perhaps she shouldn't try to go against the flow, she thought. So she sat silently, enduring Nani's ceaseless crying. She looked up at the moon and then at Nani. Sometime later, she said, "When you are done crying, let me know. I've had a long day." Mrs. Wang got up and walked toward her room.

"Mrs. Wang, please don't leave me alone," Nani squalled.

Mrs. Wang stopped and said, "Well, then, I am going to get some water. Would you like something too?"

"Yes, well, may I have some rice wine?"

Surprised, Mrs. Wang raised her eyebrows. After a moment, she went to her kitchen and brought out a jug of rice wine with two bowls. Mrs. Wang set the bowls on the bench and poured a little into one bowl for Nani and filled the other one for herself.

"Drink it," Mrs. Wang said, and she drank hers in one gulp. "Ah, that cleanses my chest—my whole soul, actually."

Nani took a sip as if drinking hot tea.

"Mrs. Wang, I am the most unfortunate girl in the whole world," Nani said. She was no longer crying.

Girls normally felt like either the most fortunate or the most unfortunate. Nothing in between. Mrs. Wang found this bizarre.

"Min has been arrested, Mrs. Wang, for having set Mr. O's house on fire. He deserves to be hanged, but I must tell you what led him to do that." Nani told her how she had met him on the west coast, and in what condition she had found him there, and how he had wanted to marry her, and that she had rejected him. Her conclusion was that she was guilty, too. If only she had agreed to marry him, he wouldn't have gone out of his mind and acted so foolishly.

Mrs. Wang listened patiently.

"Mrs. Wang, he is going to be hanged tomorrow," Nani said, trembling. She no longer cried, only because there was no more crying left in her heart. She could only fear now.

"What is your crime?" Mrs. Wang asked quietly.

Nani thought for a moment. She sighed like an old mountain, completely resigned. There was nothing she could do now. "Heartlessness toward a desperate soul. Jealousy. Arrogance," Nani replied. She wanted to do something with her life. She wasn't willing to be Min's wife and live happily ever after now. Was it because he was dumb and deaf? No. That had never bothered her. There was nothing that she meant to say that he didn't understand; there was nothing that he wanted to say that she couldn't hear. Was it because of Mirae? No.

"Nothing wrong to reject a person you don't love. Love is not charity. Love and charity flow from two different spouts. One gushes out from your heart, the other comes from your head. And your head cannot stop what your heart is doing, if you know what I mean." Mrs. Wang paused. She realized that she had skipped her dinner. Unbelievable! How had this happened? She had been too preoccupied with the shaman and so stunned by the way Mansong had fallen asleep and was still sleeping. "If you would excuse me, I need to eat something. I am going to collapse if I don't." Mrs. Wang got up and went to the kitchen.

"Mrs. Wang, can I come with you?" Nani asked, getting up.

"What for? Are you hungry too?"

"Well, I am a little scared. Your house is not near anything. I mean, it's in the forest, and there are sounds," Nani said uncomfortably.

"See, you are not in love. If you were, you wouldn't be afraid of a twelve-headed demon. So wake up from your own misunderstanding. There is no need to feel it's all your fault that Min is in jail and will be hanged tomorrow," Mrs. Wang said.

The word "hanged" pierced Nani's heart, making it difficult for her to breathe. She sighed. Tears welled up again, but she swallowed them.

In the open stove, an amber fire was still going strong. Mrs. Wang put water on the stove and waited. They both sat

on wooden stools and watched the fire. It was the only thing
that was moving.

"When you rejected him at whatever beach you mentioned,
it might very well have set his mind on fire and put him out of
his mind. Nevertheless, he is the only one responsible for his
action. The officers are not going to hear about what could
have or would have happened had the circumstances been
otherwise. So no need to go on improvising variations on the
same theme. Now, are you hungry?" Mrs. Wang asked.

"Yes, Mrs. Wang. I have eaten nothing the whole day," Nani
confessed.

Mrs. Wang poured boiling water into a large bowl with leftover rice. The water loosened and warmed up the petrified
rice. She divided the rice between two bowls and gave one
bowl to Nani. They ate the rice with kimchi. "Ah, hunger is
the best meal! Even the emperor of China doesn't know the
appetite hunger brings. How could he? He is never hungry,"
Mrs. Wang said, satisfied.

Nani ate little. Every grain of rice settled in her chest like a
stone. The world was collapsing in front of her eyes, and there
was nothing she could do.

"I love him!" Nani shouted abruptly and broke down with a
pitiful cry. "I love him, Mrs. Wang. I can't bear knowing that
he will die tomorrow. I can't live with him dead," Nani cried.
"Oh, Mother, help me!" She clasped her hands.

Mrs. Wang kept eating, ignoring Nani. When she had finished
her bowl of rice, she asked, "Aren't you going to finish yours?"

"Is this a dream? Are we in a dream? I think I am dreaming,"
Nani babbled.

Mrs. Wang clucked her tongue.

"Why don't you go to bed?" Mrs. Wang suggested. "Or do
the dishes."

Nani took the dishes and went out to the water tub in the
yard. Mrs. Wang followed. She sat on the bench and helped

herself to some more rice wine. Mrs. Wang thought for a minute, looking up at the moon.

"Come and sit here," Mrs. Wang said gently. She poured a bowl of rice wine and gave it to Nani.

Nani was not able to thank Mrs. Wang: she had lost her voice.

"Drink it and go to bed. The room is warm. It will melt your bones. Sleeping is a short death," Mrs. Wang said, wondering what she was trying to say. "Min will be hanged tomorrow," she said, enunciating every syllable, as if to see how the idea sounded if she said it slowly.

Nani covered her ears and screwed up her face.

"He will be hanged ... unless," Mrs. Wang paused. "Unless," she said and stopped again. "Unless Mr. O says he doesn't mind that his servant burned his house and all his possessions. In other words, if Mr. O says he absolves his servant who meant to kill him and his family."

"He never meant to kill anyone. He wouldn't kill a fly, Mrs. Wang," Nani wheezed.

"Don't speak. Your voice is gone," Mrs. Wang advised her.

A little while later, Nani bowed to Mrs. Wang and tried to leave. Mrs. Wang said, "Stay in my house. It's too late to walk about. All the spirits who got lost on their way to the next life inhabit this mountain. You don't want to encounter them at this hour."

Nani went in reluctantly and fell asleep next to Mansong as soon as she laid her head down.

Mrs. Wang lit another candle and looked into her chest of drawers. She pulled out her journals and examined them. She picked one out, leafed through it, and put her finger on the page where a woman named Hong by the Snake River gave birth to a son. She loosened the binding of the book to remove the page. She read the page and sat there, thinking hard. She took her brush and began to compose a letter addressed to

Mr. O. It took a while to finish the letter. When she was done, she put the page from the journal and her letter in an envelope and sealed it. Then she slept next to Nani.

At daybreak, Mrs. Wang woke up and thundered to Nani, "Wake up, child! This is the day your boy will be hanged if you don't take this letter, as soon as your legs can carry you, to Mr. O."

Nani woke with a start. She looked awful, all puffed up and her hair flying in all directions. Nani took the letter from Mrs. Wang and stared at her blankly.

"I don't have time to say more. But if Mr. O reads that letter before he goes to the government office this morning, it might help. I hope it will," Mrs. Wang said, looking at Mansong in her deep slumber. "Go, now!" Mrs. Wang waved her hand, motioning Nani to hurry.

Nani ran down the mountain as fast as she could, constantly whispering, "Mother, Mother, don't let him be hanged!"

Automatically, her feet carried her to the old house. It was a horrid sight. The workers were piling up the debris in what had been Mr. O's courtyard. Just looking at the damage, she couldn't imagine how Min could ever be forgiven. Then she ran again to the guesthouse, crying because the sun was coming up. She didn't know whether Mr. O had already left for the government office.

When she arrived, she went directly to Mr. O's room. Standing outside, she caught her breath. She exhaled to steady herself.

"Big Sister, where have you been?" Soonyi asked. She was carrying a tray of food. "Quince burned the rice," she said, lowering her voice. "I had to put in some charcoal pieces to get the burned smell out of the rice."

"Why only one bowl of rice?" Nani questioned her.

"It's for the master. The mistress is not feeling well," Soonyi said.

"Give it to me," Nani said. "I will take it to him," she said as she snatched the tray.

"Look at you, Big Sister. Your hair is not tidy," Soonyi pointed out.

"Don't bring the other tray. I will come and fetch it," Nani instructed her.

Clearing her voice, Nani announced her arrival and opened the door impatiently. Mr. O was converting his land into currency at his study table. Nani bowed and transferred the dishes from the tray onto the low table. Her hands trembled. Clearing her throat once again, she said, "Master, here is a letter for you."

Concentrating on his addition, Mr. O didn't reply. When he was done, the muscle between his eyebrows relaxed, and he said, "Put it in the basket with the other letters."

Nani's heart sank. She knew nothing about the contents of the letter, but she trusted Mrs. Wang. Nani bowed and left the room to fetch the other tray with side dishes.

In the kitchen, Quince was helping herself freely to candied chestnuts. Nani couldn't speak. She picked up the tray and left the kitchen again.

"Poor thing," Quince said to Soonyi, taking another chestnut. "But the boy deserves the punishment. What an awful way of paying back his master who's been taking care of him practically since his birth."

Soonyi snatched the lacquer box with candied chestnuts and said, "You are eating all the chestnuts."

"Well, the mistress is not well, and she doesn't want to eat anything. So I offer my mouth to eat a little of what she would have eaten were she well," Quince grumbled with her mouth full.

Nani steadied herself again before she entered Mr. O's room with the tray. She bowed and glanced at the basket full of letters. She arranged the table for Mr. O and opened the lid of the rice and soup. Steam rose to her face.

"Master, there is an urgent letter Mrs. Wang sent. She says it has something to do with," she stopped. She didn't know what to say.

Mr. O raised his eyebrows, waiting for her to finish her sentence.

"Forgive me, Master. Mrs. Wang said it was urgent. That's all she said. Do you want me to bring it to you?"

Mr. O sat in front of his table and thought briefly before he picked up his spoon. "Bring it to me," he ordered her.

Nani picked out Mrs. Wang's letter from the basket and presented it to Mr. O. She lingered there, hoping Mr. O would open it. But he tasted his soup. He put his spoon down and said, "This is too salty."

"It might have been overboiled, Master. I will go and fix the problem." Nani got up and took the soup bowl.

"I don't feel like eating anything except some soup this morning. Bring it as soon as you can. I need to go out," Mr. O said. "In the meantime, I guess I will be reading this letter."

Nani ran out and went to the kitchen. She stood there, holding the soup bowl.

"What's gotten into you, Nani? Comb your hair. You look bizarre," Quince said, frowning.

"Big Sister, why did you bring the soup back?" Soonyi asked.

"Oh, shut up, Soonyi," Nani said, sitting down, still holding the soup bowl.

"Is there something wrong with the soup?" Soonyi asked.

Quince, chewing on something, protested, "What could be wrong with the soup? I made it."

Nani went out. She couldn't hear another word from the other maids. Her mind raced to Mr. O before her legs took her there. She didn't hesitate before she entered Mr. O's room again with the same soup bowl. Mr. O was no longer at the table; he was standing by the window, looking out, holding the letter in his hand. He didn't seem to notice Nani's presence. She bowed and placed the soup on the table and left the room. Again she whispered, "Mother, Mother, don't let him be hanged!"

As she stepped down into the yard, she heard the door behind her open. Mr. O was leaving. He passed her as if she were invisible.

She went back to his room in order to remove the food. She looked about, but the letter was nowhere to be found. Something about the way Mr. O had suddenly left told her that Min wouldn't be hanged. But she couldn't trust her intuition.

In the late afternoon, she heard that Min had been let out of jail because Mr. O had confessed to arson. This news traveled faster than the wind. By the end of the day, even the Chinese were laughing about the lunatic who set his own house on fire and lost everything.

FOR HALF A DAY MR. O WALKED ALONE LIKE A VAGA-
bond. He wasn't sure where he was going, but he could not
stop his legs from dragging him wherever they wanted. He
feared he would collapse and not be able to get up again if
he stopped. He ascended a mountain and descended to the
valley on the other side. He passed a lake with willow trees.
He crossed a creek full of trout. When the mountains swallowed the orange sun, he realized that he had walked all
day. But he was neither tired nor hungry. With the sun on its
nightly retreat, his shadow was no longer following him. So
he stopped, feeling strangely less shameful in the dark. He
heard himself breathe heavily and felt the weight of his life on
his chest. All day long, he had avoided thinking about himself,
but now he could no longer push his thoughts aside. The letter
that Mrs. Wang had written was like a death sentence whispered into his ear. He hated his own father for having treated
him like an inferior, but Min had been his servant for practically all of Min's short life. Did he know that he was the son of
the master he was serving? Judging from the way the dumb
servant had looked at him as he was discharged that morning
from the local jail, he did know the secret.

At the peak of his youth, when Mr. O had hated his father's
guts, he had partied hard and gotten into a lot of trouble.
Hong had been one of his many conquests. He hardly remembered her, actually, and he wouldn't have recalled her at all
had there been no mention of the Snake River in the page that
Mrs. Wang had attached to her letter. He hadn't known that
she'd had his baby. And he couldn't remember now exactly

how and when Min had come into his family. There had been many babies in front of his gate. How many of them were *his* babies? How was he supposed to have known that Min was his son? No one had told him. A crime committed without evil intentions isn't a crime.

He walked on for a while and heard music leaking out from a large house. It was a pub. There were red lamps hanging outside to attract customers. He went inside. He was thirsty.

"Ah, Mr. O, what brings you here?" a woman greeted him from behind.

Mr. O whirled around and recognized Dimple, standing at the entrance with a group of women. Everyone had heard about the fire at Mr. O's house. Seeing him, the women whispered among themselves, estimating the value of his loss in currency.

"I happened to pass by. I am just thirsty," Mr. O, taken by surprise, said uneasily.

"I brought my girls here tonight because today is the day when my wretched mother gave me birth," Dimple said. "So, Mr. O, will you buy me a drink?"

Mr. O said nothing. He was not in the mood for a conversation. He was tired now.

"I'm teasing, Mr. O," Dimple said. "I wish you a good evening," she said and bowed low.

Mr. O was guided by a maid through a maze of hallways to a private room.

Dimple entered a room and six women followed her in. Mirae was the last in line. Dimple stopped Mirae and smiled, narrowing her eyes. And she motioned with her chin, telling Mirae to go and see Mr. O. Mirae pouted at the suggestion, theatrically, to express her regret that she couldn't then celebrate Dimple's birthday. Dimple pushed Mirae gently out of the room.

Mr. O ordered a bottle of plum wine and told the maid not to disturb him for the rest of the evening.

Mirae was looking for the maid in the hallway. Pressing her ear to each latticed door, she tried to eavesdrop. But she couldn't tell which was Mr. O's room.

Soon enough, the maid appeared with a tray of wine. Mirae inserted a silver coin in her sleeve and snatched the tray, saying, "Show me the room."

$$\text{☽ O ☾}$$

Mr. O took off his hat and set it on the low table. The small size of the room comforted him. There was a folding screen against one of the walls. He observed the embroidery. Two young women were on swings that were tied to the branches of a pine tree. One was high up in the air, the other close to the ground. Several young women were standing around the tree, chatting. A few men sat in a pavilion, looking out at the women.

Mr. O opened the closet door. Inside were several red silk cushions. He stared at them mindlessly. He sat by the low table and waited for the maid to bring in his wine. He tried very hard not to think about Mrs. Wang's letter, but it kept coming back to his mind. He frowned, feeling frustrated because he couldn't control his mind.

The door slid open quietly. Mr. O was really thirsty. He didn't look up, but sat up straight, readying himself to gulp down the wine.

A girl brought in a tray and poured the wine into a bowl.

"I'll do it myself," he said. He didn't want to be waited on. But he saw the ring on the finger of the hand that poured the wine; the piece of jewelry glittered under the candlelight.

"May I stay?" Mirae asked. Her voice sounded like an echo of a dream from the past.

Mr. O didn't reply; he was surprised to realize that he had forgotten all about Mirae.

For the first time, he saw himself in perspective. He lacked the willpower to say no to himself, he admitted reluctantly. He ate whatever looked good on his plate. He didn't even consider whether it might be poisoned or bad for him. He trusted the world and, until now, there had been no reason not to.

Here, another one of those attractions was being openly presented to him. To be fair, he didn't seek attractions out: they walked into his life.

Of course, he could tell Mirae to leave him alone. But why would he do that? She wanted to be seduced so badly. Who would say no to that? Maybe he could save himself some trouble later on. But what trouble could being with this pretty girl for an evening possibly bring to him? A baby at the gate. No, he was determined not to have that happen again. His new house was going to face west, which meant that his gate would be more exposed to the passers-by. Anyone trying to drop a baby and run would be noticed.

He was thirsty. He drank three bowls of wine without a break. And it felt good.

"Pour me another one," he said.

Mirae shot a glance at Mr. O as she poured the wine.

"How is your life?" Mr. O asked, looking at his ring on her finger.

"When I left Master's house, I thought becoming a kiseng would be the only way I could have a chance to see you again. So at the moment, I am ecstatic. But tomorrow, when you leave, I might feel differently," Mirae said.

He hadn't planned to stay overnight. Mr. O drank his wine and leaned against the side cushion. "Move the candle nearer to you."

Mirae moved the candle from his side to her side.

"You are exquisitely made."

Mirae closed her eyes briefly, her eyelashes fluttering, and then opened them to stare at Mr. O.

"What do you want from me?" he asked.

"I have it already," Mirae said boldly.

Mr. O laughed, pleased. "You are clever," he said. "Is it money you want?"

Smiling divinely, she said, "I would like a little wine."

Mr. O sat up and poured wine for her. Mirae drank it at once, like a thirsty man.

"Would you like another one?" he asked.

She stared at his lips intently. He poured another bowl of wine for her.

"I would like to taste it from your mouth," she said, looking directly into his eyes.

He didn't quite understand what she meant, but it sounded good. He smiled mischievously.

"Please, you drink it," Mirae suggested.

He drank the wine at once and crawled on his knees like a dog to Mirae. As soon as her lips met his, he forgot all about his burned house and Mrs. Wang's shocking letter. He forgot all about his wife, who might have a seizure if she found out about his clandestine meeting with her former maid. And he forgot all about his father's nasty, invisible eyes, which had seemed to watch him all day.

Life was sweet and short, after all. And it was a waste of time to worry about things that hadn't happened yet.

Life was fair. After the torture of the day, the most beautiful girl in the universe was rewarding him with the sweetest, bone-melting caresses. She was it: she personified happiness.

MISTRESS YEE'S JAW DROPPED. SHE COULDN'T SPEAK anymore. She couldn't believe what she was hearing. Min had been released. Her husband had confessed to burning the house down. And now he was missing. The ground under her feet was crumbling, but there was no one around to blame or to abuse.

Mistress Yee was now lying on her silk mat with a bandanna around her head to prevent it from exploding. Nani brought in an herb drink that Dr. Choi had recommended for calming Mistress Yee's nerves, but Mistress Yee waved it away.

Knowing that at that moment nothing would help, Nani closed the door and left her mistress alone. Walking back to the kitchen, she felt strange. What had Mrs. Wang said in the letter that made Mr. O lie about the fire?

Nani sat in the kitchen and sipped the drink meant for Mistress Yee. Her own nerves definitely needed calming.

"Big Sister, what are you drinking?" Soonyi asked, panicked.

"You have some too," Nani suggested.

"That's for the mistress," Soonyi said in a hushed voice.

"She doesn't want any."

"Do I have something on my face?" Nani asked.

"No, but what's happened to you, Big Sister?"

Nani sighed. Only the night before, she had wailed about Min. She had acted like a wild beast in front of Mrs. Wang. Min survived, as Nani had hoped. But an innocent person, her master, was now regarded as a lunatic. And her mistress was unable to throw one of her infamous fits because the shock was too great.

"I am hungry, Big Sister," Soonyi said.

"You eat with Chunshim. Take the porridge for Buwon. I need to go see Mrs. Wang. I will be back soon," Nani said, getting up.

"Big Sister, you disappeared last night too. It was real hard to fib about you being here when you weren't," Soonyi said.

"If anyone looks for me, tell the truth. I will be with Mrs. Wang. But it's not going to take long," Nani said.

"Do you think she knows where Mr. O is?" Soonyi asked. But Nani ran out of the kitchen without answering.

She ran up the hill and passed the old pine tree. By the time she reached Mrs. Wang's house, her throat was dry and she was coughing. Tiger barked from inside. Nani impatiently unlatched the door.

"Mrs. Wang, Nani is here. Mrs. Wang, are you here?"

The midwife came out of her room and said, "Is this your new job? Showing up here uninvited every night?"

"I am sorry. I came here because I didn't know where to go," Nani said.

"If you don't know where to go, don't come here. Stay where you belong until you know where you want to go," Mrs. Wang said, annoyed. She had just put Mansong to sleep. And she was ready to enjoy her time alone.

"Did you hear the news?" Nani asked.

"The birds chirped all day long," Mrs. Wang replied.

Nani knelt in front of Mrs. Wang. "Thank you, Mrs. Wang. Min has been released from jail."

"I live on the mountain because I don't want to hear every bit of news there is," Mrs. Wang said.

"But Mr. O is missing. And Mistress Yee has fallen ill." Nani said despondently.

"And you think it's all your fault, or is it mine this time?" Mrs. Wang said.

"I don't know. Min is responsible for the fire. But Mr. O is being punished now."

"Ah, you wish to go back to yesterday and do nothing about Min so that he would be hanged by now, and Mr. O would be at home, and Mistress Yee would be as healthy as a horse?" Mrs. Wang asked.

"No!" Nani shouted involuntarily. "I don't know," she whispered.

"Then let your tongue rest. Mr. O will be home soon. It would be unnatural if Mistress Yee didn't fall ill when her house had burned down and her husband was missing," Mrs. Wang said.

Nani was silent, wondering how Mrs. Wang knew all she knew.

"Mrs. Wang, I am starving," Nani said.

"Make yourself at home and eat whatever you find in my kitchen, child. I am tired," Mrs. Wang replied.

Nani bowed and went to the kitchen. Water was boiling on the stove. She took the water and poured it into the pot that held rice from breakfast.

Mrs. Wang came in and said, "There is cucumber kimchi Jaya brought today. You can have that, too, with your rice."

"Mrs. Wang, I have a wish," Nani said.

"Don't you like cucumber?"

"No. Yes, I do," Nani said. She got up and took Mrs. Wang's hand.

"What is it?" Mrs. Wang asked.

Nani knelt down, still holding Mrs. Wang's hand. "Mrs. Wang, I would like to be a midwife."

"When did this idea come to you?"

"I can't remember," Nani answered hesitantly.

"Why do you want to be a midwife?" Mrs. Wang asked.

Nani thought for a moment. She knew Mrs. Wang well. She didn't want to say anything unconvincing. Finally, she said,

"I don't want to waste my life being a maid. I want to do something more interesting."

Mrs. Wang weighed Nani's reply in her mind for a moment and asked, "Wasn't it yesterday that you professed your love for Min? Aren't you going to marry him, now that he is free?"

"No, Mrs. Wang. It turns out that I am more in love with my life than with him. I didn't want him to be hanged because he didn't deserve hanging. I cannot put the reason behind this into plain words, but if he set his master's house on fire there must be a reason for it that I don't know. And no life was harmed in the fire, so I thought he should live too. But to answer your question, I don't intend to marry him," Nani explained clearly.

"You can't have a family and have this profession too," Mrs. Wang said.

"I know, Mrs. Wang. You can't deliver your own baby," Nani said.

"That's not my point," Mrs. Wang said. "You can't have two lovers."

Nani blushed at the word.

"What I mean is that you have to choose only one. Or else you will fail in both jobs," Mrs. Wang said.

"I know," Nani said, vaguely understanding what Mrs. Wang was saying.

"You know how to read and write?" Mrs. Wang asked.

"Yes, I do. I read better than I write. But I will practice," Nani answered quickly.

"You really need to know how to write. You will be recording all you do every time you deliver a baby," Mrs. Wang said. "The first thing you do is get to know the women in the village. On a good day, I go around and visit with every pregnant woman to check the position of the fetus and the complexion of the expecting mother and so on. But all this you will learn in time. When you come next time, you will go with me to pick medicinal plants in the wild. I will teach you all I know. But again, you will have to write down the things I say."

"I will practice writing before I come," Nani said.

"Well, now, eat your dinner. And do the dishes before you go. I hate doing the dishes," Mrs. Wang said. And she went to her room to sleep.

Nani was feeling wonderful. She looked up at the velvety night sky and felt her mother was watching her. But she couldn't leave the house, for she feared the spirits in the mountain. She stealthily entered Mrs. Wang's room and lay down next to her. Mrs. Wang was snoring. Nani pulled the pillow away from Mrs. Wang, which made Mrs. Wang stop snoring immediately.

MIN WAITED OUTSIDE THE PUB THE WHOLE NIGHT. IT was getting chilly toward dawn, and he huddled under a tile awning and fell asleep briefly. He woke up worrying that Mr. O might have left the pub. He stood at the end of the alley and kept vigil.

When Mr. O finally came out, Min automatically hid himself. But when Mr. O came close, Min stepped into his path.

Surprised, Mr. O fell back onto the ground. Min groaned and helped him up.

"What brings you here?" Mr. O asked and craned his neck to see if anyone else was around. He actually felt repelled to be facing Min.

Min stood there, looking at his own feet, a servant's feet in a pair of straw shoes, and then he eyed Mr. O's cowhide shoes. Was this his father? He didn't know why he had waited all night long.

"I don't know what to say," Mr. O managed and tugged on his chin. He had no feelings toward the young man. The enormity of the newly discovered fact that his servant was his son hadn't congealed in his mind yet. Besides, his mind had traversed a different world for the night.

Mirae slipped out of the pub. She was dressed in white and iris purple. She wore a silver head covering. She spotted Mr. O next to a ragged young man in the alley. She stopped for a moment, and then she walked toward them confidently. There was nothing to be ashamed of. Mr. O was her husband. As she passed, she acknowledged Mr. O openly by bowing her head briefly. Then she noticed that the other person was Min.

Several paces away from the two men, she turned around slightly, but then changed her mind because she remembered something which made her laugh. She kept going. The only two men she had ever slept with were standing next to each other, one in rags and the other in silk. Mirae laughed aloud in the wide street, not minding the few other pedestrians.

Min didn't know what he should do. He had wanted to bow to thank Mr. O for having saved his life. But he could tell that his father was neither proud nor happy about what he had done to save him. Actually, he seemed a little uncomfortable to be standing there with him.

Min bowed quickly and then walked away.

"Come and see me another time," Mr. O said to his back. He had forgotten that Min was also deaf.

Min kept walking. From a distance he spotted a lake surrounded by tall grass. Now he moved faster with his legs stiff as if in need of emptying his bladder. He sighed in front of the lake. All of a sudden he undressed himself and plunged into the lake, shocking a duck that was sitting on the water. He swam, splashing wildly until he perspired. Then he waded the waist-deep water, crawled into the grassy area and lay on his back. His heart raced. His mind wandered off to the moment when Mr. O found him in front of the pub earlier that morning. Now it became clear that Mr. O felt nothing for him. Mr. O had not saved him out of love. Mrs. Wang had importuned Mr. O to spare his life.

But this was the way his master was. Mr. O did things on the spur of the moment, or because someone else urged him to. But Min knew that he himself was the villain of the story. He had burned down his father's house, jeopardizing many lives. He had gotten away unpunished because his father had taken the blame.

After seeing Nani on the west coast, he had followed Mistress Yee's carriage. He had wanted to talk to Nani once again, but there was no chance. He had lingered outside Mr. O's house all evening, hoping that Nani would come out and see him. As the night deepened, he was simply going mad with one idea: he wanted to set the house on fire and take Nani away. Only when the fire had become uncontrollable did he realize that he had done something very foolish.

He walked a while and arrived on top of the mountain. He would have liked to shout at the top of his lungs. But he only groaned pitifully. He looked down at Mr. O's house. From a distance, the house looked haunted, thanks to Min.

Smoke was coming out of the chimneys of the farmhouses in the valley. It was breakfast time. He descended to the valley. The gate of the burned house looked the same as before, but everything else on Mr. O's property was either burned down or blackened. When he stepped into the first courtyard, he heard something. He walked toward the noise. To his surprise, Nani was there, going through the debris. She was picking out objects and throwing them back on the pile of things, grumbling and sighing.

Nani shrieked when he came into view. She stood there on guard, ready to claw at him. She was boiling.

"Look at this! Is this how you repay your benefactor? Mr. O has fed you, clothed you, sheltered you ever since you were an infant?" Nani said, her spittle flying.

Min dropped his head, ashamed.

"You are an idiot!" she shrilled.

A little while later, Min and Nani sat on a rock behind the tool shed, where Min had once sat to sharpen the blades of sickles and mend other tools. He pulled his sleeve down to his palm and cleaned Nani's smudged face.

"You'd better disappear before the villagers stone you. No one believes Mr. O. Why on earth would he have burned down his own house? I know you did it. You should have been hanged," Nani said, tears trickling out of her eyes. She wiped her tears and her face was smudged black again.

"What are you going to do now?" Nani asked.

Min groaned and used his hands to tell Nani. She was the only one who understood his sign language.

"What are you going to do on the west coast? It's a rough place," Nani said.

Min groaned again, waving his hands in the air and jerking this way and that.

"On a ship? Where are you going to go?" Nani asked disapprovingly.

Min didn't know the name of the place where his friend Blane had gone. He pulled out the compass that Blane had given him before Blane had boarded the Chinese ship.

"What is it?" Nani asked, taking it in her hand. "It moves!" she exclaimed. She played with it for a while.

Min explained that a compass shows which way you should take.

"How does it know which way I should go?" Nani questioned. The small, round device seemed a little too superstitious. She handed it back to him. "I don't take random trips and go wherever something other than my mind tells me to go."

Min had felt exactly the same when Blane explained to him how to use it, but now he had become dependent on the little device. Even if he knew which way to go, he had to look at it to make sure he wasn't making a mistake.

"And then what?" Nani asked.

Min didn't know what he was going to do once he got where Blane lived, but he couldn't forget the tears of joy Blane had shed when he was about to board the ship. He had scribbled something on a piece of paper and given it to Min. If he ever wanted to go and visit, that was the paper he needed, perhaps. In any case, Min had carefully tucked it away in his sack. And just yesterday, he had wanted to get away from his country and go far away. He wanted to start his life all over again.

"Let me pack you some food before you go," Nani said. Soonyi and Quince would be cooking breakfast, but Mistress

Yee was always capable of mustering enormous energy, even when she was ill, to attack her maids with her sharp tongue.

"Stay here, will you? I will pack the food soon," Nani said, and ran off.

Min went over to the place where he had found Nani a little while earlier. What had she been trying to pick out? He stood there, inhaling the smell of destruction.

At the guesthouse, Quince was sitting in the kitchen, chewing on a large carrot. When she saw Nani, she got up and asked, "Where have you been?"

"Did you make breakfast for Mistress Yee?" Nani asked, panting.

"Dr. Choi is with her. Apparently her tongue isn't moving," Quince said, her cheek bulging with food.

"What do you mean?" Nani asked.

Soonyi popped in then and said, "Oh, Big Sister, something terrible has happened! Mistress Yee cannot speak! I just went and fetched Dr. Choi."

"Calm down. She is probably still overcome with shock from yesterday," Nani said.

Soonyi reported excitedly, "A little while ago, I took a breakfast tray to Mistress Yee. All I heard from inside was hissing. So I opened the door. Her room was a mess. Random articles were strewn all over the room. I asked Mistress Yee if she would like breakfast. She couldn't speak! She threw her fan at me. I was so frightened. I asked if she would like me to fetch a doctor. She threw her writing brush box at me. So I ran to fetch Dr. Choi."

Quince stopped chewing her carrot and cried theatrically, spitting bits of carrot, "Oh my gods!"

"She is probably still very angry with the master," Nani said dismissively.

"You heard what she just said. She must have had a stroke in the middle of the night, and her maid wasn't available for help," Quince said excitedly, showing the food in her mouth.

"Has Mr. O returned?" Nani asked Soonyi, ignoring Quince.

"No," Soonyi replied.

"The gods have set their minds against this household! Mr. O should have another Kut to really get rid of Mistress Kim's spirit," Quince said, clucking her tongue.

"Don't you breathe a word about this household to anyone outside! Now you can go, Quince," Nani said firmly.

"You can't 'go' and 'don't go' me as you please. I am an employee at this house," Quince said, looking sour. She got up and drank a large bowl of water, swishing it in her mouth to clean between her teeth.

"I said you go now or else you won't be coming back here after today," Nani said, clenching her teeth.

Quince looked at Soonyi, hoping for support, but she was looking at her feet. "Should I come back this afternoon, Missy?" Quince asked impertinently.

"I'll send Soonyi over to get you should the need arise," Nani said coldly.

"All right, then," Quince said and left.

Nani waited until Quince was gone. Then she said, "Let's go and clean up Mistress Yee's room and see what Dr. Choi might want us to do. I should have come back last night," Nani said, regretfully, leading the way to Mistress Yee's room.

Indeed, the room was in chaos. In the midst of all the articles that Mistress Yee had thrown, she was lying on her silk mat with her eyes closed, dozens of acupuncture needles stuck in her forehead.

"I put her out for a while so I could treat her," Dr. Choi said. "Where is Mr. O?"

"He is not home at the moment," Nani replied. "May we tidy up the room?"

Dr. Choi considered it for a moment and said, "I guess that would be all right. But when your mistress wakes up, it is absolutely crucial that she stay calm." He took Mistress Yee's wrist and felt her pulse with his eyes closed. He sighed when he put her hand back on her silk mat.

Nani and Soonyi were on their tiptoes, picking up and putting things away. When they were about to leave, Mr. O appeared in the yard, looking tired.

"Master, Dr. Choi is in Mistress Yee's room," Nani informed him.

"Bring me something to drink," he said as he took off his shoes and ascended to the anteroom.

In the kitchen, Nani prepared a tray of ginseng tea for three. And then she took away one cup, thinking that Mistress Yee wouldn't be drinking any. Suddenly, she realized that she had forgotten all about Min at the old house.

"Soonyi, I need to slip out for a few moments," she said desperately.

"No, Big Sister. You can't leave me alone here," Soonyi said, furrowing her forehead.

"All right. I guess I need to prepare lunch. You take the tea to Mr. O and then stay in the hallway to see if Dr. Choi wants anything more," Nani said.

After Soonyi had left, Nani began to grind the soaked soybeans in the millstone, adding a spoonful of water every now and then. The coarse yellow meal oozed out between the two stone plates. Nani was hoping that Min was long gone. Someday, maybe, she would see him again. She was not worried.

She put the ground soybeans in a linen pouch and squeezed the juice out. It would be the base of a noodle soup for lunch. She poured the juice into a pot and set it on the stove. While the soybean juice simmered, Nani began to practice writing, tracing characters with her wet finger on the side of the millstone.

IT TOOK MUCH LONGER TO BUILD MR. O'S HOUSE THAN he had anticipated. Twenty-five men worked on the site, even on rainy days, and five women cooked, cleaned, and finally pasted wallpaper.

On the final day when the women workers were sweeping the courtyards, Mr. O came and wept in his new quarters. He had done nothing quite so stressful in his whole life. "Well, I did it," he said out loud. He felt that his deceased father had not thought him capable of the task. But now he had proved him wrong.

He came out and looked about the place once again. Dubak appeared and congratulated him. Then Dubak accompanied Mr. O everywhere, telling him how everything was looking grand. Gradually, the villagers gathered and then the shamans arrived to perform a housewarming Kut. White rice cakes were served for good luck.

Nani, Soonyi, and Quince arranged the offering table in front of the main gate. The shamans put on their colorful robes and began slowly dancing. Some of the villagers were dancing too. All the spirits from the mountain behind them rushed down to find out what the brouhaha was about. Mrs. Wang was also coming down the mountain with Mansong. "Mansong, wait for me!" Mrs. Wang cried as she followed the little girl.

Turning around covering her ears, Mansong mumbled, "Loud."

"Listen carefully," Mrs. Wang said.

"Gongs and drums." Mansong frowned

"Listen to the voice."

Mansong stopped and listened. "Someone's shouting," she said.

"Yes, that too," Mrs. Wang said. "She is calling the spirits to come forth to hear what the people have to say."

"What do they say?"

"Who knows? People always have so much to say. Your father wants blessings on his new house," Mrs. Wang explained.

A crowd stood in front of the gate of Mr. O's magnificent new house. Mrs. Wang looked about. Mansong wanted to be lifted up over the crowd to have a look at the shamans.

Nani spotted Mrs. Wang and rushed to her.

"Ah, Nani, can you lift her up? She wants to see all the fuss," Mrs. Wang said.

"Come, my little lady," Nani said, hoisting Mansong.

"Where is Mr. O?" Mrs. Wang asked.

"Inside the house."

"You stay here with Mansong. I need to go see him."

Away from the crowd, Mrs. Wang slipped into the house. A few male workers were cleaning the rooftop, and several others were pretending to be busy doing a last-minute check-up before the move-in the next day.

A man greeted Mrs. Wang from the rooftop. He had recently become a father.

"Where is the master of the house?" Mrs. Wang asked.

"At the well behind the kitchen," he shouted.

Mrs. Wang walked to the well where Mr. O was pouring in a bowl of clear rice liquor to wish for a ceaseless stream of water to the well from the mountain. When he saw Mrs. Wang, he poured a bowl of the same wine from a jug and encouraged her to drink.

Mrs. Wang could not say no. She drank it at once and said, "I was just thinking on the way down here, looking at your beautiful house, that we are the only creatures who need a roof."

Mr. O smiled and nodded.

"Mr. O, how is Mistress Yee?"

"Ah, she is about the same. She improves slowly. She is able to sit up now and eat on her own."

"That's better," Mrs. Wang said.

"Thank you for coming to our house. Please have some food," Mr. O encouraged her. He was ready to leave the well. He was remembering the tone of the letter she had written to him about Min. It was the voice of a stern mother.

"I need to have a talk with you, Mr. O. It won't take long," Mrs. Wang said.

"Sure," he said, looking about. He led Mrs. Wang to the garden.

"Yes, Mrs. Wang," he said, politely offering her his attention.

"I brought your daughter today. I am so attached to her, and I would really like to keep her with me longer, but Mistress Kim, your deceased wife, would disagree with me. Mansong belongs here after all," Mrs. Wang said.

Mr. O thought for a moment. He was surprised. Of course, he knew that he had a daughter. But he had thought she was with another caregiver, Dubak's wife or sister, whatever her name was. His wife had said that she was in good care.

"I don't believe that is her name?" Mr. O suddenly pointed out.

"Ach, Mr. O, that is the nickname I gave her myself instead of Beautiful Flower. I hope you forgive me. I just thought she needed a name that's less susceptible to the elements, if you understand what I mean. Again, my apologies for having taken the liberty to name your daughter Ten Thousand Pine Trees. But so poetic is Beautiful Flower."

"Mrs. Wang, I thank you for all your efforts. I have been so preoccupied with building the house and with Mistress Yee that I have neglected my duty as a father," he apologized. "I should have had Mistress Yee take care of the matter," he said, and then he realized that she was in no condition to take care of any matter. So he blushed.

288 H. S. Kim

"There is nothing to worry about. I am here to ask you for a big favor, seeing as I have done you a favor by taking care of Mansong."

That simplified everything for Mr. O. He liked it when people expressed what they wanted because often he didn't even know what he wanted.

"Yes?" he said, eyeing Mrs. Wang blankly.

"I am getting old. I would like to have a maid, but I cannot afford one. But if I could borrow one of your maids once in a while to take care of some things at my house, I would be most grateful," Mrs. Wang said.

"Ah, Mrs. Wang," he said, relieved to hear her minor request, "let me arrange it for you. Let me go now and tell the first one I see to go with you. You may even keep one of my maids. Why borrow?" he said. "In fact, we are hiring more in a few days," he said, blushing again. Mrs. Wang made him nervous.

"No need for you to speak to anyone. I have picked one out already. Nani, she is called. I will ask her to come to my house after the move."

"Fine."

"But I would like you to come with me to welcome Mansong. She has been most eager to see you." Mrs. Wang walked out to the gate with Mr. O following her. The shamans were shouting shrilly to pacify the old spirits who had suffered in the fire. People were drinking and eating and gossiping about Mistress Yee's misfortune. And when they saw Mr. O, the crowd grew silent out of respect.

"Here she is," Mrs. Wang said. "My little Mansong, here is your father."

Mansong bowed deeply, and then said, "I have watched my house being built every day from the mountain. I am glad that it is finally finished. Please show me my room."

"Well, well. I am g-glad you are here," Mr. O stuttered. And he looked about. Everyone was staring at him and Mansong, even the shamans, stopping their routine temporarily. "Why don't you show Mansong her room?" he asked Nani. She hesitated because she didn't know which room was reserved for Mansong.

"No. I want you, Father," said Mansong.

The villagers clapped their hands and commented that she was the brightest girl in the whole village. One said that she was going to be the ruler of the province.

Mr. O disappeared into the house with Mansong. And the shamans resumed their dance. Mrs. Wang took Nani aside and said, "After the move, when things settle down, pack your things and come to me. Your master gave me permission to take you as my maid."

"Oh, thank you. Thank you. I have practiced writing every day, Mrs. Wang," said Nani, trying to hold her flooding emotion inside.

Mrs. Wang left the crowd to go and see a woman who was due to have a baby soon. In spite of her aching legs, Mrs. Wang felt good that she had fulfilled Mistress Kim's wish.

"When I become old and frail, remember me," Mrs. Wang said, looking back at the mountain, which loomed up beyond the crowd in front of Mr. O's gate. The mountain was beautifully dressed in its gorgeous fall colors once again.

Nani stood by the gate and watched Mrs. Wang walk away. Soon—very soon—she would go around with Mrs. Wang and learn everything there was to learn to be a midwife. She picked up a stone and wrote on the ground, "I will be a midwife." She got up and felt as though she would fly if she didn't make sure that her feet were planted firmly on the ground.

THE MOVE TOOK A WHOLE MONTH. WHENEVER THERE
was a new delivery, the villagers gathered near Mr. O's gate to
have a look at the impressive pieces of furniture. They were
built by a famous carpenter named Gong by the Snake River.
Gong would let his logs float in the river for three months and
then let them dry for another three months so that they were
seasoned before they were cut.

The first night, Mr. O slept in his quarters to let his ancestors know that he owned it so that they could feel free to come
and go. The maids and servants were in and out to clean and
to plant trees.

Some days later, Mistress Yee was carried to the new house in
a closed carriage so that no one would see her. Nani followed the
carriage with the servants. When the carriage arrived at the new
house, the servants carried Mistress Yee in on a Chinese chair.
Mistress Yee looked about and realized that the new house was
not exactly the same as the previous one. She shrieked, dissatisfied. The chair was carried to the rear of the house. Mistress Yee
trembled and turned purple when she saw where she was going
to reside. The servants carried her to her room. Nani and Soonyi
helped her sit on the mat in the room. Mistress Yee howled and
hissed.

"Big Sister, Mistress Yee is thirsty," Soonyi pointed out to
Nani. Soonyi turned to Mistress Yee to confirm this. "Am I
right, Mistress Yee? You made the same sound yesterday when
you wanted tea."

Mistress Yee raised her left hand to strike Soonyi. But Nani
pulled Soonyi away in time. Mr. O had warned the maids to
remove themselves when Mistress Yee got into one of her foul

moods and became violent. According to Dr. Choi, it was advisable not to speak to Mistress Yee at such a time.

Nani pulled Soonyi out the door.

"Don't make comments about Mistress Yee in front of her. There is nothing wrong with her hearing. She just can't say things properly right now. Dr. Choi says she will be able to speak again sometime soon, but it will take time," Nani said as she led the way to the new kitchen.

The kitchen was much more spacious, due to the high ceiling. The light came in directly through openings designed for ventilation.

"Look, Soonyi, up there!" Nani pointed her finger to one of the openings. Remarkably, there was a bird nest with baby birds.

"Oh, Big Sister, look at them!" Soonyi cooed.

"Ah, sweet!" Nani exclaimed, looking up. "Birds are a good sign," she said. Nani had broken the news the night before that she would move to Mrs. Wang's sometime soon. Soonyi had bawled like a cranky toddler. And she had said that she was going to go with Nani.

"Birds are a good sign?" Soonyi asked, looking up.

"My mother said so," Nani said.

"Maybe you will stay," Soonyi said.

There was a silence, and then Nani said, "Soonyi, I am going to Mrs. Wang's. I have moved some of my things already. But you can always come and see me. And I am sure that you and I will run into each other often."

They organized the kitchen in silence, avoiding eye contact. Only when there was a ruckus outside did they look at each other. Then they ran outside together.

Bok ran to Nani and said, "Here comes the new mistress!"

Nani looked at Soonyi meaningfully and Soonyi grimaced. They had dreaded this moment.

Mirae was coming in her carriage. She was six months pregnant and dressed exquisitely in yellow and light green. She smiled divinely, looking down at the villagers as if she were the queen of China. They had heard about Mirae's extreme good fortune, but seeing her arrive as the mistress of the house dumbfounded them. Everyone was waiting for the others to comment on the event.

"She sure is pretty," one voice finally said.

"Oh, she always has been," said another.

"As far as her beauty is concerned, the queen of China would envy her," a man said.

"Not just her beauty. Look at the life ahead of her!" his wife said and snorted.

"Great fortune has struck her," a voice said.

"'Struck' is not quite the word," a woman said. But she did not offer another word.

Mirae disappeared into the gate. She went to the mistress's quarters.

"How nice to see you again, Nani." Mirae smiled pleasantly. "Here is my maid, Kumi. I would like you to teach her. I've always thought that you were born an ideal maid."

Nani bowed slightly and found herself unable to answer. She swallowed her saliva and hoped to be dismissed.

"I have forgotten your voice. You need to speak so that I know you are the maid I remember," Mirae said sarcastically.

"Yes, Mistress," Nani said.

"There you go," Mirae said, composed like an arrogant peacock. "I would like some refreshments and tea. And then I would like you to take my maid on a tour of the house."

"Yes, Mistress." Nani led the way to the kitchen and showed the new maid how to make tea. She put the tea set on a tray and peeled a pear. Slicing it on a cutting board, Nani remembered how Mirae used to salivate over juicy winter pears. She had often picked out leftover winter pears, which bruised and browned so easily, from Mistress Yee's snack tray and devoured them in the corner of the old kitchen.

Nani asked Soonyi to take the tray to Mirae, and she took the new maid to show her around.

Mr. O was with Mirae when Soonyi brought in the tea tray with pear slices.

"Bring me another tea tray with refreshments," Mirae ordered her.

Soonyi's eyebrows shot up in surprise, but she said she would, immediately, and she left promptly.

"Why would you like another one?" Mr. O asked.

"I would like to take it to Mistress Yee," Mirae said. "She was my mistress. I am going to take care of her as long as I live."

Mr. O was moved. He took Mirae's hand and said, "You are pure gold."

"Oh, please," Mirae said, and she blushed becomingly. "I feel guilty absorbing your undivided attention," she confessed.

"Whom I give my attention to is my decision," Mr. O said, smiling.

"But would you hear my wish?" Mirae asked.

"Of course. Whatever you say."

"Will you spend time with Big Mistress?"

"I will if you wish. But she can't stand me," Mr. O grumbled.

Soonyi arrived with another tea tray.

"Shall we?" Mirae asked.

"All right. I guess I can't dissuade you from wanting to take care of her," Mr. O said, getting up. Mirae asked Soonyi to follow them with the tray. They walked by the recently planted persimmon trees.

"Ah, this is the perfect location for Big Mistress. Away from the noise of everyday life, and set back so that she is well protected and we can keep an eye on her health," Mirae said, standing in front of the small quarters behind the back corner of the house.

"Well, it was your wisdom that she is here," Mr. O said.

"Soonyi, announce Master's arrival and give me the tray. And then you may go," Mirae said.

"Master has arrived, Mistress," Soonyi announced. And she opened the door without hearing the answer from inside.

Soonyi withdrew, and Mr. O stepped in. Mirae followed him in with the tray.

Mistress Yee was drooling from the right side of her mouth. And when she saw Mirae, she groaned harshly. She waved her hand in the air to say something to Mr. O, stretching her left leg out tensely.

"Mistress Yee, calm down," Mr. O said, sitting down a few feet away from her.

Mirae kowtowed. "Mistress, your sister greets you," Mirae said as she lowered herself. She got up and sat down next to Mr. O and buried her face in his bosom. She sobbed and said, "Please tell me this is a dream. How can such misfortune have befallen my sister?"

Mistress Yee groaned wildly.

Mirae turned her face to Mistress Yee. "My sister, I am going to take good care of you. I am indebted to you deeply. I am going to pay you back for your many kindnesses. Oh, my heart breaks. Who would now know you were once the most beautiful bride in the whole province!" She turned back to Mr. O and said, "I must thank you, my husband, for bringing me here. Not only will I be serving you, but I will also be serving my sister. She used to say that I was her soul mate, because she and I think alike. She doesn't need to speak. I understand exactly what she thinks and wants."

"Thank you for your wisdom and grace. You are making everything so easy for me," Mr. O complimented her.

At that moment, from outside the door, Soonyi said, "Master, Soonyi is here. May I speak?"

"What is it?" Mr. O asked.

"I have a message from Lady Mansong. She would like the new mistress to come and introduce herself."

Mr. O guffawed, and Mirae turned pale.

"She is her mother's child," Mr. O commented, amused. "Tell her we will be there shortly."

Mirae sat there silently.

"Why don't we go and see the child?" Mr. O said, getting up. Mirae followed him out, calculating how to handle the situation.

In the courtyard, Mirae said feebly, "I am tired. I should lie down for a while. Not for me, but for your baby."

"Of course. You have had a long day," Mr. O said. He turned to Soonyi to tell her to escort Mirae to her quarters, but he hadn't thought about how Mirae should be addressed by everyone in the house.

"Take me, Soonyi," muttered Mirae, annoyed.

"Yes—" Soonyi said, breaking off her thought and silently wondering what to call Mirae.

Mirae walked slowly with Soonyi back to her new quarters. Mirae said to Soonyi, "Call me Mistress Mirae from now on because I am the mistress of this house. And do not walk next to me. Walk a few steps behind me at all times." Mirae's last name was Ma, one of the seven names that belonged to her class. She didn't want to use a working-class surname here in her new home.

"Yes, uh, Mistress Mirae."

On the other side of the house, Mr. O stood in front of Mansong's room and asked, "Who comes here?"

"The master of the house," she replied from inside.

"How did you know?" he said, opening the door and smiling.

"Because no one should come to me uninvited, unless it's my father," Mansong said.

Mr. O sat and took his daughter onto his lap. For some reason, he had fallen in love with this clever child.

"I was just with the new mistress, introducing her to Mistress Yee. You mustn't summon a grown up. That is not polite," Mr. O explained.

"But you told me to summon the maids as I pleased," Mansong said.

"Yes, you ought to, but not the mistress of the house," Mr. O said.

"But Quince told me that she had once been a maid at my house," Mansong said innocently.

Mr. O thought for a moment. He wasn't prepared to have this conversation with his daughter. "She is no longer a maid," Mr. O said.

"I see," Mansong said, confused.

"She is carrying your sibling," Mr. O said.

Mansong nodded.

"Will you give me a reading lesson today?" she asked. Her favorite pastime was studying with her father. And she had already advanced to the level he had attained at the age of ten.

"Ah, thank you for reminding me. Your father forgot because the new mistress arrived today, and he was busy with her," Mr. O said apologetically. Mansong took the book out from her drawer, opened it on the table, and they began their lesson.

Mirae sat in her room, breathing rapidly and shallowly. She was irritated because her husband hadn't returned yet. An hour later, her rage had turned to sorrow. She had been the center of attention and the envy of everyone when she became the third wife of Mr. O. But why had no one jumped to be her friend? Why didn't everyone love her when she was willing to give so much? All her relationships had resulted in betrayal.

Her baby kicked. This always scared her. She had never imagined life with a baby who resembled her. But now it was on its way. Sometimes she wanted to run back to the past, when she had been a little girl. She was pregnant by the richest man in the village, but she didn't feel happy.

At least she wasn't a maid anymore. She flashed on the worst night of her life, which she had spent in the storage room tied up, bruised, and with her mouth stuffed with a large pebble after eighty lashes of the whip. Recalling that scene always made boiling hot tears flow down her cheeks. She clenched her teeth hard and ground them in frustration.

When Soonyi announced that dinner was ready, Mirae realized that she had been sitting in the dark. She asked Soonyi to come in and light the candles.

"Where is the master?" Mirae asked.

"He will have dinner with Lady Mansong," Soonyi reported.

Mirae swallowed her saliva. Her baby kicked again. She realized that her baby must be born, whether she liked it or not. She told Soonyi to bring the dinner in. "I must eat," Mirae whispered between gritted teeth. She had to stay healthy and be strong to match up to the challenges of her life.

Soonyi came in with a large tray of food which she transferred to the low table.

"Where is my maid, Kumi?" Mirae asked.

"Oh, earlier she was helping Nani carry the dinner tray to Lady Mansong's quarters, and now I think she is feeding Mistress Yee."

"Listen carefully, Soonyi!" Mirae screeched. "From now on, serve my dinner first, before you serve the sick woman. And I want my dinner to be served by Nani. Do you understand?"

"Yes, Mistress," Soonyi said and left the room.

After Mr. O retired, Nani went into Mansong's room and asked, "Did my lady have a good day?"

"I did. I like this house. Are you ready to learn?" Mansong asked.

"Of course," Nani said, pulling out her book.

"Ah, I thought you might forget about the lesson because you were busy with the new mistress's arrival. But you are a good pupil," Mansong said and laughed pleasantly.

Nani recited a poem by Gosan that Mansong had taught her during the preceding lesson:

Mountains dressed in white
Chestnuts on amber
Summer days gone
Amber turns to ashes
Our hearts shiver in oblivion.

THE ROAD UP THE MOUNTAIN WAS FROSTY IN THE EARLY morning. Spring was just around the corner—you could almost smell it—but it was still chilly before the sun came out. Nani climbed swiftly, carrying the sack of her things on her head. She saw steam come out of her mouth and heard the swish of her starched skirt as she moved. At the old pine tree, she slowed down, as everyone else who climbed the mountain did. Then she bowed to the tree, wishing for health and the wisdom to be a good midwife like Mrs. Wang. She resumed her climb. She looked down on the valley and began to sing feebly, but as she climbed her voice got louder and louder. At the end of her song, she was shouting at the top of her lungs. She ran the rest of the way. At Mrs. Wang's gate, she was out of breath.

She stood there for a moment, expecting Mrs. Wang's dog, Tiger, to bark, but he didn't. Through the crack in the old gate, she saw Mrs. Wang sitting by the well, washing something in a bowl. The dog was wagging his tail.

"Mrs. Wang, Nani is here!" she shouted. When she caught her breath, she shouted again in her high-pitched voice, "Here I come, Mrs. Wang!" and threw her arm over the gate to unlatch it. She entered and dropped her sack on the wooden bench.

Mrs. Wang stopped cleaning the rice, turned around, and said, "What an awful mistake I made to accept you as my apprentice!"

Nani smiled, squatting next to Mrs. Wang.

"Mrs. Wang, I will try not to be so loud."

"That's the first thing you have to learn: to control what you feel. When something goes wrong, stay calm. When you deliver a deformed baby, don't gasp. When you deliver a healthy baby, don't compliment. Don't intrude on the emotional life of innocent and sometimes ignorant people," Mrs. Wang said.

"I understand, Mrs. Wang," Nani said humbly.

"It will take several seasons for you to understand that, but you are young and I am not dead yet," Mrs. Wang said, grinning. "Finish washing the rice. I am making red-bean rice and kelp soup to celebrate your commencement as my apprentice."

Nani's chest knotted. The tone of Mrs. Wang's voice reminded her of the voice of her late mother. On her birthdays, her mother had never failed to make red-bean rice and kelp soup, saying, "This is the day you came to this world to do something greater than your mother could ever do."

Nani swirled the rice in the water with her fingers and bit her lip, trying not to show her emotions. Suddenly, she got up and went to the bench. She pulled out a cloth from the sack. She ran to the kitchen and said excitedly, "Mrs. Wang, I have something for you."

"Speak in an even tone," Mrs. Wang said, and she frowned, not because of Nani, but because smoke had escaped from the stove and wafted toward her face.

"Mrs. Wang, let me handle that, please," Nani said confidently. She took the fan from Mrs. Wang's hand and skillfully tamed the fire. "I have done this most of my life, Mrs. Wang," she added proudly.

"I am glad you are good for something," Mrs. Wang said, getting up to go out to wash her hands.

After Nani fixed the fire, she went out and said, "Mrs. Wang, I have something for you."

Mrs. Wang was letting the chickens out of the cage. She turned around to see what Nani had brought. Nani unfolded a cloth she had embroidered for Mrs. Wang. It was a mountain in fall colors on a piece of coarse hemp cloth.

"I looked at the mountain this past fall, hoping I would come up here soon. And I began to embroider this, thinking that when I was done with this, I would come here to be with you," Nani said.

"Ah, Nani. Such a beautiful thing you've made!" Mrs. Wang said excitedly.

Nani was pleased to see how happy her teacher was.

"I will frame this on a wooden board and keep it on my wall as long as I live," Mrs. Wang declared.

They cooked together. The red beans bled and colored the rice purple. Kelp soup bubbled in the pot. Nani set the low table.

"How is my little Mansong?" Mrs. Wang asked.

"Ah, Mrs. Wang, she is the cleverest child I've ever seen. She amuses Mr. O so much that he says that he is getting younger every day."

"She belongs there after all," Mrs. Wang said.

After breakfast, Mrs. Wang pulled a book out of a drawer and showed it to Nani.

"What is this, Mrs. Wang?"

"It's my journal. I write in it every time I see a patient and every time I deliver a baby. It has taught me a lot. And I would like you to take over from now on. I want you to record all our visits with pregnant women."

Nani's confusion was written plainly all over her face.

Mrs. Wang explained, "First, you write the date, and then the name of the woman. Ah, never forget to record the name of the man who is involved. I mean, the father of the baby. And then you record what happens, what you see, and how you feel."

Nani was silent; she was still very confused. Mrs. Wang suggested, "Why don't you read one of my journal entries? In fact, you can read the one I wrote after Mansong was born."

"Oh yes," Nani said, still looking at the cover of the book.

"Let me find the page for you. Hand it to me," Mrs. Wang said. She took the book and flipped the pages. "I think it is in the previous book. Let me see." Mrs. Wang went to her drawer and pulled out another one.

"So many!" Nani exclaimed as she glimpsed the drawer full of journals.

"I started writing in my journals when I became a midwife. I was younger then than you are now. My grandmother told me to do so. And it is a very important part of the job. It sometimes saves lives," Mrs. Wang said, thinking of Min. But thinking of him, she remembered something. "By the way, Min stopped by some time ago. Now, where is that?" Mrs. Wang got up and opened the door to a small storage room, where she kept her money jar. She dipped her hand in and said, "Here it is!" She pulled out a knotted handkerchief.

Nani took it silently. Something was inside. She opened it and found the jade necklace she had lost in the fire. Min must have found it in the pile of debris while he waited for her to come and see him one last time. She remembered sitting in the kitchen, hoping he would leave and not wait. Before going to bed, she had gone back over to the house but had found him nowhere.

The handkerchief was smudged black from the charred necklace. She put it in her sleeve and thought of Min for a long moment. He might show up someday if she kept the necklace. Wherever he was now, she hoped that he would do something worthy with his life.

Mrs. Wang was still flipping through the pages, distracted by some of her own writings. She stopped and put her finger between two pages and handed the book to Nani.

"I believe Min was my son in a past life. He keeps returning to my mind," Mrs. Wang said.

Nani gasped. "Oh! What a coincidence! I feel exactly the same."

Mrs. Wang rolled her eyes comically and said, "You can read that page and see if it makes any sense." Then she lay down to take a nap.

Nani read what Mrs. Wang had to say about Mansong's birth:

Life is absurd. I can only sigh, feeling utterly ashamed of myself. Mistress Kim died. Even before I arrived! But she left a healthy baby girl behind. Somehow I feel responsible for this baby. I put her under the care of Jaya, who has just given birth to a boy. She has too much milk, she complains. The living have as many complaints as the dead.

Mistress Kim's house was ominously hushed. No one was present to receive the news of the death or the birth. Only two young maids, one of them practically a child herself. Earlier, a servant from that house had delivered a letter consisting of one sentence: "The mistress is in excruciating pain." I laughed. All the aristocrats are in "excruciating pain," and the peasants are about to die when the contractions begin. I told the mute servant I would come, by and by. He groaned and turned around to walk back down the mountain.

A little later, Dubak came up and said his wife would die if I didn't come immediately. I said I would come soon. He said he would carry me on his back. I snorted and scolded him, but he insisted that he wouldn't take one step from my house unless I came with him. So I walked down with him. His mother had prepared dinner for me. The newborn was enormous, so it took longer than anticipated. The happy grandmother so badly wanted me to stay to celebrate. So I had a few drinks.

Mistress Kim's house was in the dark; even the torch light at the entrance was out. As soon as I opened her door, I smelled death. I checked the woman's pulse. Too late. From now on, I shall spring up and go promptly when summoned, no matter who comes to fetch me, even if it means I will idle away half a day. Had I an assistant, it would be more efficient. Perhaps someday.

Tears welled up in Nani's eyes. She was feeling over-whelmed. She was entering a new world she knew nothing about. She was moved by what went on behind the scenes. Nani remembered very well how scared she had been when Mistress Kim had stuffed her own mouth with a cloth. Mistress Kim lay on her side and gripped whatever she could get hold of. She and Soonyi sat, feeling hopelessly worried, watching their mistress writhe in agony, groaning hideously. Mistress Kim grabbed her hand and Soonyi's in the end and wouldn't let go of them. When the baby came out with a great flop into a pool of blood on the mat, Soonyi and she looked at each other, but neither could go check to see what it was that had emerged into the world. Soonyi sobbed annoyingly. And then, Nani heard that Mrs. Wang had arrived. She went out with a lantern, trying to control her trembling hands. She wanted to say something to Mrs. Wang, but her tongue wouldn't move. She had been clenching her teeth so hard that her jaw ached. She couldn't even cry.

Mrs. Wang was sleeping. Nani decided to peruse some more of the journal. It was amazing reading. She pored over it until dusk. Mrs. Wang got up and said, "Light the candle. You are going to ruin your eyesight if you read in the dark."

"Should I start making dinner?" Nani asked. At Mr. O's house, she had to start thinking about dinner as soon as lunch was over.

"I always eat what's left from breakfast," Mrs. Wang said.

"Then I will warm up the kelp soup," Nani said, getting up. She went to the kitchen and took the jade necklace from her sleeve to wash it. It turned deep green in the water. She put it on and felt the coolness on her chest.

As she started a fire in the stove, there was a big thud from outside. Nani sprang up and went out of the kitchen. The old gate had finally given its last breath and lay collapsed on the ground.

"Big Sister!" Soonyi shouted. Bok picked up the gate and tried in vain to put it back.

"What brings you here?" Nani asked.

"Mirae—the little mistress—is in extreme pain. Her baby is on the way," Soonyi said with a broad smile, happy to see Nani.

Mrs. Wang came out to see what was going on. She thundered, "Who broke my gate?"

"It fell all by itself," Soonyi said. Bok was trying to fix it.

"There is a tool box behind the chicken cage. You can fix it. And I need to eat before I come," Mrs. Wang said. She went to the kitchen where leftover kelp soup was boiling on the stove.

Nani followed her in and said, "Mrs. Wang, I think we should go now."

"How am I going to walk all the way down to Mr. O's on an empty stomach?"

"But in your journal you regretted that you hadn't left promptly to see Mistress Kim," Nani reminded her cautiously.

Mrs. Wang clucked her tongue and said, "What an awful mistake I made to take you as my apprentice!"

Mrs. Wang went into her room and dressed herself warmly. She told Bok to finish fixing her gate, and she headed down to the valley with Nani. When they passed the old pine tree, Mrs. Wang said, "Bury me just beyond that tree when I am dead."

"Why there, Mrs. Wang?"

"So I can keep an eye on you. As you pass by, I will tell you if you are doing the right thing."

The moon rose. The two women walked by the barren rice field, talking about how the winter was almost over. Mrs. Wang said that she was going to plant cabbages and cucumbers in her backyard. Nani thought of reading all of Mrs. Wang's journals.

At the gate of Mr. O's house, Kumi came out with a lantern, looking like a frightened squirrel. Trembling, she guided the midwives to her mistress. Nani could already hear Mirae's shrieking voice. She noticed that Mrs. Wang kept a steady pace, even though Mirae's piercing cry was hard to ignore.

Mr. O was not available at the moment. He was reading a poem titled "Wheel of Fortune" with Mansong, which had been written by the country's only known female poet from the previous century. He was explaining the title to his daughter. He stopped abruptly. Life repeats itself.

"Father, what are you thinking about?" Mansong asked, looking up at him.

Mr. O came to his senses and asked, "What did you say?" His daughter's sparkling eyes stared at him intently, and he saw his reflection in her eyes. A long time before, when he was a little boy, he had stepped up to look inside a well. He saw a figure on the surface of the water. Behind it was a patch of cloud. The figure moved. He gasped, which immediately echoed in the well, sounding as if the well had gasped. A frantic maid pulled him back. He was dizzy. He told her that there was someone in the well. The maid looked in. She said, laughing, that it was his own reflection.

He had forgotten about this.

"My little one, I see myself in your eyes," Mr. O said to his daughter.

"I see myself in your eyes, too, Father."

He paused for a moment. Suddenly, the meaning of the conversation he had with the head monk some time before dawned on him. *He is you. He is I.* Mr. O pressed the middle of his eyebrows with his two fingers as if to expel a headache. But in truth he was trying to remember what else the head monk had tried to communicate with him.

Mansong yawned. She needed to be put to bed.

"Where is Soonyi?" Mr. O wondered.

"She went to fetch Mrs. Wang," she replied dreamily, leaning on his arm. She fell asleep within a moment. He put her down on the mat and covered her with a blanket. Observing her small, peaceful face, he lingered before he blew out the candle. She resembled her mother, definitely, but from a certain angle, she also looked a little like his father too.

Mr. O slipped out of his daughter's room. The moon filled the yard. Each time he walked about in his house, he was pleased that it was almost exactly the way the original was. In the dark, he knew it could fool even the spirit of his father.

A sharp cry issued from Mirae's quarters, tearing him out of his thoughts. He was about to enter the gate that led to his quarters. It took a moment for him to realize where the cry had come from. He stood in front of the stone step. Mirae must have given birth. He was going to sit in his room and wait for a maid to deliver the message.

He went in his room, lit candles, and sat in the middle of the room meditatively. He felt the weight of his life. He was an old man. And his wife, young and exceptionally beautiful, had just given birth to a baby. "Ah!" he exclaimed, remembering his haunting dream a few years before, in which he was an ancient man and his first wife was so young and beautiful. Now he knew that even dreams are made of life.

He heard footsteps rapidly approaching his quarters. It was not a maid, but a servant running fast to him, perhaps to tell him that the baby was born. Or that his wife had died while giving birth. Or that the baby was deformed. All was possible. Whatever it might be, the sun would rise again the next morning.

About the Author

AT THE AGE OF TWENTY, H. S. KIM MOVED TO THE U.S. After graduating from Teacher's College at Columbia University, she taught Creative Writing and English as a Second Language to a wide range of students, including teenagers in Harlem, prison inmates in upstate New York, businessmen in Austria, Laotian refugees in Oakland, and foreign scholars at various universities. A born storyteller, H. S. Kim began to write fiction after settling down in Berkeley, California with her husband and two children. *Waxing Moon* is her first novel. Her second novel, currently under construction, will be a depiction of the 1970s in a divided Korea through the eyes of a child.

Acknowledgements

I WOULD LIKE TO THANK THE FOLLOWING INDIVID-uals: Mary Bradford, Laura Gorjance, Cathy Hale, and Linda Wulf for proofreading and Amy McCracken, my editor at WiDō, for her excellent work and suggestions.

CPSIA information can be obtained at www.ICGtesting.com
Printed in the USA
LVOW09s1853090215

426300LV00001B/188/P